Maui has more than 80 accessible beaches of every conceivable description. Makena, one of the island's loveliest, lies on the southern end of the resort coast, offering vistas of Molokini Crater and Kahoolawe off in the distance. See chapter 6 for details on all of Maui's best beaches. © G. Brad Lewis / Tony Stone Images.

Sunrise at Haleakala National Park. See chapters 6 and 7. © *Jim Cazel / Photo Resource Hawaii.*

After viewing the sunrise at Haleakala, bikers mount up, test their brakes, and set out to cruise 37 miles down the slopes of the 10,000-ft. volcano. See chapter 6 for complete details on this and other adventure outings around the island. © *Robert Holmes Photography.*

The snaky Haleakala Crater Road climbs from sea level to 10,000 ft., where you might tower above puffy cumulus clouds like these. See chapters 6 and 7. © Robert Holmes Photography.

Lahaina, Maui's old whaling seaport, teems with restaurants, T-shirt shops, and a gallery on nearly every block, but there's still lots of real history to be found amid the tourist development. See chapter 7 for a detailed walking tour. © Chris Bryant / Tony Stone Images.

Four-mile-long Kaanapali is one of Maui's best beaches, with soft golden sand as far as the eye can see. See chapter 6. © Greg Vaughn / Tony Stone Images.

A snorkel cruise to Molokini, a natural sanctuary for tropical fish, is one of the most popular Maui adventures. See chapter 6. © Mark E. Gibson Photography.

The road to Hana winds for 50 miles past taro fields, magnificent seascapes, waterfall pools, botanical gardens, and verdant rain forests, ending at one of Hawaii's most beautiful tropical towns. See chapter 7 for a detailed driving tour. © Hollenbeck Photography.

Oheo Gulch (often called the Seven Sacred Pools) at Kipahulu, just beyond Hana. More than 20 waterfall pools and cataracts cascade into the sea. See chapter 7.
© Hollenbeck Photography.

Taro and banana patches along the Hana coast. See chapter 7. © *Greg Vaughn / Tony Stone Images.*

Iao Valley, a state park in the West Maui Mountains, offers easy trails that are perfect for family hikes. See chapter 7. © Mark E. Gibson Photography.

The highest sea cliffs in the world stretch for 14 majestic miles along Molokai's north shore, laced with waterfalls and creased by emerald valleys. See chapter 10. © Franco Salmoiraghi / Photo Resource Hawaii.

A waterfall in the lush Maui Mountains. See chapters 6 and 7. © *Randy Wells / Tony Stone Images.*

Frommer's®

Maui

with Molokai & Lanai

2004

by Jeanette Foster

Here's what the critics say about Frommer's:

"Amazingly easy to use. Very portable, very complete."

—Booklist

"Detailed, accurate, and easy-to-read information for all price ranges."
—Glamour Magazine

"Hotel information is close to encyclopedic."

—Des Moines Sunday Register

"Frommer's Guides have a way of giving you a real feel for a place."
—Knight Ridder Newspapers

WILEY

Wiley Publishing, Inc.

About the Author

A resident of the Big Island, **Jeanette Foster** has skied the slopes of Mauna Kea—during a Fourth of July ski meet, no less—and gone scuba diving with manta rays off the Kona Coast. A prolific writer widely published in travel, sports, and adventure magazines, she's also a contributing editor to *Hawaii* magazine and the editor of *Zagat's Survey to Hawaii's Top Restaurants*. In addition to this guide, Jeanette is the author of *Frommer's Hawaii, Frommer's Hawaii from $80 a Day,* and *Frommer's Honolulu, Waikiki & Oahu.*

Published by:

Wiley Publishing, Inc.

111 River St.
Hoboken, NJ 07030

ISBN   0-7645-3719-9
ISSN   1076-2817

Editor: Christine Ryan
Production Editor: M. Faunette Johnston
Cartographer: Nicholas Trotter
Photo Editor: Richard Fox
Production by Wiley Indianapolis Composition Services

For information on our other products and services or to obtain technical support, please contact our Customer Care Department within the U.S. at 800-762-2974, outside the U.S. at 317-572-3993 or fax 317-572-4002.

Wiley also publishes its books in a variety of electronic formats. Some content that appears in print may not be available in electronic formats.

Manufactured in the United States of America

5   4   3

Contents

List of Maps   vi

What's New in Maui   1

1   The Best of Maui   4

1 The Best Beaches 4   **8** The Best Bed & Breakfasts 15
2 The Best Maui Experiences 5   **9** The Best Resort Spas 17
3 The Best Adventures 9   **10** The Best Restaurants 17
4 The Best of Underwater   *Pampering in Paradise* 18
   Maui .10   *A Night to Remember:*
5 The Best Golf Courses 11   *Maui's Top Luau* 21
6 The Best Luxury Hotels   **11** The Best Shops & Galleries 21
   & Resorts 12
7 The Best Moderately Priced
   Accommodations 13

2   Planning Your Trip to Maui   23

1 The Island in Brief 23   *Flying with Film & Video* 47
2 Visitor Information   . . . . .27 *The Welcoming Lei* 50
3 Money .28   **10** Money-Saving Package Deals . . .51
4 When to Go   . . . . .29 **11** Planning Your Trip Online 52
Maui, Molokai & Lanai   *Frommers.com: The Complete*
Calendar of Events 30   *Travel Resource* 54
Ongoing Events 33   **12** The 21st-Century Traveler 55
5 Travel Insurance   . . . . .36 **13** Getting Around 56
What to Pack 36   **14** Tips on Accommodations 58
6 Health & Insurance   . . . . .37 **15** The Active Vacation Planner   . . .62
Don't Get Burned: Smart   *Fun for Less: Don't Leave Home*
Tanning Tips 39   *Without the Gold Card* 63
7 Specialized Travel Resources   . . .41   **16** Suggested Itinerary 64
8 Getting Married on Maui 43   **17** Recommended Reading 66
9 Getting There   . . . . .45 *Fast Facts: Maui* 68
Coping with Jet Lag 46

3   For International Visitors   70

1 Preparing for Your Trip 70   *Fast Facts: For International*
2 Getting to & Around the   *Visitors* 76
   United States 75

4 Where to Stay   81

1 Central Maui 81
2 West Maui 82
Family-Friendly Accommodations 88
3 South Maui 99
4 Upcountry Maui 109
5 East Maui: On the Road to Hana 114
6 At the End of the Road in East Maui: Hana 117

5 Where to Dine   123

1 Central Maui 123
2 West Maui 126
Family-Friendly Restaurants . . .130
The Tiki Terrace 134
3 South Maui 139
4 Upcountry Maui 144
5 East Maui: On the Road to Hana 148
6 At the End of the Road in East Maui: Hana 151

6 Fun in the Surf & Sun   152

1 Beaches 152
2 Watersports 158
An Expert Shares His Secrets: Maui's Best Dives 162
3 Hiking & Camping 168
4 Great Golf 175
5 Biking, Horseback Riding & Other Outdoor Pursuits 178

7 Seeing the Sights   182

1 By Air, Land & Sea: Guided Island Adventures 182
2 Central Maui 183
3 Lahaina & West Maui 186
Where to Park for Free—or Next to Free—in Lahaina 190
Walking Tour: Historic Lahaina 190
4 South Maui 197
5 House of the Sun: Haleakala National Park 199
6 More in Upcountry Maui 204
7 Driving the Road to Hana 205
8 The End of the Road: Heavenly Hana 212

8 Shops & Galleries   219

1 Central Maui 219
2 West Maui 223
3 South Maui 228
4 Upcountry Maui 229
5 East Maui 231

9 Maui After Dark   233

It Begins with Sunset... 234
1 West Maui: Lahaina 236
2 Upcountry Maui 237

10   Molokai: The Most Hawaiian Isle   238

1 Orientation 241
2 Getting Around 243
3 Accommodations 243
*Believe It or Not: High-Priced
Camping* 247
*Family-Friendly
Accommodations* 249
4 Dining 249
5 Beaches 253
6 Watersports 255
*Molokai's Best Snorkel
Spots* 256

7 Hiking & Camping 257
8 Golf & Other Outdoor
Pursuits 259
*Frommer's Favorite Molokai
Experiences* 260
9 Seeing the Sights 262
Especially for Kids 263
10 Shopping 269
11 Molokai After Dark 271
The Hot Bread Run 272

11   Lanai: A Different Kind of Paradise   273

1 Orientation 276
2 Getting Around 277
3 Accommodations 278
4 Dining 280
5 Beaches 283
6 Watersports 284
*Frommer's Favorite Lanai
Experiences* 285
7 Hiking & Camping 287

8 Golf & Other Outdoor
Pursuits 288
9 Seeing the Sights 290
Especially for Kids 291
10 Shopping 292
*"Talk Story" with the Greats:
Lanai's Visiting Artists
Program* 294
11 Lanai After Dark 295

Appendix A: Maui in Depth   296

1 History 101 296
Did You Know? 298
2 Maui Today 301
3 Life & Language 302
4 A Taste of Maui 304
*Ahi, Ono & Opakapaka:
A Hawaiian Seafood Primer* . . .306

*A Summary of Everyday
Hawaiian Food Terms* 308
5 The Natural World: An
Environmental Guide
to Maui 310

Appendix B: Useful Toll-Free Numbers & Websites   319

Index   321

General Index 321
Accommodations Index 333

Restaurant Index 335

List of Maps

Maui   6

Lahaina & Kaanapali
Accommodations   83

Accommodations & Dining from
Honokowai to Kapalua   93

South Maui Accommodations   101

Upcountry Maui
Accommodations   111

Lahaina & Kaanapali
Dining   127

South Maui Dining   141

Upcountry & East Maui
Dining & Attractions   145

Beaches & Outdoor
Pursuits   154

Lahaina   188

Walking Tour: Historic
Lahaina   191

Haleakala National Park   201

The Road to Hana   206

Hana   213

Molokai   239

Molokai Accommodations
& Dining   245

Lanai   275

An Invitation to the Reader

In researching this book, we discovered many wonderful places—hotels, restaurants, shops, and more. We're sure you'll find others. Please tell us about them, so we can share the information with your fellow travelers in upcoming editions. If you were disappointed with a recommendation, we'd love to know that, too. Please write to:

Frommer's Maui with Molokai & Lanai 2004
Wiley Publishing, Inc. • 111 River St. • Hoboken, NJ 07030

An Additional Note

Please be advised that travel information is subject to change at any time—and this is especially true of prices. We therefore suggest that you write or call ahead for confirmation when making your travel plans. The authors, editors, and publisher cannot be held responsible for the experiences of readers while traveling. Your safety is important to us, however, so we encourage you to stay alert and be aware of your surroundings. Keep a close eye on cameras, purses, and wallets, all favorite targets of thieves and pickpockets.

Other Great Guides for Your Trip:

Frommer's Hawaii
Frommer's Hawaii from $80 a Day
Frommer's Honolulu, Waikiki & Oahu
Frommer's Portable Maui
Frommer's Portable Hawaii: The Big Island
Hawaii For Dummies

Frommer's Star Ratings, Icons & Abbreviations

Every hotel, restaurant, and attraction listing in this guide has been ranked for quality, value, service, amenities, and special features using a **star-rating system.** In country, state, and regional guides, we also rate towns and regions to help you narrow down your choices and budget your time accordingly. Hotels and restaurants are rated on a scale of zero (recommended) to three stars (exceptional). Attractions, shopping, nightlife, towns, and regions are rated according to the following scale: zero stars (recommended), one star (highly recommended), two stars (very highly recommended), and three stars (must-see).

In addition to the star-rating system, we also use **seven feature icons** that point you to the great deals, in-the-know advice and unique experiences that separate travelers from tourists. Throughout the book, look for:

Finds	Special finds—those places only insiders know about
Fun Fact	Fun facts—details that make travelers more informed and their trips more fun
Kids	Best bets for kids and advice for the whole family
Moments	Special moments—those experiences that memories are made of
Overrated	Places or experiences not worth your time or money
Tips	Insider tips—great ways to save time and money
Value	Great values—where to get the best deals

The following **abbreviations** are used for credit cards:

AE	American Express	DISC	Discover	V	Visa
DC	Diners Club	MC	MasterCard		

Frommers.com

Now that you have the guidebook to a great trip, visit our website at **www.frommers.com** for travel information on more than 3,000 destinations. With features updated regularly, we give you instant access to the most current trip-planning information available. At Frommers.com, you'll also find the best prices on airfares, accommodations, and car rentals—and you can even book travel online through our travel booking partners. At Frommers.com, you'll also find the following:

- Online updates to our most popular guidebooks
- Vacation sweepstakes and contest giveaways
- Newsletter highlighting the hottest travel trends
- Online travel message boards with featured travel discussions

What's New in Maui

Ever since Captain James Cook sailed by the island of Maui some 300-plus years ago, visitors can't resist this emerald green island, bordered by sandy beaches and sapphire blue water. Venturing to Maui once makes you a visitor, twice and you're a traveler, most likely destined to return again and again, just to see what Maui is up to.

This "Valley Isle" is constantly in the processes of changing. The same white-sand beach beckons, but there are new ways to explore the exotic underwater world. The quaint cafes and bistros are there, but new eateries with innovative regional cuisine have cropped up. The resorts have spent billions to renovate, refurbish, and reinvent their rooms, their amenities, and their water features—even the beds are more comfortable than ever.

If you've been to Maui before, see it again—you won't believe the transformation. If you haven't experienced Maui, what are you waiting for?

PLANNING YOUR TRIP TO MAUI
Getting There   Today there are more direct flights to Maui from the West Coast than ever.

Aloha Airlines (© **800/367-5250** or 808/484-1111; www.alohaairlines. com) now has nonstop service from Kahului Maui to Burbank, California (closer to downtown Los Angeles than Los Angles International Airport); Orange County, California; and Phoenix, Arizona. International travelers can use Aloha's service from Vancouver, BC. If you are not taking a direct flight, beware: Since the September 11, 2001, terrorist attacks, the number of interisland connecting flights from Honolulu to Maui has dropped dramatically. Gone are the days of interisland flights every half-hour: The flights are now few and far between, so be sure to book in advance. For a list of the growing number of air carriers serving Maui, from the U.S. mainland, overseas, and interisland, see "Getting There" in chapter 2.

WHERE TO STAY   The venerable **Hotel Hana-Maui** (© **800/321-HANA** or 808/248-8211; fax 808/248-7202; www.hotelhanamaui.com) has returned. This legendary hotel has been significantly upgraded and restored in honor of its Hawaiian heritage and the unspoiled beauty that make Hana a special place. Upgrades include refurbished interiors in all Sea Ranch cottages; a remodeled main dining room, lobby, and Paniolo bar; a restored Hana Town Center and Hana Ranch Restaurant; and a redesigned garden pool pavilion. A $2.5 million spa is scheduled to open in Fall 2003. Renovations will total $10.3 million at project's end. Rates range from $295 to $725, with numerous package deals available. See p. 117.

WHERE TO DINE   On the third Saturday of each month, **Whalers Village** hosts a **live cooking demonstration** with Maui's top chefs from noon to 1pm in the shopping center courtyard. Two visitors are drawn from the assembled crowd to be served the results of the cooking demonstration at a linen-covered table. Even if you aren't chosen, there are plenty of free samples and door prizes.

If the local cuisine on Maui is a little too attractive and the local brew a bit too tempting, you now can work off any extra pounds at the Hyatt Regency Maui Resort's "**Beach Boot Camp**" (© 808/661-1234). Every Wednesday, Friday, and Saturday at 8am, you get to go through a regime of a high-impact workout on the beach, with stretching and cardio exercises (sprints in the sand, lunges through the water, and abdominal crunches along a hill). Classes are $5 for hotel guests and $7 for non-hotel guests.

For complete information on Maui's collection of eateries, see chapter 5.

SHOPPING   Power-shoppers will find plenty to do on Maui. The queen of specialty products, Maui has everything from a cornucopia of agricultural products (including Kula onions, upcountry protea, Kaanapali coffee, world-renowned potato chips, and many other tasty treats that are shipped worldwide) to a wealth of Hawaiian souvenirs (aloha shirts, CDs of ancient chants, videos of hula, hand-carved native woods, and so on). The **Shops at Wailea,** an upscale shopping and restaurant complex, on 16 acres with some 50-plus shops and a half a dozen restaurants, offers live music, restaurant specials, and fashion events during **WOW (Wailea on Wednesday),** every Wednesday, from 6:30 to 9:30pm. Many of the galleries have special exhibits with featured artists present to discuss their work.

FUN IN THE SUN   Trilogy Excursions (© 888/MAUI-800 or 888/628-4800; www.sailtrilogy.com) has added an "Eco-Enrichment Kids Camp" to its popular Discover Lanai all day adventurer. Designed for kids ages 6 to 12, this program is great for families who want an all-day activity that caters to the interests of the whole family. **Camp Trilogy,** which takes place during the major holidays and from June to August, has trained

counselors and marine naturalists on staff who make camp both educational and entertaining. Camp Trilogy kids are first taught to snorkel and then taken on a guided reef tour with a certified marine naturalist. In addition there are beach games and activities that teach team building and respect for the environment. Plus all participants receive special T-shirts, Eco-coloring books, and even their own BBQ.

Another great activity for kids is **Maui Menehune Golf,** 32-A Lono Ave., Kahului, © 808/877-5599, which recently opened a miniature golf course in the heart of central Maui, across the street from Sears and the Kaahumanu Shopping Center. It's open Monday to Friday from 3 to 7pm and Saturday and Sunday from 10am to 11pm. There's a flat admission rate of $3 on Wednesday and Friday; the rest of the week, fees range from $5 to $7 for clubs and balls.

SEEING THE SIGHTS   Kaanapali's **Whale Center of the Pacific** shows free movies daily between 9:30am and 10pm in the newly renovated theater (with padded chairs, new surround-sound, and a 50-inch screen). Popular films shown include: *Onboard the Morgan* (depicting the life of 19th-century whalers), *Red Turtle Rising* (Hawaiian folklore on turtles), and *Hawaiian Humpback: Pacific Voyager* (which follows the whales from Alaska to Hawaii). See p. 196.

MAUI AFTER DARK   Go to a wedding next time you are on Maui, no gift necessary. The Hyatt Regency Maui (© 808/667-4727) is now the site of the off-Broadway play *Tony n' Tina's Wedding.* The 2-plus hour musical comedy allows the audience to attend the wedding, then follow the cast to the reception and dinner (you really get to eat). After dinner there's the traditional toast and dancing. All the while you are watching the play, which involves two Italian families coming together for their children's wedding, along with the pregnant maid of honor, a drunken priest, and a host of other characters. Tickets are $75.

MOLOKAI The **Kaluakoi Golf Course** reopened after an extended period starting when the Kalaukoi Hotel closed in late 2000. The first 9 holes went online with $150,000 in repairs to the irrigation system and work on the fairways, tees, and greens. The back 9 holes, scheduled for completion in 2004, will cost $6 million more for development of a water supply. See p. 259.

1

The Best of Maui

Maui, also called the Valley Isle, is just a small dot in the vast Pacific Ocean, but it has the potential to offer visitors unforgettable experiences: floating weightless through rainbows of tropical fish, standing atop a 10,000-foot volcano watching the sunrise color the sky, listening to the raindrops in a bamboo forest.

Whether you want to experience the "real" Hawaii, go on a heart-pounding adventure, or simply relax on the beach, this book is designed to help you create the vacation of your dreams.

It can be bewildering to plan your trip with so many options vying for your attention; to make your task easier, this chapter highlights what we consider the very best that Maui has to offer.

1 The Best Beaches

- **D. T. Fleming Beach Park:** This quiet, out-of-the-way beach cove, located north of the Ritz-Carlton Hotel, starts at the 16th hole of the Kapalua golf course (Makalua-puna Point) and rolls around to the sea cliffs on the other side. Ironwood trees provide shade on the land side. Offshore, a shallow sandbar extends out to the edge of the surf. Generally, the waters are good for swimming and snorkeling, but sometimes, off near the sea cliffs, the waves are big enough to suit body boarders and surfers. See p. 152.

- **Kapalua Beach:** On an island of many great beaches, this one takes the prize. A golden crescent with swaying palms protected from strong winds and currents by two outstretched lava-rock promontories, Kapalua has calm waters that are perfect for snorkeling, swimming, and kayaking. Even though it borders the Kapalua Bay Hotel, the beach is long enough for everyone to enjoy. Facilities include showers, restrooms, and lifeguards. See p. 153.

- **Kaanapali Beach:** Four-mile-long Kaanapali stands out as one of Maui's best beaches, with grainy gold sand as far as the eye can see. Most of the beach parallels the sea channel, and a paved beach walk links hotels and condos, open-air restaurants, and the Whalers Village shopping center. Summertime swimming is excellent. The best snorkeling is around Black Rock, in front of the Sheraton; the water is clear, calm, and populated with brilliant tropical fish. See p. 153.

- **Wailea Beach:** This is the best gold-sand, crescent-shaped beach on Maui's sunbaked southwestern coast. One of five beaches within Wailea Resort, Wailea is big, wide, and protected on both sides by black-lava points. It serves as the front yard for the Four Seasons Wailea, Maui's most elegant hotel, and the Grand Wailea Resort Hotel & Spa, its most outrageous. From the beach, the view out to sea is magnificent, framed by neighboring Kahoolawe and Lanai and the tiny crescent of Molokini. The clear waters tumble to shore in waves just the right size for gentle riding, with or without a board. While all the beaches on the west and south coasts are great for spotting whales and watching sunsets, Wailea, with its fairly flat sandy beach that gently slopes down to the ocean, provides exceptionally good whale-watching from shore in season (Dec–Apr), as well as unreal sunsets nightly. See p. 156.

- **Maluaka Beach (Makena Beach):** On the southern end of Maui's resort coast, development falls off dramatically, leaving a wild, dry countryside punctuated by green kiawe trees. The wide, palm-fringed crescent of golden sand is set between two black-lava points and bounded by big sand dunes topped by a grassy knoll. Makena can be perfect for swimming when it's flat and placid, but it can also offer excellent bodysurfing when the waves come rolling in. Or, if you prefer, it can be a place of serenity, with vistas of Molokini Crater and Kahoolawe off in the distance. See p. 157.

- **Waianapanapa State Park:** In east Maui, a few miles from Hana, the 120 acres of this state park offer 12 cabins, a caretaker's residence, a picnic area, a shoreline hiking trail, and, best of all, a black-sand beach (actually small black pebbles). Swimming is generally unsafe, though, due to strong waves breaking offshore, which roll into the beach unchecked, and strong rip currents. But it's a great spot for picnicking, hiking along the shore, and simply sitting and relaxing. See p. 158.

- **Hamoa Beach:** This half-moon–shaped, gray-sand beach (a mix of coral and lava) in a truly tropical setting is a favorite among sunbathers, snorkelers, and body-surfers in Hana. The 100-foot-wide beach is three football fields long and sits below 30-foot black-lava sea cliffs. An unprotected beach open to the ocean, Hamoa is often swept by powerful rip currents. Surf breaks offshore and rolls ashore, making it a popular surfing and bodysurfing area. The calm left side is best for snorkeling in the summer. See p. 158.

- **Hulopoe Beach (Lanai):** This golden, palm-fringed beach off the south coast of Lanai gently slopes down to the azure waters of a Marine Life Conservation District, where clouds of tropical fish flourish and spinner dolphins come to play. A tide pool in the lava rocks defines one side of the bay, while the other is lorded over by the Manele Bay Hotel, which sits prominently on the hill above. Offshore, you'll find good swimming, snorkeling, and diving; onshore, there's a full complement of beach facilities, from restrooms to camping areas. See p. 283.

2 The Best Maui Experiences

- **Taking the Plunge:** Don mask, fins, and snorkel, and explore the magical world beneath the surface of the ocean, where kaleidoscopic clouds of tropical fish flutter by exotic corals; a sea turtle might even come over to check you out. Molokini is everyone's favorite snorkeling destination, but the shores of Maui are lined with magical spots as well. Can't swim? No problem: Hop on the **Atlantis Submarine** (© **800/548-6262**) for a plunge beneath the waves without getting wet. See "Watersports" in chapter 6 and "By Air,

Maui

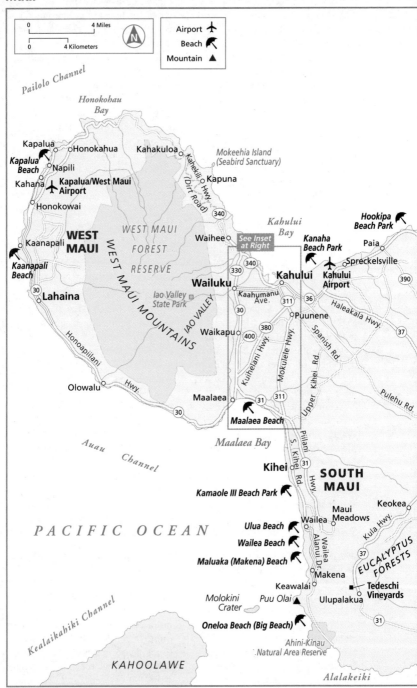

Airport ✈
Beach 🏖
Mountain ▲

0 ——— 4 Miles
0 ——— 4 Kilometers

N

Pailolo Channel

Honokohau Bay

Kapalua
Kapalua Beach
Honokahua
Kahakuloa
Napili
Kahana
Kapalua/West Maui Airport
Honokowai

Mokeehia Island (Seabird Sanctuary)
Kapuna

Kahekili Hwy. (Dirt Road)

340

Kahului Bay

See Inset at Right

WEST MAUI
Kaanapali
Kaanapali Beach
Lahaina

WEST MAUI FOREST RESERVE

WEST MAUI MOUNTAINS

Waihee

340
330

Hookipa Beach Park
Kanaha Beach Park
Paia
Spreckelsville

Wailuku
Iao Valley State Park
IAO VALLEY

Kahului
Kahului Airport

390

30

Kaahumanu Ave.
311
36
Haleakala Hwy.
37

30
Waikapu
400
380
Puunene

Kuihelani Hwy.
Mokulele Hwy.
Spanish Rd.

Upper Kihei Rd.
Pulehu Rd.

Honoapiilani Hwy.

Olowalu

Maalaea
31
311

30
Maalaea Beach

Maalaea Bay

Kihei
31

SOUTH MAUI

Auau Channel

Kamaole III Beach Park

Maui Meadows
Keokea

S. Kihei Rd.
Piilani Hwy.

Wailea

Ulua Beach
Wailea Beach
Maluaka (Makena) Beach

Wailea Alanui Dr.

Kula Hwy.
37

EUCALYPTUS FORESTS

PACIFIC OCEAN

Makena
Keawalai
Molokini Crater
Puu Olai ▲
Ulupalakua

■ **Tedeschi Vineyards**

Oneloa Beach (Big Beach)

Ahini-Kinau Natural Area Reserve

31

Kealaikahiki Channel

KAHOOLAWE

Alalakeiki

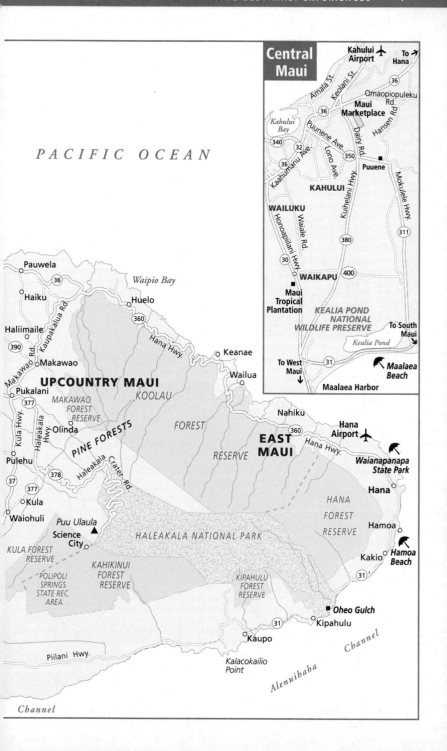

Land & Sea: Guided Island Adventures" in chapter 7.

- **Hunting for Whales on Land:** No need to shell out megabucks to go out to sea in search of humpback whales—you can watch these majestic mammals breach and spy hop from shore. We recommend scenic McGregor Point, at mile marker 9 along Honoapiilani Highway, just outside Maalaea in South Maui. The humpbacks arrive as early as November, but the majority travel through Maui's waters from mid-December to mid-April. See "Watersports" in chapter 6.

- **Watching the Windsurfers:** Sit on a grassy bluff or stretch out on the sandy beach at Hookipa, on the north shore, and watch the world's top-ranked windsurfers twirling and dancing on the wind and waves like colorful butterflies. World championship contests are held at Hookipa, one of the greatest windsurfing spots on the planet. See "Watersports" in chapter 6 and "Driving the Road to Hana" in chapter 7.

- **Experiencing Maui's History:** Wander the historic streets of the old whaling town of Lahaina, where the 1800s are alive and well thanks to the efforts of the Lahaina Restoration Society. Drive the scenic Kahekili Highway, where the preserved village of Kahakuloa looks much as it did a century ago. Stand in awe at Piilanihale, Hawaii's largest *heiau* (temple), located just outside Hana. See "Lahaina & West Maui" in chapter 7.

- **Greeting the Rising Sun from Haleakala's Summit:** Bundle up in warm clothing, fill a thermos full of hot java, and drive up to the summit to watch the sky turn from inky black to muted charcoal as a small sliver of orange forms on the horizon. Standing at 10,000 feet, breathing in the rarefied air, and watching the first rays of light streak across the sky is a mystical experience of the first magnitude. See "House of the Sun: Haleakala National Park" in chapter 7.

- **Exploring a Different Hawaii— Upcountry Maui:** On the slopes of Haleakala, cowboys, farmers, ranchers, and other country people make their homes in serene, neighborly communities like Makawao, Kula, and Ulupalakua—worlds away from the bustling beach resorts. Acres of onions, lettuce, tomatoes, carrots, cabbage, and flowers cover the hillsides. Maui's only winery is located here, offering the perfect place for a picnic and a chance to sample the tropical varieties of paradise. See "More in Upcountry Maui" in chapter 7.

- **Driving Through a Tropical Rainforest:** The Hana Highway is not just a "drive" but an adventure: Stop along the way to plunge into icy mountain ponds filled by cascading waterfalls; gaze upon vistas of waves pummeling soaring ocean cliffs; inhale the sweet aroma of blooming ginger; and take a walk back in time, catching a glimpse of what Hawaii looked like before concrete condos and fast-food joints washed ashore. See "Driving the Road to Hana" in chapter 7.

- **Taking a Day Trip to Lanai:** From Lahaina, join **Trilogy Excursions' snorkel cruise** to Lanai (© **800/ 874-2666**), or take the Expeditions Lahaina/Lanai Passenger Ferry over and rent a four-wheel-drive Jeep on your own. It's a two-for-one island experience: Board in Lahaina Harbor and admire Maui from offshore, then get off at Lanai and go snorkeling in the clear waters, tour the tiny former plantation island, and catch the last ferry home. See chapter 11.

3 The Best Adventures

Branch out while you're in Maui; do something you wouldn't normally do—after all, you're on vacation. Below is a list of adventures we highly recommend. Some are a bit pricey, but these splurges are worth every penny.

- **Scuba Diving:** You're in love with snorkeling and the chance to view the underwater world, but it's just not enough—you want to get closer and see even more. Take an introductory scuba dive; after a brief lesson on how to use the diving equipment, you'll plunge into the deep to swim with the tropical fish and go eyeball to eyeball with other marine critters. See "Watersports" in chapter 6.

- **Skimming over the Ocean in a Kayak:** Glide silently over the water, hearing only the sound of your paddle dipping beneath the surface. This is the way the early Hawaiians traveled along the coastline. You'll be eye level and up close and personal with the ocean and the coastline, exploring areas you can't get to any other way. Venture out on your own, or go with an experienced guide—either way, you won't be sorry. See "Watersports" in chapter 6.

- **Exploring a Lava Tube:** Most people come to Maui to get outdoors and soak up some Hawaiian sunshine, but don't miss the opportunity to see firsthand how volcanic islands were formed. With **Maui Cave Adventures** (© **808/248-7308**), you can hike into the subterranean passages of a huge, extinct lava tube with 40-foot ceilings—an offbeat adventure and a geology lesson you won't soon forget. See "Biking, Horseback Riding & Other Outdoor Pursuits" in chapter 6.

- **Seeing the Stars from Inside a Volcanic Crater:** Driving up to see the sunrise is a trip you'll never forget, but to *really* experience Haleakala, plan to hike in and spend the night. To get a feel for why the ancient Hawaiians considered this one of the most sacred places on the island, you simply have to wander into the heart of the dormant volcano, where you'll find some 27 miles of hiking trails, two camping sites, and three cabins. See "Hiking & Camping" in chapter 6 and "House of the Sun: Haleakala National Park" in chapter 7.

- **Hiking to a Waterfall:** There are waterfalls, and there are waterfalls; the magnificent 400-foot Waimoku Falls, in Oheo Gulch outside of Hana, are worth the long drive and the uphill hike you have to take to get there. The falls are surrounded by lush green ferns and wild orchids, and you can even stop to take a dip in the pool at the top of Makahiku Falls on the way. See "Hiking & Camping" in chapter 6.

- **Flying over the Remote West Maui Mountains:** Your helicopter streaks low over razor-thin cliffs, then flutters past sparkling waterfalls and down into the canyons and valleys of the inaccessible West Maui Mountains. There's so much beauty to absorb that it all goes by in a rush. You'll never want to stop flying over this spectacular, surreal landscape—and it's the only way to see the dazzling beauty of the prehistoric area of Maui. See "By Air, Land & Sea: Guided Island Adventures" in chapter 7.

- **Taking a Drive on the Wild Side:** Mother Nature's wild side, that is—on the Kahekili Highway on Maui's northeast coast. This back-to-nature experience will take you past ancient Hawaiian *heiau* (temples); along steep ravines; and by rolling pastures, tumbling waterfalls, exploding blowholes, crashing surf, and jagged lava coastlines. You'll wander through the tiny Hawaiian village of Kahakuloa and around the "head" of Maui to the Marine Life Conservation Area of Honolua-Mokuleia and on to the resort of Kapalua. You'll remember this adventure for years. See "Lahaina & West Maui" in chapter 7.

- **Riding a Mule to Kalaupapa:** Even if you have only 1 day to spend on Molokai, spend it on a

mule. The **Molokai Mule Ride** (© 800/567-7550) trek from "topside" Molokai to the Kalaupapa National Historic Park (Father Damien's world-famous leper colony) is a once-in-a-lifetime adventure. The cliffs are taller than 300-story skyscrapers, and the narrow 3-mile trail includes 26 dizzying switchbacks, but Buzzy Sproat has never lost one of his trustworthy mules (or any riders) on the difficult trail. The mules make the trek daily, rain or shine. See "Seeing the Sights" in chapter 10.

4 The Best of Underwater Maui

An entirely different Maui greets anyone with a face mask, snorkel, and fins. Under the sea, you'll find schools of brilliant tropical fish, green sea turtles, quick-moving game fish, slack-jawed moray eels, and prehistoric-looking coral. It's a kaleidoscope of color and wonder.

- **Black Rock:** This spot, located on the Kaanapali Beach just off the Sheraton Maui Resort, is excellent for beginner snorkelers during the day and for scuba divers at night. Schools of fish congregate at the base of the rock and are so used to snorkelers that they go about their business as if no one were around. If you take the time to look closely at the crannies of the rock, you'll find lion fish in fairly shallow water. At night (when a few outfitters run night dives here), lobsters, Spanish dancers, and eels come out. See p. 153.

- **Olowalu:** When the wind is blowing and the waves are crashing everywhere else, Olowalu, the small area 5 miles south of Lahaina, can be a scene of total calm—perfect for snorkeling and diving. You'll find a good snorkeling area around mile marker 14. You might have

to swim about 50 to 75 feet; when you get to the large field of finger coral in 10 to 15 feet of water, you're there. You'll see a turtle-cleaning station here, where turtles line up to have small cleaner wrasses pick off small parasites. This is also a good spot to see crown-of-thorns starfish, puffer fish, and lots of juvenile fish. See "Watersports" in chapter 6 and "Lahaina & West Maui" in chapter 7.

- **Hawaiian Reef:** Scuba divers love this area off the Kihei-Wailea coast because it has a good cross-section of topography and marine life typical of Hawaiian waters. Diving to depths of 85 feet, you'll see everything from lava formations and coral reef to sand and rubble, plus a diverse range of both shallow- and deep-water creatures. See the box "An Expert Shares His Secrets: Maui's Best Dives" in chapter 6.

- **Third Tank:** Scuba divers looking for a photo opportunity will find it at this artificial reef, located off Makena Beach at 80 feet. This World War II tank acts like a fish magnet—because it's the only large solid object in the area, any fish or invertebrate looking for a safe home comes here. Surrounding the tank is a cloak of schooling snappers and goatfish just waiting for a photographer with a wide-angle lens. It's small, but the Third Tank is loaded with more marine life per square inch than any site off Maui. See the box "An Expert Shares His Secrets: Maui's Best Dives" in chapter 6.

- **Molokini:** Shaped like a crescent moon, this islet's shallow concave side serves as a sheltering backstop against sea currents for tiny tropical fish; on its opposite side is a deep-water cliff inhabited by spiny lobsters, moray eels, and white-tipped sharks. Neophyte snorkelers report to the concave side; experienced scuba divers, the cliff side.

Either way, the clear water and abundant marine life make this islet off the Makena coast one of Hawaii's most popular dive spots. See "Watersports" in chapter 6.

- **Ahihi-Kinau Natural Preserve:** Fishing is strictly *kapu* (forbidden) in Ahihi Bay (at the end of the road in South Maui), and the fish know it; they're everywhere in this series of rocky coves and black-lava tide pools. The black, barren, lunarlike land stands in stark contrast to the green-blue water, which is home to a sparkling mosaic of tropical fish. Scuba divers might want to check out **La Pérouse Pinnacle** in the middle of La Pérouse Bay; clouds of damsel fish and triggerfish will greet you on the surface. See "Watersports" in chapter 6.

5 The Best Golf Courses

- **Kaanapali Courses** (© 808/661-3691): All golfers, from high handicappers to near-pros, will love these two challenging courses. The North Course is a true Robert Trent Jones, Jr. design: an abundance of wide bunkers; several long, stretched-out tees; and the largest, most contoured greens on Maui. The South Course is an Arthur Jack Snyder design; although shorter than the North Course, it does require more accuracy on the narrow, hilly fairways. Just like its sibling course, it has a water hazard on its final hole, so don't tally up your score card until the final putt is sunk. See p. 176.

- **Kapalua Resort Courses** (© 877/527-2582): Kapalua is probably the best nationally known golf resort in Hawaii, due to the PGA Kapalua Mercedes played here each January. The Bay Course and the Village Course are vintage Arnold Palmer designs; the new

Plantation Course is a strong entry from Ben Crenshaw and Bill Coore. All are situated on Maui's windswept northwestern shore, at the rolling foothills of Puu Kukui, the summit of the West Maui Mountains. See p. 176.

- **Wailea Courses** (© 888/328-MAUI): On the sunbaked south shore of Maui stands Wailea Resort, *the* hot spot for golf in the islands. You'll find great golf at these three resort courses: The Blue course is an Arthur Jack Snyder design, and the Emerald and Gold courses are both by Robert Trent Jones, Jr. All boast outstanding views of the Pacific and the mid–Hawaiian Islands. See p. 177.

- **Makena Courses** (© 808/879-3344): Here you'll find 36 holes by "Mr. Hawaii Golf"—Robert Trent Jones, Jr.—at his best. Add to that spectacular views: Molokini islet looms in the background, humpback whales gambol offshore in winter, and the tropical sunsets are spectacular. The South Course has magnificent views (bring your camera) and is kinder to golfers who haven't played for a while. The North Course is more difficult but also more spectacular. The 13th hole, located partway up the mountain, has a view that makes most golfers stop and stare. The next hole is even more memorable: a 200-foot drop between tee and green. See p. 177.

- **The Lanai Courses:** For quality and seclusion, nothing in Hawaii can touch Lanai's two golf-resort offerings. **The Experience at Koele** (© 800/321-4666), designed by Ted Robinson and Greg Norman, and **The Challenge at Manele** (© 800/321-4666), a wonderful Jack Nicklaus course with ocean views from every hole, both rate among Hawaii's best courses. Both are tremendous fun to play, with the Experience featuring the par-four 8th hole, which drops some 150 yards from tee to fairway, and the Challenge boasting the par-three 12th, which plays from one cliff side to another over a Pacific inlet—one of the most stunning holes in Hawaii. See p. 288.

6 The Best Luxury Hotels & Resorts

- **Ritz-Carlton Kapalua** (© 800/ 262-8440 or 808/669-6200; www. ritzcarlton.com): With its great location, style, and loads of hospitality, this is the best Ritz anywhere. Situated on the coast below the picturesque West Maui Mountains, this grand, breezy hotel overlooks the Pacific and Molokai across the channel. The natural setting, on an old coastal pineapple plantation, is the picture of tranquility. The service is legendary; the golf courses are daunting; and the nearby beaches are perfect for snorkeling, diving, and just relaxing. See p. 98.

- **Sheraton Maui** (© 800/782-9488 or 808/661-0031; www. sheaton-maui.com): Offering the best location on Kaanapali Beach, recent renovations, and a great "hassle-free" experience, the Sheraton is our pick of Kaanapali hotels. This is the place for travelers who just want to arrive, have everything ready for them, and get on with their vacation. (Sheraton has a "no-hassle" check-in: The valet takes you and your luggage straight to your room, which means no time wasted standing in line at registration.) See p. 87.

- **Kaanapali Alii** (© 800/642-6284 or 808/661-3330; www. kaanapali-alii.com): The height of luxury, these oceanfront condominium units (right on Kaanapali Beach) combine all the amenities of a luxury hotel (including a 24-hr. front desk) with the convenience of a condominium. One-bedroom units (1,500 sq. ft.) start at $350 for four. The beachside recreation area includes a swimming pool, plus a separate children's pool, whirlpool, gas barbecue grills and picnic areas, exercise rooms, saunas, and tennis courts. See p. 87.

- **Hyatt Regency Maui** (© 800/ 233-1234 or 808/661-1234; www. maui.hyatt.com): Spa-goers will love Hawaii's only oceanfront spa. The 806 rooms of this fantasy resort have undergone $19 million in renovations. Spread out among three towers, the rooms have very comfortable separate sitting areas and private lanais with eye-popping views. This huge place covers some 40 acres; even if you don't stay here, you might want to walk through the expansive tree-filled atrium and the parklike grounds. See p. 90.

- **Four Seasons Resort Maui at Wailea** (© **800/334 MAUI [6284]** or 808/874-8000; www. fshr.com): This is the ultimate beach hotel for latter-day royals, offering excellent cuisine, spacious rooms, gracious service, and Wailea Beach—one of Maui's best gold-sand beaches—right outside the front door. Every room has at least a partial ocean view from a private lanai. The luxury suites are as big as some Honolulu condos, and full of marble and deluxe appointments. See p. 107.

- **Grand Wailea Resort Hotel & Spa** (© **800/888-6100** or 808/ 875-1234; www.grandwailea.com): There's nothing subtle or under-stated about it, but many travelers adore this over-the-top fantasy resort. It has 10,000 tropical plants in the lobby; a fabulous pool with slides, waterfalls, and rapids; Hawaii's largest spa; plush oceanview rooms; and a superb location on a gorgeous stretch of beach. See p. 107.

- **The Fairmont Kea Lani Maui** (© **800/659-4100** or 808/875-4100; www.kealani.com): This all-suite luxury hotel in Wailea has 840-square-foot suites with kitchenette, microwave, and cof-feemaker, living room with high-tech media center and pullout sofa bed (great if you have the kids in tow), a marble wet bar, and a spacious bedroom. The oversize marble bathrooms have separate showers big enough for a party. Your own large lanai off the bedroom and living room over-looks the pools and lawns, with a view that sweeps right down to the white-sand beach. See p. 106.

- **Hotel Hana-Maui** (© **800/321-HANA** or 808/248-8211; www. hotelhanamaui.com): Picture Shangri-La, Hawaiian-style: 66 acres rolling down to the sea in a remote Hawaiian village, with a wellness center, two pools, and access to one of the best beaches in Hana. This is the atmosphere, the landscape, the culture of old Hawaii set in the latest accommo-dations of the 21st century, where every unit is excellent. A white-sand beach just a 5-minute shuttle away, top-notch wellness center, and numerous activities (horse-back riding, mountain bicycles, tennis, pitch and putt golf) all add up to make this one of the top resorts in the state. See p. 117.

7 The Best Moderately Priced Accommodations

- **Napili Kai Beach Resort** (© **800/367-5030** or 808/669-6271; www.napilikai.com): Nes-tled in its own private white-sand cove, this property gives you a chance to experience what Maui was like 30 years ago. Composed of a range of units (from hotel rooms to 2-bedroom suites), Napili Kai has all the comforts of home (including full kitchens), plus a restaurant on the property, and it's within walking distance to Kapalua's top restaurants, shops, golf, and tennis. Prices start at $190. See p. 92.

- **Kahana Sunset** (© **800/669-1488** or 808/669-8011; www. kahanasunset.com): This is a great choice for families, featuring a series of wooden condo units stair-stepping down the side of a hill to a postcard-perfect white-sand beach. The units feature full kitchens, washers/dryers, large lanais with terrific views, and sleeper sofas (starting at $130 for 4). See p. 94.

- **Lahaina Inn** (© **800/669-3444** or 808/661-0577; www.lahaina inn.com): If the romance of historic Lahaina catches your fancy, a stay here will really complete the experience. Built in 1938 as a general store, it has been restored as a charming, Victorian antique–filled inn right in the heart of town, with rooms as low as $109. Downstairs you'll find one of Hawaii's most popular storefront bistros, David Paul's Lahaina Grill. See p. 84.

- **Plantation Inn** (© **800/433-6815** or 808/667-9225; www.theplantationinn.com): Attention romantic couples: You need look no further. This charming Lahaina hotel looks like it's been here 100 years or more, but looks can be deceiving. The Victorian-style inn is actually of 1990s vintage—an artful deception. The rooms are romantic to the max, tastefully done with period furniture, hardwood floors, stained glass, ceiling fans, and four-poster canopy beds. The rooms wrap around the large pool and deck; also on site area spa and an elegant pavilion lounge, where breakfast is served, all for $152 up. See p. 84.

- **Maui Coast Hotel** (© **800/895-MAUI** or 808/874-6284; www.mauicoasthotel.com): This off-beach midrise is one of the only moderately priced hotels in Kihei (though the Kihei area has lots of affordable condo complexes). One chief advantage of this hotel is its location: It's about a block from Kamaole Beach Park I, with plenty of bars, restaurants, and shopping within walking distance (Jamison's Grill & Bar is next door). A $2.5 million renovation

of all the furniture and soft goods in the rooms plus the remodeled public areas (lobby, pool, restaurant, bar) has made this moderate hotel into a luxury resort with a reasonable price tag (starting at $155). See p. 100.

- **Punahoa Beach Apartments** (© **800/564-4380** or 808/879-2720; www.punahoa.com): This small ocean-side Kihei condo complex is hidden on a quiet side street; the grassy lawn out front rolls about 50 feet down to the beach. You'll find great snorkeling just offshore and a popular surfing spot next door, with shopping and restaurants all within walking distance. Every well-decorated unit features a lanai with fabulous ocean views, from $94. See p. 105.

- **Paniolo Hale** (Molokai; © **800/367-2984** or 808/552-2731; www.paniolohaleresort.com): This is far and away Molokai's most charming lodging, and probably its best value. The two-story Old Hawaii ranch-house design is airy and homey, with oak floors and walls of folding-glass doors that open to huge screened verandas. The whole place overlooks the Kaluakoi Golf Course, a green barrier that separates these condos (which start at $95 for 2) from the rest of Kaluakoi Resort. See p. 246.

- **Hotel Lanai** (Lanai; © **800/795-7211** or 808/565-7211; www.onlanai.com): Lanai's only budget lodging is a simple, down-home, plantation-era relic that has recently been Laura Ashley–ized. The Hotel Lanai is homey, funky, and fun—and, best of all, a real bargain (starting at $98 for 2) compared to its ritzy neighbors. See p. 279.

8 The Best Bed & Breakfasts

- **Old Wailuku Inn at Ulupono** (© 800/305-4899 or 808/244-5897; www.mauiinn.com): Located in historic Wailuku, the most charming town in central Maui, this restored 1924 former plantation manager's home is the place to stay if you're looking for a night in the old Hawaii of the 1920s. The guest rooms are wide and spacious, with exotic ohia-wood floors and traditional Hawaiian quilts, starting at $120. The morning meal is a full gourmet breakfast served on the enclosed back lanai, or on a tray delivered to your room if you prefer. See p. 81.
- **Guest House** (© 800/621-8942 or 808/661-8085; www.mauiguesthouse.com): This is one of the great bed-and-breakfast deals in Lahaina: a charming inn offering more amenities than the expensive Kaanapali hotels just down the road. The spacious home features floor-to-ceiling windows, parquet floors, and a large swimming pool. Guest rooms have quiet lanais and romantic hot tubs. Breakfasts are a gourmet affair. All units are $129 double. See p. 86.
- **Two Mermaids on the Sunnyside of Maui B&B** (© 800/262-9912 or 808/985-7488; www.bestbnb.com): Two avid scuba divers are the hosts at this very friendly Kihei B&B, professionally decorated in brilliant, tropical colors, complete with hand-painted art of the island (above and below the water) in a quiet neighborhood just a short 10-minute walk from the beach. Comfy rooms from $95 with breakfast. See p. 105.
- **What a Wonderful World B&B** (© 800/943-5804 or 808/879-9103; http://thesupersites.com/wonderfulworld): Another one of Kihei's best B&Bs offers a great central location in town—just a half mile to Kamaole II Beach Park, 5 minutes from Wailea golf courses, and convenient to shopping and restaurants. All rooms boast cooking facilities and private entrances, bathrooms, and phones. A family style breakfast (eggs Benedict, Alaskan waffles, skillet eggs with mushroom sauce, fruit blintzes) is served on the lanai, which has views of white-sand beaches, the West Maui Mountains, and Haleakala. From $75. See p. 106.
- **Nona Lani Cottages** (© 800/733-2688 or 808/879-2497; www.nonalanicottages.com): Picture this: a grassy expanse dotted with eight cottages tucked among palm, fruit, and sweet-smelling flower trees, right across the street from a white-sand beach. This is one of the great hidden deals in Kihei. The cottages are tiny but contain everything you'll need. At $75 a night, this is a deal. See p. 104.
- **Wild Ginger** (© 800/262-9912 or 808/985-7488; www.bestbnb.com): This cozy, romantic intimate cottage, hidden in Miliko Gulch, just outside of Haliimaile, overlooking a stream with a waterfall, bamboo, sweet-smelling ginger and banana trees, is perfect for honeymooners, lovers, and fans of Hawaiian art. The moment you step into this 400-square-foot artistically decorated Hawaiian cottage (with additional 156-sq.-ft. screened deck) you will be delighted at the carefully placed memorabilia throughout. Priced at $125 double. See p. 115.
- **Olinda Country Cottages & Inn** (© 800/932-3435 or 808/572-1453; www.mauibnbcottages.com): Breathe the crisp, clean air of Olinda at this charming B&B,

located on an 8½-acre protea farm on the slopes of Haleakala and surrounded by 35,000 acres of ranch lands (with miles of great hiking). The 5,000-square-foot Tudor mansion, refurbished and outfitted with priceless antiques, has large windows with incredible panoramic views of all of Maui. In addition to the guest rooms in the country house, two cozy cottages and a romantic country suite are also available. From $140 with breakfast. See p. 110.

- **Malu Manu** (© 888/878-6161 or 808/878-6111; www.maui.net/~alive/): Tucked into the side of Haleakala Volcano at 4,000 feet, in the Kula region, is this old Hawaiian estate. It offers a single-room cabin with a full kitchen, fireplace, and antiques for just $135. Built as a writer's retreat in the early 1900s, it's one of the most romantic places to stay on Maui, with a panoramic view of the entire island from the front door. See p. 112.

- **Kili's Cottage** (© 800/262-9912 or 808/985-7488; www.bestbnb.com): If you're looking for a quiet getaway in the cool upcountry elevation of Kula, this sweet three-bedroom cottage with a large lanai, situated on 2 acres, is the perfect place. Not only is the price right for families (just $105), but the amenities are numerous: full kitchen, gas barbecue, washer/dryer, views, even toys for the kids. See p. 113.

- **Ekena** (© 808/248-7047; www.ekenamaui.com): Situated on 8½ acres in the hills above Hana, this Hawaiian-style wooden pole house, with 360-degree views of the coastline, the ocean, and Hana's verdant rain forest, is perfect for those in search of a quiet, peaceful vacation. Inside, the elegantly furnished home features floor-to-ceiling sliding-glass doors

and a fully equipped kitchen (starting at $185 for 2); outside, hiking trails into the rainforest start right on the property. Beaches, waterfalls, and pools are mere minutes away. See p. 118.

- **Hamoa Bay Bungalow** (© 808/248-7884; www.hamoabay.com): This enchanting retreat sits on 4 verdant acres within walking distance of Hamoa Beach, just outside Hana. The romantic, 600-square-foot, Balinese-style cottage has a full kitchen and hot tub. This very private place is perfect for honeymooners—even the tropical breakfast of fruit, yogurt, and muffins is left out daily to eat at your leisure. The price? Just $195. See p. 118.

- **Heavenly Hana Inn** (© 808/248-8442; www.heavenlyhanainn.com): Just a stone's throw from the center of Hana is this tiny Japanese-style inn, where no attention to detail has been spared. Flowers are everywhere, ceiling fans keep the rooms cool, and the delicious gourmet breakfast is served in a setting filled with art. The 2 acres of grounds are impeccable, with tiny bridges over a meandering stream and Japanese gardens. Rooms start at $185. See p. 119.

- **Aloha Beach House** (© 888/828-1008 or 808/828-1100; www.molokaivacation.com): Nestled on the lush East End of Molokai lies this Hawaiian-style beach house sitting right on the white-sand beach of Waialua. Perfect for families, this impeccably decorated two-bedroom, 1,600-square-foot beach house has a huge open living/dining/kitchen area that opens out to an old-fashioned porch for meals or just sitting in the comfy chairs and watching the clouds roll by. Just $180 for up to five. See p. 247.

9 The Best Resort Spas

- **The Health Centre at the Four Seasons Resort Maui** (© **800/334-MAUI [6284]** or 808/874-8000; www.fshr.com): Imagine the sounds of the waves rolling on Wailea Beach as you are soothingly massaged in the privacy of your cabana, tucked into the beachside foliage. This is the place to come to be absolutely spoiled. Yes, there's an excellent workout area and tons of great classes, but their specialty is hedonistic indulgence. See p. 107 for a review of the Four Seasons.

- **Spa Grande at the Grand Wailea Resort** (© **800/888-6100** or 808/875-1234; www.grandwailea.com): This is Hawaii's biggest spa, at 50,000 square feet, with 40 treatment rooms. The spa incorporates the best of the Old World (romantic ceiling murals, larger-than-life Roman-style sculptures, mammoth Greek columns, huge European tubs), the finest Eastern traditions (a full Japanese-style traditional bath and various exotic treatments from India), and the lure of the islands (tropical foliage, ancient Hawaiian treatments, and island products). This spa has everything from a top fitness center to a menu of classes and is constantly on the cutting edge of the latest trends. See p. 107 for a review of Grand Wailea Resort.

- **Spa Kea Lani at The Fairmont Kea Lani Maui** (© **800/659-4100** or 808/875-4100; www.kealani.com): This intimate, Art Deco boutique spa (just a little over 5,000 sq. ft., with 9 treatment rooms), which opened in 1999, is the place for personal and private attention. The fitness center next door is open 24 hours (a rarity in Hawaiian resorts) with a personal trainer on duty some 14 hours a day. See p. 106 for a review of the Fairmont Kea Lani Maui.

- **Spa Moana at the Hyatt Regency Maui Resort & Spa** (© **800/233-1234** or 808/661-1234; www.maui.hyatt.com): The island's first oceanfront spa, a 9,000-square-foot facility, opened recently with a $3.5 million price tag. The new spa offers an open-air exercise lanai, wet treatment rooms, massage rooms, a relaxation lounge, sauna and steam rooms, a Roman pool illuminated by overhead skylights, and a duet treatment suite for couples. See p. 90 for a review of the Hyatt Regency Maui.

- **Spa at Ritz-Carlton Kapalua** (© **800/262-8440** or 808/669-6200; www.ritzcarlton.com): Book a massage on the beach. The spa itself is welcoming and wonderful, but there is nothing like smelling the salt in the air and feeling the gentle caressing of the wind in your hair while experiencing a true Hawaiian massage. See p. 98 for a review of the Ritz-Carlton Kapalua.

10 The Best Restaurants

- **Mañana Garage** (© **808/873-0220**): It's great fun dining here, and the food is fantastic, too. Tuck into fabulous *arepas* (cornmeal-cheese griddle cakes with smoked salmon), fried green tomatoes, excellent ceviche, and a host of new flavors in an ambience of spirited color and industrial edge. You'll dine among vertical garage doors, hubcap table bases, cobalt walls, and chrome accents, with *Buena Vista Social Club* on the sound system and very hip servers who will bring you the best desserts in this neck of the woods—Kahului, of all

Pampering in Paradise

Hawaii's spas have raised the art of relaxation and healing to a new level. The traditional Greco-Roman–style spas, with lots of marble and big tubs in closed rooms, have evolved into airy, open facilities that embrace the tropics. Spa goers in Hawaii are looking for a sense of place, seeped in the culture. They want to hear the sound of the ocean, smell the salt air, and feel the caress of the warm breeze. They want to experience Hawaiian products and traditional treatments they can get only in the islands.

The spas of Hawaii, once nearly exclusively patronized by women, are now attracting more male clients. There are special massages for children and pregnant women, and some spas have created programs to nurture and relax brides on their big day.

Today's spas offer a wide diversity of treatments. There is no longer plain, ordinary massage, but Hawaiian lomilomi, Swedish, aromatherapy (with sweet-smelling oils), craniosacral (massaging the head), shiatsu (no oil, just deep thumb pressure on acupuncture points), Thai (another oilless massage involving stretching), and hot stone (with heated, and sometimes cold, rocks). There are even side-by-side massages for couples. The truly decadent might even try a duo massage—not one, but *two* massage therapists working on you at once.

Massages are just the beginning. Body treatments, for the entire body or for just the face, involve a variety of herbal wraps, masks, or scrubs using a range of ingredients from seaweed to salt to mud, with or without accompanying aromatherapy, lights, and music.

After you have been rubbed and scrubbed, most spas offer an array of water treatments—a sort of hydromassage in a tub with jets and an assortment of colored crystals, oils, and scents.

Those are just the traditional treatments. Most spas also offer a range of alternative healthcare like acupuncture, chiropractic, and other exotic treatments like ayurvedic and siddha from India or reiki from Japan. Many places offer specialized, cutting-edge treatments, like the Grand Wailea Resort's full-spectrum color-light therapy pod (based on NASA's work with astronauts).

Once your body has been pampered, spas also offer a range of fitness facilities (weight-training equipment, racquetball, tennis, golf, and so on) and classes (yoga, aerobics, step, spinning, stretch, tai chi, kickboxing, aquacize, and so on). Several even offer adventure fitness packages (from bicycling to snorkeling). For the nonadventurous, most spas have salons dedicated to hair and nail care and makeup.

If all this sounds a bit overwhelming, not to worry; all the spas in Hawaii have individual consultants who will help you design an appropriate treatment program to fit your individual needs.

Of course, all this pampering doesn't come cheap. Massages are generally $95 to $130 for 50 minutes and $145 to $180 for 80 minutes; body treatments are in the $120 to $165 range; and alternative healthcare treatments can be as high as $150 to $220. But you may think it's worth the expense to banish your tension and stress.

places! The chef, Tom Lelli, came here from Haliimaile General Store. See p. 123.

- **A Saigon Cafe** (© 808/243-9560): Jennifer Nguyen's unmarked dining room in an odd corner of Wailuku is always packed, a tribute to her clean, crisp Vietnamese cuisine—and the Maui grapevine. Grab a round of rice paper and wrap your own Vietnamese "burrito" of tofu, noodles, and vegetables. Lemongrass shrimp, curries, and Nhung Dam, the Vietnamese version of fondue, are among the solid hits, but the spicy, crisped Dungeness crab is tops. See p. 125.

- **Café O'Lei** (© 808/244-6816): There are now five of these eateries pumping out the delicious, creative cuisine of Dana Pastula, who managed fancy restaurants on Lanai and in Wailea before opening her own. She started in Makawao and now has branches in Wailuku, Makawao, Maalaea, and Lahaina. For reasonably priced, interesting, and memorable meals, don't miss the chance to eat at the O'Leis. See p. 125.

- **David Paul's Lahaina Grill** (© 808/667-5117): Tirelessly popular and universally appreciated for its high quality, David Paul's is still most folks' favorite Maui eatery—even without David Paul. No one seems to tire of the kalua duck he turned into a Maui institution, or the Kona coffee–roasted rack of lamb, or the much-imitated tequila shrimp. The menu changes often, but thank goodness the room doesn't; its pressed-tin ceilings and 1890s decor continue to intrigue. See p. 128.

- **Gerard's** (© 808/661-8939): Proving that French is fabulous, particularly in the land of sushi and sashimi, Gerard Reversade is the Gallic gastronome who delivers ecstasy with every bite. From the rack of lamb to the spinach salad and oyster mushrooms in puff pastry, you will never forget his cooking. Like Piaf on the sound system, his food has integrity and excellence. The fairy lights on the veranda in the balmy outdoor Lahaina setting are the icing on the gâteau. See p. 128.

- **Swan Court** (© 808/661-1234): For a romantic setting with candlelight, a Japanese garden, and swans gliding by serenely, this is the ticket. It isn't often that we find a fine dining experience in a hotel that is terrific, but this is the exception to the rule. In addition to excellent seafood, impeccable service, and a dreamy ocean view, Swan Court is a wonderful change of pace, a year-round Valentine dinner where you can dress up and impress your date. See p. 133.

- **Roy's Kahana Bar & Grill/Roy's Nicolina Restaurant** (© 808/669-6999; www.roysrestaurant.com): These sibling restaurants are next door to each other, offer the same menu, and are busy, busy, busy. They bustle with young, hip servers impeccably trained to deliver blackened ahi or perfectly seared lemongrass *shutome* (broadbill swordfish) hot to your table, in rooms that sizzle with cross-cultural tastings. See p. 136.

- **The Bay Club** (© 808/669-8008): The first thing you notice is the remarkable view: The sun sets behind the rolling surf of Kapalua Bay, with the island of Molokai in the background. The view alone would be worth eating here, but luckily, the food, especially the seafood, promises a memorable dining experience. This intimate restaurant (with a piano bar at one end) features such culinary masterpieces as steamed Kona lobster in banana leaf; ahi and cured salmon sashimi; macadamia-nut-crusted mahimahi with papaya pineapple salsa and passion fruit salsa; and Hawaiian seafood bouillabaisse. Not to be missed. See p. 137.

- **Sansei Seafood Restaurant** (© 808/669-6286): Furiously fusion and relentlessly popular, Sansei serves sushi, and then some: hand rolls warm and cold, udon and ramen, and the signature Asian rock-shrimp cake with the oh-so-complex lime chile butter and cilantro pesto. This Kapalua choice is flavor central—simplicity is not the strong suit, so be prepared for some busy tasting. Another branch has opened in Kihei. See p. 138.

- **Plantation House Restaurant** (© 808/669-6299): There are teak tables, a fireplace, open sides, mountain and ocean views, and chef Alex Stanislaw's love for Mediterranean flavors and preparations. It's a friendly, comfortable restaurant with great food from breakfast to dinner, from sublime eggs Mediterranean to polenta, crab cakes, several preparations of fish, pork tenderloin, filet mignon, and other delights at dinner. The ambience is superb. See p. 138.

- **Joe's Bar & Grill** (© 808/875-7767; www.joesbarandgrill.com): The 360-degree view spans the Wailea golf course, tennis courts, ocean, and Haleakala—a worthy setting for Beverly Gannon's style of American home cooking with a regional twist (also see Haliimaile General Store below). The hearty staples include excellent mashed potatoes, lobster, fresh fish, and filet mignon, but the meatloaf (a whole loaf, like Mom used to make) seems to upstage them all. See p. 142.

- **Moanai Bakery & Café** (© 808/579-9999): In the unlikely location of Paia, the Moanai gets high marks for its stylish concrete floors, high ceilings, booths and cafe tables, and fabulous food. Don Ritchey, formerly a chef at Haliimaile General Store, has created the perfect Paia eatery, a casual bakery-cafe that highlights his stellar skills. It may not look like much from the outside, but do not miss this innovative eatery serving breakfast, lunch, and dinner and live entertainment at night. See p. 148.

- **Haliimaile General Store** (© 808/572-2666): More than a decade later, Bev Gannon, one of the 12 original Hawaii Regional Cuisine chefs, is still going strong at her foodie haven in the pineapple fields. You'll dine at tables set on old wood floors under high ceilings. The food, a blend of eclectic American with ethnic touches, bridges Hawaii with Gannon's Texas roots and puts an innovative spin on Hawaii Regional Cuisine. Examples include sashimi napoleon and the house salad, island greens with mandarin oranges, onions, toasted walnuts, and blue-cheese crumble. See p. 144.

- **Casanova Italian Restaurant** (© 808/572-0220): Yes, we still love Casanova in upcountry Makawao, and for more than one reason: garlic spinach topped with Parmesan and pine nuts, polenta with radicchio, tiramisu, and the spaghetti fradiavolo. This is pasta heaven and the center of nightlife on this half of the island. See p. 146.

- **Henry Clay's Rotisserie** (Hotel Lanai, Lanai City; © 808/565-7211): Henry Clay Richardson, a New Orleans native, has made some welcome changes to Lanai's dining landscape with his rustic inn in the middle of Lanai City.

Moments A Night to Remember: Maui's Top Luau

The **Old Lahaina Luau** (© **800/248-5828** or **808/667-1998**) has always been at the leading edge of cultural entertainment in Hawaii; it's one-third entertainment, one-third good food, and one-third ambience. At its new and more spacious location at the northern end of Lahaina, there's more of everything, particularly those qualities we've come to love: authenticity, intimacy, hospitality, cultural integrity, and sheer romantic beauty. This is Maui's top luau and one of our two favorites in the state. With the expansion of the luau in its 1-acre site just ocean-side of the Lahaina Cannery, what was peerless has become even better.

Local craftspeople display their wares only a few feet from the ocean. Seating is provided on lauhala mats for those wishing to dine as the traditional Hawaiians did, but there are tables for everyone else. Staging has been thoughtfully planned, so that the audience faces the ocean as well as the show; hidden underground dressing rooms allow the dancers dramatic entrances and exits. Thatched buildings, amphitheater seating, and the backdrop of a Lahaina sunset are among the event's unforgettable features.

The luau begins at sunset and features Tahitian and Hawaiian entertainment, including ancient hula, hula from the missionary era, modern hula, and an intelligent narrative on the dance's rocky course of survival into modern times. The sophisticated entertainment is both educational *and* riveting, even for jaded locals, and the top-quality food is as much Pacific Rim as authentically Hawaiian, served from an open-air thatched structure. No watered-down mai tais, either—these are the real thing. You won't soon forget the genuine hospitality and enthusiasm of the staff. The cost is $79 for adults, $49 for children 12 and under, plus tax.

The menu focuses on French country fare: fresh meats, seafood, and local produce in assertive preparations. The decor consists of plates on the pine-paneled walls, chintz curtains, peach table-cloths and hunter-green napkins, and a roaring fireplace. See p. 281.

- **Pele's Other Garden** (© **808/565-9628**): You do not have to spend a fortune at the high-priced eateries at the two resorts on Lanai; this charming bistro in the heart of Lanai City has a full-scale New York deli (yummy pizzas), and you can also get box lunches and picnic baskets to go. Dinner is now served on china, not paper, with tablecloths under sconces—a real dining room! See p. 283.

11 The Best Shops & Galleries

- **Summerhouse** (© **808/871-1320**): Bright and sassy tropical wear, and the jewelry and accessories to go with it, are a cut above at Kahului's Summerhouse. T-shirts are tailored and in day-to-evening colors, while dresses are good for either the office or a night out. See p. 221.
- **Bailey House Gift Shop** (© **808/244-3326**): You can travel Hawaii and peruse its past with the

assemblage of made-in-Hawaii items at this museum gift shop in Wailuku. Tropical preserves, Hawaiian music, pareus, prints by esteemed Hawaiian artists, cookbooks, hatbands, and magnificent wood bowls reflect a discerning standard of selection. Unequaled for Hawaiian treasures on Maui. See p. 221.

- **Brown-Kobayashi** (© 808/242-0804): At this quiet, tasteful, and elegant Asian shop in Wailuku, the selection of antiques and collectibles changes constantly but reflects an unwavering sense of gracious living. There are old and new European and Hawaiian objects, from koa furniture (which disappears fast) to lacquerware, Bakelite jewelry, Peking glass beads, and a few priceless pieces of antique ivory. Every square inch is a treasure trove. See p. 222.

- **Sig Zane Designs** (© 808/249-8997): This Hilo icon didn't skip a beat in winning the hearts of Maui residents when he moved to Wailuku. It's just like the time he moved to the Hilo Bayfront from his first, more obscure location; his presence brought an infusion of energy to the area and helped revitalize the entire neighborhood. Located on Wailuku's Market Street, his new shop of aloha wear and Hawaiian lifestyle treasures is a boon to historic Wailuku. See p. 222.

- **Hui No'eau Visual Arts Center** (© 808/572-6560): Half the experience is the center itself, one of Maui's historic treasures: a strikingly designed 1917 *kamaaina* (native-born or old-timer) estate on 9 acres in Makawao; two of Maui's largest hybrid Cook and Norfolk pines; and an art center with classes, exhibitions, and demonstrations. The gift shop is as memorable as the rest of it. You'll find one-of-a-kind works by local artists, from prints to jewelry and pottery. See "Upcountry Maui" in chapter 8.

- **Village Galleries** (© 808/661-4402 in Lahaina, or 808/669-1800 in Kapalua): Maui's oldest galleries have maintained high standards and the respect of a public that is increasingly impatient with clichéd island art. On exhibit are the finest contemporary Maui artists in all media, with a discerning selection of handcrafted jewelry. In Lahaina, the new contemporary gallery has a larger selection of jewelry, ceramics, glass, and gift items, as well as paintings and prints. See p. 225 and p. 227.

- **Viewpoints Gallery** (© 808/572-5979): We love this airy, well-designed Makawao gallery and its helpful staff, which complement the fine Maui art: paintings, sculpture, jewelry, prints, woods, and glass. This is Maui's only fine-arts cooperative, showcasing the work of dozens of local artists. See p. 231.

- **Hana Coast Gallery** (© 808/248-8636): This gallery is one main reason to go to Hana: It's an esthetic and cultural experience that informs as it enlightens. Tucked away in the posh hideaway hotel, the gallery is known for its high level of curatorship and commitment to the cultural art of Hawaii. The 3,000-square-foot gallery is devoted entirely to Hawaiian artists. Dozens of well-established local artists display their sculptures, paintings, prints, feather work, stonework, and carvings in displays that are so natural they could well exist in someone's home. The award-winning gallery has won accolades from the top travel and arts magazines in the country and has steered clear of trendiness and unfortunate tastes. See p. 232.

2

Planning Your Trip to Maui

Maui has so many places to explore, things to do, sights to see—where do you start? That's where we come in. In the pages that follow, we've compiled everything you need to know to plan your ideal trip to Maui: information on airlines, seasons, a calendar of events, how to make camping reservations, and much more (even how to tie the knot).

1 The Island in Brief

CENTRAL MAUI

This flat, often windy corridor between Maui's two volcanoes is where you'll most likely arrive—it's the site of the main airport. It's also home to the majority of the island's population, the heart of the business community, and the local government (courts, cops, and county/state government agencies). You'll find good shopping and dining bargains here, but very little in the way of accommodations.

KAHULUI This is "Dream City," home to thousands of former sugar cane workers who dreamed of owning their own homes away from the plantations. A couple of small hotels located just 2 miles from the airport are convenient for 1-night stays if you have a late arrival or early departure, but this is not a place to spend your vacation.

WAILUKU With its faded wooden storefronts, old plantation homes, and shops straight out of the 1940s, Wailuku is like a time capsule. Although most people race through on their way to see the natural beauty of **Iao Valley** ☆, this quaint little town is worth a brief visit, if only to see a real place where real people actually appear to be working at something other than a suntan. This is the county seat, so you'll see men and women in suits on important missions in the tropical heat. Beaches surrounding Wailuku are not great for swimming, but the old town has a spectacular view of Haleakala, a couple of hostels and an excellent historic B&B, great budget restaurants, a tofu factory, some interesting bungalow architecture, a Frank Lloyd Wright building on the outskirts of town, and the always-endearing Bailey House Museum.

WEST MAUI

This is the fabled Maui you see on postcards. Jagged peaks, green valleys, a wilderness full of native species—the majestic West Maui Mountains are the epitome of earthly paradise. The beaches here are some of the islands' best. And it's no secret: This stretch of coastline along Maui's "forehead," from Kapalua to the historic port of Lahaina, is the island's most bustling resort area (with South Maui close behind). Expect a few mainland-style traffic jams.

If you want to book into a resort or condo on this coast, first consider which community you'd like to make your base. Starting at the southern end of West Maui and moving northward, the coastal communities are as listed below.

LAHAINA ☆ This old whaling seaport teems with restaurants, T-shirt shops, and a gallery on nearly every block, but there's still lots of real history to be found amid the tourist development. This vintage village is a tame version of its former self, when whalers swaggered ashore in search of women and grog. The town is a great base for visitors: A few old hotels (like the newly restored 1901 Pioneer Inn on the harbor), quaint B&Bs, and a handful of oceanfront condos offer a variety of choices, most within walking distance to the beach as well as town. This is the place to stay if you want to be in the center of things—oodles of restaurants, shops, and nightlife—but note that the town is rather congested and doesn't have enough parking.

KAANAPALI ★★ Farther north along the West Maui coast is Hawaii's first master-planned resort. Pricey midrise hotels, which line nearly 3 miles of lovely gold-sand beach, are linked by a landscaped parkway and separated by a jungle of plants. Golf greens wrap around the slope between beachfront and hillside properties. **Whalers Village** (a seaside mall with such fancy names as Tiffany and Louis Vuitton, plus the best little whale museum in Hawaii) and other restaurants are easy to reach on foot along the waterfront walkway or via resort shuttle, which also serves the small West Maui airport just to the north. Shuttles also go to Lahaina, 3 miles to the south, for shopping, dining, entertainment, and boat tours. Kaanapali is popular with convention groups and families—especially those with teenagers, who will like all the action.

FROM HONOKOWAI TO NAPILI In the building binge of the 1970s, condominiums sprouted along this gorgeous coastline like mushrooms after a rain. Today, these older oceanside units offer excellent bargains for astute travelers. The great location—along sandy beaches, within minutes of both the Kapalua and the Kaanapali

resort areas, and close to the goings-on in Lahaina town—makes this area a great place to stay for value-conscious travelers. It feels more peaceful and residential than either Kaanapali or Lahaina.

In **Honokowai** and **Mahinahina,** you'll find mostly older units that tend to be cheaper; there's not much shopping here aside from convenience stores, but you'll have easy access to the shops and restaurants of Kaanapali.

Kahana is a little more upscale than Honokowai and Mahinahina. Most of the condos here are big high-rise types, built more recently than those immediately to the south. You'll find a nice selection of shops and restaurants in the area, and Kapalua–West Maui Airport is nearby.

Napili is a much-sought-after area for condo seekers: It's quiet; has great beaches, restaurants, and shops; and is close to Kapalua. Units are generally more expensive here (although we've found a few hidden gems at affordable prices; see the Napili Bay entry on p. 96).

KAPALUA ★ North beyond Kaanapali and the shopping centers of Napili and Kahana, the road starts to climb, and the vista opens up to fields of silver-green pineapple and manicured golf fairways. Turn down the country lane of Pacific pines toward the sea, and you could only be in Kapalua. It's the very exclusive domain of two gracious and expensive hotels, set on one of Hawaii's best gold-sand beaches, next to two bays that are marine-life preserves (with fabulous surfing in winter).

Even if you don't stay here, you're welcome to come and enjoy Kapalua. Both of the fancy hotels provide public parking and beach access. The resort champions innovative environmental programs; it also has an art school, a golf school, three golf courses, historic features, a collection of swanky condos and homes (many available for vacation rental at astronomical prices), and wide-open spaces that include a rainforest preserve—all open to the general public. Kapalua is a great place to stay put. However, if you plan to "tour" Maui, know that it's a long drive from here to get to many of the island's highlights; you might want to consider a more central place to stay, because even Lahaina is a 15-minute drive away.

SOUTH MAUI

This is the hottest, sunniest, driest coastline on Maui, and the most popular one for sun worshippers—Arizona by the sea. Rain rarely falls, and temperatures stick around 85°F (29°C) year-round. On former scrubland from Maalaea to Makena, where cacti once grew wild and cows grazed, are now four distinct areas—Maalaea, Kihei, Wailea, and Makena—and a surprising amount of traffic.

MAALAEA If the western part of Maui is a head, Maalaea is just under the chin. This windy oceanfront village centers around the small boat harbor (with a general store, a couple of restaurants, and a huge new mall) and the **Maui Ocean Center** ✦, an aquarium/ocean complex. This quaint region offers several condominium units to choose from, but visitors staying here should be aware that it is almost always very windy (all the wind from the Pacific is funneled between the West Maui Mountains and Haleakala, coming out in Maalaea).

KIHEI Kihei is less a proper town than a nearly continuous series of condos and minimalls lining South Kihei Road. This is Maui's best vacation bargain: Budget travelers flock to the eight sandy beaches along this scalloped, condo-packed, 7-mile stretch of coast. Kihei is neither charming nor quaint, but it does offer sunshine, affordability, and convenience. If you want latte in the morning, fine beaches in the afternoon, and Hawaii

Regional Cuisine in the evening, all at budget prices, head to Kihei.

WAILEA ✦ Only 2½ decades ago, this was wall-to-wall scrub kiawe trees, but now Wailea is a manicured oasis of multimillion-dollar resort hotels strung along 2 miles of palm-fringed gold coast. It's like Beverly Hills by the sea, except California never had it so good: warm, clear water full of tropical fish; year-round sunshine and clear blue skies; and hedonistic pleasure palaces on 1,500 acres of black-lava shore. Amazing what a billion dollars can do.

This is the playground of the stretch-limo set. The planned resort development—practically a well-heeled town—has a shopping village, three prized golf courses of its own and three more in close range, and a tennis complex. A growing number of large homes sprawl over the upper hillside (some offering excellent bed-and-breakfast units at reasonable prices). The resorts along this fantasy coast are spectacular, to say the least.

Appealing natural features include the coastal trail, a 3-mile round-trip path along the oceanfront with pleasing views everywhere you look—out to sea and to the neighboring islands, or inland to the broad lawns and gardens of the hotels. The trail's south end borders an extensive garden of native coastal plants, as well as ancient lava-rock house ruins juxtaposed with elegant oceanfront condos. But the chief attractions, of course, are those five outstanding beaches (the best is Wailea).

MAKENA ✦ After passing through well-groomed Wailea, suddenly the road enters raw wilderness. After Wailea's overmanicured development, the thorny landscape is a welcome relief. Although beautiful, this is an end-of-the-road kind of place: It's a long drive from Makena to anywhere on Maui. If you want to tour a lot of the island, you might want to book somewhere else, or resign yourself to spending a lot of time in your car. But if you crave a quiet, relaxing respite, where the biggest trip of the day is from your bed to the gorgeous, pristine beach, Makena is your place.

Beyond Makena you'll discover Haleakala's last lava flow, which ran to the sea in 1790; the bay named for French explorer La Perouse; and a chunky lava trail known as the King's Highway, which leads around Maui's empty south shore past ruins and fish camps. Puu Olai stands like Maui's Diamond Head on the shore, where a sunken crater shelters tropical fish, and empty golden-sand beaches stand at the end of dirt roads.

UPCOUNTRY MAUI

After a few days at the beach, you'll probably take notice of the 10,000-foot mountain in the middle of Maui. The slopes of Haleakala ("House of the Sun") are home to cowboys, farmers, and other country people who wave back as you drive by. They're all up here enjoying the crisp air, emerald pastures, eucalyptus, and flower farms of this tropical Olympus—there's even a misty California redwood grove. You can see 1,000 tropical sunsets reflected in the windows of houses old and new, strung along a road that runs like a loose hound from Makawao, an old paniolo-turned–New Age village, to Kula, where the road leads up to the crater and **Haleakala National Park** ✦✦✦. The rumpled, two-lane blacktop of Highway 37 narrows on the other side of Tedeschi Winery, where wine grapes and wild elk flourish on the Ulupalakua Ranch, the biggest on Maui. A stay upcountry is usually affordable, a chance to commune with nature, and a nice contrast to the sizzling beaches and busy resorts below.

MAKAWAO ✦   Until recently, this small, two-street upcountry town consisted of little more than a post office, gas station, feed store, bakery, and restaurant/bar serving the cowboys

and farmers living in the surrounding community; the hitching posts outside storefronts were really used to tie up horses. As the population of Maui started expanding in the 1970s, a health-food store popped up, followed by boutiques, a chiropractic clinic, and a host of health-conscious restaurants. The result is an eclectic amalgam of old paniolo Hawaii and the baby-boomer trends of transplanted mainlanders. **Hui No'eau Visual Arts Center,** Hawaii's premier arts collective, is definitely worth a peek. The only accommodations here are reasonably priced bed-and-breakfasts, perfect for those who enjoy great views and don't mind slightly chilly nights.

KULA ✦   A feeling of pastoral remoteness prevails in this upcountry community of old flower farms, humble cottages, and new suburban ranch houses with million-dollar views that take in the ocean, isthmus, West Maui Mountains, Lanai, and Kahoolawe off in the distance. At night, the lights run along the gold coast like a string of pearls, from Maalaea to Puu Olai. Kula sits at a cool 3,000 feet, just below the cloud line, and from here, a winding road snakes its way up to Haleakala National Park. Everyone here grows something—Maui onions, carnations, orchids, and proteas, those strange-looking blossoms that look like *Star Trek* props. The local B&Bs cater to guests seeking cool tropical nights, panoramic views, and a rural upland escape. Here you'll find the true peace and quiet that only rural farming country can offer—yet you're still just 30 to 40 minutes away from the beach and an hour's drive from Lahaina.

EAST MAUI

THE ROAD TO HANA ✦✦   When old sugar towns die, they usually fade away in rust and red dirt. Not **Paia.** The tangle of electrical, phone, and cable wires hanging overhead symbolizes the town's ability to adapt to the times—it may look messy, but it works. Here, trendy restaurants, eclectic boutiques, and high-tech windsurf shops stand next door to the ma-and-pa grocery, fish market, and storefronts that have been serving customers since the plantation days. Hippies took over in the 1970s; although their macrobiotic restaurants and old-style artists' co-op have made way for Hawaii Regional Cuisine and galleries featuring the works of renowned international artists, Paia still manages to maintain a pleasant vibe of hippiedom. The town's main attraction, though, is **Hookipa Beach Park,** where the wind that roars through the isthmus of Maui brings windsurfers from around the world, who come to fly over the waves on gossamer wings linked to surfboards.

Ten minutes down the road from Paia and up the hill from the Hana Highway—the connector road to the entire east side of Maui—sits **Haiku.** Once a pineapple-plantation village, complete with cannery (today a shopping complex), Haiku offers vacation rentals and B&Bs in a quiet, pastoral setting: the perfect base for those who want to get off the beaten path and experience a quieter side of Maui, but don't want to feel too removed (the beach is only 10 min. away).

About 15 to 20 minutes past Haiku is the largely unknown community of

Huelo. Every day, thousands of cars whiz by on the road to Hana. But if you take the time to stop, you'll discover a hidden Hawaii, where Mother Nature is still sensual and wild, where ocean waves pummel soaring lava cliffs, and where serenity prevails. Huelo is not for everyone, but if you want the magic of a place still largely untouched by "progress," check into a B&B or vacation rental here.

HANA ★★ Set between an emerald rainforest and the blue Pacific is a village probably best defined by what it lacks: golf courses, shopping malls, and McDonald's. Except for two gas stations and a bank with an ATM, you'll find little of what passes for progress here. Instead, you'll discover fragrant tropical flowers, the sweet taste of backyard bananas and papayas, and the easy calm and unabashed small-town aloha spirit of old Hawaii. What saved "Heavenly" Hana from the inevitable march of progress? The 52-mile **Hana Highway,** which winds around 600 curves and crosses more than 50 one-lane bridges on its way from Kahului. You can go to Hana for the day—it's a 3-hour drive (and a half century away)—but 3 days are better. The tiny town has one hotel, a handful of great B&Bs, and some spectacular vacation rentals (where else can you stay in a tropical cabin in a rainforest?).

2 Visitor Information

For advance information on traveling in Maui, contact the **Maui Visitors Bureau,** 1727 Wili Pa Loop, Wailuku, Maui, HI 96793 (© **800/525-MAUI** or 808/244-3530; fax 808/244-1337; www.visitmaui.com).

The **Kaanapali Beach Resort Association** is at 2530 Kekaa Dr., Suite 1-B, Lahaina, HI 96761 (© **800/245-9229** or 808/661-3271; fax 808/661-9431; www.maui.net/~kbra).

The state agency responsible for tourism is the **Hawaii Visitors and Convention Bureau (HVCB),** Suite 801, Waikiki Business Plaza, 2270 Kalakaua Ave., Honolulu, HI 96815 (© **800/GO-HAWAII** or 808/923-1811; www.gohawaii.com).

If you want information about working and living in Hawaii, contact **The Chamber of Commerce of Hawaii,** 1132 Bishop St., Suite 200, Honolulu, HI 96815 (© **808/545-4300**).

INFORMATION ON MAUI'S PARKS

NATIONAL PARKS   Both Maui and Molokai have one national park each: **Haleakala National Park,** P.O. Box 369, Makawao, HI 96768 (© **808/572-4400;** www.nps.gov/ hale); and **Kalaupapa National Historical Park,** P.O. Box 2222, Kalaupapa, HI 96742 (© **808/567-6802;** www.nps.gov/kala). For more information, see "Hiking & Camping" in chapters 6 and 10.

STATE PARKS   To find out more about state parks on Maui and Molokai, contact the **Hawaii State Department of Land and Natural Resources,** 54 S. High St., Wailuku, HI 96793 (© **808/984-8109;** www. hawaii.gov), which provides information on hiking and camping and will send you free topographic trail maps on request.

COUNTY PARKS   For information on Maui County Parks, contact **Maui County Parks and Recreation,** 1580-C Kaahumanu Ave., Wailuku, HI 96793 (© **808/270-7230;** www.maui mapp.com).

3 Money

ATMS

Hawaii pioneered the use of **ATMs** more than 2 decades ago, and now they're everywhere. You'll find them at most banks, in supermarkets, at Long's Drugs, and in most resorts and shopping centers. **Cirrus** (© **800/424-7787;** www.mastercard.com) and **PLUS** (© **800/843-7587;** www.visa. com) are the two most popular networks; check the back of your ATM card to see which network your bank belongs to (most banks belong to both these days).

TRAVELER'S CHECKS

Traveler's checks are something of an anachronism from the days before the ATM made cash accessible at any time. Traveler's checks used to be the only sound alternative to traveling with dangerously large amounts of cash. They were as reliable as currency, but, unlike cash, could be replaced if lost or stolen.

These days, traveler's checks are less necessary because most cities have 24-hour ATMs that allow you to withdraw small amounts of cash as needed. However, keep in mind that you will likely be charged an ATM withdrawal fee if the bank is not your own, so if you're withdrawing money every day, you might be better off with traveler's checks—provided that you don't mind showing identification every time you want to cash one.

You can get traveler's checks at almost any bank. **American Express** offers denominations of $20, $50, $100, $500, and (for cardholders only) $1,000. You'll pay a service charge ranging from 1% to 4%. You can also get American Express traveler's checks over the phone by calling © **800/221-7282;** Amex gold and platinum cardholders who use this number are exempt from the 1% fee. AAA members can obtain Visa checks without a fee at most AAA offices or by calling © **866/339-3378.**

Visa offers traveler's checks at Citibank locations nationwide, as well as at several other banks. The service charge ranges between 1.5% and 2%; checks come in denominations of $20, $50, $100, $500, and $1,000. Call © **800/732-1322** for information. **MasterCard** also offers traveler's checks. Call © **800/223-9920** for a location near you.

If you choose to carry traveler's checks, be sure to keep a record of their serial numbers separate from your checks in the event that they are stolen or lost. You'll get a refund faster if you know the numbers.

Tips   Dear Visa: I'm Off to Kapalua, Kaanapali & Kahakuloa!

Some credit card companies recommend that you notify them of any impending trip so that they don't become suspicious when the card is used numerous times in an exotic destination and your charges are blocked. Even if you don't call your credit card company in advance, you can always call the card's toll-free emergency number (see "Fast Facts" later in this chapter) if a charge is refused—a good reason to carry the phone number with you. But perhaps the most important lesson is to carry more than one card on your trip; if one card doesn't work for any number of reasons, you'll have a backup card just in case.

Credit cards are accepted all over the island. They're a safe way to carry money and they provide a convenient record of all your expenses. You can also withdraw cash advances from your credit cards at banks or ATMs, provided you know your PIN. If you've forgotten yours, or didn't even know you had one, call the number on the back of your credit card and ask the bank to send it to you. It usually takes 5 to 7 business days, though some banks will provide the number over the phone if you tell them your mother's maiden name or some other personal information. Still, be sure to keep some cash on hand for that rare occasion when a restaurant or small shop doesn't take plastic.

4 When to Go

Most visitors don't come to Maui when the weather's best in the islands; rather, they come when it's at its worst everywhere else. Thus, the **high season**—when prices are up and resorts are booked to capacity—generally runs from mid-December through March or mid-April. The last 2 weeks of December in particular are the prime time for travel to Maui; if you're planning a holiday trip, make your reservations as early as possible, count on holiday crowds, and expect to pay top dollar for accommodations, car rentals, and airfare. Whale-watching season begins in January and continues through the rest of winter, sometimes lasting into May.

The **off seasons,** when the best bargain rates are available, are spring (from mid-Apr to mid-June) and fall (from Sept to mid-Dec)—a paradox, since these are the best seasons in terms of reliably great weather. If you're looking to save money, or if you just want to avoid the crowds, this is the time to visit. Hotel rates tend to be significantly lower during these off seasons. Airfares also tend to be lower—again, sometimes substantially—and good packages and special deals are often available.

Note: If you plan to come to Maui between the last week in April and mid-May, be sure to book your accommodations, interisland air reservations, and car rental in advance. In Japan, the last week of April is called **Golden Week,** because three Japanese holidays take place one after the other; the islands are especially busy with Japanese tourists during this time.

Due to the large number of families traveling in **summer** (June–Aug), you won't get the fantastic bargains of spring and fall. However, you'll still do much better on packages, airfare, and accommodations than you will in the winter months.

THE WEATHER

Because Maui lies at the edge of the tropical zone, it technically has only two seasons, both of them warm. The dry season corresponds to summer, and the rainy season generally runs during the winter from November to March. It rains every day somewhere in the islands at any time of the year, but the rainy season can cause "gray" weather and spoil your tanning opportunities. Fortunately, it seldom rains for more than 3 days straight, and rainy days often just consist of a mix of clouds and sun, with very brief showers.

The **year-round temperature** usually varies no more than 15°F (9°C), but it depends on where you are. Maui is like a ship in that it has leeward and windward sides. The **leeward** sides (the west and south) are usually hot and dry, whereas the **windward** sides (east and north) are generally cooler and moist. If you want arid, sunbaked, desertlike weather, go leeward. If you want lush, often wet, junglelike weather, go windward. Your best bets for total year-round sun are the Kihei-Wailea and Lahaina-Kapalua coasts.

Maui is also full of **microclimates,** thanks to its interior valleys, coastal plains, and mountain peaks. If you travel into the mountains, it can change from summer to winter in a matter of hours, because it's cooler the higher up you go. In other words, if the weather doesn't suit you, go to the other side of the island—or head into the hills.

HOLIDAYS

When Hawaii observes holidays, especially those over a long weekend, travel between the islands increases, interisland airline seats are fully booked, rental cars are at a premium, and hotels and restaurants are busier than usual.

Federal, state, and county government offices are closed on all federal holidays: January 1 (New Year's Day); third Monday in January (Martin Luther King Jr. Day); third Monday in February (Presidents' Day, Washington's Birthday); last Monday in May (Memorial Day); July 4 (Independence Day); first Monday in September (Labor Day); second Monday in October (Columbus Day); November 11 (Veterans' Day); fourth Thursday in November (Thanksgiving Day); and December 25 (Christmas).

State and county offices also are closed on local holidays, including Prince Kuhio Day (Mar 26), honoring the birthday of Hawaii's first delegate to the U.S. Congress; King Kamehameha Day (June 11), a statewide holiday commemorating Kamehameha the Great, who united the islands and ruled from 1795 to 1819; and Admission Day (3rd Fri in Aug), which honors Hawaii's admission as the 50th state in the United States on August 21, 1959.

Other special days celebrated by many people in Hawaii but that do not involve the closing of federal, state, or county offices are Chinese New Year (in Jan or Feb), Girls' Day (Mar 3), Buddha's Birthday (Apr 8), Father Damien's Day (Apr 15), Boys' Day (May 5), Samoan Flag Day (in Aug), Aloha Festivals (in Sept or Oct), and Pearl Harbor Day (Dec 7).

MAUI, MOLOKAI & LANAI CALENDAR OF EVENTS

As with any schedule of upcoming events, the following information is subject to change; always confirm the details before you plan your schedule around an event. For a complete and up-to-date list of events throughout Maui, Molokai, and Lanai, point your browser to **www.visitmaui.com** or **www.calendarmaui.com.**

January

PGA Kapalua Mercedes Championship, Kapalua Resort, Maui. Top PGA golfers compete for $1 million. Call (C) **808/669-2440;** www. kapaluamaui.com. January 5 to January 11, 2004.

Ka Molokai Makahiki, Kaunakakai Town Baseball Park, Mitchell Pauole Center, Kaunakakai, Molokai. Makahiki, a traditional time of peace in ancient Hawaii, is re-created with performances by Hawaiian music groups and hula halau, ancient Hawaiian games, a sporting competition, and Hawaiian crafts and food. A wonderful chance to experience the Hawaii of yesteryear. Call ✆ **800/800-6367** or 808/553-3876; www.molokai-hawaii.com. January 17, 2004.

Chinese New Year. On Maui, Lahaina town rolls out the red carpet for this important event with a traditional lion dance at the historic Wo Hing Temple on Front Street, accompanied by fireworks, food booths, and a host of activities. Call ✆ **888/310-1117** or 808/667-9175 for details. In Wailuku, Chinese New Year is celebrated on Market Street (✆ **808/270-7414** for more info). The year of the monkey starts January 22, 2004.

Hula Bowl Football All-Star Classic, War Memorial Stadium, Maui. An annual all-star football classic featuring America's top college players. Call ✆ **808/871-4141;** www.hulabowlmaui.com; ticket orders are processed beginning April 1 for the next year's game, January 31, 2004.

Senior Skins Tournament, Golf Course, Wailea Golf Courses, Maui. Longtime golfing greats participate in this four-man tournament for $600,000 in prize money. Call ✆ **800/332-1614;** www.seniorskinswailea.com. January 31, 2004.

February

Whalefest Week, Maui. A weeklong celebration of Maui's best-known winter visitors, the humpback whales. Activities include a whale-counting day and other islandwide events like Hawaiian entertainment,

great food by Maui's top restaurants, seminars, art exhibits, sailing, snorkeling and diving tours, and numerous events for children. Call ✆ **808/667-9175** or 808/879-8860. February or March.

March

Art Maui 2004, Kahului, Maui. The 25th annual juried art show of multimedia works by Maui artists. Maui Arts and Cultural Center, ✆ **808/242-7469;** www.MauiArts.org. Mid-March through early April.

Run to the Sun, Paia to Haleakala, Maui. The world's top ultramarathoners make the journey from sea level to the top of 10,000-foot Haleakala, some 37 miles. Call ✆ **808/891-2516** or www.virr.com. March 21, 2004.

East Maui Taro Festival, Hana, Maui. Here's your chance to taste taro in its many different preparations, from poi to chips. Also on hand are Hawaiian exhibits, demonstrations, and food booths. Call ✆ **808/248-8972;** www.calendarmaui.com. March 26 to March 28, 2004.

Molokai Hawaiian Paniolo Heritage Rodeo, Molokai Rodeo Arena, Maunaloa, Molokai. A celebration of Hawaii's *paniolo* (cowboy) heritage. Call ✆ **808/552-2791.**

April

Buddha Day, Lahaina Jodo Mission, Lahaina, Maui. Each year, this historic mission holds a flower festival pageant honoring the birth of Buddha. Call ✆ **808/661-4303;** www.calendarmaui.com. First Saturday in April.

Annual Ritz-Carlton Kapalua Celebration of the Arts, Ritz-Carlton Kapalua, Maui. Contemporary and traditional artists give free hands-on lessons. Call ✆ **808/669-6200;** www.celebrationofthearts.org. The

4-day festival begins the Thursday before Easter, April 8 to April 11, 2004.

David Malo Day, Lahaina. Lahainaluna High School celebrates its famous Hawaiian scholar with a luau and hula performances. Call ② 808/662-4000; www.visitmaui. com. Usually mid- to late April.

Annual Trash Art Show, Queen Kaahumanu Center, Kahului, Maui. This whimsical show depicts art made of garbage. Call ② 808/877-3369; www.visitmaui. com. Mid-April to mid-May.

Banyan Tree Birthday Party, Lahaina. Come celebrate the 129th birthday of Lahaina's famous Banyan Tree with a weekend of activities. Call ② 888/310-1117 or 808/667-9194. April 17 to April 18, 2004.

Molokai Earth Day, Mitchell Pauole Center, Kaunakakai, Molokai. A daylong event honoring the natural resources and beauty of the island of Molokai. Call ② 808/553-5236. April 24, 2004.

That Ulupalakua Thing! Maui County Agricultural Trade Show and Sampling, Ulupalakua Ranch and Tedeschi Winery, Ulupalakua, Maui. The name may be long and cumbersome, but this event is hot, hot, hot. It features local product exhibits, food booths, and live entertainment. Call ② 808/875-0457; www.mauiag.org. April 24, 2004.

May

Outrigger Canoe Season, all islands. From May to September, nearly every weekend, canoe paddlers across the state participate in outrigger canoe races. Call ② 808/961-5797.

Annual Lei Day Celebration. May Day is Lei Day in Hawaii, celebrated with lei-making contests, pageantry, arts and crafts, and concerts throughout the islands. Call ② 800/525-6284 or 808/244-3530; www.visitmaui.org for Maui events. May 1.

Mother's Day Orchid Show, Queen Kaahumanu Center, Kahului, Maui. The Maui Orchid Society puts on their annual exotic orchid show, with corsages for sale. Call ② 808/877-3369. Mother's Day weekend.

In Celebration of Canoes, West Maui. Celebration of the Pacific islands' seafaring heritage. Events include canoe paddling and sailing regattas, a luau feast, cultural arts demonstrations, canoe-building exhibits, and music. Call ② 888/310-1117. May 8 to May 22, 2004.

Molokai Ka Hula Piko, Papohaku Beach Park, Kaluakoi, Molokai. This daylong celebration of the hula takes place on the island where it was born. It features performances by hula schools, musicians, and singers from across Hawaii, as well as local food and Hawaiian crafts, including quilting, woodworking, feather work, and deer-horn scrimshaw. Call ② 800/800-6367 or 808/553-3876; www.molokai-hawaii.com. Third Saturday in May.

June

Neil Pryde Slalom, Kahului. Annual windsurfing slalom race at Kanaha Beach Park. Call ② 808/877-2111. June 5, 2004.

King Kamehameha Celebration, statewide. It's a state holiday with a massive floral parade, *hoolaulea* (party), and much more. Call ② 888/310-1117 or 808/661-5304 for Maui events, or **808/567-6361** for Molokai events. June 12, 2004.

Maui Film Festival, Wailea Resort, Maui. Five days and nights of screenings of premieres, special

Ongoing Events

Every Friday night from 7 to 10pm, as part of **Friday Night Is Art Night** in Lahaina, the town's galleries open their doors for special shows, demonstrations, and refreshments; there are even strolling musicians wandering the streets.

On the first and third weekends of the month, Hawaiian artists sell and share culture, arts, and crafts under the famous landmark **Banyan Tree** in Lahaina. On the other weekends, the Lahaina Arts Society has an exhibit and sale of various works of art in the same place.

Every Wednesday, at 4:30 and 7:30pm, outstanding contemporary and art films are shown at the Maui Arts & Culture Center in Kahului, as part of the **Maui Film Festival.**

You don't have to spend a good chunk of change and order two drinks to experience the Hawaiian art of hula. There are **free hula performances** every week. In **Lahaina:** every Saturday and Sunday at 1pm and Tuesday and Thursday at 7pm in the Lahaina Cannery Mall; and every Wednesday at 2pm, and every Friday at 2 and 6pm at the Lahaina Center. In **Kaanapali:** every Monday, Wednesday, and Friday at 7pm at the Whalers Village. In **Kapalua:** every Thursday at 10am at the Kapalua Shops.

It's also fun to check out Maui's **outdoor markets,** where you can find good deals on gifts to bring home, try the local produce, and meet the locals. Every Wednesday and Saturday from 7am to 1pm, the **Maui Swap Meet** is held next to the Post Office on Puunene Avenue in Kahului. This is Maui's largest outdoor market, filled with everything from produce to Hawaiian art. The **Hana Farmer's and Crafter's Market,** Hasegawa Service Station, Hana Highway, Hana, is a chance to meet local artists and farmers every Thursday from 9:30am to 3:30pm. The parking lot of the **Kaahumanu Shopping Center,** Kaahumanu Avenue, Kahului, is filled with bargains every Friday from 9am to 5pm. At the **Kahului Shopping Center,** also on Kaahumanu Avenue in Kahului, you'll get great deals on produce every Wednesday morning from 7am to noon. Arrive early to get the best bargains at the **Suda Store,** on Kihei Road in Kihei, which hosts an outdoor market every Monday, Wednesday, and Friday from 1:30 to 5:30pm. On Lower Honoapiilani Road in **Honokowai,** you'll find a great farmers market and other items for sale every Monday, Wednesday, and Friday from 7 to 11am.

films, along with traditional Hawaiian storytelling, chants, hula, and contemporary music. Call ℂ **808/ 579-9996;** mauifilmfestival.com. June 16 to June 20, 2004.

Hawaiian Slack-Key Guitar Festival, Maui Arts and Cultural Center, Kahului, Maui. Great music performed by the best musicians in Hawaii. It's 5 hours long and absolutely free. Call ℂ **808/239- 4336;** kahokuproductions@yahoo. com. June 20, 2004.

July

Polo Season, Olinda Polo Field, Makawao, Maui. Polo matches featuring Hawaii's top players, often joined by famous international players. Call ☎ **808/572-7326.** Held every Sunday, 1pm, throughout the summer.

Pineapple Festival, Lanai City, Lanai. Some of Hawaii's best musicians participate in Lanai's liveliest event, celebrating the golden fruit with everything from fishing tournaments to pineapple-cooking contests, food and craft booths, water activities, entertainment, and demonstrations by well-known chefs. Call ☎ **808/565-7600.** July 3, 2004.

Fourth of July, Kaanapali. A grand ole celebration with live music, children's activities, and fireworks. Call ☎ **808/661-3271.**

Makawao Parade and Rodeo, Makawao, Maui. The annual parade and rodeo event have been taking place in this upcountry cowboy town for generations. Call ☎ **800/525-MAUI** or 808/572-9565. July 4, 2004.

Kapalua Wine and Food Festival, Kapalua, Maui. Famous wine and food experts and oenophiles gather at the Ritz-Carlton and Kapalua Bay hotels for formal tastings, panel discussions, and samplings of new releases. Call ☎ **800/KAPALUA** or 808/669-0244; www.kapaluaresort. com. July 8 to July 11, 2004.

Bon Dance and Lantern Ceremony, Lahaina. This colorful Buddhist ceremony honors the souls of the dead. Call ☎ **808/661-4304.** Usually early July.

August

Maui Onion Festival, Whalers Village, Kaanapali, Maui. Everything you ever wanted to know about the sweetest onions in the world. Food, entertainment, tasting, and Maui Onion Cook-Off. Call ☎ **808/661-4567;** www.whalersvillage.com. August 7 to August 8, 2004.

Hawaii State Windsurf Championship, Kanaha Beach Park, Kahu-

lui. Top windsurfers compete. Call ☎ **808/877-2111.** August 7, 2004.

Admission Day, all islands. Hawaii became the 50th state on August 21, 1959, so the state takes a holiday; all state-related facilities will be closed. Third Friday in August.

September

Aloha Festivals, various locations statewide. Parades and other events celebrate Hawaiian culture. Call ☎ **800/852-7690** or 808/545-1771; www.alohafestivals.com for a schedule of events.

Maui Writer's Conference, Marriott Outrigger Wailea Resort. Workshops, lectures, and panel discussions with writers, agents, and publishers. Call ☎ **888/974-8373** or 808/879-0061; www.maui writers.com. Labor Day weekend.

A Taste of Lahaina, Lahaina Civic Center, Maui. Some 30,000 people show up to sample 40 signature entrees of Maui's premier chefs during this weekend festival, which includes cooking demonstrations, wine tastings, and live entertainment. The event begins Friday night with Maui Chefs Present, a dinner/cocktail party featuring about a dozen of Maui's best chefs. Call ☎ **888/310-1117;** September 11 to September 12.

Hana Relays, Hana Highway. Hundreds of runners, in relay teams, will crowd the Hana Highway from Kahalui to Hana (you might want to avoid the road this day). Call ☎ **808/871-6441.** September 11, 2004.

Maui Marathon, Kahului to Kaanapali, Maui. Runners line up at the Maui Mall before daybreak and head off for Kaanapali. Call ☎ **808/871-6441;** www.virr.com. Sunday, September 19, 2004.

Maui County Fair, War Memorial Complex, Wailuku, Maui. The oldest county fair in Hawaii features a parade, amusement rides, live entertainment, and exhibits. Call ✆ **800/525-MAUI** or 808/244-3530; www.calendarmaui.com. September 30 to October 3.

October

Aloha Classic World Wavesailing Championship, Hookipa Beach, Maui. The top windsurfers in the world gather for this final event in the Pro Boardsailing World Tour. If you're on Maui, don't miss it—it's spectacular to watch. Call ✆ **808/575-9151.** Depending on the waves and the wind, the championship can be held in October or November.

Halloween in Lahaina, Maui. There's Carnival in Rio, Mardi Gras in New Orleans, and Halloween in Lahaina. Come to this giant costume party (some 20,000 people show up) on the streets of Lahaina; Front Street is closed off for the party. Call ✆ **888/310-1117.** October 31, 2004.

November

Hula O Na Keiki, Kaanapali Beach Hotel. Maui's only children's solo hula dance competition. The weekend-long festival includes workshops on chants and hula, arts and crafts demonstrations, and entertainment. Call ✆ **808/661-0011.** November 5 to November 7, 2004.

Hawaii International Film Festival, various locations on Maui. A cinema festival with a cross-cultural spin, featuring filmmakers from Asia, the Pacific Islands, and the United States. Call ✆ **800/752-8193** or 808/528-FILM; www.hiff.org. Mid-November.

Maui Invitational Basketball Tournament, Lahaina Civic Center, Maui. Top college teams vie in this annual preseason tournament. Call ✆ **312/755-3504.** Usually held around Thanksgiving.

December

Festival of Lights, islandwide. Festivities include parades and tree-lighting ceremonies. Call ✆ **808/667-9175** on Maui, or 808/567-6361 on Molokai. Early December.

Na Mele O Maui, Student Song and Art Competition, Maui Marriott Ballroom. Students from kindergarten to 12th grade perform traditional Hawaiian songs in a scholarship fundraiser. Call ✆ **808/667-1200.** December 3, 2004.

Festival of Art & Flowers, Lahaina, Maui. Look for cut flower displays, floral arrangements, demonstrations, lei-making contests, art exhibits, and entertainment. Call ✆ **808/667-9175.** December 4, 2004.

Old-Fashioned Holiday Celebration, Lahaina, Maui. A day of Christmas carolers, Santa Claus, live music and entertainment, a crafts fair, Christmas baked goods, and activities for children, all taking place in the Banyan Tree Park on Front Street. Call ✆ **888/310-1117.** December 4, 2004.

Tree Lighting Ceremony, Ritz-Carlton Kapalua. With the flick of a switch, more than 250,000 sparkling lights will illuminate the 25-foot holiday tree and dozens of pine and palm trees around the courtyards of The Ritz-Carlton Kapalua and throughout the resort. Call ✆ **808/669-6200;** www.kapaluaresort.com. December 5, 2004.

First Light 2004, Maui Arts and Cultural Center, Maui. Academy of Motion Pictures holds major screening of top films. Not to be missed. Call ✆ **808/579-9996;** www.mauifilmfestival.com. December 15, 2004 to January 2, 2005.

5 Travel Insurance

Check your existing insurance policies and credit-card coverage before you buy travel insurance. You may already be covered for lost luggage, canceled tickets, or medical expenses. The cost of travel insurance varies widely, depending on the cost and length of your trip, your age, health, and the type of trip you're taking.

TRIP-CANCELLATION INSUR-ANCE Trip-cancellation insurance helps you get your money back if you have to back out of a trip, if you have to go home early, or if your travel supplier goes bankrupt. Allowed reasons for cancellation can range from sickness to natural disasters to the State Department declaring your destination unsafe for travel. (Insurers usually won't cover vague fears, though, as many travelers discovered who tried to cancel their trips in October 2001 because they were wary of flying.) In this unstable world, trip-cancellation insurance is a good buy if you're getting tickets well in advance—who knows what the state of the world, or of your airline, will be in 9 months? Insurance policy details vary, so read the fine print—and especially make sure that your airline or

---

Tips What to Pack

Maui is very informal: You'll get by with shorts, T-shirts, and sneakers at most attractions and restaurants; a casual sundress or a polo shirt and khakis is fine even in the most expensive places. Dinner jackets for men are required only at very few resorts, such as the Lodge at Koele on Lanai, and they'll cordially provide a jacket if you don't bring your own. Don't forget a long-sleeved coverup (to throw on at the beach when you've had enough sun for the day), rubber water shoes or flip-flops, and hiking shoes and several pairs of good socks if you plan to do any hiking. You might also want to bring binoculars for whale-watching.

Be sure to bring **sun protection:** sunglasses, strong sunscreen, a light hat (like a baseball cap or a sun visor), and a canteen or water bottle if you'll be hiking—you'll easily dehydrate on the trail in the tropic heat. Experts recommend carrying a gallon of water per person per day on any hike. Campers should bring water purification tablets or devices. Also see "Staying Healthy" below.

Don't bother overstuffing your suitcase with 2 whole weeks' worth of shorts and T-shirts: Maui has **laundry facilities** everywhere. If your accommodation doesn't have a washer and dryer or laundry service (most do), there will most likely be a laundry nearby. The only exception to this is Hana; the tiny town has no Laundromat, so either check with the place you're staying beforehand, or do a load of laundry before you arrive.

One last thing: **It really can get cold on Maui.** If you plan to see the sunrise from the top of Haleakala, bring a warm jacket; even in summer, when it's 80°F (27°C) at the beach, 40°F (4°]C) upcountry temperatures are not uncommon. It's always a good idea to bring long pants and a windbreaker, sweater, or light jacket. And be sure to bring along rain gear if you'll be in Maui from November to March.

cruise line is on the list of carriers covered in case of bankruptcy. For information, contact one of the following insurers: **Access America** (© **800/284-8300;** www.accessamerica.com); **Travel Guard International** (© **800/826-1300;** www.travelguard.com); **Travel Insured International** (© **800/243-3174;** www.travelinsured.com); and **Travelex Insurance Services** (© **800/228-9792;** www.travelex-insurance.com).

MEDICAL INSURANCE Most health insurance policies cover you if you get sick away from home—but check, particularly if you're insured by an HMO.

LOST-LUGGAGE INSURANCE On domestic flights, checked baggage is covered up to $2,500 per ticketed passenger. On international flights (including U.S. portions of international trips), baggage is limited to approximately $9.07 per pound, up to approximately $635 per checked bag. If you plan to check items more valuable than the standard liability, see if your valuables are covered by your homeowner's policy, get baggage insurance as part of your comprehensive travel-insurance package, or buy Travel Guard's "Bag-Trak" product. Don't buy insurance at the airport, as it's usually overpriced. Be sure to take any valuables or irreplaceable items with you in your carry-on luggage, as many valuables (including books, money, and electronics) aren't covered by airline policies.

If your luggage is lost, immediately file a lost-luggage claim at the airport, detailing the luggage contents. For most airlines, you must report delayed, damaged, or lost baggage within 4 hours of arrival. The airlines are required to deliver luggage, once found, directly to your house or destination free of charge.

6 Health & Insurance

STAYING HEALTHY
If you suffer from a chronic illness, consult your doctor before your departure. For conditions like epilepsy, diabetes, or heart problems, wear a **Medic Alert Identification Tag** (© **888/633-4298;** www.medicalert.org), which will immediately alert doctors to your condition and give them access to your records through Medic Alert's 24-hour hot line.

Pack prescription medications in your carry-on luggage. Carry written prescriptions in generic, not brand name, form and dispense all prescription medications from their original labeled vials. If you wear contact lenses, pack an extra pair in case you lose one.

ON LAND
As in any tropical climate, there are lots of bugs in Maui. Most of them won't harm you; however, three insects—mosquitoes, centipedes, and scorpions—do sting, and they can cause anything from mild annoyance to severe swelling and pain.

MOSQUITOES These pesky insects aren't native to Hawaii, but arrived as larvae stowed away in the water barrels on the ship *Wellington* in 1826. There's not a whole lot you can do about them, except to apply repellent, or burn mosquito punk or citronella candles to keep them out of your area. If they've bitten you, head to the drugstore for sting-stopping ointments (antihistamine creams like Benadryl or homeopathic creams like Sting Stop or Florasone); they'll ease the itching and swelling. Most bites disappear in anywhere from a few hours to a few days.

CENTIPEDES These segmented insects with a jillion legs come in two varieties: 6- to 8-inch brown ones and the smaller 2- to 3-inch blue guys; both can really pack a wallop with their sting. Centipedes are generally found in damp places, like under wood piles or compost heaps; wearing closed-toe shoes can help prevent stings if you accidentally unearth a centipede. If you're stung, the reaction can range from something similar to a mild bee sting to severe pain; apply ice at once to prevent swelling. See a doctor if you experience extreme pain, swelling, nausea, or any other severe reaction.

SCORPIONS Rarely seen, scorpions are found in arid, warm regions; their stings can be serious. Campers in dry areas should always check their boots before putting them on, and shake out sleeping bags and bedrolls. Symptoms of a scorpion sting include shortness of breath, hives, swelling, and nausea. In the unlikely event that you're stung, apply diluted household ammonia and cold compresses to the area of the sting and seek medical attention immediately.

Hiking Safety

In addition to taking the appropriate cautions regarding Maui's bug population (see above), hikers should always let someone know where they're heading, when they're going, and when they plan to return; too many hikers get lost on Maui because they don't inform others of their basic plans.

Always check weather conditions with the **National Weather Service** (✆ **808/877-5111**) before you go. Hike with a pal, never alone. Wear hiking boots, a sun hat, clothes to protect you from the sun and from getting scratches, and high-SPF sunscreen on all exposed areas of skin. Take water. Stay on the trail. Watch your step. It's easy to slip off precipitous trails and into steep canyons, with often disastrous, even fatal, results. Incapacitated hikers are often plucked to safety by fire and rescue squads, who must use helicopters to gain access to remote sites. Many experienced hikers and boaters today pack a cellular phone in case of emergency; just dial ✆ **911.**

Vog

The volcanic haze dubbed "vog" is caused by gases released when molten lava—from the continuous eruption of the volcano on the flank of Kilauea on the Big Island—pours into the ocean. This hazy air, which looks like urban smog, limits viewing from scenic vistas and wreaks havoc with photographers trying to get clear panoramic shots. Some people claim that long-term exposure to vog has even caused bronchial ailments.

There actually is a "vog" season in Hawaii: the fall and winter months, when the trade winds that blow the fumes out to sea die down. The vog is felt not only on the Big Island, but also as far away as Maui and Oahu.

OCEAN SAFETY

Because most people coming to Maui are unfamiliar with the ocean environment, they're often unaware of the natural hazards it holds. But with just a few precautions, your ocean experience can be a safe and happy one. An excellent book to get is *All Stings Considered: First Aid and Medical Treatment of Hawaii's Marine Injuries* (University of Hawaii Press, 1997), by Craig Thomas (an emergency-medicine doctor) and Susan Scott (a registered nurse). These avid water people have put together the authoritative book on first aid for Hawaii's marine injuries.

SEASICKNESS The waters off Maui can range from calm as glass to downright frightening (in storm conditions), and they usually fall somewhere in between; in general, expect rougher conditions in winter than in summer.

Some 90% of the population tends toward seasickness. If you've never been out on a boat or if you've gotten seasick in the past, you might want to heed the following suggestions:

- The day before you go out on the boat, avoid alcohol; caffeine; citrus

Tips Don't Get Burned: Smart Tanning Tips

Tanning just ain't what it used to be. Hawaii's Caucasian population has a higher incidence of deadly skin cancer, malignant melanoma, than anywhere else in the United States. But none of us are safe from the sun's harmful rays: People of all skin types and races can burn when exposed to the sun too long.

To ensure that your vacation won't be ruined by a painful, throbbing sunburn, here are some helpful tips on how to tan safely and painlessly:

- **Wear a strong sunscreen at all times, and use lots of it.** Use a sunscreen with a sun-protection factor (SPF) of 15 or higher; people with a light complexion should use 30. Apply sunscreen as soon as you get out of the shower in the morning, and at least 30 minutes before you're exposed to the sun. No matter what the label says—even if the sunscreen is waterproof—reapply it every 2 hours and immediately after swimming.

- **Read the labels.** To avoid developing allergies to sunscreens, avoid those that contain para-aminobenzoic acid (PABA). Look for a sunscreen with zinc oxide, talc, or titanium dioxide, which reduce the risk of developing skin allergies. For the best protection from UVA rays (which can cause wrinkles and premature aging), check the label for zinc oxide, benzophenone, oxybenzone, sulisobenzone, titanium dioxide, or avobenzone (also known as Parsol 1789).

- **Wear a hat and sunglasses.** And make sure that your sunglasses have UV filters.

- **Avoid being in the sun between 9am and 3pm.** Use extra caution during these peak hours. Remember that a beach umbrella is not protection enough from the sun's harmful UV rays; in fact, with the reflection from the water, the sand, and even the sidewalk, some 85% of the ultraviolet rays are still bombarding you.

- **Protect children from the sun, and keep infants out of the sun altogether.** Infants under 6 months should not be in the sun at all. Older babies need zinc oxide to protect their fragile skin, and children should be slathered with sunscreen every hour. The burns that children get today predict what their future will be with skin cancer tomorrow.

If you start to turn red, **get out of the sun.** Contrary to popular belief, you don't have to turn red to tan; if your skin is red, it's burned—and that's serious. The redness from a burn may not show until 2 to 8 hours after you get out of the sun, and the full force of that burn may not appear for 24 to 36 hours. During that time, you can look forward to pain, itching, and peeling. The best **remedy** for a sunburn is to get out of the sun immediately and stay out of the sun until all the redness is gone. Aloe vera (straight from the plant or from a commercial preparation), cool compresses, cold baths, and anesthetic benzocaine may also help with the pain of sunburn.

If you've decided to get a head start on your tan by using a self-tanning lotion that dyes your skin a darker shade, remember that this will not protect you from the sun. You'll still need to generously apply sunscreen when you go out.

and other acidic juices; and greasy, spicy, or hard-to-digest foods.

- Get a good night's sleep the night before.
- Take or use whatever seasickness prevention works best for you—medication, an acupressure wrist-band, gingerroot tea or capsules, or any combination—*before* you board; once you set sail, it's generally too late.
- Once you're on the water, stay as low and as near the center of the boat as possible. Avoid the fumes (especially if it's a diesel boat); stay out in the fresh air and watch the horizon. Do not read.
- If you start to feel queasy, drink clear fluids like water, and eat something bland, such as a soda cracker.

STINGS The most common stings in Hawaii come from jellyfish, particularly Portuguese man-of-war and box jellyfish. Since the poisons they inject are very different, you need to treat each sting differently.

A bluish-purple floating bubble with a long tail, the **Portuguese man-of-war** causes thousands of stings a year. Stings, although painful and a nuisance, are rarely harmful; fewer than one in a thousand requires medical treatment. The best prevention is to watch for these floating bubbles as you snorkel (look for the hanging tentacles below the surface). Get out of the water if anyone near you spots these jellyfish.

Reactions to stings range from mild burning and redness to severe welts and blisters. *All Stings Considered* recommends the following treatment: First, pick off any visible tentacles with a gloved hand, a stick, or anything handy; rinse the sting with fresh or salt water; and apply ice to prevent swelling and to help control pain.

Hawaiian folklore advises using vinegar, meat tenderizer, baking soda, papain, or alcohol, or even urinating on the wound. Studies have shown that these remedies may actually cause further damage. Most Portuguese man-of-war stings will disappear by themselves within 15 to 20 minutes if you do nothing to treat them. Still, be sure to see a doctor if pain persists or if a rash or other symptoms develop.

Box jellyfish, transparent, square-shaped bell jellyfish, are nearly impossible to see in the water. Fortunately, they seem to follow a monthly cycle: 8 to 10 days after the full moon, they appear in the waters on the leeward side of the island and hang around for about 3 days. Also, they seem to sting more in the morning hours, when they're on or near the surface. The best prevention is to get out of the water.

Stings range from no visible marks to red, hivelike welts, blisters, and pain (a burning sensation) lasting from 10 minutes to 8 hours. *All Stings Considered* recommends the following course of treatment: First, pour regular household vinegar on the sting; this may not relieve the pain, but it will stop additional burning. Do not rub the area. Pick off any vinegar-soaked tentacles with a stick. For pain, apply an ice pack. Seek additional medical treatment if you experience shortness of breath, weakness, palpitations, muscle cramps, or any other severe symptoms. Again, ignore any folk remedies. Most box jellyfish stings disappear by themselves without treatment.

PUNCTURES Most sea-related punctures come from stepping on or brushing against the needlelike spines of sea urchins (known locally as *wana*). Be careful when you're in the water; don't put your foot down (even if you have booties or fins on) if you cannot clearly see the bottom. Waves can push you into wana in a surge zone in shallow water (the wana's spines can even puncture a wet suit).

A sea urchin sting can result in burning, aching, swelling, and discoloration (black or purple) around the area where the spines have entered your skin. The best thing to do is to pull out any protruding spines. The body will absorb the spines within 24 hours to 3 weeks, or the remainder of the spines will work themselves out. Again, contrary to popular wisdom, do not urinate or pour vinegar on the embedded spines—this will not help.

CUTS All cuts obtained in the marine environment must be taken seriously, because the high level of bacteria present can quickly cause the cut to become infected. The most common cuts are from **coral.** Contrary to popular belief, coral cannot grow inside your body. However, bacteria can—and very often does—grow inside a cut. The best way to prevent cuts is to wear a wet suit, gloves, and reef shoes. Never, under any circumstances, should you touch a coral head; not only can you get cut, but you can also damage a living organism that took decades to grow.

The symptoms of a coral cut can range from a slight scratch to severe welts and blisters. *All Stings Considered* recommends gently pulling the edges of the skin open and removing any embedded coral or grains of sand with tweezers, or rinsing well with fresh water. Next, scrub the cut well with fresh water. Never use ocean water to clean a cut. If the wound is bleeding, press a clean cloth against it until it stops. If bleeding continues, or the edges of the injury are jagged or gaping, seek medical treatment.

WHAT TO DO IF YOU GET SICK AWAY FROM HOME

In most cases, your existing health plan will provide the coverage you need. But double-check; you may want to buy **travel medical insurance** instead. (See the section on insurance above.) Bring your insurance ID card with you when you travel.

If you suffer from a chronic illness, consult your doctor before your departure. For conditions like epilepsy, diabetes, or heart problems, wear a **Medic Alert Identification Tag** (© 800/825-3785; www.medicalert.org), which will immediately alert doctors to your condition and give them access to your records through Medic Alert's 24-hour hot line.

Pack **prescription medications** in your carry-on luggage, and carry prescription medications in their original containers, with pharmacy labels—otherwise, they won't make it through airport security. Also bring along copies of your prescriptions in case you lose your pills or run out. Don't forget an extra pair of contact lenses or prescription glasses.

7 Specialized Travel Resources

FOR TRAVELERS WITH DISABILITIES

Travelers with disabilities are made to feel very welcome in Maui. Hotels are usually equipped with wheelchair-accessible rooms, and tour companies provide many special services. The **Hawaii Center for Independent Living,** 414 Kauwili St., Suite 102, Honolulu, HI 96817 (© **808/522-5400;** fax 808/586-8129; www.hawaii.gov/health; cpdppp@aloha.net), can provide information and send you a copy of the *Aloha Guide to Accessibility* ($15).

Moss Rehab ResourceNet (www.mossresourcenet.org) is a great source for information, tips, and resources relating to accessible travel. You'll find links to a number of travel agents who specialize in planning trips for travelers with disabilities here and through **Access-Able Travel Source** (© 303/232-2979; www.access-able.com), another excellent online source. You'll also find relay and voice numbers for hotels, airlines, and car-rental companies on Access-Able's user-friendly site, as well as links to accessible accommodations, attractions, transportation, tours, local medical resources and equipment repair, and much more.

For travelers with disabilities who wish to do their own driving, hand-controlled cars can be rented from **Avis** (*©* 800/331-1212; www.avis.com) and **Hertz** (*©* 800/654-3131; www. hertz.com). The number of hand-controlled cars in Hawaii is limited, so be sure to book well in advance. For wheelchair-accessible vans, contact **Accessible Vans of Hawaii,** 186 Mehani Circle, Kihei (*©* 800/303-3750 or 808/879-5521; fax 808/879-0640; www.accessiblevans.com). Maui recognizes other states' windshield placards indicating that the driver of the car is disabled, so be sure to bring yours with you.

Vision-impaired travelers who use a Seeing Eye dog can now come to Hawaii without the hassle of quarantine. A recent court decision ruled that visitors with Seeing Eye dogs only need to present documentation that the dog is a trained Seeing Eye dog and has had rabies shots. For more information, contact the **Animal Quarantine Facility** (*©* 808/483-7171; www.hawaii.gov).

FOR GAY & LESBIAN TRAVELERS

Known for its acceptance of all groups, Hawaii welcomes gays and lesbians just as it does anybody else.

To get a sense of the local gay and lesbian community on the island of Maui, contact **Both Sides Now** (*©* 808/244-4566; fax 808/874-6221), which publishes a monthly newspaper on issues and events for Maui's gay, lesbian, bisexual, and transgender community.

For the latest information on the gay marriage issue, contact the **Hawaii Marriage Project** (*©* 808/532-9000).

Pacific Ocean Holidays, P.O. Box 88245, Honolulu, HI 96830 (*©* 800/735-6600 or 808/923-2400; www.gayhawaii.com), offers vacation packages that feature gay-owned and gay-friendly lodgings. It also publishes the *Pocket Guide to Hawaii: A Guide for Gay Visitors & Kamaaina,* a list of gay-owned and gay-friendly businesses throughout the islands. Send $5 for a copy (mail order only; no phone orders, please), or access the online version on the website.

If you want help planning your trip, the **International Gay & Lesbian Travel Association (IGLTA;** *©* 800/448-8550 or 954/776-2626; www. iglta.org) can link you up with the appropriate gay-friendly service organization or tour specialist. With around 1,200 members, it offers quarterly newsletters, marketing mailings, and a membership directory that's updated quarterly. Members are kept informed of gay and gay-friendly hoteliers, tour operators, and airline and cruise-line representatives. **GayWired Travel Services (www.gaywired.com)** is another great trip-planning resource; click on "Travel Services."

Out and About (*©* 800/929-2268 or 415/486-2591; www.outandabout. com) offers a monthly newsletter packed with good information on the global gay and lesbian scene. Its website features links to gay and lesbian tour operators and other gay-themed travel links, plus extensive online travel information to subscribers only. Out and About's guidebooks are available at most major bookstores and through www.adlbooks.com.

FOR SENIORS

Discounts for seniors are available at almost all of Maui's major attractions, and occasionally at hotels and restaurants. Always inquire when making hotel reservations, and especially when you're buying your airline ticket—most major domestic airlines offer senior discounts.

Members of **AARP** (© **800/424-3410** or 202/434-2277; www.aarp.org) are usually eligible for such discounts; AARP also puts together organized tour packages at moderate rates.

Some great, low-cost trips to Hawaii are offered to people 55 and older through **Elderhostel,** 75 Federal St., Boston, MA 02110 (© **617/426-8056;** www.elderhostel.org), a nonprofit group that arranges travel and study programs around the world. You can obtain a complete catalog of offerings by writing to Elderhostel, P.O. Box 1959, Wakefield, MA 01880-5959.

If you're planning to visit Haleakala National Park, you can save sightseeing dollars if you're 62 or older by picking up a **Golden Age Passport** from any national park, recreation area, or monument. This lifetime pass has a one-time fee of $10 and provides free admission to all of the parks in the system, plus a 50% savings on camping and recreation fees. You can pick one up at any park entrance; be sure to have proof of your age with you.

FOR FAMILIES

Maui is paradise for children: beaches to frolic on, water to splash in, unusual sights to see, and a host of new foods to taste. Be sure to check out the boxes "Family-Friendly Accommodations" in chapter 4, "Family-Friendly Restaurants" in chapter 5, and "Especially for Kids" in chapter 7.

The larger hotels and resorts have supervised programs for children and can refer you to qualified babysitters. You can also contact **People Attentive to Children** (PATCH; © **808/242-9232;** www.patch-hi.org), which will refer you to individuals who have taken their training courses on child care.

Baby's Away (© **800/942-9030** or 808/875-9093; www.babysaway.com) rents cribs, strollers, highchairs, playpens, infant seats, and the like, to make your baby's vacation (and yours) much more enjoyable.

Remember that Maui's sun is probably much stronger than what you're used to at home, so it's important to protect your kids, and keep infants out of the sun altogether. Infants under 6 months should not be in the sun at all. Older babies need zinc oxide to protect their fragile skin, and children should be slathered with sunscreen every hour.

Condo rentals are a great option for families; the convenience of having your own kitchen is great for mom and dad. See "Types of Accommodations" later in this chapter. Our favorite condo complexes are reviewed throughout that chapter.

8 Getting Married on Maui

Whatever your budget, Maui is a great place for a wedding. Not only does the entire island exude romance and natural beauty, but after the ceremony, you're only a few steps away from the perfect honeymoon. And the members of your wedding party will most likely be delighted, since you've given them the perfect excuse for their own island vacation.

More than 20,000 marriages are performed each year on the islands, and nearly half of the couples married here are from somewhere else. This booming business has spawned dozens of companies that can help you organize a long-distance event and stage an unforgettable wedding, Hawaiian style or your style.

The easiest way to plan your wedding is to let someone else handle it at the resort or hotel where you'll be staying. All of the major resorts and hotels (and even most of the small ones) have wedding coordinators, whose job is to make sure that your wedding day is everything you've dreamed about. They can plan everything from a simple (relatively) low-cost wedding to an extravaganza that people will remember and talk about for years. Remember that resorts can be pricey—catering, flowers, musicians, and so on, may cost more in a resort than outside a resort, but sometimes you can save money because the resort will not charge a room rental fee if they get to do the catering. Be frank with your wedding coordinator if you want to keep costs down. However, you can also plan your own island wedding, even from afar, and not spend a fortune doing it.

THE PAPERWORK

The state of Hawaii has some very minimal procedures for obtaining a marriage license. The first thing you should do is contact the **Marriage License Office,** State Department of Health Building, 54 S. High St., Wailuku, HI 96793 (© **808/984-8210;** www.state. hi.us/doh/records/vr_marri.html), open Monday through Friday from 8am to 4pm. The staff will mail you a brochure, *Getting Married,* and direct you to the marriage licensing agent closest to where you'll be staying on Maui.

Once on Maui, the prospective bride and groom must go together to the marriage licensing agent to get a license. A license costs $60 and is good for 30 days; if you don't have the ceremony within the time allotted, you'll have to pay another $60 for another license. The only requirements for a marriage license are that both parties are 15 years of age or older (couples 15–17 years old must have proof of age, written consent of both parents, and the written approval of the judge of the family court) and are not more closely related than first cousins. That's it.

Contrary to some reports from the media, gay couples cannot marry in Hawaii. After a protracted legal battle, and much discussion in the state legislature, in late 1999 the Hawaii Supreme Court ruled the state won't issue a marriage license to a couple of the same sex. For the latest information on this issue, contact the **Hawaii Marriage Project** (© **808/532-9000).**

PLANNING THE WEDDING

DOING IT YOURSELF   The marriage licensing agents, which range from the governor's satellite office to private individuals, are usually friendly, helpful people who can steer you to a nondenominational minister or someone who's licensed by the state of Hawaii to perform the ceremony. These marriage performers are great sources of information for budget weddings. They usually know great places to have the ceremony for free or for a nominal fee.

If you don't want to use a wedding planner (see below) but want to make arrangements before you arrive on Maui, our best advice is to get a copy of the daily newspaper, the *Maui News,* P.O. Box 550, Wailuku, HI 96793 (© **808/244-7691;** www.maui news.com). People willing and qualified to conduct weddings advertise in the classifieds. They're great sources of information, because they know the best places to have the ceremony and can recommend caterers, florists, and everything else you'll need.

USING A WEDDING PLANNER Wedding planners—many of whom are marriage licensing agents as well—can arrange everything for you, from a small, private, outdoor affair to a full-blown formal ceremony in a tropical setting. They charge anywhere from $450 to a small fortune—it all depends on what you want.

Planners on Maui include **A Wedding Made in Paradise** (© 800/453-3440 or 808/879-3444; fax 808/874-1278; www.wedinparadise.com); **A Dream Wedding: Maui Style** (© 800/743-2777 or 808/661-1777; fax 808/667-2042; www.maui.net/~dreamwed/dream.html); **A Romantic Maui Wedding** (© 800/808-4144 or

808/874-6444; fax 808/879-5525; www.justmauied.com); **Dolphin Dream Weddings** (© 800/793-2-WED or 808/661-8535; www.maui. net/~dolphin); and **Simply Married** (© 800/291-0110 or 808/572-7898; fax 800/368-6933 or 808/572-1240; www.maui.net/~married).

9 Getting There

If possible, fly directly to Maui; doing so can save you a 2-hour layover in Honolulu and another plane ride. If you're headed for Molokai or Lanai, you'll have to connect through Honolulu.

If you think of the island of Maui as the shape of a head and shoulders of a person, you'll probably arrive on its neck, at **Kahului Airport.**

At press time, six airlines fly directly from the U.S. mainland to Kahului: **United Airlines** (© 800/241-6522; www.ual.com) offers daily nonstop flights from San Francisco and Los Angeles; **Aloha Airlines** (© 800/367-5250; www.alohaair.com) has nonstop service from Kahului Maui to Burbank, California (closer to downtown Los Angeles than Los Angles International Airport), Orange County, California, and Phoenix, Arizona. International travelers can use Aloha's service from Vancouver, BC; **Hawaiian Airlines** (© 800/367-5320; www.hawaiianair.com) has direct flights from Los Angeles, San Francisco, Portland, and Seattle; **American Airlines** (© 800/433-7300; www.aa. com) flies direct from Los Angeles and San Jose; **Delta Airlines** (© 800/221-1212; www.delta.com) offers direct flights from San Francisco and Los Angeles; and **American Trans Air** (© 800/435-9282; www.ata.com) has direct flights from Los Angeles, San Francisco, and Phoenix.

The other carriers—including **Continental** (© 800/525-0280; www. continental.com), which offers nonstop service from Newark to Honolulu, and **Northwest Airlines** (© 800/225-2525; www.nwa.com), which has a daily nonstop from Detroit—fly to Honolulu, where you'll have to pick up an interisland flight to Maui. (The airlines listed in the paragraph above also offer many more flights to Honolulu from additional cities on the mainland.) Both **Aloha Airlines** and **Hawaiian Airlines** offer jet service from Honolulu. See "Interisland Flights" later in this chapter.

For information on airlines serving Hawaii from places other than the U.S. mainland, see chapter 3, "For International Visitors."

FLY FOR LESS: TIPS FOR GETTING THE BEST AIRFARES

- Keep your eye out for periodic **sales.** You'll almost never see a sale during the peak winter vacation months, and especially not around the holidays. But during the rest of the year, you can find deals. *Note:* The lowest-priced fares are often nonrefundable, require advance purchase of 1 to 3 weeks and a certain length of stay, and carry penalties for changing dates of travel. Make sure you know exactly what the restrictions are before you commit.
- If your schedule is flexible, you can almost always get a cheaper fare by **staying over a Saturday night** or by **flying during midweek.**
- **Consolidators,** also known as bucket shops, are a good place to find low fares, often below even the airlines' discounted rates. There's nothing shady about the reliable ones—basically, they're just big travel agents that get discounts for buying in bulk and pass some of the savings on to you. But be aware that consolidator tickets

Tips   Coping with Jet Lag

Jetlag is a pitfall of traveling across time zones. If you're flying north-south and you feel sluggish when you touch down, your symptoms will be caused by dehydration and the general stress of air travel. When you travel east to west, like going to Hawaii, however, your body becomes thoroughly confused about what time it is, and everything from your digestion to your brain gets knocked for a loop. Traveling east, say, from Maui to Los Angeles, is more difficult on your internal clock than traveling west, say, from Atlanta to Hawaii, as most peoples' bodies find it more acceptable to stay up late than to fall asleep early.

Here are some tips for combating jet lag:

- **Reset your watch** to your destination time before you board the plane.
- **Drink lots of water** before, during, and after your flight. Avoid alcohol.
- **Exercise and sleep well** for a few days before your trip.
- If you have trouble sleeping on planes, **fly eastward on morning flights.**
- **Daylight** is the key to resetting your body clock. At the website for **Outside In** (www.bodyclock.com), you can get a customized plan of when to seek and avoid light.
- If you need help getting to sleep earlier than you usually would, doctors recommend taking either the hormone **melatonin** or the sleeping pill **Ambien**—but not together. Take 2 to 5 milligrams of melatonin about 2 hours before your planned bedtime.

are usually nonrefundable or come with stiff cancellation penalties.

We've gotten great deals on many occasions from **Cheap Tickets** ✪ (© **800/377-1000;** www.cheaptickets.com). **Council Travel** (© **800/226-8624;** www.counciltravel.com) caters especially to young travelers, but their bargain-basement prices are available to people of all ages. Other reliable consolidators include **Lowestfare.com** (© **888/278-8830;** www.lowestfare.com); **Cheap Seats** (© **800/451-7200;** www.cheapseatstravel.com); and **1-800-FLY-CHEAP** (www.flycheap.com).

- **Search the Internet for cheap fares,** though it's still best to compare your findings with the research of a dedicated travel agent,

if you're lucky enough to have one, especially when you're booking more than just a flight. Three of the best-respected virtual travel agents are **Expedia** (**www.expedia.com**), **Travelocity** (**www.travelocity.com**), and **Yahoo! Travel** (**http://travel.yahoo.com**).

- Join **frequent-flier clubs.** Accrue enough miles, and you'll be rewarded with free flights and elite status. It's free. You don't need to fly to build frequent-flier miles—**frequent-flier credit cards** can provide thousands of miles for doing your everyday shopping.

GETTING THROUGH THE AIRPORT

With the federalization of airport security, security procedures at U.S.

airports are more stable and consistent than ever. When you leave Maui, allow 90 minutes before your flight. The airport was not designed or built with the new security measures in mind, and you have to stand in four different lines before you get to your gate (agricultural inspection, ticket line, baggage inspection, and security), where you will stand in line for your flight. Believe me, it will take you at least 90 minutes to get through all these lines.

Your airline carrier will tell you when to show up for your flight from your departing city. Some carriers are now recommending 90 minutes due to the addition of random vehicle inspections at the airport.

Bring a **current, government-issued photo ID** such as a driver's license or passport, and if you've got an E-ticket, print out the **official confirmation page;** you'll need to show your confirmation at the security checkpoint, and your ID at the ticket counter or the gate. (Children under 18 do not need photo IDs for domestic flights, but the adults checking in with them need them.)

If you want to speed up security, **do not wear metal objects** such as big belt buckles or clanky earrings. Most boots and many shoes have a steel shaft in them that will set of metal detectors. Save yourself some trouble by taking them off and run them through the X-ray machines along with your carry-on luggage. If you've got metallic body parts, a note from your doctor can prevent a long chat with the security screeners.

Federalization has stabilized **what you can carry on** and **what you can't.** The general rule is that sharp things are out, nail clippers are okay, and food and beverages must be passed through the X-ray machine—but that security screeners can't make you drink from your coffee cup. Bring

---

 Flying with Film & Video

Never pack film—developed or undeveloped—in checked bags, as the new, more powerful scanners in U.S. airports can fog film. The film you carry with you can be damaged by scanners as well. X-ray damage is cumulative; the slower the film, and the more times you put it through a scanner, the more likely the damage. Film under 800 ASA is usually safe for up to five scans. If you're taking your film through additional scans, U.S. regulations permit you to demand hand inspections.

Most photo supply stores sell protective pouches designed to block damaging X-rays. The pouches fit both film and loaded cameras. They should protect your film in checked baggage, but they also may raise alarms and result in a hand inspection.

An organization called **Film Safety for Traveling on Planes, FSTOP** (© 888/301-2665; www.f-stop.org), can provide additional tips for traveling with film and equipment.

Carry-on scanners will not damage **videotape** in video cameras, but the magnetic fields emitted by the walk-through security gateways and handheld inspection wands will. Always place your loaded camcorder on the screening conveyor belt or have it hand-inspected. Be sure your batteries are charged, as you will probably be required to turn the device on to ensure that it's what it appears to be. Bring food in your carry-on rather than checking it, as explosive-detection machines used on checked luggage have been known to mistake food (especially chocolate, for some reason) for bombs. Travelers in the U.S. are allowed one carry-on bag, plus a "personal item" such as a purse, briefcase, or laptop bag. Carry-on hoarders can stuff all sorts of things into a laptop bag; as long as it has a laptop in it, it's still considered a personal item. The Transportation Security Administration (TSA) has issued a list of restricted items; check its website (http://www.tsa.gov/public/index.jsp) for details.

Passengers with E-tickets and without checked bags can still beat the ticket-counter lines by using **electronic kiosks** or even **online check-in.** Ask your airline which alternatives are available, and if you're using a kiosk, bring the credit card you used to book the ticket. If you're checking bags, you will still be able to use most airlines' kiosks; again, call your airline for up-to-date information. **Curbside check-in** is also a good way to avoid lines, although a few airlines still ban curbside check-in entirely; call before you go.

At press time, the TSA is also recommending that you **not lock your checked luggage** so screeners can search it by hand if necessary. The agency says to use plastic "zip ties"

instead, which can be bought at hardware stores and can be easily cut off.

LONG-HAUL FLIGHTS: HOW TO STAY COMFORTABLE

Long flights can be trying; stuffy air and cramped seats can make you feel as if you're being sent parcel post in a small box. But with a little advance planning, you can make an otherwise unpleasant experience almost bearable.

- Your choice of airline and airplane will definitely affect your leg room. Among U.S. airlines, American Airlines has the best average seat pitch (the distance between a seat and the row in front of it). Find more details at www.seatguru.com, which has extensive details about almost every seat on six major U.S. airlines.

- Emergency exit seats and bulkhead seats typically have the most leg room. Emergency exit seats are usually held back to be assigned the day of a flight (to ensure that the seat is filled by someone able-bodied); it's worth getting to the ticket counter early to snag one of these spots for a long flight. Keep in mind that bulkheads are where airlines often put baby bassinets, so you may be sitting next to an infant.

- To have two seats for yourself, try for an aisle seat in a center section toward the back of coach. If you're

---

traveling with a companion, book an aisle and a window seat. Middle seats are usually booked last, so chances are good you'll end up with three seats to yourselves. And in the event that a third passenger is assigned the middle seat, he or she will probably be more than happy to trade for a window or an aisle.

- To sleep, avoid the last row of any section or a row in front of an emergency exit, as these seats are the least likely to recline. Avoid seats near highly trafficked toilet areas. You also may want to reserve a window seat so that you can rest your head and avoid being bumped in the aisle.

- Get up, walk around, and stretch every 60 to 90 minutes to keep your blood flowing. This helps avoid deep vein thrombosis, or "economy-class syndrome," a rare and deadly condition that can be caused by sitting in cramped conditions for too long.

- Drink water before, during, and after your flight to combat the lack of humidity in airplane cabins—which can be drier than the Sahara. Bring a bottle of water on board. Avoid alcohol, which will dehydrate you.

- If you're flying with kids, don't forget to carry on toys, books, pacifiers, and chewing gum to help them relieve ear pressure buildup during ascent and descent. Let each child pack his or her own backpack with favorite toys.

LANDING AT KAHULUI AIRPORT

If there's a long wait at baggage claim, step over to the state-operated **Visitor Information Center,** where you can pick up brochures and the latest issue of *This Week Maui,* which features great regional maps of the islands, and ask about island activities. After collecting your bags from the poky, automated carousels, step out, take a deep breath, proceed to the curbside rental-car pickup area, and wait for the appropriate rental-agency shuttle van to take you a half mile away to the rental-car checkout desk. (All major rental companies have branches at Kahului; see "Getting Around" later in this chapter.)

If you're not renting a car, the cheapest way to get to your hotel is **Speedi Shuttle** (© 808/875-8070; www. speedishuttle.com), which can take you between Kahului Airport and all the major resorts between 5am and 11pm daily. Rates vary, but figure on $30 for one to Wailea (one-way), $41 for one to Kaanapali (one-way), and $57 one-way to Kapalua. Be sure to call before your flight to arrange pickup.

You'll see taxis outside the airport terminal, but note that they are quite expensive—expect to spend around $60 to $75 for a ride from Kahului to Kaanapali and $50 from the airport to Wailea.

If possible, avoid landing on Maui between 3 and 6pm, when the working stiffs on Maui are "pau work" (finished with work) and a major traffic jam occurs at the first intersection.

AVOIDING KAHULUI If you're planning to stay at any of the hotels in Kapalua or at the Kaanapali resorts, you might consider flying **Island Air** (© 800/323-3345; www.islandair. com) from Honolulu to **Kapalua–West Maui Airport.** From this airport, it's only a 10- to 15-minute drive to most hotels in West Maui, as opposed to an hour from Kahului. **Pacific Wings** (© 888/873-0877 or 808/575-4546; fax 808/873-7920; www.pacificwings.com) flies eight-passenger, twin-engine Cessna 402C aircraft into tiny **Hana Airport,** and also flies into Kahului.

INTERISLAND FLIGHTS

Don't expect to jump a ferry between any of the Hawaiian islands. Today, everyone island-hops by plane. Before

The Welcoming Lei

Nothing makes you feel more welcome than a lei. The tropical beauty of the delicate garland, the deliciously sweet fragrance of the blossoms, the sensual way the flowers curl softly around your neck—there's no doubt about it: Getting lei'd in Hawaii is a sensuous experience.

Leis are much more than just a decorative necklace of flowers; they're also one of the nicest ways to say hello, goodbye, congratulations, I salute you, my sympathies are with you, or I love you. The custom of giving leis can be traced back to Hawaii's very roots: According to chants, the first lei was given by Hiiaka, the sister of the volcano goddess, Pele, who presented Pele with a lei of lehua blossoms on a beach in Puna.

During ancient times, leis given to *alii* (royalty) were accompanied by a bow, since it was *kapu* (forbidden) for a commoner to raise his arms higher than the king's head. The presentation of a kiss with a lei didn't come about until World War II; it's generally attributed to an entertainer who kissed an officer on a dare, then quickly presented him with her lei, saying it was an old Hawaiian custom. It wasn't then, but it sure caught on fast.

Lei-making is a tropical art form. All leis are fashioned by hand in a variety of traditional patterns; some are sewn of hundreds of tiny blooms or shells, or bits of ferns and leaves. Some are twisted, some braided, some strung. Every island has its own special flower lei. On Oahu, the choice is *ilima,* a small orange flower. Big Islanders prefer the *lehua,* a large, delicate red puff. Maui likes the *lokelani,* a small rose. On Kauai, it's the *mokihana,* a fragrant green vine and berry. Molokai prefers the *kukui,* the white blossom of a candlenut tree. Lanai's lei is made of *kaunaoa,* a bright yellow moss, while Niihau uses its abundant seashells to make leis that were once prized by royalty and are now worth a small fortune.

Leis are available at the Kahului Airport, from florists, and even at supermarkets.

Leis are the perfect symbol for Hawaii: They're given in the moment, their fragrance and beauty are enjoyed in the moment, but when they fade, their spirit of aloha lives on. Welcome to the islands!

the September 11, 2001, terrorist attacks, there used to be flights between Honolulu and Maui almost every 20 minutes of every day from just before sunrise to well after sunset.

Those days are gone. There are fewer and fewer interisland flights, so be sure to book your interisland connection from Honolulu to Maui in advance.

Aloha Airlines (© **800/367-5250** or 808/244-9071; www.alohaair.com) is the state's largest provider of interisland air transport service. It offers 15 regularly scheduled daily jet flights a day from Honolulu to Maui on their all-jet fleet of Boeing 737 aircraft. Aloha's sibling company, **Island Air** (© **800/323-3345** or 808/484-2222; www.alohaair.com), operates deHavilland DASH-8 and DASH-6 turboprop aircraft and serves Hawaii's small interisland airports on Maui, Molokai, and Lanai, with flights connecting them to Oahu.

Hawaiian Airlines (✆ **800/367-5320** or 808/871-6132; www.hawaiianair.com) is Hawaii's other interisland airline featuring jet planes.

A newcomer on the interisland commuter scene is Kahului-based **Pacific Wings** (✆ **888/873-0877** or 808/575-4546; www.pacificwings.com), which flies eight-passenger, twin-engine Cessna 402C aircraft. It currently offers flights between Kahului and Hana, Molokai, Lanai, and Honolulu.

10 Money-Saving Package Deals

Booking an all-inclusive travel package that includes some combination of airfare, accommodations, rental car, meals, airport and baggage transfers, and sightseeing can be the most cost-effective way to travel to Maui.

Package tours are not the same as escorted tours. They are simply a way to buy airfare and accommodations (and sometimes extras like sightseeing tours and rental cars) at the same time. When you're visiting Hawaii, a package can be a smart way to go. You can sometimes save so much money by buying all the pieces of your trip through a packager that your transpacific airfare ends up, in effect, being free. That's because packages are sold in bulk to tour operators, who then resell them to the public at a cost that drastically undercuts standard rates.

Packages, however, vary widely. Some offer a better class of hotels than others. Some offer the same hotels for lower prices. With some packagers, your choice of accommodations and travel days may be limited. Which package is right for you depends entirely on what you want.

Start out by **reading this guide.** Do a little homework, and read up on Maui so that you can be a smart consumer. Compare the rack rates that we've published to the discounted rates being offered by the packagers to see what kinds of deals they're offering—if you're actually being offered a substantial savings, or if they've just gussied up the rack rates to make their offer *sound* like a deal. If you're being offered a stay in a hotel we haven't recommended, do more research to learn about it, especially if it isn't a reliable franchise. It's not a deal if you end up at a dump.

Be sure to **read the fine print.** Make sure you know *exactly* what's included in the price you're being quoted, and what's not. Are hotel taxes and airport transfers included, or will you have to pay extra? Before you commit to a package, make sure you know how much flexibility you have, say, if your kid gets sick or your boss suddenly asks you to adjust your vacation schedule. Some packagers require ironclad commitments, while others will go with the flow, charging only minimal fees for changes or cancellations.

The best place to start looking for a package deal is in the travel section of your local Sunday newspaper. Also check the ads in the back of such national travel magazines as *Arthur Frommer's Budget Travel* and *Travel Holiday.* **Liberty Travel** (✆ **888/271-1584;** www.libertytravel.com), for instance, one of the biggest packagers in the Northeast, usually boasts a full-page ad in Sunday papers. **American Express Travel** (✆ **800/AXP-6898;** www.americanexpress.com/travel) can also book you a well-priced Hawaiian vacation; it also advertises in many Sunday travel sections.

Excellent deals, like a rental car and 7 nights in a Maui condo starting at $420 per person (based on double occupancy), can be found at **More Hawaii For Less** (© 800/967-6687; www.hawaii4less.com), a California-based company that specializes in air-condominium packages at unbelievable prices.

Other reliable packagers include the airlines themselves, which often package their flights with accommodations. Among the airlines offering good-value package deals to Hawaii are **American Airlines FlyAway Vacations** (© 800/321-2121; www.aa.com), **Continental Airlines Vacations** (© 800/634-5555 or 800/301-3800; www.cool vacations.com), **Delta Dream Vacations** (© 800/872-7786; www.delta vacations.com), and **United Vacations** (© 800/328-6877; www.unitedvacations. com). If you're traveling to the islands from Canada, ask your travel agent about package deals through **Air Canada Vacations** (© 800/776-3000; www.air canada.ca).

GREAT DEALS AT HAWAII'S TOP HOTEL CHAINS

Hawaii's major hotel chains—which together represent nearly 100 hotels, condominiums, resorts, a historic B&B, and even restored plantation homes—have a host of packages that will save you money.

With five properties on Maui, **Outrigger Hotels and Resorts** (© 800/OUTRIGGER; fax 800/622-4852; www.outrigger.com) offers excellent, moderately priced, luxury-resort accommodations. Package deals include a car package, bed-and-breakfast, golf packages, deals on multinight stays, family plans, cut rates for seniors, and even a package for island hopping where you save up to 20% when you stay 7 nights at any Outrigger resort on any island.

The **Aston** chain (© 800/92-ASTON; fax 808/922-8785; www. astonhotels.com), which celebrated 50 years in Hawaii in 1998, has some 37 hotels, condominiums, and resort properties scattered throughout the islands, with 10 on Maui. They range dramatically in price and style, from the elegant Whaler on Kaanapali Beach to the moderate Aston at Maui Banyans. Aston offers package deals galore, including family plans; discounted senior rates; car, golf, and shopping packages; and deals on multinight stays, including a wonderful "Island Hopper" deal that allows you to hop from island to island and get 25% off on 7 nights or more at Aston properties.

11 Planning Your Trip Online

SURFING FOR AIRFARES

The "big three" online travel agencies, **Expedia.com**, **Travelocity.com**, and **Orbitz.com**, sell most of the air tickets bought on the Internet. (Canadian travelers should try expedia.ca and Travelocity.ca; U.K. residents can go for expedia.co.uk and opodo.co.uk.) Each has different business deals with the airlines and may offer different fares on the same flights, so it's wise to shop around. Expedia and Travelocity will also send you **e-mail notification** when a cheap fare to your favorite destination becomes available. Of the smaller travel agency websites, **Side-**

Step (www.sidestep.com) has gotten the best reviews from Frommer's authors. It's a browser add-on that purports to "search 140 sites at once," but in reality only beats competitors' fares as often as other sites do.

Also remember to check **airline websites,** especially those for low-fare carriers such as Southwest, JetBlue, AirTran, WestJet, or Ryanair, whose fares are often misreported or simply missing from travel agency websites. Even with major airlines, you can often shave a few bucks from a fare by booking directly through the airline and avoiding a travel agency's

---

Tips **Package-Buying Tip**

For one-stop shopping on the Web, go to **Pleasant Hawaiian Holidays** (© **800/2-HAWAII** or 800/242-9244; www.pleasantholidays.com), by far the biggest and most comprehensive packager to Hawaii; it offers an extensive, high-quality collection of 50 condos and hotels in every price range. Just as we went to press, they had a package deal that included air from Los Angeles or San Francisco to Maui, 7 nights in Lahaina (based on double occupancy), and 7 days car rental for $499.

---

transaction fee. But you'll get these discounts only by **booking online:** Most airlines now offer online-only fares that even their phone agents know nothing about. For the websites of airlines that fly to and from your destination, go to "Getting There" earlier in this chapter.

Great **last-minute deals** are available through free weekly e-mail services provided directly by the airlines. Most of these are announced on Tuesday or Wednesday and must be purchased online. Most are only valid for travel that weekend, but some (such as Southwest's) can be booked weeks or months in advance. Sign up for weekly e-mail alerts at airline websites or check mega-sites that compile comprehensive lists of last-minute specials, such as **Smarter Living** (smarter living.com). For last-minute trips, **site59.com** in the U.S. and **last-minute.com** in Europe often have better deals than the major-label sites.

If you're willing to give up some control over your flight details, use an **opaque fare service** like **Priceline** (www.priceline.com; www.priceline. co.uk for Europeans) or **Hotwire** (www.hotwire.com). Both offer rock-bottom prices in exchange for travel on a "mystery airline" at a mysterious time of day, often with a mysterious change of planes en route. The mystery airlines are all major, well-known carriers—and the possibility of being sent from Philadelphia to Chicago via Tampa is remote; the airlines' routing computers

have gotten a lot better than they used to be. But your chances of getting a 6am or 11pm flight are pretty high. Hotwire tells you flight prices before you buy; Priceline usually has better deals than Hotwire, but you have to play their "name our price" game. If you're new at this, the helpful folks at **BiddingForTravel** (www.biddingfor travel.com) do a good job of demystifying Priceline's prices. Priceline and Hotwire are great for flights within North America and between the U.S. and Europe. But for flights to other parts of the world, consolidators will almost always beat their fares.

For much more about airfares and savvy air-travel tips and advice, pick up a copy of *Frommer's Fly Safe, Fly Smart* (Wiley Publishing).

SURFING FOR HOTELS

Shopping online for hotels on Maui is easy; nearly every single accommodation in this book has its own website and most offer online-only discounts where you can save by booking online. Check the hotel/B&B of your choice to see if there is a deal. If you go to the "big three" sites, they may not list all the smaller hotels and B&Bs we have listed here. So shop around. **Expedia** may be the best choice, thanks to its long list of special deals. **Travelocity** runs a close second. Hotel specialist sites **hotels.com** and **hoteldiscounts. com** are also reliable. An excellent free program, **TravelAxe** (www.travelaxe. net), can help you search multiple hotel

Frommers.com: The Complete Travel Resource

For an excellent travel-planning resource, we highly recommend **Frommers.com** (www.frommers.com). We're a little biased, of course, but we guarantee that you'll find the travel tips, reviews, monthly vacation giveaways, and online-booking capabilities thoroughly indispensable. Among the special features are our popular **Message Boards,** where Frommer's readers post queries and share advice (sometimes even our authors show up to answer questions); **Frommers.com Newsletter,** for the latest travel bargains and inside travel secrets; and Frommer's **Destinations Section,** where you'll get expert travel tips, hotel and dining recommendations, and advice on the sights to see for more than 2,500 destinations around the globe. When your research is done, the **Online Reservation System** (www.frommers.com/booktravelnow) takes you to Frommer's favorite sites for booking your vacation at affordable prices.

sites at once, even ones you may never have heard of.

Priceline and Hotwire are even better for hotels than for airfares; with both, you're allowed to pick the neighborhood and quality level of your hotel before offering up your money. *Note:* Hotwire overrates its hotels by one star—what Hotwire calls a four-star is a three-star anywhere else.

SURFING FOR RENTAL CARS

For booking rental cars online, the best deals are usually found at rental-car company websites, although all the major online travel agencies also offer rental-car reservations services. Priceline and Hotwire work well for rental cars, too; the only "mystery" is which major rental company you get, and for most travelers the difference between Hertz, Avis, and Budget is negligible. Don't forget to check package deals. Sometimes you can get an air/car rental package or an air/car/accommodation package where the rental car is virtually free.

SMART E-SHOPPING

The savvy traveler is armed with insider information. Here are a few tips to help you navigate the Internet successfully and safely.

- **Know when sales start.** Last-minute deals may vanish in minutes. If you have a favorite booking site or airline, find out when last-minute deals are released to the public. (For example, Southwest's specials are posted every Tues at 12:01am central time.)
- **Shop around.** If you're looking for bargains, compare prices on different sites and airlines—and against a travel agent's best fare. Try a range of times and alternative airports before you make a purchase.
- **Stay secure.** Book only through secure sites (some airline sites are not secure). Look for a key icon (Netscape) or a padlock (Internet Explorer) at the bottom of your Web browser before you enter credit card information or other personal data.
- **Avoid online auctions.** Sites that auction airline tickets and frequent-flier miles are the number-one perpetrators of Internet fraud, according to the National Consumers League.
- **Maintain a paper trail.** If you book an E-ticket, print out a confirmation, or write down your

confirmation number, and keep it safe and accessible—or your trip could be a virtual one!

HAWAII ON THE WEB

Below are some of the best Hawaii-specific websites for planning your trip.

- **Hawaii Visitors & Convention Bureau (HVCB; www.gohawaii. com):** An excellent, all-around guide to activities, tours, lodging, and events, plus a huge section on weddings and honeymoons. But keep in mind that only members of the HVCB are listed.
- **Planet Hawaii (www.planet-hawaii.com):** Click on "Island" for an island-by-island guide to activities, lodging, shopping, culture, the surf report, weather, and more. Mostly, you'll find short listings with links to companies' own websites. Click on "Hawaiian Eye" for live images from around the islands.
- **Internet Hawaii Radio (www. hotspots.hawaii.com):** A great way to get into the mood, this eclectic site features great Hawaiian music, with opportunities to order a CD or cassette. You can also purchase a respectable assortment of Hawaiian historical and cultural books.
- **Maui Island Currents (www. islandcurrents.com):** Specializing in arts and culture, Island Currents gives the most detailed lowdown on current exhibitions and performance art. Gallery listings are organized by town, while in-depth articles highlight local artists. Consult restaurant reviews from the *Maui News* "Best of Maui" poll for suggestions and prices.
- **Maui Net (www.maui.net):** The clients of this Internet service provider are featured in this extensive directory of links to accommodations, activities, and shopping. The activities section has links to golf, hiking, airborne activities, and ocean adventures, such as scuba and snorkeling. These links lead to outfitters' sites, where you can learn more and set up excursions before you arrive in paradise.
- **Molokai: The Most Hawaiian Island (www.molokai-hawaii. com):** This is a very complete site for activities, events, nightlife, accommodations, and family vacations. Enjoy the landscape by viewing a virtual photo tour, get driving times between various points, and learn about local history.
- **The Hawaiian Language Website (http://hawaiianlanguage. com):** This fabulous site not only has easy lessons on learning the Hawaiian language, but also a great cultural calendar, links to other Hawaiian websites, a section on the hula, and lyrics (and translations) to Hawaiian songs.

12 The 21st-Century Traveler

INTERNET ACCESS AWAY FROM HOME

Travelers have any number of ways to check their e-mail and access the Internet on the road. Of course, using your own laptop—or even a PDA (personal desk assistant) or electronic organizer with a modem—gives you the most flexibility. But even if you don't have a computer, you can still access your e-mail and even your office computer from cybercafes.

WITHOUT YOUR OWN COMPUTER

It's hard nowadays to find a city that *doesn't* have a few cybercafes, and Maui is no exception. Although there's no definitive directory for cybercafes— these are independent businesses, after all—some good places to start are www.cybercaptive.com, www.netafe guide.com, and www.cybercafe.com.

In Kihei, you can get Internet access at the **Hale Imua Internet Café,** in the Kamaole Center, © **808/891-9219** (they also have a cafe in Wailuku, 1980 Main St., © **808/242-1896**). In Lahaina, drop by **Buns of Maui,** 878 Front St., © **808/661-5407.**

Aside from formal cybercafes, all **public libraries** on Maui offer free access if you have a library card, which you can purchase for a $10 fee. All hotels on Maui have **in-room dataports** and **business centers,** but the charges can be exorbitant.

To retrieve your e-mail, ask your **Internet Service Provider (ISP)** if it has a Web-based interface tied to your existing e-mail account. If your ISP doesn't have such an interface, you can use the free **mail2web** service (www. mail2web.com) to view (but not reply to) your home e-mail. For more flexibility, you may want to open a free, Web-based e-mail account with **Yahoo! Mail** (mail.yahoo.com). (Microsoft's Hotmail is another popular option, but Hotmail has severe spam problems.) Your home ISP may be able to forward your e-mail to the Web-based account automatically.

WITH YOUR OWN COMPUTER

Major Internet Service Providers (ISPs) have **local access numbers** allowing you to go online by simply placing a local call in Maui. Check your ISP's website or call its toll-free number and ask how you can use your current account away from home, and how much it will cost.

Wherever you go, bring a **connection kit** of the right power and phone adapters, a spare phone cord, and a spare Ethernet network cable.

All hotels on Maui (and even some of the B&Bs) offer dataports for laptop modems, and a few have high-speed Internet access using an Ethernet network cable. You'll have to bring your own cables either way, so **call your hotel in advance** to find out what the options are.

USING A CELLPHONE

Just because your cellphone works at home doesn't mean it'll work in Maui (thanks to our nation's fragmented cellphone system). Take a look at your wireless company's coverage map on its website before heading out—T-Mobile, Sprint, and Nextel are particularly weak in Maui's rural areas. If you need to stay in touch at a destination where you know your phone won't work, **rent** a phone that does from **InTouch USA** (© **800/ 872-7626;** www.intouchglobal.com) or a rental-car location, but beware that you'll pay $1 a minute or more for airtime.

13 Getting Around

The only way to really see Maui is by rental car. There's no real islandwide public transit.

Maui has only a handful of major roads: One follows the coastline around the two volcanoes that form the island, Haleakala and Puu Kukui; one goes up to Haleakala's summit; one goes to Hana; one goes to Wailea; and one goes to Lahaina. It sounds simple, right? Well, it isn't, because the names of the few roads change en route. Study the foldout map in the back included with this book before you set out. Also, you should expect to encounter a traffic jam or two in the major resort areas.

The best and most detailed road maps are published by *This Week Magazine,* a free visitor publication available on Maui. Most rental-car maps are pretty good, too.

Tips **Traffic Advisory**

The road from central Maui to Kihei and Wailea, **Mokulele Highway (Hwy. 311)**, is a dangerous strip that's often the scene of head-on crashes involving intoxicated and speeding drivers; be careful. Also, be alert on the **Honoapiilani Highway (Hwy. 30)** en route to Lahaina, because drivers who spot whales in the channel between Maui and Lanai often slam on the brakes and cause major tie-ups and accidents.

If you get into trouble on Maui's highways, look for the flashing blue strobe lights on 12-foot poles; at the base are emergency, solar-powered call boxes (programmed to dial 911 as soon as you pick up the handset). There are 29 emergency call boxes on the island's busiest highways and remote areas, including along the Hana and Haleakala highways and on the north end of the island in the remote community of Kahakuloa.

Another traffic note: Buckle up your seat belt—Hawaii has stiff fines for noncompliance.

CAR RENTALS

Maui has one of the least expensive car-rental rates in the country. The average nondiscounted, unlimited-mileage rate for a 1-day rental for an intermediate-size car was $41 in 2001 (plus the $3 state tax). That's one of the lowest rates in the country; the national average is $53.50 a day. Cars are usually plentiful on Maui, except on holiday weekends, which in Hawaii also means King Kamehameha Day, Prince Kuhio Day, and Admission Day (see "When to Go" earlier in this chapter). Rental cars are usually at a premium on Molokai and Lanai, so be sure to book well ahead.

Maui is a great place to tool around in a convertible! You might ask your car-rental company about rates and try to reserve one in advance.

All the major car-rental agencies have offices on Maui, usually at both Kahului and West Maui Airports. They include: **Alamo** (© 800/327-9633; www.goalamo.com), **Avis** (© 800/321-3712; www.avis.com), **Budget** (© 800/935-6878; https://rent.drivebudget.com/Home.jsp), **Dollar** (© 800/800-4000; www.dollarcar.com), **Hertz** (© 800/654-3011; www.hertz.com), and **National** (© 800/227-7368; www.nationalcar.com).

There are also a few frugal car-rental agencies offering older cars at discount prices. **Word of Mouth Rent-a-Used-Car** ✮, in Kahului (© 800/533-5929 or 808/877-2436; www.mauirentacar.com), offers an older, four-door compact without air-conditioning for $120 a week, plus tax; with air-conditioning, it's $140 a week, plus tax. **Discount Car Rental,** 1993 S. Kihei Rd., Suite 214-B Kihei (© 877/874-4800 or 808/874-4800), rents used economy cars at a weekly rate of $115 to $140, plus tax. They do not provide airport pickup, however; you'll have to make your own way to Kihei (it's about $28 via taxi; see "Other Transportation Options" below, for details).

To rent a car in Hawaii, you must be at least 25 years old and have a valid driver's license and a credit card. Your valid home-state license will be recognized here.

INSURANCE   Hawaii is a no-fault state, which means that if you don't have collision-damage insurance, you are required to pay for all damages before you leave the state, whether or not the accident was your fault. Your personal car insurance back home may provide rental-car coverage; read your policy or call your insurer before you leave home. Bring your insurance identification card if you decline the optional insurance, which usually costs from $12 to $20 a day. Obtain the name of your company's local claim representative before you go. Some credit-card companies also provide collision-damage insurance for their customers; check with yours before you rent.

EASY RIDING AROUND MAUI

Don black denim and motorcycle boots and ride around Maui on a hog, available for $99 for 6 hours and $149 a day at **Island Riders,** 126 Hinau St. (by Pizza Hut), Lahaina (✆ **800/ 529-2925** or 808/661-9966; www. islandriders.com) and in Kihei at 1975 S. Kihei Rd. (✆ 808/874-0311). Forget the greasy Hell's Angels image; latter-day Wild Ones are buttoned-down corporate types, or California Highway Patrol officers on holiday. Whether you blast up Haleakala's grand corniche or haul ass to Hana, it's the most fun you can have on two wheels. This toy store for big boys and girls also rents exotic cars (Dodge Vipers, Prowlers, and Corvettes), which start at about $169 for 5 hours and $249 a day. Island Riders offers free pickup from most Maui hotels—convenient if you're throwing caution to the wind for just a day. They also have 4×4 Jeeps starting at $69 for 8 hours and $79 for 24 hours.

MOPEDS

Mopeds are available for rent from **Wheels USA** at either of their two locations: 741 Wainee St., Lahaina (✆ **808/667-7751;** http://www.maui. net/~rentals/wheels.html) and 75 Kaahumanu Ave., Kahului (✆ **808/ 871-6858**). Mopeds, which start at $26 a day (from 8am–4:30pm), are little more than motorized bicycles that get up to around 35 miles per hour (with a good wind at your back), so we suggest using them only locally (to get to the beach or to go shopping). Don't take them out on the highway, because they can't keep up with the traffic. They also rent motorcycles and dune buggies.

OTHER TRANSPORTATION OPTIONS

TAXIS For islandwide 24-hour service, call **Alii Cab Co.** (✆ 808/ 661-3688 or 808/667-2605). You can also try **Kihei Taxi** (✆ 808/879-3000), **Wailea Taxi** (✆ 808/874-5000), or **Maui Central Cab** (✆ 808/ 244-7278) if you need a ride.

SHUTTLES SpeediShuttle (✆ **808/875-8070;** www.speedishuttle. com) can take you between Kahului Airport and all the major resorts from 5am to 11pm daily (for details, see "Landing at Kahului Airport" under "Getting There" earlier in this chapter).

Free shuttle vans operate within the resort areas of Kaanapali, Kapalua, and Wailea; if you're staying in those areas, your hotel can fill you in on exact routes and schedules.

14 Tips on Accommodations

Maui offers a tremendous variety of accommodations, from ritzy resorts to simple bed-and-breakfasts. Read this section to find out what each option typically has to offer before booking a room. We've also included some tips on how to get the best rates.

TYPES OF ACCOMMODATIONS

HOTELS In Hawaii, the term *hotel* can indicate a wide range of options, from few or no on-site amenities to enough extras to qualify as a resort. Generally, a hotel offers daily maid service and has a restaurant, on-site laundry facilities, a pool, and a sundries/convenience-type shop (as opposed to the shopping arcades that most resorts have). Top hotels also provide activities desks, concierge service, business centers, a bar and/or lounge, and perhaps a few more shops. The advantages of staying in a hotel are privacy and convenience; the disadvantage is generally noise—either thin walls between rooms or loud music from a lobby lounge late into the night.

RESORTS   In Hawaii, a resort offers everything a hotel offers and more. What you get varies from property to property, of course, but expect facilities, services, and amenities such as direct beach access, with cabanas and chairs; pools (often more than one) and a Jacuzzi; a spa and fitness center; restaurants, bars, and lounges; a 24-hour front desk; concierge, valet, and bell services; room service (often around the clock); an activities desk; tennis and golf (some of the world's best courses are at Hawaii resorts); ocean activities; a business center; children's programs; and more.

The advantage of staying at a resort is that you have everything you could possibly want in the way of services and things to do; the disadvantage is that the price generally reflects this. Don't be misled by a name—just because a place is called "ABC Resort" doesn't mean it actually *is* a resort. Make sure you're getting what you pay for.

CONDOS   The roominess and convenience of a condo—usually a fully equipped, multibedroom apartment—makes this a great choice for families. Condominium properties in Hawaii are generally several apartments set in either a single high-rise or a cluster of low-rise units. Condos generally have amenities such as some degree of maid service (ranging from daily to weekly; it may or may not be included in your rate, so be sure to ask), a pool, laundry facilities (either in your unit or in a central location),

and an on-site front desk or a live-in property manager. The advantages of a condo are privacy, space, and conveniences—which usually include a fully equipped kitchen, a washer and dryer, a private phone, and perhaps your own lanai or balcony. The downsides include the absence of an on-site restaurant and the density of the units (perhaps more private than a B&B or hotel, but not quite like renting your own cottage, villa, or house, either).

Condos vary in price according to size, location, and amenities. Many of them are located on or near the beach, and they tend to be clustered in resort areas. While there are some very high-end condos, most tend to be quite affordable, especially if you're traveling in a group that's large enough to require more than one bedroom.

BED & BREAKFASTS   Maui has a wide variety of places that fall under this category: everything from the traditional B&B—several bedrooms in a home (which may or may not share a bathroom), with breakfast served in the morning—to what is essentially a vacation rental on an owner's property that comes with fixings for you to make your own breakfast. Make sure that the B&B you're booking matches your own mental picture. Would you prefer conversation around a big dining-room table as you eat a hearty breakfast, or just a muffin and juice to enjoy in your own private place? Laundry facilities, televisions, and private phones are not always available at B&Bs. We've reviewed lots of wonderful places in chapter 4. If you have to share a bathroom, we've spelled it out in the listings; otherwise, you can assume that you will have a private bathroom.

The advantage of a traditional B&B is its individual style and congenial atmosphere. B&Bs are great places to meet other visitors, and the host is generally very happy to act as your own private concierge, offering tips on where to go and what to do. In addition, B&Bs

Tips What to Do If Your Dream Hotel Turns Out to Be a Nightmare

To avoid any unpleasant surprises, ask lots of questions when you make your reservation. Find out exactly what the accommodation is offering you, particularly the cost, minimum stay, and included amenities. Ask if there's a penalty fee for leaving early. Read the small print in the contract—especially the part on cancellation fees. Discuss the cancellation policy ahead of time with the B&B, vacation rental, condominium agent, or booking agency so you'll know what your options are if the accommodation doesn't meet your expectations. Get this in writing (so there are no misunderstandings later).

When you arrive, if the room you're given doesn't meet your expectations, notify the front desk, rental agent, or booking agency immediately. Approach the management in a calm, reasonable manner, and suggest a constructive solution (such as moving to another unit). Be reasonable and be willing to compromise. Do not make threats or leave; if you leave, it may be harder to get your deposit returned.

are usually an affordable way to go (though fancier ones can run $150 or more a night). The disadvantages are lack of privacy, usually a set time for breakfast, few amenities, generally no maid service, and the fact that you'll have to share the quarters beyond your bedroom with others. In addition, B&B owners usually require a minimum stay of 2 or 3 nights, and it's often a drive to the beach.

VACATION RENTALS This is another great choice for families, as well as for long-term stays. The term *vacation rental* usually means there will be no one on the property where you're staying. The actual accommodation can range from an apartment in a condominium building to a two-room cottage on the beach to an entire fully equipped house. Generally, vacation rentals are the kinds of places you can settle into for a while: They have kitchen facilities (sometimes a full kitchen, sometimes just a microwave, minifridge, stovetop, and coffeemaker), on-site laundry facilities, and phone; some also have such extras as TV, VCR, and stereo. The advantages of a vacation rental are complete privacy, your own kitchen (which can save you

money on meals), and lots of conveniences. The disadvantages are a lack of an on-site property manager, no organized ocean activities, and generally no maid service; often, a minimum stay is required (sometimes as much as a week). If you book a vacation rental, be sure you have a 24-hour contact so that when the toilet won't flush or you can't figure out how to turn on the air-conditioning, you'll have someone to call.

BARGAINING ON PRICES

Rates can sometimes be bargained down, but it depends on the place. In general, each type of accommodation allows a different amount of latitude in bargaining on its rack (or published) rates.

The best bargaining can be had at **hotels** and **resorts.** Hotels and resorts regularly pay travel agents as much as 30% of the rate they're getting for sending clients their way; if business is slow, some hotels might give you the benefit of at least part of this commission if you book directly instead of going through an airline or travel agent. Most also have *kamaaina* or "local" rates for islanders, which they might extend to visitors during slow periods. It never hurts to ask politely for a discounted or local rate; a host of special rates are also available for the military, seniors, members of the travel industry, families, corporate travelers, and long-term stays.

Ask about package deals, which might include a car rental or free breakfast for the same price as a room. Hotels and resorts offer packages for everyone: golfers, tennis players, families, honeymooners, and more. See "Money-Saving Package Deals" earlier in this chapter.

We've found that it's worth the extra few cents to make a local call to the hotel; sometimes the local reservationist knows about package deals that the toll-free operators are unaware of.

If all else fails, try to get the hotel or resort to upgrade you to a better room for the same price as a budget room, or to waive the parking fee or the extra fees for children. Persistence and polite inquiries can pay off.

It's harder to bargain at **bed-and-breakfasts.** You may be able to bargain down the minimum stay, or negotiate a discount if you're staying a week or longer. But generally, a B&B owner has only a few rooms and has already priced the property at a competitive rate, so expect to pay what's asked.

You have somewhat more leeway to negotiate on **vacation rentals** and **condos.** In addition to asking for a discount on multinight stays, also ask whether the condo or vacation rental can throw in a rental car to sweeten the deal; believe it or not, they often will.

USING A BOOKING AGENCY VERSUS DOING IT YOURSELF

Sometimes you can save money by making arrangements yourself—not only can you bargain on the phone, but some accommodations may also be willing to pass on a percentage of the commission they would normally have to pay a travel agent or a booking agency.

However, if you don't have the time or money to call several places to make sure they offer the amenities you'd like and to bargain for a price you're comfortable with, then you might consider using a booking agency. The time the agency spends on your behalf might well be worth any fees you'll have to pay.

The top reservations service in the state is **Hawaii's Best Bed & Breakfasts,** P.O. Box 758, Volcano, HI 96785 (© **800/262-9912** or 808/985-7488; fax 808/967-8610; www.best bnb.com). This service charges $15 to book the first two locations and $5 for each additional location. The staff personally selects the traditional homestays, cottages, and inns, based on each one's hospitality, distinctive charm, and attention to detail.

Ann and Bob Babson, 3371 Keha Dr., Kihei, HI 96753 (© **800/824-6409** or 808/874-1166; fax 808/879-7906; www.mauibnb.com), run

---

Tips Safety Tips

Be sure to see "Health & Insurance" earlier in this chapter, before setting out on any adventure; it includes useful information on hiking, camping, and ocean safety. Even if you just plan to lie on the beach, check out the box called "Don't Get Burned: Smart Tanning Tips" on p. 39, to learn how to protect yourself against the sun's harmful rays.

When planning sunset activities, be aware that Hawaii, like other places close to the equator, has a very short (5–10 min.) twilight period after the sun sets. After that, it's dark. If you hike out to watch the sunset, be sure you can make it back quickly, or take a flashlight.

another great statewide booking agency; they can steer you in the right direction for both accommodations and car rentals. Not only do they personally inspect the units they recommend, but the Babsons are also impeccably honest and dedicated to matching you up with the place that's right for you.

For vacation rentals, contact **Hawaii Beachfront Vacation Homes** (© 808/247-3637 or 808/235-2644; www.hibeach.com). **Hawaii Condo Exchange** (© 800/442-0404; www.hawaiicondoexchange.com) acts as a consolidator for condo and vacation-rental properties.

15 The Active Vacation Planner

If you want nothing more on your vacation than a fabulous beach and a perfectly mixed mai tai, you're in luck—Maui has some of the most spectacular beaches (not to mention the best mai tais) in the world. But Maui's wealth of natural wonders is hard to resist; the year-round tropical climate and spectacular scenery tend to inspire even the most committed desk jockeys and couch potatoes to get outside and explore.

If you have your own snorkel gear or other watersports equipment, bring it if you can. If not, don't fret; everything you'll need is available for rent. We'll list all kinds of places to rent or buy gear in chapter 6, "Fun in the Surf & Sun."

SETTING OUT ON YOUR OWN VERSUS USING AN OUTFITTER

There are two ways to go: Plan all the details before you go and schlepp your gear 2,500 miles across the Pacific, or go with an outfitter or a guide and let them worry about the details.

Experienced outdoor enthusiasts can follow their noses to coastal campgrounds or even trek into the rainforest on their own, but it's often preferable to go with a local guide who is familiar with the conditions at both sea level and the summit, knows the land and its flora and fauna in detail, and has all the gear you'll need. It's also good to go with a guide if time is an issue. If you really want to see native birds, for instance, an experienced guide will take you directly to

the best areas for sightings. And many forests and valleys in the interior of the islands are either on private property or in wilderness preserves that are accessible only on guided tours. If you go with a guide, plan on spending at least $100 a day per person; we recommend the best local outfitters and tour-guide operators in chapter 6.

But if you have the time, already own the gear, and love doing the research and planning, try exploring on your own. Chapter 6 discusses the best spots to set out on your own, from the best offshore snorkel and dive spots to great daylong hikes, as well as the federal, state, and county agencies that can help you with hikes on public property; we also list references for spotting birds, plants, and sea life. We recommend that you always use the resources available and inquire about weather, trail or surf conditions, water availability, and other conditions before you take off on your adventure.

For hikers, a great alternative to hiring a private guide is taking one of the guided hikes offered by the **Nature Conservancy of Hawaii,** 1116 Smith St., Honolulu, HI 96817 (© 808/573-4147 on Maui, 808/553-5236 on Oahu, or 808/524-0779 on Molokai), and the **Hawaii Chapter of the Sierra Club,** P.O. Box 2577, Honolulu, HI 96803 (© 808/573-4147 on Maui; www.hi.sierraclub.org). Both organizations offer guided hikes on preserves and special places during the year, as well as 1- to 7-day work trips to restore habitats and trails and root out invasive

> **Value Fun for Less: Don't Leave Home Without the Gold Card**
>
> Almost any activity you can think of, from submarine rides to Polynesian luaus, can be purchased at a discount by using the **Activities and Attractions Association of Hawaii Gold Card**, 355 Hukilike St., no. 202, Kahului, HI 96732 (© **800/398-9698** or 808/871-7947; fax 808/877-3104; www.hawaiifun.org). The Gold Card, accepted by members on Oahu, the Big Island, Maui, Molokai, Lanai, and Kauai, offers a discount of 10% to 25% off activities and meals for up to four people; it's good for a year from the purchase date and costs $30.
>
> You can save big bucks with the Gold Card. For example, if you have your heart set on taking a helicopter ride that goes for $149, you'll pay only $119.20 with your Gold Card, saving you nearly $30 per person—almost $120 in savings for a family of four. With just one activity alone, you've gotten the cost of the card back in savings. And there are hundreds of activities to choose from: air tours, attractions, bicycling tours, dinner cruises, fishing, guided tours, helicopter tours, horseback riding, kayaking, luaus, snorkeling, rafting, sailing, scuba diving, submarine rides, and more. It even gets you discounts on rental cars, restaurants, and golf!
>
> Here's how it works: You contact Activities and Attractions Association via mail, e-mail, fax, phone, or Internet (see above). They issue you the card, good for discounts for 1 year after the date you purchased it. You contact the activity (restaurant, rental car, and so on) directly, give them your Gold Card number, and get discounts ranging from 10% to 25%.

plants like banana poka, New Zealand flax, nonnative gorse, and wild ginger. It might not sound like a dream vacation to everyone, but it's a chance to see the "real" Maui—including wilderness areas that are usually off-limits.

All Nature Conservancy hikes are free. However, you must reserve a spot, and a deposit is required for guided hikes to ensure that you'll show up; your deposit is refunded once you do. The hikes are generally offered once a month on Maui, Molokai, and Lanai (call the Oahu office for reservations). There's also no charge for the trips to restore habitats. Write for a schedule of guided hikes and other programs.

The Sierra Club offers weekly hikes on Maui. Hikes are led by certified Sierra Club volunteers and are classified as easy, moderate, or strenuous. These half-day or all-day affairs cost $1 for Sierra Club members, $3 for nonmembers (bring exact change). For a copy of the newsletter, which lists all outings and trail repair work, send $2 to the address above.

USING ACTIVITIES DESKS TO BOOK YOUR ISLAND FUN

If you're interested in an activity that requires an outfitter or a guide, such as horseback riding, whale-watching, or sportfishing, you might want to consider booking through a discount activities center or activities desk. These agents—who act as a clearinghouse for activities, just as a consolidator functions as a discount clearinghouse for airline tickets—can often get you a better price than you'd get by booking an activity directly with the outfitter yourself.

Discount activities centers will, in effect, split their commission with you, giving themselves a smaller commission to get your business—and passing, on average, a 10% discount on to you. In addition to saving you money, good activities centers should be able to help you find, say, the snorkel cruise that's right for you, or the luau that's most suitable for both you *and* the kids.

But it's in the activity agent's best interest to sign you up with outfitters from which they earn the most commission, and some agents have no qualms about booking you into any old activity if it means an extra buck for them. If an agent tries to push a particular outfitter or activity too hard, be skeptical. Conversely, they'll try to steer you away from outfitters that don't offer big commissions. For example, Trilogy, the company that offers Maui's most popular snorkel cruises to Lanai (and the only one with rights to land at Lanai's Hulupoe Beach), offers only minimal commissions to agents and does not allow agents to offer any discounts at all; as a result, most activities desks on Maui will automatically try to steer you away from Trilogy even if you say you want to book with it.

Another important word of warning: Be careful to avoid those activities centers offering discounts as fronts for timeshare sales presentations. Using a free snorkel cruise or luau tickets as bait, they'll suck you into a 90-minute presentation—and try to get you to buy into a Maui timeshare in the process. Not only will they try to sell you a big white elephant you never wanted in the first place, but—since their business is timeshares, not activities—they also won't be as interested, or as knowledgeable, about which activities might be right for you. These shady deals seem to be particularly rampant on Maui. Just do yourself a favor and avoid them altogether.

On Maui, we recommend **Tom Barefoot's Cashback Tours** ⍟, 834 Front St., Lahaina (℡ **888/222-3601** or 808/661-8889; www.barefoot hawaii.com). Tom offers a 10% discount on all tours, activities, and adventures when you pay in cash or with traveler's checks. If you pay with a credit card or personal check, he'll give you a 7% discount. The two showrooms are loaded with pictures and maps of all the activities the company books. We found Tom's to be very reliable and honest.

OUTDOOR ETIQUETTE

Carry out what you carry in. Find a trash container for all your litter (including cigarette butts). Litterbugs anger the gods.

Observe *kapu* (taboo) and NO TRESPASSING signs. Don't climb on ancient Hawaiian *heiau* (temple) walls or carry home rocks, all of which belong to the Hawaiian volcano goddess, Pele. Some say it's just a silly superstition, but each year the national and state park services get boxes of lava rocks in the mail, sent back to Hawaii by visitors who have experienced unusually bad luck.

16 Suggested Itinerary

If you only have a week on Maui and want to do everything, we've suggested a jammed-packed 7-day/6-night itinerary below. However, you might want to skip a few suggestions and just veg out on the beach, or substitute your own interests like sailing, scuba diving, or golf.

Day 1 Arrive in Maui and head towards the closest **beach** (see our recommendations for the best beaches in Chapter 1). Don't forget the sunscreen.

Enjoy a Hawaiian dinner at the **Old Lahaina Luau** (p. 236) to get in the spirit of your Hawaiian vacation (be sure to book this before you leave home for Maui).

Day 2   Since you're probably still on mainland time and will be wide awake before the break of dawn on Maui, you might as well get up and see the sunrise atop **Haleakala** (p. 199).

If you don't feel like joining the crowds at the top, wait until after dawn (5:30am in the summer and 6:30am in the winter) and make your way slowly from your hotel to the top of 10,000-foot Haleakala.

Stop for breakfast in Kula at either the **Kula Lodge** (p. 146) or the **Kula Sandalwoods Restaurant** (p. 147) and enjoy the view of the Valley Isle. Plan to spend several hours in **Haleakala National Park** (p. 199) before wandering down the mountain to take in the quaint old town of **Paia,** where there are numerous restaurants and shops.

You can eat in Paia or continue into the Wailuku-Kahului area for lunch. In Kahului we recommend **Mañana Garage** (p. 123); if you're in Wailuku, try **Café O'Lei on Main** (p. 125). You'll find great shopping in the malls in Kahului and the quaint boutiques in Wailuku.

After lunch head out to **Iao Valley** (p. 185) to experience this natural wonder. Then take a drive on the wild side, on the "back way" to Lahaina via the **Kahekili Highway** (p. 196).

Take some time to explore the resorts and shops at Kapalua. **The Bay Club** (p. 137), overlooking Kapalua Bay, would be a great place for dinner or a sunset drink. Or continue down the coast to Roy's two restaurants, **Roy's Kahana Bar & Grill** and **Roy's Nicolina Restaurant** (p. 136). There's no sunset view, but, as we say in Hawaii, "ono grinds" (good food).

Day 3   Time to hit the ocean and spend the day at the beach—the beach on **Lanai** that is. Sail on the 50-foot catamaran from **Trilogy Ocean Sports** from Lahaina Harbor to the island of Lanai (p. 160), where you'll spend the day on one of Hawaii's most beautiful beaches, **Hulopoe,** enjoy a barbecued lunch, and sail back to Lahaina in the afternoon.

After you get back to **Lahaina,** take the rest of the afternoon and explore this old whaling town (see p. 190 for a **historic walking tour**). In the evening take in a show, **Ulalena,** a combination of hula, myth, and modern dance (p. 236), and then dinner at one of Lahaina's best restaurants: **Gerard's, David Paul's Lahaina Grill, Pacific'O, I'o,** or a host of others (see chapter 5).

Day 4   To explore an entirely different side of Maui, take a trip to **Hana.** Rise early and get breakfast in Paia either at **Charlie's** (p. 148) or **Moanai Bakery & Café** (p. 148). Get a picnic lunch at **Pic-nics** (p. 149) and spend the entire day exploring the **Road to Hana** (p. 205). Stop off at waterfalls, swim in cool mountain stream pools, pull over and take photos, smell the ginger, and let everyone else rush off to Hana; you're on vacation and want to enjoy one of Hawaii's best adventures.

Book a place in Hana (see Chapter 4) and plan to stay a couple of nights; you didn't come all the way to Maui to miss out on this most-Hawaiian place.

Dinner options in Hana are the **Hotel Hana-Maui** dining room or the **Hana Ranch Restaurant** (p. 151). Otherwise, stop in at **Hasegawa's General Store** and get your own fixings for dinner.

Day 5   You have the entire day to **explore Hana.** Start with the tiny town and wander through the **Hana Museum Cultural Center** and out to **Hana Bay** to **Kauiki Hill,** where Queen Kaahumanu was born. If you are not staying there, plan to have at least one meal at the **Hotel Hana-Maui** and don't miss out on the terrific **Hana Coast Gallery** there, and book a massage or an array of other treatments at the Spa.

There's a wide range of activities in Hana from hiking to exploring fresh water pools to relaxing on a red-sand beach (yes, red!) to a host of ocean activities; check out p. 212–217 for more information on what to do in Hana.

Day 6   Time to head off on another adventure; instead of returning via the Hana Highway, continue on to **Oheo Gulch** and the **Haleakala National Park** (p. 199). Stop for a swim in the fresh-water pools, then head out to **Kaupo** and the arid side of the island.

When you reach the **Tedeschi Vineyards and Winery** (p. 204) in Ulupalakua, a couple of hours later, get out and stretch your legs, make a bathroom stop, and explore the winery. As you drive back down the mountain, spend some time exploring Maui's **Upcountry** area of **Kula** and **Makawao,** with their restaurants, unique shops, and points of interest.

Plan to have lunch at the **Haliimaile General Store** (p. 144), just down the street from Makawao. Either spend the rest of the afternoon at the beach or take in the **Maui Ocean Center** (p. 197) in Maalaea.

Day 7   If this is your last day, and you have a late-night flight back home, get up early and drive to either **Makena** to see **Maluaka Beach** (p. 157) or further on to **La Perouse Bay** and the **Ahihi-Kinau Preserve** (p. 164).

After snorkeling, swimming, or just soaking up the rays, head over to the **Shops at Wailea** and eat a hearty breakfast at **Longhi's** (p. 143). Now's the time to get in the last of your shopping, especially for souvenirs or gifts for those back home who weren't lucky enough to come to Maui (see chapter 8 on Shops and Galleries).

If you have one more day   Get over to **Molokai** (by ferry or by plane) and experience the **Molokai Mule Ride** (p. 265), a once-in-a-lifetime memorable experience of descending down the several thousand-foot cliffs via a sure-footed mule into the historic Kalaupapa Peninsula, now a National Historic Park, but once the home to some 11,000 lepers.

17 Recommended Reading

In addition to the books discussed below, those planning an extended trip to other islands in Hawaii should check out *Frommer's Hawaii 2004, Frommer's Hawaii from $80 a Day,* and *Frommer's Honolulu, Waikiki & Oahu.*

FICTION

The first book people think about is James A. Michener's *Hawaii* (Fawcett Crest, 1974). This epic novel is a fictionalization of Hawaii's history. It manages to put the island's history into chronological order, but remember, it is still fiction, and very sanitized fiction, too. For a more contemporary look at life in Hawaii today, one of the best novels is *Shark Dialogue* by Kiana Davenport (Plume, 1995). The novel tells the story of Pono, the larger-than-life matriarch, and her four daughters of mixed races. Davenport skillfully weaves legends and myths of Hawaii into the "real life" reality that Pono and her family face in the complex Hawaii of today. Lois-Ann Yamanaka, a recent emerging writer from Hawaii, uses a very "local" voice and stark depictions of life in the islands in her fabulous novels *Wild Meat and the Bully Burgers* (Farrar, Straus, Giroux, 1996), *Blu's Hanging* (Avon, 1997), and *Heads by Harry* (Avon, 1999).

NONFICTION

Mark Twain's writing on Hawaii in the 1860s offers a wonderful introduction to Hawaii's history. One of his best books is *Mark Twain in Hawaii: Roughing It in the Sandwich Islands* (Mutual Publishing, 1990). Another great depiction of Hawaii of 1889 is

Travels in Hawaii (University of Hawaii Press, 1973) by Robert Louis Stevenson. For contemporary voices on Hawaii's unique culture, one of the best books to get is *Voices of Wisdom: Hawaiian Elders Speak* by M. J. Harden (Aka Press, 1999). Some 24 different *kahuna* (experts) in their fields were interviewed about their talent, skill, or artistic practice. These living treasures talk about how Hawaiians of yesteryear viewed nature, spirituality and healing, preservation and history, dance and music, arts and crafts, canoes, and the next generation.

FLORA & FAUNA

Because Hawaii is so lush with nature and blessed with plants, animals, and reef fish seen nowhere else on the planet, a few reference books can help you identify what you're looking at and make your trip more interesting. In the botanical world, Angela Kay Kepler's *Hawaiian Heritage Plants* (A Latitude 20 Book, University of Hawaii Press, 1998) is the standard for plant reference. In a series of essays, Kepler weaves culture, history, geography, botany, and even spirituality into her vivid descriptions of plants. You'll never look at plants the same way. There are great color photos and drawings to help you sort thorough the myriad species. Another great plant book is *Tropicals* (Timber Press, 1988) by Gordon Courtright, which is filled with color photos identifying everything from hibiscus and heliconia to trees and palms. As Courtright puts it, "This book is intended to be a visual plant dictionary."

The other necessary reference guide to have in Hawaii is a book identifying the colorful reef fish you will see snorkeling. The best reference book is John E. Randall's *Shore Fishes of Hawaii* (University of Hawaii Press, 1998). Randall is the expert on everything that swims underwater, and his book is one of the best. Two other books on reef fish identification, with easy-to-use

spiral bindings, are *Hawaiian Reef Fish—The Identification Book* (Blue Kirio Publishing, 1993) by Casey Mahaney and *Hawaiian Reef Fish* (Island Heritage, 1998) by Astrid Witte and Casey Mahaney.

For birders or those who just wonder about Hawaii's unique birds, H. Douglas Pratt's *A Pocket Guide to Hawaii's Birds* (Mutual Publishing, 1996) gives you everything you need to identify Hawaii's birds.

HISTORY

There are many great books on Hawaii's history, but one of the best places to start is with the formation of the Hawaiian islands, vividly described in David E. Eyre's *By Wind, By Wave: An Introduction to Hawaii's Natural History* (Bess Press, 2000). In addition to chronicling the natural history of Hawaii, Eyre also describes the complex interrelationships among the plants, animals, ocean, and people that are necessary. Eyre points out that Hawaii has become the "extinction capital of the world," but rather than dwelling on that fact, he urges readers to do something about it and carefully spells out how.

For history of "precontact" Hawaii (before Westerners arrived), David Malo's *Hawaiian Antiquities* (Bishop Museum Press, 1976) is the preeminent source. Malo was born around 1793, and wrote about the Hawaiian lifestyle at that time, as well as the beliefs and religion of his people. It's an excellent reference book, but not a fast read. For more readable books on old Hawaii, try *Stories of Old Hawaii* (Bess Press, 1997) by Roy Kakulu Alameide on myths and legends; *Hawaiian Folk Tales* (Mutual Publishing, 1998) by Thomas G. Thrum; and *The Legends and Myths of Hawaii* (Charles E. Tuttle Company, 1992) by His Hawaiian Majesty King David Kalakaua.

The best book on the overthrow of the Hawaiian monarchy in 1898 is told by the woman who experienced it, Queen Liliuokalani, in her book *Hawaii's Story by Hawaii's Queen Liliuokalani* (Mutual Publishing, 1990). When it was written at the turn of the 19th century, it was an international plea for justice for her people, but it is a poignant read even today. It's also a "must-read" for people interested in current events and the recent rally in the 50th state for sovereignty. Two contemporary books on the question of Hawaii's sovereignty are Tom Coffman's *Nation Within—The Story of America's Annexation of the Nation of Hawaii* (Epicenter, 1998) and *Hawaiian Sovereignty: Do the Facts Matter?* (Goodale, 2000) by Thurston

Twigg-Smith, which explores the opposite view. Twigg-Smith, former publisher of the statewide newspaper *The Honolulu Advertiser,* is the grandson of Lorrin A. Thurston, one of the architects of the 1893 overthrow of the monarchy. His so-called "politically incorrect" views present a different look on this hotly debated topic.

For more recent history, Lawrence H. Fuchs' *Hawaii Pono* (Bess Press, 1991) is a carefully researched tome on the contributions of each of Hawaii's main immigrant communities (Chinese, Japanese, and Filipino) made between 1893 and 1959.

 FAST FACTS: Maui

American Express For 24-hour traveler's check refunds and purchase information, call ✆ **800/221-7282.** Local offices are located in South Maui at the **Grand Wailea Resort** (✆ **808/875-4526**) and the **Westin Maui** at Kaanapali Beach (✆ **808/661-7155**).

Area Code All of the islands are in the **808** area code. Note that if you're calling one island from another, you must dial 1-808 first, and you'll be billed at long-distance rates (which can be more expensive than calling the mainland).

Business Hours Most offices are open from 8am to 5pm. The morning commute usually runs from 6 to 8am, and the evening rush is from 4 to 6pm. Bank hours are Monday through Thursday from 8:30am to 3pm, Friday from 8:30am to 6pm; some banks are open on Saturday. Shopping centers are open Monday through Friday from 10am to 9pm, Saturday from 10am to 5:30pm, and Sunday from 10am to 5 or 6pm.

Dentists Emergency dental care is available at **Kihei Dental Center,** 1847 S. Kihei Rd., Kihei (✆ **808/874-8401**) or in Lahaina at the **Aloha Lahaina Dentists,** 134 Luakini St. (in the Maui Medical Group Building), Lahaina (✆ **808/661-4005**).

Doctors No appointment is necessary at **West Maui Healthcare Center,** Whalers Village, 2435 Kaanapali Pkwy., Suite H-7 (near Leilani's Restaurant), Kaanapali (✆ **808/667-9721**), which is open 365 days a year, nightly until 10pm. In Kihei, call **Urgent Care,** 1325 S. Kihei Rd., Suite 103 (at Lipoa St., across from Star Market), Kihei (✆ **808/879-7781**), open daily from 6am to midnight; doctors are on call 24 hours a day.

Emergencies Dial ✆ **911** for the police, ambulance, and fire department. District stations are located in Lahaina (✆ **808/661-4441**) and in Hana (✆ **808/248-8311**). For the **Poison Control Center,** call ✆ **800/362-3585.**

Hospitals For medical attention, go to **Maui Memorial Hospital,** in Central Maui at 221 Mahalani, Wailuku (© **808/244-9056**); and East Maui's **Hana Medical Center,** on Hana Highway (© **808/248-8924**).

Liquor Laws The legal drinking age in Hawaii is 21. Beer, wine, and liquor are sold in grocery and convenience stores at any hour, 7 days a week. It's illegal (though rarely prosecuted) to have an open container on the beach.

Newspapers The *Honolulu Advertiser* and the *Honolulu Star Bulletin* are circulated statewide. The *Maui News* is the island's daily paper.

Post Offices To find the nearest post office, call © **800/ASK-USPS.** In Lahaina, there are branches at the Lahaina Civic Center, 1760 Honoapiilani Hwy.; in Kahului, there's a branch at 138 S. Puunene Ave.; and in Kihei, there's one at 1254 S. Kihei Rd.

Radio The most popular stations are KHPR (88.1 or 90.7 FM), the **National Public Radio** station; KPOA (93.5 FM) for **Hawaiian music;** KAOI (95.1 FM) for **contemporary music;** KLHI (99 FM) for **oldies music;** and KMVI (550 AM) for the **pop-music station** and the top morning-drive DJs.

Safety Although Hawaii is generally a safe tourist destination, visitors have been crime victims, so stay alert. The most common crime against tourists is rental car break-ins. Never leave any valuables in your car, not even in your trunk. Thieves can be in and out of your trunk faster than you can open it with your own key. Be especially careful at high-risk areas such as beaches and resorts. Never carry large amounts of cash with you. Stay in well-lighted areas after dark. Don't hike on deserted trails alone. See also section 6 of this chapter, "Health & Insurance," for other safety tips.

Smoking It's against the law to smoke in public buildings, including airports, grocery stores, retail shops, movie theaters, banks, and all government buildings and facilities. Hotels have no-smoking rooms available, restaurants have no-smoking sections, and car-rental agencies have smoke-free cars. Most bed-and-breakfasts prohibit smoking indoors.

Taxes Hawaii's sales tax is 4%. Hotel occupancy tax is 7.25%, and hoteliers are allowed by the state to tack on an additional .001666% excise tax. Thus, expect taxes of about 11.42% to be added to every hotel bill.

Time Hawaii Standard Time is in effect year-round. Hawaii is 2 hours behind Pacific Standard Time and 5 hours behind eastern standard time. In other words, when it's noon in Hawaii, it's 2pm in California and 5pm in New York during standard time on the mainland. There's no daylight saving time here, so when daylight saving time is in effect on the mainland, Hawaii is 3 hours behind the West Coast and 6 hours behind the East Coast—so in summer, when it's noon in Hawaii, it's 3pm in California and 6pm in New York.

Hawaii is east of the international date line, putting it in the same day as the U.S. mainland and Canada, and a day behind Australia, New Zealand, and Asia.

Weather For the current weather, call © **808/871-5111;** for recreational activities, call © **808/871-5054;** for Haleakala National Park weather, call © **808/871-5111;** for marine weather and surf and wave conditions, call © **808/877-3477.**

3

For International Visitors

Whether it's your first visit or your 10th, a trip to the United States may require additional planning. The pervasiveness of American culture around the world may make the United States feel like familiar territory to foreign visitors, but leaving your own country for the States—especially the unique island of Maui—still requires some arrangements before you leave home. This chapter will provide you with essential information, helpful tips, and advise for the more common problems that some visitors encounter.

1 Preparing for Your Trip

ENTRY REQUIREMENTS

Check at any U.S. embassy or consulate for current information and requirements. You can also obtain a visa application and other information online at the **U.S. State Department**'s website, at **www.travel.state.gov**.

VISAS The U.S. State Department has a **Visa Waiver Program** allowing citizens of certain countries to enter the United States without a visa for stays of up to 90 days. At press time these included Andorra, Australia, Austria, Belgium, Brunei, Denmark, Finland, France, Germany, Iceland, Ireland, Italy, Japan, Liechtenstein, Luxembourg, Monaco, the Netherlands, New Zealand, Norway, Portugal, San Marino, Singapore, Slovenia, Spain, Sweden, Switzerland, the United Kingdom, and Uruguay. Citizens of these countries need only a valid passport and a round-trip air or cruise ticket in their possession upon arrival. If they first enter the United States, they may also visit Mexico, Canada, Bermuda, and/or the Caribbean islands and return to the United States without a visa. Further information is available from any U.S. embassy or consulate. Canadian citizens may enter the

United States without visas; they need only proof of residence.

Citizens of all other countries must have (1) a valid passport that expires at least 6 months later than the scheduled end of their visit to the United States and (2) a tourist visa, which may be obtained without charge from any U.S. consulate.

To obtain a visa, the traveler must submit a completed application form (either in person or by mail) with a 1½-inch-square photo, and must demonstrate binding ties to a residence abroad. Usually you can obtain a visa at once or within 24 hours, but it may take longer during the summer rush from June through August. If you cannot go in person, contact the nearest U.S. embassy or consulate for directions on applying by mail. Your travel agent or airline office may also be able to provide you with visa applications and instructions. The U.S. consulate or embassy that issues your visa will determine whether you will be issued a multiple- or single-entry visa and any restrictions regarding the length of your stay.

British subjects can obtain up-to-date passport and visa information by calling the **U.S. Embassy Visa**

Information Line (📞 0891/200-290) or the **London Passport Office** (📞 0990/210-410 for recorded information), or they can find the visa information on the U.S. Embassy Great Britain website at ww.passport.gov.uk.

Irish citizens can obtain up-to-date passport and visa information through the **Embassy of USA Dublin,** 42 Elgin Rd., Dublin 4, Ireland (📞 353/1-668-8777) or check the visa page on the website at www.usembassy.ie.

Australian citizens can obtain up-to-date passport and visa information by calling the **U.S. Embassy Canberra,** Moonah Place, Yarralumla, ACT 2600 (📞 02/6214-5600) or check the website's visa page at www.usis-australia.gov/consular/niv.html.

Citizens of **New Zealand** can obtain up-to-date passport and visa information by calling the **U.S. Embassy New Zealand,** 29 Fitzherbert Terr., Thorndon, Wellington, New Zealand (📞 644/472-2068) or get the information directly from the website at http://usembassy.org.nz.

MEDICAL REQUIREMENTS

Unless you're arriving from an area known to be suffering from an epidemic (particularly cholera or yellow fever), inoculations or vaccinations are not required for entry into the United States. If you have a medical condition that requires **syringe-administered medications,** carry a valid signed prescription from your physician—the Federal Aviation Administration (FAA) no longer allows airline passengers to pack syringes in their carry-on baggage without documented proof of medical need. If you have a disease that requires treatment with **narcotics,** you should also carry documented proof with you—smuggling narcotics aboard a plane is a serious offense that carries severe penalties in the U.S.

For **HIV-positive visitors,** requirements for entering the United States are somewhat vague and change frequently. According to the latest publication of *HIV and Immigrants: A Manual for AIDS Service Providers*, the Immigration and Naturalization Service (INS) doesn't require a medical exam for entry into the United States, but INS officials may stop individuals because they look sick or because they are carrying AIDS/HIV medicine.

If an HIV-positive noncitizen applies for a non-immigrant visa, the question on the application regarding communicable diseases is tricky no matter which way it's answered. If the applicant checks "no," INS may deny the visa on the grounds that the applicant committed fraud. If the applicant checks "yes" or if INS suspects the person is HIV-positive, it will deny the visa unless the applicant asks for a special waiver for visitors. This waiver is for people visiting the United States for a short time, to attend a conference, for instance, to visit close relatives, or to receive medical treatment. It can be a confusing situation. For further up-to-the-minute information, contact the Centers for Disease Control's **National Center for HIV** (📞 404/332-4559; www.hivatis.org) or the **Gay Men's Health Crisis** (📞 212/367-1000; www.gmhc.org).

DRIVER'S LICENSES Foreign driver's licenses are mostly recognized in the U.S., although you may want to get an international driver's license if your home license is not written in English.

PASSPORT INFORMATION

Safeguard your passport in an inconspicuous, inaccessible place like a money belt. Make a copy of the critical pages, including the passport number, and store it in a safe place, separate from the passport itself. If you lose your passport, visit the nearest consulate of your native country as soon as possible for a replacement. Passport applications are downloadable from the Internet sites listed below.

Note that the International Civil Aviation Organization (ICAO) has recommended a policy requiring that *every* individual who travels by air have his or her own passport. In response, many countries are now requiring that children must be issued their own passport to travel internationally, where before those under 16 or so may have been allowed to travel on a parent or guardian's passport.

FOR RESIDENTS OF CANADA

You can pick up a passport application at one of 28 regional passport offices or most travel agencies. As of December 11, 2001, Canadian children who travel will need their own passport. However, if you hold a valid Canadian passport issued before December 11, 2001, that bears the name of your child, the passport remains valid for you and your child until it expires. Passports cost C$85 for those 16 years and older (valid 5 years), C$35 for children 3 to 15 (valid 5 years), and C$20 for children under 3 (valid for 3 years). Applications, which must be accompanied by two identical passport-size photographs and proof of Canadian citizenship, are available at travel agencies throughout Canada or from the central **Passport Office, Department of Foreign Affairs and International Trade,** Ottawa, ON K1A 0G3 (☎ **800/ 567-6868;** www.dfait-maeci.gc.ca/ passport). Processing takes 5 to 10 days if you apply in person, or about 3 weeks by mail.

FOR RESIDENTS OF THE UNITED KINGDOM

To pick up an application for a regular 10-year passport (the Visitor's Passport has been abolished), visit your nearest passport office, major post office, or travel agency. You can also contact the **London Passport Office** at ☎ **0171/271-3000,** or search its website at www.ukpa.gov.uk. Passports are £21 for adults and £11 for children under 16.

FOR RESIDENTS OF IRELAND

You can apply for a 10-year passport, costing €45, at the **Passport Office,** Setanta Centre, Molesworth Street, Dublin 2 (☎ **01/671-1633;** www.irl gov.ie/iveagh). Those under age 18 and over 65 must apply for an €10 3-year passport. You can also apply at 1A South Mall, Cork (☎ **021/272-525**) or over the counter at most main post offices.

FOR RESIDENTS OF AUSTRALIA

Apply at your local post office or passport office or search the government website at **www.dfat.gov.au/passports**. Passports for adults are A$126 and for those under 18 are A$63.

FOR RESIDENTS OF NEW ZEALAND

You can pick up a passport application at any travel agency or Link Centre. For more info, contact the **Passport Office,** P.O. Box 805, Wellington (☎ **0800/225-050**). Passports for adults are NZ$80 and for those under 16 they're NZ$40.

CUSTOMS
WHAT YOU CAN BRING IN

Every visitor over 21 years of age may bring in, duty-free, the following: (1) 1 liter of wine or hard liquor; (2) 200 cigarettes, 150 cigars (but not from Cuba), or 3 pounds of smoking tobacco; and (3) $100 worth of gifts. These exemptions are offered to travelers who spend at least 72 hours in the United States and who have not claimed them within the preceding 6 months. In addition, you cannot bring fresh fruits and vegetables into Hawaii, even if you're coming from the U.S. mainland and have no need to clear Customs. Every passenger is asked shortly before landing to sign a certificate declaring that he or she does not have fresh fruits and vegetables in his or her possession.

Foreign tourists may bring in or take out up to $10,000 in U.S. or foreign currency with no formalities; larger sums must be declared to U.S. Customs upon entering or leaving, which includes filing form CM 4790.

Declare any medicines you are carrying and be prepared to present a letter or prescription from your doctor demonstrating you need the drugs; you may bring in no more than you would normally use in the duration of your visit.

For many more details on what you can and cannot bring, check the informative U.S. Customs website at **www.customs.ustreas.gov** and click "Traveler Information," or call ✆ **202/927-1770.**

WHAT YOU CAN TAKE HOME

U.K. citizens returning from a non-EU country have a Customs allowance of: 200 cigarettes; 50 cigars; 250 grams of smoking tobacco; 2 liters of still table wine; 1 liter of spirits or strong liqueurs (over 22% volume); 2 liters of fortified wine, sparkling wine, or other liqueurs; 60cc (ml) perfume; 250cc (ml) of toilet water; and £145 worth of all other goods, including gifts and souvenirs. People under 17 cannot have the tobacco or alcohol allowance. For more information, contact HM Customs & Excise at ✆ **0845/010-9000** (from outside the U.K., 020/8929-0152), or consult their website at www.hmce.gov.uk.

For a clear summary of **Canadian** rules, request the booklet *I Declare,* issued by the **Canada Customs and Revenue Agency** (✆ **800/461-9999** in Canada, or 204/983-3500; www.ccra-adrc.gc.ca). Canada allows its citizens a C$750 exemption, and you're allowed to bring back duty-free 1 carton of cigarettes, 1 can of tobacco, 40

imperial ounces of liquor, and 50 cigars (if you're bringing tobacco or alcohol products back, you must meet local age restrictions). In addition, you're allowed to mail gifts to Canada valued at less than C$60 a day, provided they're unsolicited and don't contain alcohol or tobacco (write on the package "Unsolicited gift, under $60 value"). All valuables should be declared on the Y-38 form before departure from Canada, including serial numbers of valuables you already own, such as expensive foreign cameras. *Note:* The $750 exemption can only be used once a year and only after an absence of 7 days.

The duty-free allowance in **Australia** is A$400 or, for those under 18, A$200. Citizens age 18 and over can bring in 250 cigarettes or 250 grams of loose tobacco, and 1,125 milliliters of alcohol. If you're returning with valuables you already own, such as foreign-made cameras, you should file form B263. A helpful brochure available from Australian consulates or Customs offices is *Know Before You Go.* For more information, call the **Australian Customs Service** at ✆ **1300/363-263,** or log on to www.customs.gov.au.

The duty-free allowance for **New Zealand** is NZ$700. Citizens over 17 can bring in 200 cigarettes, 50 cigars, or 250 grams of tobacco (or a mixture of all 3 if their combined weight doesn't exceed 250g); plus 4.5 liters of wine and beer, or 1.125 liters of liquor. New Zealand currency does not carry import or export restrictions. Fill out a certificate of export, listing the valuables you are taking out of the country; that way, you can bring them back without paying duty. Most questions are answered in a free pamphlet available at New Zealand consulates and Customs offices: *New Zealand Customs Guide for Travellers, Notice no. 4.* For more information, contact **New Zealand Customs,** The Customhouse, 17–21 Whitmore St., Box 2218,

Wellington (© **0800/428-786** or 04/ 473-6099; www.customs.govt.nz).

HEALTH INSURANCE

Although it's not required of travelers, health insurance is highly recommended. Unlike many European countries, the United States does not usually offer free or low-cost medical care to its citizens or visitors. Doctors and hospitals are expensive, and in most cases will require advance payment or proof of coverage before they render their services. Policies can cover everything from the loss or theft of your baggage and trip cancellation to the guarantee of bail in case you're arrested. Good policies will also cover the costs of an accident, repatriation, or death. See "Health & Insurance" in chapter 2 for more information. Packages such as **Europ Assistance's "Worldwide Healthcare Plan"** are sold by European automobile clubs and travel agencies at attractive rates. **Worldwide Assistance Services,** Inc. (© **800/821-2828;** www.worldwide assistance.com) is the agent for Europ Assistance in the United States.

Though lack of health insurance may prevent you from being admitted to a hospital in nonemergencies, don't worry about being left on a street corner to die: The American way is to fix you now and bill the living daylights out of you later.

INSURANCE FOR BRITISH TRAVELERS Most big travel agents offer their own insurance and will probably try to sell you their package when you book a holiday. Think before you sign. **Britain's Consumers' Association** recommends that you insist on seeing the policy and reading the fine print before buying travel insurance. **The Association of British Insurers** (© 020/7600-3333; www.abi.org.uk) gives advice by phone and publishes *Holiday Insurance,* a free guide to policy provisions and prices. You might also shop around for better deals: Try **Columbus Direct** (© **020/7375-0011;** www.columbusdirect.net).

INSURANCE FOR CANADIAN TRAVELERS Canadians should check with their provincial health plan offices or call **Health Canada** (© **613/957-2991;** www.hc-sc.gc.ca) to find out the extent of their coverage and what documentation and receipts they must take home in case they are treated in the United States.

MONEY

CURRENCY The most common **bills** (all ugly, all green) are the $1 (colloquially, a "buck"), $5, $10, and $20 denominations. There are also $2 bills (seldom encountered), $50 bills, and $100 bills (the last two are usually not welcome as payment for small purchases). Note that redesigned bills were introduced in the last few years, but the old-style bills are still legal tender.

There are seven denominations of coins: 1¢ (1 cent, or a penny); 5¢ (5 cents, or a nickel); 10¢ (10 cents, or a dime); 25¢ (25 cents, or a quarter); 50¢ (50 cents, or a half dollar); the new gold "Sacagawea" coin worth $1; and, prized by collectors, the rare, older silver dollar.

EXCHANGING CURRENCY Exchanging foreign currency for U.S. dollars is usually painless in Oahu. Generally, the best rates of exchange are available through major banks, most of which exchange foreign currency. In Waikiki, go to **A-1 Foreign Exchange,** which has offices in the Royal Hawaiian Shopping Center, 2301 Kalakaua Ave., and in the Hyatt Regency Waikiki Tower, 2424 Kalakaua Ave. (© **808/922-3327**), or **Pacific Money Exchange,** 339 Royal Hawaiian Ave. (© **808/924-9318**). There also are currency services at **Honolulu International Airport.** Most of the major hotels offer currency-exchange services, but generally the rate of exchange is not as good as what you'll get at a bank.

On the other islands, it's not so easy. None of the other airports have currency-exchange facilities. You'll need to either go to a bank (call first to see if currency exchange is available) or use your hotel.

TRAVELER'S CHECKS Though traveler's checks are widely accepted at most hotels, restaurants, and large stores, *make sure that they're denominated in U.S. dollars,* as foreign-currency checks are often difficult to exchange. The three traveler's checks that are most widely recognized—and least likely to be denied—are **Visa, American Express,** and **Thomas Cook/MasterCard.** Be sure to record the numbers of the checks, and keep that information separately in case they get lost or stolen. Most businesses are pretty good about taking traveler's checks, but you're better off cashing them in at a bank (in small amounts, of course) and paying in cash. *Remember:* You'll need identification, such as a driver's license or passport, to change a traveler's check. It's generally easier to use ATMs than to bother with traveler's checks.

CREDIT CARDS Credit cards are widely used in Hawaii. You can save yourself trouble by using plastic rather than cash or traveler's checks in most hotels, restaurants, retail stores, and a growing number of food and liquor stores. You must have a credit card to rent a car in Hawaii.

SAFETY
GENERAL SAFETY Although tourist areas are generally safe, visitors should always stay alert. It's wise to ask the island tourist office if you're in doubt about which neighborhoods are safe. Avoid deserted areas, especially at night. Generally speaking, you can feel safe in areas where there are many people and open establishments.

Avoid carrying valuables with you on the street, and don't display expensive cameras or electronic equipment. Hold onto your pocketbook, and place your billfold in an inside pocket. In theaters, restaurants, and other public places, keep your possessions in sight.

Remember also that hotels are open to the public and that, in a large hotel, security may not be able to screen everyone entering. Always lock your room door—don't assume that once inside your hotel, you're automatically safe.

DRIVING SAFETY Safety while driving is particularly important. Ask your rental agency about personal safety, or request a brochure of traveler safety tips when you pick up your car. Get written directions or a map with your route clearly marked in red showing you how to get to your destination.

Recently, crime has involved more burglary of tourist rental cars in hotel parking structures and at beach parking lots. Park in well-lighted and well-traveled areas if possible. Never leave any packages or valuables visible in the car. If someone attempts to rob you or steal your car, do not try to resist the thief or carjacker—report the incident to the police department immediately.

For more information on driving rules and getting around by car in Hawaii, see "Getting Around" in chapter 2.

2 Getting to & Around the United States

The only airline with direct flights from foreign cities to Maui is **Air Canada** (© 800/776-3000; www.air canada.ca). Because of Maui's short runway, most international visitors will have to fly to Honolulu first to clear Customs, then get an interisland flight to Kahului, Maui.

Airlines serving Hawaii from places other than the U.S. mainland include

Air Canada (© 800/776-3000; www. aircanada.ca); **Air New Zealand** (© 0800/737-000 in Auckland, 64-3/379-5200 in Christchurch, 800/ 926-7255 in the U.S.; www.airnew zealand.com), which runs 40 flights per week between Auckland and Hawaii; **Qantas** (© 008/177-767 in Australia, 800/227-4500 in the U.S.; www. qantas.com.au), which flies between Sydney and Honolulu daily (plus additional flights 4 days a week); **Japan Air Lines** (© 03/5489-1111 in Tokyo, 800/525-3663 in the U.S.; www.japan air.com); **All Nippon Airways (ANA)** (© 03/5489-1212 in Tokyo, 800/ 235-9262 in the U.S.; www.fly-ana. com); **China Airlines** (© 02/715-1212 in Taipei, 800/227-5118 in the U.S.; www.china-airlines.com); **Air Pacific,** serving Fiji, Australia, New Zealand, and the South Pacific (© 800/227-4446; www.airpacific. com); **Korean Airlines** (© 02/656-2000 in Seoul, 800/223-1155 on the East Coast, 800/421-8200 on the West Coast, 800/438-5000 from Hawaii; www.koreanair.com); and **Philippine Airlines** (© 631/816-6691 in Manila, 800/435-9725 in the U.S.; www. philippineair.com).

Operated by the European Travel Network, **www.discount-tickets.com** is a great online source for regular and discounted airfares to destinations around the world. You can also use this site to compare rates and book accommodations, car rentals, and tours. Click on "Special Offers" for the latest package deals. Students should also try

Campus Travel (© **0870/240-1010** in England, 0131/668-3303 in Scotland; www.usitcampus.com).

If you're traveling in the United States beyond Hawaii, some large American airlines—such as **American, Delta, Northwest,** and **United**—offer travelers on transatlantic or transpacific flights special discount tickets under the name **Visit USA,** allowing travel between any U.S. destinations at reduced rates. These tickets must be purchased before you leave your foreign point of departure. This system is the best, easiest, and fastest way to see the United States at low cost. You should obtain information well in advance from your travel agent or the office of the airline concerned, since the conditions attached to these discount tickets can change without advance notice.

Visitors arriving by air should cultivate patience and resignation before setting foot on U.S. soil. Getting through immigration control may take as long as 2 hours on some days, especially summer weekends. Add the time it takes to clear Customs, and you'll see that you should make a very generous allowance for delay in planning connections between international and domestic flights—an average of 2 to 3 hours at least.

After you have cleared Customs in Honolulu, hop a short, 20-minute interisland flight. For further information about travel to Hawaii, see "Getting There" and "Getting Around" in Chapter 2.

 FAST FACTS: For International Visitors

Automobile Organizations Auto clubs will supply maps, suggested routes, guidebooks, accident and bail-bond insurance, and emergency road service. The major auto club in the United States, with 955 offices nationwide, is the **American Automobile Association** (AAA; often called "Triple A"). Members of some foreign auto clubs have reciprocal arrangements with AAA and enjoy its services at no charge. If you belong to an auto club, inquire about AAA reciprocity before you leave. AAA can also provide you with an **International Driving Permit** validating your foreign license. You may be able to join AAA even if you are not a member of a reciprocal club. To inquire, call ✆ **800/736-2886** or visit www.aaa.com.

Some car-rental agencies now provide automobile club–type services, so inquire about their availability when you rent your car.

Automobile Rentals To rent a car in the United States, you need a valid driver's license, a passport, and a major credit card. The minimum age is usually 25, but some companies will rent to younger people and add a surcharge. It's a good idea to buy maximum insurance coverage unless you're positive your own auto or credit-card insurance is sufficient. Rates vary, so it pays to call around.

Business Hours See "Fast Facts: Maui" in chapter 2.

Climate See "When to Go" in chapter 2.

Electricity Hawaii, like the U.S. mainland and Canada, uses 110–120 volts (60 cycles), compared to the 220–240 volts (50 cycles) used in most of Europe and in other areas of the world, including Australia and New Zealand. Small appliances of non-American manufacture, such as hair dryers or shavers, will require a plug adapter with two flat, parallel pins; larger ones will require a 100-volt transformer.

Embassies & Consulates All embassies are in Washington, D.C. Some countries have consulates general in major U.S. cities, and most have a mission to the United Nations in New York City. If your country isn't listed below, call for directory information in Washington, D.C. (✆ **202/555-1212**), or point your Web browser to **www.embassy.org/embassies** for the location and phone number of your national embassy.

The embassy of **Australia** is at 1601 Massachusetts Ave. NW, Washington, D.C. 20036 (✆ **202/797-3000**; www.austemb.org). There is also an Australian consulate in Hawaii at 1000 Bishop St., Penthouse Suite, Honolulu, HI 96813 (✆ 808/524-5050).

The embassy of **Canada** is at 501 Pennsylvania Ave. NW, Washington, D.C. 20001 (✆ **202/682-1740**; www.canadianembassy.org). Canadian consulates are also at 1251 Avenue of the Americas, New York, NY 10020 (✆ 212/596-1628), and at 550 South Hope St., 9th floor, Los Angeles, CA 90071 (✆ 213/346-2700).

The embassy of **Japan** is at 2520 Massachusetts Ave. NW, Washington, D.C. 20008 (✆ **202/238-6700**; www.embjapan.org). The consulate general of Japan is located at 1742 Nuuanu Ave., Honolulu, HI 96817 (✆ 808/543-3111).

The embassy of **New Zealand** is at 37 Observatory Circle NW, Washington, D.C. 20008 (✆ **202/328-4800**; www.nzemb.org). The only New Zealand consulate in the United States is at 780 Third Ave., New York, NY 10017 (✆ 202/328-4800).

The embassy of the **Republic of Ireland** is at 2234 Massachusetts Ave. NW, Washington, D.C. 20008 (✆ **202/462-3939**; www.irelandemb.org). There's a consulate office in San Francisco at 44 Montgomery St., Suite 3830, San Francisco, CA 94104 (✆ 415/392-4214).

The embassy of the **United Kingdom** is at 3100 Massachusetts Ave. NW, Washington, D.C. 20008 (✆ **202/588-6640**; www.fco.gov.uk/directory). British consulates are at 845 Third Ave., New York, NY 10022

(✆ 212/745-0200), and 11766 Wilshire Blvd., Suite 400, Los Angeles, CA 90025 (✆ 310/477-3322).

Emergencies   Call ✆ **911** to report a fire, call the police, or get an ambulance.

Gasoline (Petrol)   One U.S. gallon equals 3.8 liters, while 1.2 U.S. gallons equal 1 Imperial gallon. You'll notice there are several grades (and price levels) of gasoline available at most gas stations. You'll also notice that their names change from company to company. The ones with the highest octane are the most expensive, but most rental cars take the least expensive "regular" gas, with an octane rating of 87.

Holidays   See "When to Go" in chapter 2.

Legal Aid   The ordinary tourist will probably never become involved with the American legal system. If you're pulled over for a minor infraction (for example, driving faster than the speed limit), never attempt to pay the fine directly to a police officer; you may wind up arrested on the much more serious charge of attempted bribery. Pay fines by mail or directly into the hands of the clerk of the court. If accused of a more serious offense, it's wise to say and do nothing before consulting a lawyer (under the U.S. Constitution, you have the rights both to remain silent and to consult an attorney). Under U.S. law, an arrested person is allowed one telephone call to a party of his or her choice; call your embassy or consulate.

Mail   Mailboxes, which are generally found at intersections, are blue with a blue-and-white eagle logo and carry the inscription U.S. POSTAL SERVICE. If your mail is addressed to a U.S. destination, don't forget to add the five-figure postal code, or ZIP code, after the two-letter abbreviation of the state to which the mail is addressed. The abbreviation for Hawaii is HI.

At press time, domestic postage rates were 23¢ for a postcard and 37¢ for a letter. For international mail, a first-class letter of up to 1 ounce costs 80¢ (60¢ to Canada and Mexico); a first-class postcard costs 70¢ (50¢ to Canada and Mexico); and a preprinted postal aerogramme costs 70¢. Point your Web browser to **www.usps.com** for complete U.S. postal information, or call ✆ **800/275-8777** for information on the nearest post office. Most branches are open Monday through Friday from 8am to 5 or 6pm, and Saturday from 9am to noon or 3pm.

Taxes   The United States has no VAT (value-added tax) or other indirect taxes at a national level. Every state, and every city in it, has the right to levy its own local tax on all purchases, including hotel and restaurant checks, airline tickets, and so on. In Hawaii, sales tax is 4%; there's also a 7.25% hotel-room tax and a small excise tax, so the total tax on your hotel bill will be 11.42%.

Telephone & Fax   The telephone system in the United States is run by private corporations, so rates, particularly for long-distance service and operator-assisted calls, can vary widely—especially on calls made from public telephones. Local calls—that is, calls to other locations on the island you're on—made from public phones in Hawaii cost 50¢.

Generally, hotel surcharges on long-distance and local calls are astronomical. You are usually better off using a **public pay telephone,** which you will find clearly marked in most public buildings and private establishments as well as on the street. Many convenience stores and news-stands sell **prepaid calling cards** in denominations up to $50.

Most **long-distance** and **international calls** can be dialed directly from any phone. **For calls within the United States and to Canada,** dial 1 followed by the area code and the seven-digit number. **For other international calls,** dial 011 followed by the country code, city code, and the telephone number of the person you are calling. Some country and city codes are as follows: **Australia** 61, Melbourne 3, Sydney 2; **Ireland** 353, Dublin 1; **New Zealand** 64, Auckland 9, Wellington 4; **United Kingdom** 44, Belfast 232, Birmingham 21, Glasgow 41, London 71 or 81.

If you're calling the **United States from another country,** the country code is 01.

In Hawaii, interisland phone calls are considered long-distance and are often as costly as calling the U.S. mainland. The international country code for Hawaii is 1, just as it is for the rest of the United States and Canada.

For **reversed-charge** or **collect calls,** and for **person-to-person calls,** dial 0 (zero, not the letter "O"), followed by the area code and number you want; an operator will then come on the line, and you should specify that you are calling collect, person-to-person, or both. If your operator-assisted call is international, ask for the overseas operator.

Note that all phone numbers with the area code 800, 888, 866, and 877 are toll-free. However, calls to numbers in area codes 700 and 900 (chat lines, "dating" services, and so on) can be very expensive—usually a charge of 95¢ to $3 or more per minute.

For **local directory assistance** ("information"), dial 411. For **long-distance information,** dial 1, then the appropriate area code and 555-1212; for **directory assistance for another island,** dial 1, then 808, then 555-1212.

Fax facilities are widely available and can be found in most hotels and many other establishments. Try **Mail Boxes, Etc.** or **Kinko's** (check the local Yellow Pages) or any photocopying shop.

Telephone Directories There are two kinds of telephone directories in the United States. The general directory, the so-called White Pages, lists private and business subscribers in alphabetical order. The inside front cover lists the emergency numbers for police, fire, and ambulance, along with other vital numbers. The first few pages are devoted to community-service numbers, including a guide to long-distance and international calling, complete with country codes and area codes.

The second directory, printed on yellow paper (hence its name, Yellow Pages), lists all local services, businesses, and industries by type of activity, with an index at the front. The listings cover not only such obvious items as automobile repairs and drugstores (pharmacies), but also restaurants by type of cuisine and geographical location, bookstores by special subject and/or language, places of worship by religious denomination, and other information that the visitor might not otherwise readily find. The Yellow Pages also include detailed maps, postal ZIP codes, and a calendar of events.

Time Zone See "Fast Facts: Maui" in chapter 2.

Tipping It's part of the American way of life to tip. Many service employees receive little direct salary and must depend on tips for their income. The following are some general rules:

In **hotels,** tip bellhops at least $1 per piece of luggage ($2 to $3 if you have a lot of luggage), and tip the housekeeping staff $1 per person, per day. Tip the doorman or concierge only if he or she has provided you with some specific service (for example, calling a cab for you or obtaining difficult-to-get theater tickets). Tip the valet-parking attendant $1 to $2 every time you get your car.

In **restaurants, bars,** and **nightclubs,** tip service staff 15% to 20% of the check, tip bartenders 10% to 15%, and tip valet-parking attendants $1 to $2 per vehicle. Tip the doorman only if he or she has provided you with some specific service (such as calling a cab for you). Tipping is not expected in cafeterias and fast-food restaurants.

Tip **cab drivers** 15% of the fare.

As for **other service personnel,** tip skycaps at airports at least $1 per piece ($2-$3 if you have a lot of luggage), and tip hairdressers and barbers 15% to 20%. Tipping ushers at theaters is not expected.

Toilets Foreign visitors often complain that public toilets are hard to find in most U.S. cities. True, there are none on the streets, but visitors can usually find one in a bar, fast-food outlet, restaurant, hotel, museum, or department store—and it will probably be clean. (The cleanliness of toilets at service stations, parks, and beaches is more open to question.) Note, however, a growing practice in some restaurants and bars of displaying a notice that toilets are for the use of patrons only. You can ignore this sign or, better yet, avoid arguments by paying for a cup of coffee or soft drink, which will qualify you as a patron.

4

Where to Stay

Maui has accommodations to fit every taste and budget, from luxury oceanfront suites and historic bed-and-breakfasts to reasonably priced condos that will sleep a family of four.

Remember to consider *when* you will be traveling to the islands. The high season, during which rooms are always booked and rates are at the top end, runs from mid-December to March. A second high season, when rates are high but reservations are somewhat easier to get, is summer (late June–early Sept). The low seasons, with fewer tourists and cheaper rates, are April to early June and late September to mid-December.

Remember to add Maui's 11.42% accommodations tax to your final bill. Parking is free unless otherwise noted.

Important note: Before you book, be sure to read "The Island in Brief," in chapter 2, which will help you choose your ideal location, as well as "Tips on Accommodations" also in chapter 2. Also check out the accommodations categories in chapter 1, "The Best of Maui," for a quick look at our favorites.

1 Central Maui

KAHULUI

If you're arriving late at night or you have an early morning flight out, the best choice near Kahului Airport is the **Maui Beach Hotel,** 170 Kaahumanu Ave. (© **888/649-3222**). The nondescript, motel-like rooms go for $98 to $175 and include free airport shuttle service. It's okay for a night, but not a place to spend your vacation.

WAILUKU
Moderate

Old Wailuku Inn at Ulupono ★★ *Finds*   This 1924 former plantation manager's home, lovingly restored by innkeepers Janice and Thomas Fairbanks, offers a genuine old Hawaii experience. The theme is Hawaii of the 1920s and '30s, with decor, design, and landscaping to match. The spacious rooms are gorgeously outfitted with exotic ohia-wood floors, high ceilings, and traditional Hawaiian quilts. The mammoth bathrooms (some with claw-foot tubs, others with Jacuzzis) have plush towels and earth-friendly toiletries on hand. A full gourmet breakfast is served on the enclosed back lanai or, if you prefer, delivered to your room. You'll feel right at home lounging on the generously sized living-room sofa or watching the world go by from an old wicker chair on the lanai. The inn is located in the old historic area of Wailuku, just a few minutes' walk from the Maui County Seat Government Building, the courthouse, and a wonderful stretch of antiques shops.

2199 Kahookele St. (at High St., across from the Wailuku School), Wailuku, HI 96732. © **800/305-4899** or 808/244-5897. Fax 808/242-9600. www.mauiinn.com. 7 units. $120–$180 double. Rates include full breakfast. Extra person $20. AE, DISC, MC, V. **Amenities:** Jacuzzi; laundry service; dry cleaning. *In room:* A/C, TV, dataport.

Inexpensive

Backpackers, head for **Banana Bungalow Maui,** a funky Happy Valley hostel at 310 N. Market St., Wailuku, HI 96793 (✆ **800/846-7835** or 808/244-5090; fax 808/244-3678; www.mauihostel.com), with $17.50 dorm rooms and some private rooms ($32 single, $45 double). Dorm-style accommodations ($15.95) and private rooms ($28.95 single, $39.95 double) are also available at the **Northwind Inn,** in old Wailuku, at 2080 Vineyard St., Wailuku, HI 96793 (✆ **800/9HOS-TEL,** phone and fax 808/242-1448; www.northwind-hostel.com). Note, however, that women traveling alone might not feel safe here after dark.

2 West Maui

LAHAINA

MODERATE

If you dream of an oceanfront condo but your budget is on the slim side, consider **Lahaina Roads,** 1403 Front St. (a block north of the Lahaina Cannery Shopping Center). Reservations can be made c/o Klahani Travel, Lahaina Cannery Mall, 1221 Honoapiilani Hwy., Lahaina, HI 96761 (✆ **800/669-MAUI** or 808/667-2712; fax 808/661-5875; www.klahani-travel.com). The 17 units here go for $125 for a one-bedroom unit (for up to 4). There's a 3-night minimum.

In addition to the following choices, you may want to consider the oceanfront condos at **Lahaina Shores Beach Resort,** 475 Front St. (✆ **800/628-6699;** www.lahaina-shores.com); studio and one-bedroom units go for $180 to $315.

Best Western Pioneer Inn   This once-rowdy home away from home for sailors now seems almost respectable—even charming. The hotel is a two-story plantation-style structure with big verandas that overlook the streets of Lahaina and the harbor, a short distance away. All rooms have been totally remodeled, with vintage bathrooms and new curtains and carpets. The quietest rooms face either the garden courtyard—devoted to refined outdoor dining accompanied by live (but quiet) music—or the square-block–size banyan tree next door. We recommend room no. 31, over the banyan court, with a view of the ocean and the harbor. If you want a front-row seat for all the Front Street action, book no. 49 or 36.

658 Wharf St. (in front of Lahaina Pier), Lahaina, HI 96761. ✆ **800/457-5457** or 808/661-3636. Fax 808/667-5708. www.pioneerinnmaui.com. 34 units. $115–$200 double. Extra person $10. AE, DC, DISC, MC, V. Parking $4 in lot 2 blocks away. **Amenities:** Restaurant (good for breakfast); bar with live music; outdoor pool; big shopping arcade; laundry service. *In room:* A/C, TV/VCR, fridge, coffeemaker, hair dryer, iron, safe.

House of Fountains Bed & Breakfast *(Finds*   This 7,000-square-foot contemporary home, in a quiet residential subdivision at the north end of town, is popular with visitors from around the world. This place is immaculate (hostess Daniela Atay provides daily maid service). The oversize rooms are fresh and quiet, with white ceramic-tile floors, handmade koa furniture, Hawaiian quilt bedspreads, and Hawaiiana theme; the four downstairs rooms all open onto flower-filled private patios. In fact in 2002, Daniela won the prestigious "Most Hawaiian Accommodation" award from the Hawaii Visitors and Convention Bureau. Guests share the fully equipped guest kitchen and barbecue area, and are welcome to curl up on the living-room sofa facing the fireplace (not really needed in Lahaina) with a book from the library. The nearest beach is about a 5-minute drive away, and tennis courts are nearby. Around the pool is a thatch hut for weekly hula performances, an imu pit for luaus, and an area that's perfect for Hawaiian weddings.

Lahaina & Kaanapali Accommodations

Best Western Pioneer Inn **18**

Garden Gate Bed and
Breakfast **10**

Guest House **11**

House of Fountains Bed
& Breakfast **13**

Hyatt Regency Maui **9**

Kaanapali Alii **6**

Kaanapali Beach Hotel **4**

Lahaina Inn **16**

Lahaina Roads **14**

Lahaina Shores Beach
Resort **21**

Maui Eldorado Resort **2**

Maui Marriott Resort
and Ocean Club **8**

Ohana Maui Islander **19**

Old Lahaina House **20**

Penny's Place **15**

The Plantation Inn **17**

Puamana **22**

Royal Lahaina Resort **1**

Sheraton Maui **3**

Wai Ola Vacation Paradise
on Maui **12**

Westin Maui **7**

The Whaler on Kaanapali
Beach **5**

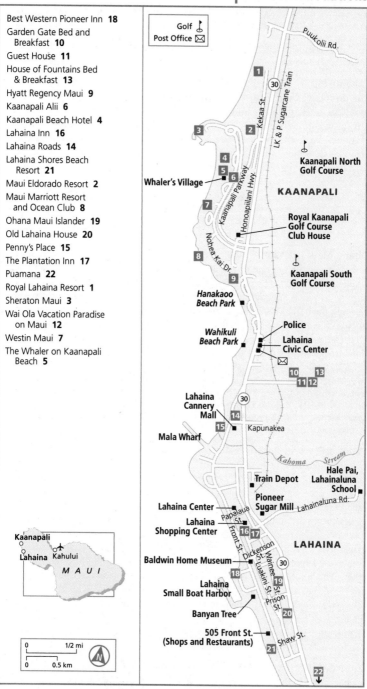

1579 Lokia St. (off Fleming Rd., north of Lahaina town), Lahaina, HI 96761. ② **800/789-6865** or 808/667-2121. Fax 808/667-2120. www.alohahouse.com. 6 units (shower only). $95–$145 double. Rates include full breakfast. Extra person $20. DISC, MC, V (additional 5% charge if using credit card). From Hwy. 30, take the Fleming Rd. exit; turn left on Ainakea; after 2 blocks, turn right on Malanai St.; go 3 blocks, and turn left onto Lokia St. **Amenities:** Outdoor pool; Jacuzzi; washer/dryers. *In room:* A/C, TV, fridge, hair dryer, no phone.

Lahaina Inn ✿ If you like old hotels that have genuine historic touches, you'll love this place. As in many old hotels, some of these Victorian antique–stuffed rooms are small; if that's a problem for you, ask for a larger unit. All come with private bathrooms and lanais. The best room in the house is no. 7 ($109), which overlooks the beach, the town, and the island of Lanai; you can watch the action below or close the door and ignore it. There's an excellent, though unaffiliated, restaurant in the same building (David Paul's Lahaina Grill, p. 128), with a bar downstairs.

127 Lahainaluna Rd. (near Front St.), Lahaina, HI 96761. ② **800/669-3444** or 808/661-0577. Fax 808/667-9480. www.lahainainn.com. 12 units (most bathrooms have shower only). $109–$169 double. Rates include continental breakfast. AE, DC, MC, V. Next-door parking $5. No children under age 15. **Amenities:** Concierge; activity desk. *In room:* A/C.

Ohana Maui Islander ✿ *(Value)* This wooden complex's units, especially those with kitchenettes, are one of Lahaina's great buys. The larger ones are great for families on a budget. The property isn't on the beach, but on a quiet side street (a rarity in Lahaina) and within walking distance of restaurants, shops, attractions, and, yes, the beach (just 3 blocks away). All of the good-size rooms, decorated in tropical-island style, are comfortable and quiet. The entire complex is spread across 10 landscaped acres and includes a sun deck, a barbecue, and a picnic area. The aloha-friendly staff will take the time to answer all of your questions.

660 Wainee St. (between Dickenson and Prison sts.), Lahaina, HI 96761. ② **800/462-6262** or 808/667-9766. Fax 808/661-3733. www.ohanahotels.com. 317 units. $149 double; $179 studio with kitchenette; $199 1-bedroom with kitchen (sleeps up to 4); $279 2-bedroom with kitchen (sleeps 6). Extra rollaway bed $18, cribs free. AE, DC, DISC, MC, V. Parking $3. **Amenities:** Outdoor pool; tennis courts (lit for night play until 10pm); activity desk; coin-op washer/dryers. *In room:* A/C, TV, kitchenettes (in some units), fridge, coffeemaker, hair dryer, iron, safe.

Penny's Place in Paradise *(Finds)* No attention to detail has been spared in this Victorian-style bed-and-breakfast, just 50 feet from the water, with a fabulous view from the front porch of Molokai and Lanai. Each of the four rooms is uniquely decorated, with themes ranging from contemporary Hawaii (with a canopy bed and a traditional island quilt) to formal Victorian (with a four-poster cherry bed and an antique gentleman's night chest). Guests are welcome to use the balcony kitchenette (fridge, microwave, toaster, coffeemaker, and ice machine). Only the location is a problem—Penny's is located in a small island bounded by Honoapiilani Highway on one side and busy Front Street on the other. The house is sound-proof, and air-conditioning in each room helps drown out the noise inside, but not when you step outside to enjoy that beautiful view. Penny showed us plans to enclose the outside lanai area to drown out the highway noise.

1440 Front St., Lahaina, HI 96761. ② **877/431-1235** or 808/661-1068. Fax 808/667-7102. www.pennys place.net. 4 units. $88–$124 double. Rates include continental breakfast. MC, V. *In room:* A/C,, TV.

The Plantation Inn ✿✿ *(Finds)* Attention, romance-seeking couples: Look no further. This charming Victorian-style inn, located a couple of blocks from the water, looks like it's been here 100 years or more, but it's actually of 1990s vintage—an artful deception. The rooms are romantic to the max, tastefully done

Tips **B&B Etiquette**

In Hawaii, it is traditional and customary to remove your shoes before entering anyone's home. The same is true for most bed-and-breakfast facilities. Most hosts post signs or will politely ask you to remove your shoes before entering the B&B. Not only does this keep the B&B clean, but you'll be amazed how relaxed you feel walking around barefoot. If this custom is unpleasant to you, a B&B may not be for you. Consider a condo or hotel, where no one will be particular about your shoes.

Hotels, resorts, condos, and vacation rentals generally allow smoking in the guest rooms (most also have nonsmoking rooms available), but the majority of bed-and-breakfast units forbid smoking in the rooms. If this matters to you, be sure to check the policy of your accommodation before you book.

with period furniture, hardwood floors, stained glass, and ceiling fans. There are four-poster canopy beds and armoires in some rooms, brass beds and wicker in others. All units are soundproof (a plus in Lahaina) and come with a private lanai; the suites have kitchenettes. The rooms wrap around the large pool and deck. Also on the property is **Gerard's** (p. 128), an outstanding French restaurant (it can be pricey, but hotel guests get a discount on dinner). Breakfast is served around the pool and in the elegant pavilion lounge.

174 Lahainaluna Rd. (between Wainee and Luakini sts. 1 block from Hwy. 30), Lahaina, HI 96761. © 800/433-6815 or 808/667-9225. Fax 808/667-9293. www.theplantationinn.com. 19 units (some bathrooms w/shower only). $152–$245 double. Rates include full breakfast. Extra person $20. AE, DC, DISC, MC, V. **Amenities:** Acclaimed restaurant and bar; large outdoor pool and Jacuzzi; concierge; activity desk; coin-op washer/dryers. *In room:* A/C, TV/VCR, kitchenettes (in suites), fridge, hair dryer, iron, safe.

Puamana   These 28 acres of town houses set right on the water are ideal for those who want to retreat from the crowds and cacophony of downtown Lahaina into the serene quiet of an elegant neighborhood. Private and peaceful are apt descriptions for this complex: Each unit is a privately owned individual home, with no neighbors above or below. Most are exquisitely decorated, and all come with full kitchen, lanai, barbecue, and at least two bathrooms. Puamana was once a private estate in the 1920s, part of the sugar plantations that dominated Lahaina; the plantation manager's house has been converted into a clubhouse with an oceanfront lanai, library, card room, sauna, table-tennis tables, and office. *One warning:* The rental office is not on-site, which has caused some problems with guests getting assistance.

Front St. (at the extreme southern end of Lahaina, ½ mile from downtown). Reservations c/o Klahani Travel, Lahaina Cannery Mall, 1221 Honoapiilani Hwy., Lahaina, HI 96761. © 800/669-6284 or 808/667-2712. Fax 808/661-5875. www.klahani-travel.com. 40 units. $125–$200 1-bedroom unit; $150–$275 2-bedroom; $300–$500 3-bedroom. 3-night minimum. AE, DC, DISC, MC, V. **Amenities:** 3 pools (1 for adults only); tennis court; Jacuzzi; game room; activity desk; on-site laundry. *In room:* TV, kitchen, fridge, coffeemaker, hair dryer, iron, washer/dryer (in some units).

Wai Ola Vacation Paradise on Maui ⋞   Just 2 blocks from the beach, in a quiet, residential development behind a tall concrete wall, lies this lovely retreat, with shade trees, sitting areas, gardens, a pool, an ocean mural, and a range of accommodations (a suite inside the 5,000 sq. ft. home, a separate studio cottage, a 1-bedroom apartment, or the entire house). Hostess Julie Frank is a veteran innkeeper who knows how to provide comfortable accommodations and memorable vacations. You'll also find a deck, barbecue facilities, and an outdoor wet bar on the property; tennis courts are nearby. Ask about her honeymoon package.

Kuuipo St. (P.O. Box 12580), Lahaina, HI 96761. © 800/492-4652 or 808/661-7901. Fax 808/661-7901. www.waiola.com. 5 units. $135 suite; $150 1-bedroom apt.; $175 cottage; $550-$850 house. 5-night minimum. Extra person $15. AE, DC, DISC, MC, V. **Amenities:** Outdoor pool; Jacuzzi; complimentary use of watersports equipment; free self-service washer/dryers. *In room:* A/C, TV/DVD/VCR, dataport, kitchenette, fridge, coffeemaker, hair dryer, iron.

INEXPENSIVE

In addition to the following choices, also consider value-priced **Old Lahaina House** (© **800/847-0761** or 808/667-4663; fax 808/667-5615; www.old lahaina.com), which features comfy twin- and king-bedded doubles for just $69 to $115, plus a one-bedroom apartment across the street for $125 to $150; it's about a 2-minute walk to the water just across Front Street.

Garden Gate Bed and Breakfast *(Finds)* This oasis of a B&B, located on a quiet residential street just outside of Lahaina town, is just 5 minutes from the beach by car. The four units all have fridges, microwaves, private entrances, private bathrooms, plus a garden or ocean view; the deluxe suites have a deck and a separate pullout sofa for kids. Continental breakfast is served in the garden, and hosts Jamie and Bill Mosley are available to answer any questions about things to do or places to eat. Bicycles, Boogie Boards, beach chairs, and mats are available at no charge. The barbecue area and adjacent laundry facilities are available for guests' use. About a 5-minute drive to the beach.

67 Kaniau Rd., Lahaina, HI 96761. © 800/939-3217 or 808/661-8800. Fax 808/661-0209. www.garden gatebb.com. 4 units. $79–$125. 3 nights minimum. Extra person $15. Rates include continental breakfast. AE, DC, DISC, MC, V. *In room:* A/C, TV, VCR available on request, fridge, coffeemaker, microwave, hair dryer, iron.

Guest House *(★★)* *(Finds)* This is one of Lahaina's great bed-and-breakfast deals: a charming house with more amenities than the expensive Kaanapali hotels just down the road. The roomy home features parquet floors and floor-to-ceiling windows; its swimming pool—surrounded by a deck and comfortable lounge chairs—is larger than some at high-priced condos. Every guest room has a quiet lanai and a romantic hot tub. The large kitchen (with every gadget imaginable) and high-speed Internet access computers are available for guests' use. The Guest House also operates Trinity Tours and offers discounts on car rentals and just about every island activity. Tennis courts are nearby, and the nearest beach is about a block away.

1620 Ainakea Rd. (off Fleming Rd., north of Lahaina town), Lahaina, HI 96761. © **800/621-8942** or 808/661-8085. Fax 808/661-1896. www.mauiguesthouse.com. 4 units. $129 double. Rates include full breakfast. AE, DC, DISC, MC, V. Take Fleming Rd. off Hwy. 30; turn left on Ainakea; it's 2 blocks down. **Amenities:** Huge outdoor pool; watersports equipment rentals; concierge; activity desk; car-rental desk; self-service washer/dryers. *In room:* A/C, TV/VCR, fridge, Jacuzzi.

KAANAPALI
VERY EXPENSIVE

Another option to consider, in addition to those below, is the **Royal Lahaina Resort** (© **800/44-ROYAL** or 808/661-3611; fax 808/661-6150; www.hawaiian hotels.com). But skip the overpriced hotel rooms; only stay here if you can get one of the 122 cottages tucked among the well-manicured grounds. *Tip:* book on the Internet where rates are $195 to $250 double; rack racks are double that price.

The **Maui Marriott Resort and Ocean Club** (© **800/228-9290** or 808/ 667-1200; fax 808/667-8300; www.marriott.com) is wonderful if you like the

Marriott style, not so wonderful if you're looking for something a little more Hawaiian. It's a big hit with conventions and incentive groups. Recently part of the property became a timeshare, but there are still hotel rooms, too. Rates are $269 to $550 double; ask about packages. Both properties are located right on the beach.

Kaanapali Alii ⭐⭐ *(Kids* The height of luxury, these oceanfront condominium units sit on 8 landscaped acres right on Kaanapali Beach. Kaanapali Alii combines all the amenities of a luxury hotel (including a 24-hr. front desk) with the convenience of a condominium to make a memorable stay. Each of the one-bedroom (1,500 sq. ft.) and two-bedroom (1,900 sq. ft.) units is impeccably decorated and comes with all the comforts of home (fully equipped kitchen, washer/dryer, lanai, 2 full bathrooms) and then some (room service, daily maid service, complimentary local newspaper). The beachside recreation area includes a swimming pool, plus a separate children's pool, whirlpool, gas barbecue grills and picnic areas, exercise rooms, saunas, and tennis courts.

50 Nohea Kai Dr., Lahaina, HI 96761. © 800/642-6284 or 808/661-3330. Fax 808/667-1145. www.kaanapali-alii.com. 264 units. $350–$525 1-bedroom for 4; $475–$740 2-bedroom for 6; $900 suite. AE, DC, DISC, MC, V. Free parking. **Amenities:** Poolside cafe; 2 outdoor pools; 36-hole golf course; 3 lighted tennis courts; fitness center; Jacuzzi; watersports equipment rentals; children's program; game room; concierge; activity desk; room service; in-room massage; babysitting; same-day dry cleaning. *In room:* A/C, TV, dataport, kitchen, fridge, coffeemaker, hair dryer, iron, safe, washer/dryers.

Sheraton Maui ⭐⭐ *(Kids* Terrific facilities for families and fitness buffs and a premier beach location make this beautiful resort an all-around great place to stay. The grande dame of Kaanapali Beach is built into the side of a cliff on the curving, white-sand cove next to Black Rock (a lava formation that rises 80 ft. above the beach), where there's excellent snorkeling. After its recent renovation, the resort is virtually new, with six buildings of six stories or less set in well-established tropical gardens. The lobby has been elevated to take advantage of panoramic views, while a new lagoonlike pool features lava-rock waterways, wooden bridges, and an open-air whirlpool. But not everything has changed, thankfully. Cliff divers still swan dive off the torch-lit lava-rock headland in a traditional sunset ceremony—a sight to see. And the views of Kaanapali Beach, with Lanai and Molokai in the distance, are some of the best around. Sheraton Maui offers a unique dining option in addition to its more traditional restaurants: "Dinner Under the Stars," outdoor dining with three fixed-price menus served by a private butler at your choice of location on the grounds.

The new emphasis is on family appeal, with a class of rooms dedicated to those traveling with kids. Every unit is outfitted with amenities galore, right down to toothbrushes and toothpaste. Other pluses include a "no-hassle" check-in policy: The valet takes you and your luggage straight to your room—no time wasted standing in line at registration. One downside is the "resort fee," which is outrageous on top of these high prices.

2605 Kaanapali Pkwy., Lahaina, HI 96761. © 800/782-9488 or 808/661-0031. Fax 808/661-0458. www.sheraton-maui.com. 510 units. $350–$750 double; from $825 suite. Extra person $50; children 17 and under stay free in parent's room using existing bedding. "Resort fee" of $10 for self-parking, "free" local calls and credit-card calls, in-room safe, lei greeting, daily coffee and newspaper, use of fitness center, and kids' program. AE, DC, DISC, MC, V. Valet parking $5. **Amenities:** 3 restaurants; snack bar; 3 bars; 2 huge outdoor pools; 36-hole golf course; 3 tennis courts; fitness center; Jacuzzi; watersports equipment rentals; children's program; game room; concierge; activity desk; car-rental desk; business center; shopping arcade; salon; limited room service (6:30am–10:30pm); in-room massage; babysitting; coin-op washer/dryers; same-day laundry service and dry cleaning. *In room:* A/C, TV, dataport, fridge, coffeemaker, hair dryer, iron, safe.

Kids Family-Friendly Accommodations

If you're traveling with the kids, you'll be welcomed with open arms at many of Maui's accommodations. Our favorites are listed below, but other kid-friendly spots include Kaanapali Alii, Westin Maui, Hyatt Regency Maui, Maui Eldorado Resort, Kahana Sunset, Kapalua Bay Hotel & Ocean Villas, and Kula Lynn Farm Bed & Bath, all reviewed in this chapter. Note that by state law, hotels that offer supervised activity programs can accept only children ages 5 to 12.

WEST MAUI

Hale Kai (p. 92)   This small condo complex is ideally located for families: right on the beach, next door to a county park, and a 10-minute drive from Lahaina's attractions. Kids can hang out at the pool, swim in the ocean, or play in the park. There's a TV and VCR in every unit, and the well-equipped kitchens (with dishwasher, microwave, and even a blender) allow Mom and Dad to save money on eating out.

Noelani Condominium Resort (p. 95)   If your kids love to swim, head to this Kahana condo on the ocean. Right next door is great snorkeling at a sandy cove, frequented by spinner dolphins and turtles in summer and humpback whales in winter. On site are two freshwater pools (1 heated for night swimming). The units feature complete kitchens and entertainment centers.

Ritz-Carlton Kapalua (p. 98)   The Ritz Kids is a year-round daytime activities center that features both educational programs (from exploring the ecosystems in streams to learning the hula) and sports (from golf to swimming). The cost, for kids ages 5 to 12, is $15 for hotel guests for a full day (9am–4pm) and includes lunch, and $70 for Kapalua Villa guests for a full day (with the second child $35). The half-day program (9am–noon or 1–4pm) is complimentary for hotel guests (covered by the $12 daily resort fee) and $35 for Kapalua Villa guests ($17.50 for the second child).

Sheraton Maui (p. 87)   In addition to one of the best beaches on Kaanapali, the Sheraton offers "family suites," which have three beds (2 double beds and 1 pull-down double wall bed), a sitting room with full-size couch, and two TVs, both equipped with Nintendo. In addition, there's the Keiki Aloha program for children ages 5 to 12, costing $45 for full day (including lunch and a T-shirt on the first day), with fun activities ranging from Hawaiian games to visits to nearby attractions.

Westin Maui 🌟 Kids   In addition to having a great location on the beach, the Westin Maui is a great place to sleep. The rooms are outfitted with fabulous new beds (Westin's custom-designed, pillow-top "heavenly beds"), plus a choice of five different pillows. If that doesn't give you sweet dreams, nothing will. Once you get up, you'll find the "aquatic playground"—an 87,000-square-foot pool area with five amazing free-form heated pools joined by swim-through grottoes, waterfalls, and a 128-foot-long water slide—sets this resort apart from its peers along lovely Kaanapali Beach. This is the Disney World of water-park resorts,

Children 12 and younger enjoy free meals (breakfast, lunch, and dinner) when dining with one adult in the Kids Eat Free program.

SOUTH MAUI

Koa Resort (p. 100)   Right across the street from the ocean in Kihei, this deluxe condo complex is great for active families, with its two tennis courts, pool, hot tub, and 18-hole putting green. The spacious, privately owned units are fully equipped and have plenty of room for even a large brood.

Mana Kai Maui Resort (p. 104)   This complex, an unusual combination of hotel and condominium, sits on a beautiful white-sand cove that's one of the best snorkeling beaches on the south coast. Families will like the condo units, which have full kitchens and open living rooms; sliding-glass doors lead to small lanais overlooking the sandy beach and ocean.

Our Favorite: The Four Seasons Resort Maui at Wailea (p. 107)   This is a real standout, the most kid-friendly hotel on Maui. The *keiki* will feel welcome with such amenities as free milk and cookies on the first day, children's menus in all restaurants (including room service), and complimentary infant needs (crib, stroller, highchair, playpen, car seats) and child-safety features (toilet-seat locks, plug covers, security gates). The resort can also prepurchase a range of necessities (such as diapers and baby food) for you before your arrival. Kids and teens have a huge list of recreational activities and equipment to choose from, including a game room (with Super Nintendo, Sony PlayStation, foosball, and more); a free scuba clinic (for ages 12 and up); children's videos; and a host of sailing, snorkeling, and whale-watching activities.

UPCOUNTRY

Kili's Cottage (p. 113)   In the cool elevation of Kula, this sweet three-bedroom/two-bathroom cottage, situated on 2 acres, is a great place for families. The price is right—$105 double—and the amenities are numerous: a large lanai, a full kitchen, a gas barbecue, a washer/dryer, great views, and even toys for the kids. The hostess, Kili Namau'u, who is the director of a Hawaiian language immersion school, greets each guest with royal aloha, from a house filled with flowers (picked from the garden) to the welcome basket filled with tropical produce grown on the property.

and your kids will be in water-hog heaven. The fantasy theme extends from the estate-like grounds into the interior's public spaces, which are filled with the shrieks of tropical birds and the splash of waterfalls. The oversize architecture, requisite colonnade, and $2 million art collection make a pleasing backdrop for all the action. Most of the rooms in the two 11-story towers overlook the aquatic playground, the ocean, and the island of Lanai in the distance. Like the Sheraton, the Westin has instituted a not-very-hospitable "resort fee."

2365 Kaanapali Pkwy., Lahaina, HI 96761. ☎ 800/WESTIN-1 or 808/667-2525. Fax 808/661-5764. 758 units. www.westinmaui.com. $350–$630 double; from $800 suite. Extra person $45. "Resort fee" of $10 for "free" local calls, use of fitness center, coffee and tea, and local paper. Parking $5. AE, DC, DISC, MC, V. **Amenities:** 5 restaurants; 3 bars; 5 free-form outdoor pools; 36-hole golf course; tennis courts; health club and spa with aerobics, steam baths, sauna, massage, and body treatments; Jacuzzi; watersports equipment rentals; bike rental; children's program; game room; concierge; activity desk; car-rental desk; business center; shopping arcade; salon; limited room service; massage; babysitting; coin-op washer/dryers; same-day laundry/dry cleaning; concierge-level rooms. *In room:* A/C, TV, dataport, minibar, fridge, coffeemaker, hair dryer, iron, safe.

EXPENSIVE

Hyatt Regency Maui ★★ *Kids*   Spa-goers will love this resort. Hawaii's first oceanfront spa, the Spa Moana, opened here in 2000 with some 9,000 square feet of facilities, including an exercise floor with an ocean view, 11 treatment rooms, sauna and steam rooms, and a huge menu of massages, body treatments, and therapies. Book your treatment before you leave home—this place is popular.

The management has poured some $19 million in renovations to rooms in this fantasy resort, the southernmost of the Kaanapali beachfront properties. It certainly has lots of imaginative touches: a collection of exotic species (flaming pink flamingoes, unhappy-looking penguins, and an assortment of loud parrots and macaws in the lobby), nine waterfalls, and an eclectic Asian and Pacific art collection. This huge place covers some 40 acres; even if you don't stay here, you might want to walk through the expansive tree-filled atrium and the parklike grounds, with their dense riot of plants and the half-acre outdoor pool with a 150-foot lava tube slide, a cocktail bar under the falls, a "honeymooner's cave," and a swinging rope bridge. There's even a children-only pool with its own beach, tidal pools, and fountains.

The rooms, spread out among three towers, are pleasantly outfitted with an array of amenities, and have very comfortable separate sitting areas and private lanais with eye-popping views. The latest, most comfortable bedding is now standard in every room (you will sleep like a baby in these fluffy, feather beds). The very romantic Swan Court (p. 133) is not to be missed for a special dinner. Two Regency Club floors have a private concierge, complimentary breakfast, sunset cocktails, and snacks.

200 Nohea Kai Dr., Lahaina, HI 96761. ☎ 800/233-1234 or 808/661-1234. Fax 808/667-4714. www.maui.hyatt.com. 806 units. $345–$565 double; $585–$650 Regency Club; from $850 suite. All rooms are charged a mandatory $12 "resort fee" for access to spa, local phone calls, daily local paper, in-room coffee and tea, in-room safe, and 1-hr. tennis court time. Extra person $35 ($50 in Regency Club rooms). Children 18 and under stay free in parent's room using existing bedding. Packages available. AE, DC, DISC, MC, V. Valet parking $10, free self-parking. **Amenities:** 5 restaurants; 2 bars; a half-acre-size outdoor pool; 36-hole golf course; 6 tennis courts; health club with weight room; brand-new, state-of-the-art spa; Jacuzzi; watersports equipment rentals; bike rental; Camp Hyatt kids' program, offering supervised activities for 5- to 12-year-olds; game room; concierge; activity desk; car-rental desk; business center; big shopping arcade; salon; 24-hr. room service; in-room or spa massage; babysitting; coin-op washer/dryers; laundry service; dry cleaning; concierge-level rooms. *In room:* A/C, TV, dataport, 2-line phone, minibar, fridge (on request), coffeemaker, hair dryer, iron, safe.

Maui Eldorado Resort ★ *Kids*   These spacious condominium units—each with a full kitchen and daily maid service—were built when land in Kaanapali was cheap, contractors took pride in their work, and visitors expected large, spacious units with views from every window. You'll find it hard to believe that this was one of Kaanapali's first properties in the late 1960s, as this first-class choice still looks like new. The Outrigger chain has managed to keep prices down to reasonable levels, especially if you come in spring or fall. This is a great choice for families, with its big units, grassy areas that are perfect for running off excess energy, and a beachfront (with beach cabanas and a barbecue area) that's usually safe for swimming. Tennis courts are nearby.

2661 Kekaa Dr., Lahaina, HI 96761. *©* **800/688-7444** or 808/661-0021. Fax 808/667-7039. www.outrigger. com. 98 units. $195–$240 studio double; $245–$295 1-bedroom (rates for up to 4); $355–$425 2-bedroom (rates for up to 6). Numerous packages available, including 5th night free, rental-car packages, senior rates, and more. AE, DC, DISC, MC, V. **Amenities:** 3 outdoor pools; 36-hole golf course; concierge; activity desk; car-rental desk; some business services; babysitting; coin-op washer/dryers. *In room:* A/C, TV, dataport, kitchen, fridge, coffeemaker, hair dryer, iron, safe, washer/dryer (in some units).

The Whaler on Kaanapali Beach ★★   In the heart of Kaanapali, right on the world-famous beach, lies this oasis of elegance, privacy, and luxury. The relaxing atmosphere strikes you as soon as you enter the open-air lobby, where light reflects off the dazzling koi in the meditative lily pond. No expense has been spared on these gorgeous accommodations; each unit has a full kitchen, washer/dryer, marble bathroom, 10-foot beamed ceilings, and blue-tiled lanai. Every unit boasts spectacular views of Kaanapali's gentle waves or the humpback peaks of the West Maui Mountains. Next door is Whalers Village, with numerous restaurants, bars, and shops; Kaanapali Golf Club's 36 holes are across the street.

2481 Kaanapali Pkwy. (next to Whalers Village), Lahaina, HI 96761. *©* **800/922-7866** or 808/661-4861. Fax 808/661-8315. www.whalermaui.com. 360 units. High season $235–$255 studio double; $330–$485 1-bedroom (rate for up to 4 people); $535–$700 2-bedroom (up to 6). Low season $205–$230 studio double; $275–$415 1-bedroom; $435–$570 2-bedroom. Check Internet for specials. Extra person $20; crib $12. 2-night minimum. AE, DC, DISC, MC, V. **Amenities:** Outdoor pool; 5 tennis courts; fitness room; Jacuzzi; watersports equipment rentals; concierge; activity desk; car-rental desk; babysitting; coin-op washer/dryers; laundry service; dry cleaning. *In room:* A/C, TV, dataport, kitchen, fridge, coffeemaker, hair dryer, iron, safe, washer/dryer.

MODERATE

Kaanapali Beach Hotel ★ *Value*   It's older and less high-tech than its upscale neighbors, but the Kaanapali has an irresistible local style and a real Hawaiian warmth that's missing from many other Maui hotels. Three low-rise wings, bordering a fabulous stretch of beach, are set around a wide, grassy lawn with coco palms and a whale-shaped pool. The spacious, spotless motel-like rooms are done in wicker and rattan, with Hawaiian-style bedspreads and a lanai that looks toward the courtyard and the beach. The beachfront rooms are separated from the water only by Kaanapali's landscaped walking trail.

Old Hawaii values and customs are always close at hand, and the service is some of the friendliest around. Tiki torches, hula, and Hawaiian music create a festive atmosphere in the expansive open courtyard every night. As part of the hotel's extensive Hawaiiana program, you can learn to cut pineapple, weave lauhala, even dance the *real* hula. There's also an arts-and-crafts fair 3 days a week, a morning welcome reception on weekdays, and a Hawaiian library.

2525 Kaanapali Pkwy., Lahaina, HI 96761. *©* **800/262-8450** or 808/661-0011. Fax 808/667-5978. www.kbhmaui.com. 430 units. $195–$290 double; from $235 suite. Extra person $25. Car, golf, bed-and-breakfast, and romance packages available, as well as senior discounts. AE, DC, DISC, MC, V. Valet parking $7, self-parking $5. **Amenities:** 3 restaurants; 2 bars (including a poolside bar that fixes a mean piña colada); outdoor pool; 36-hole golf course; access to tennis courts; Jacuzzi; watersports equipment rentals; children's program; game room; concierge; activity desk; car-rental desk; business center; convenience shops; salon; limited room service; babysitting; coin-op washer/dryers. *In room:* A/C, TV, fridge, coffeemaker, iron, safe.

HONOKOWAI, KAHANA & NAPILI
EXPENSIVE

Also consider **Sands of Kahana** (*©* **800/326-9874** or 808/669-0423; www. sands-of-kahana.com), an eight-story condo/timeshare complex that's great for families. The one- to three-bedroom units have small kitchens and washer/dryers. The property is loaded with kid-friendly extras, including a large children's pool, a playground, and a stretch of beach that's safe for swimming. Rates start at $130 for one bedroom, $180 for two bedrooms, and $275 for three bedrooms (5-night minimum).

Napili Kai Beach Resort ★★ *Finds*   Just south of the Bay Club restaurant in Kapalua, nestled in a small white-sand cove, lies this comfortable oceanfront complex. The one- and two-story units with double-hipped Hawaii-style roofs face their very own gold-sand beach, which is safe for swimming.

Many units have a view of the Pacific, with Molokai and Lanai in the distance. The older beachfront Lahaina Building units—with ceiling fans only—are a good buy starting at $225. Those who prefer air-conditioning should book into the Honolua Building, where, for the same price, you'll get a fully air-conditioned room set back from the shore around a grassy, parklike lawn and pool. Every unit (except 8 hotel rooms) has a fully stocked kitchenette with full-size fridge, cooktop, microwave, toaster oven, washer/dryer, and coffeemaker; some have dishwashers as well.

On-site pluses include daily maid service, even in the condo units; two shuffleboard courts; barbecue areas; complimentary coffee at the beach pagoda every morning; free tea in the lobby every afternoon; weekly lei making, hula lessons, and horticultural tours; and a free weekly mai tai party. There are three nearby championship golf courses and excellent tennis courts at next-door Kapalua Resort.

5900 Honoapiilani Rd. (at the extreme north end of Napili, next to Kapalua), Lahaina, HI 96761. © 800/367-5030 or 808/669-6271. Fax 808/669-0086. www.napilikai.com. 163 units. $190–$225 hotel room double; $220–$305 studio double; $360–$410 1-bedroom suite (sleeps up to 4); $525–$675 2-bedroom (sleeps 6). Packages available. Extra person $15. AE, MC, V. **Amenities:** Well-recommended restaurant (Sea House, p. 136); bar; 4 outdoor pools; 2 18-hole putting greens (w/free golf putters for guest use); complimentary use of tennis racquets; good-size fitness room, filled with the latest equipment; Jacuzzi; complimentary watersports equipment; free children's activities at Easter, June 15–Aug 31, and at Christmas; concierge; activity desk; babysitting; coin-op washer/dryers; laundry service; dry cleaning. *In room:* A/C (in most units, but not all), TV, kitchenette, fridge, coffeemaker, hair dryer, iron, safe.

MODERATE

Another option is **Polynesian Shores,** 3975 Lower Honoapiilani Rd. (near Kahana, and just 2 min. from the Kapalua–West Maui Airport), Lahaina, HI 96761 (© **800/433-6284** or 808/669-6065; fax 808/669-0909; www.maui.net/~polyshor). Every unit (1–3 bedrooms, from $135–$245) has floor-to-ceiling sliding-glass doors that open onto a private lanai with an ocean view; there's great snorkeling off the beach out front.

Hale Kai ★ *Kids*   This small, two-story condo complex is ideally located, right on the beach and next door to a county park. Shops, restaurants, and ocean activities are all within a 6-mile radius. The units are older but in excellent shape, and come with well-equipped kitchens (with dishwasher, disposal, microwave, even a blender), and louvered windows that open to the trade winds. Lots of guests clamor for the oceanfront pool units, but we find the park-view units cooler, and they still have ocean views (upstairs units also have cathedral ceilings). This place fills up fast, so book early; repeat guests make up most of the clientele.

3691 Lower Honoapiilani Rd. (in Honokowai), Lahaina, HI 96761. © **800/446-7307** or 808/669-6333. Fax 808/669-7474. www.halekai.com. 23 units. High season $120 1-bedroom double; $150–$155 2-bedroom (rates for up to 4); $200 3-bedroom (up to 6). Low season $105 1-bedroom; $135–$140 2-bedroom; $200 3-bedroom. Extra person $15. 3-night minimum. MC, V. **Amenities:** Outdoor pool; concierge; car-rental desk; coin-op washer/dryers. *In room:* TV/VCR, kitchen, fridge, coffeemaker, hair dryer, iron.

Honokeana Cove *Value*   These large, secluded units—cozily set around a pool in a lush tropical setting—have fabulous views of Honokeana Cove. The beach

Accommodations & Dining from Honokowai to Kapalua

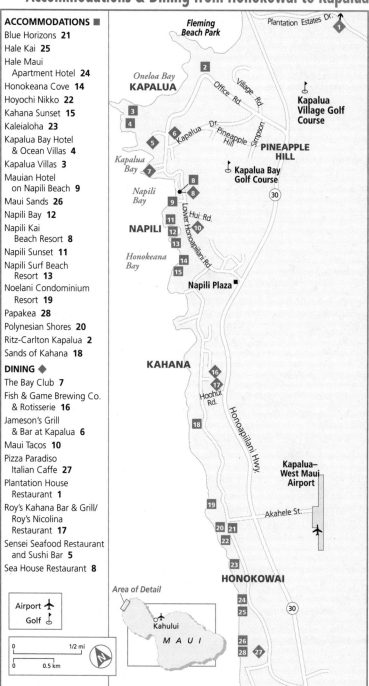

ACCOMMODATIONS ■

Blue Horizons **21**
Hale Kai **25**
Hale Maui
  Apartment Hotel **24**
Honokeana Cove **14**
Hoyochi Nikko **22**
Kahana Sunset **15**
Kaleialoha **23**
Kapalua Bay Hotel
  & Ocean Villas **4**
Kapalua Villas **3**
Mauian Hotel
  on Napili Beach **9**
Maui Sands **26**
Napili Bay **12**
Napili Kai
  Beach Resort **8**
Napili Sunset **11**
Napili Surf Beach
  Resort **13**
Noelani Condominium
  Resort **19**
Papakea **28**
Polynesian Shores **20**
Ritz-Carlton Kapalua **2**
Sands of Kahana **18**

DINING ◆

The Bay Club **7**
Fish & Game Brewing Co.
  & Rotisserie **16**
Jameson's Grill
  & Bar at Kapalua **6**
Maui Tacos **10**
Pizza Paradiso
  Italian Caffe **27**
Plantation House
  Restaurant **1**
Roy's Kahana Bar & Grill/
  Roy's Nicolina
  Restaurant **17**
Sensei Seafood Restaurant
  and Sushi Bar **5**
Sea House Restaurant **8**

Airport ✈
Golf ⛳

0 _____ 1/2 mi
0 _____ 0.5 km

Fleming
Beach Park

Plantation Estates Dr.

Oneloa Bay
KAPALUA

Office Rd.

Village Rd.

Kapalua
Village Golf
Course

Kapalua Dr.
Pineapple Hill

Simpson

**PINEAPPLE
HILL**

Kapalua
Bay

Kapalua Bay
Golf Course

Napili
Bay

(30)

NAPILI

Lower Honoapiilani Rd.

Hui Rd.

Honokeana
Bay

Napili Plaza ■

KAHANA

Hoohui
Rd.

Honoapiilani Hwy.

Kapalua–
West Maui
Airport

Akahele St.

✈

HONOKOWAI

(30)

Area of Detail

Kahului
✈

M A U I

93

here isn't sandy (it's composed of smooth round rocks), but the water just off-shore is excellent for snorkeling (turtles have been spotted just offshore) and for whale-watching in winter. The well-appointed units all come with full kitchens and lanais. Amenities include laundry, barbecues, and deck chairs. The management holds weekly pupu-parties so you can meet the other guests. All in all, a well-priced option in an expensive neighborhood.

5255 Lower Honoapiilani Rd. (in Napili), Lahaina, HI 96761. ✆ **800/237-4948** or 808/669-6441. Fax 808/669-8777. www.honokeana-cove.com. 34 units. $127–$137 1-bedroom; $146–$175 2-bedroom (sleeps up to 4); $204–$207 3-bedroom (sleeps up to 6). 3-night minimum. Extra person $10–$15. MC, V. **Amenities:** Outdoor pool; concierge; coin-op washer/dryers. *In room:* TV/VCR, kitchen, fridge, coffeemaker, iron.

Kahana Sunset ★★ *Kids* Lying in the crook of a sharp horseshoe curve on Lower Honoapiilani Road is this series of wooden condo units, stair-stepping down the side of a hill to a postcard-perfect white-sand beach. The unique location, nestled between the coastline and the road above, makes this a very private place to stay. In the midst of the buildings sits a grassy lawn with a small pool and Jacuzzi; down by the sandy beach are gazebos and picnic areas with barbecues. The units feature full kitchens (complete with dishwashers), washer/dryers, large lanais with terrific views, and sleeper sofas. This is a great complex for families: The beach is safe for swimming, the grassy area is away from traffic, and the units are roomy. The two-bedroom units have parking just outside, making carrying luggage and groceries that much easier.

4909 Lower Honoapiilani Hwy. (at the northern end of Kahana, almost in Napili). c/o P.O. Box 10219 Lahaina, HI 96761. ✆ **800/669-1488** or 808/669-8011. Fax 808/669-9170. www.kahanasunset.com. 79 units, 49 in rental pool. $130–$240 1-bedroom (sleeps up to 4); $175–$370 2-bedroom (sleeps 6). 2-night minimum. AE, MC, V. From Hwy. 30, turn *makai* (toward the ocean) at the Napili Plaza (Napilihau St.), then left on Lower Honoapiilani Rd. **Amenities:** 2 outdoor pools (1 just for children); concierge. *In room:* TV, kitchen, coffeemaker, hair dryer, iron, safe (in some units), washer/dryer.

Maui Sands The Maui Sands was built back when property wasn't as expensive and developers took the extra time and money to surround their condos with lush landscaping. It's hard to get a unit with a bad view: All face either the ocean (with views of Lanai and Molokai) or tropical gardens blooming with brilliant heliconia, flowering hibiscus, and sweet-smelling ginger. Each roomy unit has a big lanai and a full kitchen. With two big bedrooms, plus space in the living room for a fifth person (or even a sixth), the larger units are good deals for families. There's a narrow beach out front.

Maui Resort Management, 3600 Lower Honoapiilani Rd. (in Honokowai), Lahaina, HI 96761. ✆ **800/367-5037** or 808/669-1902. Fax 808/669-8790. www.mauigetaway.com. 76 units. $105–$145 1-bedroom (sleeps up to 3); $150–$210 2-bedroom (sleeps 5). Extra person $10. 7-night minimum. MC, V. **Amenities:** Outdoor pool; coin-op washer/dryer. *In room:* A/C, TV, kitchen, fridge, coffeemaker.

Mauian Hotel on Napili Beach ★ The family that built this low-rise hotel in 1961 now owns it again, and they've restored the studio units to their original old Hawaiian style. The Mauian is perched above a beautiful half-mile long white-sand beach with great swimming and snorkeling; there's a pool with chaise lounges, umbrellas, and tables on the sun deck; and the verdant grounds are bursting with tropical color. The rooms feature hardwood floors, Indonesian-style furniture, and big lanais with great views. Thoughtful little touches include fresh flowers in rooms upon arrival, plus chilled champagne for guests celebrating a special occasion. There are no phones and no TVs in the rooms (this place really is about getting away from it all), but the large Ohana (family) room does have a TV with a VCR and an extensive library for those who can't bear the solitude.

There's complimentary coffee; phones and fax service are available in the business center. Great restaurants are just a 5-minute walk away, and Kapalua Resort is up the street. The nightly sunsets off the beach are spectacular.

5441 Lower Honoapiilani Rd. (in Napili), Lahaina, HI 96761. ☏ 800/367-5034 or 808/669-6205. Fax 808/669-0129. www.mauian.com. 44 units. High season $165–$195 double; low season $145–$180 double. Rates include continental breakfast. Extra 3rd person $10; 4th person $15. Children under 5 stay free in parent's room. AE, DISC, MC, V. **Amenities:** Outdoor pool; golf course; tennis courts; concierge; activity desk; business center; coin-op washer/dryer. In room: Kitchen, fridge, coffeemaker; no phone.

Napili Surf Beach Resort ⭐ (Finds) This well-maintained, superbly land-scaped condo complex has a great location on Napili Beach. Facilities include two pools, three shuffleboard courts, and three gas barbecue grills. The well-furnished units (all with full kitchens) were renovated in 1997. Free daily maid service, a rarity in condo properties, keeps the units clean. Management encourages socializing: In addition to weekly mai tai parties and coffee socials, the resort hosts annual shuffleboard and golf tournaments, as well as get-togethers on July 4th, Thanksgiving, Christmas, and New Year's. Many guests arrange their travel plans around these events at the Napili Surf.

50 Napili Place (off Lower Honoapiilani Rd., in Napili), Lahaina, HI 96761. ☏ 800/541-0638 or 808/669-8002. Fax 808/669-8004. www.napilisurf.com. 53 units (some w/shower only). $135–$195 studio (sleeps up to 3); $210–$285 1-bedroom (sleeps up to 4). Extra person $15. No credit cards. **Amenities:** 2 freshwater swimming pools; washer/dryers. In room: TV/VCR, kitchen, fridge, coffeemaker, iron, safe, washer/dryer (in larger units).

Noelani Condominium Resort ⭐⭐ (Finds) (Kids) This oceanfront condo is a great value, whether you stay in a studio or a three-bedroom unit (ideal for large families). Everything is first-class, from the furnishings to the oceanfront location. Though it's on the water, there's no sandy beach here (despite the photos posted on their website)—but next door is a sandy cove at the new county park, opened in 2001. All units feature complete kitchens, entertainment centers, and spectacular views (the 1-, 2-, and 3-bedroom units also have their own washer/dryers and dishwashers). Our favorites are in the Anthurium Building, where the condos have oceanfront lanais just 20 feet from the water. Frugal travelers will love the deluxe studios in the Orchid Building, with great ocean views and all the amenities for just $107 in the low season and $122 in high season. Guests are invited to mai tai parties at night; there are also oceanfront barbecue grills for guest use.

4095 Lower Honoapiilani Rd. (in Kahana), Lahaina, HI 96761. ☏ 800/367-6030 or 808/669-8374. Fax 808/669-7904. www.noelani-condo-resort.com. 50 units. $107–$135 studio double; $147–$165 1-bedroom (sleeps up to 4); $217 2-bedroom (sleeps 4); $267 3-bedroom (sleeps 6). Rates include continental breakfast on first morning. Extra person $10. Children under 18 stay free in parent's room. Packages for honeymooners, seniors, and AAA members available. 3-night minimum. AE, MC, V. **Amenities:** 2 freshwater swimming pools (1 heated for night swimming); access to nearby health club; oceanfront Jacuzzi; concierge; activity desk; car-rental desk; coin-op washer/dryers. In room: TV/VCR, kitchen, fridge, coffeemaker, hair dryer, iron, safe, washer/dryer (in larger units).

INEXPENSIVE

Another option is **Hoyochi Nikko,** 3901 Lower Honoapiilani Rd. (in Honokowai), Lahaina, HI 96761 (☏ **800/487-6002** or 808/669-8343; fax 808/669-3937; www.mauilodging.com), which has just 17 older (but well-maintained) one- and two-bedroom units sharing 180 feet of oceanfront ($100–$125 double for 1-bedroom and $131–$168 for 2-bedrooms).

Frugal travelers should also consider the **Hale Maui Apartment Hotel** (☏ **808/669-6312;** fax 808/669-1302; www.maui.net/~halemaui), a wonderful tiny apartment hotel run by Hans and Eva Zimmerman, whose spirit is 100%

aloha. All their one-bedroom suites, which run $85 to $95 double, come with ceiling fans, private lanai, and complete kitchens. There's no pool, but a private path leads to a great swimming beach.

Blue Horizons *(Finds)* This is the only bed-and-breakfast on this stretch of West Maui, about a 10-minute drive to Lahaina and about a 5-minute walk to sandy beaches. The four units, in a custom-built home in a subdivision, range from compact to spacious suites with separate bedrooms and a living-room area with sofa bed. Three units have kitchenettes, and all four are air-conditioned, which helps not only with the heat but also with the noise of the subdivision. A lavish breakfast is served in the screened dining area, where the ocean view may distract you from the banana pancakes. Amenities on site include a tile lap pool, washer/dryer, gas barbecue, and video library.

3894 Mahinahina Dr. (in Kahana, 1 block from Honoapiilani Hwy.), Lahaina, HI 96761. © 800/669-1948 or 808/669-1965. Fax 808/665-1615. www.bluehorizonsmaui.com. 4 units. $89–$129 double. 2-night minimum. Rates include breakfast Mon–Sat. Extra person $15. AE, MC, V. **Amenities:** Small outdoor pool; free use of washer/dryers. *In room:* A/C, TV/VCR, kitchenette (in 3 rooms), fridge, coffeemaker (some rooms).

Kaleialoha *(Value)* This condo complex for the budget-minded has recently been upgraded, with new paint, bedspreads, and drapes in each apartment. The one-bedroom units each have a sofa bed in the living room, which allows you to sleep four comfortably. All of the island-style units feature fully equipped kitchens that include dishwashers. There's great ocean swimming just off the rock wall (sandy beach at low tide); a protective reef mows waves down and allows even timid swimmers to relax.

3785 Lower Honoapiilani Rd. (in Honokowai), Lahaina, HI 96761. © 800/222-8688 or 808/669-8197. Fax 808/669-2502. www.maui.net. 26 units. $95 or $125 1-bedroom double. Extra person $10. 3-night minimum; cleaning fee $50 if less than 7 nights. MC, V. **Amenities:** Outdoor pool; concierge; activity desk; coin-op washer/dryers. *In room:* TV, kitchen, fridge, coffeemaker, washer/dryer.

Napili Bay *(★ (Finds)* One of Maui's best secret bargains is this small, two-story complex right on Napili's beautiful half-mile white-sand beach. It's perfect for a romantic getaway: The atmosphere is comfortable and relaxing, the ocean lulls you to sleep at night, and birdsong wakes you in the morning. The beach here is one of the best on the coast, with great swimming and snorkeling—in fact, it's so beautiful that people staying at much more expensive resorts down the road frequently haul all their beach paraphernalia here for the day. The studio apartments are definitely small, but they pack in everything you need to feel at home, from a full kitchen to a comfortable queen bed, and a roomy lanai that's great for watching the sun set over the Pacific. There's no air-conditioning, but louvered windows and ceiling fans help keep the units cool during the day. There are lots of restaurants and a convenience store within walking distance, and you're about 10 to 15 minutes away from Lahaina and some great golf courses. All this for as little as $110 a night—unbelievable! Book early, and tell 'em Frommer's sent you.

33 Hui Dr. (off Lower Honoapiilani Hwy., in Napili). c/o Maui Beachfront Rentals, 256 Papalaua St., Lahaina, HI 96767. © 888/661-7200 or 808/661-3500. Fax 808/661-5210. www.mauibeachfront.com. 33 units. $110–$140 studio for up to 4. 5-night minimum. MC, V. **Amenities:** Coin-op washer/dryers. *In room:* TV, kitchen, fridge, coffeemaker.

Napili Sunset *(Value)* Housed in three buildings (2 on the ocean and 1 across the street) and located just down the street from Napili Bay (see above), these clean, older, but well-maintained units offer good value. At first glance, the plain two-story structures don't look like much, but the location, the bargain prices, and the friendly staff are the real hidden treasures here. In addition to daily maid service, the units all have full kitchens (with dishwashers), ceiling fans, sofa beds, small dining areas, and small bedrooms. The beach, one of Maui's best, can get a little crowded, as the public beach access is through this property (and everyone on Maui seems to want to come here). The studio units are all located in the building off the beach and a few steps up a slight hill; they're good-size, with a full kitchen and either a sofa bed or a Murphy bed, and they overlook the small pool and garden. The one- and two-bedroom units are all on the beach (the downstairs units have lanais that lead right to the sand). The staff makes sure each unit has the basics—paper towels, dishwasher soap, coffee filters, condiments—to get your stay off to a good start. There are restaurants within walking distance.

46 Hui Rd. (in Napili), Lahaina, HI 96761. ℂ 800/447-9229 or 808/669-8083. Fax 808/669-2730. www.napilisunset.com. 42 units. High season $120 studio double; $225 1-bedroom double; $315 2-bedroom (sleeps up to 4). Low season $105 studio; $205 1-bedroom; $265 2-bedroom. Extra person $12. Children under 3 stay free in parent's room. 3-night minimum. MC, V. **Amenities:** Small outdoor pool; coin-op washer/dryers (free detergent supplied). *In room:* TV, kitchen, fridge, coffeemaker.

Papakea *(Value)*   Just a mile down the beach from Kaanapali lie these low-rise buildings, surrounded by manicured, landscaped grounds and ocean views galore. Palm trees and tropical plants dot the property, a putting green wraps around two kidney-shaped pools, and a footbridge arches over a lily pond brimming with carp. Each pool has its own private cabana with sauna, Jacuzzi, and barbecue grills; a poolside shop rents snorkel gear for exploring the offshore reefs. All units have big lanais and dishwashers, and some units have their own washer/dryers. The studios have pull-down beds to save space during the day. Definitely a good value.

Maui Resort Management, 3600 Lower Honoapiilani Rd. (in Honokowai), Lahaina, HI 96761. ℂ 800/367-5037 or 808/669-1902. Fax 808/669-8790. www.mauigetaway.com. 364 units. $115–$135 studio double; $135–$200 1-bedroom (sleeps up to 4); $155–$220 2-bedroom (sleeps up to 6). 7-night minimum. Extra person $10. MC, V. **Amenities:** 2 outdoor pools; 3 tennis courts; 2 Jacuzzis; watersports equipment rentals, coin operated laundry. *In room:* TV/VCR, dataport, kitchen, fridge, coffeemaker.

KAPALUA
VERY EXPENSIVE

Kapalua Bay Hotel & Ocean Villas *(★★)* *(Kids)*   Few Hawaiian resorts have so much open space. The Kapalua Bay sits seaward of 23,000 acres of green fields lined with spiky Norfolk pine windbreaks. The 1970s-style rectilinear building, down by the often-windy shore, is full of angles that frame stunning views of the

---

Nickel-&-Dime Charges at High-Priced Hotels

Several upscale resorts in Hawaii have begun a practice that we find distasteful, dishonest, and downright discouraging: charging a so-called "resort fee." This daily fee is added on to your bill (and can range from $8–$15 a day), for such "complimentary" items as a daily newspaper, local phone calls, use of the fitness facilities, and so on. Amenities that the resort has been happily providing its guests for years are now tacked on to your bill under the guise of a "fee." In most cases, you do not have an option to decline the resort fee—in other words, this is a sneaky way to further increase the prices without telling you. We are very opposed to this practice and urge you to voice your complaints to the resort management. Otherwise, what'll be next—a charge for using the tiny bars of soap or miniature shampoo bottles?

ocean, mountains, and blue sky. The tastefully designed maze of oversize rooms fronts a palm-fringed gold-sand beach that's one of the best in Hawaii, and there's an excellent Ben Crenshaw golf course. Each guest room has a sitting area with sofa, a king or two double beds, and an entertainment center. Plantation-style shutter doors open onto private lanais with views of Molokai across the channel. The renovated bathrooms feature two granite vanities, a large soaking tub, and a glass-enclosed shower.

The good news is that unlike some other luxury resorts, the Kapalua Bay has waved the obnoxious and not-very-hospitable "resort fee"; the bad news is that they now charge for parking (self or valet) at the outrageous rate of $15 a day (the highest not only on Maui, but the highest rate of all the neighbor islands, rivaling parking in Waikiki).

1 Bay Dr., Kapalua, HI 96761. ⓒ 800/367-8000 or 808/669-5656. Fax 808/669-4694. www.kapaluabayhotel. com. 206 units. $350–$600 double; from $500 1- and 2-bedroom bay villas; from $1200 suites. Extra person $75. Children 17 and under stay free in parent's room using existing bedding. Parking $15. AE, DC, MC, V. **Amenities:** 3 restaurants; 3 bars; 2 outdoor pools; access to the Kapalua Resort's acclaimed trio of golf courses (each with its own pro shop); 10 Plexi-pave tennis courts for day and night play; 24-hr. fitness facilities; small spa; Jacuzzi; watersports equipment rentals; children's program for kids age 5–12, offering activities ranging from snorkeling and surfing to lei-making and cookie-baking; concierge; activity desk; car-rental desk; business center; shopping arcade; salon; 24-hr. room service; in-room and spa massage; babysitting; same-day laundry service and dry cleaning; concierge-level rooms. *In room:* A/C, TV, dataport, minibar, fridge, coffeemaker, hair dryer, iron, safe.

Ritz-Carlton Kapalua 𝒦𝒦 *(Kids*   In our opinion, this is the best Ritz-Carlton in the world. It's in the best place (Hawaii), near the best beach (Kapalua), and has a friendly staff that goes above and beyond the call of duty. The Ritz is a complete universe, one of those resorts where you can happily sit by the ocean with a book for 2 whole weeks and never leave the grounds. It rises proudly on a knoll, in a singularly spectacular setting between the rainforest and the sea. During construction, the burial sites of hundreds of ancient Hawaiians were discovered in the sand, so the hotel was moved inland to avoid disrupting the graves. The setback improved the hotel's outlook, which now has a commanding view of Molokai.

The style is fancy plantation, elegant but not imposing. The public spaces are open, airy, and graceful, with plenty of tropical foliage and landscapes by artist Sarah Supplee that recall the not-so-long-ago agrarian past. Rooms are up to the usual Ritz standard, outfitted with marble bathrooms, private lanais, and in-room fax capability. Hospitality is the keynote here; you'll find the exemplary service you expect from Ritz-Carlton seasoned with good old-fashioned Hawaiian aloha. The Club Floor 𝒦𝒦𝒦 offers the best amenities in the state (and you'll pay for them), from French roast coffee in the morning to a buffet at lunch to cookies in the afternoon to pupu and drinks at sunset. The Ritz Kids program offers a variety of activities and is very reasonable for hotel guests—only $15 for a full day, including lunch. Our only complaint about this fabulous property is the "resort fee" you're charged on top of the already-high room rates.

1 Ritz-Carlton Dr., Kapalua, HI 96761. ⓒ 800/262-8440 or 808/669-6200. Fax 808/665-0026. www.ritzcarlton. com. 548 units. $375–$535 double; from $635 suite. Extra person $50 ($125 in Club Floor rooms). "Resort fee" of $15 for "complimentary" use of fitness center and children's program. Wedding/honeymoon, golf, and other packages available. AE, DC, DISC, MC, V. Valet parking $10, free self-parking. **Amenities:** 4 restaurants; 4 bars (including 1 serving drinks and light fare on the sand); outdoor pool; access to the Kapalua Resort's 3 championship golf courses (each with its own pro shop) and its deluxe tennis complex; fitness room; spa; Jacuzzi; watersports equipment rentals; bike rental; children's program; game room; concierge; activity desk; car-rental desk; business center; shopping arcade; salon; room service; in-room and spa massage; babysitting; same-day laundry and dry cleaning; concierge-level rooms (some of Hawaii's best, with top-drawer service and amenities). *In room:* A/C, TV, dataport, minibar, coffeemaker, hair dryer, iron, safe.

EXPENSIVE

If you're interested in a luxurious condo or town house, consider **Kapalua Villas** (© **800/545-0018** or 808/669-8088; www.kapaluavillas.com). The palatial units dotting the oceanfront cliffs and fairways of this idyllic coast are a (relative) bargain, especially if you're traveling with a group. The one- bedroom condos go for $199 to $279; two-bedrooms for $299 to $469; plus numerous package deals (which include golf, tennis, honeymoon amenities, and car) save you even more money.

3 South Maui

MAALAEA

We recommend two booking agencies that rent a host of condominiums and unique vacation homes in the Kihei/Wailea/Maalaea area: **Kihei Maui Vacation** (© **800/541-6284** or 808/879-7581; www.kmvmaui.com) and **Condominium Rentals Hawaii** (© **800/367-5242** or 808/879-2778; www.crhmaui.com).

KIHEI
EXPENSIVE

In addition to the choices below, also consider the **Aston at the Maui Banyan** (© **800/92-ASTON** or 808/875-0004; www.aston-hotels.com), a condo property across the street from Kamaole Beach Park II. The one- to three-bedroom units are very nicely done and feature full kitchens, air-conditioning, and washer/dryers. Rates start at $145 for hotel rooms, $180 for one-bedroom units, and $245 for two-bedroom units; be sure to ask about packages.

Maalaea Surf Resort Come here for a quiet, relaxing vacation on a well-landscaped property, with a beautiful white-sand beach right outside. Located at the quiet end of Kihei Road, this two-story complex sprawls across 5 acres of lush tropical gardens. The luxury town houses all have ocean views, big kitchens (with dishwashers), cable TV, and VCRs. Amenities include maid service (Mon–Sat), shuffleboard, barbecue grills, discounts on tee times at nearby golf courses, and restaurants and shops within a 5-minute drive.

12 S. Kihei Rd. (at S. Kihei Rd. and Hwy. 350), Kihei, HI 96753. © **800/423-7953** or 808/879-1267. Fax 808/874-2884. www.maalaeasurfresort.com. 34 units in rental pool. $205–$230 1-bedroom unit; $277–$307 2-bedroom (sleeps up to 6). Extra person $15. MC, V. **Amenities:** 2 outdoor pools; 2 tennis courts; concierge; activity desk; car-rental desk; coin-op washer/dryers. *In room:* A/C, TV/VCR, kitchen, fridge, coffeemaker, hair dryer, iron, safe.

Maui Hill If you can't decide between the privacy of a condo and the conveniences of a hotel, try this place. Managed by the respected Aston chain, Maui Hill gives you the best of both worlds. Located on a hill above the heat of Kihei town, this large, Spanish-style resort (with stucco buildings, red-tile roofs, and arched entries) combines all the amenities and activities of a hotel (pool, hot tub, tennis courts, Hawaiiana classes, maid service, and more) with large luxury condos that have full kitchens and plenty of privacy. Nearly all units have ocean views, dishwashers, washer/dryers, queen sofa beds, and big lanais. Beaches, restaurants, and shops are within easy walking distance, and a golf course is nearby. The management here goes out of its way to make sure your stay is perfect.

2881 S. Kihei Rd. (across from Kamaole Park III, between Keonekai St. and Kilohana Dr.), Kihei, HI 96753. © **800/92-ASTON** Aston Hotels and Resorts or 808/879-6321. Fax 808/879-8945. www.aston-hotels.com. 140 units. High season $280 1-bedroom apt; $365 2-bedroom; $495 3-bedroom. Low season $215 1-bedroom; $280 2-bedroom; $385 3-bedroom. AE, DC, DISC, MC, V. **Amenities:** Outdoor pool; putting green; tennis courts; Jacuzzi; concierge; activity desk; car-rental desk; coin-op washer/dryers; laundry service; dry cleaning. *In room:* A/C, TV, kitchen, fridge, coffeemaker, hair dryer, iron, safe, washer/dryer (in most units).

MODERATE

The **Kihei Beach Resort,** 36 S. Kihei Rd., Kihei, HI 96753 (© **888/875-9366** or 808/879-2744; fax 808/875-0306; www.kiheibeachresort.com), has spacious condos right on the beach. The downside is the constant traffic noise from Kihei Road. Rates are $120 to $185 for a one-bedroom, $180 to $250 for a two-bedroom; there's a 4-night minimum.

Kamaole Nalu Resort   This six-story condominium complex is located between two beach parks: Kamaole I and Kamaole II, and right across the street from a shopping complex. Units have fabulous ocean views, large living rooms, and private lanais; the kitchens are a bit small but come fully equipped. We recommend no. 306 for its wonderful bird's-eye view. The property also has an ocean-side pool and great barbecue facilities. Restaurants, bars, a golf course, and tennis courts are nearby; shopping is across the street. *Be warned:* Because the building is right on Kihei Road, it can be noisy.

2450 S. Kihei Rd. (between Kanani and Keonekai rds., next to Kamaole Beach Park II), Kihei, HI 96753. © **800/ 767-1497** or 808/879-1006. Fax 808/879-8693. www.kamaolenalu.com. 36 units. High season $155–$215 double. Low season $135–$195 double. Extra person $15. 5-night minimum. MC, V. **Amenities:** Outdoor pool; activity desk; car-rental desk. *In room:* TV, kitchen, fridge, coffeemaker, hair dryer, iron, safe, washer/dryer.

Koa Resort (★ (Value (Kids   Located just across the street from the ocean, Koa Resort consists of five two-story wooden buildings on more than 5½ acres of landscaped grounds. The spacious, privately owned one-, two-, and three-bedroom units are decorated with care, large enough for families, and come fully equipped, right down to the dishwasher and disposal in the kitchens. The larger condos have both showers and tubs; the smaller units have showers only. All feature large lanais, ceiling fans, and washer/dryers. For maximum peace and quiet, ask for a unit far from Kihei Road. Bars, restaurants, and a golf course are nearby; these, along with the beach, putting green, pool, and tennis courts, should be enough to keep the whole family busy.

811 S. Kihei Rd. (between Kulanihakoi St. and Namauu Place), c/o Bello Realty, P.O. Box 1776, Kihei, HI 96753. © **800/541-3060** or 808/879-3328. Fax 808/875-1483. www.bellomaui.com. 54 units (some w/shower only). High season $110 1-bedroom; $120-$130 2-bedroom; $155-$180 3-bedroom. Low season $85 1-bedroom; $100-$110 2-bedroom; $135-$160 3-bedroom. No credit cards. **Amenities:** Outdoor pool; 18-hole putting green; 2 tennis courts; Jacuzzi. *In room:* TV, kitchen, fridge, coffeemaker, hair dryer, iron, safe, washer/dryer.

Maui Coast Hotel (★★   This place stands out as one of the only moderately priced hotels in Kihei (which is largely full of affordable condo complexes rather than traditional hotels or resorts). That's big news—especially on Maui, where luxury abounds. Ask about packages: For slightly more than the regular price of a room, the Maui Coast's Room and Car package gives you a rental car. The other chief advantage of this hotel is its location, about a block from Kamaole Beach Park I, with plenty of bars, restaurants, and shopping within walking distance and a golf course nearby. A $2.5 million renovation of all the furniture, linens, and upholstery in the rooms has this moderately priced hotel looking better than ever. The rooms offer extras such as sitting areas, whirlpool tubs, ceiling fans, and private lanais.

2259 S. Kihei Rd. (1 block from Kamaole Beach Park I), Kihei, HI 96753. © **800/895-MAUI** or 808/874-6284. Fax 808/875-4731. www.mauicoasthotel.com. 265 units. $155–$165 double; $175–$195 alcove suite; $230 1-bedroom suite (sleeps up to 4). Children 17 and under stay free in parent's room using existing bedding. Rollaway bed $20. Packages including rental car available. AE, DC, DISC, MC, V. **Amenities:** Restaurant; pool bar with nightly entertainment; outdoor pool (plus children's wading pool); 2 night-lit tennis courts; fitness room; concierge; activity desk; limited room service; free use of self-serve washer/dryers; laundry service; dry cleaning. *In room:* A/C, TV, fridge, coffeemaker, hair dryer, iron, safe.

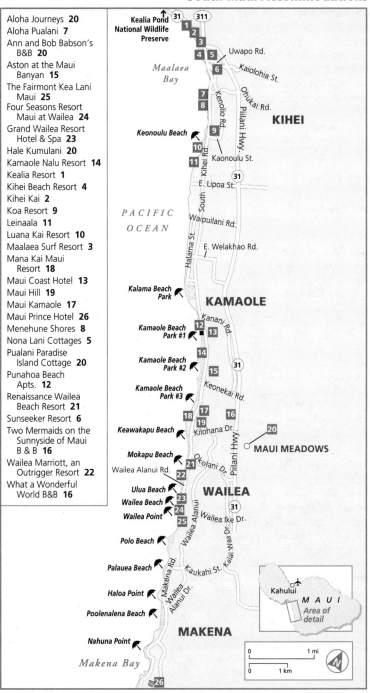

South Maui Accommodations

Aloha Journeys **20**
Aloha Pualani **7**
Ann and Bob Babson's
B&B **20**
Aston at the Maui
Banyan **15**
The Fairmont Kea Lani
Maui **25**
Four Seasons Resort
Maui at Wailea **24**
Grand Wailea Resort
Hotel & Spa **23**
Hale Kumulani **20**
Kamaole Nalu Resort **14**
Kealia Resort **1**
Kihei Beach Resort **4**
Kihei Kai **2**
Koa Resort **9**
Leinaala **11**
Luana Kai Resort **10**
Maalaea Surf Resort **3**
Mana Kai Maui
Resort **18**
Maui Coast Hotel **13**
Maui Hill **19**
Maui Kamaole **17**
Maui Prince Hotel **26**
Menehune Shores **8**
Nona Lani Cottages **5**
Pualani Paradise
Island Cottage **20**
Punahoa Beach
Apts. **12**
Renaissance Wailea
Beach Resort **21**
Sunseeker Resort **6**
Two Mermaids on the
Sunnyside of Maui
B & B **16**
Wailea Marriott, an
Outrigger Resort **22**
What a Wonderful
World B&B **16**

Kealia Pond
National Wildlife
Preserve

Maalaea
Bay

Uwapo Rd.

Kaiolohia St.

Ohukai Rd.

Kenolio Rd.

Piilani Hwy.

KIHEI

Keonoulu Beach

Kaonoulu St.

South Kihei Rd.

E. Lipoa St.

PACIFIC
OCEAN

Waipuilani Rd.

Halama St.

E. Welakhao Rd.

Kalama Beach
Park

KAMAOLE

Kanani Rd.

Kamaole Beach
Park #1

Kamaole Beach
Park #2

Kamaole Beach
Park #3

Keonekai Rd.

Keawakapu Beach

Kilohana Dr.

MAUI MEADOWS

Mokapu Beach

Okolani Dr.

Wailea Alanui Rd.

Piilani Hwy.

Ulua Beach

WAILEA

Wailea Beach

Wailea Point

Wailea Alanui

Wailea Ike Dr.

Polo Beach

Palauea Beach

Makena Rd.

Kaukahi St.

Wailea
Alanui Dr.

Kaiai Waa Dr.

Haloa Point

Poolenalena Beach

Nahuna Point

MAKENA

Makena Bay

Kahului

MAUI
Area of
detail

0   1 mi
0   1 km

Maui Kamaole You'll find this condo complex right across the street from the Kihei Public Boat Ramp and beautiful Kamaole Beach Park III, which is great for swimming, snorkeling, and beachcombing. Each roomy, fully furnished unit comes with a private lanai, two bathrooms (even in the 1-bedroom units), and an all-electric kitchen. The one-bedroom units—which can comfortably accommodate four—are quite a deal, especially if you're traveling in the off season. The grounds are nicely landscaped and offer barbecues. Restaurants and bars are within walking distance; a golf course and tennis courts are also nearby.

2777 S. Kihei Rd. (between Keonekai and Kilohana rds., at the Wailea end of Kihei), Kihei, HI 96753. ⓒ 800-822-4409 or 808/874-8467. Fax 808/875-9117. www.mauikamaole.com. 210 units. High season $170–$195 1-bedroom double (sleeps up to 4); $220–$250 2-bedroom (rates for 4, sleeps up to 6). Low season $135–$150 1-bedroom; $175–$200 2-bedroom. 4-night minimum. AE, MC, V. **Amenities:** 2 outdoor pools; Jacuzzi; concierge; laundry service; dry cleaning. *In room:* A/C, TV, kitchen, fridge, coffeemaker, iron, safe, washer/dryer.

INEXPENSIVE

In addition to the choices below, six suites are available at **Aloha Pualani** (ⓒ 800/ **PUALANI** or 808/874-9265; www.alohapualani.com), which manages to combine the personal service of a B&B with the independent living arrangements of a condo—and the beach is just across the street. Rates are $89 to $150 (3-night minimum).

Luana Kai Resort, 940 S. Kihei Rd., Kihei, HI 96753 (ⓒ **800/669-1127** or 808/879-1268; fax 808/879-1455; www.luanakai.com), is an older condo complex with 113 one- and two-bedroom units ($89–$149 for a 1-bedroom, $109–$169 for a 2-bedroom; 4-night minimum).

Kihei Kai, 61 N. Kihei Rd., Kihei, HI 96753 (ⓒ **800/735-2357** or 808/879-2357; fax 808/874-4960; www.maui.net/~kiheikai), has one-bedroom apartments ($95–$130) that are ideal for families.

Finally, the **Sunseeker Resort,** 551 S. Kihei Rd., P.O. Box 276, Kihei, HI 96753 (ⓒ **800/532-MAUI** or 808/879-1261; fax 808/874-3877; www.maui.net/~sunseekr), offers older, sometimes noisy budget units with great ocean views—somewhat of a rarity on Maui. Rates are $60 to $70 for a studio, $90 to $110 for a one-bedroom, or $175 for a two-bedroom; there's a 3-night minimum.

Aloha Journeys ⚡ *Finds* Tucked into the residential neighborhood of Maui Meadows (and a 5-min. drive from the nearest good beach) is an oasis of fruit trees, a flower garden, and a sun deck with picnic table, chairs, and a hot tub overlooking the ocean. Both rental cottages have their own TVs, VCRs, CD players, and washer/dryers. The two-bedroom Ginger Cottage is best for families, with full kitchen, two separate bedrooms and an enclosed lanai. The one-bedroom Palm Cottage makes a cozy honeymoon cottage (it also has a sofa bed). Guests are welcome to gather fresh fruits for their breakfast. Other great amenities for guests: yoga classes, free bicycles, and numerous beach toys. Occasionally owner/hostess Karen will waive the 5-night minimum for last-minute bookings. They also rent a three-bedroom million-dollar vacation home for just $220 a night ($73 and change per couple).

490 Mikioi Place (Maui Meadows), Kihei, HI 96753. ⓒ 800/871-5032 or 808/875-4840. Fax 808/879-3998. www.alohajourneys.com. 2 units. Apr 16–Dec 14 $80 double (plus $50 cleaning fee), extra person $15; Dec 15–Apr 15 $100 double (plus $50 cleaning fee), extra person $20. 5-night minimum. MC, V. **Amenities:** Jacuzzi; laundry facilities. *In room:* TV/VCR, answering machine, kitchen, fridge, coffeemaker, hair dryer, washer/dryer.

Ann and Bob Babson's Bed & Breakfast and Sunset Cottage ⚡ *Value* We highly recommend staying on this spacious landscaped lot, which boasts

180 degree views of the islands of Lanai, Kahoolawe, and Molokini; sunsets are not to be missed. Accommodations include two rooms in the main house (1 with panoramic ocean views, skylights, and a whirlpool tub), a one-bedroom suite downstairs, and a two-bedroom cottage with a kitchen. The Babsons have three adorable cats—if you're allergic, you might want to book elsewhere.

3371 Keha Dr. (in Maui Meadows), Kihei, HI 96753. © **800/824-6409** or 808/874-1166. Fax 808/879-7906. www.mauibnb.com. 4 units. $100–$130 double (including breakfast Mon–Sat); $135 cottage double (sleeps up to 4). Extra person $15. 5-night minimum in house, 7-night minimum for cottage. MC, V. *In room:* TV, kitchen (in cottage only), fridge, coffeemaker.

Hale Kumulani ★ *Finds*   At the top of Maui Meadows subdivision, right on the Wailea border and about a 5-minute drive to the beach, lies this half acre (chemical-free) property, surrounded by a 40,000 acre wilderness area with two quaint units. The first is a darling, one-room cottage with full kitchen, wood flooring, high beam ceilings, living room area (with TV/VCR, stereo, and full-size guest sofa/futon), large deck, and outdoor shower. Underneath the main house, but with private entrance and complete privacy, is the waterfall suite with a kitchenette (2-burner stove, microwave, toaster oven, blender, coffeemaker, and so on) and a giant outdoor patio with an overhang that provides shade and is landscaped with a waterfall plus banana and papaya trees. Both units have access to the organic vegetable garden, numerous fruit trees, and beach equipment. Hosts Ron and Merry couldn't be more gracious in helping you navigate around the island. They also accommodate children with both a full-size crib and junior beds available (as well as a stroller).

Kumulani Dr., Maui Meadows, Kihei, HI 96753. Reservations c/o Hawaii's Best Bed & Breakfasts, P.O. Box 758, Volcano, HI 96785. © **800/262-9912** or 808/985-7488. Fax 808/967-8610. www.bestbnb.com. 2 units. $100 double suite; $135 cottage double. $50 cleaning fee. 3- night minimum. No credit cards. **Amenities:** 6 championship golf courses within 5 miles; aquatic center with 3 pools nearby (a 7-min. drive). *In room:* TV/VCR, kitchen (in cottage), kitchenette (in suite), fridge, coffeemaker, washer/dryer, hair dryer, iron.

Kealia Resort *Value*   This oceanfront property at the northern end of Kihei is well maintained and nicely furnished—and the price is excellent. But as tempting as the $75 studio units may sound, don't give in: They face noisy Kihei Road and are near a major junction, so you'll be listening to big trucks downshifting all night. Instead, go for one of the oceanview units, which all have full kitchens and private lanais. The grounds face a 5-mile stretch of white-sand beach. The management goes out of its way to provide opportunities for guests to meet; social gatherings include free coffee-and-doughnut get-togethers every Friday morning and pupu parties on Wednesdays.

191 N. Kihei Rd. (north of Hwy. 31, at the Maalaea end of Kihei), Kihei, HI 96753. © **800/265-0686** or 808/879-0952. Fax 808/875-1540. www.apmimaui.com. 51 units. $75–$99 studio double; $100–$150 1-bedroom double; $165–$195 2-bedroom (sleeps up to 4). Children 12 and under stay free in parent's room. Extra person $10. 4-night minimum. MC, V. **Amenities:** Recently retiled outdoor pool. *In room:* TV, kitchen, fridge, coffeemaker, hair dryer, iron, washer/dryer.

Leinaala ★ *Value*   From Kihei Road, you can't see Leinaala amid the jumble of buildings, but this oceanfront boutique condo offers excellent accommodations at 1980s prices. The building is set back from the water, with a county park—an oasis of green grass and tennis courts—in between. A golf course lies nearby. The units are compact, but filled with everything you need: a full kitchen, sofa bed, and oceanview lanai. (Hideaway beds are available if you need one.)

998 S. Kihei Rd., Kihei, HI 96753. ℂ **800/822-4409** or 808/879-2235. Fax 808/879-8366. www.maui condo.com. 24 units. $135 1-bedroom double; $180 2-bedroom (sleeps up to 4). 4-night minimum. Extra person $10. No credit cards. **Amenities:** Outdoor pool; coin-op washer/dryers. *In room:* A/C, TV, kitchen, fridge, coffeemaker.

Mana Kai Maui Resort ★ *Kids*   This eight-story complex, situated on a beautiful white-sand cove, is an unusual combination of hotel and condominium. The hotel rooms, which account for half of the total number of units, are small but nicely furnished. The condo units feature full kitchens and open living rooms with sliding-glass doors that lead to small lanais overlooking the sandy beach and ocean. Some units are beginning to show their age (the building is more than 30 years old), but they're all clean and comfortable. One of the best snorkeling beaches on the coast is just steps away; a golf course and tennis courts are nearby.

2960 S. Kihei Rd. (between Kilohana and Keonekai rds., at the Wailea end of Kihei), Kihei, HI 96753. ℂ **800/ 367-5242** or 808/879-2778. Fax 808/879-7825. www.crhmaui.com. 105 units. $95–$135 hotel room double; $175–$245 1-bedroom (sleeps up to 4); $234–$300 2-bedroom (up to 6). AE, DC, DISC, MC, V. **Amenities:** Restaurant; bar; outdoor pool; concierge; coin-op washer/dryers. *In room:* A/C (in hotel rooms only), TV, kitchen (in condo units), fridge, coffeemaker, safe.

Menehune Shores *Value*   If you plan to stay on Maui for a week, you might want to look into the car/condo packages here; they're a real deal, especially for families on a budget. The six-story Menehune Shores is more than 30 years old and is showing its age in some places, but all units are well maintained and have ocean views. The design is straight out of the 1970s, but the view from the private lanai is timeless. The kitchens are fully equipped, all units have washer/dryers, and the oceanfront location guarantees a steady breeze that keeps the rooms cool (there's no air-conditioning). The building sits in front of the ancient Hawaiian fish ponds of Kalepolepo; some Hawaiians still fish them using traditional throw nets, but generally the pond serves as protection from the ocean waves, making it safe for children (and those unsure of their ability) to swim in the relatively calm waters. There's also a heated pool, shuffleboard courts, and a whale-watching platform on the roof garden.

760 S. Kihei Rd. (between Kaonoulu and Hoonani sts.), P.O. Box 1327, Kihei, HI 96753. ℂ **800/558-9117** or 808/879-3428. Fax 808/879-5218. www.menehunereservations.com. 70 units. $105–$130 1-bedroom double ($839/week w/car); $120–$155 2-bedroom double ($989/week w/car); $135–$180 2-bedroom for 4 ($1,129/week w/car); $170–$220 3-bedroom for up to 6 ($1,539/week w/car). 3-night minimum. Extra person $7.50. No credit cards. **Amenities:** Restaurant (Hawaiian/Pacific Rim) and bar; outdoor pool; room service (8am–9pm). *In room:* TV/VCR, kitchen, fridge, coffeemaker, washer/dryers.

Nona Lani Cottages ★ *Finds*   Picture this: a grassy expanse dotted with eight cottages tucked among palm, fruit, and sweet-smelling flower trees, right across the street from a white-sand beach. This is one of the great hidden deals in Kihei. The cottages are tiny, but contain everything you'll need: a small but complete kitchen, twin beds that double as couches in the living room, a separate bedroom with a queen bed, and a lanai with table and chairs. The cottages were renovated in 2002 with new ceramic flooring. The real attraction, however, is the garden setting next to the beach. There are no phones in the cabins (a blessing if you're trying to escape civilization), but there's a public one by the registration/check-in area.

If the cabins are booked, or if you want a bit more luxury, you might opt for one of the private guest rooms, with private entrance and private bath. These beautiful units feature plush carpet, koa bed frames, lanais, and private entrances. As we went to press, the industrious Kong family, hosts here, were working on hostel accommodations on the other side of the island in Happy Valley, next to Wailuku, with very low rates.

455 S. Kihei Rd. (just south of Hwy. 31), P.O. Box 655, Kihei, HI 96753. © **800/733-2688** or 808/879-2497. www.nonalanicottages.com. 11 units. $75–$85 double; $90–$99 cottage. Extra person $12–$15. 3-night minimum for rooms, 4-night minimum for cottages. No credit cards. **Amenities:** Coin-op washer/dryers. *In room:* TV, kitchen (in cottages), fridge, coffeemaker, no phone.

Pualani Paradise Island Cottage *(Finds)*   Hidden away on a quiet street in the residential area above Wailea known as Maui Meadows (about a 5-min. drive from the nearest good beach), you'll find this quaint cottage, surrounded by lush landscaped grounds and a large swimming pool. The cozy cottage, with a fully equipped kitchen, has all the comforts of home, including a VCR, stereo, and phones. Some guests return again and again to the immaculate grounds, the charming cottage, and the cool pool. Host Jack St. Germain also has a real estate company specializing in vacation rentals (condos, cottages, and homes). Check the website for details.

3134 Hoomua Dr. (in Maui Meadows), Kihei, HI 96753. © **800/800-8608** or 808/874-1048. Fax 808/879-6932. www.mauisuncoast.com. 1 cottage. $75–$95 double. 4-night minimum. MC, V. **Amenities:** Pool; laundry service. *In room:* TV/VCR, kitchen, fridge, coffeemaker, iron.

Punahoa Beach Apartments *(★) (Value)*   Book this place! We can't put it any more simply than that. The location—off noisy, traffic-ridden Kihei Road, on a quiet side street with ocean frontage—is fabulous. A grassy lawn rolls about 50 feet down to the beach, where there's great snorkeling just offshore and a popular surfing spot next door; shopping and restaurants are all within walking distance. All of the beautifully decorated units in this small, four-story building have fully equipped kitchens and lanais with great ocean views. Rooms go quickly in winter, so reserve early.

2142 Iliili Rd. (off S. Kihei Rd., 100 yards from Kamaole Beach I), Kihei, HI 96753. © **800/564-4380** or 808/879-2720. Fax 808/875-9147. www.punahoa.com. 13 units. High season $130 studio double; $185–$198 1-bedroom double; $220 2-bedroom double. Low season $94 studio; $130–$145 1-bedroom; $160 2-bedroom. Extra person $15. 5-night minimum. AE, MC, V. **Amenities:** Coin-op washer/dryer. *In room:* TV, kitchen, fridge, coffeemaker, iron.

Two Mermaids on the Sunnyside of Maui B&B *(★) (Finds)*   The two mermaids, Juddee and Miranda, both avid scuba divers, have a friendly accommodation, professionally decorated in brilliant, tropical colors, complete with hand-painted art of the island in a quiet neighborhood just a 10-minute walk from the beach. Our favorite is the "ocean ohana," a large one-bedroom apartment (with option of a second connecting bedroom), complete with kitchenette (full-size fridge, microwave, coffeemaker), huge private deck, private entryway, and your own giant hot tub. Equally cute is the "poolside suite," with private entry next to the outdoor pool. This studio (with the option of a connecting separate bedroom) is a living room during the day, and at night it converts to a bedroom with a pull-down hide-a-bed. Continental breakfast, with some of the best homemade bread on the island, is placed on your doorstep every morning (so you can sleep in). The many amenities include guitars in every unit (in case you get the urge to strum a few songs), a range of complimentary beach equipment, microwave popcorn, barbecue area, and swimming pool. Juddee is also a licensed minister and performs weddings and vow renewal.

Kihei. Reservations c/o Hawaii's Best Bed & Breakfasts, P.O. Box 758, Volcano, HI 96785. © **800/262-9912** or 808/985-7488. Fax 808/967-8610. www.bestbnb.com. 2 units. $95 studio double; $150 studio plus connecting bedroom double; $135 1-bedroom apartment; $175 with connecting 2nd bedroom. Rates include continental breakfast. No credit cards. **Amenities:** Outdoor pool; golf nearby; tennis courts nearby; massage available; babysitting available. *In room:* TV/VCR, kitchen, fridge, coffeemaker, hair dryer, iron, free local phone calls.

What a Wonderful World B&B ★ *(Value)* We couldn't believe what we discovered here: an impeccably done B&B with a great location, excellent rates, and thought and care put into every room. Then we met hostess Eva Tantillo, who has not only a full-service travel agency, but also a master's degree—along with several years of experience—in hotel management. The result? One of Maui's finest bed-and-breakfasts, centrally located in Kihei (½ mile to Kamaole II Beach Park, 5 min. from Wailea golf courses, and convenient to shopping and restaurants). Choose from one of four units: the master suite (with small fridge, coffeemaker, and barbecue grill on the lanai), studio apartment (with fully equipped kitchen), or two one-bedroom apartments (also with full kitchens). All come with private bathroom, phone, and entrance. You're also welcome to use the communal barbecue. Eva serves a family-style full breakfast on her lanai, which boasts views of white-sand beaches, the West Maui Mountains, and Haleakala.

2828 Umalu Place (off Keonakai St., near Hwy. 31), Kihei, HI 96753. ⓒ **800/943-5804** or 808/879-9103. Fax 808/874-9352. www.amauibedandbreakfast.com. 4 units. $75 double; $89 studio double; $99 1-bedroom apt. (5% discount for cash). Rates include full breakfast. Children 11 and under stay free in parent's room. AE, MC, V. **Amenities:** Hot tub; laundry facilities. *In room:* AC, TV, kitchenette, fridge, coffeemaker, hair dryer, iron.

WAILEA

For a complete selection of condo units throughout Wailea and Makena, contact **Destination Resorts Hawaii** (ⓒ **800/367-5246** or 808/879-1595; fax 808/874-3554; www.destinationresortshi.com). Its luxury units include studio doubles starting at $180; one-bedroom doubles from $170; two-bedrooms from $205; and three-bedrooms from $585. Children under 16 stay free; minimum stays vary by property.

VERY EXPENSIVE

The Fairmont Kea Lani Maui ★★★ At first glance, this blinding white complex of arches and turrets may look a bit out of place in tropical Hawaii (it's actually a close architectural cousin of Las Hadas, the Arabian Nights fantasy resort in Manzanillo, Mexico). But once you enter the flower-filled lobby and see the big blue Pacific outside, there's no doubt you're in Hawaii.

The prices are high, but you get what you pay for here, plus a few extras. Each unit in this all-suite luxury hotel has a kitchenette (with microwave and coffeemaker), a living room with entertainment center and sofa bed (great if you have the kids in tow), a marble wet bar, an oversize marble bathroom with separate shower big enough for a party, a spacious bedroom, and a large lanai that overlooks the pools, lawns, and white-sand beach.

The villas are definitely out of a fantasy. The rich and famous stay in these 2,000-square-foot, two- and three-bedroom beach bungalows, each with its own plunge pool and gourmet kitchen.

4100 Wailea Alanui Dr., Wailea, HI 96753. ⓒ **800/659-4100** or 808/875-4100. Fax 808/875-1200. www.kealani.com. 450 units. $339–$729 suite (sleeps up to 4); from $1,400 villa. AE, DC, DISC, MC, V. **Amenities:** 4 restaurants (see reviews for Nick's Fishmarket Maui on p. 143 and Caffé Ciao on p. 143); 3 bars (w/sunset cocktails and nightly entertainment at the Lobby Lounge); 2 large swimming "lagoons" connected by a 140-ft. water slide and swim-up bar, plus an adult lap pool; use of Wailea Golf Club's 3 18-hole championship golf courses, as well as the nearby Makena and Elleair golf courses; use of Wailea Tennis Center's 11 courts (3 lit for night play and a pro shop); fine 24-hr. fitness center; excellent full-service spa offering the latest in body treatments, facials, and massage; Jacuzzi; watersports equipment rentals; bike rental; children's program; game room; concierge; activity desk; car-rental desk; business center; shopping arcade; salon; 24-hr. room service; in-room and spa massage; babysitting; same-day laundry service and dry cleaning. *In room:* A/C, TV, dataport, kitchenette, minibar, fridge, coffeemaker, hair dryer, iron, safe.

Four Seasons Resort Maui at Wailea ★★★ *Kids*   If money's no object, this is the place to spend it. It's hard to beat this modern version of a Hawaiian palace by the sea, with a relaxing, casual atmosphere. Although it sits on a glorious beach between two other hotels, you won't feel like you're on resort row: The Four Seasons inhabits its own separate world, thanks to an open courtyard of pools and gardens. Amenities are first-rate here, including outstanding restaurants, an excellent spa, and a complete activities program for kids (complimentary, of course).

The spacious (about 600 sq. ft.) rooms feature furnished lanais (nearly all with ocean views) that are great for watching whales in winter and sunsets year-round. The grand bathrooms contain deep marble tubs, showers for two, and lighted French makeup mirrors.

Service is attentive but not cloying. At the pool, guests lounge in casbah-like tents, pampered with special touches like iced Evian and chilled towels. And you'll never see a housekeeping cart in the hall: The cleaning staff works in teams, so they're as unobtrusive as possible and in and out of your room in minutes.

Wolfgang Puck recently opened his Spago Restaurant (p. 142) at the resort featuring a fusion of Hawaiian and California cuisine in a dreamy open-air setting. Ferraro's at Seaside Restaurant offers a casual atmosphere overlooking the Pacific by day; by night, it's transformed into a romantic atmosphere featuring authentic Italian cucina rustica with great sunset views and dining under the stars. The poolside Pacific Grill offers lavish breakfast buffets and dinners featuring Pacific Rim cuisine.

The ritzy neighborhood surrounding the hotel is home to great restaurants and shopping, the Wailea Tennis Center (known as Wimbledon West), and six golf courses—not to mention that great beach, with gentle waves and islands framing the view on either side.

3900 Wailea Alanui Dr., Wailea, HI 96753. ℂ **800/334-MAUI** or 808/874-8000. Fax 808/874-2222. www. fourseasons.com/maui. 380 units. $335–$590 double; from $630 suite. Packages available. Extra person $90 ($160 in Club Floor rooms). Children under 18 stay free in parent's room. AE, DC, MC, V. **Amenities:** 3 restaurants; 3 bars (w/nightly entertainment); 3 fabulous outdoor pools; putting green; use of Wailea Golf Club's 3 18-hole championship golf courses, as well as the nearby Makena and Elleair golf courses; 2 on-site tennis courts (lit for night play); use of Wailea Tennis Center's 11 courts (3 lit for night play and a pro shop); health club featuring outdoor cardiovascular equipment (w/individual TV/VCR); excellent spa (offering a variety of treatments in the spa, in-room, and ocean side); 2 whirlpools (1 for adults only); beach pavilion with watersports gear rental and 1 hr. free use of snorkel equipment; complimentary use of bicycles; fabulous year-round kids' program, plus a teen recreation center and a children's video library and toys; game room (w/shuffleboard, pool tables, jukebox, big-screen TV, and video games); one of Maui's best concierge desks; activity desk; car-rental desk; business center; shopping arcade; salon; 24-hr. room service; in-room, spa, or oceanside massage; babysitting; same-day laundry service and dry cleaning; concierge-level rooms. *In room:* A/C, TV, dataport, minibar, fridge, coffeemaker, hair dryer, iron, safe.

Grand Wailea Resort Hotel & Spa ★★   Here's where grand becomes grandiose. The pinnacle of Hawaii's brief fling with fantasy megaresorts, this monument to excess is extremely popular with families, incentive groups, and conventions; it's the grand prize in Hawaii vacation contests and the dream of many honeymooners. It has a Japanese restaurant decorated with real rocks hewn from the slopes of Mount Fuji; 10,000 tropical plants in the lobby; an intricate pool system with slides, waterfalls, rapids, and a water-powered elevator to take you up to the top; Hawaii's largest and most elaborate spa; a restaurant in a man-made tide pool; a floating New England–style wedding chapel; and nothing but oceanview rooms, outfitted with every amenity you could ask for. And it's all crowned with a $30 million collection of original art, much of it created expressly for the hotel by Hawaii artists and sculptors. Though minimalists may be put off, there's no denying that the Grand Wailea is plush, professional, and pampering, with all the diversions you could imagine. Oh, and did we mention the fantastic beach out front?

3850 Wailea Alanui Dr., Wailea, HI 96753. (C) **800/888-6100** or 808/875-1234. Fax 808/874-2442. www. grandwailea.com. 780 units. $450–$760 double; from $1575 suite. Concierge tower from $800. Resort fee $15 for "complimentary" lei greeting on arrival; welcome drink; local calls; coffee in room; use of spa; admission to scuba diving clinics and water aerobics; art and garden tours; nightly turndown service; self parking; and shuttle service to Wailea area. Extra person $25 ($75 in concierge tower). AE, DC, DISC, MC, V. **Amenities:** 6 restaurants; 12 bars (including a nightclub w/laser-light shows and a hydraulic dance floor); 2,000-foot-long Action Pool, featuring a 10-min. swim/ride through mountains and grottoes; use of Wailea Golf Club's 3 18-hole championship golf courses, as well as the nearby Makena and Elleair golf courses; use of Wailea Tennis Center's 11 courts (3 lit for night play and a pro shop); complete fitness center; Hawaii's largest spa, the 50,000-square-foot Spa Grande, with a blend of European-, Japanese-, and American-style techniques; Jacuzzi; watersports equipment rentals; complimentary dive and windsurf lessons; bike rental; children's program (including a computer center, video game room, arts and crafts, children's theater, outdoor playground, and infant-care center); game room; concierge; activity desk; car-rental desk; business center; shopping arcade; salon; 24-hr. room service; in-room and spa massage; babysitting; same-day laundry service and dry cleaning; concierge-level rooms. *In room:* A/C, TV, dataport, kitchenette, minibar, fridge ($25 per stay fee), coffeemaker, hair dryer, iron, safe.

Renaissance Wailea Beach Resort 🏨🏨   This is the place for visitors in search of Wailea-style luxury, but in a smaller, more intimate setting. Located on 15 acres of rolling lawn and tropical gardens, the Renaissance Wailea has the air of a small boutique hotel. Perhaps it's the resort's U-shaped design, the series of small coves and beaches, or the spaciousness of the rooms—whatever the reason, you just don't feel crowded here.

Each room has a sitting area, a large lanai, and three phones. The bathrooms include such extras as double vanities (one with lighted makeup mirror) and *hapi* coats (Japanese-style cotton robes). All bedspreads, drapes, and towels have been recently upgraded. Rooms in the Mokapu Beach Club, an exclusive two-story building just steps from a crescent-shaped beach, feature such extras as private check-in, in-room continental breakfast, and access to a private pool and beach cabanas.

3550 Wailea Alanui Dr., Wailea, HI 96753. (C) **800/9-WAILEA** or 808/879-4900. Fax 808/874-5370. www. renaissancehotels.com. 345 units. $360–$600 double; from $1,050 suite. Extra person $40. Children 18 and under stay free in parent's room using existing bedding. Package rates available. AE, DC, DISC, MC, V. Parking $4. **Amenities:** 3 restaurants (the casual, open-air Palm Court offers buffets and oven-baked pizzas; Hana Gion features a sushi bar and teppanyaki grill; and Maui Onion is a poolside breakfast and lunch spot surrounded by lush gardens and a cascading waterfall); 2 bars; 2 freshwater outdoor pools; use of Wailea Golf Club's 3 18-hole championship golf courses, as well as the nearby Makena and Elleair golf courses; use of Wailea Tennis Center's 11 courts (3 lit for night play and a pro shop); fitness center; small spa; 2 Jacuzzis; watersports equipment rentals; children's program; game room; concierge; activity desk; car-rental desk; business center; shopping arcade; salon; room service (6am–11pm); massage; babysitting; laundry service; dry cleaning; concierge-level rooms. *In room:* A/C, TV/VCR, dataport, fridge, coffeemaker, hair dryer, iron, safe.

EXPENSIVE

Wailea Marriott, an Outrigger Resort 🏨🏨   Yes, it is confusing and yes, it seems ridiculous to have two brand names tacked on to a Hawaiian resort, but it seems that the Outrigger people entered into a "franchise agreement" with Marriott in 2002 to increase sales (through Marriott), yet still retain the same management (Outrigger). The bottom line: This classic open-air, 1970s-style hotel in a tropical garden by the sea gives you a sense of what Maui was like before the big resort boom. It was the first resort built in Wailea (in 1976), yet it remains the most Hawaiian of them all; airy and comfortable, with touches of Hawaiian art throughout.

What's truly special about this hotel is how it fits into its environment without overwhelming it. Eight buildings, all low-rise except for an eight-story tower, are spread along 22 gracious acres of lawns and gardens spiked by coco palms, with lots of open space and a half mile of oceanfront on a point between Wailea and Ulua beaches. The vast, parklike expanses are a luxury on this now-crowded coast.

In 2000, the resort went through a $25 million renovation that expanded the entrance into an open-air courtyard with a waterfall and carp pond, transformed the south pool into a water-activities area complete with two water slides, added a fabulous spa, and refurbished and upgraded the guest rooms.

3700 Wailea Alanui Dr., Wailea, HI 96753. © 800/367-2960 or 808/879-1922. Fax 808/874-8331. www.out riggerwailea.com. 524 units. $325–$525 double. Suites from $650. Extra person $40. Packages available. AE, DC, DISC, MC, V. **Amenities:** 2 restaurants; 2 bars; 3 outdoor pools; use of Wailea Golf Club's 3 18-hole championship golf courses, as well as the nearby Makena and Elleair golf courses; use of Wailea Tennis Center's 11 courts (3 lit for night play and a pro shop); fitness room; Mandora Spa; Jacuzzi; watersports equipment rentals; children's program (plus kids-only pool and recreation center); game room; concierge; activity desk; business center; shopping arcade; salon; room service (6am–11pm); in-room and spa massage; babysitting; coin-op washer/dryers; same-day laundry service and dry cleaning; concierge-level rooms. *In room:* A/C, TV, dataport, fridge, coffeemaker, hair dryer, iron, safe.

MAKENA
EXPENSIVE

Maui Prince Hotel ★★   If you're looking for a vacation in a beautiful, tranquil spot with a golden-sand beach, here's your place. But if you plan to tour Maui, you might prefer another hotel. The Maui Prince is at the end of the road, far, far away from anything else on the island, so sightseeing in other areas would require a lot of driving.

When you first see the stark-white hotel, it looks like a high-rise motel stuck in the woods—but only from the outside. Inside, you'll discover an atrium garden with a koi-filled waterfall stream, an ocean view from every room, and a simplicity to the furnishings that makes some people feel uncomfortable and others blissfully clutter-free. Rooms are small but come with private lanais with great views.

5400 Makena Alanui, Makena, HI 96753. © 800/PRINCE-4 or 808/874-1111. Fax 808/879-8763. www.maui princehotel.com. 310 units. $310–$480 double; from $600 suite. Extra person $40. Packages available. AE, DC, MC, V. **Amenities:** 4 restaurants (including the excellent Prince Court, p. 144); 2 bars with local Hawaiian music nightly; 2 outdoor pools (adults' and children's); 36 holes of golf (designed by Robert Trent Jones); 6 Plexi-pave tennis courts (2 lit for night play); fitness room; Jacuzzi; watersports equipment rental; children's program; concierge; activity desk; business center; shopping arcade; salon; room service; in-room massage; babysitting; same-day laundry service and dry cleaning. *In room:* A/C, TV, dataport, fridge, hair dryer, iron, safe.

4 Upcountry Maui

MAKAWAO, OLINDA & HALIIMAILE

When you stay in the cooler upcountry climate of Makawao, Olinda, and Haliimaile, on the slopes of Maui's 10,000-foot Haleakala volcano, you'll be (relatively) close to Haleakala National Park. Makawao and Olinda are approximately 90 minutes from the entrance to the park at the 7,000-foot level (you still have 3,000 ft. and another 30–45 min. to get to the top). Haliimaile, which is about 10 to 15 minutes driving time from Makawao, adds additional time to your drive up to the summit. Accommodations in Kula are the only other options that will get you closer to the summit so you can make the sunrise.

MODERATE

Olinda Country Cottages & Inn ★★ *(Finds)*   This charming B&B is set on the slopes of Haleakala in the crisp, clean air of Olinda, on an 8½-acre protea farm, surrounded by 35,000 acres of ranch lands (with miles of great hiking trails). The 5,000-square-foot country home, outfitted with a professional eye to detail, has large windows with incredible panoramic views of all of Maui. Upstairs are two guest rooms with antique beds, private full bathrooms, and separate entryways. Connected to the main house but with its own private entrance, the Pineapple Sweet has a full kitchen, an antique-filled living room, a marble-tiled full bathroom, and a comfy bedroom area. A separate 1,000-square-foot cottage is the epitome of cozy country luxury, with a fireplace, bedroom with queen-size bed, cushioned window seats (with great sunset views), and cathedral ceilings. The 950-square-foot Hidden Cottage (located in a truly secluded spot surrounded by protea flowers) features three decks, French glass doors, a full kitchen, a washer/dryer, and a private tub for two on the deck.

Restaurants are a 15-minute drive away in Makawao, and beaches are another 15 minutes beyond that. Once ensconced, however, you may never want to leave this enchanting inn.

2660 Olinda Rd. (near the top of Olinda Rd., a 15-min. drive from Makawao), Makawao, HI 96768. ⓒ 800/932-3435 or 808/572-1453. Fax 808/573-5326. www.mauibnbcottages.com. 5 units. $140 double (includes continental breakfast); $140 suite double (includes 1st morning's breakfast in fridge); $195–$245 cottage for 2 (sleeps up to 5; includes 1st morning's breakfast in fridge). Extra person $25. 2-night minimum for rooms and suite, 3-night minimum for cottages. No credit cards. *In room:* TV, kitchen (in cottages), fridge, coffeemaker.

INEXPENSIVE

If you'd like your own private cottage, consider **Peace of Maui,** 1290 Haliimaile Rd. (just outside Haliimaile town), Haliimaile, HI 96768 (ⓒ 888/475-5045 or 808/572-5045; www.peaceofmaui.com), which has a full kitchen, a bedroom, a day bed, and a large deck. The cottage goes for $85, and children are welcome. The owners also have rooms in the main house (with shared bathroom and kitchen facilities) from $50.

Banyan Tree House ★ *(Finds)*   Huge monkeypod trees (complete with swing and hammock) extend their branches over this property like a giant green canopy. The restored 1920s plantation manager's house is decorated with Hawaiian furniture from the 1930s. It can accommodate a big family or a group of friends; it has three spacious bedrooms with big, comfortable beds and three private, marble-tiled bathrooms. A fireplace stands at one end of the huge living room, a large lanai runs the entire length of the house, and the hardwood floors shine throughout. The four smaller guest cottages have been totally renovated and also feature hardwood floors and marble bathrooms. The small cottage has a queen bed, private bathroom, microwave, coffee pot, and access to the fridge in the laundry room. Each of the larger cottages has two beds, a private bathroom, and a TV. One cottage has a kitchenette, the other a full kitchen.

New additions to this grand property include a full-size, saltwater swimming pool and Jacuzzi with a fabulous ocean view. The quiet neighborhood and old Hawaii ambience give this place a comfortable, easygoing atmosphere. Restaurants and shops are just minutes away in Makawao, and the beach is a 15-minute drive—but this place is so relaxing that you may find yourself wanting to do nothing more than lie in the hammock and watch the clouds float by.

3265 Baldwin Ave. (next to Veteran's Cemetery, less than a mile below Makawao), Makawao, HI 96768. ⓒ 808/572-9021. Fax 808/573-5072. www.banyantreehouse.com. 1 house, 4 cottages. $85–$110 cottage for 2; $300

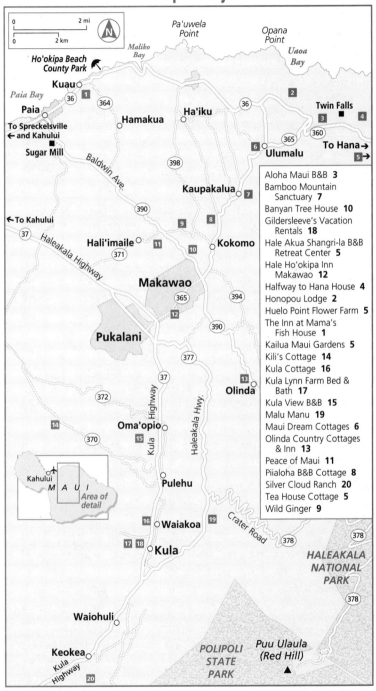

Upcountry Maui Accommodations

Aloha Maui B&B **3**
Bamboo Mountain Sanctuary **7**
Banyan Tree House **10**
Gildersleeve's Vacation Rentals **18**
Hale Akua Shangri-la B&B Retreat Center **5**
Hale Ho'okipa Inn Makawao **12**
Halfway to Hana House **4**
Honopou Lodge **2**
Huelo Point Flower Farm **5**
The Inn at Mama's Fish House **1**
Kailua Maui Gardens **5**
Kili's Cottage **14**
Kula Cottage **16**
Kula Lynn Farm Bed & Bath **17**
Kula View B&B **15**
Malu Manu **19**
Maui Dream Cottages **6**
Olinda Country Cottages & Inn **13**
Peace of Maui **11**
Piialoha B&B Cottage **8**
Silver Cloud Ranch **20**
Tea House Cottage **5**
Wild Ginger **9**

3-bedroom house (sleeps up to 9). Extra person $15. Children age 12 and under stay free in parent's room. Cleaning deposit for house of $150 if less than 7-day stay. MC, V. **Amenities:** Outdoor pool; Jacuzzi; babysitting; small charge for self-serve washer/dryer. *In room:* Kitchen or kitchenette, fridge, coffeemaker.

Hale Ho'okipa Inn Makawao ★ *(Finds* Step back in time at this 1924 plantation-style home, rescued by owner Cherie Attix in 1996 and restored to its original charm (on the State and National Historic Registers). Cherie lovingly refurbished the old wooden floors, filled the rooms with furniture from the 1920s, and hung works by local artists on the walls. The result is a charming, serene place to stay, just a 5-minute walk from the shops and restaurants of Makawao, 15 minutes from beaches, and a 1½-hour drive from the top of Haleakala. The guest rooms have separate outside entrances and private bathrooms. The house's front and back porches are both wonderful for sipping tea and watching the sunset. The Kona Wing is a two-bedroom suite with private bathroom and use of the kitchen.

32 Pakani Place, Makawao, HI 96768. (*© **808/572-6698**. www.maui-bed-and-breakfast.com. 3 units (2 w/shower only). $95–$110 double; $145–$165 suite with full kitchen. Rates include continental breakfast. Extra person $5–$10. MC, V. From Haleakala Hwy., turn left on Makawao Ave., then turn right on the fifth street on the right off Makawao Ave. (Pakani Place); second to the last house on the right (green house w/white picket fence and water tower). *In room:* TV, hair dryer.

KULA

Lodgings in Kula are the closest options to the entrance of Haleakala National Park (about 60 min. away).

MODERATE

Malu Manu ★★ *(Finds* This is one of the most romantic places to stay on Maui, with a panoramic view of the entire island from the front door. Tucked into the side of Haleakala Volcano at 4,000 feet is this old Hawaiian estate with a single-room log cabin (built as a writer's retreat in the early 1900s) and a 30-year-old family home. The writers' cabin has a full kitchen, a fireplace, and antiques galore. The two-bedroom, 2½-bathroom home also has antiques, koa walls, and beautiful eucalyptus floors. It's an ideal retreat for a romantic couple, a family, or two couples traveling together. The 7-acre property is filled with native forest, organic gardens (help yourself to lemons, avocados, and whatever else is ripe), a paddle tennis court, and a Japanese-style outdoor soaking tub. If you're a dog person, the resident golden retriever, Alohi, may come over and make your acquaintance. This is one of the closest accommodations to Haleakala; restaurants are about a 15-minute drive away.

446 Cooke Rd. (mailing address: P.O. Box 175, Kula, HI 96790). (*© **888/878-6161** or 808/878-6111. www.maui. net/~alive/index.html. 2 units. $135 double in log cabin; $170 double in 2-bedroom house. Extra person $10. MC. V. **Amenities:** Hot tub; paddle tennis court; in-room massage; laundry facilities. *In room:* Kitchen, fridge, coffeemaker, iron.

Silver Cloud Ranch Old Hawaii lives on at Silver Cloud Ranch, founded in 1902 by a sailor who jumped ship when he got to Maui. The former working cattle spread has a commanding view of four islands, the West Maui Mountains, and the valley and beaches below. The Lanai Cottage, a honeymoon favorite nestled in a flower garden, has an oceanview lanai, claw-foot tub, full kitchen, and wood-burning stove to warm chilly nights; a futon is available for a third person. The best rooms in the main house are on the second floor: the King Kamehameha Suite (with king bed) and the Queen Emma Suite (with queen sleigh bed). One-lane Thompson Road makes an ideal morning walk (about 3 miles round-trip), and you can go horseback riding next door at Thompson Ranch. There's a TV available if you feel visually deprived, but after a few Maui sunsets, you won't even remember why you bothered to ask.

Old Thompson Rd. (1¼ miles past Hwy. 37). RR 2, Box 201, Kula, HI 96790. © **800/532-1111** or 808/ 878-6101. Fax 808/878-2132. www.silvercloudranch.com. 12 units. $110–$162 double in main house; $136–$188 double studio in mauka hale; $195 double cottage. Rates include full breakfast. Extra person $15. 2 night minimum or $15 surcharge. AE, DC, DISC, MC, V. *In room:* TV, kitchen (in cottage), fridge (in cottage), coffeemaker (in cottage); no phone.

INEXPENSIVE

In addition to the options below, also consider **Gildersleeve's Vacation Rentals,** formerly known as Elaine's Upcountry Guest Rooms (© **808/878-6623;** fax 808/878-2619; m.gildersleeve@verizon.net); the warm and welcoming hosts rent three rooms in their spacious pole house ($80 double; 3-night minimum).

Kili's Cottage ★ *Value* *Kids* If you're looking for a quiet getaway in the cool elevation of Kula, this sweet cottage, situated on 2 acres, is the place. The amenities are numerous: large lanai, full kitchen, gas barbecue, washer/dryer, views, even toys for the kids. The hostess, Kili Namau'u, who is the director of a Hawaiian-language immersion school, greets each guest with royal aloha—from the flowers (picked from the garden) that fill the house to the welcome basket filled with tropical produce grown on the property.

Kula. Reservations c/o Hawaii's Best Bed & Breakfasts, P.O. Box 758, Volcano, HI 96785. © **800/262-9912** or 808/985-7488. Fax 808/967-8610. www.bestbnb.com. 1 3-bedroom/2-bathroom house. $105 double. Extra person $15. 2-night minimum. No credit cards. *In room:* TV, kitchen, fridge, coffeemaker, washer/dryer.

Kula Cottage ★ *Finds* We can't imagine having a less-than-fantastic vacation here. Tucked away on a quiet street amid blooming papaya and banana trees, Cecilia and Larry Gilbert's romantic honeymoon cottage is very private—it even has its own driveway and carport. The 700-square-foot cottage has a full kitchen (complete with dishwasher), and three huge closets that offer enough storage space for you to move in permanently. An outside lanai has a big gas barbecue and an umbrella table and chairs. Cecilia delivers a continental breakfast daily. Groceries and a small take-out lunch counter are within walking distance; it's a 30-minute drive to the beach.

40 Puakea Place (off Lower Kula Rd.), Kula, HI 96790. © **808/878-2043** or 808/871-6230. Fax 808/871-9187. www.gilbertadvertising.com/kulacottage. 1 cottage. $95 double. Rate includes continental breakfast. 2-night minimum. No credit cards. *In room:* TV, kitchen, fridge, coffeemaker, washer/dryer.

Kula Lynn Farm Bed & Bath ★ *Kids* The Coons, the same great family that runs Maui's best sailing adventure on the *Trilogy,* offer this spectacular 1,600-square-foot unit on the ground floor of a custom-built pole house. From its location on the slopes of Haleakala, the panoramic view—across Maui's central valley, with the islands of Lanai and Kahoolawe in the distance—is worth the price alone. Wall-to-wall windows and high ceilings add to the feeling of spaciousness throughout. The two bedrooms, two bathrooms, and two queen sofa beds in the living room make this the perfect place for a family. No expense has been spared in the European-style kitchen, with top appliances and Italian marble floors. This place should appeal to those who enjoy a quiet location and such activities as barbecuing on the lanai and watching the sun set.

P.O. Box 847, Kula, HI 96790. © **800/874-2666,** ext. 211, or 808/878-6176. Fax 808/878-6320. capt coon@gte.net. 1 unit. $95 double. 3-night minimum. Rate includes breakfast fixings. Extra person $15. AE, MC, V. *In room:* TV/VCR, kitchen, fridge, coffeemaker, iron.

Kula View B&B *(Finds)* Hostess and gardener extraordinaire Susan Kauai has this cute private suite (with its own deck and private entrance) upstairs in her home. You are greeted on arrival by George, the world's biggest, fluffiest tabby cat. The roomy studio has a huge deck with a panoramic view of Haleakala. Inside are a reading area with a comfy lounge chair and an eating area with table and chairs, toaster oven, coffeemaker, and electric tea kettle. Susan serves breakfast in your suite (or will pack a picnic breakfast if you are out early) of tasty breads or muffins, fruit, juice, and tea and coffee. Because her 2 acre property is located so close to Haleakala, she has plenty of warm jackets, sweaters and blankets to make your trip to the top of the 10,000 foot mountain warm. There is a phone in the studio, but no TV, so you can entertain yourself with a stroll in her magical garden.

P.O. Box 322, Kula, Hi 96790. © 808/878-6736. www.kulaview.com. 1 suite $85 double. Rate includes continental breakfast. 2 night minimum. *In room:* fridge, coffeemaker.

5 East Maui: On the Road to Hana
KUAU
MODERATE

The Inn at Mama's Fish House *(*) The fabulous location (nestled in a coconut grove on secluded Kuau Beach), beautifully decorated interior (with island-style rattan furniture and works by Hawaiian artists), full kitchen, and extras (Weber gas barbecue, big-screen TVs, and all the beach toys you can think of) make this place a gem for those seeking a centrally-located vacation rental. It has everything, even Mama's Fish House next door, where guests get a discount off lunch and dinner. The one-bedrooms are nestled in tropical jungle (red ginger surrounds the garden patio), while the two-bedrooms face the beach. Both have terra-cotta floors, complete kitchens (even dishwashers), sofa beds, and laundry facilities.

799 Poho Place (off the Hana Hwy. in Kuau), Paia, HI 96779. © 800/860-HULA or 808/579-9764. Fax 808/579-8594. www.mamasfishhouse.com. 6 units. $140–$160 1-bedroom (sleeps up to 4); $350 2-bedroom (up to 6). 3-night minimum stay. AE, DISC, MC, V. *In room:* A/C, TV/VCR, answering machine, kitchen, fridge, coffeemaker, hair dryer, iron, safe, washer/dryer.

HAIKU
MODERATE

Honopou Lodge *(* (Finds)* Hidden on Maui's north shore, next door to a 750-acre ranch, is this upscale vacation retreat. The Lodge is a unique 4,000 square foot, architect-designed, octagonal house with native ohia posts and cedar wood. The three rooms in the house can be rented separately or the entire complex as a whole. Two spacious octagonal studios downstairs share the deluxe, gourmet kitchen. Upstairs is a smaller studio with its own private entrance and a small kitchenette. Outside is a huge (32 ft. by 16 ft.), ozone-filtered swimming pool, and Jacuzzi. The hotel also offers satellite TV. Awe-inspiring ocean views beckon from every room, and sculptures and painting by the owners decorate the house. It's minutes from hiking trails and waterfalls.

Honopou Rd., Haiku. Reservations c/o Hawaii's Best Bed & Breakfasts, P.O. Box 758, Volcano, HI 96785. © 800/ 262-9912 or 808/985-7488. Fax 808/967-8610. www.bestbnb.com. 3 units. $125–$150 studio double; $300 2-bedroom downstairs of house; $400 entire house. Additional person $25. 3-night minimum. No credit cards. **Amenities:** Outdoor pool; Jacuzzi. *In room:* TV, kitchen (downstairs), kitchenette (upstairs), fridge, coffeemaker, hair dryer, iron.

Pilialoha B&B Cottage *(* (Finds)* The minute you arrive at this split-level country cottage, located on 2 acres of half-century-old eucalyptus trees, you'll see owner Machiko Heyde's artistry at work. Just in front of the quaint cottage (which is great for couples but can sleep up to 5) is a garden blooming with some 200 varieties of roses. You'll find more of Machiko's handiwork inside. There's a queen bed in the master bedroom, a twin bed in a small adjoining room, and a queen sofa bed in the living room. A large lanai extends from the master bedroom. There's a great movie collection for rainy days or cool country nights, and a garage. Machiko delivers breakfast daily; if you plan on an early morning ride to the top of Haleakala, she'll make sure you go with a thermos of coffee and her homemade bread.

2512 Kaupakalua Rd. (¾ mile from Kokomo intersection), Haiku, HI 96708. ℂ 808/572-1440. Fax 808/ 572-4612. www.pilialoha.com. 1 cottage. $130 double. Rates include continental breakfast. Extra person $20. 3-night minimum. MC, V. **Amenities:** Complimentary use of beach gear (including snorkel equipment); complimentary use of washer/dryer. *In room:* TV/VCR, kitchen, fridge, coffeemaker.

Wild Ginger ✶✶ *(Finds*   This cozy, romantic intimate cottage, hidden in Miliko Gulch, overlooking a stream with a waterfall, bamboo, sweet smelling ginger and banana trees, is perfect for honeymooners, lovers, and fans of Hawaiian art. The moment you step into this 400-square-foot, artistically decorated Hawaiian cottage (with additional 156-sq.-ft. screened deck), you will be delighted at the carefully placed memorabilia (ukulele tile, canoe paddle, and so on) found throughout. The cottage has a full kitchen with everything you could possibly need for cooking. The Hawaiian theme carries into the living room with VCR behind a tropical painted cabinet and stereo. The comfy queen bed opens to the living area. The screened porch has table, chairs, and couch, perfect for curling up with a good book. Outside there's a barbecue, plus all the beach toys you could want to borrow. Your hosts are Bob, a ceramic artist (you'll see his creations throughout the cottage) and his wife, Sonny, who manages Dolphin Galleries (where she has selected the best artwork for the cottage).

Haiku. Reservations c/o Hawaii's Best Bed & Breakfasts, P.O. Box 758, Volcano, HI 96785. ℂ 800/262-9912 or 808/985-7488. Fax 808/967-8610. www.bestbnb.com. 1 unit. $125 double, 3-night minimum. No credit cards. *In room:* VCR, kitchen, fridge, coffeemaker, hair dryer, iron, washer/dryer.

INEXPENSIVE

For a peaceful retreat, try the **Bamboo Mountain Sanctuary,** 1111 Kaupakalua Rd., Haiku, HI 96708 (ℂ **808/572-4897;** www.maui.net/~bamboomt), a 1940s plantation house that has served as a Zen monastery for 17 years; it offers seven rooms (all with shared bathroom) on the edge of the Koolau Forest Reserve ($80 double), plus a two-bedroom apartment ($180 double).

Aloha Maui B&B   On 2 acres of jungle, tucked away in the Twin Falls area, this budget traveler accommodation of four separate bungalows offers a back-to-nature experience. The rustic but clean and well-outfitted cabins are all landscaped to offer privacy and offer good value for the price. The cabins range from the $110 Mango cottage with hardwood floors, full kitchen, big bedroom with ocean view, with continental breakfast included (for an extra $5 a night, you can get satellite TV) to the Banana Room, a small room with kitchenette (2 burners, full fridge, microwave, toaster, coffeemaker), a CD player, and even a phone, all for $65, including breakfast (the only drawback to this room is a shared bathroom). Host Ken knows all the hiking and biking trails and how to get to the secret waterfalls (he will loan you his mountain bikes to go exploring). This is the perfect place if you are on a tight budget and looking for a vacation in Maui's rainforest.

P.O. Box 790210, Paia, HI 96779. ℂ 808/572-0298. kenred101@yahoo.com. 4 units. $65–$110, including continental breakfast. Extra person $5 plus $5 for breakfast. 3 night minimum. No credit cards. *In room:*TV on request ($5 per night)CD player, voice mail.

Maui Dream Cottages (Value) Essentially a vacation rental, this country estate is located atop a hill overlooking the ocean. The spacious grounds are dotted with fruit trees (bananas, papayas, and avocados, all free for the picking), and the front lawn is comfortably equipped with a double hammock, chaise lounges, and table and chairs. One cottage has two bedrooms, a full kitchen, a washer/dryer, and an entertainment center. The other is basically the same, but with only one bedroom (plus a sofa bed in the living room). They're both very well maintained and comfortably outfitted with furniture that's attractive but casual. The Haiku location is quiet and restful and offers the opportunity to see how real islanders live. However, you'll have to drive a good 20 to 25 minutes to restaurants in Makawao or Paia. Hookipa Beach is about a 20-minute drive, and Baldwin Beach (which has good swimming) is 25 minutes away.

265 W. Kuiaha Rd. (1 block from Pauwela Cafe), Haiku, HI 96708. ℂ 808/575-9079. Fax 808/575-9477. http://planet-hawaii.com/haiku. 2 cottages (shower only). $70 for 4. 7-night minimum. MC, V. *In room:* TV, kitchen, fridge, coffeemaker, washer/dryer.

TWIN FALLS
INEXPENSIVE
Also consider the off-the-beaten-path **Tea House Cottage** (ℂ 808/572-5610; www.mauiteahouse.com): You park your car and follow a fern-lined path to a secluded hideaway in the jungle, powered by alternative energy (no power poles!). Here's your chance to get away from it all while still having utilities, phone, and TV—you can even plug in your laptop. Rates are $120 double, and the seventh night is free.

Budget travelers might consider the very affordable **Halfway to Hana House** (ℂ 808/572-1176; www.halfwaytohana.com), an adorable studio (complete with kitchenette), nestled among the ferns and flowers in the jungle, just past Twin Falls, with rates starting at $85 double ($100 with breakfast).

HUELO/WAILUA
EXPENSIVE
Huelo Point Flower Farm (R) (Finds) Here's a peaceful retreat by the sea on a spectacular, remote 300-foot sea cliff near a waterfall stream. This large estate overlooking Waipio Bay has two guest cottages, a guesthouse, and a main house available for rent. The studio-size Gazebo Cottage has a floor-to-ceiling glass wall that overlooks a spectacular ocean view. Inside the intimate cabin are a koa-wood captain's bed, a TV, a stereo, a kitchenette, a private ocean-side patio, a private hot tub, and a half-bathroom with outdoor shower. The 900-square-foot Carriage House apartment sleeps four and has glass walls facing the mountain and sea, plus a kitchen, a den, decks, and a loft bedroom. The four-bedroom main house contains a fireplace, a sunken Roman bath, cathedral ceilings, and other extras. On-site is a natural pool with a waterfall and an oceanfront hot tub. You're welcome to pick fruit, vegetables, and flowers from the extensive garden. Homemade scones, tree-ripened papayas, and fresh-roasted coffee start your day. Despite its seclusion, off the crooked road to Hana, it's just a half-hour to Kahului, or about 20 minutes to Paia's shops and restaurants.

Off Hana Hwy., between mile markers 3 and 4. P.O. Box 791808, Paia, HI 96779. ℂ 808/572-1850. www.maui flowerfarm.com. 4 units. $150 cottage double; $175 carriage house double; $325 guesthouse double; $425 main house double (sleeps 6). Extra person $20–$35. 7-night minimum for main house; 2-night minimum for other units. No credit cards. **Amenities:** Outdoor pool; 3 Jacuzzis; self-serve washer/dryer. *In room:* TV, kitchenette (in cottage), kitchen (in houses), fridge, coffeemaker, hair dryer.

MODERATE

Kailua Maui Gardens *(Finds)*   In the middle of nowhere lies this nearly 2-acre tropical botanical garden with four bungalows dotting the property. Just a couple of miles down the serpentine Hana Highway from Huelo, in the remote area of Kailua, is an unlikely place for accommodations (it's a 30-min. drive to the nearest beach and 1 hr. to Hana), but for those who want to get away from it all, this could be your place. The small cabanas range from one-room studios with a futon and full kitchen to compact accommodations with basic kitchenette amenities. They all face out into gorgeous gardens. In the midst of the botanical garden is a pool, with cabana and covered barbecue area, and a hot tub. The garden sits right on the Hana Highway, so ask for a unit away from the road. Even if you don't stay here, stop by and visit the garden; hosts Kirk and Shelley love to show people their piece of paradise.

Located between mile marker 5 and 6 on the Hana Hwy. S.R. 1, Box 9, Haiku, HI 96708. © **800/258-8588** or 808/572-9726. Fax 808/575-2966. www.kailuamauigardens.com. 4 units. $90–$145 double. 2-night minimum. No credit cards. **Amenities:** Outdoor pool; 2 hot tubs; laundry facilities. *In room:* TV/VCR, CD/stereo, kitchen or kitchenette, fridge, coffeemaker.

INEXPENSIVE

Hale Akua Shangri-la B&B Retreat Center *(Value)*   This place isn't for everyone; the hang-loose atmosphere might not be your style. Way off the beaten path, Hale Akua is a collection of eclectic buildings where, at certain times of the year, guests can choose to go "clothing optional" (translation: nude) outdoors. The main house on the property has breathtaking ocean views and private lanais off most rooms; guests share the living room, bathroom, and kitchen. The Cabana building, next to the 60-foot pool, is a two-story house with five separate rooms, two kitchens, and a dining area. Also on the property is a cottage with two rooms, one pyramid-shaped. Other on-site features include a hot tub, fountain, lily pond, hammock, trampoline, and maze formed by panex trees. Yoga classes are available.

Star Rte. 1, Box 161 (off Hana Hwy., between mile markers 3 and 4), Haiku, HI 96708. © **888/368-5305** or 808/572-9300. Fax 808/572-6666. www.haleakua.com. 13 units (some w/shared bathroom). $55–$155 double. Rates include breakfast. Extra person $25. AE, DISC, MC, V. **Amenities:** Giant pool; hot tub; yoga classes; massage; coin-operated laundry; Internet access; use of kitchen.

6 At the End of the Road in East Maui: Hana

To locate the following accommodations, see the "Hana" map on p. 213.

EXPENSIVE

Hotel Hana-Maui *(★★★)*   Picture Shangri-La, Hawaiian-style: 66 acres rolling down to the sea in a remote Hawaiian village, with a wellness center, two pools, and access to one of the best beaches in Hana. This is the atmosphere, the landscape, and the culture of old Hawaii set in the accommodations of the 21st century. Every unit is excellent, but our favorites are the Sea Ranch Cottages (especially units 215–218 for the best views of turtles frolicking in the ocean), where individual duplex bungalows look out over the craggy shoreline to the rolling surf. The oversize, open, airy units (with floor-to-ceiling sliding doors) step out on a huge lanai with views that will stay with you long after your tan has faded. These comfy units have been totally redecorated with every amenity you can think of (with no nickle-and-diming you with charges for coffee, water, and so on—everything from the homemade banana bread to the bottled water is complimentary). Cathedral ceilings, plush feather bed, giant-size soaking tub, Hawaiian art work, bamboo hardwood floors—this is the vacation of luxury. A white-sand beach just a 5-minute shuttle away, a top-notch wellness center with some of the best massage therapists in Hawaii, and numerous activities (horseback riding, mountain bicycles, tennis, pitch and putt golf) all add up to make this one of the top resorts in the state. There are no TVs in the rooms, but the Club Room has a giant screen TV, plus VCR and Internet access. We highly recommend this little slice of paradise; it's the Hawaii vacation of your dreams.

Hana, Maui 96713. Ⓒ/ **800/321-HANA** or 808/248-8211. Fax 808/248-7202. www.hotelhanamaui.com. 78 units. $295–$365 Bay Cottages double; $395–$725 Sea Ranch Cottages double; 2-bedroom Plantation Guest House from $1,500. $50 extra person. AE, DC, DISC, MC, V. **Amenities:** Restaurant (w/Hawaiian entertainment twice a week); bar (w/nightly entertainment); 2 outdoor pools; complimentary use of the 3-hole practice golf course (clubs are complimentary as well); complimentary tennis courts; fitness center; game room; concierge; activity desk; car-rental desk; business center; small shopping arcade; salon; room service; in-room and spa massage; babysitting; laundry service. *In room:* Dataport, kitchenette, fridge, coffeemaker, hair dryer, iron, safe.

MODERATE

Ekena ⭐ *Finds*   With just one glance at the 360 degree view, you'll understand why hosts Robin and Gaylord gave up their careers on the mainland and moved here. This 8½-acre piece of paradise in rural Hana boasts ocean and rainforest views; the floor-to-ceiling glass doors in the spacious Hawaiian-style pole house bring the outside in. The elegant two-story home is exquisitely furnished, from the comfortable U-shaped couch that invites you to relax and take in the view to the top-of-the-line mattress on the king bed. The kitchen is fully equipped with every high-tech convenience you can imagine (guests have made complete holiday meals here). Only one floor (and 1 two-bedroom unit) is rented at any one time to ensure privacy. The grounds are impeccably groomed and dotted with tropical plants and fruit trees. Hiking trails into the rainforest start right on the property, and beaches and waterfalls are just minutes away. Robin places fresh flowers in every room and makes sure you're comfortable; after that, she's available to answer questions, but she also respects your privacy.

P.O. Box 728 (off Hana Hwy., above Hana Airport), Hana, HI 96713. Ⓒ **808/248-7047**. Fax 808/248-7047. www.ekenamaui.com. 2 units. $185 for 2; $250–$350 for 4. Extra person $25. 3-night minimum. No credit cards. **Amenities:** Complimentary use of washer/dryers. *In room:* TV, kitchen, fridge, coffeemaker, iron.

Hamoa Bay Bungalow ⭐ *Finds*   Down a country lane guarded by two Balinese statues stands a little bit of Indonesia in Hawaii: a carefully crafted bungalow and an Asian-inspired two-bedroom house overlooking Hamoa Bay. This enchanting retreat is just 2 miles beyond Hasegawa's general store on the way to Kipahulu. It sits on 4 verdant acres within walking distance of Hamoa Beach (which James Michener considered one of the most beautiful in the Pacific). The 600-square-foot Balinese-style cottage is distinctly tropical, with giant bamboo furniture from Indonesia, batik prints, a king bed, a full kitchen, and a screened porch with hot tub and shower. Hidden from the cottage is a 1,300-square-foot home with a soaking tub and private outdoor stone shower. It offers a bamboo king bed in one room, a queen bed in another, a screened-in sleeping porch, a full kitchen, and wonderful ocean views.

P.O. Box 773, Hana, HI 96713. Ⓒ **808/248-7884**. Fax 808/248-7047. www.hamoabay.com. 2 units. $195 cottage (sleeps only 2); $250 house for 2, $350 house for 4. 3-night minimum. No credit cards. **Amenities:** Hot tub, complimentary use of washer/dryers. *In room:* TV, kitchen, fridge, coffeemaker, iron.

Hana Hale Malamalama *(Finds)*   Hana Hale Malamalama sits on a historic site with ancient fish ponds and a cave mentioned in ancient chants. Host John takes excellent care of the ponds (you're welcome to watch him feed the fish at 5pm daily) and is fiercely protective of the hidden cave ("It's not a tourist attraction, but a sacred spot"). There's access to a nearby rocky beach, which isn't good for swimming but makes a wonderful place to watch the sunset. All accommodations include fully equipped kitchens, bathrooms, bedrooms, living/dining areas, and private lanais. Next to the fish pond, the Royal Lodge, a 2600-square-foot architectural masterpiece built entirely of Philippine mahogany, has large skylights the entire length of the house and can be rented as a house or two separate units. The oceanfront Bamboo Inn contains two units (a studio and a 1- or 2-bedroom unit). The cottages range from a separate two-level Tree House cottage, with Jacuzzi tub for two, a Balinese bamboo bed, small kitchen/living area, and deck upstairs, to the Pond Side Bungalow, which features a private outdoor Jacuzzi tub and shower.

P.O. Box 374, Hana, HI 96713. (*C*) **808/248-7718.** www.hanahale.com. 7 units. $125–$225 double. Extra person $15. 2-night minimum. No credit cards. **Amenities:** Jacuzzi. *In room:* TV/VCR, kitchen, fridge, coffeemaker.

Hana Kai Maui Resort   Hana's only vacation condo complex, Hana Kai offers studio and one-bedroom units overlooking Hana Bay. All units have a large kitchen and private lanai. The one-bedroom units each have a sliding door that separates the bedroom from the living room, plus a sofa bed that sleeps two additional guests. There are no phones or TVs in the units (a pay phone is located on the property), so you can really get away from it all. Ask for a corner unit with wraparound ocean views.

1533 Uakea Rd. (P.O. Box 38), Hana, HI 96713. (*C*) **800/346-2772** or 808/248-8426. Fax 808/248-7482. www.hanakaimaui.com. 17 units. $125–$195 studio double; $145–$195 1-bedroom (sleeps up to 4). Children under 8 stay free in parent's room. AE, MC, V. *In room:* Kitchen, fridge, coffeemaker, no phone.

Hana Oceanfront *(★★)*   Just across the street from Hamoa Bay, Hana's premier white-sand beach, lie these two plantation-style units, impeccably decorated in old Hawaii decor. Our favorite unit is the romantic cottage, complete with an old-fashioned front porch where you can sit and watch the ocean; separate bedroom (with a bamboo sleigh bed), plus pullout sofa for extra guests; top notch kitchen appliances (Jenn-Air stove); and comfy living room. The 1,000 square foot vacation suite, located downstairs from hosts Dan and Sandi's home (but totally soundproof—you'll never hear them) has an elegant master bedroom with polished bamboo flooring; spacious bath with custom hand-painted tile, and a fully-appointed gourmet kitchen. Outside is a 320-square foot lanai. The units sit on the road facing Hana's most popular beach, so there is traffic during the day. At night, the traffic disappears, the stars come out, and the sound of the ocean soothes you to sleep.

Hana. Reservations c/o Hawaii's Best Bed & Breakfasts, P.O. Box 758, Volcano, HI 96785. (*C*) **800/262-9912** or 808/985-7488. Fax 808/967-8610. www.bestbnb.com. 2 units. $190–$225 double; 2-night minimum. No credit cards. *In room:* TV/VCR, kitchen, fridge, coffeemaker, hair dryer, iron.

Heavenly Hana Inn *(★★)* *(Finds)*   Owners Robert and Sheryl Filippi humbly describe their B&B as a "Japanese-style inn." That's like saying a Four Seasons Hotel is a big building with rooms. This place on the Hana Highway, just a stone's throw from the center of Hana town, is a little bit of heaven, where no attention to detail has been spared. Each suite has a sitting room with futon and couch, polished hardwood floors, and separate bedroom with a raised platform bed (with an excellent, firm mattress). The black-marble bathrooms have huge tubs. Flowers are everywhere, ceiling fans keep the rooms cool, and the delicious gourmet breakfast—worth splurging for—is served in a setting filled with art. The spacious grounds are done in Japanese style with a bamboo fence, tiny bridges over a meandering stream, and Japanese gardens.

P.O. Box 790, Hana, HI 96713. ℂ and fax 808/248-8442. www.heavenlyhanainn.com. 3 units. $185–$250 suite. Full gourmet breakfast available for $15 per person. Ask about special rates. 2-night minimum. AE, DISC, MC, V. No children under age 15 accepted. **Amenities:** Laundry service. *In room:* TV, no phone.

Papalani These luxurious, romantic accommodations are hidden from the road, offering privacy and quiet in a gorgeous setting. There's only one drawback: mosquitoes. A stream runs through the property, and although hostess Cybil has done everything possible to eliminate this nuisance (like providing screened-in lanais so you can enjoy the outdoors without experiencing these biting pests), definitely bring your insect repellent. Otherwise, Papalani lives up to its name, which means "heaven and all the spiritual powers." The apartment and the cottage, both professionally decorated, have white leather couches, wood floors, Berber carpets, and serious artwork. The great location means you're just a 5-minute walk to Waioka Stream (where there's good swimming in the pools), a mile from beautiful Hamoa Beach, and 5 minutes from Hana. Cybil asks that guests not smoke on the property and that you cook your meat on a barbecue outside.

Star Rte. 27 (3 miles past Hasegawa's General Store, before the bridge at mile marker 48), Hana, HI 96713. ℂ **808/248-7204.** Fax 808/248-7285. 2 units. $160 double. Extra person $20. 2-night minimum. No credit cards. *In room:* Kitchen, fridge, coffeemaker.

INEXPENSIVE

Mrs. Nakamura has been renting her **Aloha Cottages** (ℂ **808/248-8420**) since the 1970s. Located in residential areas near Hana Bay, these five budget rentals are simple but adequately furnished, varying in size from a roomy studio with kitchenette to a three-bedroom, two-bathroom unit. They're all fully equipped, clean, and fairly well kept. Rates run from $62 to $95 double. Not all units have TVs, and none have phones, but Mrs. N. is happy to take messages.

Baby Pigs Crossing Bed & Breakfast ★★ (Finds) If you are looking for a quiet, romantic little cottage, nestled away from it all in Old Hawaii but close enough to drive into Hana for dinner, this is your place. International artist Gail Bakutis has created this lovely retreat on a one-acre property, landscaped in a "fragrance" garden featuring Hawaii's best sweet-smelling plants carefully planted throughout the property. The separate guesthouse, with an ocean view from the lanai, is professionally decorated with comfort in mind, from the very cozy rattan furniture to the king-size sofa bed. There's a separate bedroom with a queen bed and a small kitchenette (fridge, microwave, toaster, and coffeemaker). But the surprise is the unique bathroom with glass ceiling and walls (with discreet privacy curtains) which opens out to a garden area.

P.O. Box 667, Hana, HI 96713. ℂ **808/248-8890.** Fax 808/248-4865. www.mauibandb.com. 1 unit. $125 double. 2-night minimum. AE, DISC, MC, V. *In-room* TV/VCR, kitchenette, fridge, coffeemaker, cellphone.

Hana's Heaven Just outside of Hana, at 500 feet elevation, with a million-dollar panoramic view, is this just-opened vacation rental on the ground level of a new home, surrounded by 6½ acres of tropical jungle. The large (720-sq.-ft.) studio, with waterfall and pond just outside, is decorated in brilliant white with hardwood floors and rattan furniture. Giant picture windows run down the length of the studio (perfect for watching the humpback whales Nov–Mar). A

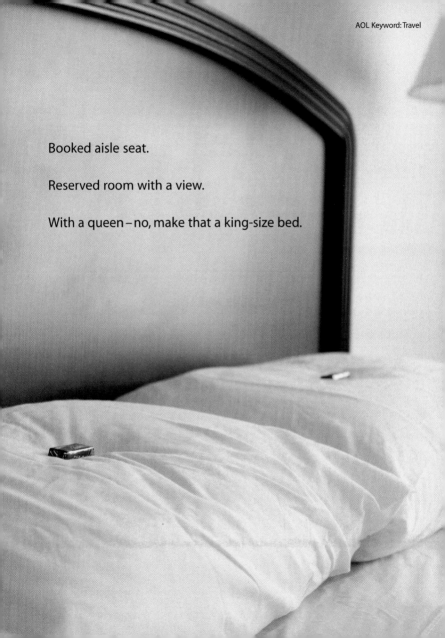

Booked aisle seat.

Reserved room with a view.

With a queen – no, make that a king-size bed.

full kitchen with everything you need to cook gourmet meals (no worries about the lack of dining opportunities in this neck of the woods), large living area, and king-size bed complete the studio. Through French double doors is a screened lanai with a double bed that can sleep extra guests or serve as a great nook to curl up with a good book. The entire house is off the grid and runs totally on solar power. Hosts Michael and Cathy live upstairs and are very willing to direct you to Hana's secret hidden treasures. This is a great location, just a couple of miles from Hamoa Beach, about a mile from Waioka Pond (also known as Venus Pool), 3.5 miles from Hana and 6 miles from Oheo Gulch and the Kipahulu end of Haleakala National Park. However, the property is ¾ mile off the Hana Highway, up a partially dirt road (which could be tricky during the rainy season; their website recommends a four-wheel drive vehicle to "enhance your Hana adventure").

P.O. Box 1006, Hana, HI 96713. © **888/205-3030** or 808/248-7628. www.hanasheaven.com. 1 unit. $150 double. Extra person $20. No credit cards. *In room:* TV/VCR, kitchen, fridge, coffeemaker, laundry facilities, no phone.

Hana's Tradewinds Cottage ⭐ *Value*   Nestled among the ginger and heliconias on a 5-acre flower farm are two separate cottages, each with full kitchen, carport, barbecue, private hot tub, TV, ceiling fans, and sofa bed. The studio cottage sleeps up to four; a bamboo shoji blind separates the sleeping area (with queen bed) from the sofa bed in the living room. The Tradewinds cottage has two bedrooms (with a queen bed in one room and 2 twins in the other), one bathroom (shower only), and a huge front porch. The atmosphere is quiet and relaxing, and hostess Rebecca Buckley, who has been in business for a decade, welcomes families (she has 2 children, a cat, and a very sweet golden retriever). You can use the laundry facilities at no extra charge.

135 Alalele Place (the airport rd.), P.O. Box 385, Hana, HI 96713. © **800/327-8097** or 808/248-8980. Fax 808/248-7735. www.hanamaui.net. 2 cottages. $120 studio double; $145 2-bedroom double. Extra person $10. 2-night minimum. AE, DISC, MC, V. *In room:* TV, kitchen, fridge, coffeemaker, no phone.

Joe's Place *Value*   This is as close to a hostel as you can get in Hana. Joe's is a large rambling house located just spitting distance from Hana Bay. Seven spartan but immaculately clean bedrooms share showers and bathroom; one has private facilities. All the guests are welcome to use the large living room with TV and adjoining communal kitchen (free coffee available all day). Other facilities include a rec room, barbecue, and owner Ed Hill himself. He'll tell you the long story about the name if you ask, and can also talk about what to do and see in Hana all day if you let him.

4870 Ua'kea Rd. (Reservations: P.O. Box 746), Hana, HI 96713. © **808/248-7033.** www.joesrentals.com. 8 units (7 w/shared bathroom). $45 double (shared bathroom); $55 double (private bathroom). Extra person $10. MC. V.

Kulani's Hideaway in Hana, Maui ⭐ *Value*   On the road to Waianapanapa State Park is the "deal" of Hana—two one-bedroom units, each with pullout sofa beds in the living room, full kitchen, cable TV (a plus in Hana), and washer/dryer, within walking distance of a fabulous black-sand beach. Outside is a large lanai for watching the clouds go by, with a barbecue area with picnic table in the yard. Book early; this is one of Maui's best deals for the budget traveler.

P.O. Box 483, Hana, HI 96713. © and fax **808/248-8234** or 808/268-9248. kulanis@maui.net. 2 units. $65 double. Extra person $15. **Amenities:** Complimentary coffee. *In room:* TV, kitchen, fridge, coffeemaker; washer/dryer; no phone.

Waianapanapa State Park Cabins *Value*   These 12 rustic cabins are the best lodging deal on Maui. Everyone knows it, too—so make your reservations early

(up to 6 months in advance). The cabins are warm and dry and come complete with kitchen, living room, bedroom, and bathroom with hot shower; furnishings include bedding, linen, towels, dishes, and very basic cooking and eating utensils. Don't expect luxury—this is a step above camping, albeit in a beautiful tropical jungle setting. The key attraction at this 120-acre state beach park is the unusual horseshoe-shaped black-sand beach on Pailoa Bay, popular for shore fishing, snorkeling, and swimming. The park has a caretaker on-site, along with restrooms, showers, picnic tables, shoreline hiking trails, and historic sites. But bring mosquito protection—this *is* the jungle, after all.

Off Hana Hwy. c/o State Parks Division, 54 S. High St., Rm. 101, Wailuku, HI 96793. ℂ **808/984-8109.** 12 cabins. $45 for 4 (sleeps up to 6). Extra person $5. 5-night maximum. No credit cards. *In room:* Kitchen, fridge, coffeemaker, no phone.

Where to Dine

With soaring visitor statistics and a glamorous image, the Valley Isle is fertile ground for Hawaii's famous enterprising chefs (like Roy Yamaguchi from Roy's and Nicolina; Gerard Reversade of Gerard's; James McDonald of I'o and Pacific 'O; Peter Merriman of Hula Grill; Mark Ellman of Maui Taco; D.K. Kodoma of Sansei Seafood; and Beverly Gannon of Haliimaile General Store and Joe's Bar and Grill), as well as an international name or two (Wolfgang Puck of Spago). Plus a few newcomers who are cooking up a storm and getting a well-deserved following (Jennifer Nguyen of A Saigon Café, Tom Lelli of Mañana Garage, Dana Pastula of Café O'Lei, and Don Ritchey of Moana Bakery and Café), dining on Maui has become a culinary treat able to hold its own against most major metropolitan areas.

In this dizzying scenario, some things haven't changed: You can still dine well at Lahaina's open-air waterfront watering holes, where the view counts for 50% of the experience. There are still budget eateries, but not many; Maui's old-fashioned, multigenerational mom-and-pop diners are disappearing, eclipsed by the flashy newcomers, or clinging to the edge of existence in the older neighborhoods of central Maui, such as lovable Wailuku. Although you'll have to work harder to find them in the resort areas, you won't have to go far to find creative cuisine, pleasing style, and stellar dining experiences.

In the listings below, reservations are not necessary unless otherwise noted.

1 Central Maui

KAHULUI

MODERATE

Mañana Garage ★★ *Finds* LATIN AMERICAN   Chef Tom Lelli, formerly of Haliimaile General Store, is serving up some incomparable fare at this central Maui hot spot. The industrial motif features table bases like hubcaps, a vertical garage door as a divider for private parties, blown-glass chandeliers, and gleaming chrome and cobalt walls with orange accents. The brilliantly conceived and executed menu includes fried green tomatoes, done just right and served with slivered red onions; a ceviche with the perfectly balanced flavors and textures of lime, cilantro, chile, coconut, and fresh fish; and arepas (cornmeal and cheese griddle cakes with smoked salmon and wasabi sour cream) that meld the flavors and textures of many traditions. We're sold on Mañana Garage—it has really raised the bar and introduced exciting new flavors to Maui's dining options.

33 Lono Ave., Kahului. © **808/873-0220.** Reservations recommended. Lunch main courses $6.95–$13; dinner main courses $12–$26. AE, DC, DISC, MC, V. Mon 11am–9pm; Tues–Fri 11am–10:30pm; Sat 5–10:30pm; Sun 5–9pm.

Marco's Grill & Deli ★ ITALIAN   Located in central Maui, where the roads to Upcountry, West, and South Maui converge, Marco's is popular among area residents for its homemade Italian fare and friendly informality. Everything—from the meatballs, sausages, and burgers to the sauces, salad dressings, and ravioli—is made in-house. The 35 different choices of hot and cold sandwiches and entrees are served all day, and they include vodka rigatoni with imported prosciutto; pasta e' fasio (a house specialty: smoked ham hock simmered for hours in tomato sauce, with red and white beans); and simple pasta with marinara sauce. This is one of those comfortable neighborhood fixtures favored by all generations. Locals stop here for breakfast, lunch, and dinner; before and after movies; on the way to and from baseball games and concerts. The antipasto salad, vegetarian lasagna, and roasted peppers are taste treats, but the meatballs and Italian sausage are famous in central Maui.

Dairy Center, 395 Dairy Rd., Kahului. ℂ **808/877-4446.** Main courses $11–$26. AE, DC, DISC, MC, V. Daily 7:30am–10pm.

INEXPENSIVE

The **Kaahumanu Center,** the structure that looks like a white *Star Wars* umbrella in the center of Kahului, at 275 Kaahumanu Ave. (5 min. from Kahului Airport on Hwy. 32), has a very popular food court. Busy shoppers seem more than willing to dispense with fine china and other formalities to enjoy a no-nonsense meal on foam plates. **Edo Japan** teppanyaki is a real find, its flat Benihana-like grill dispensing marvelous, flavorful mounds of grilled fresh vegetables and chicken teriyaki for $4.15. **Maui Mixed Plate** dishes out "local style" cuisine of meat with rice and macaroni salad in the $5 to $7 range. **Yummy Korean B-B-Q** offers the assertive flavors of Korea; **Panda Cuisine** serves tasty Chinese food; and the **Coffee Store** (p. 140) sells sandwiches, salads, pasta, and nearly 2 dozen different coffee drinks. There's also a branch of **Maui Tacos** (p. 137). When you leave Kaahumanu Center, take a moment to gaze at the West Maui Mountains to your left from the parking lot. They are one of Maui's wonders.

Ichiban *(Finds* JAPANESE/SUSHI   What a find: an informal neighborhood restaurant that serves inexpensive, home-cooked Japanese food *and* good sushi at realistic prices. Local residents consider Ichiban a staple for breakfast, lunch, or dinner and a haven of comforts: egg-white omelets; great saimin; combination plates of teriyaki chicken, teriyaki beef, *tonkatsu* (pork cutlet), rice, and pickled cabbage; chicken yakitori; and sushi—everything from unagi and scallop to California roll. The sushi items may not be inexpensive, but like the specials, such as steamed opakapaka, they're a good value. We love the tempura, miso soup, and spicy ahi hand roll.

Kahului Shopping Center, 47 Kaahumanu Ave., Kahului. ℂ **808/871-6977.** Main courses $4.25–$5.25 breakfast; $5.50–$9.50 lunch (combination plates $8); $5.95–$28 dinner (combination dinner $12, dinner specials from $8.95). AE, DC, MC, V. Mon–Fri 6:30am–2pm and 5–9pm; Sat 10:30am–2pm and 5–9pm; closed 2 weeks around Christmas and New Year.

Restaurant Matsu JAPANESE/LOCAL   Customers have come from Hana (more than 50 miles away) just for Matsu's California rolls, while regulars line up for the cold saimin (julienned cucumber, egg, Chinese-style sweet pork, and red ginger on noodles) and for the bento plates, various assemblages of chicken, teriyaki beef, fish, and rice. The nigiri sushi items are popular, especially among the don't-dally lunch crowd. The katsu pork and chicken, breaded and deep-fried, are other specialties of this casual Formica-style diner. We love the tempura udon and the saimin, steaming mounds of wide and fine noodles swimming in homemade broths and topped with condiments. The daily specials are a changing lineup of home-cooked classics: oxtail soup, roast pork with gravy, teriyaki ahi, miso butterfish, and breaded mahimahi.

Maui Mall, 161 Alamaha St., Kahului. ℭ 808/871-0822. Most items less than $6. No credit cards. Mon–Sat 10am–8pm.

WAILUKU
MODERATE

A Saigon Cafe ★★ VIETNAMESE   Jennifer Nguyen has stuck to her guns and steadfastly refused to erect a sign, and diners come anyway. Fans drive from all over the island for her crisped, spiced Dungeness crab, her steamed opakapaka with ginger and garlic, and her wok-cooked Vietnamese specials tangy with spices, herbs, and lemongrass. There are a dozen different soups, cold and hot noodles (including the popular beef noodle soup called *pho*), and chicken and shrimp cooked in a clay pot. You can create your own Vietnamese "burritos" from a platter of tofu, noodles, and vegetables that you wrap in rice paper and dip in garlic sauce. Among our favorites are the shrimp lemongrass, savory and refreshing, and the tofu curry, swimming in herbs and vegetables straight from the garden. The Nhung Dam, the Vietnamese version of fondue—a hearty spread of basil, cucumbers, mint, romaine, bean sprouts, pickled carrots, turnips, and vermicelli, wrapped in rice paper and dipped in a legendary sauce—is cooked at your table.

1792 Main St., Wailuku. ℭ 808/243-9560. Main courses $6.50–$17. DC, MC, V. Mon–Sat 10am–9:30pm; Sun 10am–8:30pm. Heading into Wailuku from Kahului, go over the bridge and take the first right onto Central Ave, then the first right on Nani St. At the next stop sign, look for the building with the neon sign that says "Open."

INEXPENSIVE

Café O'Lei on Main ★ AMERICAN/ISLAND   Dana Pastula, who managed fancy restaurants on Lanai and in Wailea before opening her own, has cloned her wonderful Makawao eatery for lucky Wailuku diners. The menu is expanded here, with seating for 50 and daily lunch specials that have the same imaginative, attentive touches of her Makawao gem. The cafe is on the main street of Wailuku, with a menu that features fresh Island ingredients: taro salad with crisp Molokai sweet potato, seared ahi sandwich with wasabi mayonnaise, fresh fish, and Aloha Friday crab cakes with sweet chile aioli. Sandwiches (crab club, roast turkey breast, roasted Maui vegetables) and salads (including our favorite, curry chicken: hot chicken with peanuts, chiles, ginger, and veggies) complement daily specials such as chicken fettuccine and blackened mahimahi. The plate lunch, at $5.50, is always a surprise—and a terrific deal. *Tip:* You can get a great picnic lunch here for your outing in Iao Valley. Look for sister restaurants in Makawao, Maalaea, and Lahaina.

2051 Main St., Wailuku. ℭ 808/244-6816. Sandwiches $4.95–$6.95; lunch specials $5.50–$7.50. No credit cards. Mon–Fri 10:30am–2:30pm.

Class Act ★ GLOBAL   Part of a program run by the distinguished Food Service Department of Maui Community College (soon to be housed in a new state-of-the-art, $15 million culinary facility), this restaurant has a following. Student chefs show their stuff with a flourish in their "classroom," where they pull out all the stops. Linen, china, servers in ties and white shirts, and a four-course lunch make this a unique value. The appetizer, soup, salad, and dessert are set, but you can choose between the regular entrees and a heart-healthy main course prepared in the culinary tradition of the week. The menu roams the globe with highlights of Italy, Mexico, Maui, Napa valley, France, New Orleans, and other locales. The filet mignon of French week is popular, as are the New Orleans gumbo and Cajun shrimp; the sesame-crusted mahimahi on taro leaf pasta; the polenta flan with eggplant; and the bean- and green-chile chilaquile. Tea and soft drinks are offered—and they can get pretty fancy, with fresh fruit and spritzers—but otherwise it's BYOB.

Maui Community College, 310 Kaahumanu Ave., Wailuku. ✆ 808/984-3485. Reservations recommended. 5-course lunch $15. No credit cards. Wed and Fri 11am–12:15pm (last seating); closed June–Aug for summer vacation. Menu and cuisine type change weekly.

Maui Bake Shop BAKERY/DELI   Sleepy Vineyard Street has seen many a mom-and-pop business come and go, but Maui Bake Shop is here to stay. Maui native Claire Fujii-Krall and her husband, baker Jose Krall (who was trained in the south of France), turn out buttery brioches, healthy nine-grain and two-tone rye breads, focaccia, strudels, sumptuous fresh-fruit gâteaux, puff pastries, and dozens of other baked goods and confections. The breads are baked in one of Maui's oldest brick ovens, installed in 1935; a high-tech European diesel oven handles the rest. The front window displays more than 100 bakery and deli items, among them salads, a popular eggplant marinara focaccia, homemade quiches, and an inexpensive calzone filled with chicken, pesto, mushroom, and cheese. Homemade soups (clam chowder, minestrone, cream of asparagus) team up nicely with sandwiches on freshly baked bread. The food here is light enough (well, almost) to justify the Ultimate Dessert: white-chocolate macadamia-nut cheesecake.

2092 Vineyard St., Wailuku. ✆ 808/242-0064. Most items under $5. AE, DISC, MC, V. Mon–Fri 6am–4pm; Sat 7am–2pm.

Sam Sato's NOODLES/PLATE LUNCHES   Sam Sato's is a Maui institution, not only for its noodles (saimin, dry noodles, chow fun), but also its flaky baked *manju,* filled with sweetened lima beans or adzuki beans. Sam opened his family eatery in 1933, and his daughter, Lynne Toma, still makes the broth the old-fashioned way: from scratch. The saimin and the dry noodles, with broth that comes in a separate bowl, are big sellers. One regular comes to the counter, with its wooden stools and homemade salt and pepper shakers, for his "usual": two barbecued meat sticks, two scoops of rice, and three macaroni salads. The peach, apple, coconut, and pineapple turnovers fly out the door, too, as do takeout noodles by the tray. *Tip:* If you want them to hold the MSG, be sure to make your request early.

Millyard, 1750 Wili Pa Loop, Wailuku. ✆ 808/244-7124. Plate lunches $5.75–$6.75. No credit cards. Mon–Sat 7am–2pm.

Wei Wei BBQ and Noodle House CHINESE/NOODLES   Noodles are rapidly gaining on Big Macs as the fast-food choice of Hawaii, and Wei Wei is the darling of Maui's on-the-go, noodle-loving crowd. You order at the counter, fast-food style, from a menu that includes Chinese classics: saimin with roast duck, shrimp-vegetable chow mein, dim sum, and the extremely popular house-fried noodles. American favorites—hamburgers, a teriyaki chicken burger, a turkey sandwich, and the popular chicken katsu burger—win fans, too.

Millyard Plaza, 210 Imi Kala St., Wailuku. ✆ 808/242-7928. Combination plates $4.95–$6.95; main courses $5.95–$8.50. No credit cards. Daily 10am–9pm.

2 West Maui

LAHAINA

There's a **Maui Tacos** (p. 137) in Lahaina Square (✆ 808/661-8883). Maui's branch of the **Hard Rock Cafe** is in Lahaina at 900 Front St. (✆ 808/667-7400).

Lahaina & Kaanapali Dining

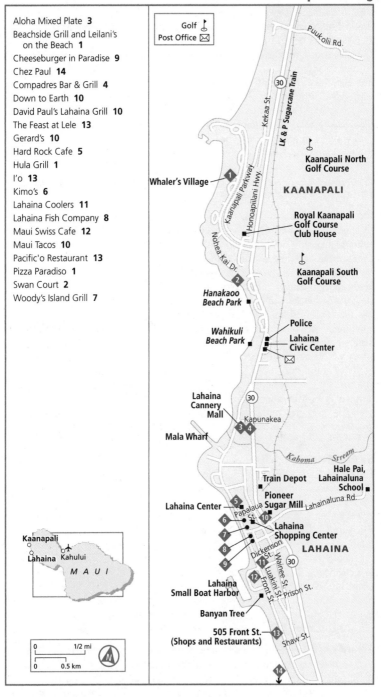

Aloha Mixed Plate **3**

Beachside Grill and Leilani's on the Beach **1**

Cheeseburger in Paradise **9**

Chez Paul **14**

Compadres Bar & Grill **4**

Down to Earth **10**

David Paul's Lahaina Grill **10**

The Feast at Lele **13**

Gerard's **10**

Hard Rock Cafe **5**

Hula Grill **1**

I'o **13**

Kimo's **6**

Lahaina Coolers **11**

Lahaina Fish Company **8**

Maui Swiss Cafe **12**

Maui Tacos **10**

Pacific'o Restaurant **13**

Pizza Paradiso **1**

Swan Court **2**

Woody's Island Grill **7**

Golf
Post Office

Puukolii Rd.

Kekaa St.

LK & P Sugarcane Train

30

Kaanapali North
Golf Course

KAANAPALI

Whaler's Village **1**

Kaanapali Parkway

Honoapiilani Hwy.

Royal Kaanapali
Golf Course
Club House

Nohea Kai Dr.

Kaanapali South
Golf Course

2

Hanakaoo
Beach Park

Wahikuli
Beach Park

Police

Lahaina
Civic Center

Lahaina
Cannery
Mall

30

Kapunakea

Mala Wharf

3 **4**

Kahoma Stream

Hale Pai,
Lahainaluna
School

Train Depot

Pioneer
Sugar Mill

Lahaina Center

5

Papalaua St.

6

7

8

9

10

Lahainaluna Rd.

Lahaina
Shopping Center

LAHAINA

Dickenson St.

11

Wainee St.

30

12

Luakini St.

Front St.

Prison St.

Lahaina
Small Boat Harbor

Banyan Tree

505 Front St.
(Shops and Restaurants)

13

Shaw St.

14

Kaanapali

Lahaina

Kahului

M A U I

0   1/2 mi

0   0.5 km

N

127

VERY EXPENSIVE

David Paul's Lahaina Grill (★) (Kids) NEW AMERICAN   Even after David Paul Johnson's departure, this Lahaina hot spot has maintained its popularity. It's still filled with chic, tanned diners in stylish aloha shirts, and there's still attitude aplenty at the entrance. The signature items remain: tequila shrimp and firecracker rice, Kona coffee–roasted rack of lamb, kalua duck, and an excellent eggplant napoleon. As always, a special custom-designed chef's table can be arranged with 72-hour notice for larger parties. The ambience—black-and-white tile floors, pressed tin ceilings, eclectic 1890s decor—is striking, and the bar, even without an ocean view, is the busiest spot in Lahaina. The children's menu is more sophisticated than usual (no burgers or hot dogs), but offers plenty of options for the little ones; entrees are $12.

127 Lahainaluna Rd. (© **808/667-5117.** www.lahainagrill.com. Reservations required. Main courses $26–$38. AE, DC, DISC, MC, V. Daily 5:30–10pm. Bar daily 5:30pm–midnight.

The Feast at Lele (★★) POLYNESIAN   The owners of Old Lahaina Luau (see "A Night to Remember: Maui's Top Luau on p. 21), have teamed up with Chef James McDonald's culinary prowess (I'o and Pacific'o), placed it in a perfect outdoor oceanfront setting, and added the exquisite dancers of the Old Lahaina Luau; the result: a culinary and cultural experience that sizzles. As if the sunset weren't heady enough, dances from Hawaii, Tonga, Tahiti, and Samoa are presented, up close and personal, in full costumed splendor. Chanting, singing, drumming, dancing, the swish of ti-leaf skirts, the scent of plumeria—it's a full culinary-cultural adventure. Guests sit at white-clothed, candlelit tables set on the sand (unlike the luau, where seating is en masse) and dine on kalua pig, tasty steamed moi, and savory pohole ferns and hearts of palm. From Tonga come lobster-ogo (seaweed) salad and grilled steak, from Tahiti steamed chicken and taro leaf in coconut milk, and from Samoa grilled fish in banana leaf. Particularly mesmerizing is the evening's opening: A softly lit canoe carries three people ashore to the sound of conch shells.

505 Front St. (© **886/244-5353** or 808/667-5353. www.feastatlele.com. Reservations a must. Set 5-course menu $89 for adults, $59 for children 2–12; gratuity not included. AE, MC, V. Apr 1–Sept 30, Tues–Sat 6–9pm; Oct 1–Mar 31, 5:30–8:30pm.

EXPENSIVE

Chez Paul (★★) (Finds) FRENCH   Chez Paul is located in the middle of nowhere. Well, actually it's in the heart of Olowalu Village (a blip on the highway—if you blink you'll miss it), next to the Olowalu Store. But it's worth the drive to this classic French restaurant, now that Chef Patrick Callarec (formerly of the Ritz-Carlton's Anuenue Room) has taken over the cooking. Look forward to such delights as wild mushroom and goat cheese pastry in an aged Port wine sauce, just to get started. Or choose their signature dish of crispy duck with local fruits or fresh island fish in a champagne and cream sauce. Don't leave without the pineapple and vanilla crème brûlée, served in a pineapple shell. The dress here is Maui casual, which means anything (short of tank tops, shorts, and slippers) will be seen.

Olowalu Village, Honoapiilani Hwy., Olowalu. (© **808/661-3843.** Reservations recommended. Main courses $22–$45. AE, MC, V. Daily (except summer when they close on Sun nights) 6–8:30pm.

Gerard's (★★★) (Finds) FRENCH   The charm of Gerard's—soft lighting, Edith Piaf on the sound system, excellent service—is matched by a menu of uncompromising standards. Gerard Reversade never runs out of creative offerings, yet stays true to his French roots. A frequent winner of the *Wine Spectator* Award of Excellence, Gerard's offers roasted opakapaka with star anise, fennel fondue, and hints of orange and ginger, a stellar entree on a menu of winners. If you're feeling extravagant, the Kona lobster ragout with pasta and morels promises ecstasy, and the spinach salad with scallops is among the finest we've tasted. Gerard's has an excellent appetizer menu, with shiitake and oyster mushrooms in puff pastry, fresh ahi and smoked salmon carpaccio, and a very rich, highly touted escargot ragout with burgundy butter and garlic cream.

In the Plantation Inn, 174 Lahainaluna Rd. ℭ **808/661-8939.** www.gerardsmaui.com. Reservations recommended. Main courses $27–$33. AE, DC, DISC, MC, V. Daily 6–9pm.

I'o ⚔ PACIFIC RIM   I'o is a fantasy of sleek curves and etched glass, co-owned by chef James McDonald. He offers an impressive selection of appetizers (his strong suit) and some lavish Asian-Polynesian interpretations of seafood, such as stir-fried lobster with mango-Thai curry sauce, fresh ahi in a nori panko crust, and lemongrass coconut fish. Unless you're sold on entrees, our advice is to go heavy on the superb appetizers, especially the silken purse, a brilliant concoction of tricolored pot stickers stuffed with roasted peppers, mushrooms, spinach, macadamia nuts, and silken tofu. Oyster lovers, take heed: The memorable Pan-Asian Rockefellers are baked on a bed of spinach and served with a hint of star anise coconut cream.

505 Front St. ℭ **808/661-8422.** www.iomaui.com. Reservations recommended. Main courses $18–$30. AE, DC, MC, V. Daily 5:30–10pm.

Pacific'o Restaurant ⚔ PACIFIC RIM/CONTEMPORARY PACIFIC   You can't get any closer to the ocean than the tables here, which are literally on the beach. With good food complementing this sensational setting, foodies and aesthetes have much to enjoy. The split-level dining starts at the top, near the entrance, with a long bar (where you can also order lunch or dinner) and a few tables along the railing. Steps lead to the outdoor tables, where the award-winning seafood dishes come to you with the backdrop of Lanai across the channel. The prawn and basil wontons, fresh fish over wilted arugula and bean sprouts, and ahi and ono tempura with miso and lime-basil sauce are among Pacific'o's memorable offerings. The vegetarian special, a marinated, roasted tofu steak crowned with quinoa, Maui onions, red lentils and a heavenly dose of shiitake mushrooms, is a longtime favorite. If you like seafood, sunsets, and touches of India and Indonesia in your fresh-from-the-sea dining choices, you should be happy here.

505 Front St. ℭ **808/667-4341.** www.pacificomaui.com. Reservations recommended. Main courses $9–$14 lunch, $19–$38 dinner. AE, DC, MC, V. Daily 11am–4pm and 5:30–10pm.

MODERATE

Compadres Bar & Grill MEXICAN   Despite its concrete floor and high industrial ceilings, Compadres exudes good cheer. And that cheer has burgeoned lately with a new open-air seating area and a take-out taqueria window for diners on the run. The food is classic Tex-Mex, good any time of the day, beginning with huevos rancheros, egg burritos, hotcakes, and omelets (the Acapulco is heroic) and progressing to enchiladas and appetizers for the margarita-happy crowd. Stay spare (vegetable enchilada in fresh spinach tortilla) or get hefty (Texas T-bone and enchiladas). This is a carefree place with a large capacity for merrymaking.

Lahaina Cannery Mall, 1221 Honoapiilani Hwy. ℭ **808/661-7189.** Main courses $10–$20. AE, DC, DISC, MC, V. Daily 8am–10pm.

Kimo's STEAK/SEAFOOD   Kimo's has a loyal following that keeps it from falling into the faceless morass of waterfront restaurants serving surf-and-turf with great sunset views. It's a formula restaurant (sibling to Leilani's and Hula

Family-Friendly Restaurants

In addition to Kahului's **Food Court at Kaahumanu Center,** where children have their pick of everything from tacos to teriyaki chicken, here's a sampling of places that go the extra mile for families:

CENTRAL MAUI

Koho Grill & Bar (Kaahumanu Center, 275 Kaahumanu Ave.; ℂ **808/877-5588**) A family of four can eat inexpensively here, and the kids have their own menus (with drawings for coloring) that change regularly. Sandwiches (grilled cheese, cheeseburger, hamburger) and fries go for $3.50 and under, and the ever-popular keiki quesadilla is a friendly $3.75. It's casual, a good value, and crayons are provided for the artists-in-the-making.

WEST MAUI

David Paul's Lahaina Grill (p. 128) You won't find a cheeseburger on the sophisticated menu, but kids get more than their share of attention. The food is terrific, and the keiki (children's) menu offers soup, salad, and a choice of pasta marinara (spaghetti), excellent fried-chicken strips with french fries, beef kabobs, mahimahi and shrimp sautéed or baked, and other entree choices—for $12. If they have the ingredients (no hamburger or hot dog buns in the pantry), the kitchen will accommodate special requests. Crayons, a coloring sheet, and the usual boosters and highchairs are part of the package.

Hula Grill (p. 134) Behind the scenes, children sort of run this place. Chef Peter Merriman, who put Hula Grill on the map, is the father of three, and the general manager's 12-year-old keeps him on his toes and the menu sensitive to keiki wants and needs. Children can play freely on the grassy lawn and the sandy beach in front of the restaurant, in full view of the outdoor tables. Besides free pasta for kids under 4, the menu (a coloring page of a gecko surfing, a smiling sun, and a hula girl under a palm tree) includes keiki cheese pizza, grilled

Grill) that works not only because of its oceanfront patio and upstairs dining room, but also because, for the price, there are some satisfying choices. It's always crowded, buzzing with people on a deck offering views of Molokai, Lanai, and Kahoolawe. Burgers and sandwiches are affordable and consistent, and the fresh catch baked in a garlic, lemon, and sweet basil glaze is a top seller. The waistline-defying hula pie—macadamia-nut ice cream in a chocolate-wafer crust with fudge and whipped cream—originated here.

845 Front St. ℂ **808/661-4811.** www.kimosmaui.com. Reservations recommended for dinner. Main courses $6.95–$11 lunch, $15–$24 dinner. AE, DC, DISC, MC, V. Daily 11am–3pm and 5–10:30pm; bar open 11am–1:30am.

Lahaina Fish Company SEAFOOD   The open-air dining room is literally over the water, with flickering torches after sunset and an affordable menu that covers the seafood-pasta basics. Head to an oceanside table and order a cheeseburger, chicken burger, fish burger, generous basket of peel-and-eat shrimp, or chicken and fries, cheeseburger and fries, fish and chips, pasta with Parmesan and butter, and other choices for $3.95 to $8.95.

Maui Tacos (p. 137)   The four locations of Maui Tacos on Maui are all kid-friendly. The place is largely takeout, but those who eat in have a fast-food type of environment that goes with the keiki menu: $2.75 keiki burritos; $3 for the tacos with churro (pastry) and a small drink; $4 for the ever-popular cheese quesadilla without lettuce or tomatoes, and minisize combination plates. In all Maui Tacos except Kaahumanu Center, there's a candy machine with everything from Chiclets to Gummi Bears.

SOUTH MAUI

Peggy Sue's (p. 140)   Since this is a malt, burger, and fries kind of place, kids fit in naturally. There are highchairs and booster seats, of course, but the real draw is the food: $3.95 for a choice of half of Peggy Sue's famous hamburger, a small hot dog, or a peanut-butter-and-jelly or grilled-cheese sandwich, each served with fries, a small drink, and a junior sundae for dessert. The atmosphere is carefree, with a tongue-in-cheek, teenybopper quality. The keiki menu has a full page of coloring ("Surf's Up at Peggy Sue's!") with a find-a-word game for fun.

UPCOUNTRY MAUI

Haliimaile General Store (p. 144)   A beautiful drawing of the plantation storefront is great coloring material for kids, who are given crayons and a pleasing keiki menu for lunch and dinner. From "kid cocktails" (chocolate and banana with milk; strawberry, banana, and cherry soda; kiwi soda; and lemonade) to the cheese pizza, barbecue ribs, chicken, and spaghetti and meatballs, this is the mother lode for families. With the ice-cream-and-cookie dessert, these are splashy choices for $8 at lunch, $15 at dinner.

sashimi—lingering is highly recommended. The light lunch/grill menu offers appetizers (sashimi, seared ahi, spring rolls, and pot stickers), salads, and soups. The restaurant has spiffed up its dinner selections to include hand-carved steaks, several pasta choices, and local fare such as stir-fry dishes, teriyaki chicken, and luau-style ribs. The specialty, though, remains the fresh seafood: four types of fresh fish are offered nightly, in three preparations, and Pacific Rim specials include fresh ahi, seared spicy or cooked in a sweet ginger-soy sauce.

831 Front St. ✆ **808/661-3472.** Main courses $10–$26. AE, MC, V. Daily 11am–midnight.

Woody's Island Grill AMERICAN   The owners of Cheeseburger in Paradise closed Aloha Cantina and replaced it with Woody's, a big improvement. You'll walk through an aloha-shirt shop to enter the open-air oceanfront room, where a wood-burning grill cooks fresh ono, mahimahi (with mango ginger butter), ribs, New York steak, and other surf-and-turf choices. Other options include sandwiches, such as an excellent blackened ahi with wasabi aioli, Cajun fish tacos, and coconut shrimp with sweet-and-sour sauce. The grilled opakapaka, with a lemon-caper-butter sauce and coconut shrimp, is $20 and very popular.

839 Front St. ② **808/661-8788**. Reservations recommended. Main courses $8–$22. AE, DISC, MC, V. Daily 11am–10pm.

INEXPENSIVE

Aloha Mixed Plate ⭐ ✓Value PLATE LUNCHES/BEACHSIDE GRILL Look for the festive turquoise-and-yellow, plantation-style front with the red corrugated-iron roof and adorable bar, tiny and busy, directly across from the Lahaina Cannery Mall. Grab a picnic table at ocean's edge, in the shade of large kiawe and milo trees, where you can watch the bobbing sailboats and two islands on the near horizon. (On the upper level, there are umbrellas and plumeria trees—just as charming.) Then tuck into inexpensive mahimahi, kalua pig and cabbage, shoyu chicken, teriyaki beef, and other local plate-lunch specials, all at budget-friendly prices, served with macaroni salad and rice. The shoyu chicken is the best we've had, fork tender and tasty, and the spicy chicken drumettes come from a fabled family recipe. (The bestsellers are the coconut prawns and Aloha Mixed Plate of shoyu chicken, teriyaki beef, and mahimahi.) We don't know of anywhere else where you can order a mai tai with a plate lunch and enjoy table service with an ocean view.

1285 Front St. ② **808/661-3322**. www.alohamixedplate.com. Main courses $4.95–$9.95. MC, V. Daily 10:30am–10pm.

Cheeseburger in Paradise AMERICAN   Wildly successful, always crowded, highly visible, and very noisy with its live music in the evenings, Cheeseburger is a shrine to the American classic. The home of three-napkin cheeseburgers with attitude, this is burger country, tropical style, with everything from tofu and garden burgers to big, juicy beef and chicken burgers, served on whole-wheat and sesame buns baked fresh daily. There are good reasons why the two-story green-and-white building next to the seawall is always packed: good value, good grinds, and a great ocean view. The Cheeseburger in Paradise is a hefty hunk with Jack and cheddar cheeses, sautéed onions, lettuce, fresh tomatoes, and Thousand Island dressing. You can build your own burger by adding sautéed mushrooms, bacon, grilled ortega chiles, and other condiments for an extra charge. Onion rings, chili-cheese fries, and cold beer complete the carefree fantasy.

811 Front St. ② **808/661-4855**. www.cheeseburgermaui.com. Burgers $7.50–$8.50. AE, DISC, MC, V. Daily 8am–10pm.

Down to Earth ✓Value ORGANIC HEALTH FOOD   This is one of the best deals in West Maui. Healthy organic ingredients, 90% vegan, appear in scrumptious salads, lasagna, chili, curries, and dozens of tasty dishes, presented at hot-and-cold serve-yourself stations. Stools line the abundant windows in the simple dining area, where a few tables are available for those who don't want takeout. (For all you cyberjunkies, there's Internet access, too.) The food is great, and includes millet cakes, mock tofu chicken, curried tofu, and Greek salad, everything organic and tasty, with herb-tamari marinades and pleasing condiments such as currants or raisins, apples, and cashews. (The tofu curry has apples, raw cashews, and raisins, and is fabulous.) Because the food is sold by the pound, you can buy a hearty, wholesome plate for $7. Vitamin supplements, health food products, fresh produce, and cosmetics fill the rest of the store.

193 Lahainaluna Rd. ② **808/667-2855**. Self-serve hot buffet and salad bar; food sold by the pound. Average $6–$8 for a plate. AE, MC, V. Mon–Sat 7:30am–9pm; Sun 8:30am–8pm.

Lahaina Coolers AMERICAN/INTERNATIONAL   A huge marlin hangs above the bar, epic wave shots and wall sconces made of surfboard fins line the walls, and open windows on three sides of this ultracasual indoor/outdoor restaurant take advantage of the shade trees to create a cheerful ambience. This is a great breakfast joint, with feta-cheese Mediterranean omelets, huevos rancheros, fried jasmine rice, Kula vegetables, and Portuguese sausage. There are three types of eggs Benedict—the classic, a vegetarian version (with Kula vegetables, excellent), and the local, with Portuguese sausage and sweetbread. At lunch, burgers rule and the sandwiches, from grilled portobellos to the classic tuna melt, are ideal for casual Lahaina. Made fresh daily, the pasta is prepared Asian style (chicken breast in a spicy Thai peanut sauce), with pesto, and vegetarian, in a spicy creole sauce. Pizzas, fresh catch, steak, and enchiladas round out the entrees, and everything can be prepared vegetarian upon request.

180 Dickensen St. (℃ 808/661-7082. www.lahainacoolers.com. Lunch main courses $7.50–$11; dinner main courses $11–$19. AE, DC, DISC, MC, V. Daily 8am–2am (full menu until midnight).

Maui Swiss Cafe SANDWICHES/PIZZA   Newly renovated and double its original size (which was tiny), Swiss Cafe now has five Internet stations (3 of them with flat-screen monitors) and continues to serve excellent sandwiches and continental breakfast. Having gone from a sandwich-and-pizza shop to a European-style sidewalk Internet cafe, it still serves $5 lunch specials and $2 ice cream and remains a welcome stop in hot Lahaina. Top-quality breads baked fresh daily, Dijon mustard, good Swiss cheese, and keen attention to sandwich fillings and pizza toppings make this a very special sandwich shop. The Swiss owner, Dominique Martin, has imbued this corner of Lahaina with a European flavor, down to the menus printed in English and German and the Swiss breakfast of sliced ham, Emmentaler cheese, hard-boiled egg, and freshly baked croissant. *Tip:* The "signature melt" sandwiches, with imported Emmentaler cheese baked on an Italian Parmesan crust, are something to watch for, and there are excellent vegetarian and turkey sandwiches.

640 Front St. (℃ 808/661-6776. www.swisscafe.net. Sandwiches and 8-inch pizzas $5.95–$7.95. No credit cards. Daily 9am–6pm.

KAANAPALI
EXPENSIVE

Swan Court ⭐⭐ CONTINENTAL   What could be better than a fantasy restaurant in a fantasy resort? It's not exactly a hideaway (this is, after all, a Hyatt), but Swan Court is wonderful in a resorty sort of way, with a dance floor, waterfalls, flamingos, and an ocean view adding to the package. Come here as a splurge or on a bottomless expense account, and enjoy Pacific lobster coconut soup, rock shrimp crab cake, Maui sugar cane skewered ahi, and sautéed opakapaka in striking surroundings. The menu sticks to the tried-and-true, making Swan Court a safe choice for those who like a respectable and well-executed selection in a romantic setting with candlelight, a Japanese garden, and swans gliding by serenely. A year-round Valentine dinner.

In the Hyatt Regency Maui, 200 Nohea Kai Dr. (℃ 808/661-1234. Reservations recommended for dinner. Main courses $30–$38. AE, DC, DISC, MC, V. Daily 6:30–11:30am; Tues–Sat 6–10pm.

MODERATE

Beachside Grill and Leilani's on the Beach STEAK/SEAFOOD   The Beachside Grill is the informal, less-expensive room downstairs on the beach, where folks wander in off the sand for a frothy beer and a beachside burger. Leilani's is the dinner-only room, with more expensive but still not outrageously

The Tiki Terrace

Bravo to the Kaanapali Beach Hotel for the low-salt, employee-tested Native Hawaiian Diet served in its **Tiki Terrace,** 2525 Kaanapali Pkwy. (ⓒ **808/667-0124**). Titled Kulaiwi Cuisine, the menu features the healthy, traditional Hawaiian diet of fresh fish and taro greens, flavored with herbs and spices. Salt is kept to a minimum, but you can always add your own. The Kulaiwi menu consists of pohole fern shoots from Keanae Valley (on the way to Hana), marinated with onions and seaweed and served with ginger-tomato dressing. (We think that with their freshness, pleasing crunch, and mild flavor, fern shoots are one of the most underused greens of Hawaii.)

Entree choices might be oven-poached chicken breast or fresh catch, served with pureed taro tops (like spinach, but better), grilled bananas, steamed sweet potato, taro, and fresh poi made on the premises (the poi is well known on Maui, and sells out regularly). Entrees run from $17 to $39, and include chilled Hana papaya with lemon.

The use of taro greens is a noteworthy touch in the a la carte menu as well, where baked crab and taro leaf dip, spiced up with Maui onions, artichoke hearts, shallots, garlic, Parmesan cheese, and homemade mayonnaise, is served with focaccia bread. The pohole ferns with smoked salmon and fresh poke with roasted kukui nut are special Hawaiian touches. If this is too tame for you, the a la carte menu offers everything from steak and lobster to tiger shrimp basted in Hawaiian chile pepper and seaweed sauce, served in a laulau pouch. The dining room is old-fashioned Hawaii, not fancy, with tables on a terrace ringed with plumeria

priced steak and seafood offerings. At Leilani's, you can order everything from affordable spinach, cheese, and mushroom ravioli to lobster and steak. Children can get a quarter-pound hamburger for under $5 or a broiled chicken breast for a couple of dollars more—a value, for sure. Pasta, rack of lamb, filet mignon, and Alaskan king crab at market price are among the choices in the upstairs room. Although the steak-and-lobster combinations can be pricey, the good thing about Leilani's is the strong middle range of entree prices, especially the fresh fish for around $20 to $25. All of this, of course, comes with an ocean view. There's live Hawaiian music every afternoon except Fridays, when the Rock 'n' Roll Aloha Friday set gets those decibels climbing. Free concerts are usually offered on a stage outside the restaurant on the last Sunday of the month.

In Whalers Village, 2435 Kaanapali Pkwy. ⓒ **808/661-4495.** www.leilanis.com. Reservations suggested for dinner. Lunch and dinner (Beachside Grill) $6.95–$13; dinner (Leilani's) from $18. AE, DC, DISC, MC, V. Beachside Grill daily 11am–11pm (bar daily until 12:30am); Leilani's daily 5–10pm.

Hula Grill ⭐ *Kids* HAWAII REGIONAL/SEAFOOD   Who wouldn't want to be tucking into crab-and-corn cakes, banana-glazed opah, macadamia-nut-roasted opakapaka, or crab won tons under a thatched umbrella, with a sand floor and palm trees at arm's length and a view of Lanai across the channel? Peter Merriman, one of the originators of Hawaii Regional Cuisine, segued seamlessly from his smallish, Big Island upcountry enclave to this large, high-volume, open-air dining and palm trees and a nightly Hawaiian trio (6–9pm in the courtyard, visible from the Tiki Terrace).

The regular Tiki Terrace breakfast menu presents a good opportunity to sample Hawaiian food in a familiar context: taro hash browns; three-egg lomi salmon omelet with sweet-potato home fries; a fruit plate of banana baked in ti leaf with lehua honey and macadamia nuts, served with yogurt; and French toast made with taro bread. There are even Hawaiian taro pancakes, and they're wonderful. The Hawaiian Sunday Champagne Brunch ($29) features Hawaiian music to go with the Hawaiian food, along with Belgian waffles and great desserts.

At the buffet-style **Mixed Plate** on the same property, the Hawaiian Friday lunch is widely touted among residents, who voted this the best Hawaiian food in the *Maui News:* fresh poi, lomi salmon, laulau, kalua pig, ahi poke, and pohole fern salad for $9.50. Dinner includes all of the above and prime rib (early bird, $11 from 4–6pm). The hotel also sponsors **Aunty Aloha's Breakfast Luau** at 8am weekdays, with live music, hula, breakfast (scrambled eggs, Portuguese sausage, and rice), and the inimitable and hilarious Aunty Aloha, who does a fire-knife dance with cigarette lighters and will tell you how to save money on your Maui vacation. Her slide show of Maui activities lasts about 1½ hours. The emphasis on Hawaiian food is only one part of a pervasive spirit of aloha that distinguishes this hotel. Reservations are recommended for dining in the Tiki Terrace. American Express, Discover, MasterCard, and Visa are accepted. Dinner is served daily from 5:30 to 9pm.

room on the beach. Hula Grill offers a wide range of prices and choices; it can be expensive but doesn't have to be. The menu includes Merriman's signature fire-cracker mahimahi, seafood pot stickers, and several different fresh-fish preparations, including his famous ahi poke rolls—lightly sautéed rare ahi wrapped in rice paper with Maui onions. At lunch the menu is more limited, with a choice of sandwiches, entrees, pizza, appetizers, and salads. There's happy-hour entertainment and Hawaiian music daily. For those wanting a more casual atmosphere, the Barefoot Bar, located on the beach, offers burgers, fish, pizza, and salads.

In Whalers Village, 2435 Kaanapali Pkwy. © 808/667-6636. www.hulagrill.com. Reservations recommended for dinner. Lunch and Barefoot Bar menus $5.95–$12; dinner main courses from $13. AE, DC, DISC, MC, V. Daily 11am–11pm.

INEXPENSIVE

Whalers Village has a food court where you can buy pizza, very good Japanese food (including tempura, soba, and other noodle dishes), Korean plates, and fast-food burgers at serve-yourself counters and courtyard tables. It's an inexpensive alternative and a quick, handy stop for shoppers and Kaanapali beachgoers.

Pizza Paradiso PIZZA   Pizza Paradiso took over the ice cream counter next door and expanded to include a full menu of pastas, pizzas, and desserts, including smoothies, coffee, and ice cream. This is a welcome addition to the Kaanapali scene, where casual is king and good food doesn't have to be fancy. The pizza reflects a simple and effective formula that has won acclaim through the years: good crust, true-blue sauces, and toppings loyal to tradition but with just enough edge for those who want it. Create your own pizza with roasted eggplant, mushrooms, anchovies, artichoke hearts, spicy sausages, cheeses, and a slew of other toppings. Pizza Paradiso offers some heroic choices, from the "Veg Wedge" to the "Maui Wowie" (ham and Maui pineapple) and the "God Father" (roasted chicken, artichoke hearts, sun-dried tomatoes). Also popular is Pizza Paradiso's Honokowai location (p. 137), where award-winning pastas are part of the draw.

In Whalers Village, 2435 Kaanapali Pkwy. ⓒ 808/667-0333. www.pizzaparadiso.com. Gourmet pizza $3.65–$4.45 (by the slice); whole pizzas $12–$26. MC, V. Daily 11am–10pm.

HONOKOWAI, KAHANA & NAPILI
EXPENSIVE
Roy's Kahana Bar & Grill/Roy's Nicolina Restaurant ✪ EURO-ASIAN
These sibling restaurants are next door to each other, offer the same menu, and are busy, busy, busy. They bustle with young, hip servers impeccably trained to deliver blackened ahi or perfectly seared lemongrass *shutome* (broadbill swordfish) hot to your table, in rooms that sizzle with cross-cultural tastings. Both are known for their rack of lamb and fresh seafood (usually 8 or 9 choices), and for their large, open kitchens that turn out everything from pizza to sake-grilled New York steak. If polenta is on the menu, don't resist; on my last visit, the polenta was fabulous and rich, with garlic, cream, spinach, and wild mushrooms. Large picture windows open up Roy's Kahana but don't quell the noise, another tireless trait long ago established by Roy's Restaurant in Honolulu, the flagship of Yamaguchi's burgeoning empire. The restaurant has banquet facilities for up to 70 people, while Roy's Nicolina features dining on the lanai.

In the Kahana Gateway Shopping Center, 4405 Honoapiilani Hwy. ⓒ 808/669-6999. www.roysrestaurant. com. Reservations strongly recommended. Main courses $14–$31. AE, DC, DISC, MC, V. Roy's Kahana daily 5:30–10pm; Roy's Nicolina daily 5:30–9:30pm.

Sea House Restaurant ASIAN/PACIFIC   The Sea House is not glamorous, famous, or hip, but it's worth mentioning for its gorgeous view of Napili Bay. It is spectacular. The Napili Kai Beach Club, where Sea House is located, is a charming throwback to the days when hotels blended in with their surroundings, had lush tropical foliage, and were sprawling rather than vertical. Dinner entrees come complete with soup or salad, vegetables, and rice or potato. The lighter appetizer menu is a delight—more than a dozen choices ranging from sautéed or blackened crab cake to crisp Pacific Rim sushi of ahi capped in nori and cooked tempura-style. On Friday nights, a Polynesian dinner show features the children of the Napili Kai Foundation, an organization devoted to supporting Hawaiian culture. They share top billing with the million-dollar view.

In Napili Kai Beach Resort, 5900 Honoapiilani Hwy. ⓒ 808/669-1500. Reservations required for dinner. Main courses $18–$49; appetizer menu $5–$14. AE, DISC, MC, V. Sun–Fri 8–10:30am, and noon–2pm; pupu menu Sat–Thurs 2–9pm, Fri 2–7:30pm, and 5:30–9pm (6–9pm in summer); Fri Polynesian Show 6–9pm.

MODERATE
Fish & Game Brewing Co. & Rotisserie SEAFOOD/STEAK   The restaurant consists of an oyster bar, deli counter and retail section, and tables. The small retail section sells fresh seafood, while the sit-down menu covers basic tastes: salads (Caesar, Asian chicken with wontons), fish and chips, fresh-fish sandwiches, cheeseburgers, and beer—lots of it. At dinner, count on heavier meats and the fresh catch of the day (ahi, mahimahi, ono), with rotisserie items

such as grilled chicken, steaks, and duck. The late-night menu offers shrimp, cheese fries, quesadillas, and lighter fare.

In the Kahana Gateway Shopping Center, 4405 Honoapiilani Hwy. Ⓒ **808/669-3474**. Reservations recommended for dinner. Main courses $6.95–$13 lunch, $14–$31 dinner. AE, DC, DISC, MC, V. Daily 11am–10pm; late-night menu 10:30pm–1am. During football season (Sept–Jan) brunch Sat–Sun 7:30am–3pm.

INEXPENSIVE

Maui Tacos *Kids* MEXICAN   Mark Ellman's Maui Tacos chain has grown faster than you can say "Haleakala." Ellman put gourmet Mexican on paper plates and on the island's culinary map long before the island became known as Hawaii's center of salsa and chimichangas. Barely more than a take-out counter with a few tables, this and the six other Maui Tacos in Hawaii (4 on Maui alone) are the rage of hungry surfers, discerning diners, burrito buffs, and Hollywood glitterati, like Sharon Stone, whose picture adorns a wall or two. Choices include excellent fresh-fish tacos (garlicky and flavorful), chimichangas, and mouth-breaking compositions such as the Hookipa, a "surf burrito" of fresh fish, black beans, and salsa and a personal favorite. The green-spinach burrito contains four kinds of beans, rice, and potatoes—it's a knockout, requiring a siesta afterward.

In Napili Plaza, 5095 Napili Hau St. Ⓒ **808/665-0222**. www.mauitacos.com. Items range from $1.65–$7. No credit cards. Daily 9am–9pm.

Pizza Paradiso Italian Caffe PIZZA/ITALIAN   Owner Paris Nabavi had such success with his Pizza Paradiso in Whalers Village (p. 135) that he opened up in the marketplace—and can hardly keep up with demand. Order at the counter (pastas, gourmet pizza whole or by the slice, salads, and desserts) and find a seat at one of the few tables. The pasta sauces—marinara, pescatore, Alfredo, Florentine, and pesto, with options and add-ons—are as popular as the pizzas and panini sandwiches. The Massimo, a pesto sauce with artichoke hearts, sun-dried tomatoes, and capers, comes with a choice of chicken, shrimp, or clams, and is so good it was a Taste of Lahaina winner in 1999. Take out or dine in, this is a hot spot in the neighborhood, with free delivery.

In the Honokowai Marketplace, 3350 Lower Honoapiilani Rd. Ⓒ **808/667-2929**. www.pizzaparadiso.com. Pastas $6.95–$8.95; pizzas $12–$26. MC, V. Daily 11am–10pm.

KAPALUA
EXPENSIVE

The Bay Club ★★ SEAFOOD   The first thing you notice is the remarkable view: The sun sets behind the rolling surf of Kapalua Bay, with the island of Molokai in the background. The view alone would be worth eating here, but luckily, the food, especially the seafood, promises a memorable dining experience. This intimate restaurant (with a piano bar at one end), originally designed as a private club, features such culinary masterpieces as steamed Kona lobster in banana leaf; ahi and cured salmon sashimi; macadamia-nut-crusted mahimahi with papaya pineapple salsa and passion fruit salsa; and Hawaiian seafood bouillabaisse (with lobsters, prawns, and local fish in a saffron broth). Save room for dessert (try the guava, mango, and litchi napoleon for an island-style treat). Service is impeccable, the wine list extensive. For those that just can't make up their minds, the chef can prepare a four-course tasting of the Bay Club's signature dishes.

1 Bay Dr., Kapalua Ⓒ **808/669-8008**. Reservations recommended. Main courses $33–$38. AE, DC, DISC, MC, V. Daily 6–9pm.

Plantation House Restaurant ★★ SEAFOOD/HAWAIIAN-MEDITER-RANEAN   With its teak tables, fireplace, and open sides, Plantation House gets stellar marks for atmosphere. The 360 degree view from high among the resort's pine-studded hills takes in Molokai and Lanai, the ocean, the rolling fairways and greens, the northwestern flanks of the West Maui Mountains, and the daily sunset spectacular. Readers of the *Maui News* have given it the island's "Best Ambience" award—a big honor on an island of wonderful views. It's the best place for breakfast in West Maui, hands down, and one of my top choices for dinner. The menu changes constantly but may include fresh fish prepared several ways—among them, Mediterranean (seared), Upcountry (sautéed with Maui onions and vegetable sauté), Island (pan-seared in sweet sake and macadamia nuts), and Rich Forest (with roasted wild mushrooms), the top seller. At breakfast, the Eggs Mediterranean is superb, and at lunch, sandwiches (open-faced smoked turkey, roasted vegetable, and goat cheese wrap) and salads rule. When the sun sets, the menu expands to marvelous starters such as polenta and scampi-style shrimp, crab cakes, Kula and Mediterranean salads, and a hearty entree selection of fish, pork tenderloin, roast duck, and filet mignon with apple-smoked Maui onion.

2000 Plantation Club Dr. (at Kapalua Plantation Golf Course). ℭ **808/669-6299.** www.theplantation house.com. Reservations recommended. Main courses $19–$30. AE, DC, MC, V. Daily 8am–3pm and 5:30–10pm.

MODERATE

Jameson's Grill & Bar at Kapalua AMERICAN   This is the quintessential country-club restaurant, open-air with mountain and ocean views. The glass-enclosed room is across from the Kapalua pro shop, a short lob from the tennis courts and golf course. The familiar Jameson's mix of fresh fish (sautéed, wok-seared, or grilled), stuffed shrimp, prawns, rack of lamb, ahi steak, and other basic surf-and-turf selections prevail at dinner. At lunch, duffers dashing to make tee time can opt for inexpensive "golf sandwiches" (like roast beef, turkey, or tuna salad). Other choices: fish and chips, crab cakes, and an affordable cafe menu of gourmet appetizers. Breakfasts are terrific—eggs Benedict, eggs Elizabeth (marlin on a muffin with all the trimmings), or eggs Kapalua (crab cakes topped with poached egg and wild-mushroom sauce).

200 Kapalua Dr. (at the 18th hole of the Kapalua Golf Course). ℭ **808/669-5653.** Reservations recommended for dinner. Lunch $5.95–$12; cafe menu (3–10pm) $6.95–$13; dinner main courses $18–$33. AE, DC, DISC, MC, V. Daily 8am–10pm.

Sansei Seafood Restaurant and Sushi Bar ★★ PACIFIC RIM   Perpetual award-winner Sansei proffers an extensive menu of Japanese and East-West delicacies. Furiously fusion, part Hawaii Regional Cuisine, and all parts sushi, Sansei is tirelessly creative, with a menu that scores higher with adventurous palates than with purists (although there are endless traditional choices as well). Maki is the mantra here. If you don't like cilantro, watch out for those complex spicy crab rolls. Other choices include Panko-crusted ahi sashimi, sashimi trio, ahi carpaccio, noodle dishes, lobster, Asian rock-shrimp cakes, traditional Japanese tempura, and sauces that surprise, in creative combinations such as ginger-lime chile butter and cilantro pesto. But there's simpler fare as well, such as shrimp tempura, noodles, and wok-tossed upcountry vegetables. Desserts are not to be missed. If it's autumn, don't pass up persimmon crème brûlée, made with Kula persimmons. In other seasons, opt for tempura-fried ice cream with chocolate sauce.

At the Kapalua Shops, 115 Bay Dr. ℭ **808/669-6286.** www.sanseihawaii.com. Reservations recommended. Main courses $19–$29. AE, DISC, MC, V. Daily 5:30–10pm.

3 South Maui

KIHEI/MAALAEA

There's a **Maui Tacos** at Kamaole Beach Center in Kihei (© **808/879-5005**).

EXPENSIVE

Buzz's Wharf AMERICAN   Buzz's is another formula restaurant that offers a superb view, substantial sandwiches, meaty french fries, and surf-and-turf fare—in a word, satisfying but not sensational. Still, this bright, airy dining room is a fine way station for whale-watching over a cold beer and a fresh mahimahi sandwich with fries. Some diners opt for several appetizers (stuffed mushrooms, steamer clams, clam chowder, onion soup) and a salad, then splurge on dessert. Buzz's prize-winning Tahitian Baked Papaya is a warm, fragrant melding of fresh papaya with vanilla and coconut—the pride of the house.

Maalaea Harbor, 50 Hauoli St. © **808/244-5426**. Reservations recommended. Main courses $20–$33. AE, DC, DISC, MC, V. Daily 11am–9pm.

Five Palms ✿ PACIFIC RIM   This is the best lunch spot in Kihei—open-air, with tables a few feet from the beach and up-close-and-personal views of Kahoolawe and Molokini. You'll have to walk through a nondescript parking area and the modest entrance of the Mana Kai Resort to reach this unpretentious place. At lunch, salads, sandwiches, and pasta are the hot items: Kula greens; burgers; sandwiches on homemade focaccia; capellini with shiitake mushrooms, sun-dried tomatoes, and white wine sauce; and other appealing choices, including a perfectly grilled vegetable platter. At dinner, with the torches lit on the beach and the main dining room open, the ambience shifts to evening romantic, but still casual.

In the Mana Kai Resort, 2960 S. Kihei Rd. © **808/879-2607**. Reservations recommended for dinner. Main courses $19–$49. AE, DC, MC, V. Daily 8am–2:30pm and 5–9pm.

The Waterfront at Maalaea ✿✿ SEAFOOD   The family owned Waterfront has won many prestigious awards for wine excellence, service, and seafood, but its biggest boost is word of mouth. Loyal diners rave about the friendly staff and seafood, fresh off the boat in nearby Maalaea Harbor and prepared with care. The bay and harbor view is one you'll never forget, especially at sunset. You have nine choices of preparations for the several varieties of fresh Hawaiian fish, ranging from *en papillote* (baked in buttered parchment) to Southwestern (smoked chile and cilantro butter) to Cajun spiced and Island style (sautéed, broiled, poached, or baked and paired with tiger prawns). Other choices include Kula onion soup, an excellent Caesar salad, the signature lobster chowder, and grilled eggplant layered with Maui onions, tomatoes, and spinach, served with red-pepper coulis and Big Island goat cheese. Like the seafood, it's superb.

Maalaea Harbor, 50 Hauoli St. © **808/244-9028**. Reservations recommended. Main courses $18–$35. AE, DC, DISC, MC, V. Opens daily at 5pm; last seating at 8:30pm.

MODERATE

Stella Blues Cafe AMERICAN   Stella Blues gets going at breakfast and continues through to dinner with something for everyone—vegetarians, kids, pasta and sandwich lovers, hefty steak eaters, and sensible diners who go for the inexpensive fresh Kula green salad. Grateful Dead posters line the walls, and a covey of gleaming motorcycles is invariably parked outside. It's loud and lively, irreverent, and unpretentious. Sandwiches are the highlight, ranging from Tofu Extraordinaire to Mom's Egg Salad on croissant to garden burgers and grilled chicken.

Tofu wraps and mountain-size Cobb salads are popular, and for the reckless, large coffee shakes with mounds of whipped cream. Daily specials include fresh seafood and other surprises—all home-style cooking, made from scratch, down to the pesto mayonnaise and herb bread. At dinner, selections are geared toward good-value family dining, from affordable full dinners to pastas and burgers.

In Long's Center, 1215 S. Kihei Rd. ℂ 808/874-3779. Main courses $9.95–$18. DISC, MC, V. Daily 8am–9pm.

INEXPENSIVE

Bubba's Burgers BURGERS   On the heels of his remarkable success on Kauai, Bubba has sprouted in South Maui. Half-pound Big Bubbas, Budweiser chili, and Hubba Bubbas (with rice, hot dogs, and chili) are among the heroic offerings fueling the beach-going crowd from this roadside cafe in Kihei. Fish and chips, tempeh burgers, and fresh fish specials are among the offerings of this house of Bubba, where plate lunches, burgers, and attitude aplenty provide good grinds with irreverent entertainment. (Bubba T-shirts are hilarious.)

1945 S. Kihei Rd. ℂ 808/891-2600. www.bubbaburger.com. Burgers $2.75–$6.75. MC, V. Daily 10:30am–9pm.

The Coffee Store COFFEEHOUSE   This simple, classic coffeehouse for caffeine connoisseurs serves 2 dozen different types of coffee and coffee drinks, from mochas and lattes to cappuccinos, espressos, and toddies. Breakfast items include smoothies, lox and bagels, quiches, granola, and assorted pastries. Pizza, salads, vegetarian lasagna, veggie-and-shrimp quesadillas, and sandwiches (garden burger, tuna, turkey, ham, grilled veggie panini) also move briskly from the take-out counter. The turkey-and-veggie wraps are a local legend. There are only a few small tables and they fill up fast, often with musicians and artists who've spent the previous evening entertaining at the Wailea and Kihei resorts.

In Azeka Place II, 1279 Kihei Rd. ℂ 808/875-4244. www.mauicoffee.com. All items less than $8.50. AE, MC, V. Daily 6am–6pm.

Peggy Sue's *Kids* AMERICAN   Just for a moment, forget that diet and take a leap. It's Peggy Sue's to the rescue! This 1950s-style diner has oodles of charm and is a swell place to spring for the best chocolate malt on the island. You'll also find sodas, shakes, floats, egg creams, milkshakes, and 14 flavors of made-on-Maui Roselani brand gourmet ice cream. Old-fashioned soda-shop stools, an Elvis Presley Boulevard sign, and jukeboxes on every Formica table serve as a backdrop for the famous burgers (and garden burgers), brushed with teriyaki sauce and served with all the goodies. The fries are great, too.

In Azeka Place II, 1279 S. Kihei Rd. ℂ 808/875-8944. Burgers $6–$11; plate lunches $5–$12. DC, MC, V. Sun–Thurs 11am–9pm; Fri–Sat 11am–10pm.

Shaka Sandwich & Pizza PIZZA   How many "best pizzas" are there on Maui? It depends on which shore you're on, the west or the south. At this south-shore old-timer, award-winning pizzas share the limelight with New York–style heroes and Philly cheese steaks, calzones, salads, homemade garlic bread, and homemade meatball sandwiches. Shaka uses fresh Maui produce, long-simmering sauces, and homemade Italian bread. Choose thin or Sicilian thick crust with gourmet toppings: Maui onions, spinach, anchovies, jalapeños, and a spate of other vegetables. Don't be misled by the whiteness of the white pizza; with the perfectly balanced flavors of olive oil, garlic, and cheese, you won't even miss the tomato sauce. Clam-and-garlic pizza, spinach pizza (with olive oil, spinach, garlic, and mozzarella), and the Shaka Supreme (with at least 10 toppings!) will satisfy even the insatiable.

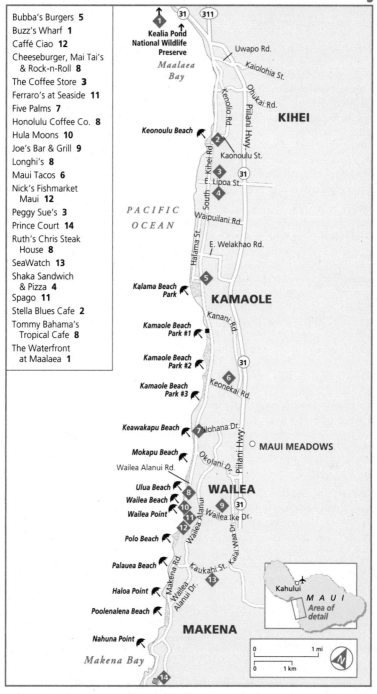

Bubba's Burgers **5**

Buzz's Wharf **1**

Caffé Ciao **12**

Cheeseburger, Mai Tai's
& Rock-n-Roll **8**

The Coffee Store **3**

Ferraro's at Seaside **11**

Five Palms **7**

Honolulu Coffee Co. **8**

Hula Moons **10**

Joe's Bar & Grill **9**

Longhi's **8**

Maui Tacos **6**

Nick's Fishmarket
Maui **12**

Peggy Sue's **3**

Prince Court **14**

Ruth's Chris Steak
House **8**

SeaWatch **13**

Shaka Sandwich
& Pizza **4**

Spago **11**

Stella Blues Cafe **2**

Tommy Bahama's
Tropical Cafe **8**

The Waterfront
at Maalaea **1**

1295 S. Kihei Rd. © **808/874-0331.** Sandwiches $4.35–$11; pizzas $13–$26. No credit cards. Daily 10:30am–9pm.

WAILEA

The Shops at Wailea, a sprawling location between the Grand Wailea Hotel and Outrigger Wailea Resort, has added a spate of new shops and restaurants to this stretch of south Maui. Five restaurants and dozens of shops, most of them upscale, are among the new tenants of this complex. **Ruth's Chris Steak House** is here, as well as **Tommy Bahama's Tropical Cafe & Emporium, Honolulu Coffee Company, Cheeseburger, Mai Tai's and Rock-n-Roll,** and **Longhi's.** Next door at the Outrigger Wailea, **Hula Moons,** the retro-Hawaiian-themed restaurant, has reopened after a $3 million renovation and moved to the upper level of the lobby building, where it serves midpriced steak and seafood with an ocean view.

VERY EXPENSIVE

Spago ★★ HAWAIIAN/CALIFORNIA/PACIFIC REGIONAL   California meets Hawaii in this open air, contemporary-designed eatery featuring fresh, local Hawaii ingredients prepared under the culinary watch of master chef Wolfgang Puck. The room, formerly Seasons Dining Room, has been stunningly transformed into a sleek modern layout using stone and wood in the open-air setting overlooking the Pacific Ocean. The cuisine lives up to Puck's reputation of using traditional Hawaiian dishes with his own brand of cutting-edge innovations. Open for dinner only, the menu features an unbelievable coconut soup with local lobster, keffir, chile, and galangal. For entrees, try the whole steamed fish served with chile, ginger, and baby choy sum; the incredible Kona lobster with sweet-and-sour banana curry, coconut rice, and dry-fried green beans; or the grilled côte de bouef with braised celery, armagnac, peppercorns, and pommes aligot. The wine and beverage list is well thought out and extensive. Save room for dessert (don't pass up the warm guanaja chocolate tart with Tahitian vanilla bean ice cream). Make reservations as soon as you land on the island, if not before—this place is popular.

Four Seasons Resort Maui, 3900 Wailea Alanui Dr., Wailea, 96753. © **808/879-2999.** www.wolf gangpuck.com. Reservations required. Dinners average $75 per person. AE, DC, DISC, MC, V. Daily 5:30–9pm; bar with pupu daily 5–11pm.

EXPENSIVE

Ferraro's at Seaside ★ ITALIAN   This was a master stroke for Four Seasons: authentic Italian fare in a casual outdoor tropical setting, with a drop-dead gorgeous view of the ocean and the West Maui Mountains. Ferraro's is not inexpensive, but the food is first-rate, whether you try the oregano-marinated shrimp with avocado or the linguine puttanesca. Mango margaritas, generous salads such as the Maine lobster with avocado and toasted sourdough, and sandwiches and half-pound burgers cater to the poolside crowd at lunch, but at dinnertime, the choices intensify. The fish selection is noteworthy: pepper-crusted ahi, grilled sea scallops and steamed mussels with saffron risotto cake, and poached snapper with red onion–orange marmalade. It won't be easy to choose.

In the Four Seasons Resort Maui at Wailea, 3900 Wailea Alanui Dr. © **808/874-8000.** Reservations recommended. Main courses $21–$39. AE, DC, DISC, MC, V. Daily 11:30am–3pm, 3–6pm (pupu menu), and 6–9pm.

Joe's Bar & Grill ★★ AMERICAN GRILL   The 360 degree view spans the golf course, tennis courts, ocean, and Haleakala—a worthy setting for Beverly Gannon's style of American home cooking with a regional twist. The hearty staples include excellent mashed potatoes, lobster, fresh fish, and filet mignon, but the meat loaf (a whole loaf, like Mom used to make) seems to upstage them all. The Tuscan white bean soup is superb, and the tenderloin, with roasted portobellos, mashed potatoes with whole garlic, and a pinot noir demiglace, is American home cooking at its best. Daily specials could be grilled ahi with white truffle–Yukon mashed potatoes or sautéed mahimahi with shrimp bisque and sautéed spinach. If chocolate cake is on the menu, you should definitely spring for it.

In the Wailea Tennis Club, 131 Wailea Ike Place. ℂ 808/875-7767. www.joesbarandgrill.com. Reservations recommended. Main courses $17–$30. AE, DC, DISC, MC, V. Daily 5:30–9pm.

Longhi's ★★ ITALIAN   This is a great alternative to the high-priced restaurants in the surrounding resorts. The open-air restaurants, with restaurateur Bob Longhi's trademark black and white checkered floor, provide a great way to start the day. Breakfasts here are something you want to wake up to: perfect baguettes, fresh baked cinnamon rolls (1 is enough for 2 people), and eggs Benedict or Florentine (with hollandaise for those not counting calories). Lunch is either an Italian banquet (ahi torino prawns amaretto and a wide variety of pastas) or fresh salads and sandwiches. Dinner (overlooking the water) is where Longhi shines, with a long list of fresh-made pasta dishes, seafood platters, and beef and chicken dishes (like filet mignon with béarnaise or veal sauté). Leave room for the daily dessert specials. Unlike Longhi's restaurant in Lahaina, this is not a verbal menu recited by your waitperson, but a real menu that you can hold and study as you plan your culinary adventure. If you come on Saturday night, stay for the live music; the place rocks until 1:30am.

The Shops at Wailea, 3750 Wailea Alanui Dr., Wailea ℂ 808/891-8883. www.longhi-maui.com. Reservations for dinner recommended. Main courses $18–$30. AE, DC, MC, V. Mon–Fri 8am–10pm; Sat 7:30am–1:30am; Sun 7:30am–10pm.

Nick's Fishmarket Maui ★★★ SEAFOOD   Hawaii's newest Nick's has the perfect balance of visual sizzle and memorable food. A private room with attractive murals seats 50, and the round bar, where you can sit facing the ocean, is highlighted with minimalist dangling amber lights, one of the friendliest touches in Wailea. Stephanotis vines create shade on the terrace, and the sunset views are superb. This is a classic seafood restaurant that sticks to the tried and true (*not* an overwrought menu) but stays fresh with excellent ingredients and a high degree of professionalism in service and preparation. The Greek Maui Wowie salad gets my vote as one of the top salads in Hawaii. The opakapaka has been a Nick's signature for eons; other choices include fresh salmon, scallops, Hawaiian lobster tails, and chicken, beef, and lamb dishes. I love the onion vichyssoise with taro swirl and a hint of *tobiko* (flying-fish roe), and the bow-tied servers bearing almond-scented cold towels.

In the Fairmont Kea Lani Hotel, 4100 Wailea Alanui. ℂ 808/879-7224. www.tri-star-restaurants.com. Reservations recommended. Main courses $25–$50. Prix fixe dinners $55–$85. AE, DC, DISC, MC, V. Mon–Thurs 5:30–10pm; Fri–Sat 5:30–10:30pm, bar until 11pm.

MODERATE

Caffe Ciao ★ ITALIAN   There are two parts to this charming trattoria: the deli and take-out section, and the tables under the trees, next to the bar. Rare and wonderful wines, such as Vine Cliff, are sold in the deli, along with ultraluxe rose soaps and other bath products, assorted pastas, pizzas, roasted potatoes, vegetable panini, vegetable lasagna, abundant salads, and an appealing selection of microwavable and take-out goodies. On the terrace under the trees, the tables are cheerfully accented with Italian herbs growing in cachepots. *A fave:* the linguine pomodoro, with fresh tomatoes, spinach-tomato sauce, and a dollop of mascarpone.

In the Kea Lani Hotel, 4100 Wailea Alanui. © **808/875-4100.** Reservations recommended. Lunch main courses $14–$20; dinner main courses $16–$38; pizzas $15–$23. AE, DC, DISC, MC, V. Daily 11am–10pm, bar until 10pm.

SeaWatch ⭐ ISLAND CUISINE   Under the same ownership as Kapalua's Plantation House Restaurant (p. 138), SeaWatch is a good choice from morning to evening, and it's one of the more affordable stops in tony Wailea. You'll dine on the terrace or in a high-ceilinged room, on a menu that carries the tee-off-to-19th-hole crowd with ease. From breakfast on, it's a celebration of island bounty, from the Maui onions on the bagels and lox to kalua pork and Maui onions in the scrambled eggs. We also like the crab cake Benedict with roasted pepper hollandaise. Lunchtime sandwiches, pastas, salads, wraps, and soups are moderately priced, and you get 360 degree views to go with them. The cashew chicken wrap with mango chutney is a winner, but if that's too Pan-Asian for you, try the tropical fish quesadilla or the grilled fresh-catch sandwich with Kula lime aioli. Save room for the bananas Foster.

100 Wailea Golf Club Dr. © **808/875-8080.** www.seawatchrestaurant.com. Reservations required for dinner. Breakfast $3–$10; lunch $6.50–$12; dinner main courses $23–$28. AE, MC, V. Daily 8am–10pm.

MAKENA
Prince Court ⭐⭐ CONTEMPORARY ISLAND   Half of the Sunday brunch experience here is the head-turning view of Makena Beach, Molokini islet, and Kahoolawe island. The other half is the fabled Sunday buffet, bountiful and sumptuous, spread over several tables: pasta, omelets, cheeses, pastries, sashimi, crab legs, smoked salmon, fresh Maui produce, and a smashing array of ethnic and continental foods. The dinner menu changes regularly; recent winners are the steamed Manila Clams Scampi with roasted garlic, diced tomatoes, and fried basil; Dungeness crab and goat cheese wonton with Maui onion guacamole; and the Prince Court Sampler with Kona lobster cakes, kalua duck lumpia, and sugar-cane-speared grilled prawns. Game entrees (venison, rack of lamb, breast of duck) come in highly acclaimed preparations, such as poha (gooseberry) compote and black cherry Cabernet sauce.

In the Maui Prince Hotel, 5400 Makena Alanui. © **808/874-1111.** Reservations recommended. Main courses $17–$30; Fri prime rib and seafood buffet $38 ($23 child); Sun brunch $36. AE, MC, V. Sun 9am–1pm; daily 6–9:30pm.

4 Upcountry Maui
HALIIMAILE (ON THE WAY TO UPCOUNTRY MAUI)
EXPENSIVE
Haliimaile General Store ⭐⭐⭐ *(Kids)* AMERICAN   More than a decade later, Bev Gannon, one of the 12 original Hawaii Regional Cuisine chefs, is still going strong at her foodie haven in the pineapple fields. You'll dine at tables set on old wood floors under high ceilings (sound ricochets fiercely here), in a peach-colored room emblazoned with works by local artists. The food, a blend of eclectic American with ethnic touches, puts an innovative spin on Hawaii Regional Cuisine. Even the fresh-catch sandwich on the lunch menu is anything but prosaic. The sashimi napoleon and the house salad—island greens with mandarin oranges, onions, toasted walnuts, and blue-cheese crumble—are notable items on a menu that bridges Hawaii with Gannon's Texas roots.

Upcountry & East Maui Dining & Attractions

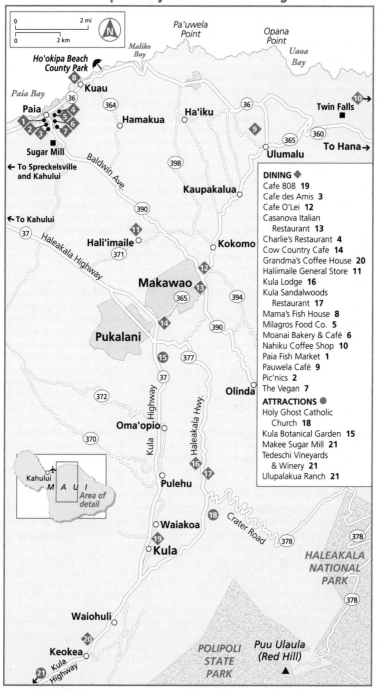

0   2 mi
0   2 km

N

Pa'uwela Point

Opana Point

Uaoa Bay

Maliko Bay

Ho'okipa Beach County Park
8
Kuau
36
Paia
36
364
Hamakua
Ha'iku
36
Twin Falls
10
Paia Bay
1 2 3 4 5 6 7
Sugar Mill
9
365
360
Ulumalu
← To Spreckelsville and Kahului
To Hana →
398
Kaupakalua
Baldwin Ave.
← To Kahului
37
Haleakala Highway
11
Hali'imaile
371
Kokomo
12
Makawao
13
365
394
14
390
Pukalani
15
377
37
Olinda
372
16
Oma'opio
370
17
Pulehu
18
Waiakoa
Crater Road
19
Kula
378
378
HALEAKALA NATIONAL PARK
378
Waiohuli
20
Keokea
21
Kula Highway

Kahului M A U I Area of detail

Puu Ulaula (Red Hill)

POLIPOLI STATE PARK

DINING ◆
Cafe 808 **19**
Cafe des Amis **3**
Cafe O'Lei **12**
Casanova Italian Restaurant **13**
Charlie's Restaurant **4**
Cow Country Cafe **14**
Grandma's Coffee House **20**
Haliimaile General Store **11**
Kula Lodge **16**
Kula Sandalwoods Restaurant **17**
Mama's Fish House **8**
Milagros Food Co. **5**
Moanai Bakery & Café **6**
Nahiku Coffee Shop **10**
Paia Fish Market **1**
Pauwela Café **9**
Pic'nics **2**
The Vegan **7**
ATTRACTIONS ●
Holy Ghost Catholic Church **18**
Kula Botanical Garden **15**
Makee Sugar Mill **21**
Tedeschi Vineyards & Winery **21**
Ulupalakua Ranch **21**

Haliimaile Rd., Haliimaile. © 808/572-2666. www.haliimailegeneralstore.com. Reservations recommended. Lunch $7–$14; dinner $14–$28. DC, MC, V. Mon–Fri 11am–2:30pm; daily 5:30–9:30pm.

MAKAWAO & PUKALANI
MODERATE

Casanova Italian Restaurant ⭐ ITALIAN   The nexus of upcountry dining and nightlife, Casanova is Makawao's citadel of hip. It's casual, too, with terrific food and music and a tiny veranda with a few stools, always full, in front of a deli at Makawao's busiest intersection. The restaurant contains a stage, dance floor, restaurant, and bar—and food to love and remember. This is pasta heaven; try the spaghetti fradiavolo or the spinach gnocchi in a fresh tomato-Gorgonzola sauce. Other choices include a huge pizza selection, grilled lamb chops in an Italian mushroom marinade, every possible type of pasta, and luscious desserts. Our personal picks on a stellar menu: fresh Kula spinach sautéed with butter, pine nuts, and Parmesan; polenta with radicchio (the mushrooms and cream sauce are fabulous!); and tiramisu, the best on the island.

1188 Makawao Ave. © 808/572-0220. Reservations recommended for dinner. Main courses $10–$24; 12-inch pizzas from $10. DC, MC, V. Mon–Sat 11:30am–2pm and 5:30–9pm; Sun 5:30–9pm; dancing Wed–Sat 9:45pm–1am. Lounge daily 5:30pm–12:30am or 1am; deli daily 8am–6:30pm.

INEXPENSIVE

Cafe O 'Lei ⭐ AMERICAN/ISLAND   Dana Pastula managed restaurants at Lanai's Manele Bay Hotel and the Four Seasons Resort Wailea before opening her tiny, charming outdoor cafe in this sunlit sliver of Makawao. And the alfresco dining is just part of it: From the sandwiches (roast chicken breast, turkey breast, prosciutto) and salads to the soup of the day, the offerings are homemade and excellent. The chic Makawao shopkeepers who lunch here never tire of the quinoa salad, the ginger chicken soup, the roasted-beet-and-potato soup, the curry chicken salad, and the talk of the town—a towering Asian salad of Oriental vegetables, tofu, and baby greens, tossed in a sesame vinaigrette with fresh mint, ginger, and lemongrass, and served over Chinese noodles. Our favorite? The shiitake mushroom soup with chicken long rice and the snow crab–avocado sandwich—too good to be true.

In the Paniolo Courtyard, 3673 Baldwin Ave. © 808/573-9065. Sandwiches and salads $4.95–$6.95. No credit cards. Mon–Sat 11am–4pm.

Cow Country Cafe AMERICAN/LOCAL   Pukalani's inexpensive, casual, and very popular cafe features cows everywhere—on the walls, chairs, menus, aprons, even the exterior. But the real draw is the simple, home-cooked comfort food, such as meat loaf, roast pork, and humongous hamburgers, plus home-baked bread, oven-fresh muffins, and local faves such as saimin and Chinese chicken salad. Soups (homemade cream of mushroom), salads, and shrimp scampi with bow-tie pasta are among the cafe's other pleasures. The signature dessert is the cow pie, a naughty pile of chocolate cream cheese with macadamia nuts in a cookie crust, shaped like you-know-what.

In the Andrade Building, 7–2 Aewa Place (just off Haleakala Hwy.), Pukalani. © 808/572-2395. Lunch $5.95–$8.95; most dinner items less than $15. MC, V. Mon–Sat 7am–3pm and 5:30–9pm; Sun 7am–1pm.

KULA (AT THE BASE OF HALEAKALA NATIONAL PARK)
EXPENSIVE

Kula Lodge HAWAII REGIONAL/AMERICAN   Don't let the dinner prices scare you; the Kula Lodge is equally enjoyable, if not more so, at breakfast and lunch, when the prices are lower and the views through the picture windows have an eye-popping intensity. The million-dollar vista spans the flanks of Haleakala, rolling 3,200 feet down to central Maui, the ocean, and the West Maui Mountains. The Kula Lodge has always been known for its breakfasts: fabulous eggs Benedict, including a vegetarian version with Kula onions, shiitake mushrooms, and scallions; legendary banana–macadamia nut pancakes; and a highly recommended tofu scramble with green onions, Kula vegetables, and garlic chives. If possible, go for sunset cocktails and watch the colors change into deep end-of-day hues. When darkness descends, a roaring fire and lodge atmosphere add to the coziness of the room. The dinner menu features "small plates" of Thai summer rolls, seared ahi, and other starters. Sesame-seared ono, Cuban-style spicy swordfish with rum-soaked bananas, and miso salmon with wild mushrooms are seafood attractions, but there's also pasta, rack of lamb, filet mignon, and free-range chicken breast.

Haleakala Hwy. (Hwy. 377). ℂ **808/878-2517.** Reservations recommended for dinner. Breakfast $7.50–$18; lunch $11–$18; dinner main courses $14–$28. AE, MC, V. Daily 6:30am–9pm.

INEXPENSIVE

Cafe 808 AMERICAN/LOCAL   Despite its out-of-the-way location (or perhaps because of it), Cafe 808 has become the universal favorite among upcountry residents of all ages. The breakfast coffee group, the lunchtime crowd, kids after school, and dinner regulars all know it's the place for tasty home-style cooking with no pretensions: chicken lasagna, smoked-salmon omelet, famous burgers (teriyaki, hamburger, cheeseburger, garden burger, mahimahi, and taro), roast pork, smoked turkey, and a huge selection of local-style specials. Regulars rave about the chicken katsu, saimin, and beef stew. The few tables are sprinkled around a room with linoleum-tile floors, hardwood benches, plastic patio chairs, and old-fashioned booths—rough around the edges in a pleasing way, and very camp.

Lower Kula Rd., past Holy Ghost Church, across from Morihara Store. ℂ **808/878-6874.** Burgers from $3.50; main courses $4.50–$9.95. No credit cards. Daily 6am–8pm.

Grandma's Coffee House COFFEEHOUSE/AMERICAN   Alfred Franco's grandmother started what is now a five-generation coffee business back in 1918, when she was 16 years old. Today, this tiny wooden coffeehouse, still fueled by homegrown Haleakala coffee beans, is the quintessential roadside oasis. Grandma's offers espresso, hot and cold coffees, home-baked pastries, inexpensive pasta, sandwiches (including sensational avocado and garden burgers), homemade soups, fresh juices, and local plate-lunch specials that change daily. Rotating specials include Hawaiian beef stew, ginger chicken, saimin, chicken curry, lentil soup, and sandwiches piled high with Kula vegetables. While the coffee is legendary, we think the real standouts are the lemon squares and the pumpkin bread.

At the end of Hwy. 37, Keokea (about 6 miles before the Tedeschi Vineyards in Ulupalakua). ℂ **808/878-2140.** Most items less than $8.95. MC, V. Daily 7am–5pm.

Kula Sandalwoods Restaurant ⟨ AMERICAN   Chef Eleanor Loui, a graduate of the Culinary Institute of America, makes hollandaise sauce every morning from fresh upcountry egg yolks, sweet butter, and Myers lemons, which her family grows in the yard above the restaurant. This is Kula cuisine, with produce from the backyard and everything made from scratch, including French toast with home-baked Portuguese sweet bread; hotcakes or Belgian waffles with fresh fruit; baguettes; open-faced country omelets; hamburgers drenched in a special cheese sauce made with grated sharp cheddar; and an outstanding veggie burger. The grilled chicken breast sandwich is marvelous, served with soup of the day and Kula mixed greens. Dine in the gazebo or on the terrace, with dazzling views in all directions, including, in the spring, a yard dusted with lavender jacaranda flowers and a hillside ablaze with fields of orange akulikuli blossoms.

15427 Haleakala Hwy. (Hwy. 377). *©* **808/878-3523.** Breakfast $6.95–$9.75; lunch $7.25–$13; Sun brunch $6.95–$9.75. MC, V. Mon–Sat 6:30am–2pm; Sun brunch 6:30am–noon.

5 East Maui: On the Road to Hana

PAIA
MODERATE

Charlie's Restaurant ⚐ AMERICAN/MEXICAN   Although Charlie's (named after Charlie P. Woofer, a Great Dane) is open for breakfast, lunch, and dinner, breakfast is really the time to come here. Located in downtown Paia, Charlie's is a cross between a 1960s hippie hangout, a windsurfer power breakfast spot, and a honky-tonk bar (which does get going after dark). Before you head out to Hana, head for Charlie's for a larger-than-life breakfast (eggs, potatoes, toast, and coffee will set you back only $7, and your probably won't be able to eat it all). They have plenty of fancy espresso drinks, but the plain ole coffee is excellent. Lunch is burgers, sandwiches, calzones, and pizza. Dinner is grilled fish and steak—hearty, but nothing to write home about. You will see all walks of life here, from visitors on their way to Hana at 7am to buff windsurfers eating mounds of food at noon to Willy Nelson on his way to the bar to play a tune.

142 Hana Hwy., Paia *©* **808/579-9453.** Breakfast items around $7; lunch items $10; dinner main courses $12–$25. AE, DC, DISC, MC, V. Daily 7am–10pm.

Moanai Bakery & Cafe ⚐ LOCAL/EUROPEAN   Moanai gets high marks for its stylish concrete floors, high ceilings, booths and cafe tables, and fabulous food. Don Ritchey, formerly a chef at Haliimaile General Store, has created the perfect Paia eatery, a casual bakery-cafe that highlights his stellar skills. All the bases are covered: saimin, omelets, wraps, pancakes, and fresh-baked goods in the morning; soups, sandwiches, pasta, and satisfying salads for lunch; and for dinner, varied selections with Asian and European influences and fresh island ingredients. The lemongrass-grilled prawns with green papaya salad are an explosion of flavors and textures, the roasted vegetable napoleon is gourmet fare, and the Thai red curry with coconut milk, served over vegetables, seafood, or tofu, comes atop jasmine rice with crisp rice noodles and fresh sprouts to cool the fire. Ritchey's Thai-style curries are richly spiced and intense. We also vouch for his special gift with fish: The nori-sesame crusted opakapaka, with wasabi beurre blanc, is cooked, like the curry, to perfection.

71 Baldwin Ave. *©* **808/579-9999.** Reservations recommended for dinner. Breakfast $4.60–$9.95; lunch $5.95–$9.95; dinner main courses $7.95–$24. MC, V. Daily 8am–9pm.

INEXPENSIVE

Cafe des Amis ⚐ CREPES/SALADS   This Paia newcomer quickly became known as the place for healthy and tasty lunches that are kind to the pocketbook. Crepes are the star here, and they are popular: spinach with feta cheese; scallops with garlic and chipotle chile; shrimp curry with coconut milk; and dozens more choices, including breakfast crepes and dessert crepes (like banana/chocolate, strawberries and cream, or caramelized apples with rum). Equally popular are the salads (including niçoise, Greek, and Caesar) and smoothies (like peach/banana/raspberry and mango/banana/pineapple). The crepes come with a house salad, and at $5.90 to $7.50, that's a deal.

42 Baldwin Ave. ℂ **808/579-6323.** Crepes $5.90–$7.50. DISC, MC, V. Mon–Sat 8:30am–8:30pm.

Milagros Food Company ⭐ SOUTHWESTERN/SEAFOOD Milagros has gained a following with its great home-style cooking, upbeat atmosphere, and highly touted margaritas. Sit outdoors and watch the parade of Willie Nelson look-alikes ambling by as you tuck into the ahi creation of the evening, a combination of Southwestern and Pacific Rim styles and flavors accompanied by fresh veggies and Kula greens. Blackened ahi taquitos, pepper-crusted ono pasta, blue shrimp tostadas, and sandwiches, salads, and combination plates are some of the offerings here. For breakfast, the Olive Oyl spinach omelet or the huevos rancheros, served with home fries, is recommended. We love Paia's tie-dyes, beads, and hippie flavor, and this is the front-row seat for it all. Watch for happy hour, with its cheap and fabulous margaritas.

Hana Hwy. and Baldwin Ave., Paia. ℂ **808/579-8755.** Breakfast around $7; lunch $6–$10; dinner $15–$20. DC, MC, V. Daily 8am–11pm.

Paia Fish Market SEAFOOD This really is a fish market, with fresh fish to take home and cooked seafood, salads, pastas, fajitas, and quesadillas to take out or enjoy at the few picnic tables inside the restaurant. It's an appealing and budget-friendly selection: Cajun-style fresh catch, fresh-fish specials (usually ahi or salmon), fresh-fish tacos and quesadillas, and seafood and chicken pastas. You can also order hamburgers, cheeseburgers, fish and chips (or shrimp and chips), and wonderful lunch and dinner plates, cheap and tasty. Peppering the walls are photos of the number one sport here, windsurfing.

110 Hana Hwy. ℂ **808/579-8030.** Lunch and dinner plates $6.95–$20. DISC, MC, V. Daily 11am–9:30pm.

Pic-nics SANDWICHES/PICNIC LUNCHES Breakfast is terrific here—omelets, eggs made to order, Maui Portuguese sausage, Hawaiian pancakes—and so is lunch. Pic-nics is famous for many things, among them the spinach-nut burger, an ingenious vegetarian blend topped with vegetables and cheddar cheese. Stop here to refresh yourself with a plate lunch or smoothie for the drive to Hana or upcountry Maui. The gourmet sandwiches (Kula vegetables, home-baked breast of turkey, Cajun chicken, Cajun fish) are worthy of the most idyllic picnic spot. The rosemary herb-roasted chicken can be ordered as a plate lunch or as part of the Hana Bay picnic, which includes sandwiches, meats, Maui-style potato chips, and home-baked cookies and muffins. You can order old-fashioned fish and chips, too, or shrimp and chips. Fresh breads and pastries add to the appeal, and several coffee drinks made with Maui-blend coffee may give you the jolt you need for the drive ahead.

30 Baldwin Ave. ℂ **808/579-8021.** Most items less than $6.95. MC, V. Daily 7am–5pm.

The Vegan GOURMET VEGETARIAN/VEGAN Wholesome foods with ingenious soy substitutes and satisfying flavors appear on a menu that dares you to feel healthy without feeling deprived. Pad Thai noodles are the best-selling item, cooked in a creamy coconut sauce and generously seasoned with garlic and spices. Curries, grilled polenta, pepper steak made of seitan (a meat substitute), and organic hummus are among the items that draw vegetarians from around the island. Proving that desserts are justly deserved, Vegan offers a carob cake and coconut milk–flavored tapioca pudding that hint of Thailand yet are dairy-free.

115 Baldwin Ave. ℂ **808/579-9144.** Main courses $7.95–$9.95. MC, V. Daily 11am–9pm.

ELSEWHERE ON THE ROAD TO HANA

Mama's Fish House ★★   The restaurant's entrance, a cove with windsurfers, tide pools, white sand, and a canoe resting under palm trees, is a South Seas fantasy worthy of Gauguin. The interior features curved lauhala-lined ceilings, walls of split bamboo, lavish arrangements of tropical blooms, and picture windows to let in the view. With servers wearing Polynesian prints and flowers behind their ears, and the sun setting in Kuau Cove, Mama's mood is hard to beat. The fish is fresh (the fishermen are even credited by name on the menu) and prepared Hawaiian style, with tropical fruit or baked in a macadamia nut and vanilla bean crust, or in a number of preparations involving ferns, seaweed, Maui onions and roasted kukui nut. Menu items include mahimahi laulau with luau leaves (taro greens) and Maui onions, baked in ti leaves and served with kalua pig and Hanalei poi—the best. Deepwater ahi could be seared with coconut and lime, while ono "caught by Keith Nakamura along the 40-fathom ledge near Hana" comes in Hana ginger teriyaki with macadamia nuts and crisp Maui onion. Other special touches include the use of Molokai sweet potato, Hana breadfruit, organic lettuces, Haiku bananas, and fresh coconut, which evoke the mood and tastes of old Hawaii.

799 Poho Place, just off the Hana Hwy., Kuau. (*C*) **808/579-8488.** Reservations recommended for lunch, required for dinner. Main courses $29–$59. AE, DC, DISC, MC, V. Daily 11am–3pm; light menu 3–4:45pm; and 4:45–9pm last seating.

Nahiku Coffee Shop, Smoked Fish Stand, and Ti Gallery ★ (Finds)
SMOKED KABOBS   What a delight to stumble across this trio of comforts on the long drive to Hana! The small coffee shop purveys locally made baked goods, several flavors of Maui-grown coffee, banana breads made in the neighborhood, organic tropical fruit smoothies, and the Original and Best Coconut Candy made by Hana character Jungle Johnny. Next door, the Ti Gallery sells locally made Hawaiian arts and crafts, such as pottery and koa wood vessels.

The barbecue smoker, though, is our favorite part of the operation. It puts out superb smoked and grilled fish, fresh and locally caught, sending seductive aromas out into the moist Nahiku air. These are not jerky-like smoked meats; the process keeps the kabobs moist while retaining the smoke flavor. The breadfruit—sliced, wrapped in banana leaf, and baked—can be bland and starchy (like a baked potato), but it's a stroke of genius to give visitors a taste of this important Polynesian staple. The teriyaki-based marinade, made by the owner, adds a special touch to the fish (ono, ahi, marlin). One of the biggest sellers is the kalua pig sandwich. Also a hit are the island-style, two-hand tacos of fish, beef, and chicken, served with about six condiments, including cheese, jalapeños, and salsa. When available, fresh corn on the cob from Kipahulu is served, and grabbed up apace. There are a few roadside picnic tables, or you can take your lunch to go for a beachside picnic in Hana.

Hana Hwy. (¾ mile past mile marker 28). No phone. Kabobs $3 each. No credit cards. Coffee shop daily 9am–5:30pm; fish stand Fri–Wed 10am–5pm; gallery daily 10am–5pm.

Pauwela Cafe ★ (Finds) INTERNATIONAL   It's easy to get lost while searching out this wonderful cafe, but it's such a find. We never dreamed you could dine so well with such pleasing informality. The tiny cafe with a few tables indoors and out has a strong local following for many reasons. Becky Speere, a gifted chef, and her husband, Chris, a former food-service instructor at Maui Community College and a former sous chef at the Maui Prince Hotel, infuse every sandwich, salad, and muffin with finesse.

All breads are prepared in-house, including rosemary potato, Scottish country, French baguette, and green onion and cheese. The scene-stealing kalua turkey sandwich is one success layered upon another: moist, smoky shredded turkey, served with cheese on home-baked French bread and covered with a green-chile and cilantro sauce. For breakfast, eggs chilaquile are a good starter, with layers of corn tortillas, pinto beans, chiles, cheese, and herbs, topped with egg custard and served hot with salsa and sour cream. At lunch, the Greek salad and veggie burrito are excellent. Because this cafe is located in an industrial center of sailboard and surfboard manufacturers, you may find a surf legend dining at the next table. The cafe is 1.4 miles past the Haiku turnoff and a half-mile up on the left.

375 W. Kuiaha Rd., off Hana Hwy., past Haiku Rd., Haiku. ℂ 808/575-9242. Most items less than $6.50. No credit cards. Mon–Sat 7am–3pm; Sun 8am–2pm.

6 At the End of the Road in East Maui: Hana

Hana Ranch Restaurant *Overrated* AMERICAN   Part of the Hotel Hana-Maui operation, the Hana Ranch Restaurant is the informal alternative to the hotel's dining room. Dinner choices include New York steak, prawns and pasta, and Pacific Rim options like spicy shrimp wontons or the predictable fresh-fish poke. The warmly received Wednesday Pizza Night and the luncheon buffets are the most affordable prospects: baked mahimahi, pita sandwiches, chicken stir-fry, cheeseburgers, and club and fresh-catch sandwiches. It's not an inspired menu, and the service can be practically nonexistent when the tour buses descend during lunch rush. There are indoor tables as well as two outdoor pavilions that offer distant ocean views. At the adjoining take-out stand, fast-food classics prevail: teriyaki plate lunch, mahimahi sandwich, cheeseburgers, hot dogs, and ice cream.

Hana Hwy. ℂ 808/248-8255. Reservations required Fri–Sat. Main courses $18–$33. AE, DC, DISC, MC, V. Daily 7–10am and 11am–2pm; Fri–Sat 6–8pm. Take-out counter daily 6–10am and 11am–4pm.

6

Fun in the Surf & Sun

This is why you've come to Maui—the sun, the sand, and the surf. In this chapter, we'll tell you about the best beaches, from where to soak up the rays to where to plunge beneath the waves for a fish's-eye view of the underwater world. We've covered a range of ocean activities on Maui, as well as our favorite places and outfitters for these marine adventures. Also in this chapter are things to do on dry land, including the best spots for hiking and camping and the greatest golf courses.

1 Beaches

Maui has more than 80 accessible beaches of every conceivable description, from rocky black-sand beaches to powdery golden ones; there's even a rare red-sand beach. What follows is a personal selection of the finest of Maui's beaches, carefully chosen to suit a variety of needs, tastes, and interests.

Hawaii's beaches belong to the people. All beaches (even those in front of exclusive resorts) are public property, and you are welcome to visit. Hawaii state law requires all resorts and hotels to offer public right-of-way access (across their private property) to the beach, along with public parking. So just because a beach fronts a hotel doesn't mean that you can't enjoy the water. It does mean that the hotel may restrict certain areas on private property for hotel guests' use only. Generally, hotels welcome nonguests to their facilities. They frown on nonguests using the beach chairs reserved for guests, but if a nonguest has money and wants to rent gear, buy a drink, or eat a sandwich, well, money is money, and they will gladly accept it from anyone. For beach toys and equipment, contact the **Activity Warehouse** (© 800/343-2087; www.travelhawaii.com), which has branches in Lahaina at 578 Front St., near Prison Street (© 808/667-4000), and in Kihei at Azeka Place II, on the mountain side of Kihei Road near Lipoa Street (© 808/875-4000). Beach chairs rent for $2 a day, coolers (with ice) for $2 a day, and a host of toys (Frisbees, volleyballs, and more) for $1 a day.

WEST MAUI

D. T. FLEMING BEACH PARK ★★

This quiet, out-of-the-way beach cove, named after the man who started the commercial growing of pineapple on the Valley Isle, is a great place to take the family. The crescent-shaped beach, located north of the Ritz-Carlton Hotel, starts at the 16th hole of the Kapalua golf course (Makaluapuna Point) and rolls around to the sea cliffs at the other side. Ironwood trees provide shade on the land side. Offshore, a shallow sandbar extends to the edge of the surf. The waters are generally good for swimming and snorkeling; sometimes, off on the right side near the sea cliffs, the waves build enough for body boarders and surfers to get a few good rides in. This park has lots of facilities: restrooms, showers, picnic tables, barbecue grills, and a paved parking lot.

KAPALUA BEACH ★★★

The beach cove that fronts the Kapalua Bay Hotel is the stuff of dreams: a golden crescent bordered by two palm-studded points. The sandy bottom slopes gently to deep water at the bay mouth; the water is so clear that you can see where the gold sands turn to green, and then deep blue. Protected from strong winds and currents by the lava-rock promontories, Kapalua's calm waters are great for snorkelers and swimmers of all ages and abilities, and the bay is big enough to paddle a kayak around without getting into the more challenging channel that separates Maui from Molokai. Waves come in just right for riding. Fish hang out by the rocks, making it great for snorkeling.

The beach is accessible from the hotel on one end, which provides sun chairs with shades and a beach-activities center for its guests, and a public access way on the other. It isn't so wide that you'll burn your feet getting in or out of the water, and the inland side is edged by a shady path and cool lawns. Outdoor showers are stationed at both ends. You'll also find restrooms, lifeguards, a rental shack, and plenty of shade.

Parking is limited to about 30 spaces in a small lot off Lower Honoapiilani Road, by Napili Kai Beach Club, so arrive early; next door is a nice but somewhat pricey oceanfront restaurant, Kapalua's Bay Club.

KAANAPALI BEACH ★★

Four-mile-long Kaanapali is one of Maui's best beaches, with grainy gold sand as far as the eye can see. The beach parallels the sea channel through most of its length, and a paved beach walk links hotels and condos, open-air restaurants, and Whalers Village shopping center. Because Kaanapali is so long, and because most hotels have adjacent swimming pools, the beach is crowded only in pockets—there's plenty of room to find seclusion. Summertime swimming is excellent.

There's fabulous snorkeling around **Black Rock,** in front of the Sheraton; the water is clear, calm, and populated with clouds of tropical fish. You might even spot a turtle or two.

Facilities include outdoor showers; you can use the restrooms at the hotel pools. Various beach-activity vendors line up in front of the hotels, offering nearly every type of water activity and equipment.

Parking is a problem, though. There are two public entrances: At the south end, turn off Honoapiilani Highway into the Kaanapali Resort, and pay for parking there, or continue on Honoapiilani Highway, turn off at the last Kaanapali exit at the stoplight near the Maui Kaanapali Villas, and park next to the beach signs indicating public access (this is a little tricky to find and limited to only a few cars, so to save time you might want to just head to the Sheraton or Whalers Village and plunk down your money).

WAHIKULI COUNTY WAYSIDE PARK

This small stretch of beach, adjacent to Honoapiilani Highway between Lahaina and Kaanapali, is one of Lahaina's most popular beach parks. It's packed on weekends, but during the week it's a great place for swimming, snorkeling, sunbathing, and picnics. Facilities include paved parking, restrooms, showers, and small covered pavilions with picnic tables and barbecue grills.

LAUNIUPOKO COUNTY WAYSIDE PARK

Families with children will love this small park off Honoapiilani Highway, just south of Lahaina. A large wading pool for kids fronts the shady park, with giant boulders protecting the wading area from the surf outside. Just to the left is a

Beaches & Outdoor Pursuits

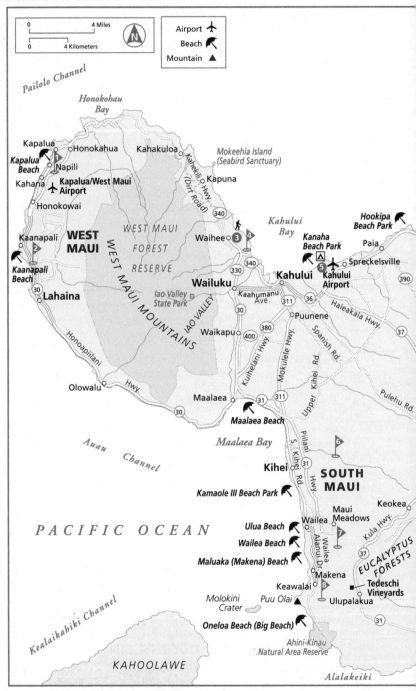

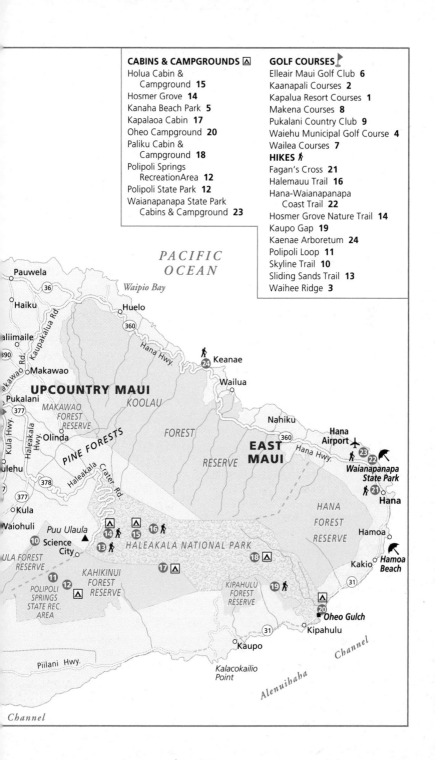

CABINS & CAMPGROUNDS ⛺
Holua Cabin &
    Campground **15**
Hosmer Grove **14**
Kanaha Beach Park **5**
Kapalaoa Cabin **17**
Oheo Campground **20**
Paliku Cabin &
    Campground **18**
Polipoli Springs
    RecreationArea **12**
Polipoli State Park **12**
Waianapanapa State Park
    Cabins & Campground **23**

GOLF COURSES ⛳
Elleair Maui Golf Club **6**
Kaanapali Courses **2**
Kapalua Resort Courses **1**
Makena Courses **8**
Pukalani Country Club **9**
Waiehu Municipal Golf Course **4**
Wailea Courses **7**
HIKES 🚶
Fagan's Cross **21**
Halemauu Trail **16**
Hana-Waianapanapa
    Coast Trail **22**
Hosmer Grove Nature Trail **14**
Kaupo Gap **19**
Kaenae Arboretum **24**
Polipoli Loop **11**
Skyline Trail **10**
Sliding Sands Trail **13**
Waihee Ridge **3**

PACIFIC
OCEAN

Pauwela

Waipio Bay

Haiku

Huelo

aliimaile

Kaupakalua Rd

36

akawao Rd

390

Makawao

Hana Hwy.

360

Keanae

24

Wailua

UPCOUNTRY MAUI

KOOLAU

Pukalani

MAKAWAO
FOREST
RESERVE

377

FOREST

Nahiku

Hana
Airport

360

EAST
MAUI

Hana Hwy.

23
22

Olinda

Kula Hwy.

Haleakala Hwy.

PINE FORESTS

RESERVE

Waianapanapa
State Park

ulehu

378

Haleakala

Crater Rd.

21

7

377

HANA

Hana

Kula

HALEAKALA NATIONAL PARK

FOREST

Waiohuli

Puu Ulaula

10   Science
      City

14

15   16

RESERVE

Hamoa

ULA FOREST
RESERVE

13

17

18

Kakio

Hamoa
Beach

11   KAHIKINUI
      FOREST
      RESERVE

12

KIPAHULU
FOREST
RESERVE

19

31

POLIPOLI
SPRINGS
STATE REC.
AREA

20   Oheo Gulch

31   Kipahulu

Piilani Hwy.

Kaupo

Channel

Kalacokailio
Point

Alenuihaha

Channel

small sandy beach with good swimming when conditions are right. Offshore, the waves are occasionally big enough for surfing. The view from the park is one of the best: You can see the islands of Kahoolawe, Lanai, and Molokai in the distance. Facilities include paved parking lot, restrooms, showers, picnic tables, and barbecue grills. It's crowded on weekends.

SOUTH MAUI

KAMAOLE III BEACH PARK 𝔊

Three beach parks—Kamaole I, II, and III—stand like golden jewels in the front yard of the funky seaside town of Kihei, which all of a sudden is exploding with suburban sprawl. The beaches are the best things about Kihei. All three are popular with local residents and visitors because they're easily accessible. On weekends they're jam-packed with fishermen, picnickers, swimmers, and snorkelers.

The most popular is Kamaole III, or "Kam-3," as locals say. The biggest of the three beaches, with wide pockets of golden sand, it's the only one with a playground for children and a grassy lawn that meets the sand. Swimming is safe here, but scattered lava rocks are toe stubbers at the water line, and parents should watch to make sure that kids don't venture too far out, because the bottom slopes off quickly. Both the north and south shores are rocky fingers with a surge big enough to attract fish and snorkelers, and the winter waves attract bodysurfers. Kam-3 is also a wonderful place to watch the sunset. Facilities include restrooms, showers, picnic tables, barbecue grills, and lifeguards. There's also plenty of parking on South Kihei Road, across from the Maui Parkshore condos.

WAILEA BEACH 𝔊𝔊

Wailea is the best golden-sand crescent on Maui's sunbaked southwestern coast. One of five beaches within Wailea Resort, Wailea is big, wide, and protected on both sides by black lava points. It's the front yard of the Four Seasons Wailea and the Grand Wailea Resort Hotel and Spa. From the beach, the view out to sea is magnificent, framed by neighboring Kahoolawe and Lanai and the tiny crescent of Molokini, probably the most popular snorkel spot in these parts. The clear waters tumble to shore in waves just the right size for gentle riding, with or without a board. From shore, you can see Pacific humpback whales in season (Dec–Apr), and unreal sunsets nightly. Facilities include restrooms, outdoor showers, and limited free parking at the blue SHORELINE ACCESS sign, on Wailea Alanui Drive, the main drag of this resort. Wailea Resort's beaches might seem off-limits, hidden from plain view by an intimidating wall of luxury resorts, but they're all open to the public.

ULUA BEACH 𝔊

One of the most popular beaches in Wailea, Ulua is a long, wide, crescent-shaped gold-sand beach between two rocky points. When the ocean is calm, Ulua offers Wailea's best snorkeling; when it's rough, the waves are excellent for bodysurfers. The ocean bottom is shallow and gently slopes down to deeper waters, making swimming generally safe. The beach is usually occupied by guests of nearby resorts; in high season (Christmas–Mar and June–Aug), it's carpeted with beach towels. Facilities include showers and restrooms. A variety of equipment is available for rent at the nearby Wailea Ocean Activity Center. To find Ulua, look for the blue SHORELINE ACCESS sign on South Kihei Road, near Stouffer Wailea Beach Resort. A tiny parking lot is nearby.

MALUAKA BEACH (MAKENA BEACH) ★★

On the southern end of Maui's resort coast, development falls off dramatically, leaving a wild, dry countryside of green kiawe trees. The Maui Prince sits in isolated splendor, sharing Makena Resort's 1,800 acres with only a couple of first-rate golf courses and a necklace of perfect beaches. The strand nearest the hotel is Maluaka Beach, often called Makena, notable for its beauty and its views of Molokini Crater, the offshore islet, and Kahoolawe, the so-called "target" island. It's a short, wide, palm-fringed crescent of golden, grainy sand set between two black-lava points and bounded by big sand dunes topped by a grassy knoll. Swimming in this mostly calm bay is considered the best on Makena Bay, which is bordered on the south by Puu Olai cinder cone and historic Keawala'i Congregational Church. Facilities include restrooms, showers, a landscaped park, lifeguards, and roadside parking. Along Makena Alanui, look for the SHORELINE ACCESS sign near the hotel, turn right, and head down to the shore.

ONELOA BEACH (BIG BEACH) ★★

Oneloa, which means "long sand" in Hawaiian, is one of the most popular beaches on Maui. Locals call it Big Beach—it's 3,300 feet long and more than 100 feet wide. Mauians come here to swim, fish, sunbathe, surf, and enjoy the view of Kahoolawe and Lanai. Snorkeling is good around the north end at the foot of Puu Olai, a 360-foot cinder cone. During storms, however, big waves lash the shore and a strong rip current sweeps the sharp drop-off, posing a danger for inexperienced open-ocean swimmers. There are no facilities except portable toilets, but there's plenty of parking. To get here, drive past the Maui Prince Hotel to the second dirt road, which leads through a kiawe thicket to the beach.

On the other side of Puu Olai is **Little Beach,** a small pocket beach where assorted nudists work on their all-over tans, to the chagrin of uptight authorities who take a dim view of public nudity. You can get a nasty sunburn and a lewd-conduct ticket, too.

EAST MAUI
BALDWIN PARK

Located off the Hana Highway between Sprecklesville and Paia, this beach park draws lots of Maui residents, especially body board enthusiasts. It's easy to see why this place is so popular: The surf breaks along the entire length of the white-sand beach, creating perfect conditions for body boarding. On occasion, the waves get big enough for surfing. A couple of swimming areas are safe enough for children: one in the lee of the beach rocks near the large pavilion, and another at the opposite end of the beach, where beach rocks protect a small swimming area. There's a large pavilion with picnic tables and kitchen facilities, barbecue grills, additional picnic tables on the grassy area, restrooms, showers, a semipaved parking area, a baseball diamond, and a soccer field. The park is well used on weekends; weekdays are much quieter.

HOOKIPA BEACH PARK ★

Two miles past Paia, on the Hana Highway, you'll find one of the most famous windsurfing sites in the world. Due to its constant winds and endless waves, Hookipa attracts top windsurfers and wave jumpers from around the globe. Surfers and fishermen also enjoy this small, gold-sand beach at the foot of a grassy cliff, which provides a natural amphitheater for spectators. Except when international competitions are being held, weekdays are the best time to watch the daredevils fly over the waves. When the water is flat, snorkelers and divers explore the reef. Facilities include restrooms, showers, pavilions, picnic tables, barbecue grills, and a parking lot.

WAIANAPANAPA STATE PARK 🏊

Four miles before Hana, off the Hana Highway, is this beach park, which takes its name from the legend of the Waianapanapa Cave, where Chief Kaakea, a jealous and cruel man, suspected his wife, Popoalaea, of having an affair. Popoalaea left her husband and hid herself in a chamber of the Waianapanapa Cave. She and her attendant ventured out only at night, for food. Nevertheless, a few days later, Kaakea was passing by the area and saw the shadow of the servant. Knowing he had found his wife's hiding place, Kaakea entered the cave and killed her. During certain times of the year, the water in the tide pool turns red as a tribute to Popoalaea, commemorating her death. (Scientists claim, however, that the change in color is due to the presence of small red shrimp.)

Waianapanapa State Park's 120 acres have 12 cabins (see chapter 4), a caretaker's residence, a beach park, picnic tables, barbecue grills, restrooms, showers, a parking lot, a shoreline hiking trail, and a black-sand beach (it's actually small black pebbles). This is a wonderful area for both shoreline hikes (mosquitoes are plentiful, so bring insect repellent) and picnicking. Swimming is generally unsafe due to powerful rip currents and strong waves breaking offshore, which roll into the beach unchecked. Waianapanapa is crowded on weekends with local residents and their families, as well as tourists; weekdays are generally a better bet.

HAMOA BEACH 🏊🏊

This half-moon–shaped, gray-sand beach (a mix of coral and lava) in a truly tropical setting is a favorite among sunbathers seeking rest and refuge. The Hotel Hana-Maui maintains the beach and acts as though it's private, which it isn't—so just march down the lava-rock steps and grab a spot on the sand. James Michener said of Hamoa, "Paradoxically, the only beach I have ever seen that looks like the South Pacific was in the North Pacific—Hamoa Beach . . . a beach so perfectly formed that I wonder at its comparative obscurity." The 100-foot-wide beach is three football fields long and sits below 30-foot black-lava sea cliffs. An unprotected beach open to the ocean, Hamoa is often swept by powerful rip currents. Surf breaks offshore and rolls ashore, making this a popular surfing and bodysurfing area. The calm left side is best for snorkeling in summer. The hotel has numerous facilities for guests; there's an outdoor shower and restrooms for nonguests. Parking is limited. Look for the Hamoa Beach turnoff from Hana Highway.

2 Watersports

Activity Warehouse (© **800/343-2087**; www.travelhawaii.com), which has branches in Lahaina at 578 Front St., near Prison Street (© **808/667-4000**), and in Kihei at Azeka Place II, on the mountain side of Kihei Road near Lipoa Street (© **808/875-4000**), rents everything from beach chairs and coolers to kayaks, Boogie Boards, and surfboards.

Snorkel Bob's (www.snorkelbob.com) has snorkel gear, boogie boards, and other ocean toys at three locations: 1217 Front St., Lahaina (© **808/661-4421**); Napili Village, 5425-C Lower Honoapiilani Hwy., Napili (© **808/669-9603**); and Kamaole Beach Center, 2411 S. Kihei Rd., Kihei (© **808/879-7449**). All locations are open daily from 8am to 5pm. If you're island hopping, you can rent from a Snorkel Bob's location on one island and return to a branch on another.

> ⌒Tips **Safety Tip**
>
> Be sure to see the section "Staying Healthy" in chapter 2, before setting out on your Maui adventures. It includes useful information on hiking, camping, and ocean safety, plus how to avoid seasickness and sunburn, and what to do should you get stung by a jellyfish.

BOATING & SAILING

To really appreciate Maui, you need to get off the land and get on the sea. Trade winds off the Lahaina Coast and the strong wind that rips through Maui's isthmus make sailing around the island exciting. Many different boats, from a three-masted schooner to spacious trimarans, offer day cruises from Maui.

For information on snorkel cruises to Molokini, see "Snorkeling" on p. 164. For fishing charters, see "Sportfishing" on p. 165. For trips that combine snorkeling with whale-watching, see "Whale-Watching Cruises" on p. 166.

America II    This U.S. contender in the 1987 America's Cup race is a true racing boat, a 65-foot sailing yacht offering 2-hour **morning sails, afternoon sails,** and **sunset sails** year-round, plus **whale-watching** in winter. These are sailing trips, so there's no snorkeling—just the thrill of racing with the wind. Complimentary bottled water, soda, and chips are available.

Lahaina Harbor, slip 5. ℂ **888/667-2133** or 808/667-2195. www.galaxymall.com/stores/americaii. Trips $33 adults, $16 children under 13; whale-watching $30 adults, $15 children.

***Scotch Mist* Sailing Charters**   This 50-foot Santa Cruz sailboat offers 2-hour sailing adventures. Prices include snorkel gear, juice, fresh pineapple spears, Maui chips, beer, wine, and soda.

Lahaina Harbor, slip 2. ℂ **808/661-0386**. www.scotchmistsailingcharters.com. Sail trips $35 adults, $18 children 5–12; sunset sail $45.

DAY CRUISES TO MOLOKAI

You can travel across the seas by ferry from Maui's Lahaina Harbor to Molokai's Kaunakakai Wharf on the ***Molokai Princess*** (ℂ **800/275-6969** or 808/667-6165; www.mauiprincess.com). The 100-foot yacht, certified for 149 passengers, is fitted with the latest generation of gyroscopic stabilizers, making the ride smoother. The ferry makes the 90-minute journey from Lahaina to Kaunakakai daily; the cost is $40 adult one-way and $20 children one-way. Or you can choose to tour the island from two different package options: Cruise-Drive, which includes round-trip passage and a rental car for $149 for the driver, $80 per additional adult passenger and $40 for children; or the Alii Tour, which is a guided tour in an air-conditioned van plus lunch for $149 for adults and $89 for children.

They also offer ferry transportation and a hike-tour of the Kalaupapa Leprosy Settlement for $215 per person. See "The Legacy of Father Damien: Kalaupapa National Historic Park" in chapter 10 for more information about the settlement.

DAY CRUISES TO LANAI

Expeditions Lahaina/Lanai Passenger Ferry ⌒Value   The cheapest way to Lanai is the ferry, which runs five times a day, 365 days a year. It leaves Lahaina at 6:45am, 9:15am, 12:45pm, 3:15pm, and 5:45pm; the return ferry from Lanai's Manele Bay Harbor leaves at 8am, 10:30am, 2pm, 4:30pm, and 6:45pm. The 9-mile channel crossing takes between 45 minutes and an hour, depending on sea conditions. Reservations are strongly recommended. Baggage is limited to two checked bags and one carry-on. Call **Lanai City Service** (✆ **800/800-4000** or 808/565-7227) to arrange a car rental or bus ride when you arrive.

Boat: Lahaina Harbor, office: 658 Front St., Suite 127, Lahaina, HI 96761. ✆ 808/661-3756. www.go-lanai.com. Round-trip from Maui to Lanai $52 adults, $42 children 2–11 (children under 2 free).

Trilogy ★★★ *Kids*   Trilogy offers our favorite **snorkel-sail trips.** Hop aboard its 50-foot catamaran for a 90-mile sail from Lahaina Harbor to **Lanai's Hulopoe Beach,** a terrific marine preserve, for a fun-filled day of sailing, snorkeling, swimming, and **whale-watching** (in season, of course). This is the only cruise that offers a personalized ground tour of the island, and the only one with rights to take you to Hulopoe Beach. The full-day trip costs $169 for adults, half-price for children ages 3 to 12. Ask about overnighters to Lanai.

Trilogy also offers snorkel-sail trips to **Molokini,** one of Hawaii's best snorkel spots. This half-day trip leaves from Maalaea Harbor and costs $95 for adults, half-price for kids 3 to 12, including breakfast and a barbecue lunch. There's also a late-morning half-day snorkel-sail off Kaanapali Beach for the same price.

These are the most expensive sail-snorkel cruises on Maui, but they're worth every penny. The crews are fun and knowledgeable, and the boats are comfortable and well equipped. All trips include breakfast (Mom's homemade cinnamon buns) and a very good barbecue lunch (shipboard on the half-day trip, on land on the Lanai trip). Note, however, that you will be required to wear a flotation device no matter how good your swimming skills are; if this bothers you, go with another outfitter.

✆ **888/MAUI-800** or 888/628-4800. www.sailtrilogy.com. Prices and departure points vary with cruise.

BODY BOARDING (BOOGIE BOARDING) & BODYSURFING

Bodysurfing—riding the waves without a board, becoming one with the rolling water—is a way of life in Hawaii. Some bodysurfers just rely on their hands to ride the waves; others use hand boards (flat, paddlelike gloves). For additional maneuverability, try a Boogie Board or body board (also known as belly boards or *paipo* boards). These 3-foot-long boards support the upper part of your body, and are easy to carry and very maneuverable in the water. Both bodysurfing and body boarding require a pair of open-heeled swim fins to help propel you through the water. Both kinds of wave riding are very popular in the islands because the equipment is inexpensive and easy to carry, and both sports can be practiced in the small, gentle waves.

Baldwin Beach, just outside of Paia, has great bodysurfing waves nearly year-round. In winter, Maui's best bodysurfing spot is **Mokuleia Beach,** known locally as Slaughterhouse because of the cattle slaughterhouse that once stood here, not because of the waves—although they are definitely for expert bodysurfers only. To get to Mokuleia, take Honoapiilani Highway just past Kapalua Bay Resort; various hiking trails will take you down to the pocket beach. Storms from the south bring fair bodysurfing conditions and great Boogie Boarding to the lee side of Maui: **Oneloa** (Big Beach) in Makena, **Ulua** and **Kamaole III** in Kihei, and **Kapalua** beaches are all good choices.

OCEAN KAYAKING

Gliding silently over the water, propelled by a paddle, seeing Maui from the sea the way the early Hawaiians did—that's what ocean kayaking is all about. One of Maui's best kayak routes is along the **Kihei Coast,** where there's easy access to calm water. Early mornings are always best, because the wind comes up around 11am, making seas choppy and paddling difficult.

The island's cheapest kayak rentals are at the **Activity Warehouse** (© **800/ 343-2087;** www.travelhawaii.com), which has branches in Lahaina at 578 Front St., near Prison Street (© **808/667-4000**), and in Kihei at Azeka Place II, on the mountain side of Kihei Road near Lipoa Street (© **808/875-4000**), where one-person kayaks are $10 a day, and two-person kayaks are $15 a day.

For the uninitiated, our favorite kayak-tour operator is **Makena Kayak Tours** (© **877/879-8426** or 808/879-8426; makenakyak@aol.com). Professional guide Dino Ventura leads a 2½-hour trip from Makena Landing and loves taking first-timers over the secluded coral reefs and into remote coves. His wonderful tour will be a highlight of your vacation. It costs $55, including refreshments and snorkel and kayak equipment.

South Pacific Kayaks, 2439 S. Kihei Rd., Kihei (© **800/776-2326** or 808/875-4848; www.mauikayak.com), is Maui's oldest kayak-tour company. Its expert guides lead ocean-kayak trips that include lessons, a guided tour, and snorkeling. Tours run from 2½ to 5 hours and range in price from $55 to $89. South Pacific also offers kayak rentals starting at $30 a day.

In Hana, **Hana-Maui Sea Sports** (© **808/248-7711**) runs 2-hour tours of Hana's coastline on wide, stable "no roll" kayaks for $118 per person.

OCEAN RAFTING

If you're semiadventurous and looking for a more intimate experience with the sea, try ocean rafting. The inflatable rafts hold 6 to 24 passengers. Tours usually include snorkeling and coastal cruising. One of the best (and most reasonable) outfitters is **Hawaiian Ocean Raft** (© **888/677-RAFT** or 808/667-2191; www.hawaiioceanrafting.com), which operates out of Lahaina Harbor. The best deal is the 5-hour morning tour for $70 for adults, $50 for children 5 to 12; it includes three snorkeling stops and time spent searching for dolphins, not to mention continental breakfast and mid-morning snacks.

PARASAILING

Soar high above the crowds (at around 400 ft.) for a bird's-eye view of Maui. This ocean adventure sport, which is something of a cross between skydiving and water-skiing, involves sailing through the air, suspended under a large parachute attached by a towline to a speedboat. Keep in mind, though, that parasailing tours don't run during whale season, which is roughly December through May.

We recommend **UFO Parasail** (© **800/FLY-4-UFO** or 808/661-7-UFO; www.ufoparasail.net), which picks you up at Kaanapali Beach. UFO offers parasail rides daily from 8am to 2pm. The cost is $47 for the standard flight of 7 minutes of air time at 400 feet, $57 for a deluxe 10-minute ride at 800 feet and for the very adventurous, $67 for 10 minutes at 1,200 feet. You can go up alone or with a friend; no experience is necessary. *Tip:* Take the early bird special (when the light is fantastic and the price is right) at 8am for just $42 for 400 feet, or $52 for 800 feet.

SCUBA DIVING

Some people come to Maui for the sole purpose of plunging into the tropical Pacific and exploring the underwater world. You can see the great variety of tropical marine life (more than 100 endemic species found nowhere else on the planet), explore sea caves, and swim with sea turtles and monk seals in the clear tropical waters off the island. We recommend going early in the morning. Trade

An Expert Shares His Secrets: Maui's Best Dives

Ed Robinson, of Ed Robinson's Diving Adventures (see above), knows what makes a great dive. Here are five of his favorites on Maui:

Hawaiian Reef   This area off the Kihei-Wailea Coast is so named because it hosts a good cross-section of Hawaiian topography and marine life. Diving to depths of 85 feet, you'll see everything from lava formations and coral reef to sand and rubble, plus a diverse range of both shallow- and deep-water creatures. It's clear why this area was so popular with ancient Hawaiian fishermen: Large helmet shells, a healthy garden of antler coral heads, and big schools of snapper are common.

Third Tank   Located off Makena Beach at 80 feet, this World War II tank is one of the most picturesque artificial reefs you're likely to see around Maui. It acts like a fish magnet: Because it's the only large solid object in the area, any fish or invertebrates looking for a safe home come here. Surrounding the tank is a cloak of schooling snappers and goatfish just waiting for a photographer with a wide-angle lens. It's fairly small, but the Third Tank is loaded with more marine life per square inch than any site off Maui.

Molokini Crater   The backside of the crater is always done as a live boat-drift dive. The vertical wall plummets from more than 150 feet above sea level to around 250 feet below. Looking down to unseen depths gives you a feeling for the vastness of the open ocean. Pelagic fish and sharks are often sighted, and living coral perches on the wall, which is home to lobsters, crabs, and a number of photogenic black-coral trees at 50 feet.

There are actually two great dive sites around Molokini Crater. Named after common chub or rudderfish, **Enenue Side** gently slopes from the surface to about 60 feet, then drops rapidly to deeper waters.

winds often rough up the seas in the afternoon, so most dive operators schedule early morning dives that end at noon, and then take the rest of the day off.

Unsure about scuba diving? Take an introductory dive; most operators offer no-experience-necessary dives, ranging from $95 to $125. You can learn from this glimpse into the sea world whether diving is for you.

Everyone dives **Molokini,** a marine-life park and one of Hawaii's top dive spots. This crescent-shaped crater has three tiers of diving: a 35-foot plateau inside the crater basin (used by beginning divers and snorkelers), a wall sloping to 70 feet just beyond the inside plateau, and a sheer wall on the outside and backside of the crater that plunges 350 feet. This underwater park is very popular thanks to calm, clear, protected waters and an abundance of marine life, from manta rays to clouds of yellow butterfly fish.

Ed Robinson's Diving Adventures ✦ (② **800/635-1273** or 808/879-3584; www.mauiscuba.com) is the only Maui company rated one of *Scuba Diver* magazine's top 10 best dive operators for 5 years straight. Ed, a widely published underwater photographer, offers specialized charters for small groups. Two-tank dives range from $110 to $120 ($5–$15 extra for equipment); his dive boats depart from Kihei Boat Ramp.

The shallower area is an easy dive, with lots of tame butterfly fish. It's also the home of Morgan Bentjaw, one of our friendliest moray eels. Enenue Side is often done as a live boat-drift dive to extend the range of the tour. Diving depths vary. Divers usually do a 50-foot dive, but on occasion, advanced divers drop to the 130-foot level to visit the rare boarfish and the shark condos.

Almost every kind of fish found in Hawaii can be seen in the crystalline waters of **Reef's End.** It's an extension of the rim of the crater, which runs for about 200 yards underwater, barely breaking the surface. Reef's End is shallow enough for novice snorkelers and exciting enough for experienced divers. The end and outside of this shoal drop off in dramatic terraces to beyond diving range. In deeper waters, there are shark ledges at varying depths and dozens of eels, some of which are tame, including moray, dragon, snowflake, and garden eels. The shallower inner side is home to Garbanzo, one of the largest and first eels to be tamed. The reef is covered with cauliflower coral; in bright sunlight, it's one of the most dramatic underwater scenes in Hawaii.

La Pérouse Pinnacle   In the middle of scenic La Pérouse Bay, site of Haleakala's most recent lava flow, is a pinnacle rising from the 60-foot bottom to about 10 feet below the surface. Getting to the dive site is half the fun: The scenery above water is as exciting as that below the surface. Underwater, you'll enjoy a very diversified dive. Clouds of damselfish and triggerfish will greet you on the surface. Divers can approach even the timid bird wrasse. There are more porcupine puffers here than anywhere else, as well as schools of goatfish and fields of healthy finger coral. La Pérouse is good for snorkeling and long, shallow second dives.

If Ed is booked, call **Severns Diving** ✦ (© **808/879-6596;** www.mike severnsdiving.com), for small (maximum 12 people, divided into 2 groups of 6), personal diving tours on a 38-foot Munson/Hammerhead boat with freshwater shower. Pauline Fiene-Severns is a biologist who makes diving in Hawaii not only fun but also educational (check out her spectacular underwater photography book, *Molokini Island*). In her 25-plus years of operation, the company has been accident-free. Two-tank dives are $120 (with equipment).

Stop by any location of the **Maui Dive Shop** ✦ (www.mauidiveshop.com), Maui's largest diving retailer, which offers everything from rentals to scuba-diving instruction to dive-boat charters. They'll give you a free copy of the 24-page *Maui Dive Guide,* which has maps and details about the 20 best shoreline and offshore dives and snorkeling sites, all ranked for beginner, intermediate, or advanced snorkelers/divers. This operation has locations in Kihei at Azeka Place II Shopping Center, 1455 S. Kihei Rd. (© **808/879-3388**), and at the Kamaole Shopping Center (© **808/879-1533**); in Lahaina at the Lahaina Cannery Mall (© **808/661-5388**); and in the Honokowai Market Place (© **808/661-6166**). Other locations include Whalers Shopping Village, Kaanapali (© **808/661-5117**), and Kahana Gateway, Kahana (© **808/669-3800**).

SNORKELING

Snorkeling is the main attraction in Maui—and almost anyone can do it. All you need are a mask, a snorkel, fins, and some basic swimming skills. Floating over underwater worlds through colorful clouds of tropical fish is like a dream. In many places, all you have to do is wade into the water and look down. If you've never snorkeled before, most resorts and excursion boats offer instruction, but it's plenty easy to figure it out for yourself.

Some snorkel tips: Always go with a buddy. Look up every once in a while to see where you are, how far offshore you are, and whether there's any boat traffic. Don't touch anything; not only can you damage coral, but camouflaged fish and shells with poisonous spines might surprise you. Always check with a dive shop, lifeguards, and others on the beach about the area in which you plan to snorkel: Are there any dangerous conditions you should know about? What are the current surf, tide, and weather conditions? If you're not a good swimmer, wear a life jacket or other flotation device, which you can rent at most places offering watersports gear.

Snorkel Bob's ✿ (www.snorkelbob.com) and the **Activity Warehouse** will rent you everything you need; see the introduction to this section for locations. Also see "Scuba Diving" (above) for Maui Dive Shop's free booklet on great snorkeling sites.

Maui's best snorkeling beaches include **Kapalua Beach; Black Rock,** at Kaanapali Beach, in front of the Sheraton; along the Kihei coastline, especially at **Kamaole III Beach Park;** and along the Wailea coastline, particularly at **Ulua Beach.** Mornings are best, because local winds don't kick in until around noon. **Olowalu** has great snorkeling around the **14-mile marker,** where there is a turtle cleaning station about 50 to 75 yards out from shore. Turtles line up here to have cleaner wrasses pick off small parasites.

Ahihi-Kinau Natural Preserve is another terrific place; it requires more effort to reach it, but it's worth it, because it's home to Maui's tropical marine life at its best. You can't miss in Ahihi Bay, a 2,000-acre state natural area reserve in the lee of Cape Kinau, on Maui's rugged south coast, where Haleakala spilled red-hot lava that ran to the sea in 1790. Fishing is strictly *kapu* here, and the fish know it; they're everywhere in this series of rocky coves and black-lava tide pools. The black, barren, lunarlike land stands in stark contrast to the green-blue water. After you snorkel, check out La Pérouse Bay on the south side of Cape Kinau, where the French admiral La Pérouse became the first European to set foot on Maui. A lava-rock pyramid known as Pérouse Monument marks the spot. To get here, drive south of Makena past Puu Olai to Ahihi Bay, where the road turns to gravel and sometimes seems like it'll disappear under the waves. At Cape Kinau, there are three four-wheel-drive trails that lead across the lava flow; take the shortest one, nearest La Pérouse Bay. If you have a standard car, drive as far as you can, park, and walk the remainder of the way

If you'd like to head over to Lanai for a day of snorkeling in its pristine waters, see **"Day Cruises to Lanai"** on p. 159.

SNORKEL CRUISES TO MOLOKINI

Like a crescent moon fallen from the sky, the crater of **Molokini** ✿ sits almost midway between Maui and the uninhabited island of Kahoolawe. Tilted so that only the thin rim of its southern side shows above water in a perfect semicircle, Molokini stands like a scoop against the tide, and it serves, on its concave side, as a natural sanctuary for tropical fish and snorkelers, who commute daily in a fleet of dive boats to this marine-life preserve. Note that in high season, Molokini can be crowded with dozens of boats, each carrying scores of snorkelers.

Maui Classic Charters ⭑⭑   Maui Classic Charters offers morning and afternoon **snorkel-sail cruises to Molokini** on *Four Winds II,* a 55-foot, glass-bottom catamaran, for $72 adults ($47 children 3–12) for the morning sail and $40 adults ($30 children) in the afternoon. *Four Winds* trips include a continental breakfast; a barbecue lunch; complimentary beer, wine, and soda; complimentary snorkeling gear and instruction; and sportfishing along the way.

Those looking for speed should sign up for a trip on the fast, state-of-the-art catamaran *Maui Magic.* The company offers a 5-hour snorkel journey to both Molokini and La Pérouse for $99 for adults and $79 for children ages 5 to 12, including a continental breakfast, barbecue lunch, beer, wine, soda, snorkel gear, and instruction. During **whale season** (Dec 22–Apr 22), the Maui Magic Whale Watch, a 1½-hour trip with beverages, is $29 for adults and $24 for children 3 to 12.

Maalaea Harbor, slip 55 and slip 80. ℂ **800/736-5740** or 808/879-8188. www.mauicharters.com. Prices vary depending on cruise.

Ocean Activities Center ⭑   In season, this activities center runs 2-hour **whale-watching cruises** on its own spacious 65-foot catamaran; trips range from $25 to $32 for adults and $15 to $20 for children ages 3 to 12. The best deal to **Molokini** is the 5-hour Maka Kai cruise, which includes a continental breakfast, deli lunch, snorkel gear, and instruction; it's $60 for adults, $50 for teenagers, and $40 for children ages 3 to 12. Trips leave from Maalaea Harbor, slip 62. They also have a sportfishing charter boat (6-hr. shared boat starts at $135) and bottom fishing cruises for $95 per angler.

1847 S. Kihei Rd., Kihei. ℂ **800/798-0652** or 808/879-4485. www.mauioceanactivities.com. Prices vary depending on cruise.

Pride of Maui   For a high-speed, action-packed snorkel-sail experience, consider the *Pride of Maui.* These 5½-hour **snorkel cruises** take in not only **Molokini,** but also Turtle Bay and Makena for more snorkeling. Continental breakfast, barbecue lunch, gear, and instruction are included.

Maalaea Harbor. ℂ **877/TO-PRIDE** or 808/875-0955. www.gopride.com. Trips $86 adults, $53 children 3–12.

SPORTFISHING

Marlin (as big as 1,200 lb.), tuna, ono, and mahimahi await the baited hook in Maui's coastal and channel waters. No license is required; just book a sportfishing vessel out of Lahaina or Maalaea harbors. Most charter boats that troll for big-game fish carry a maximum of six passengers. You can walk the docks, inspecting boats and talking to captains and crews, or book through an activities desk or one of the outfitters recommended below.

Shop around: Prices vary widely according to the boat, the crowd, and the captain. A shared boat for a half day of fishing starts at $100; a shared full day of fishing starts at around $140. A half-day exclusive (you get the entire boat) is around $400 to $700; a full-day exclusive boat can range from $500 to $1000. Also, many boat captains tag and release marlin or keep the fish for themselves (sorry, that's Hawaii style). If you want to eat your mahimahi for dinner or have your marlin mounted, tell the captain before you go.

The best way to book a sportfishing charter is through the experts, the best booking desk in the state is **Sportfish Hawaii** ⭑ (ℂ **877/388-1376** or 808/ 396-2607; www.sportfishhawaii.com), which not only books boats on Maui, but on all islands. These fishing vessels have been inspected and must meet rigorous criteria to guarantee that you will have a great time. Prices range from $800 to $1,000 for a full-day exclusive charter (you, plus 5 friends, get the entire boat to yourself), $600 to $675 for a half-day exclusive.

SURFING

The ancient Hawaiian sport of *hee nalu* ("wave sliding") is probably the sport most people picture when they think of the islands. You, too, can do some wave sliding—just sign up at any one of the recommended surfing schools listed below.

Always wanted to learn to surf, but didn't know whom to ask? Call the **Nancy Emerson School of Surfing** (② 808/244-SURF or 808/874-1183; www.surf clinics.com). Nancy has been surfing since 1961, and has even been a stunt performer for various movies, including *Waterworld*. She's pioneered a new instructional technique called "Learn to Surf in One Lesson"—you can, really. It's $70 per person for a 2-hour group lesson; private 2-hour classes are $140.

In Hana, **Hana-Maui Sea Sports** (② 808/248-7711) has private lessons taught by a certified ocean lifeguard for $79 for a 2-hour lesson.

Expert surfers visit Maui in winter when the surf's really up. The best surfing beaches include **Honolua Bay, Lahaina Harbor** (in summer, there'll be waves just off the channel entrance with a south swell), **Maalaea** (a clean, world-class left), and **Hookipa Beach,** where surfers get the waves until noon; after that—in a carefully worked-out compromise to share this prized surf spot—the windsurfers take over.

WHALE-WATCHING

Every winter, pods of Pacific humpback whales make the 3,000-mile swim from the chilly waters of Alaska to bask in Maui's summery shallows, fluking, spy hopping, spouting, and having an all-around swell time.

The humpback is the star of the annual whale-watching season, which usually begins in January and lasts until April or sometimes May. About 1,500 to 3,000 humpback whales appear in Hawaii waters each year. Humpbacks are one of the world's oldest, most impressive inhabitants. Adults grow to be about 45 feet long and weigh a hefty 40 tons (40,642kg). Humpbacks are officially an endangered species; in 1997, some of the waters around the state were designated the Hawaiian Islands Humpback Whale National Marine Sanctuary, the country's only federal single-species sanctuary.

WHALE-WATCHING FROM SHORE

Between mid-December and April, you can just look out to sea. There's no best time of day for whale-watching, but the whales seem to appear when the sea is glassy and the wind calm. Once you see one, keep watching in the same vicinity; they might stay down for 20 minutes. Bring a book—and binoculars, if you can. You can rent binoculars for $2 a day at the **Activity Warehouse** (② 800/343-2087; www.travelhawaii.com), which has branches in Lahaina at 578 Front St., near Prison Street (② 808/667-4000), and in Kihei at Azeka Place II, on the mountain side of Kihei Road near Lipoa Street (② 808/875-4000). Some good whale-watching points on Maui are:

McGregor Point   On the way to Lahaina, there's a scenic lookout at mile marker 9 (just before you get to the Lahaina Tunnel); it's a good viewpoint to scan for whales.

Outrigger Wailea Resort   On the Wailea coastal walk, stop at this resort to look for whales through the telescope installed as a public service by the Hawaiian Islands Humpback Whale National Marine Sanctuary.

Olowalu Reef Along the straight part of Honoapiilani Highway, between McGregor Point and Olowalu, you'll often spot whales leaping out of the water. Sometimes, their appearance brings traffic to a screeching halt: People abandon their cars and run down to the sea to watch, causing a major traffic jam. If you stop, pull off the road so that others can pass.

Puu Olai It's a tough climb up this coastal landmark near the Maui Prince Hotel, but you're likely to be well rewarded: This is the island's best spot for off-shore whale-watching. On the 360-foot cinder cone overlooking Makena Beach, you'll be at the right elevation to see Pacific humpbacks as they dodge Molokini and cruise up Alalakeiki Channel between Maui and Kahoolawe. If you don't see one, you'll at least have a whale of a view.

WHALE-WATCHING CRUISES

For a closer look, take a whale-watching cruise. The **Pacific Whale Foundation,** 101 N. Kihei Rd., Kihei (© **800/942-5311** or 808/879-8811; www.pacific whale.org), is a nonprofit foundation in Kihei that supports its whale research by offering cruises and snorkel tours, some to Molokini and Lanai. They operate a 65-foot power catamaran called the *Ocean Spirit,* a 50-foot sailing catamaran called the *Manute'a,* and a sea kayak. They have 15 daily trips to choose from, and their rates for a 2-hour whale-watching cruise would make Captain Ahab smile (starting at $20 for adults, $15 for children). Cruises are offered from December through May, out of both Lahaina and Maalaea harbors.

The **Ocean Activities Center** ⚓ (© **800/798-0652** or 808/879-4485), in season, runs 2-hour **whale-watching cruises** on its own spacious 65-foot catamaran; trips range from $25 to $32 for adults and $15 to $20 for children ages 3 to 12. The best deal to **Molokini** is the 5-hour Maka Kai cruise, which includes a continental breakfast, deli lunch, snorkel gear, and instruction; it's $60 for adults, $50 for teenagers, and $40 for children ages 3 to 12. Trips leave from Maalaea Harbor, slip 62. They also have a sportfishing charter boat (6-hr. shared boat starts at $135) and bottom fishing cruises for $95 per angler.

If you want to combine ocean activities, then a snorkel or dive cruise to Molokini, the sunken crater off Maui's south coast, might be just the ticket. You can see whales on the way there, at no extra charge. See "Scuba Diving" and "Boating & Sailing" earlier in this section.

WHALE-WATCHING BY KAYAK & RAFT

Seeing a humpback whale from an ocean kayak or raft is awesome. The best budget deal for rafting is **Capt. Steve's Rafting Excursions** (© **808/667-5565;** www.captainsteves.com), which offers 2-hour whale-watching excursions out of Lahaina Harbor. Take the early bird trip at 7:30am and spot some whales for only $35 per person (regular rates are $45 for adults, $35 for children 12 and under).

WINDSURFING

Maui has Hawaii's best windsurfing beaches. In winter, windsurfers from around the world flock to the town of **Paia** to ride the waves; **Hookipa Beach,** known all over the globe for its brisk winds and excellent waves, is the site of several world-championship contests. **Kanaha,** west of Kahului Airport, also has dependable winds. When the winds turn northerly, **Kihei** is the spot to be; some days, you can spot whales in the distance behind the windsurfers. The northern end of Kihei is best: **Ohukai Park,** the first beach as you enter South Kiehi Road from the northern end, has not only good winds, but also parking, a long strip of grass to assemble your gear, and good access to the water. Experienced windsurfers here are

---

Tips **Not So Close! They Hardly Know You**

In your excitement at seeing a whale or a school of dolphins, don't get too close—both are protected under the Marine Mammals Protection Act. Swimmers, kayakers, and windsurfers must stay at least 100 yards away from all whales, dolphins, and other marine mammals. And yes, they have prosecuted visitors for swimming with dolphins! If you have any questions, call the **National Marine Fisheries Service** (© **808/541-2727**) or the **Hawaiian Islands Humpback Whale National Marine Sanctuary** (© **800/831-4888**).

---

found in front of the **Maui Sunset** condo, 1032 S. Kihei Rd., near Waipuilani Street (a block north of McDonald's), which has great windsurfing conditions but a very shallow reef (not good for beginners).

Hawaiian Island Surf and Sport, 415 Dairy Rd., Kahului (© **800/231-6958** or 808/871-4981; www.hawaiianisland.com), offers lessons, rentals, and repairs. Other shops that offer rentals and lessons are **Hawaiian Sailboarding Techniques,** 425 Koloa St., Kahului (© **800/968-5423** or 808/871-5423; www.hst windsurfing.com), with 2½-hour lessons from $69 and equipment rental from $46 a day; and **Maui Windsurf Co.,** 22 Hana Hwy., Kahului (© **800/872-0999** or 808/877-4816; www.maui-windsurf.com), which has complete equipment rental (board, sail, rig harness, and roof rack) from $45 and 1½- or 2½-hour lessons ranging from $69 to $75.

For daily reports on wind and surf conditions, call the **Wind and Surf Report** at © **808/877-3611.**

3 Hiking & Camping

In the past 3 decades, Maui has grown from a rural island to a fast-paced resort destination, but its natural beauty largely remains; there are still many places that can be explored only on foot. Those interested in seeing the backcountry—complete with virgin waterfalls, remote wilderness trails, and quiet meditative settings—should head for Haleakala's upcountry or the tropical Hana coast.

Camping on Maui can be extreme (inside a volcano) or benign (by the sea in Hana). It can be wet, cold, and rainy, or hot, dry, and windy—often all on the same day. If you're heading for Haleakala, remember that U.S. astronauts trained for the moon inside the volcano; bring survival gear. Don't forget both your swimsuit and your rain gear if you're bound for Waianapanapa.

Rental gear (as well as gear for sale) is available from **The Base Camp,** 3619 Baldwin Ave. (on the way to Haleakala), Makawao (© **808/573-2267**).

For more information on Maui camping and hiking trails and to obtain free maps, contact **Haleakala National Park,** P.O. Box 369, Makawao, HI 96768 (© **808/572-4400;** www.nps.gov/hale), and the **State Division of Forestry and Wildlife,** 54 S. High St., Wailuku, HI 96793 (© **808/984-8100;** www.hawaii.gov). For information on trails, hikes, and camping, and permits for state parks, contact the **Hawaii State Department of Land and Natural Resources,** State Parks Division, P.O. Box 621, Honolulu, HI 96809 (© **808/587-0300;** www.state.hi.us/dlnr); note that you can get information from the website but cannot obtain permits there. For information on Maui County Parks, contact **Maui County Parks and Recreation,** 1580-C Kaahumanu Ave., Wailuku, HI 96793 (© **808/243-7380;** www.mauimapp.com).

TIPS ON SAFE HIKING & CAMPING Water might be everywhere in Hawaii, but it more than likely isn't safe to drink. Most stream water must be treated because cattle, pigs, and goats have probably contaminated the water upstream. The department of health continually warns campers of bacterium leptospirosis, which is found in freshwater streams throughout the state and enters the body through breaks in the skin or through the mucous membranes. It produces flulike symptoms and can be fatal. Make sure that your drinking water is safe by vigorously boiling it, or if boiling is not an option, use tablets with hydroperiodide; portable water filters will not screen out the bacterium leptospirosis. Since firewood isn't always available, it's a good idea to carry a small, light backpacking stove, which you can use both to boil water and to cook meals for your hiking and camping adventures.

Remember, the island is not crime-free: Never leave your valuables (wallet, airline ticket, and so on) unprotected. Carry a day pack if you have a campsite, and never camp alone. Some more do's and don'ts: Do bury personal waste away from streams, don't eat unknown fruit, do carry your trash out, and don't forget there is very little twilight in Maui when the sun sets—it gets dark quickly.

GUIDED HIKES If you'd like a knowledgeable guide to accompany you on a hike, call **Maui Hiking Safaris** ✪ (© 888/445-3963 or 808/573-0168; www.mauihikingsafaris.com). Owner Randy Warner takes visitors on half- and full-day hikes into valleys, rainforests, and coastal areas. Randy's been hiking around Maui for more than 15 years and is wise in the ways of Hawaiian history, native flora and fauna, and volcanology. His rates are $49 for a half day and $79 to $89 for a full day and include day packs, rain parkas, snacks, water, and, on full-day hikes, sandwiches.

Maui's oldest hiking guide company is **Hike Maui** ✪ (© 808/879-5270; www.hikemaui.com), headed by Ken Schmitt, who pioneered guided hikes on the Valley Isle. Hike Maui offers five different hikes a day, ranging from an easy 2-mile stroll in the rainforest, leading to five different pools and waterfalls ($85 for adults, $65 for children 15 and under), to a strenuous, full-day hike in Haleakala Crater ($135 for adults, $110 for children). All prices include equipment and transportation.

Venture into the lush West Maui Mountains with an experienced guide on one of the numerous hikes offered by **Maui Eco-Adventures** (© 877/661-7720 or 808/661-7720; www.ecomaui.com). After a continental breakfast, you'll hike by streams and waterfalls, through native trees and plants, and on to breathtaking vistas. The tour stops for a picnic lunch, swims in secluded pools, and memorable photo ops. The 6-hour excursion costs $110 per person, including meals, a fanny pack with bottled water, and rain gear if necessary. No children under 13 are allowed. For those wanting to take it easy, an easy hour jaunt costs $70.

About 1,500 years ago, the verdant Kahakuloa Valley was a thriving Hawaiian village. Today, only a few hundred people live in this secluded hamlet, but old Hawaii still lives on here. Explore the valley with **Ekahi Tours** ✪ (© 888/292-2422 or 808/877-9775). Your guide, a Kahakuloa resident and a Hawaiiana expert, walks you through a taro farm, explains the mystical legends of the valley, and provides you with a peek into ancient Hawaii. The 7½-hour Kahakuloa Valley Tour is $65 for adults, $50 for children under 12; snacks, beverages, and hotel pickup are included.

For information on hikes given by the **Hawaii Sierra Club** on Maui, call © 808/573-4147 (www.hi.sierraclub.org).

HALEAKALA NATIONAL PARK ★★★

For complete coverage of the national park, see "House of the Sun: Haleakala National Park" in chapter 7.

INTO THE WILDERNESS: SLIDING SANDS & HALEMAUU TRAILS

Hiking into Maui's dormant volcano is really the best way to see it. The terrain inside the wilderness area of the volcano, which ranges from burnt-red cinder cones to ebony-black lava flows, is simply spectacular. Inside the crater, there are some 27 miles of hiking trails, two camping sites, and three cabins.

The best route takes in two trails: into the crater along **Sliding Sands Trail** ★, which begins on the rim at 9,800 feet and descends into the belly of the beast, to the valley floor at 6,600 feet, and back out along **Halemauu Trail** ★. Hardy hikers can consider making the 11-mile one-way descent, which takes 9 hours, and the equally long return ascent in 1 day. The rest of us will need to extend this steep but wonderful hike to 2 days. The descending and ascending trails aren't loops; the trailheads are miles (and several thousand feet in elevation) apart, so you'll need to make advance transportation arrangements to get back to your car, which you'll leave at the beginning of the hike, about a 30- to 45-minute drive from where the Halemauu trail ends. You either arrange with someone to pick you up, hitchhike back up to your car, or hook up with other people doing the same thing and drop off one car at each trailhead. More than a few lifetime friendships have been forged this way.

Arrange to stay at least 1 night in the park; 2 or 3 nights will allow you more time to actually explore the fascinating interior of the volcano. See below for details on the cabins and campgrounds in the wilderness area in the valley. Before you set out, stop at park headquarters to get camping and hiking updates. There is no registration for day hikers.

The trailhead for Sliding Sands is well marked and the trail is easy to follow over lava flows and cinders. As you descend, look around: The view is breathtaking. In the afternoon, waves of clouds flow into the Kaupo and Koolau gaps. Vegetation is sparse to nonexistent at the top, but the closer you get to the valley floor, the more vegetation you'll see: bracken ferns, pili grass, shrubs, even flowers. On the floor, the trail travels across rough lava flows, passing rare silversword plants, volcanic vents, and multicolored cinder cones.

The Halemauu Trail goes over red and black lava and past vegetation, such as evening primrose, as it begins its ascent up the valley wall. Occasionally, riders on horseback use this trail as an entry and exit from the park. The proper etiquette is to step aside and stand quietly next to the trail as the horses pass.

Tips A Word of Warning About the Weather

The weather at nearly 10,000 feet can change suddenly and without warning. Come prepared for cold, high winds, rain, and even snow in winter. Temperatures can range from 77°F (25°C) down to 26°F (-3°C, and it feels even lower when you factor in the wind chill), and high winds are frequent. Rainfall varies from 40 inches a year on the west end of the crater to more than 200 inches on the eastern side. Bring boots, waterproof gear, warm clothes, extra layers, and lots of sunscreen—the sun shines very brightly up here.

DAY HIKES FROM THE MAIN ENTRANCE

Aside from the difficult hike into the crater, the park has a few shorter and easier options. Anyone can take a half-mile walk down the **Hosmer Grove Nature Trail** (☆), or you can start down **Sliding Sands Trail** for a mile or two to get a hint of what lies ahead. Even this short hike can be exhausting at the high altitude. A good day hike is **Halemauu Trail** to Holua Cabin and back, an 8-mile, half-day trip. A 20-minute orientation presentation is given daily in the Summit Building at 9:30, 10:30, and 11:30am. The park rangers offer two **guided hikes.** The 2-hour, 2-mile **Cinder Desert Hike** takes place Tuesday and Friday at 10am and starts from the Sliding Sands Trailhead at the end of the Haleakala Visitor Center parking lot. The 3-hour, 3-mile **Waikamoi Cloud Forest Hike** leaves every Monday and Thursday at 9am; it starts at the Hosmer Grove, just inside the park entrance, and traverses through the Nature Conservancy's Waikamoi Preserve.

CAMPING NEAR THE MAIN ENTRANCE

Most people stay at one of two tent campgrounds, unless they get lucky and win the lottery—the lottery, that is, for one of the three wilderness cabins. For more information, contact **Haleakala National Park,** P.O. Box 369, Makawao, HI 96768 (© **808/572-4400;** www.nps.gov/hale).

CABINS   It can get really cold and windy down in the valley (see "A Word of Warning About the Weather" above), so try for a cabin. They're warm, protected from the elements, and reasonably priced. Each has 12 padded bunks (but no bedding; bring your own), a table, chairs, cooking utensils, a two-burner propane stove, and a wood-burning stove with firewood (you might also have a few cockroaches). The cabins are spaced so that each one is an easy walk from the other: Holua cabin is on the Halemauu Trail, Kapalaoa cabin on Sliding Sands Trail, and Paliku cabin on the eastern end by the Kaupo Gap. The rates are $40 a night for groups of one to six and $80 a night for groups of 7 to 12. The cabins are so popular that the National Park Service has a lottery system for reservations. Requests for cabins must be made 3 months in advance (be sure to request alternate dates). You can request all three cabins at once; you're limited to no more than 2 nights in one cabin and no more than 3 nights within the wilderness per month.

CAMPGROUNDS   If you don't win the cabin lottery, all is not lost—there are three tent-camping sites that can accommodate you: two in the wilderness, and one just outside at Hosmer Grove. There is no charge for tent camping.

Hosmer Grove, located at 6,800 feet, is a small, open grassy area surrounded by a forest. Trees protect campers from the winds, but nights still get quite cold. Hard to believe, but sometimes there's ice on the ground up here. This is the best place to spend the night in a tent if you want to see the Haleakala sunrise, and you don't have to take a long, grueling hike to get here (it's close to the road). Come up the day before, enjoy the park, take a day hike, and then turn in early. The enclosed-glass summit building opens at sunrise for those who come to greet the dawn—a welcome windbreak. Facilities include a covered pavilion with picnic tables and grills, chemical toilets, and drinking water. No permits are needed at Hosmer Grove, and there's no charge—but you can stay for only 3 nights in a 30-day period.

The two tent-camping areas inside the volcano are **Holua,** just off Halemauu at 6,920 feet; and **Paliku,** just before the Kaupo Gap at the eastern end of the valley, at 6,380 feet. Facilities at both campgrounds are limited to pit toilets and nonpotable catchment water. Water at Holua is limited, especially in summer. No open fires are allowed inside the volcano, so bring a stove if you plan to cook. Tent camping is restricted to the signed area. No camping is allowed in the horse pasture. The inviting grassy lawn in front of the cabin is *kapu.* Camping is free, but limited to 2 consecutive nights, and no more than 3 nights a month inside the volcano. Permits are issued daily at park headquarters on a first-come, first-served basis. Occupancy is limited to 25 people in each campground.

THE EAST MAUI SECTION OF THE PARK AT KIPAHULU (NEAR HANA)

In the East Maui section of Haleakala National Park, you can set up at **Oheo Campground,** a first-come, first-served, drive-in campground with tent sites for 100 near the ocean, a few tables, barbecue grills, and chemical toilets. No permit is required, but there's a 3-night limit. No food or drinking water is available, so bring your own. Bring a tent as well—it rains 75 inches a year here. Contact **Kipahulu Ranger Station,** Haleakala National Park, HI 96713 (© **808/ 248-7375;** www.nps.gov/hale).

HIKING FROM THE SUMMIT   If you hike from the crater rim down **Kaupo Gap** to the ocean, more than 20 miles away, you'll pass through climate zones ranging from arctic to tropical. On a clear day, you can see every island except Kauai on the trip down.

APPROACHING KIPAHULU FROM HANA   If you drive to Kipahulu, you'll have to approach it from the Hana Highway—it's not accessible from the summit. Always check in at the ranger station before you begin your hike; the staff can inform you of current conditions and share their wonderful stories about the history, culture, flora, and fauna of the area.

There are two hikes you can take here. The first is a short, easy half-mile loop along the **Kaloa Point Trail** (Kaloa Point is a windy bluff overlooking **Oheo Gulch**), which leads toward the ocean along pools and waterfalls and back to the ranger station. The clearly marked path leaves the parking area and rambles along the flat, grassy peninsula. Crashing surf and views of the Big Island of Hawaii are a 5-minute walk from the ranger station. Along the way you'll see the remnants of an ancient fishing shrine, a house site, and a lauhala-thatched building depicting an earlier time. The loop stops at the bridge you drove over when you entered the park; this is the best place for a photo opportunity. The pools are above and below the bridge; the best for swimming are usually above the bridge.

The second hike is for the more hardy. Although just a 4-mile round-trip, the trail is steep and you'll want to stop and swim in the pools, so allow 3 hours. You'll be climbing over rocks and up steep trails, so wear hiking boots. Take water, snacks, swim gear, and insect repellent (to ward off the swarms of mosquitoes). Always be on the lookout for flash-flood conditions. This walk will pass two magnificent waterfalls, the 181-foot **Makahiku Falls** and the even bigger 400-foot **Waimoku Falls** ✿. The trail starts at the ranger station, where you'll walk uphill for a half mile to a fence overlook at the thundering Makahiku Falls. If you're tired you can turn around here; true adventurers should press on. Behind the lookout, the well-worn trail picks up again and goes directly to a pool on the top of the Makahiku Falls. The pool is safe to swim in as long as the waters aren't rising; if they are, get out and head back to the ranger station. Back on the trail, you'll cross a meadow and then a creek, where you'll scramble up the rocky bank and head into a bamboo forest jungle. At the edge of the jungle is another creek, but the trail doesn't cross this one. A few minutes more, and the vertical Waimoku Falls will be in sight.

GUIDED HIKES   The rangers at Kipahulu conduct a 1-mile hike to the **Bamboo Forest** ✿ at 9am daily; half-mile hikes or orientation talks are given at noon, 1:30, 2:30, and 3:30pm daily; and a 4-mile round-trip hike to **Waimoku Falls** takes place on Saturday at 9:30am. All programs and hikes begin at the ranger station.

SKYLINE TRAIL, POLIPOLI SPRINGS STATE RECREATION AREA ✪

This is some hike—strenuous but worth every step if you like seeing the big picture. It's 8 miles, all downhill, with a dazzling 100-mile view of the islands dotting the blue Pacific, plus the West Maui Mountains, which seem like a separate island.

The trail is located just outside Haleakala National Park at Polipoli Springs National Recreation Area; however, you access it by going through the national park to the summit. The Skyline Trail starts just beyond the Puu Ulaula summit building on the south side of Science City and follows the southwest rift zone of Haleakala from its lunarlike cinder cones to a cool redwood grove. The trail drops 3,800 feet on a 4-hour hike to the recreation area, in the 12,000-acre Kahikinui Forest Reserve. If you'd rather drive, you'll need a four-wheel-drive vehicle to access the trail.

There's a **campground** at the recreation area, at 6,300 feet. No fee or reservations are required, but your stay must be limited to 5 nights. Tent camping is free, but you'll need a permit. One 10-bunk cabin is available for $45 a night for one to four guests ($5 for each additional guest); it has a cold shower, a gas stove, and no electricity. There is no drinking water available, so bring your own. To reserve, contact the **State Parks Division,** 54 S. High St., Rm. 101, Wailuku, HI 96793 (✆ **808/984-8109** 8am–4pm Mon–Fri; www.hawaii.gov).

POLIPOLI STATE PARK ✪

One of the most unusual hiking experiences in the state can be found at Polipoli State Park, part of the 21,000-acre Kula and Kahikinui Forest Reserve on the slope of Haleakala. At Polipoli, it's hard to believe that you're in Hawaii. First of all, it's cold, even in summer, because the loop is up at 5,300 to 6,200 feet. Second, this former forest of native koa, ohia, and mamane trees, which was overlogged in the 1800s, was reforested in the 1930s with introduced species: pine, Monterey cypress, ash, sugi, red adler, redwood, and several varieties of eucalyptus. The result is a cool area, with muted sunlight filtered by towering trees.

The **Polipoli Loop** ✪ is an easy, 5-mile hike that takes about 3 hours; dress warmly for it. To get here, take the Haleakala Highway (Hwy. 37) to Keokea and turn right onto Highway 337; after less than a half mile, turn on Waipoli Road, which climbs swiftly. After 10 miles, Waipoli Road ends at the Polipoli State Park campground. The well-marked trailhead is next to the parking lot, near a stand of Monterey cypress; the tree-lined trail offers the best view of the island.

The Polipoli Loop is really a network of three trails: Haleakala Ridge, Plum Trail, and Redwood Trail. After a half mile of meandering through groves of eucalyptus, blackwood, swamp mahogany, and hybrid cypress, you'll join the Haleakala Ridge Trail, which, about a mile into the trail, joins with the Plum Trail (named for the plums that ripen in June and July). It passes through massive redwoods and by an old Conservation Corps bunkhouse and a rundown cabin before joining up with the Redwood Trail, which climbs through Mexican pine, tropical ash, Port Orford cedar, and—of course—redwood.

Camping is allowed in the park with a $5-per-night permit from the **Division of State Parks,** 54 S. High St., Rm. 101, Wailuku, HI 96793 (✆ **808/984-8109;** www.hawaii.gov). There's one cabin, available by reservation.

KANAHA BEACH PARK CAMPING

One of the few Maui County camping facilities on the island is Kanaha Beach Park, located next to the Kahului Airport. The county has two separate areas for camping: seven tent sites on the beach and an additional 10 tent sites inland. This well-used park is a favorite of windsurfers, who take advantage of the strong winds that roar across this end of the island. Facilities include a paved parking lot, portable toilets, outdoor showers, barbecue grills, and picnic tables. Camping is limited to no more than 3 consecutive days; the permit fee is $3 per adult and 50¢ for children, per night, and can be obtained from the **Maui County Parks and Recreation Department,** 1580-C Kaahumanu Ave., Wailuku, HI 96793 (© **808/243-7389;** www.mauimapp.com). The 17 sites book up quickly; reserve your dates far in advance (the county will accept reservations a year in advance).

WAIANAPANAPA STATE PARK 🏝🏝

Tucked in a tropical jungle, on the outskirts of the little coastal town of Hana is Waianapanapa State Park, a black-sand beach set in an emerald forest.

HANA-WAIANAPANAPA COAST TRAIL 🏝 This is an easy, 6-mile hike that takes you back in time. Allow 4 hours to walk along this relatively flat trail, which parallels the sea, along lava cliffs and a forest of lauhala trees. The best time of day is in either the early morning or the late evening, when the light on the lava and surf makes for great photos. Midday is the worst time; not only is it hot (lava intensifies the heat), but there's no shade or potable water available. There's no formal trailhead; join the route at any point along the Waianapanapa Campground and go in either direction.

Along the trail, you'll see remains of an ancient *heiau* (temple), stands of lauhala trees, caves, a blowhole, and a remarkable plant, *naupaka,* that flourishes along the beach. Upon close inspection, you'll see that the naupaka has only half-blossoms; according to Hawaiian legend, a similar plant living in the mountains has the other half of the blossoms. One ancient explanation is that the two plants represent never-to-be-reunited lovers: As the story goes, the two lovers bickered so much that the gods, fed up with their incessant quarreling, banished one lover to the mountain and the other to the sea.

CAMPING Waianapanapa has 12 cabins and a tent campground. Go for the cabins, as it rains torrentially here, sometimes turning the campground into a mud-wrestling arena. Tent-camping is $5 per night but limited to 5 nights in a 30-day period. Permits are available from the **State Parks Division,** 54 S. High St., Rm. 101, Wailuku, HI 96793 (© **808/984-8109;** www.hawaii.gov). Facilities include restrooms, outdoor showers, drinking water, and picnic tables.

HANA: THE HIKE TO FAGAN'S CROSS

This 3-mile hike to the cross erected in memory of Paul Fagan, the founder of Hana Ranch and Hotel Hana-Maui, offers spectacular views of the Hana Coast, particularly at sunset. The uphill trail starts across Hana Highway from the Hotel Hana-Maui. Enter the pastures at your own risk; they're often occupied by glaring bulls with sharp horns and cows with new calves. Watch your step as you ascend this steep hill on a Jeep trail across open pastures to the cross and the breathtaking view.

KEANAE ARBORETUM 🏝

About 47 miles from Kahului, along the Hana Highway and just after the Keanae YMCA Camp (and just before the turnoff to the Keanae Peninsula), is an easy family walk through the Keanae Arboretum, which is maintained by the State Department of Land and Natural Resources, Division of Forestry and Wildlife. The walk, which is just over 2 miles, passes through a forest with both native and introduced plants. Allow 1 to 2 hours, longer if you take time out to swim. Take rain gear and mosquito repellent.

Park at the Keanae Arboretum and pass through the turnstile. Walk along the fairly flat Jeep road to the entrance. For a half mile, you will pass by plants introduced to Hawaii (ornamental timber, pomelo, banana, papaya, hibiscus, and more), all with identifying tags. At the end of this section is a taro patch showing the different varieties that Hawaiians used as their staple crop. After the taro, a 1-mile trail leads through a Hawaiian rainforest. The trail crisscrosses a stream as it meanders through the forest. Our favorite swimming hole is just to the left of the first stream crossing, at about 100 yards.

WAIHEE RIDGE ★

This strenuous 3- to 4-mile hike, with a 1,500-foot climb, offers spectacular views of the valleys of the West Maui Mountains. Allow 3 to 4 hours for the round-trip hike. Pack a lunch, carry water, and pick a dry day, as this area is very wet. There's a picnic table at the summit with great views.

To get here from Wailuku, turn north on Market Street, which becomes the Kahekilii Highway (Hwy. 340) and passes through Waihee. Go just over 2½ miles from the Waihee Elementary School and look for the turnoff to the Boy Scouts' Camp Maluhia on the left. Turn into the camp and drive nearly a mile to the trailhead on Jeep road. About a third of a mile in, there will be another gate, marking the entrance to the West Maui Forest Reserve. A foot trail, kept in good shape by the State Department of Land and Natural Resources, begins here. The trail climbs to the top of the ridge, offering great views of the various valleys. The trail is marked by a number of switchbacks and can be extremely muddy and wet. In some areas, it's so steep that you have to grab onto the trees and bushes for support. There's temporary relief to this climb after about 1½ miles, when the trail crosses a flat area (which can be so wet that it's impassable). After the swampy area, the trail ascends again for about a mile to **Lanilili Peak,** where a picnic table and magnificent views await.

4 Great Golf

In some circles, Maui is synonymous with golf. The island's world-famous golf courses start at the very northern tip of the island and roll right around to Kaanapali, jumping down to Kihei and Wailea in the south. There are also some lesser-known municipal courses that offer challenging play for less than $100.

Golfers new to Maui should know that it's windy here, especially between 10am and 2pm, when winds of 10 to 15 mph are the norm. Play two to three clubs up or down to compensate for the wind factor. We also recommend bringing extra balls—the rough is thicker here and the wind will pick your ball up and drop it in very unappealing places (like water hazards).

If your heart is set on playing on a resort course, book at least a week in advance. For the ardent golfer on a tight budget: Play in the afternoon, when discounted twilight rates are in effect. There's no guarantee you'll get 18 holes in, especially in winter when it's dark by 6pm, but you'll have an opportunity to experience these world-famous courses at half the usual fee.

If you don't bring your own, rent clubs from the **Activity Warehouse** (© **800/ 343-2087;** www.travelhawaii.com), which has branches in Lahaina at 602 Front St., near Prison Street (© **808/667-4000**), and in Kihei at Azeka Place II, on the mountain side of Kihei Road near Lipoa Street (© **808/875-4000**). Top-quality clubs go for $15 a day; not-so-top-quality for $10 a day. **Golf Club Rentals** (© **808/665-0800;** www.maui.net/~rentgolf) offers custom-built clubs for men, women, and juniors in both right- and left-handed versions. Their rates are just $15 to $25 a day. The company also offers lessons with pros starting at $125 for nine holes plus green fees.

For last-minute and discount tee times, call **Stand-by Golf** (© **888/645- BOOK,** or 808/874-0600, www.stand-by-golf.com) between 7am and 9pm, Hawaii standard time. Stand-by offers discounted (by 10%–40%) and guaranteed tee times for same-day or next-day golfing.

CENTRAL MAUI

Waiehu Municipal Golf Course *Value*   This public, ocean-side, par-72 golf course is like playing two different courses: The first nine holes, built in 1930, are set along the dramatic coastline, while the back nine holes, added in 1966, head toward the mountains. It's a fun course that probably won't challenge your handicap. The only hazard here is the wind, which can rip off the ocean and play havoc with your ball. The only hole that can raise your blood pressure is the 511-yard, par five, fourth hole, which is very narrow and very long. To par here, you have to hit a long accurate drive, then another long and accurate fairway drive, and finally a perfect pitch over the hazards to the greens (yeah, right).

Facilities include a snack bar, driving range, practice greens, golf-club rental, and clubhouse. Because this is a public course, the greens fees are low—but getting a tee time is tough.

P.O. Box 507, Wailuku, HI 96793. © **808/244-5934.** Greens fees $25 Mon–Fri; $30 Sat–Sun and holidays. From the Kahului Airport, turn right on the Hana Hwy. (Hwy. 36), which becomes Kaahumanu Ave. (Hwy. 32). Turn right at the stoplight at the junction of Waiehu Beach Rd. (Hwy. 340). Go another 1½ miles, and you'll see the entrance on your right.

WEST MAUI

Kaanapali Courses ⚐   Both courses at Kaanapali offer a challenge to all golfers, from high handicappers to near-pros. The par-72, 6,305-yard **North Course** is a true Robert Trent Jones design: an abundance of wide bunkers, several long, stretched-out tees, and the largest, most contoured greens on Maui. The tricky 18th hole (par 4, 435 yd.) has a water hazard on the approach to the green. The par-72, 6,250-yard **South Course** is an Arthur Jack Snyder design; although shorter than the North Course, it requires more accuracy on the narrow, hilly fairways. It also has a water hazard on its final hole, so don't tally up your scorecard until the final putt is sunk.

Facilities include a driving range, putting course, and clubhouse with dining. Weekday tee times are best.

Off Hwy. 30, Kaanapali. © **808/661-3691.** www.kaanapali-golf.com. Greens fees $150 (North Course), $142 (South Course); Kaanapali guests pay $130 (North), $117 (South); twilight rates for the South Course are $85 after noon for everyone; after 2pm twilight rates are $77 (North), $74 (South) for everyone. At the first stoplight in Kaanapali, turn onto Kaanapali Pkwy.; the first building on your right is the clubhouse.

Kapalua Resort Courses ⚐⚐⚐   The views from these three championship courses are worth the greens fees alone. The par-72, 6,761-yard **Bay Course** (© **808/669-8820**) was designed by Arnold Palmer and Ed Seay. This course is a bit forgiving, with its wide fairways; the greens, however, are difficult to read. The well-photographed fifth overlooks a small ocean cove; even the pros have trouble with this rocky par-3, 205-yard hole. The par-71, 6,632-yard **Village Course** (𝒞 808/669-8830), another Palmer/Seay design, is the most scenic of the three courses. The hole with the best vista is the sixth, which overlooks a lake with the ocean in the distance. But don't get distracted by the view—the tee is between two rows of Cook pines. The **Plantation Course** (𝒞 808/669-8877), site of the Mercedes Championships, is a Ben Crenshaw/Bill Coore design. This 6,547-yard, par-73 course, set on a rolling hillside, is excellent for developing your low shots and precise chipping.

Facilities for all three courses include locker rooms, a driving range, and an excellent restaurant. Weekdays are your best bet for tee times.

Off Hwy. 30, Kapalua. 𝒞 877/KAPALUA. Greens fees $180 ($125 for hotel guests) at the Village and Bay courses ($80 after 2pm); $220 ($135 for guests) at the Plantation Course ($85 after 2pm).

SOUTH MAUI

Elleair Maui Golf Club   Sitting in the foothills of Haleakala, just high enough to afford spectacular ocean vistas from every hole, this course (formerly known as the Silversword Golf Club) is for golfers who love the views as much as the fairways and greens. It's very forgiving. ***Just one caveat:*** Go in the morning. Not only is it cooler, but more important, it's also less windy. In the afternoon, the winds bluster down Haleakala with great gusto. This is a fun course to play, with some challenging holes (the par-5, 2nd hole is a virtual minefield of bunkers, and the par-5, 8th hole shoots over a swale and then uphill).

1345 Piilani Hwy. (near Lipoa St. turnoff), Kihei. 𝒞 808/874-0777. Greens fees $85; twilight rates (after 2pm) are $65; 9-hole rates (after 3:30pm) are $45.

Makena Courses ⭐⭐   Here you'll find 36 holes of "Mr. Hawaii Golf"—Robert Trent Jones, Jr.—at its best. Add to that spectacular views: Molokini islet looms in the background, humpback whales gambol offshore in winter, and the tropical sunsets are spectacular. The par-72, 6,876-yard **South Course** has a couple of holes you'll never forget. The view from the par-four 15th hole, which shoots from an elevated tee 183 yards downhill to the Pacific, is magnificent. The 16th hole has a two-tiered green that's blind from the tee 383 yards away (that is, if you make it past the gully off the fairway). The par-72, 6,823-yard **North Course** is more difficult and more spectacular. The 13th hole, located partway up the mountain, has a view that makes most golfers stop and stare. The next hole is even more memorable: a 200-foot drop between tee and green.

Facilities include a clubhouse, a driving range, two putting greens, a pro shop, lockers, and lessons. Beware of weekend crowds.

On Makena Alanui Dr., just past the Maui Prince Hotel. 𝒞 808/879-3344. Greens fees $125 ($90 for Makena Resort guests). Twilight fees (after 2pm) are $85 ($75 for guests).

Wailea Courses ⭐⭐   There are three courses to choose from at Wailea. The **Blue Course,** a par-72, 6,758-yard course designed by Arthur Jack Snyder and dotted with bunkers and water hazards, is for duffers and pros alike. The wide fairways appeal to beginners, while the undulating terrain makes it a course everyone can enjoy. A little more difficult is the par-72, 7,078-yard championship **Gold Course,** with narrow fairways, several tricky dogleg holes, and the classic Robert Trent Jones, Jr. challenges: natural hazards, like lava-rock walls, and native Hawaiian grasses. The **Emerald Course,** also designed by Robert Trent Jones, Jr., is Wailea's newest, with tropical landscaping and a player-friendly design.

With 54 holes to play, getting a tee time is slightly easier on weekends than at other resorts, but weekdays are best (the Emerald Course is usually the toughest to book). Facilities include two pro shops, restaurants, locker rooms, and a complete golf training facility.

Wailea Alanui Dr. (off Wailea Iki Dr.), Wailea. (C) **888/328-MAUI** or 808/875-7450. Greens fees $140 Blue Course ($115 resort guests), twilight $95 ($80 resort guests); $160 Gold Course ($115 resort guests); $150 Emerald Course ($125 resort guests).

UPCOUNTRY MAUI

Pukalani Country Club   This cool, par-72, 6,962-yard course at 1,100 feet offers a break from the resorts' high greens fees, and it's really fun to play. The third hole offers golfers two different options: a tough iron shot from the tee (especially into the wind), across a gully (yuck!) to the green; or a shot down the side of the gully across a second green into sand traps below. (Most people choose to shoot down the side of the gully; it's actually easier than shooting across a ravine.) High handicappers will love this course, and more experienced players can make it more challenging by playing from the back tees. Facilities include club and shoe rentals, practice areas, lockers, a pro shop, and a restaurant.

360 Pukalani St., Pukalani. (C) **808/572-1314.** Greens fees, including cart, $55 for 18 holes before 11am; $45 11am–2pm; $35 after 2pm. Take the Hana Hwy. (Hwy. 36) to Haleakala Hwy. (Hwy. 37) to the Pukalani exit; turn right onto Pukalani St. and go 2 blocks.

5 Biking, Horseback Riding & Other Outdoor Pursuits

BIKING

It's not even close to dawn, but here you are, rubbing your eyes awake, riding in a van up the long, dark road to the top of Maui's sleeping volcano. It's colder than you ever thought possible for a tropical island. The air is thin. You stomp your chilly feet while you wait, sipping hot coffee. Then comes the sun, exploding over the yawning Haleakala Crater, which is big enough to swallow Manhattan whole—it's a mystical moment you won't soon forget, imprinted on a palette of dawn colors. Now you know why Hawaiians named it the House of the Sun. But there's no time to linger: Decked out in your screaming yellow parka, you mount your steed and test its most important feature, the brakes—because you're about to coast 37 miles down a 10,000-foot volcano.

Cruising down Haleakala, from the lunarlike landscape at the top, past flower farms, pineapple fields, and eucalyptus groves, is quite an experience—and you don't have to be an expert cyclist to do it; you just have to be able to ride a bike. This is a safe, comfortable, no-strain bicycle trip, although it requires some stamina in the colder, wetter months between November and March. Wear layers of warm clothing, because there may be a 30°F (16°C) change in temperature from the top of the mountain to the ocean. Generally, tour groups will not take riders under 12, but younger children can ride along in the van that accompanies the groups, as can pregnant women. The trip usually costs between $100 and $140, which includes hotel pickup, transport to the top, bicycle and safety equipment, and meals.

Maui's oldest outfitter is **Maui Downhill** ⚓ ((C) **800/535-BIKE** or 808/871-2155; www.mauidownhill.com), which offers a sunrise safari bike tour, including continental breakfast and brunch, starting at $100. If it's all booked up, try **Maui Mountain Cruisers** ((C) **800/232-6284** or 808/871-6014; www.maui mountaincruisers.com) or **Mountain Riders Bike Tours** ((C) **800/706-7700** or 808/242-9739), each of which offer sunrise rides for $120 to $125.

If you want to avoid the crowd, call **Haleakala Bike Company** (© 888/
922-2453; www.bikemaui.com), which will outfit you with the latest gear and
take you up to the top, but after making sure you are secure on the bike will let
you ride down by yourself at your own pace. Trips range from $55 to $75; they
also have bicycle rentals to tour other parts of Maui on your own.

If you want to venture out on your own, cheap rentals—$10 a day for cruis-
ers and $20 a day for mountain bikes—are available from the **Activity Ware-
house** (© 800/343-2087; www.travelhawaii.com), which has branches in
Lahaina at 602 Front St., near Prison Street (© 808/667-4000), and in Kihei at
Azeka Place II, on the mountain side of Kihei Road near Lipoa Street (© 808/
875-4000).

For information on bikeways and maps, get a copy of the Maui County Bicycle Map, which has information on road suitability, climate, trade winds,
mileage, elevation changes, bike shops, safety tips, and various bicycling routes.
The map is available for $7.50 ($6.25 for the map and $1.25 postage), bank
checks or money orders only, from: Tri Isle R, C, and D Council, Attn: Bike
Map Project, 200 Imi Kala St., Suite 208, Wailuku, HI 96793.

A great book for mountain bikers who want to venture out on their own is
John Alford's *Mountain Biking the Hawaiian Islands,* published by Ohana Publishing (www.bikehawaii.com).

HORSEBACK RIDING

Maui offers spectacular adventure rides through rugged ranchlands, into tropical
forests, and to remote swimming holes. For a 5½-hour tour on horseback—complete with swimming and lunch—call **Adventure on Horseback** ⚡ (© 808/
242-7445 or 808/572-6211; www.mauihorsewhisperer.com); the cost is $185
per person, including a hearty lunch. The day begins over coffee and pastries,
while owner Frank Levinson matches the horses to the riders in terms of skill and
personality. Frank leads small groups across pastures, through thick rainforests,
alongside streams, and up to waterfalls and pools. Frank recently added a "Maui
Horse Whisperer Experience," which includes a seminar on the language of the
horse, a morning snack, a big lunch, and an afternoon trail ride for $300 per per-
son ($200 for ½ day; both versions can be extended with an optional ride for
$50). No horse lover should pass it up.

If you're out in Hana, **Oheo Stables,** Kipahulu Ranch (a mile past Oheo
Gulch), Kipahulu (© 808/667-2222; www.mauihorse.com), offers two daily
rides through the mountains above Oheo Gulch (Seven Sacred Pools). The best
deal is the 10:30am ride ($119), which includes a snack during the 3-hour adven-
ture (2½ hr. in the saddle) into Haleakala National Park. You'll stop at scenic
spots like Pipiwai Lookout, where you can glimpse the 400-foot Waimoku Falls.
If you enjoy your ride, remember to kiss your horse and tip your guide.

HALEAKALA ON HORSEBACK If you'd like to ride down into Haleakala's
crater, contact **Pony Express Tours** ⚡ (© 808/667-2200 or 808/878-6698;
www.ponyexpresstours.com), which offers a variety of rides down to the crater
floor and back up, from $155 to $190 per person. Shorter 1- and 2-hour rides
are also offered at Haleakala Ranch, located on the beautiful lower slopes of the
volcano, for $60 and $105. If you book via the Internet, you get 10% off. Pony
Express provides well-trained horses and experienced guides, and accommodates
all riding levels. You must be at least 10 years old, weigh no more than 230
pounds, and wear long pants and closed-toe shoes.

WAY OUT WEST ON MAUI: RANCH RIDES   We recommend riding with **Mendes Ranch & Trail Rides** ✦, 3530 Kahekili Hwy., 4 miles past Wailuku (✆ **808/244-7320;** www.maui.net/~mendes). The 300-acre Mendes Ranch is a real-life working cowboy ranch that has the essential elements of an earthly paradise—rainbows, waterfalls, palm trees, coral-sand beaches, lagoons, tide pools, a rainforest, and its own volcanic peak (more than a mile high). Allan Mendes, a third-generation wrangler, will take you from the edge of the rainforest out to the sea. On the way, you'll cross tree-studded meadows where Texas longhorns sit in the shade and pass a dusty corral where Allan's father, Ernest, a champion roper, may be breaking in a wild horse. Allan keeps close watch, turning often in his saddle to make sure everyone is happy. He points out flora and fauna and fields questions, but generally just lets you soak up Maui's natural splendor in golden silence. The morning ride, which lasts 3 hours and ends with a barbecue back at the corral (the perfect ranch-style lunch after a morning in the saddle), is $130; the 2½-hour afternoon ride costs $85, including snacks.

SPELUNKING

Don't miss the opportunity to see how the Hawaiian Islands were made by exploring a million-year-old underground lava tube/cave. Chuck Thorne, of **Maui Cave Adventures** ✦ (✆ **808/248-7308;** www.mauicave.com), offers several tours of this unique geological feature. After more than 10 years of leading scuba tours through underwater caves around Hawaii, Chuck discovered some caves on land that he wanted to show visitors. When the land surrounding the largest cave on Maui went on the market in 1996, Chuck snapped it up and started his own tour company. His 75-minute walking tour ($29; no children under 8) is a fun, safe, and easy stroll through a huge, extinct lava tube with 40-foot ceilings. This is a geology lesson you won't soon forget—Chuck is a longtime student of the science of volcano-speleology and can discuss every little formation in the cave, how it came to be, and what its purpose is. He supplies all the equipment you'll need: lights, hard hats, gloves, and water bottles. For those looking for a longer experience, his "Wild Adventure Tours" are 2½ hours and cost $69 (no one under 15). Wear long pants and closed shoes, and bring your camera.

If you want to combine caving with a tour of Hana, contact **Temptation Tours** (✆ **808/877-8888**). Their "Cave Quest" tour offers not only a 2-hour cave tour, but also an air-conditioned van tour from your hotel to Hana; the $169 cost includes continental breakfast, beachside picnic lunch, and a stop for a swim.

TENNIS

Maui has excellent public tennis courts; all are free and available from daylight to sunset (a few are even lit for night play until 10pm). The courts are available on a first-come, first-served basis; when someone's waiting, limit your play to 45 minutes. For a complete list of public courts, call **Maui County Parks and Recreation** (✆ **808/243-7230**). Because most public courts require a wait and are not conveniently located near the major resort areas, most visitors pay a fee to play at their own hotels. The exceptions to that rule are in Kihei (which has courts in Kalama Park on S. Kihei Rd., and in Waipualani Park on W. Waipualani Rd., behind the Maui Sunset Condo), in Lahaina (courts are in Malu'uou o lele Park, at Front and Shaw sts.), and Hana (courts are in Hana Park, on the Hana Hwy.).

Private tennis courts are available at most resorts and hotels on the island. The **Kapalua Tennis Garden and Village Tennis Center,** Kapalua Resort (✆ **808/ 669-5677;** www.kapaluamaui.com), is home to the Kapalua Open, which features the largest purse in the state, on Labor Day weekend. Court rentals are $10 an hour for resort guests and $12 an hour for nonguests. The staff will match you up with a partner if you need one. In Wailea, try the **Wailea Tennis Club,** 131 Wailea Iki Place (© **808/879-1958**), with 11 Plexi-pave courts. Court fees are $27 for Wailea resort guests and $35 for nonguests.

Seeing the Sights

After a few days of just relaxing on the beach, the itch to explore the rest of Maui sets in: What's on top of Haleakala, looming in the distance? Is the road to Hana really the tropical jungle everyone raves about? What does the inside of a 19th-century whaling boat look like?

There is far more to the Valley Isle than just sun, sand, and surf. Get out and see for yourself the otherworldly interior of a 10,000-foot volcanic crater; watch endangered sea turtles make their way to nesting sites in a wildlife sanctuary; wander back in time to the days when whalers and missionaries fought for the soul of Lahaina; and feel the energy of a thundering waterfall cascade into a serene mountain pool.

1 By Air, Land & Sea: Guided Island Adventures

Admittedly, the adventures below aren't cheap. However, each one offers such a wonderful opportunity to see Maui from a unique perspective that, depending on your interests, you might make one of them the highlight of your trip—it'll be worth every penny.

FLYING HIGH: HELICOPTER RIDES

Only a helicopter can bring you face-to-face with remote sites like Maui's little-known Wall of Tears, up near the summit of Puu Kukui in the West Maui Mountains. A helicopter ride on Maui isn't a wild ride; it's more like a gentle gee-whiz zip into a seldom-seen Eden. You'll glide through canyons etched with 1,000-foot waterfalls, and over dense rainforests; you'll climb to 10,000 feet, high enough to glimpse the summit of Haleakala, and fly by the dramatic vistas at Molokai.

The first chopper pilots in Hawaii were good ol' boys on their way back from Vietnam—hard-flying, hard-drinking cowboys who cared more about the ride than the scenery. But not anymore. Today, pilots, like the ones at Blue Hawaiian (see below), are an interesting hybrid: part Hawaiian historian, part DJ, part tour guide, and part amusement-ride operator. As you soar through the clouds, absorbing Maui's scenic terrain, you'll learn about the island's flora, fauna, history, and culture.

Among the many helicopter-tour operators on Maui, the best is **Blue Hawaiian** ★★, at Kahului Airport (✆ **800/745-BLUE** or 808/871-8844; www.blue hawaiian.com), which not only takes you on the ride of your life, but also entertains, educates, and leaves you with an experience you'll never forget. Blue Hawaiian also is the only helicopter company in the state to have the latest, high-tech, environmentally friendly (and quiet) Eco-Star helicopter, specially designed for air-tour operators. Flights vary from 30 to 100 minutes and range from $150 to $335. A keepsake video of your flight is available for $20 (so your friends at home can ooh and aah).

If Blue Hawaiian is booked, try **Sunshine Helicopters** (✆ **800/544-2520** or 808/871-0722; www.sunshinehelicopters.com), which offers a variety of flights from short hops around the West Maui Mountains to island tours. Prices range from $125 to $235.

GOING UNDER: SUBMARINE RIDES

Plunge 100 feet under the sea in a state-of-the-art, high-tech submarine and meet swarms of vibrant tropical fish up close and personal as they flutter through the deep blue waters off Lahaina. **Atlantis Submarines,** 665 Front St., Lahaina (© **800/548-6262** or 808/667-7816), offers trips out of Lahaina Harbor every hour on the hour from 9am to 1pm; tickets range from $70 to $80 for adults and $40 for children under 12 (children must be at least 3 ft. tall). Allow 2 hours for this underwater adventure.

ECOTOURS

Venture into the lush West Maui Mountains with an experienced guide on one of the numerous hikes offered by **Maui Eco-Adventures** (© **877/661-7720** or 808/661-7720; www.ecomaui.com). After a continental breakfast, you'll hike by streams and waterfalls, through native trees and plants, and on to breathtaking vistas. The tour stops for a picnic lunch, swims in secluded pools, and memorable photo ops. The 6-hour excursion costs $110 per person, including meals, a fanny pack with bottled water, and rain gear if necessary. No children under 13 are allowed.

About 1,500 years ago, the verdant Kahakuloa Valley was a thriving Hawaiian village. Today, only a few hundred people live in this secluded hamlet, but old Hawaii still lives on here. Explore the valley with **Ekahi Tours** (© **888/292-2422** or 808/877-9775). Your guide, a Kahakuloa resident and a Hawaiiana expert, walks you through a taro farm, explains the mystical legends of the valley, and provides you with a peek into ancient Hawaii. The 7½-hour Kahakuloa Valley Tour is $65 for adults, $50 for children under 12; snacks, beverages, and hotel pickup are included.

2 Central Maui

Central Maui isn't exactly tourist central; this is where real people live. You'll most likely land here and head directly to the beach. However, there are a few sights worth checking out if you need a respite from the sun and surf.

KAHULUI

Under the airport flight path, next to Maui's busiest intersection and across from Costco and Kmart in Kahului's new business park, is the most unlikely place: **Kanaha Wildlife Sanctuary,** Haleakala Highway Extension and Hana Highway (© **808/984-8100**). Look for a parking area off Haleakala Highway Extension (behind the mall, across the Hana Hwy. from Cutter Automotive), and you'll find a 50-yard trail that meanders along the shore to a shade shelter and lookout. Watch for the sign proclaiming this the permanent home of the endangered black-neck Hawaiian stilt, whose population is now down to between 1,000 and 1,500. Naturalists say this is a good place to see endangered Hawaiian Koloa ducks, stilts, coots, and other migrating shorebirds. For a quieter, more natural-looking wildlife preserve, try the **Kealia Pond National Wildlife Preserve** in Kihei (p. 198).

PUUNENE

This town, located in the middle of the central Maui plains, is nearly gone. Once a thriving sugar-plantation town with hundreds of homes, a school, a shopping area, and a community center, today Puunene is little more than the sugar mill, a post office, and a museum. The Hawaiian Commercial & Sugar

Co., owner of the land and the mill, has slowly phased out the rental plantation housing to open up more land to plant sugar.

Alexander & Baldwin Sugar Museum   This former sugar-mill superintendent's home has been converted into a museum that tells the story of sugar in Hawaii. Exhibits explain how sugar is grown, harvested, and milled. An eye-opening display shows how Samuel Alexander and Henry Baldwin managed to acquire huge chunks of land from the Kingdom of Hawaii and how they ruthlessly fought to gain access to water on the other side of the island, making sugarcane an economically viable crop. Allow about a half hour to enjoy the museum.

Puunene Ave. (Hwy. 350) and Hansen Rd. ⓒ **808/871-8058.** Admission $5 adults, $2 children 6–17, free for children 5 and under. Daily 9:30am–4:30pm.

WAIKAPU

Across the sugar cane fields from Puunene, and about 3 miles south of Wailuku on the Honoapiilani Highway, lies the tiny, one-street village of Waikapu, which has two attractions that are worth a peek, especially if you're trying to kill time before your flight out.

Relive Maui's past by taking a 40-minute narrated tram ride around fields of pineapple, sugar cane, and papaya trees at **Maui Tropical Plantation,** 1670 Honoapiilani Hwy,, Waikapu (ⓒ **800/451-6805** or 808/244-7643), a real working plantation open daily from 9am to 5pm. A shop sells fresh and dried fruit, and a restaurant serves lunch. Admission is free; the tram tours, which start at 10am and leave about every 45 minutes, are $9.50 for adults, $4.50 for kids 3 to 12.

Marilyn Monroe and Frank Lloyd Wright meet for dinner every night (well, sort of) at the **Waikapu Golf and Country Club,** 2500 Honoapiilani Hwy. (ⓒ **808/244-2011**), one of Maui's most unusual buildings. Neither actually set foot on Maui, but these icons of glamour and architecture share a Hawaiian legacy. Wright designed this place for a Pennsylvania family in 1949, but it was never constructed. In 1957, Marilyn and husband Arthur Miller wanted it built for them in Connecticut, but they separated the following year. When Tokyo billionaire Takeshi Sekiguchi went shopping at Taliesen West for a signature building to adorn his 18-hole golf course, he found the blueprints and had Marilyn's Wright house cleverly redesigned as a clubhouse. A horizontal in a vertical landscape, it doesn't quite fit the setting, but it's still the best-looking building on Maui today. You can walk in and look around at Wright's architecture and the portraits of Marilyn in Monroe's, the restaurant.

WAILUKU

This historic gateway to Iao Valley (see below) is worth a visit, if only for a brief stop at the Bailey House Museum and some terrific shopping (see chapter 8).

Bailey House Museum ⭐   Missionary and sugar planter Edward Bailey's 1833 home—an architectural hybrid of stones laid by Hawaiian craftsmen and timbers joined in a display of Yankee ingenuity—is a treasure trove of Hawaiiana. Inside, you'll find an eclectic collection, from precontact artifacts like scary temple images, dog-tooth necklaces, and a rare lei made of tree-snail shells to latter-day relics like Duke Kahanamoku's 1919 redwood surfboard and a koa-wood table given to Pres. Ulysses S. Grant, who had to refuse it because he couldn't accept gifts from foreign countries. There's also a gallery devoted to a few of Bailey's landscapes, painted from 1866 to 1896, which capture on canvas a Maui we can only imagine today.

2375-A Main St. ⓒ **808/244-3326.** Admission $4 adults, $3.50 seniors, $1 children 7–12, free for children 6 and under. Mon–Sat 10am–4pm.

IAO VALLEY

A couple of miles north of Wailuku, past the Bailey House Museum, where the little plantation houses stop and the road climbs ever higher, Maui's true nature begins to reveal itself. The transition between suburban sprawl and raw nature is so abrupt that most people who drive up into the valley don't realize they're suddenly in a rainforest. The walls of the canyon begin to close around them, and a 2,250-foot needle pricks gray clouds scudding across the blue sky. After the hot tropic sun, the air is moist and cool, and the shade a welcome comfort. This is Iao Valley, a 6-acre state park whose great nature, history, and beauty have been enjoyed by millions of people from around the world for more than a century.

Iao ("Supreme Light") Valley, 10 miles long and encompassing 4,000 acres, is the eroded volcanic caldera of the West Maui Mountains. The head of the Iao Valley is a broad circular amphitheater where four major streams converge into Iao Stream. At the back of the amphitheater is rain-drenched Puu Kukui, the West Maui Mountains' highest point. No other Hawaiian valley lets you go from seacoast to rainforest so easily. This peaceful valley, full of tropical plants, rainbows, waterfalls, swimming holes, and hiking trails, is a place of solitude, reflection, and escape for residents and visitors alike.

From Wailuku, take Main Street, then turn right on Iao Valley Road to the entrance to the state park. The park is open daily from 7am to 7pm. Go early in the morning or late in the afternoon, when the sun's rays slant into the valley and create a mystical atmosphere. You can bring a picnic and spend the day, but be prepared at any time for a tropical cloudburst, which often soaks the valley and swells both waterfalls and streams.

For information, contact **Iao Valley State Park,** State Parks and Recreation, 54 S. High St., Rm. 101, Wailuku, HI 96793 (© **808/984-8109;** www.hawaii.gov). The **Hawaii Nature Center** ✿, 875 Iao Valley Rd. (© **808/244-6500;** www. hawaiinaturecenter.org), home of the Iao Valley Nature Center, features hands-on, interactive exhibits and displays relating the story of Hawaiian natural history; it's an important stop for all who want to explore Iao Valley. Hours are daily from 10am to 4pm; admission is $6 for adults and $4 for children 4 to 12, under 4 free.

Two paved walkways loop into the massive green amphitheater, across the bridge of Iao Stream, and along the stream itself. The one-third-mile loop on a paved trail is an easy walk—you can even take your grandmother on this one. A leisurely stroll will allow you to enjoy lovely views of the Iao Needle and the lush vegetation. Others often proceed beyond the state park border and take two trails deeper into the valley, but the trails enter private land, and NO TRESPASS-ING signs are posted.

The feature known as **Iao Needle** is an erosional remnant composed of basalt dikes. The phallic rock juts an impressive 2,250 feet above sea level. Youngsters play in **Iao Stream,** a peaceful brook that belies its bloody history. In 1790, King Kamehameha the Great and his men engaged in the bloody battle of Iao Valley to gain control of Maui. When the battle ended, so many bodies blocked Iao Stream that the battle site was named Kepaniwai, or "damming of the waters." An architectural heritage park of Hawaiian, Japanese, Chinese, Filipino, and New England–style houses stands in harmony by Iao Stream at **Kepaniwai Heritage Garden.** This is a good picnic spot, as there are plenty of picnic tables and benches. You can see ferns, banana trees, and other native and exotic plants in the **Iao Valley Botanic Garden** along the stream.

3 Lahaina & West Maui

OLOWALU

Most people drive right by Olowalu, on the Honoapiilani Highway 5 miles south of Lahaina; there's little to mark the spot but a small general store and Chez Paul, an expensive, but excellent, French restaurant. Olowalu ("many hills") was the scene of a bloody massacre in 1790. The Hawaiians, fascinated with iron nails and fittings, stole a skiff from the U.S.S. *Eleanora,* took it back to shore here, and burned it for the iron parts. The captain of the ship, Simon Metcalf, was furious and tricked the Hawaiians into sailing out in their canoes to trade with the ship. As the canoes approached, he mowed them down with his cannons, killing 100 people and wounding many others.

Olowalu has great snorkeling around **mile marker 14,** where there is a turtle-cleaning station about 50 to 75 yards out from shore. Turtles line up here to have cleaner wrasses (small bony fish) pick off small parasites.

HISTORIC LAHAINA

Located between the West Maui Mountains and the deep azure ocean offshore, Lahaina stands out as one of the few places in Hawaii that has managed to preserve its 19th-century heritage while still accommodating 21st-century guests.

In ancient times, powerful chiefs and kings ruled this hot, dry ocean-side village. At the turn of the 19th century, after King Kamehameha united the Hawaiian Islands, he made Lahaina the royal capital—which it remained until 1845, when Kamehameha III moved the capital to the larger port of Honolulu.

In the 1840s, the whaling industry was at its peak: Hundreds of ships called into Lahaina every year. The streets were filled with sailors 24 hours a day. Even Herman Melville, who later wrote *Moby-Dick,* was among the throngs of whalers in Lahaina.

Just 20 years later, the whaling industry was waning, and sugar had taken over the town. The Pioneer Sugar Mill Co., which still stands but no longer operates today, reigned over Lahaina for the next 100 years.

Today the drunken and derelict whalers who wandered through Lahaina's streets in search of bars, dance halls, and brothels have been replaced by hordes of tourists crowding into the small mile-long main section of town in search of

---

Day Trips to Molokai

It's possible to visit Molokai's famous leper colony (officially known as Kalaupapa National Historic Park) as a day trip from Maui. You won't be able to squeeze in the exhilarating mule ride down the 1,600-foot cliffs (they start at 8am), but you didn't want to sit on your own ass all day long anyway, now did you? (Sorry, bad pun.) **Pacific Wings** (© 808/873-0877; www.pacificwings.com) offers daily scheduled flights to Kalaupapa from Honolulu for $163 roundtrip or check out **Paragon Air** (© 808/244-3356; www.paragon-air.com), which offers a $210 package deal that includes round-trip airfare from Kahului Airport to Molokai's Kalaupapa airport, a 4-hour tour, lunch, and drinks. All visitors must be at least 16 years old. Or you can take a ferry ride over to Molokai and then hike down to Kalaupapa and tour the legendary peninsula on the **Molokai Princess** (© 800/275-6969 or 808/667-6165 or www.mauiprincess.com) for $215 per person, including lunch.

boutiques, art galleries, and chic gourmet eateries. Lahaina's colorful past continues to have a profound influence today. This is no quiet seaside village, but a vibrant, cutting-edge kind of place, filled with a sense of history—but definitely with its mind on the future.

See chapter 6 for details on the various cruises and outfitters operating out of Lahaina.

Baldwin Home Museum ☆   The oldest house in Lahaina, this coral-and-rock structure was built in 1834 by Rev. Dwight Baldwin, a doctor with the fourth company of American missionaries to sail round the Horn to Hawaii. Like many missionaries, he came to Hawaii to do good—and did very well for himself. After 17 years of service, Baldwin was granted 2,600 acres in Kapalua for farming and grazing. His ranch manager experimented with what Hawaiians called *hala-kahiki,* or pineapple, on a 4-acre plot; the rest is history. The house looks as if Baldwin has just stepped out for a minute to tend a sick neighbor down the street.

Next door is the **Masters' Reading Room,** Maui's oldest building. This became visiting sea captains' favorite hangout once the missionaries closed down all of Lahaina's grog shops and banned prostitution; but by 1844, once hotels and bars started reopening, it lost its appeal. It's now the headquarters of the **Lahaina Restoration Foundation** (✆ **808/661-3262**), a plucky band of historians who try to keep this town alive and antique at the same time. Stop in and pick up a self-guided walking-tour map, which will take you to Lahaina's most historic sites.

120 Dickenson St. (at Front St.). ✆ **808/661-3262**. Admission $3 adults, $2 seniors, $5 family. Daily 10am–4:30pm.

Banyan Tree (Kids)   Of all the banyan trees in Hawaii, this is the greatest of all—so big that you can't get it in your camera's viewfinder. It was only 8 feet tall when it was planted in 1873 by Maui Sheriff William O. Smith to mark the 50th anniversary of Lahaina's first Christian mission; now the big old banyan from India is more than 50 feet tall, has 12 major trunks, and shades two-thirds of an acre in Courthouse Square.

At the Courthouse Building, 649 Wharf St.

The Brig Carthaginian ☆ (Kids)   This restored square-rigged brigantine, an authentic replica of a 19th-century whaling ship, the kind that brought the first missionaries to Hawaii, was closed for "repairs" when we went to press. Apparently the old vessel has become a liability, and the people in charge were leaning towards getting rid of the old boat versus repairing her. As we went to press, history lovers were frantically trying to raise funds to either restore the old ship or purchase another replica of the same era. If you don't see her proud masts at the foot of the Lahaina Pier, then you know her fate. If the ship is still there, drop by; the floating museum features exhibits on whales and 19th-century whaling life. You won't believe how cramped the living quarters were—they make today's cruise-ship cabins look downright roomy.

Lahaina Harbor. ✆ **808/661-8527**. Admission $3 adults, $2 seniors, $5 family. Daily 10am–4:30pm.

Hale Pai   When the missionaries arrived in Hawaii to spread the word of God, they found the Hawaiians had no written language. They quickly rectified the situation by converting the Hawaiian sounds into a written language. They then built the first printing press in order to print educational materials that would assist them on their mission. Hale Pai was the printing house for the Lahainaluna Seminary, the oldest American school west of the Rockies. Today Lahainaluna is the public high school for the children of West Maui.

Lahaina

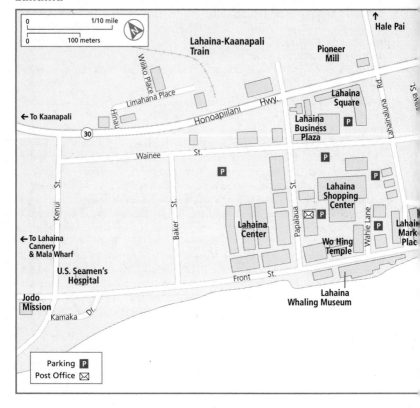

Lahainaluna High School Campus, 980 Lahainaluna Rd. (at the top of the mountain). © **808/661-3262**. Free admission. Mon–Fri by appointment only.

Lahaina Jodo Mission   This site has long been held sacred. The Hawaiians called it Puunoa Point, which means "the hill freed from taboo." Once a small village named "Mala" ("garden"), this peaceful place was a haven for Japanese immigrants, who came to Hawaii in 1868 as laborers for the sugar cane plantations. They eventually built a small wooden temple to worship here. In 1968, on the 100th anniversary of the Japanese in Hawaii, a Great Buddha statue, the largest outside of Japan (some 12 ft. high and weighing 3½ tons) was brought here from Japan. The immaculate grounds also contain a replica of the original wooden temple and a 90-foot-tall pagoda.

12 Ala Moana St. (off Front St., near the Mala Wharf). © **808/661-4304**. Free admission. Daily during daylight hours.

Maluuluolele Park (Kids)   At first glance, this Front Street park appears to be only a hot, dry, dusty softball field. But under home plate is the edge of Mokuula, where a royal compound once stood more than 100 years ago, now buried under tons of red dirt and sand. Here, Prince Kauikeaolui, who ascended the throne as King Kamehameha III when he was only 10, lived with the love of his life, his sister Princess Nahienaena. Missionaries took a dim view of incest, which was acceptable to Hawaiian nobles in order to preserve the royal bloodlines. Torn between love for

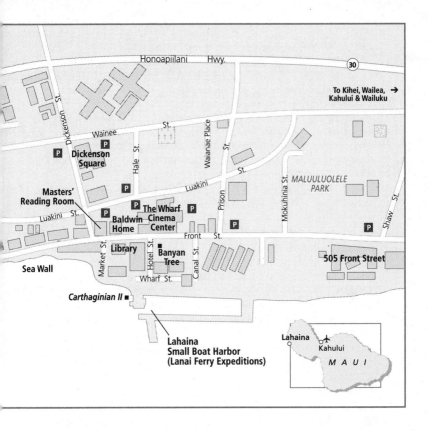

her brother and the new Christian morality, Nahienaena grew despondent and died at the age of 21. King Kamehameha III, who reigned for 29 years—longer than any other Hawaiian monarch—presided over Hawaii as it went from kingdom to constitutional monarchy, and absolute power over the islands began to transfer from island nobles to missionaries, merchants, and sugar planters. Kamehameha died in 1854 at the age of 39. In 1918, his royal compound, containing a mausoleum and artifacts of the kingdom, was demolished and covered with dirt to create a public park. The baseball team from Lahainaluna School now plays games on the site of this royal place, still considered sacred to many Hawaiians.

Front and Shaw sts.

Wo Hing Temple ✿ The Chinese were among the various immigrants brought to Hawaii to work in the sugar cane fields. In 1909, several Chinese workers formed the Wo Hing society, a chapter of the Chee Kun Tong society, which dates from the 17th century. In 1912, they built this social hall for the Chinese community. Completely restored, the Wo Hing Temple contains displays and artifacts on the history of the Chinese in Lahaina; next door in the old cookhouse is a theater with movies of Hawaii taken by Thomas Edison in 1898 and 1903.

Front St. (between Wahie Lane and Papalaua St.). © **808/661-3262.** Admission by donation. Daily 10am–4pm.

Where to Park for Free—or Next to Free—in Lahaina

Lahaina is the worst place on Maui for parking. The town was created and filled with shops, restaurants, and historic sites before the throngs of tourists (and their cars) invaded. Street parking is hit-or-miss. You can either drive around the block for hours looking for a free place to park on the street or park in one of the nearly 20 parking lots. We've divided the lots into four classes: free; free for customers; discount with validation; and pay.

Free: Of the free lots, the best is the public lot on the south side of Prison Street, between Front and Luakini streets (the lot across the street is pay), which offers 3 hours of free parking. Another free lot is on the corner of Front and Shaw streets, for the users of Maluuluolele Park.

Free for Customers: The three lots on Papalaua Street are all free for customers. The largest is the Lahaina Shopping Center lot, with 2 free hours. Next in size is the Lahaina Center, across the street (which allows 4 hr. free, but you must get validation from a store in the Lahaina Center); the smallest is the Lahaina Square lot on Papalaua and Wainee streets, which offers 2 free hours for customers.

Discount with Validation: Customers of the Wharf Cinema Center, located on Front Street, can get a discount by parking at either of the theater's two lots: one on Wainee Street, between Dickenson and Prison streets; and the other on Luakini Street, between Dickenson and Prison streets.

Pay: Lahaina is filled with pay lots ranging from 50¢ for a half hour to all-day parking for $8 to $10. Pay lots on Front Street are located between Papalaua and Lahainaluna streets, on the corner of Dickenson Street, and underground at the 505 Front Street shopping center. Pay lots on Luakini Street are located near the Prison Street intersection and near the Lahainaluna Road intersection. Lahainaluna Road has several pay lots between Wainee and Front streets. Dickenson Street has three pay lots between Wainee and Luakini streets.

WALKING TOUR   **HISTORIC LAHAINA**

Getting There:	From the Kahului Airport, take the Kuihelani Highway (Hwy. 38) to the intersection of Honoapiilani Highway (Hwy. 30), where you turn left. Follow Honoapiilani Highway to Lahaina and turn left on Lahainaluna Road. When Lahainaluna Road ends, make a left on Front Street. Dickenson Street is a block down (see the box on parking, above).
Start:	Front and Dickenson streets.
Finish:	Same location.
Time:	About an hour.

Back when "there was no God west of the Horn," Lahaina was the capital of Hawaii and the Pacific's wildest port. Today it's a mild, mollified version of its old self—mostly a hustle-bustle of whale art, timeshares, and "Just Got Lei'd" T-shirts.

1 Masters' Reading Room
2 Baldwin Home
3 Richards House
4 Taro Patch
5 Hauola Stone
6 Brick Palace
7 Carthaginian II
8 Pioneer Inn
9 Banyan Tree

10 Courthouse
11 Fort
12 Canal
13 Government Market
14 Innocents Episcopal Church
15 Hale Piula
16 Maluuluolele Park
17 Wainee Church

18 Waihee Cemetery
19 Hongwanji Mission
20 David Malo's Home
21 Old Prison
22 Episcopal Cemetery
23 Hale Aloha
24 Buddhist Church
25 Luakini Street

We're not sure the rowdy whalers would have been pleased. But, if you look hard, you'll still find the historic port town they loved, filled with the kind of history that inspired James Michener to write his best-selling epic novel *Hawaii.*

Members of the Lahaina Restoration Foundation have worked for 3 decades to preserve Lahaina's past. They have marked a number of historical sites with brown-and-white markers; below, we've provided explanations of the significance of each site as you walk through Lahaina's historic past.

Begin your tour at the:

❶ Masters' Reading Room

This coral-and-stone building looks just as it did in 1834, when Rev. William Richards and Rev. E. Spaulding convinced the whaling-ship captains that they needed a place for the ships' masters and captains, many of whom traveled with their families, to stay while they were ashore. The bottom floor was used as a storage area for the mission; the top floor, from which you could see the ships at anchor in the harbor, was for the visiting ships' officers.

Next door is the:

❷ Baldwin Home

Harvard-educated physician Rev. Dwight Baldwin, with his wife of just a few weeks, sailed to Hawaii from New England in 1830. Baldwin was first assigned to a church in Waimea, on the Big Island, and then to Lahaina's Wainee Church in 1838. He and his family lived in this house until

1871. The Baldwin Home and the Masters' Reading Room are the oldest standing buildings in Lahaina, made from thick walls of coral and hand-milled timber. Baldwin also ran his medical office and his missionary activities out of this house. (See the Baldwin Home Museum, p. 187, for information on hours and admission.)

On the other side of the Baldwin Home is the former site of the:

❸ Richards House

The open field is empty today, but it represents the former home of Lahaina's first Protestant missionary, Rev. William Richards, who had quite an influence on the Kingdom of Hawaii. Richards went on to become the chaplain, teacher, and translator to Kamehameha III. He was also instrumental in drafting Hawaii's constitution and acted as the king's envoy to the United States and England, seeking recognition of Hawaii as an independent nation. After his death in 1847, he was buried in the Wainee Churchyard.

From here, cross Front Street and walk toward the ocean, with the Lahaina Public Library on your right and the green Pioneer Inn on your left, until you see the:

❹ Taro Patch

The lawn in front of the Lahaina Library was once a taro patch stretching back to the Baldwin Home. The taro plant was a staple of the Hawaiian diet: The root was used to make poi, and the leaves were used in cooking. At one time, Lahaina looked like Venice of the tropics, with streams, ponds, and waterways flooding the taro fields. As the population of the town grew, the water was siphoned off for drinking water.

Walk away from the Lahaina Harbor toward the edge of the lawn, where you'll see the:

❺ Hauola Stone

Hawaiians believed that certain stones placed in sacred places had the power to heal. Kahuna (priests) of medicine used stones like this to help cure illnesses.

Turn around and walk back toward the Pioneer Inn; look for the concrete depression in the ground, which is all that's left of the:

❻ Brick Palace

This structure was begun in 1798 as the first Western-style building in Hawaii. King Kamehameha I had this 20-by-40-foot, two-story brick structure built for his wife, Queen Kaahumanu (who is said to have preferred a grass thatched house nearby). Inside, the walls were constructed of wood and the windows were glazed glass. Kamehameha I lived here from 1801 to 1802, when he was building his war canoe, *Peleleu,* and preparing to invade Kauai. A handmade stone seawall surrounded the palace to protect it from the surf. The building stood for 70 years; in addition to being a royal compound, it was also used as a meeting house, storeroom, and warehouse.

Behind you, dockside of the loading pier of the Lahaina Harbor, is the:

❼ *Carthaginian*

This is a replica of a 19th-century brig, which carried commerce back and forth to Hawaii. It also serves as a museum and exhibit of 19th-century boating and whaling. (For details on hours and fees, see the listing for the Brig *Carthaginian* on p. 187.)

Directly opposite the Carthaginian is the:

❽ Pioneer Inn

Lahaina's first hotel was the scene of some wild parties at the turn of the 20th century. George Freeland, of the Royal Canadian Mounted Police, tracked a criminal to Lahaina and then fell in love with the town. He built the hotel in 1901 but soon discovered that Lahaina wasn't the tourist mecca it is today. To make ends meet, Freeland built a movie theater, which was wildly successful. The Pioneer Inn remained the only hotel in all of West Maui until the 1950s. You can stay at this restored building today (see chapter 4).

From the Pioneer Inn, cross Hotel Street and walk along Wharf Street, which borders the harbor. On your left is the:

9 Banyan Tree

This ancient tree has witnessed decades of luaus, dances, concerts, private chats, public rallies, and resting sojourners under its mighty boughs. Hard to believe that this huge tree was only 8 feet tall when it was planted here. (See p. 187 for a complete listing.)

Continue along Wharf Street; near the edge of the park is the:

10 Courthouse

In 1858, a violent windstorm destroyed about 20 buildings in Lahaina, including Hale Piula, which served as the courthouse and palace of King Kamehameha III. It was rebuilt immediately, using the stones from the previous building; it served not only as courthouse, but also as custom house, post office, tax collector's office, and government offices.

Continue down Wharf Street to Canal Street. On the corner are the remains of the:

11 Fort

This structure once covered an acre and had 20-foot-high walls. In 1830, some whalers fired a few cannonballs into Lahaina in protest of Rev. William Richards's meddling in their affairs. (Richards had convinced Governor Hoapili to create a law forbidding the women of Lahaina from swimming out to greet the whaling ships.) The fort was constructed from 1831 to 1832 with coral blocks taken from the ocean where the Lahaina Harbor sits today. As a further show of strength, cannons were placed along the waterfront, where they remain today. Historical accounts seem to scoff at the "fort," saying it appeared to be more for show than force. It was later used as a prison, until it was finally torn down in the 1850s; its stones were used for construction of the new prison, Hale Paahao (see no. 21 below).

Cross Canal Street to the:

12 Canal

Unlike Honolulu with its natural deepwater harbor, Lahaina was merely a roadstead with no easy access to the shore. Whalers would anchor in deep water offshore, then board smaller boats (which they used to chase down and harpoon whales) to make the passage over the reef to shore. If the surf was up, coming ashore could be dangerous. In the 1840s, the U.S. consular representative recommended digging a canal from one of the freshwater streams that ran through Lahaina and charging a fee to the whalers who wanted to obtain fresh water. In 1913, the canal was filled in to construct Canal Street.

Up Canal Street is the:

13 Government Market

A few years after the canal was built, the government built a thatched marketplace with stalls for Hawaiians to sell goods to the sailors. Merchants quickly took advantage of this marketplace and erected drinking establishments, grog shops, and other pastimes of interest nearby. Within a few years, this entire area became known as "Rotten Row."

Make a right onto Front Street and continue down the street, past Kamehameha III Elementary School. Across from the park is:

14 Holy Innocents Episcopal Church

When the Episcopal missionaries first came to Lahaina in 1862, they built a church across the street from the current structure. In 1909, the church moved to its present site, which was once a thatched house built for the daughter of King Kamehameha I. The present structure, built in 1927, features unique paintings of a Hawaiian Madonna and endemic birds and plants to Hawaii, executed by DeLos Blackmar in 1940.

Continue down Front Street, and at the next open field look for the white stones by the ocean, marking the former site of the "iron-roofed house":

⑮ Hale Piula

In the 1830s, the two-story stone building with a large surrounding courtyard was built for King Kamehameha III. However, the king preferred sleeping in a small thatched hut nearby, so the structure was never really completed. In the 1840s, Kamehameha moved his capital to Honolulu and wasn't using Hale Piula, so it became the local courthouse. The wind storm of 1858, which destroyed the Courthouse on Wharf Street (see no. 10 above), also destroyed the iron-roofed house. The stones from Hale Piula were used to rebuild the Courthouse on Wharf Street.

Continue down Front Street; across from the 505 Front Street complex is:

⑯ Maluuluolele Park

This sacred spot to Hawaiians is now the site of a park and ball field. This used to be a village, Mokuhinia, with a sacred pond that was the home of a *moo* (a spirit in the form of a lizard), which the royal family honored as their personal guardian spirit. In the middle of the pond was a small island, Mokuula, home to Maui's top chiefs. After conquering Maui, Kamehameha I claimed this sacred spot as his own; he and his two sons, Kamehameha II and III, lived here when they were in Lahaina. In 1918, in the spirit of progress, the pond was drained and the ground leveled for a park.

Make a left onto Shaw Street and then another left onto Wainee Street; on the left side, just past the cemetery, is:

⑰ Wainee Church

This was the first stone church built in Hawaii (1828–32). At one time the church could seat some 3,000 people, albeit tightly packed together, complete with "calabash spittoons" for the tobacco-chewing Hawaiian chiefs and the ship captains. That structure didn't last long—the 1858 wind storm that destroyed several buildings in Lahaina also blew the roof off the original church, knocked over the belfry, and picked up the church's bell and deposited it 100 feet away. The structure was rebuilt, but that, too, was destroyed—this time by Hawaiians protesting the 1894 overthrow of the monarchy. Again the church was rebuilt, and again it was destroyed—by fire, in 1947. The next incarnation of the church was destroyed by yet another windstorm, in 1951. The current church has been standing since 1953, and so far, so good. Be sure to walk around to the back of the church: The row of palm trees on the ocean side includes some of the oldest palm trees in Lahaina.

Wander next door to the first Christian cemetery in Hawaii:

⑱ Waihee Cemetery

Established in 1823, this cemetery tells a fascinating story of old Hawaii, with graves of Hawaiian chiefs, commoners, missionaries and their families (infant mortality was high then), and sailors. Enter this ground with respect because Hawaiians consider it sacred—many members of the royal family were buried here, including Queen Keopuolani, who was wife of King Kamehameha I, mother of Kings Kamehameha II and III, and the first Hawaiian baptized as a Protestant. Among the other graves are Rev. William Richards (the first missionary in Lahaina) and Princess Nahienaena (sister of kings Kamehameha II and III).

Continue down Waihee Street to the corner of Luakini Street and the:

⑲ Hongwanji Mission

The temple was originally built in 1910 by members of Lahaina's Buddhist sect. The current building was constructed in 1927, housing a temple and language school. The public is welcome to attend the New Year's Eve celebration, Buddha's birthday in

April (see "Maui, Molokai & Lanai Calendar of Events" in chapter 2), and O Bon Memorial Services in August.

Continue down Wainee Street; just before the intersection with Prison Street, look for the historical marker for:

⑳ David Malo's Home

Although no longer standing, the house that once stood here was the home of Hawaii's first scholar, philosopher, and well-known author. Educated at Lahainaluna School, his book on ancient Hawaiian culture, *Hawaiian Antiquities,* is considered *the* source on Hawaiiana today. His alma mater celebrates David Malo Day every year in April in recognition of his contributions to Hawaii.

Cross Prison Street; on the corner of Prison and Waihee is the:

㉑ Old Prison

The Hawaiians called the prison Hale Paahao ("stuck in irons house"). Sailors who refused to return to their boats at sunset used to be arrested and taken to the old fort (see no. 11 above). In 1851, however, the fort physician told the government that sleeping on the ground at night made the prisoners ill, costing the government quite a bit of money to treat them—so the Kingdom of Hawaii used the prisoners to build a prison from the coral block of the old fort. Most prisoners here had terms of a year or less (those with longer terms were shipped off to Honolulu) and were convicted of crimes like deserting ship, being drunk, or working on Sunday. Today the grounds of the prison have a much more congenial atmosphere, as they are rented out to community groups for parties.

Continue down Waihee Street, just past Waianae Place, to the small:

㉒ Episcopal Cemetery

This burial ground tells another story in Hawaii's history. During the reign of King Kamehameha IV, his wife, Queen Emma, formed close ties with the British royalty. She encouraged Hawaiians to join the Anglican Church after asking the Archbishop of Canterbury to form a church in Hawaii. This cemetery contains the burial sites of many of those early Anglicans.

Next door is:

㉓ Hale Aloha

This "house of love" was built in 1858 by Hawaiians in "commemoration of God's causing Lahaina to escape the smallpox," while it desolated Oahu in 1853, carrying off 5,000 to 6,000 of its population. The building served as a church and school until the turn of the 20th century, when it fell into disrepair.

Turn left onto Hale Street and then right onto Luakini Street to the:

㉔ Buddhist Church

This green wooden Shingon Buddhist temple is very typical of myriad Buddhist churches that sprang up all over the island when the Japanese laborers were brought to work in the sugar cane fields. Some of the churches were little more than elaborate false "temple" fronts on existing buildings.

On the side of Village Galleries, on the corner of Luakini and Dickenson streets, is the historical marker for:

㉕ Luakini Street

"Luakini" translates as a *heiau* or temple where the ruling chiefs prayed and where human sacrifices were made. This street received its unforgettable name after serving as the route for the funeral procession of Princess Harriet Naiehaena, sister of King Kamehameha III. The princess was a victim of the rapid changes in Hawaiian culture. A convert to Protestantism, she had fallen in love with her brother at an early age. Just 20 years earlier, their relationship would have been nurtured in order to preserve the purity of the royal bloodlines. The missionaries, however, frowned on brother and sister marrying. In August 1836, the couple had a son, who only lived a few short hours. Nahienaena never recovered and died in December of that same year (the king was said to mourn her death for years, frequently visiting her grave at the Waihee Cemetery; see no. 18 above). The route of her funeral procession through the breadfruit and koa trees to the cemetery became known as "Luakini," in reference to the gods "sacrificing" the beloved princess.

Turn left on Dickenson and walk down to Front Street, where you'll be back at the starting point.

WINDING DOWN
Ready for some refreshment after your stroll? Head to **Maui Swiss Cafe**, at 640 Front St. (across the street from the Baldwin Home and the library; ☎ **808/661-6776**), for tropical smoothies, great espresso, and affordable snacks. Sit in the somewhat funky garden area, or get your drink to go and wander over to the seawall to watch the surfers.

A WHALE OF A PLACE IN KAANAPALI

Heading north from Lahaina, the next resort area you'll come to is Kaanapali, which boasts a gorgeous stretch of beach. If you haven't seen a real whale yet, go to **Whalers Village**, 2435 Kaanapali Pkwy., a shopping center that has adopted the whale as its mascot. You can't miss it: A huge, almost life-size metal sculpture of a mother whale and two nursing calves greets you. A few more steps, and you're met by the looming, bleached-white bony skeleton of a 40-foot sperm whale; it's pretty impressive.

On the second floor of the mall is the **Whale Center of the Pacific** (☎ **808/661-5992**), a museum celebrating the "Golden Era of Whaling" (1825–60). Harpoons and scrimshaw are on display; the museum has even re-created the cramped quarters of a whaler's seagoing vessel. Open during mall hours, daily from 9:30am to 10pm; admission is free.

THE SCENIC ROUTE FROM WEST MAUI TO CENTRAL OR UPCOUNTRY MAUI: THE KAHEKILI HIGHWAY

The usual road from West Maui to Wailuku is the Honoapiilani Highway (Hwy. 30), which runs along the coast and then turns inland at Maalaea. But those in search of a back-to-nature driving experience should go the other way, along the **Kahekili Highway** ✦ (Hwy. 340). (*Highway* is a bit of a euphemism for this paved but somewhat precarious narrow road; check your rental-car agreement before you head out. If it is raining or has been raining, skip this road due to mud and rock slides.) It was named after the great chief Kahekili, who built houses from the skulls of his enemies.

You'll start out on the Honoapiilani Highway (Hwy. 30), which becomes the Kahekili Highway (Hwy. 340) after Honokohau, at the northernmost tip of the island. Around this point are **Honolua** ✦ and **Mokuleia** ✦ bays, which have been designated as Marine Life Conservation Areas (the taking of fish, shells, or anything else is prohibited).

From this point, the quality of the road deteriorates, and you may share the way with roosters, goats, cows, and dogs. The narrow, winding road that weaves along for the next 20 miles, following an ancient Hawaiian coastal footpath, will show you the true wild nature of Maui. If you want views, these are photo opportunities from heaven: steep ravines, rolling pastoral hills, tumbling waterfalls, exploding blowholes, crashing surf, jagged lava coastlines, and a tiny Hawaiian village straight off a postcard.

Just before mile marker 20, look for a small turnoff on the mauka side of the road (just before the guardrail starts). Park here and walk across the road, and on your left you'll see a spouting **blowhole.** In winter, this is an excellent spot to look for whales.

About 3 miles farther along the road, you'll come to a wide turnoff providing a great photo op: a view of the jagged coastline down to the crashing surf.

Less than half a mile farther along, just before mile marker 16, look for the POHAKU KANI sign, marking the huge, 6-by-6-foot, bell-shaped stone. To "ring" the bell, look on the side facing Kahakuloa for the deep indentations, and strike the stone with another rock.

Along the route, nestled in a crevice between two steep hills, is the picturesque village of **Kahakuloa** ☆ ("the tall hau tree"), with a dozen weather-worn houses, a church with a red-tile roof, and vivid green taro patches. From the northern side of the village, you can look back at the great view of Kahakuloa, the dark boulder beach, and the 636-foot Kahakuloa Head rising in the background.

At various points along the drive are artists' studios, nestled into the cliffs and hills. One noteworthy stop is the **Kaukini Gallery,** which features work by more than two dozen local artists, with lots of gifts and crafts to buy in all price ranges. (You may also want to stop here to use one of the few restrooms along the drive.)

When you're approaching Wailuku, stop at the **Halekii and Pihanakalani Heiau,** which visitors rarely see. To get here from Wailuku, turn north from Main Street onto Market Street. Turn right onto Mill Street and follow it until it ends; then make a left on Lower Main Street. Follow Lower Main until it ends at Waiehu Beach Road (Hwy. 340), and turn left. Turn left on Kuhio Street and again at the first left onto Hea Place, and drive through the gates and look for the Hawaii Visitor's Bureau marker.

These two heiau, built in 1240 from stones carried up from the Iao Stream below, sit on a hill with a commanding view of central Maui and Haleakala. Kahekili, the last chief of Maui, lived here. After the bloody battle at Iao Stream, Kamehameha I reportedly came to the temple here to pay homage to the war god, Ku, with a human sacrifice. Halekii ("House of Images") is made of stone walls with a flat grassy top, whereas Pihanakalani ("gathering place of supernatural beings") is a pyramid-shaped mount of stones. If you sit quietly nearby (never walk on any heiau—it's considered disrespectful), you'll see that the view alone explains why this spot was chosen.

4 South Maui

MAALAEA

At the bend in the Honopiilani Highway (Hwy. 30), Maalaea Bay runs along the south side of the isthmus between the West Maui Mountains and Haleakala. This is the windiest area on Maui: Trade winds blowing between the two mountains are funneled across the isthmus, and by the time they reach Maalaea, gusts of 25 to 30 miles per hour are not uncommon.

This creates ideal conditions for **windsurfers** out in Maalaea Bay. Surfers are also seen just outside the small boat harbor in Maalaea, which has one of the fastest breaks in the state.

Maui Ocean Center ☆☆ *Kids*   This 5-acre facility houses the largest aquarium in Hawaii and features one of Hawaii's largest predators: the tiger shark. Exhibits are geared toward the residents of Hawaii's ocean waters. As you walk past the three dozen or so tanks and countless exhibits, you'll slowly descend from the "beach" to the deepest part of the ocean, without ever getting wet. Start at the surge pool, where you'll see shallow-water marine life like spiny urchins and cauliflower coral, then move on to the reef tanks, turtle pool, "touch" pool (with starfish and urchins), and eagle-ray pool before reaching the star of the show: the 100-foot-long, 600,000-gallon main tank featuring tiger, gray, and white-tip sharks, as well as tuna, surgeonfish, triggerfish, and numerous other tropicals. The most phenomenal thing about this tank is that the walkway goes right through it—so you'll be surrounded on three sides by marine creatures. A very cool place, and well worth the time.

Maalaea Harbor Village, at the triangle between Honoapiilani Hwy. and Maalaea Rd. *(C)* **808/270-7000.** Fax 808/270-7070. www.mauioceancenter.com. Admission $19 adults, $17 seniors, $13 children 3–12. Daily 9am–5pm.

KIHEI

Capt. George Vancouver landed at Kihei in 1778, when it was only a collection of fisherman's grass shacks on the hot, dry, dusty coast (hard to believe, eh?). A **totem pole** stands today where he's believed to have landed, across from Aston Maui Lu Resort, 575 S. Kihei Rd. Vancouver sailed on to what later became British Columbia, where a great international city and harbor now bear his name.

West of the junction of Piilani Highway (Hwy. 31) and Mokulele Highway (Hwy. 350) is **Kealia Pond National Wildlife Preserve** (*(C)* **808/875-1582**), a 700-acre U.S. Fish and Wildlife wetland preserve where endangered Hawaiian stilts, coots, and ducks hang out and splash. These ponds work two ways: as bird preserves and as sedimentation basins that keep the coral reefs from silting from runoff. You can take a self-guided tour along a boardwalk dotted with interpretive signs and shade shelters, through sand dunes, and around ponds to Maalaea Harbor. The boardwalk starts at the outlet of Kealia Pond on the ocean side of North Kihei Road (near mile marker 2 on Piilani Hwy.). Among the Hawaiian waterbirds seen here are the black-crowned high heron, Hawaiian coot, Hawaiian duck, and Hawaiian stilt. There are also shorebirds like sanderling, Pacific golden plover, ruddy turnstone, and wandering tattler. From July to December, the hawksbill turtle comes ashore here to lay her eggs. *Tip:* If you're bypassing Kihei, take the Piilani Highway (Hwy. 31), which parallels strip-mall laden South Kihei Road, and avoid the hassle of stoplights and traffic.

WAILEA

The dividing line between arid Kihei and artificially green Wailea is distinct. Wailea once had the same kiawe-strewn, dusty landscape as Kihei until Alexander & Baldwin, Inc. (of sugar cane fame) began developing a resort here in the 1970s (after piping water from the other side of the island to the desert terrain of Wailea). Today, the manicured 1,450 acres of this affluent resort stand out like an oasis along the normally dry leeward coast.

The best way to explore this golden resort coast is to rise with the sun and head for Wailea's 1½-mile **coastal nature trail** ✦, stretching between the Kea Lani Hotel and the kiawe thicket just beyond the Renaissance Wailea. It's a great morning walk, a serpentine path that meanders uphill and down past native plants, old Hawaiian habitats, and a billion dollars' worth of luxury hotels. You can pick up the trail at any of the resorts or from clearly marked SHORELINE ACCESS points along the coast. The best time to go is when you first wake up; by midmorning, the coastal trail is too often clogged with joggers, and it grows crowded with beachgoers as the day wears on. As the path crosses several bold black-lava points, it affords new vistas of islands and ocean; benches allow you to pause and contemplate the view across Alalakeiki Channel, which jumps with **whales** in season. Sunset is another good time to hit the trail.

MAKENA

A few miles south of Wailea, the manicured coast turns to wilderness; now you're in Makena ("abundance").

In the 1800s, cattle were driven down the slope from upland ranches, lashed to rafts, and sent into the water to swim to boats that waited to take them to market. Now **Makena Landing** ✯ is a beach park with boat-launching facilities, showers, toilets, and picnic tables. It's great for snorkeling and for launching kayaks bound for Pérouse Bay and Ahihi-Kinau preserve.

From the landing, go south on Makena Road; on the right is **Keawali Congregational Church** ✯ (© **808/879-5557**), built in 1855 with walls 3 feet thick. Surrounded by ti leaves, which by Hawaiian custom provides protection, and built of lava rock with coral used as mortar, this Protestant church sits on its own cove with a gold-sand beach. It always attracts a Sunday crowd for its 9:30am Hawaiian-language service. Take some time to wander through the cemetery; you'll see great examples of the old custom of having a ceramic picture of the deceased on the tombstone.

A little farther south on the coast is **La Pérouse Monument** ✯, a pyramid of lava rocks that marks the spot where French explorer Admiral Comte de La Pérouse set foot on Maui in 1786.

The first Westerner to "discover" the island, he described the "burning climate" of the leeward coast, observed several fishing villages near Kihei, and sailed on into oblivion, never to be seen again; some believe he may have been eaten by cannibals in what is now Vanuatu. To get here, drive south past Puu Olai to Ahihi Bay, where the road turns to gravel. Go another 2 miles along the coast to La Pérouse Bay; the monument sits amid a clearing in black lava at the end of the dirt road.

The rocky coastline and sometimes rough seas contribute to the lack of appeal for water activities here; **hiking** opportunities, however, are excellent. Bring plenty of water and sun protection, and wear hiking boots that can withstand walking on lava. From La Pérouse Bay, you can pick up the old King's Highway trail, which at one time circled the island. Walk along the sandy beach at La Pérouse and look for the trail indentation in the lava, which leads down to the lighthouse at the tip of Cape Hanamanioa, about a three-quarter-mile round-trip. Or you can continue on the trail as it climbs up the hill for 2 miles, then ventures back toward the ocean, where there are quite a few old Hawaiian home foundations and rocky/coral beaches.

5 House of the Sun: Haleakala National Park ✯✯✯

At once forbidding and compelling, **Haleakala National Park** ("House of the Sun") is Maui's main natural attraction. More than 1.3 million people a year go up the 10,023-foot-high mountain to peer down into the crater of the world's largest dormant volcano. (Haleakala is officially considered to be "active, but not currently erupting," even though it has not rumbled or spewed lava since 1790.) That hole would hold Manhattan: 3,000 feet deep, 7½ miles long by 2½ miles wide, and encompassing 19 square miles.

The Hawaiians recognized the mountain as a sacred site. Ancient chants tell of Pele, the volcano goddess, and one of her siblings doing battle on the crater floor where Kawilinau ("Bottomless Pit") now stands. Commoners in ancient Hawaii didn't spend much time here, though. The only people allowed into this sacred area were the kahunas, who took their apprentices to live for periods of

Impressions

There are few enough places in the world that belong entirely to them-selves. The human passion to carry all things everywhere, so that every place is home, seems well on its way to homogenizing our planet, save for the odd unreachable corner. Haleakala crater is one of those corners.
                               —Barbara Kingsolver, the *New York Times*

time in this intensely spiritual place. Today, New Agers also revere Haleakala as one of the earth's powerful energy points, and even the U.S. Air Force has a not-very-well-explained presence here.

But there's more to do here than simply stare in a big black hole: Just going up the mountain is an experience in itself. Where else on the planet can you climb from sea level to 10,000 feet in just 37 miles, or a 2-hour drive? The snaky road passes through big, puffy, cumulus clouds to offer magnificent views of the isthmus of Maui, the West Maui Mountains, and the Pacific Ocean.

Many drive up to the summit in predawn darkness to watch the **sunrise** over Haleakala; writer Mark Twain called it "the sublimest spectacle" of his life. Others take a trail ride inside the bleak lunar landscape of the wilderness inside the crater, or coast down the 37-mile road from the summit on a bicycle with special brakes (see "Biking" and "Horseback Riding" in chapter 6). Hardy adventurers hike and camp inside the crater's wilderness (see "Hiking & Camping" in chapter 6). Those bound for the interior bring their survival gear, because the terrain is raw, rugged, and punishing—not unlike the moon. However you choose to experience Haleakala National Park, it will prove memorable—guaranteed.

JUST THE FACTS

Haleakala National Park extends from the summit of Mount Haleakala into the crater, down the volcano's southeast flank to Maui's eastern coast, beyond Hana. There are actually two separate and distinct destinations within the park: **Haleakala Summit** and the **Kipahulu** coast (see "Just Beyond Hana" on p. 217). The summit gets all the publicity, but Kipahulu draws crowds, too—it's lush, green, and tropical, and home to Oheo Gulch (also known as Seven Sacred Pools). No road links the summit and the coast; you have to approach them separately, and you need at least a day to see each place.

WHEN TO GO   At the 10,023-foot summit, weather changes fast. With wind chill, temperatures can be below freezing any time of year. Summer can be dry and warm, winters wet, windy, and cold. Before you go, get current weather conditions from the park (© **808/572-4400**) or the **National Weather Service** (© **808/871-5054**).

From sunrise to noon, the light is weak, but the view is usually free of clouds. The best time for photos is in the afternoon, when the sun lights the crater and clouds are few. Go on full-moon nights for spectacular viewing. As with all natural attractions, there are no schedules or guarantees, however. Even when the forecast is promising, the weather at Haleakala can change in an instant; be prepared.

ACCESS POINTS   **Haleakala Summit** is 37 miles, or about a 2-hour drive, from Kahului. To get here, take Highway 37 to Highway 377 to Highway 378. For details on the drive, see "The Drive to the Summit" below. Pukalani is the last town for water, food, and gas.

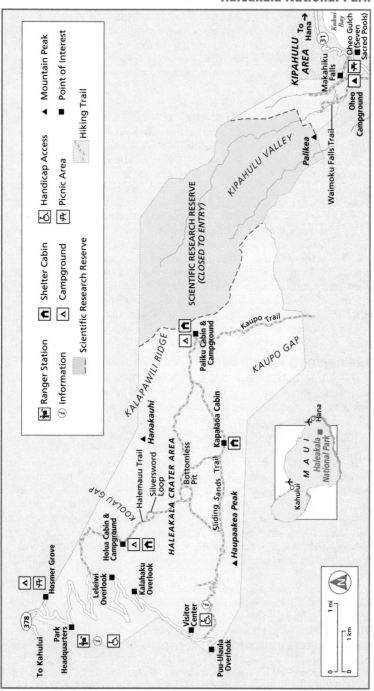

Haleakala National Park

Legend:
- Ranger Station
- Information
- Shelter Cabin
- Campground
- Handicap Access
- Picnic Area
- Mountain Peak
- Point of Interest
- Hiking Trail
- Scientific Research Reserve

To Kahului • 378 • Park Headquarters • Hosmer Grove • Leleiwi Overlook • Kalahaku Overlook • Holua Cabin & Campground • KOOLAU GAP • Halemauu Trail • Silversword Loop • Hanakauhi • KALAPAWILI RIDGE • HALEAKALA CRATER AREA • Bottomless Pit • Sliding Sands Trail • Kapalaoa Cabin • Visitor Center • Puu-Ulaula Overlook • Haupaakea Peak • Paliku Cabin & Campground • Kaupo Trail • KAUPO GAP • SCIENTIFIC RESEARCH RESERVE (CLOSED TO ENTRY) • KIPAHULU VALLEY • Palikea • Waimoku Falls Trail • KIPAHULU AREA • Makahiku Falls • Oheo Campground • Oheo Gulch (Seven Sacred Pools) • To Hana • 31 • Kipahulu Bay

MAUI • Kahului • Hana • Haleakala National Park

N

1 mi

1 km

201

The **Kipahulu** section of the national park is on Maui's east end near Hana, 60 miles from Kahului on Highway 36 (the Hana Hwy.). Due to traffic and rough road conditions, plan on 4 hours for the drive from Kahului (see "Driving the Road to Hana" below). Hana is the only nearby town for services, water, gas, food, and overnight lodging; some facilities may not be open after dark.

At both entrances to the park, the admission fee is $5 per person or $10 per car, good for a week of unlimited entry.

INFORMATION, VISITOR CENTERS & RANGER PROGRAMS   For information before you go, contact **Haleakala National Park,** P.O. Box 369, Makawao, HI 96768 (© **808/572-4400;** www.nps.gov.hale).

One mile from the park entrance, at 7,000 feet, is **Haleakala National Park Headquarters** (© **808/572-4400**), open daily from 7am to 4pm. You can pick up information on park programs and activities, get camping permits, and, occasionally, see a *nene* (Hawaiian goose)—one or more are often here to greet visitors. Restrooms, a pay phone, and drinking water are available.

The **Haleakala Visitor Center,** open daily from sunrise to 3pm, is near the summit, 11 miles from the park entrance. It offers a panoramic view of the volcanic landscape, with photos identifying the various features, and exhibits that explain its history, ecology, geology, and volcanology. Park staff members are often handy to answer questions. The only facilities are restrooms and water.

Rangers offer excellent, informative, and free **naturalist talks** at 9:30, 10:30, and 11:30am daily in the summit building. For information on **hiking** (including guided hikes) and **camping,** including cabins and campgrounds in the wilderness itself, see "Hiking & Camping" in chapter 6.

THE DRIVE TO THE SUMMIT

If you look on a Maui map, almost in the middle of the part that resembles a torso, there's a black wiggly line that looks like this: WWWWW. That's **Highway 378,** also known as **Haleakala Crater Road**—one of the fastest-ascending roads in the world. This grand corniche has at least 33 switchbacks; passes through numerous climate zones; goes under, in, and out of clouds; takes you past rare silversword plants and endangered Hawaiian geese sailing through the clear, thin air; and offers a view that extends for more than 100 miles.

Going to the summit takes about 2 hours from Kahului. No matter where you start out, you'll follow Highway 37 (Haleakala Hwy.) to Pukalani, where you'll pick up Highway 377 (which is also Haleakala Hwy.), which you take to Highway 378. Along the way, expect fog, rain, and wind. You might encounter stray cattle and downhill bicyclists. Fill up your gas tank before you go—the only gas available is 27 miles below the summit at Pukalani. There are no facilities beyond the ranger stations—not even a coffee urn in sight. Bring your own food and water.

Remember, you're entering a high-altitude wilderness area. Some people get dizzy due to the lack of oxygen; you might also suffer lightheadedness, shortness of breath, nausea, or worse: severe headaches, flatulence, and dehydration. People with asthma, pregnant women, heavy smokers, and those with heart conditions should be especially careful in the rarefied air. Bring water and a jacket or a blanket, especially if you go up for sunrise. Or you might want to go up to the summit for sunset, which is also spectacular.

As you go up the slopes the temperate drops about 3°F every 1,000 feet, so the temperature at the top can be 30°F (17°C) cooler than it was at sea level. Come prepared with sweaters, jackets, and rain gear.

At the **park entrance,** you'll pay an entrance fee of $10 per car (or $2 for a bicycle). About a mile from the entrance is **Park Headquarters,** where an endangered **nene,** or Hawaiian goose, might greet you with its unique call. With its black face, buff cheeks, and partially webbed feet, the gray-brown bird looks like a small Canada goose with zebra stripes; it brays out "nay-nay" (thus its name), doesn't migrate, and prefers lava beds to lakes. The unusual goose clings to a precarious existence on these alpine slopes. Vast populations of more than 25,000 once inhabited Hawaii, but hunters, pigs, feral cats and dogs, and mongooses preyed on the nene; coupled with habitat destruction, these predators nearly caused its extinction. By 1951, there were only 30 left. Now protected as Hawaii's state bird, the wild nene on Haleakala numbers fewer than 250—and the species remains endangered.

Beyond headquarters are **two scenic overlooks** on the way to the summit. Stop at Leleiwi on the way up and Kalahaku on the way back down, if only to get out, stretch, and get accustomed to the heights. Take a deep breath, look around, and pop your ears. If you feel dizzy or drowsy, or get a sudden headache, consider turning around and going back down.

Leleiwi Overlook ✦ is just beyond mile marker 17. From the parking area, a short trail leads you to a panoramic view of the lunarlike crater. When the clouds are low and the sun is in the right place, usually around sunset, you can experience a phenomenon known as the "Specter of the Brocken"—you can see a reflection of your shadow, ringed by a rainbow, in the clouds below. It's an optical illusion caused by a rare combination of sun, shadow, and fog that occurs in only three places on the planet: Haleakala, Scotland, and Germany.

Two miles farther along is **Kalahaku Overlook** ✦, the best place to see a rare **silversword.** You can turn into this overlook only when you are descending from the top. The silversword is the punk of the plant world, its silvery bayonets displaying tiny purple bouquets—like a spacey artichoke with attitude. This botanical wonder proved irresistible to humans, who gathered them in gunnysacks for Chinese potions, for British specimen collections, and just for the sheer thrill of having something so rare. Silverswords grow only in Hawaii, take from 4 to 50 years to bloom, and then, usually between May and October, send up a 1- to 6-foot stalk with a purple bouquet of sunflower-like blooms. They're now very rare, so don't even think about taking one home.

Fun Fact **The Legend of the House of the Sun**

According to ancient legend, Haleakala got its name from a very clever trick that the demigod Maui pulled on the sun. Maui's mother, the goddess Hina, complained one day that the sun sped across the sky so quickly that her tapa cloth couldn't dry.

Maui, known as a trickster, devised a plan. The next morning, he went to the top of the great mountain and waited for the sun to poke its head above the horizon. Quickly, Maui lassoed the sun, bringing its path across the sky to an abrupt halt.

The sun begged Maui to let go, and Maui said he would on one condition: that the sun slow its trip across the sky to give the island more sunlight. The sun assented. In honor of this agreement, the Hawaiians call the mountain Haleakala, or "House of the Sun."

To this day, the top of Haleakala has about 15 minutes more sunlight than the communities on the coastline below.

Continue on, and you'll quickly reach the **Haleakala Visitor Center** ⚡, which offers spectacular views. You'll feel as if you're at the edge of the earth. But don't turn around here; the actual summit's a little farther on, at **Puu Ulaula Overlook** ⚡ (also known as Red Hill), the volcano's highest point, where you'll find a mysterious cluster of buildings officially known as Haleakala Observatories, but unofficially called **Science City.** If you do go up for sunrise, the building at Puu Ulaula Overlook, a triangle of glass that serves as a windbreak, is the best viewing spot. After the daily miracle of sunrise—the sun seems to rise out of the vast crater (hence the name "House of the Sun")—you can see all the way across Alenuihaha Channel to the often snowcapped summit of Mauna Kea on the Big Island.

MAKING YOUR DESCENT   Put your car in low gear; that way, you won't destroy your brakes by riding them the whole way down.

6 More in Upcountry Maui

Come upcountry and discover a different side of Maui: On the slopes of Haleakala, cowboys, planters, and other country people make their homes in serene, neighborly communities like **Makawao** and **Kula,** a world away from the bustling beach resorts. Even if you can't spare a day or 2 in the cool upcountry air, there are some sights that are worth a look on your way to or from the crater. Shoppers and gallery hoppers might really want to make the effort; see chapter 8 for details. For a map of this area, turn to the "Upcountry Maui Dining & Attractions" map on p. 145.

On the slopes of Haleakala, Maui's breadbasket has been producing vegetables since the 1800s. In fact, during the gold rush in California, the Hawaiian farmers in Kula shipped so many potatoes that it was nicked named Nu Kaleponi, a sort of pidgin Hawaiian pronunciation of "New California." In the late 1800s, Portuguese and Chinese immigrants, who had fulfilled their labor contracts with the sugarcane companies, moved to this area, drawn by the rural agricultural lifestyle. That lifestyle continues today, among the fancy gentlemen's farms that have sprung up in the past 2 decades. Kula continues to grow the well-known onions, lettuce, tomatoes, carrots, cauliflower, and cabbage. It is also a major source of cut flowers for the state: Most of Hawaii's proteas, as well as nearly all the carnations used in leis, come from Kula.

To experience a bit of the history of Kula, turn off the Kula Highway (Hwy. 37) onto Lower Kula Road. Well before the turnoff, you'll see a white octagonal building with a silver roof, the **Holy Ghost Catholic Church** (*C* **808/878-1091**). Hawaii's only eight-sided church, it was built between 1884 and 1897 by Portuguese immigrants. It's worth a stop to see the hand-carved altar and works of art for the stations of the cross, with inscriptions in Portuguese.

Kula Botanical Garden ⚡   You can take a self-guided, informative, leisurely stroll through more than 700 native and exotic plants—including three unique collections of orchids, proteas, and bromeliads—at this 5-acre garden. It offers a good overview of Hawaii's exotic flora in one small, cool place.

Hwy. 377, south of Haleakala Crater Rd. (Hwy. 378), ½ mile from Hwy. 37. *C* **808/878-1715.** Admission $5 adults, $1 children 6–12. Daily 9am–4pm.

Tedeschi Vineyards and Winery ⚡   On the southern shoulder of Haleakala is **Ulupalakua Ranch,** a 20,000-acre spread once owned by legendary sea captain James Makee, celebrated in the Hawaiian song and dance *Hula O Makee.*

Wounded in a Honolulu waterfront brawl in 1843, Makee moved to Maui and bought Ulupalakua. He renamed it Rose Ranch, planted sugar as a cash crop, and grew rich. Still in operation, the ranch is now home to Maui's only winery, established in 1974 by Napa vintner Emil Tedeschi, who began growing California and European grapes here and producing serious still and sparkling wines, plus a silly wine made of pineapple juice. The rustic grounds are the perfect place for a picnic. Pack a basket before you go, but don't BYOB: There's plenty of great wine to enjoy at Tedeschi. Settle in under the sprawling camphor tree, pop the cork on a Blanc du Blanc, and toast your good fortune in being here.

Across from the winery are the remains of the three smokestacks of the **Makee Sugar Mill,** built in 1878. This is home to Maui artist Reems Mitchell, who carved the mannequins on the front porch of the Ulupakalua Ranch Store: a Filipino with his fighting cock, a cowboy, a farmhand, and a sea captain, all representing the people of Maui's history.

Off Hwy. 37 (Kula Hwy.). 🕿 **808/878-6058.** www.mauiwine.com. Daily 9am–5pm. Free tastings; tours given 10:30am–1:30pm.

7 Driving the Road to Hana ★★★

Top down, sunscreen on, radio tuned to a little Hawaiian music on a Maui morning: It's time to head out to Hana along the Hana Highway (Hwy. 36), a wiggle of a road that runs along Maui's northeastern shore. The drive takes at least 3 hours, but plan to take all day. Going to Hana is about the journey, not the destination.

There are wilder roads and steeper roads and even more dangerous roads, but in all of Hawaii no road is more celebrated than this one. It winds for 50 miles past taro patches, magnificent seascapes, waterfall pools, botanical gardens, and verdant rainforests, and it ends at one of Hawaii's most beautiful tropical places.

The outside world discovered the little village of Hana in 1926, when the narrow coastal road, carved by pickax-wielding convicts, opened with 56 bridges and 600 hairpin switchbacks. The mud-and-gravel road, often subject to landslides and washouts, was paved in 1962, when tourist traffic began to increase; it now sees more than 1,000 cars and dozens of vans a day, according to storekeeper Harry Hasegawa. That equals about 500,000 people a year on this road, which is way too many. Go at the wrong time, and you'll be stuck in a bumper-to-bumper rental-car parade—peak traffic hours are midmorning and midafternoon year-round, especially on weekends.

In the rush to "do" Hana in a day, most visitors spin around town in 10 minutes flat and wonder what all the fuss is about. It takes time to take in Hana, play in the waterfalls, sniff the tropical flowers, hike to bamboo forests, and take in the spectacular scenery; stay overnight if you can, and meander back in a day or 2.

However, if you really must do the Hana Highway in a day, go just before sunrise and return after sunset: On a full-moon night, the sea and the waterfalls glow in soft white light, with mysterious shadows appearing in the jungle. And you'll have the road almost to yourself on the way back.

Akamai tips: Forget your mainland road manners. Practice aloha: Give way at the one-lane bridges, wave at oncoming motorists, let the big guys in four-by-fours with pig-hunting dogs in the back have the right of way—it's just common sense, brah. If the guy behind you blinks his lights, let him pass. Oh, yeah, and don't honk your horn—in Hawaii, it's considered rude.

THE JOURNEY BEGINS IN PAIA Before you even start out, fill up your gas tank. Gas in Paia is very expensive (even by Maui standards), and it's the last

The Road to Hana

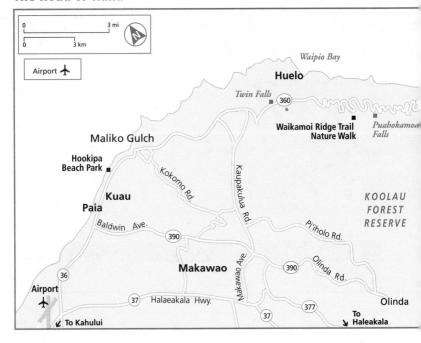

place for gas until you get to Hana, some 42 miles, 54 bridges, and 600 hairpin turns down the road.

The former plantation village of Paia was once a thriving sugar-mill town. The mill is still here, but the population shifted to Kahului in the 1950s when subdivisions opened there, leaving Paia to shrivel up and die. But the town refused to give up, and it has proven its ability to adapt to the times. Now chic eateries and trendy shops stand next door to the mom-and-pop establishments that have been serving generations of Paia customers.

Plan to be here early, around 7am, when **Charley's** ✺, 142 Hana Hwy. (℗ **808/579-9453**), opens. Enjoy a big, hearty breakfast for a reasonable price. After your meal, head up Baldwin Avenue; about a half block from the intersection of the Hana Highway and Baldwin Avenue, stop by **Pic-nics** ✺, 30 Baldwin Ave. (℗ **808/579-8021**), to stock up for a picnic lunch for the road (p. 149).

After you leave Paia, just before the bend in the road, you'll pass the Kuau Mart on your left; a small general store, it's the only reminder of the once-thriving sugar plantation community of **Kuau.** The road then bends into an S-turn; in the middle of the **S** is the entrance to **Mama's Fish House,** marked by a restored boat with Mama's logo on the side. Just past the truck on the ocean side is the entrance to Mama's parking lot and adjacent small sandy cove in front of the restaurant. Mainly surfers use this treacherous ocean access over very slippery rocks into strong surf, but the beach is a great place to sit and soak up some sun.

WINDSURFING MECCA   A mile from Mama's, just before mile marker 9, is a place known around the world as one of the greatest windsurfing spots on the planet, **Hookipa Beach Park** ✺. Hoopika ("hospitality") is where the top-ranked windsurfers come to test themselves against the forces of nature: thunderous surf and forceful wind. World-championship contests are held here (see

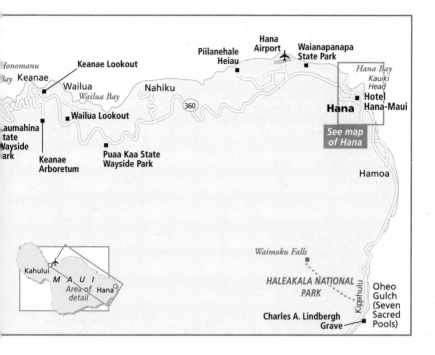

"Maui, Molokai & Lanai Calendar of Events" in chapter 2), but on nearly every windy afternoon (the board surfers have the waves in the morning), you can watch dozens of windsurfers twirling and dancing in the wind like colored butterflies. To watch the windsurfers, do not stop on the highway, but go past the park and turn left at the entrance on the far side of the beach. You can either park on the high grassy bluff or drive down to the sandy beach and park alongside the pavilion. The park also has restrooms, a shower, picnic tables, and a barbecue area.

INTO THE COUNTRY   Past Hookipa Beach, the road winds down into **Maliko ("Budding") Gulch** at mile marker 10. At the bottom of the gulch, look for the road on your right, which will take you out to **Maliko Bay.** Take the first right, which goes under the bridge and past a rodeo arena (scene of competitions by the Maliko Roping Club in summer) and on to the rocky beach. There are no facilities here except a boat-launch ramp. In the 1940s, Maliko had a thriving community at the mouth of the bay, but its residents rebuilt farther inland after a strong tidal wave wiped it out. The bay may not look that special, but if the surf is up, it's a great place to watch the waves.

Back on the Hana Highway, as you leave Maliko Gulch, around mile marker 11, you'll pass through the rural area of **Haiku,** with banana patches, cane grass blowing in the wind, and forests of guava trees, avocados, kukui trees, palms, and Christmas berry. Just before mile marker 15 is the **Maui Grown Market and Deli** (© **808/572-1693**), a good stop for drinks or snacks for the ride.

At mile marker 16, the curves begin, one right after another. Slow down and enjoy the view of bucolic rolling hills, mango trees, and vibrant ferns. After mile marker 16, the road is still called the Hana Highway, but the number changes from Highway 36 to Highway 360, and the mile markers go back to 0.

A GREAT PLUNGE ALONG THE WAY A dip in a waterfall pool is every-body's tropical-island fantasy. The first great place to stop is **Twin Falls** ⍟, at mile marker 2. Just before the wide, concrete bridge, pull over on the mountain side and park (but not in front of the sign that says DO NOT BLOCK DRIVEWAY). Remember that there have been thefts in this area. Ignore the NO TRESPASSING sign (no one will mind, but you're liable if you stub your toe) and hop over the ladder on the right side of the red gate. From here you can walk 3 to 5 minutes to the waterfall and pool, or continue on another 10 to 15 minutes to the second, larger waterfall and pool (don't go in if it has been raining). If you're lucky, there will be a fruit stand set up here, making fabulous fresh smoothies. What a way to start the trip to Hana.

HIDDEN HUELO Just before mile marker 4 on a blind curve, look for a double row of mailboxes on the left-hand side by the pay phone. Down the road lies a hidden Hawaii: a Hawaii of an earlier time, where ocean waves pummel soaring lava cliffs and where serenity prevails.

Protruding out of Maui's tumultuous northern coastline, hemmed in by Waipo and Hoalua bays, is the remote, rural community of **Huelo** ⍟. Once, this fertile area supported a population of 75,000; today, only a few hundred live among the scattered homes on this windswept land, where a handful of bed-and-breakfasts and exquisite vacation rentals are known only to a select few travelers (see chapter 4).

The only reason Huelo is even marked is the historic 1853 **Kaulanapueo Church,** which sits in the center of a putting-green–perfect lawn, bordered with hog-wire fence and accessible through a squeaky, metal turnstile. Reminiscent of New England architecture, this coral-and-cement church, topped with a planta-tion-green steeple and a cloudy gray tin roof, is still in use, although services are held just once or twice a month. It still has the same austere, stark interior of 1853: straight-backed benches, a no-nonsense platform for the minister, and nothing on the walls to distract you from the sermon.

Next to the church is a small graveyard, a personal history of this village in concrete and stone. The graves, facing the setting sun and bleached white over the decades, are the community's garden of memories, each well tended and oft visited.

KOOLAU FOREST RESERVE After Huelo, the vegetation seems lusher, as though Mother Nature had poured Miracle-Gro on everything. This is the edge of the **Koolau Forest Reserve** ⍟. Koolau means "windward," and this certainly is one of the greatest examples of a lush windward area: The coastline here gets about 60 to 80 inches of rain a year, and farther up the mountain, the rainfall is 200 to 300 inches a year.

Here you will see 20- to 30-foot-tall guava trees, their branches laden with green (not ripe) and yellow (ripe) fruit. The skin is peeled and the fruit inside of the guava eaten raw, squeezed for juice, or cooked for jams or jellies. Also in this prolific area are mangos, java plums, and avocados the size of softballs. The spiny, long-leafed plants you see are hala trees, which the Hawaiians used for roofing material and for weaving baskets, mats, and even canoe sails.

The very tall trees, up to 200 feet tall, are eucalyptus, brought to Hawaii from Australia to supply the sugar cane mills with power for the wood-burning engines. Unfortunately, in the nearly 100 years since the fast-growing tree was first introduced, it has quickly taken over Hawaiian forests, forcing out native plants and trees.

The copious rainfall up the mountain means a waterfall (and 1-lane bridge) around nearly every turn in the road from here on out, so drive slowly and be prepared to stop and yield to oncoming cars.

DANGEROUS CURVES   About a half mile after mile marker 6, there's a sharp U-curve in the road, going uphill. The road is practically one lane here, with a brick wall on one side and virtually no maneuvering room. Sound your horn at the start of the U-curve to let approaching cars know you are coming. Take this curve, as well as the few more coming up in the next several miles, very slowly.

Just before mile marker 7 is a forest of waving **bamboo.** The sight is so spectacular that drivers are often tempted to take their eyes off the road. Be very cautious. Wait until just after mile marker 7, at the **Kaaiea ("Breathtaking") Bridge,** to pull over and take a closer look at the hand-hewn stone walls. Then turn around to see the vista of bamboo, a photo opportunity that certainly qualifies as "breathtaking."

A GREAT FAMILY HIKE   At mile marker 9, there's a small state wayside area with restrooms, a pavilion, picnic tables, and a barbecue area. The sign says KOOLAU FOREST RESERVE, but the real attraction here is the **Waikamoi Ridge Trail** ⍟, an easy three-quarter-mile loop that the entire family can do. The start of the trail is just behind the QUIET TREES AT WORK sign. The well-marked trail meanders through eucalyptus (including the unusual paper-bark eucalyptus), ferns, and hala trees.

MORE GREAT PLUNGES   Another great waterfall is **Puohokamoa Falls** ⍟, a 30-foot waterfall that spills into an idyllic pool in a fern-filled amphitheater. Naturalist Ken Schmidt says that its name, loosely translated, means "valley of the chickens bursting into flight"—which is what hot, sweaty hikers look like as they take the plunge.

Park at the bridge at mile marker 11 and take the short walk up the trail, which is lined with stone walls. The spectacular waterfall and deep swimming pool are surrounded by banana trees, colorful heliconias, and sweet-smelling ginger. Bring mosquito repellent. There's a picnic table at the pool.

Back at your car, be sure to check out the view toward the ocean from the bridge: Dozens of varieties of heliconias blanket the valley below.

CAN'T-MISS PHOTO OPPORTUNITIES   Just past mile marker 12 is the **Kaumahina ("Moonrise") State Wayside Park.** Not only is this a good pit stop (restrooms are available here) and a wonderful place for a picnic under the tall eucalyptus trees (with tables and barbecue area), but it's also a great vista. The view of the rugged coastline makes an excellent photo—you can see all the way down to the jutting Keanae Peninsula. Just past the park on the ocean side, there's another scenic turnoff (be careful crossing the oncoming traffic) and great photo opportunity.

Another mile and a couple of bends in the road, and you'll enter the Honomanu Valley ("valley of the bird"), with its beautiful bay. To get down to the **Honomanu Bay County Beach Park** ⍟, look for the turnoff on your left, just after mile marker 14, as you begin your ascent up the other side of the valley. The rutted dirt-and-cinder road takes you down to the rocky black-sand beach. There are no facilities here, except for a stone fire pit someone has made in the sand. This is a popular site among surfers and net fishermen. There are strong rip currents offshore, so swimming is best in the stream inland from the ocean. You'll consider the drive down worthwhile as you stand on the beach, well away from the ocean, and turn to look back on the steep cliffs covered with vegetation.

MAUI'S BOTANICAL WORLD   Farther along the winding road, between mile markers 16 and 17, is a cluster of bunkhouses composing the YMCA Camp Keanae. A quarter-mile down is the **Keanae Arboretum** 🐾🐾, where the region's botany is divided into three parts: native forest; introduced forest; and traditional Hawaiian plants, food, and medicine. You can swim in the pools of Piinaau Stream, or press on along a mile-long trail into Keanae Valley, where a lovely tropical rainforest waits at the end (see "Hiking & Camping" in chapter 6).

KEANAE PENINSULA   The old Hawaiian village of **Keanae** 🐾🐾 stands out against the Pacific like a place time forgot. Here, on an old lava flow graced by an 1860 stone church and swaying palms, is one of the last coastal enclaves of native Hawaiians. They still grow taro in patches and pound it into poi, the staple of the old Hawaiian diet; they still pluck *opihi* (limpet) from tide pools along the jagged coast and cast throw-nets at schools of fish.

The turnoff to the Keanae Peninsula is on the left, just after the arboretum. The road passes by farms and banana bunches as it hugs the peninsula. Where the road bends, there's a small beach where fishermen gather to catch dinner. A quarter-mile farther is the **Kaenae Congregational Church (✆ 808/248-8040),** built in 1860 of lava rocks and coral mortar, standing out in stark contrast to the green fields surrounding it. Beside the church is a small beachfront park, with false kamani trees against a backdrop of black lava and a roiling turquoise sea.

For an experience in an untouched Hawaii, follow the road until it ends. Park by the white fence and take the short, 5-minute walk along the shoreline over the black lava. Continue along the footpath through the tall California grass to the black rocky beach, separating the freshwater stream, **Pinaau,** which winds back into the Keanae Peninsula, nearly cutting it off from the rest of Maui. This is an excellent place for a picnic and a swim in the cool waters of the stream. There are no facilities here, so be sure you leave no evidence that you were here (carry everything out with you and use restroom facilities before you arrive). As you make your way back, notice the white PVC pipes sticking out of the rocks—they're fishing-pole holders for fishermen, usually hoping to catch ulua.

ANOTHER PHOTO OP: KEANAE LOOKOUT   Just past mile marker 17 is a wide spot on the ocean side of the road, where you can see the entire Keanae Peninsula's checkerboard pattern of green taro fields and its ocean boundary etched in black lava. Keanae was the result of a postscript eruption of Haleakala, which flowed through the Koolau Gap and down Keanae Valley and added this geological punctuation to the rugged coastline.

FRUIT & FLOWER STANDS   Around mile marker 18, the road widens; you'll start to see numerous small stands selling fruit or flowers. Many of these stands work on the honor system: You leave your money in the basket and select your purchase. We recommend stopping at **Uncle Harry's,** which you'll find just after the Keanae School around mile marker 18. Native Hawaiian Harry Kunihi Mitchell was a legend in his time. An expert in native plants and herbs, he devoted his life to the Hawaiian-rights and nuclear-free movements. His family sells a variety of fruit and juices here, Monday through Saturday from 9am to 4pm.

WAILUA   Just after Uncle Harry's, look for the Wailua Road off on the left. This will take you through the hamlet of homes and churches of Wailua, which also contains a shrine depicting what the community calls a "miracle." Behind the pink **St. Gabriel's Church** is the smaller, blue and white **Coral Miracle Church,** home of the **Our Lady of Fatima Shrine.** According to the story, in 1860, the men of this village were building a church by diving for coral to make the stone. But the coral offshore was in deep water and the men could only come up with a few pieces at a time, making the construction of the church an arduous project. A freak storm hit the area and deposited the coral from the deep on a nearby beach. The Hawaiians gathered what they needed and completed the church. This would make a nice enough miracle story, but there's more—after the church was completed, another freak storm hit the area and swept all the remaining coral on the beach back out to sea.

If you look back at Haleakala from here, on your left you can see the spectacular, near-vertical **Waikani Falls.** On the remainder of the dead-end road is an eclectic collection of old and modern homes. Turning around at the road's end is very difficult, so we suggest you just turn around at the church and head back for the Hana Highway.

Back on the Hana Highway, just before mile marker 19, is the **Wailua Valley State Wayside Park**, on the right side of the road. Climb up the stairs for a view of the Keanae Valley, waterfalls, and Wailua Peninsula. On a really clear day, you can see up the mountain to the Koolau Gap.

For a better view of the Wailua Peninsula, continue down the road about a quarter-mile; on the ocean side, there will be a pull-off area with parking.

PUAA KAA STATE WAYSIDE PARK   You'll hear this park long before you see it, about halfway between mile markers 22 and 23. The sound of waterfalls provides the background music for this small park area with restrooms, a phone, and a picnic area. There's a well-marked path to the falls and to a swimming hole. Ginger plants are everywhere: Pick some flowers and put them in your car so that you can travel with that sweet smell.

OLD NAHIKU   Just after mile marker 25 is a narrow 3-mile road leading from the highway, at about 1,000 feet elevation, down to sea level—and to the remains of the old Hawaiian community of **Nahiku.** At one time, this was a thriving village of thousands; today, the population has dwindled to fewer than a hundred—including a few Hawaiian families, but mostly extremely wealthy mainland residents who jet in for a few weeks at a time to their luxurious vacation homes. At the turn of the 20th century, this site saw brief commercial activity as home of the Nahiku Rubber Co., the only commercial rubber plantation in the United States. You can still see rubber trees along the Nahiku Road. However, the amount of rainfall, coupled with the damp conditions, could not support the commercial crop; the plantation closed in 1912, and Nahiku was forgotten until the 1980s, when multimillionaires "discovered" the remote and stunningly beautiful area.

At the end of the road, you can see the remains of the old wharf from the rubber-plantation days. Local residents come down here to shoreline fish; there's a small picnic area off to the side. Dolphins are frequently seen in the bay.

HANA AIRPORT   After mile marker 31, a small sign points to the Hana Airport, down Alalele Road on the left. Newly formed commuter airline **Pacific Wings** (© 888/575-4546; www.pacificwings.com) offers three flights daily to and from Hana, with connecting flights from Kahului and traveling on to Honolulu. There is no public transportation in Hana. Car rentals are available through **Dollar Rent A Car** (© 800/800-4000 or 808/248-8237).

WAIANAPANAPA STATE PARK   At mile marker 32, just on the outskirts of Hana, shiny black-sand Waianapanapa Beach appears like a vivid dream, with bright-green jungle foliage on three sides and cobalt-blue water lapping at its feet. The 120-acre park on an ancient *aa* lava flow includes sea cliffs, lava tubes, arches, and the beach, plus 12 cabins, tent camping, picnic pavilions, rest-rooms, showers, drinking water, and hiking trails. If you're interested in staying here, see chapter 4; also see "Beaches" and "Hiking & Camping" in chapter 6.

8 The End of the Road: Heavenly Hana ★★

Green, tropical Hana is a destination all its own, a small coastal village that's probably what you came to Maui in search of. Here you'll find a rainforest dot-ted with cascading waterfalls and sparkling blue pools, skirted by red- and black-sand beaches.

Beautiful Hana enjoys more than 90 inches of rain a year—more than enough to keep the scenery lush. Banyans, bamboo, breadfruit trees—everything seems larger than life in this small town, especially the flowers, such as wild ginger and plumeria. Several roadside stands offer exotic blooms for $1 a bunch. Just "put money in box." It's the Hana honor system.

A LOOK AT THE PAST

The Hana coast is rich in Hawaiian history and the scene of many turning points in Hawaiian culture. The ancient chants tell of rulers like the 15th-cen-tury **Piilani,** who united the island of Maui and built fish ponds, irrigation fields, paved roads, and the massive **Piilanihale Heiau,** which still stands today. It was Piilani's sons and grandson who finished the heiau and built the first road to Hana from West Maui, not only along the coast, but also up the Kaupo Gap and through the Haleakala Crater.

In 1849, the cantankerous sea captain **George Wilfong** brought commerce to this isolated village when he started the first sugar plantation on some 60 acres. Because his harsh personality and set demands for plantation work did not sit well with the Hawaiians, Wilfong brought in the first Chinese immigrants to work his fields.

In 1864, two Danish brothers, **August and Oscar Unna,** contributed to the growth of the local sugar industry when they established the Hana Plantation. Four years later, they brought in Japanese immigrants to labor in the fields.

By the turn of the 20th century, sugar wasn't the only crop booming in Hana (there were some 6 plantations in the area): Rubber was being commercially grown in Nahiku, wheat in Kaupo, pineapple in Kipahulu, and tobacco in Ulupalakua.

In the 1920s and 1930s, several self-sufficient towns lined the coast, each with its own general store, school, and churches; some had movie theaters as well. Hana has all of the above plus some 15 stores, a pool hall, and several restaurants.

We can only guess what those towns would have been like today if tragedy hadn't struck. On April 1, 1946, a huge tidal wave hit the state. The damage along the Hana coast was catastrophic: The Keanae Peninsula was swept clear (only the stone church remained), Hamoa was totally wiped out, and entire vil-lages completely disappeared.

After World War II, the labor movement became a powerful force in Hawaii. **C. Brewer,** owner of the largest sugar plantation in Hana, decided to shut down his operation instead of fighting the labor union. The closure of the plantation meant not only the loss of thousands of jobs, but also the loss of plantation-sup-plied homes and the entire plantation lifestyle. Thankfully, **Paul I. Fagan,** an entrepreneur from San Francisco who had purchased the Hana Sugar Co. from the Unna Brothers in the 1930s, became the town's guardian angel.

Fagan wanted to retire here, so he focused his business acumen on the tiny town with big problems. Recognizing that sugar in isolated Hana was no longer

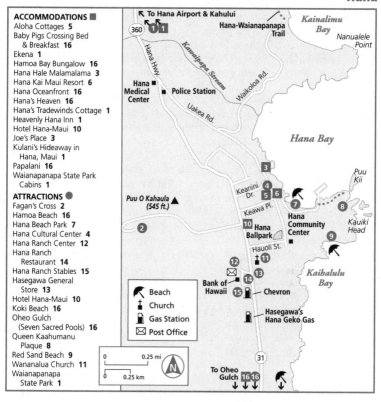

ACCOMMODATIONS ■
Aloha Cottages **5**
Baby Pigs Crossing Bed
& Breakfast **16**
Ekena **1**
Hamoa Bay Bungalow **16**
Hana Hale Malamalama **3**
Hana Kai Maui Resort **6**
Hana Oceanfront **16**
Hana's Heaven **16**
Hana's Tradewinds Cottage **1**
Heavenly Hana Inn **1**
Hotel Hana-Maui **10**
Joe's Place **3**
Kulani's Hideaway in
Hana, Maui **1**
Papalani **16**
Waianapanapa State Park
Cabins **1**

ATTRACTIONS ●
Fagan's Cross **2**
Hamoa Beach **16**
Hana Beach Park **7**
Hana Cultural Center **4**
Hana Ranch Center **12**
Hana Ranch
Restaurant **14**
Hana Ranch Stables **15**
Hasegawa General
Store **13**
Hotel Hana-Maui **10**
Koki Beach **16**
Oheo Gulch
(Seven Sacred Pools) **16**
Queen Kaahumanu
Plaque **8**
Red Sand Beach **9**
Wananalua Church **11**
Waianapanapa
State Park **1**

economically feasible, he looked at the community and saw other opportunities. He bought 14,000 acres of land in Hana, stripped it of sugar cane, planted grass, and shipped in cattle from his ranch on Molokai.

Next he did something that was years ahead of his time: He thought tourism might have a future in Hana, so he established an inn in 1946 that later became the **Hotel Hana-Maui.** Fagan also pulled off a public-relations coup: He brought the entire San Francisco Seals baseball team (which he happened to own) to Hana for spring training, and, more important, he brought out the sportswriters as well. The writers loved Hana and wrote glowing reports about the town; one even gave the town a nickname that stuck: "Heavenly Hana."

In 1962, the state paved the Hana Highway. By the 1970s, tourists had not only "discovered" Maui, but they also were willing to make the long trek out to Hana.

The biggest change to the local lifestyle came in December 1977, when television finally arrived—after a local cable operator spent 6 months laying cable over cinder cones, mountain streams, and cavernous gulches from one side of the island to the other. Some 125 homes tuned in to the tube—and the rural Hawaiian community was never the same. Today Hana is inhabited by 2,500 people, many part Hawaiian.

SEEING THE SIGHTS

Most visitors will zip through Hana, perhaps taking a quick look out their car windows at a few sights before buzzing on down the road. They might think they've "seen" Hana, but they definitely haven't "experienced" Hana. Allow at least 2 or 3 days to really let this land of legends show you its beauty and serenity.

As you enter Hana, the road splits about a half mile past mile marker 33, at the police station. Both roads will take you to Hana, but the lower road, Uakea Road, is more scenic. Just before you get to Hana Bay, you'll see the old wood-frame **Hana District Police Station and Courthouse.** Next door is the **Hana Museum Cultural Center** ✯, on Uakea Road (© **808/248-8622;** www.planet-hawaii.com/hana), open daily from 10am to 4pm (most of the time). This small building has an excellent collection of Hawaiian quilts, artifacts, books, and photos. Also on the grounds are Kauhala O Hana, composed of four *hale* (houses) for living, meeting, cooking, and canoe building or canoe storage.

Cater-cornered from the cultural center is the entrance to **Hana Bay** ✯. You can drive right down to the pier and park. There are restrooms, showers, picnic tables, barbecue areas, and even a snack bar here. The 386-foot, red-faced cinder cone beside the bay is **Kauiki Hill,** the scene of numerous fierce battles in ancient Hawaii and the birthplace of Queen Kaahumanu in 1768. A short, 5-minute walk will take you to the spot. Look for the trail along the hill on the wharf side, and follow the path through the ironwood trees; the lighthouse on the point will come into view, and you'll see pocket beaches of red cinder below. Grab onto the ironwood trees for support, because the trail has eroded in some areas. This is a perfect place for a secluded picnic, or you can continue on the path out to the lighthouse. To get to the lighthouse, which sits on a small island, watch the water for about 10 minutes to get a sense of how often and from which direction the waves are coming. Between wave sets, either swim or wade in the shallow, sandy bottom channel or hop across the rocks to the island.

To get to the center of town, leave Hana Bay, cross Uakea Road, and drive up Keawa Place; turn left on Hana Highway, and on the corner will be the **Hotel Hana-Maui,** the once-luxurious hotel established by Paul Fagan in 1946. It has been neglected of late, but new management has taken over, and we're hoping this historic hotel gets the care and maintenance it deserves. On the green hills above Hotel Hana-Maui stands a 30-foot-high white cross made of lava rock. Citizens erected the cross in memory of Paul Fagan, who founded the Hana Ranch as well as the hotel, and helped keep the town alive. The hike up to **Fagan's Cross** provides a gorgeous view of the Hana coast, especially at sunset, when Fagan himself liked to climb this hill (see p. 174, for details).

Back on the Hana Highway, just past Hauoli Road, is the majestic **Wananalua Congregation Church.** It's on the National Historic Register not only because of its age (it was built in 1838–42 from coral stones), but also because of its location, atop an old Hawaiian heiau.

Just past the church on the right side of the Hana Highway is the turnoff to the **Hana Ranch Center,** the commercial center for Hana, with a post office, bank, general store, the Hana Ranch Stables, and a restaurant and snack bar (see chapter 5). But the real shopping experience is across the Hana Highway at the **Hasegawa General Store** ✯, a Maui institution (see chapter 8), which carries oodles of merchandise from soda and fine French wines to fishing line to name-brand clothing, plus everything you need for a picnic or a gourmet meal. This is also the place to find out what's going on in Hana: The bulletin board at the entrance has fliers and handwritten notes advertising everything from fundrais-ing activities to classes to community-wide activities. You cannot make a trip to Hana without a stop at this unique store.

Note your gas tank. If you need gas before heading back, **Chevron Service Station** sits on the right side of the Hana Highway as you leave town.

OUTDOOR PURSUITS

Most day-trippers to Hana don't think there's much to do in this tiny community. They couldn't be more wrong. One of the best areas on Maui for ocean activities, it also boasts a wealth of nature hikes, remote places to explore on horseback, waterfalls to discover, and even lava tube caves to investigate.

For more information on the lava tubes, see **Maui Cave Adventures** (© 808/ 248-7308) on p. 180; for details on horseback riding, see **Oheo Stables** (© 808/ 667-2222) on p. 179. If you're a tennis player, you can take advantage of the free public courts located next to the Hotel Hana-Maui, available on a first-come, first-served basis.

BEACHES & OCEAN ACTIVITIES

Hana's beaches come in numerous varieties—white, black, gray, or red sand; perfectly shaped coves, crescents, or long stretches—and they're excellent for just about every kind of ocean activity you can think of. Call **Hana-Maui Sea Sports** (© 808/248-7711; www.hana-maui-seasports.com) if you'd like to snorkel or kayak, or venture out on your own at our favorite beaches:

HANA The waters in the Hana Bay are calm most of the time and great for swimming. There's excellent snorkeling and diving by the lighthouse. Strong currents can run through here, so don't venture farther than the lighthouse. See Hana Bay, above, for more details on the facilities and hikes here.

RED SAND BEACH 🐟🐟 The Hawaiian name for this beach is Kaihalulu Beach, which means "roaring sea." It's truly a sight to see. The beach is on the ocean side of Kauiki Hill, just south of Hana Bay, in a wild, natural setting on a pocket cove, where the volcanic cinder cone lost its seaward wall to erosion and spilled red cinders everywhere to create the red sands. Before you put on your bathing suit, there are two things to know about this beach: You have to trespass to get here (remember, trespassing is against the law), and nudity (also illegal in Hawaii—arrests have been made) is common here.

To reach the beach, put on solid walking shoes (no flip-flops) and walk south on Uakea Road, past Haoli Street and the Hotel Hana-Maui, to the parking lot for the hotel's Sea Ranch Cottages. Turn left and cross the open field next to the Hana Community Center. Look for the dirt trail and follow it to the huge ironwood tree, where you turn right (do not go ahead to the old Japanese cemetery). Use the ironwood trees to maintain your balance as you follow the ever-eroding cinder footpath a short distance along the shoreline, down the narrow cliff trail (do not attempt this if it's wet). The trail suddenly turns the corner, and into view comes the burnt-red beach, set off by the turquoise waters, black lava, and vivid green ironwood trees.

The lava outcropping protects the bay and makes it safe for swimming. Snorkeling is excellent and there's a natural whirlpool area on the Hana Bay side of the cove. Stay away from the surge area where the ocean enters the cove.

KOKI BEACH 🐟 One of the best surfing and Boogie Boarding beaches on the Hana Coast lies just a couple of miles from the Hasegawa General Store in the Oheo Gulch direction. There is a very strong rip current here, so unless it is dead calm and you are a strong swimmer, do not attempt swimming here. In fact, a sign on the emergency call box, installed after a drowning in 1996, warns of the strong currents. It's a great place, though, to sit on the white sand and watch the surfers. The only facility is a big parking area. To get here, drive toward Oheo Gulch from Hana, where Highway 36 changes to Highway 31. About 1½ miles outside of Hana, turn left at Haneoo Road.

HAMOA BEACH ★★ For one of Hana's best beaches—great for swimming, Boogie Boarding, and sunbathing—continue another half mile down the Haneoo Road loop to Hamoa Beach. There is easy access from the road down to the sandy beach, and facilities include a small restroom and an outdoor shower. The large pavilion and beach accessories are for the guests of the Hotel Hana-Maui.

WAIOKA POND Locally, this swimming hole in a series of waterfalls and pools is called Venus Pool, and the rumor is that in ancient Hawaii, only royalty were allowed to use this exquisite site. The freshwater swimming area is a great place to spend a secluded day. Only two warnings here: Don't go to the pond if it has been raining (flash floods), and don't go near the surf at the ocean end of the stream (strong undertow). To get here, park your car well off the Hana Highway at mile marker 48, before the bridge. Hop over the fence on the ocean side of the bridge, and follow the well-worn footpath that parallels the stream. At the stream, turn to your right to take the path down to the smooth rocks above the stream. There's a huge pond just off the white-rock waterfall with a little island you can swim to in the middle.

HIKING

Hana is woven with hiking trails along the shoreline, through the rainforest, and up in the mountains. See "Hiking & Camping" in chapter 6, for a discussion of hiking in Waianapanapa and up to Fagan's Cross.

Another excellent hike leads you to **Piilanihale Heiau** ★★ and **Blue Pool** ★. This easy, 3-mile round-trip takes you to a freshwater, ocean-side waterfall and swimming pool at the halfway point. On the way back, you can tour a tropical botanical garden and see the largest heiau in the state. The hike is on a Jeep trail with some climbing over boulders, so wear good hiking boots or tennis shoes (no flip-flops) and bring a swimsuit and mosquito repellent. Go in the morning, when the sun lights up the ocean-side pool, and you'll have plenty of time for a picnic lunch before seeing the garden and heiau in the afternoon.

Turn toward the ocean on Ulaino Road, by mile marker 31. Drive down the paved road (which turns into a dirt road but is still drivable) to the first stream (about 1½ miles). If the stream is flooded, turn around and go back. If you can forge the stream, cross it and park on the right side of the road by the huge bread-fruit trees. The trees are part of the 122-acre **Kahanu Garden** ★★ (© **808/ 248-8912**), owned and operated by the National Tropical Botanical Garden (www.ntbg.org), which also has two gardens on Kauai. Open Monday through Friday, 10am to 2pm, admission is $5 for adults and free for children 12 and under, guided tours by reservation. Allow at least an hour to explore the gardens and heiau.

The 122 acres encompass plant collections from the Pacific Islands, concentrating on plants of value to the people of Polynesia, Micronesia, and Melanesia. Kahanu Garden contains the largest known collection of breadfruit cultivars from more than 17 Pacific Island groups and Indonesia, the Philippines, and the Seychelles.

The real draw here is the **Piilanihale Heiau** ("House of Piilani," one of Maui's greatest chiefs—see "A Look at the Past" earlier in this chapter). Believed to be the largest in the state, it measures 340 feet by 415 feet, and it was built in a unique terrace design not seen anywhere else in Hawaii. The walls are some 50 feet tall and 8 to 10 feet thick. Historians believe that Piilani's two sons and his grandson built the mammoth temple, which was dedicated to war, sometime in the 1500s.

You can park your car here and walk down the Jeep road that parallels the Kahanu Gardens. You'll have to forge two more streams before the road ends at the beach. Cross the rock-and-gravel beach. If it has been dry, you can just walk along the shoreline. If there has been rain, you will need to cross over the big boulders in the stream. Continue walking down the beach to the 100-foot waterfall on your left with its deep freshwater pool, known locally as **Blue Pool.** After a dip in the bracing spring water, you can sun yourself and eat a picnic lunch on the large boulders.

JUST BEYOND HANA
TROPICAL HALEAKALA: OHEO GULCH AT KIPAHULU 🦀🦀
If you're thinking about heading out to the so-called Seven Sacred Pools, out past Hana at the Kipahulu end of Haleakala National Park, let's clear this up right now: There are more than seven pools—about 24, actually—and *all* water in Hawaii is considered sacred. It's all a PR scam that has spun out of control into contemporary myth. Folks here call the attraction by its rightful name, **Oheo Gulch,** and visitors sometimes refer to it as Kipahulu, which is actually the name of the area where Oheo Gulch is located. No matter what you call it, it's a beautiful sight. The dazzling series of waterfall pools and cataracts cascading into the sea is so popular that it now has its own roadside parking lot.

Even though Oheo is part of Haleakala National Park, you cannot drive here from the summit. Even hiking from Halekala to Oheo is tricky: The access trail out of Haleakala is down Kaupo Gap, which ends at the ocean, a good 6 miles down the coast from Oheo. To drive to Oheo, head for Hana, some 60 miles from Kahului on the Hana Highway (Hwy. 36). Oheo is about 30 to 50 minutes beyond Hana, along Highway 31. The Highway 31 bridge passes over pools near the ocean; the other pools, plus magnificent 400-foot Waimoku falls, are reachable via an often-muddy but rewarding, hour-long uphill hike (see "Hiking & Camping" in chapter 6). Expect showers on the Kipahulu coast. The admission fee is $5 per person or $10 per car.

The **Kipahulu Ranger Station** (© **808/248-7375**) is staffed from 9am to 5pm daily. Restrooms are available, but no drinking water. Kipahulu rangers offer safety information, exhibits, books, and a variety of walks and hikes year-round; check at the station for current activities.

There are a number of hikes in the park, and tent camping is allowed. See "Hiking & Camping" in chapter 6, for details.

Check with the Haleakala Park rangers before hiking up to or swimming in the pools, and always keep one eye on the water in the streams; the sky can be sunny near the coast, but floodwaters travel 6 miles down from 8,000 acres of Kipahulu Valley and can rise 4 feet in less than 10 minutes.

LINDBERGH'S GRAVE
A mile past Oheo Gulch on the ocean side of the road is **Lindbergh's Grave.** First to fly across the Atlantic Ocean, Charles A. Lindbergh (1902–74) found peace in the Pacific; he settled in Hana, where he died of cancer in 1974. The famous aviator is buried under river stones in a seaside graveyard behind the 1857 **Palapala Hoomau Congregational Church,** where his tombstone is engraved with his favorite words from the 139th Psalm: "If I take the wings of the morning and dwell in the uttermost parts of the sea . . ."

EVEN FARTHER AROUND THE BEND

About 2½ miles past Oheo Gulch, Kaupo Road, or Old Piilani Highway (Hwy. 31), turns rough and unpaved in parts, often full of potholes and ruts. In the spring, this is a beautiful drive. But if it has rained recently, this narrow, winding road washes out and becomes treacherous. Many car-rental companies forbid you from taking their cars on this road (not because they're worried about your safety, but because they don't want to send their tow trucks all the way out here); check your rental agreement before setting out on this road. Ask around about road conditions, or call the **Maui Public Works Department** (© **808/248-8254**) or the **Police Department** (© **808/248-8311**). Note that Kaupo Road links back to upcountry Maui, not South Maui. If you're heading back to the beaches after your visit to Hana, you're better off retracing your route on the Hana Highway.

The road is unpaved all the way to the fishing village of **Kaupo,** one lane at times, wandering in and out of valleys with sharp rock walls and blind bends hugging the ocean cliffs. You may encounter wild pigs and stray cows. About 6 miles and about 60 minutes from Oheo Gulch, you'll see the restored **Huialoha Congregationalist "Circuit" Church,** originally constructed in 1859. Across from the church and down the road a bit is the **Kaupo Store** (© **808/248-8054**), which marks the center of the ranching community of Kaupo. Store hours are officially Monday through Friday from 7:30am to 4:30pm, but in this arid cattle country, posted store hours often prove meaningless. The Kaupo Store is the last of the Soon family stores, which at one time stretched from Kaupo to Keanae.

From the Kaupo Store, the landscape turns into barren, dry desert. In the lee of Haleakala, this area gets little rain. There are no phones or services until you reach **Ulupalakua Ranch** (p. 204), where there's a winery, general store, and gas station, which is likely to be closed.

Between mile markers 29 and 30, look for the ancient lava flow that created an arch as it rolled down Haleakala. Keep an eye peeled for cattle, because this is open range country. Eventually the road will wind uphill, and suddenly the forest and greenery of Ulupalakula come into sight. From here, you're about 45 minutes from Kahului.

8

Shops & Galleries

Maui is a shopaholic's dream as well as an arts center, with a large number of resident artists who show their works in dozens of galleries and countless gift shops. Maui is also the queen of specialty products, an agricultural cornucopia that includes Kula onions, upcountry protea, Kaanapali coffee, world-renowned potato chips, and many other tasty treats that are shipped worldwide.

As with any popular visitor destination, you'll have to wade through bad art and mountains of trinkets, particularly in Lahaina and Kihei, where touristy boutiques line the streets between rare pockets of treasures. If you shop in South or West Maui, expect to pay resort prices, clear down to a bottle of Evian or sunscreen.

With a well-heeled flourish, **The Shops at Wailea,** an upscale shopping and restaurant complex, opened in South Maui in 2001. The 16-acre complex features more than 50 shops and five restaurants, everything from an ABC store to Louis Vuitton, Tiffany, Gap, Banana Republic, and the ever-popular local retailers Martin & MacArthur and Ki'i Gallery. This is resort shopping much in the vein of Whalers Village in Kaanapali, where shopping and restaurant activity is concentrated in a single oceanfront complex. The Shops at Wailea signals a repositioning of the resort as a place of heightened commercial activity.

Don't ignore central Maui, home to some first-rate boutiques. Watch Wailuku, which is poised for a resurgence—if not now, soon. The town has its own antiques alleys, the new Sig Zane Designs has brought a delightful infusion of creative and cultural energy, and a major promenade/emporium on Main Street is in the works. The Kaahumanu Center, in neighboring Kahului, is becoming more fashionable by the month.

Upcountry, Makawao's boutiques are worth seeking out, despite some attitude and high prices. The charm of shopping on Maui has always rested in the small, independent shops and galleries that crop up in surprising places.

1 Central Maui

KAHULUI

Kahului's best shopping is concentrated in two places. Almost all of the shops listed below are at one of the following centers:

The once rough-around-the-edges **Maui Mall,** 70 E. Kaahumanu Ave. (© **808/877-7559**), is the talk of Kahului. Newly renovated, it's now bigger and better, and has retained some of our favorite stores while adding a 12-screen movie megaplex that features current releases as well as art-house films. The mall is still a place of everyday good things, from **Long's Drugs** to **Star Market** to **Tasaka Guri Guri,** the decades-old purveyor of inimitable icy treats, neither ice cream nor shave ice but something in between.

Queen Kaahumanu Center, 275 Kaahumanu Ave. (© 808/877-3369), 5 minutes from the Kahului Airport on Highway 32, offers more than 100 shops, restaurants, and theaters. Its second-floor Plantation District offers home furnishings and accessories, fabulous Naot and Kenneth Cole shoes (**Native Soles**), and gift and accessories shops. Kaahumanu covers all the bases, from the arts and crafts to a **Foodland Supermarket** and everything in between: a thriving food court; the island's best beauty supply, **Lisa's Beauty Supply & Salon** (© 808/877-6463), and its sister store for cosmetics, **Madison Avenue Day Spa and Boutique** (© 808/873-0880); mall standards like **Sunglass Hut, Radio Shack,** and **Local Motion** (surf and beach wear—including the current fad, women's board shorts, a combination of hot pants and men's surf trunks); attractive gift shops such as **Maui Hands** and standard department stores like **Macy's** and **Sears.**

Apricot Rose   The former Caswell-Massey has changed its name but still offers the same selection of products for beauty and home: unique Maui-made soaps and bath products that use tropical fragrances and botanicals. America's oldest perfume company, established in 1752, Caswell-Massey triple-mills all of its soaps (so they last longer), scents them with natural oils, and uses old-fashioned, tried-and-true methods and ingredients. Choose from hundreds of specialty products, from decadent bath salts with 23-karat gold flakes to Damask rose shampoo and bath gels, body lotions, sachets, candles, perfume bottles, potpourris, room mists, and more. You can also get handsome, custom-designed baskets at no extra charge. In the Kaahumanu Center. © 808/877-7761.

Cost Less Imports   Natural fibers are ubiquitous in this newly expanded corner of the Maui Mall. Household accessories include lauhala, bamboo blinds, grassy floor and window coverings, shoji-style lamps, burlap yardage, baskets, Balinese cushions, Asian imports, and top-of-the-line, made-on-Maui soaps and handicrafts. Japanese folk curtains, called *noreng,* are among the diverse items you'll find here; it's a good source of tropical and Asian home decor. In the Maui Mall. © 808/877-0300.

Lightning Bolt Maui Inc.   Here's an excellent selection of women's board shorts, aloha shirts, swimwear, sandals and shoes, and all necessary accouterments for fun in the sun. Quality labels such as Patagonia and high-tech, state-of-the-art outdoor gear and moccasins attract adventurers heading for the chilly hinterlands as well as the sun-drenched shores. 55 Kaahumanu Ave. © 808/877-3484.

Maui Hands   Maui hands have made most of the items in this shop/gallery. Because it's a consignment shop, you'll find Hawaii-made handicrafts and prices that aren't inflated. The selection includes paintings, prints, jewelry, glass marbles, native-wood bowls, and tchotchkes for every budget. This is an ideal stop for made-on-Maui products and crafts of good quality; 90% of what's sold here was made on the island. The original **Maui Hands** remains in Makawao at the Courtyard, 3620 Baldwin Ave. (© 808/572-5194); another Maui Hands can be found in Paia, at 84 Hana Hwy. (© 808/579-9245). In the Kaahumanu Center. © 808/877-0368.

Maui Swap Meet   The Maui Swap Meet, the pioneer of neighbor-island markets, is a large and popular event. After Thanksgiving and throughout December, the number of booths explodes into the hundreds and the activity reaches fever pitch. The colorful Maui specialties include vegetables from Kula and Keanae, fresh taro, plants, proteas, crafts, household items, homemade ethnic foods, and baked goods, including some fabulous fruit breads. Every Saturday from 7am to noon, vendors spread out their wares in booths and under tarps, in a festival-like atmosphere that is pure Maui with a touch of kitsch. Between the cheap Balinese imports and New Age crystals and incense, you may find some vintage John Kelly prints and 1930s collectibles. Admission is 50¢, and if you go early while the vendors are setting up, no one will turn you away. S. Puunene Ave. (next to the Kahului Post Office). ⓒ **808/877-3100.**

Summerhouse   Sleek and chic, tiny Summerhouse is big on style: casual and party dresses, separates by Russ Berens, FLAX, Kiko, and Tencel jeans by Signatur—the best. During the holiday season the selection gets dressy and sassy, but it's a fun browse year-round. We adore the hats, accessories, easy-care clothing, and up-to-the-minute evening dresses that Summerhouse carries in abundance. The high-quality T-shirts are always a cut above. The casual selection is well suited to the island lifestyle. In the Dairy Center, 395 Dairy Rd. ⓒ **808/871-1320.**

EDIBLES

The **Star Market** and **Long's Drugs** in the Maui Mall, **Foodland** in the Kaahumanu Center, and **Safeway** at 170 E. Kamehameha Ave. will satisfy your ordinary grocery needs. On Saturday, you may want to check out the **Maui Swap Meet** (see above).

Down to Earth Natural Foods, 305 Dairy Rd. (ⓒ **808/877-2661**), a health-food staple for many years, has fresh organic produce, a bountiful salad bar, sandwiches and smoothies, vitamins and supplements, fresh-baked goods, chips and snacks, whole grains, and several packed aisles of vegetarian and health foods.

Maui's produce has long been a source of pride for islanders, and **Ohana Farmers Market** (ⓒ **808/871-8347**), Kahului Shopping Center, is the place to find a fresh, inexpensive selection of Maui-grown fruit, vegetables, flowers, and plants. Crafts and gourmet foods add to the event, and the large monkeypod trees provide welcome shade.

WAILUKU

Located at the gateway to Iao Valley, Wailuku is the county seat, the part of Maui where people live and work. Wailuku's attractive vintage architecture, smattering of antiques shops, and mom-and-pop eateries imbue the town with a down-home charm noticeably absent in the resort areas of West, South, and upcountry Maui. The community spirit fuels festivals throughout the year and is slowly attracting new businesses, but Wailuku is still a work in progress. It's a mixed bag—of course there's junk, but a stroll along Main and Market streets usually turns up a treasure or two.

Bailey House Gift Shop   For made-in-Hawaii items, Bailey House is a must-stop. It offers a thoroughly enjoyable browse through authoritative Hawaiiana, in a museum that's one of the finest examples of missionary architecture, dating from 1833. Gracious gardens, rare paintings of early Maui, wonderful programs in Hawaiian arts and culture, and a restored hand-hewn koa canoe await visitors. The shop, a small space of discriminating taste, packs a wallop with its selection of remarkable gift items, from Hawaiian music to exquisite woods, traditional Hawaiian games to pareus and books. Prints by the legendary Hawaii artist Madge Tennent, lauhala hats hanging in midair, hand-sewn pheasant hatbands, jams and jellies, Maui cookbooks, and an occasional Hawaiian quilt are some of the treasures to be found here. In the Bailey House Museum, 2375-A Main St. ⓒ **808/244-3326.**

Bird of Paradise Unique Antiques   Owner Joe Myhand loves furniture, old Matson liner menus, blue willow china, kimono for children, and anything nostalgic that happens to be Hawaiian. The furniture in the strongly Hawaiian collection ranges from 1940s rattan to wicker and old koa—those items tailor-made for informal island living and leisurely moments on the lanai. The collection ebbs and flows with his finds, keeping buyers waiting in the wings for Depression glass, California pottery from the 1930s and 1940s, old dinnerware, perfume bottles, vintage aloha shirts, and vintage Hawaiian music on cassettes. 56 N. Market St. ✆ 808/242-7699.

Brown-Kobayashi From self-adornment to interior design, graceful living is the theme here. Prices range from a few dollars to the thousands in this 750-square-foot treasure trove. The owners have added a fabulous selection of antique stone garden pieces that mingle quietly with Asian antiques and old and new French, European, and Hawaiian objects. Although the collection is eclectic, there is a strong cohesive aesthetic that sets Brown-Kobayashi apart from other Maui antiques stores. Japanese kimono and obi, Bakelite and Peking glass beads, breathtaking Japanese lacquerware, cricket carriers, and cloisonné are among the delights here. Exotic and precious Chinese woods (purple sandalwood and huanghauali) glow discreetly from quiet corners, and an occasional monarchy-style lidded milo bowl comes in and flies out. 160-A N. Market St. ✆ 808/242-0804.

Gottling Ltd. Karl Gottling's shop specializes in Asian antique furniture, but you can also find smaller carvings, precious stones, jewelry, opium weights, and finds in all sizes. To give you an idea of the range of possibilities here: On a recent visit, we saw a cabinet with 350-year-old doors, a 17th-century Buddha lending an air of serenity next to a 150-year-old Chinese cabinet, and Ming dynasty ceramics. The prices vary as widely, from carved wooden apples for $15 to a Persian rug for $65,000. 34 N. Market St. ✆ 808/244-7779.

Old Daze Nineteenth-century Americana and Hawaiian collectibles are nicely wedded in this charming shop. The collection features a modest furniture selection, Hawaiian pictures, 1960s ashtrays, Depression glass, old washboards, and souvenir plates from county fairs. Choices range from hokey to rustic to pleasantly nostalgic, with many items for the kitchen. Some recent finds: an 1850s German sideboard, a Don Blanding teapot, Royal Worcester china, antique kimono, and framed vintage music sheets. Owner Geni Dowling's love of nostalgia fills every corner of this tiny shop. 7 North Market St. (close to Main St.). ✆ 808/249-0014.

Sig Zane Designs Wailuku Here is a designer with a graphic sense and personal integrity that never wanes, who integrates visual sense with cultural sensibility in a way that is inimitable. Whether it's a T-shirt, golf shirt, pareu, duffel bag, aloha shirt, or muumuu, a Sig Zane design has depth and sizzle. That is why, when Hilo-based Sig Zane Designs opened on Wailuku's Market Street, near Iao Theater, the entire island perked up. Zane and co-owner Punawai Rice have redefined Hawaiian wear by creating an inimitable style in clothing, textiles, furnishings, bedding, and lifestyle accessories, and this, their Maui store, has proven enormously successful. Zane's strong, graphic fabrics are made into aloha shirts and women's wear and used in interiors and furnishings that evoke the gracious Hawaii of an earlier time. The staff is helpful and willing to share the background of each design, so you will learn much about the culture, botany, mythology, and beauty of the Islands. 53 Market St. ✆ 808/249-8997.

EDIBLES

Established in 1941, the **Ooka Super Market,** 1870 Main St., Wailuku (✆ **808/244-3931**), Maui's ultimate homegrown supermarket, is a mom-and-pop business that has grown by leaps and bounds but still manages to keep its neighborhood flavor. Ooka sells inexpensive produce (fresh Maui mushrooms for a song), fresh island seafood, certified Angus beef, and Maui specialties such as manju and mochi. Proteas cut the same day, freesias in season, hydrangeas, fresh leis, torch ginger from Hana, upcountry calla lilies in season, and multicolored anthuriums are offered at what is one of Maui's finest and most affordable retail flower selections. Prepared foods are also a hit: bentos and plate lunches, roast chicken and laulau, and specialties from all the islands. The fish is fresh, and the seaweed, poi, Kula persimmons in fall, fresh Haiku mushrooms, and dried marlin from Kona are among the local delicacies that make Ooka a Maui favorite.

Located in the northern section of Wailuku, **Takamiya Market,** 359 N. Market St. (© **808/244-3404**), is much loved by local folks and visitors with adventurous palates, who often drive all the way from Kihei to stock up on picnic fare and mouthwatering ethnic foods for sunset gatherings. Unpretentious home-cooked foods from East and West are prepared daily and served on plastic-foam plates. From the chilled-fish counter come fresh sashimi and poke, and in the renowned assortment of prepared foods are mounds of shoyu chicken, tender fried squid, roast pork, kalua pork, laulau, Chinese noodles, fiddlehead ferns, and Western comfort foods, such as corn bread and potato salad. Fresh produce and paper products are also available, but it's the prepared foods and fresh-fish counter that have made Takamiya's a household name in central Maui.

2 West Maui

LAHAINA

Lahaina's merchants and art galleries go all out from 7 to 9pm on Friday, when **Art Night** brings an extra measure of hospitality and community spirit. The Art Night openings are usually marked with live entertainment, refreshments, and a livelier-than-usual street scene.

If you're in Lahaina on the second or last Thursday of the month, stroll by the front lawn of the **Baldwin Home,** 120 Dickenson St. (at Front St.), for a splendid look at lei-making and an opportunity to meet the gregarious seniors of Lahaina. In a program sponsored by AARP, they gather from 10am to 4pm to demonstrate lei-making, to sell their floral creations, and, equally important, to socialize.

What was formerly a big, belching pineapple cannery is now a maze of shops and restaurants at the northern end of Lahaina town, known as the **Lahaina Cannery Mall,** 1221 Honoapiilani Hwy. (© **808/661-5304**). Find your way through the T-shirt and sportswear shops to **Lahaina Printsellers,** home of antique originals, prints, paintings, and wonderful 18th- to 20th-century cartography, representing the largest collection of engravings and antique maps in Hawaii. Follow the scent of coffee to **Sir Wilfred's Coffee House,** where you can unwind with espresso and croissants, or head for **Compadres Bar & Grill,** where the margaritas flow freely and the Mexican food is tasty (see chapter 5). For film, water, aspirin, groceries, sunscreen, and other things you can't live without, nothing beats **Long's Drugs** and **Safeway,** two old standbys. **Roland's** may surprise you with its selection of footwear, everything from Cole-Haan sophisticates to inexpensive sandals. At the recently expanded food court, the new **Compadres Taquería** sells Mexican food to go, while **L & L Drive-Inn** sells plate lunches near Greek, pizza, Vietnamese, and Japanese food booths.

The **Lahaina Center,** 900 Front St. (© **808/667-9216**), is still a work in progress. It's located north of Lahaina's most congested strip, where Front Street begins. Across the street from the center, the seawall is a much-sought-after front-row seat to the sunset. There's plenty of free validated parking and easy access to more than 30 shops, a salon, restaurants, a nightclub, and a four-plex movie-theater complex. **Ruth's Chris Steak House** has opened its doors in Lahaina Center, and **Maui Brews** serves lunch and dinner and offers live music nightly except weekends. Among the shopping stops: **Banana Republic,** the **Hilo Hattie Fashion Center** (a dizzying emporium of aloha wear), **ABC Discount Store,** and a dozen other recreational, dining, and entertainment options.

The conversion of 10,000 square feet of parking space into the re-creation of a traditional Hawaiian village is a welcome touch of Hawaiiana at Lahaina Center. With the commercialization of modern Lahaina, it's easy to forget that it was once the capital of the Hawaiian kingdom and a significant historic site. The village, called **Hale Kahiko,** features three main houses, called *hale:* a sleeping house; the men's dining house; and the crafts house, where women pounded hala (pandanus) strips to weave into mats and baskets. Construction of the houses consumed 10,000 square feet of ohia wood from the island, 20 tons of pili grass, and more than 4 miles of hand-woven coconut sennit for the lashings. Artifacts, weapons, a canoe, and indigenous trees are among the authentic touches in this village, which can be toured privately or with a guide.

David Lee Galleries This gallery is devoted to the works of David Lee, who uses natural powder colors to paint on silk. The pigments and technique create a luminous, ethereal quality. 712 Front St. ℂ **808/667-7740.**

Gary's Island What a pleasant place to shop. Gary's cranks up the fun factor in aloha wear with this abundant, well-displayed selection of aloha shirts featuring the hot and up-and-coming labels of the genre. Lahaina was number 11 in the Gary's chain of brightly colored resort shops—its first venture outside of California and Las Vegas. You must go through Gary's to enter Woody's, a restaurant hanging over the ocean, and you won't be sorry. We've found fantastic hula-girl silk ties here by Tommy Bahama, and some offbeat shirt styles by Toes on the Nose and the usual top-drawer lines, such as Kamehameha, Tori Richard, Reyn's, Avanti, and Kahala. This tiny but dynamic shop also carries shoes for men and women, from Cole-Haan to gel-soled Sensis. 839-A Front St. ℂ **808/662-0424.**

Lahaina Arts Society Galleries With its membership of more than 185 Maui artists, the nonprofit Lahaina Arts Society is an excellent community resource. Changing monthly exhibits in the Banyan Tree and Old Jail galleries offer a good look at the island's artistic well: two-dimensional art, fiber art, ceramics, sculpture, prints, jewelry, and more. In the shade of the humongous banyan tree in the square across from Pioneer Inn, "Art in the Park" fairs are offered every second and fourth weekend of the month. 648 Wharf St. ℂ **808/661-3228.**

Lei Spa Maui Expanded to include two massage rooms and shower facilities, this is a day spa offering facials and other therapies. It's a good sign that 95% of the beauty and bath products sold are made on Maui, and that includes Hawaiian Botanical Pikake shower gel; kukui and macadamia-nut oils; Hawaiian potpourris; mud masks with Hawaiian seaweed; and a spate of rejuvenating, cleansing, skin-soothing potions for hair and skin. Aromatherapy body oils and perfumes are popular, as are the handmade soaps and fragrances of torch ginger, plumeria, coconut, tuberose, and sandalwood. Scented candles in coconut shells, inexpensive and fragrant, make great gifts. 505 Front St. ℂ **808/661-1178.**

Martin Lawrence Galleries   The front is garish, with pop art, kinetic sculptures, and bright, carnivalesque glass objects. Toward the back of the gallery, however, there's a sizable inventory of two-dimensional art and some plausible choices for collectors of Keith Haring, Andy Warhol, and other pop artists. The originals, limited-edition graphics, and sculptures also include works by Marc Chagall, Pablo Picasso, Joan Miró, Roy Lichtenstein, and other noted artists. The focus is pop art and national and international artists. In Lahaina Market Place, 126 Lahainaluna Rd. ✆ 808/661-1788.

Na Mea Hawaii   The best of Hawaii can be found here, if not in the striking Tutuvi silk-screened dresses and shirts, then in the delicately patterned shawls and scarves of Maile Andrade that depict Hawaiian scenes and traditions on velvet. Arts, crafts, gifts, and clothing, all made by Hawaii artists, fill this cozy niche of Lahaina in the historic Baldwin House on Front Street. You might find a beautifully made lauhala bag, a colorful muumuu, a Hawaii-themed book, or a pheasant hat lei made by master feather lei makers Mary Lou Kekuewa and Paulette Kahalepuna. The shop is tiny, filled with the colors, fibers, and spirit of Hawaii. Lahaina Cannery Mall, 1221 Honoapiilani Hwy. ✆ 808/667-5345.

The Old Lahaina Book Emporium   What a bookstore! Chockablock with used books in stacks, shelves, counters, and aisles, this bookstore is a browser's dream. More than 25,000 quality used books are lovingly housed in this shop, where owner JoAnn Carroll treats books and customers well. The store is 95% used books and 100% delight. Specialties include Hawaiiana, fiction, mystery, sci-fi, and military history, with substantial selections in cookbooks, children's books, and philosophy/religion. You could pay as little as $2 for a quality read, or a whole lot more for that rare first edition. Books on tape, videos, the classics, and old guitar magazines are among the treasures of this two-story emporium. 505 Front St. ✆ 808/661-1399.

Totally Hawaiian Gift Gallery   This gallery makes a good browse for its selection of Niihau shell jewelry, excellent Hawaiian CDs, Norfolk pine bowls, and Hawaiian quilt kits. Hawaiian quilt patterns sewn in Asia (at least they're honest about it) are labor-intensive, less expensive, and attractive, although not totally Hawaiian. Hawaiian-quilt-patterned gift wraps and tiles, perfumes and soaps, handcrafted dolls, and koa accessories are of good quality, and the artists, such as Kelly Dunn (Norfolk wood bowls), Jerry Kermode (wood), and Pat Coito (wood), are among the tops in their fields. In the Lahaina Cannery Mall, 1221 Honoapiilani Hwy. ✆ 808/667-2558.

Village Galleries in Lahaina   The nearly 30-year-old Village Galleries is the oldest continuously running gallery on Maui, and it's highly esteemed as one of the few galleries with consistently high standards. Art collectors know this as a respectable showcase for regional artists; the selection of mostly original two- and three-dimensional art offers a good look at the quality of work originating on the island. The newer contemporary gallery offers colorful gift items and jewelry. 120 and 180 Dickenson St. ✆ 808/661-4402 or 808/661-5559. Also the Ritz-Carlton Kapalua, 1 Ritz-Carlton Dr. ✆ 808/669-1800.

Down to Earth   A longtime Lahaina staple, Down to Earth is serious about providing tasty food that's healthy and affordable. Its excellent food bar offers vegetarian lasagna, marinated tofu strips, vegetarian pot-pie, crisp salads, grains, curries, and gorgeous organic produce. The selection changes regularly, and the products section covers produce, cosmetics, and healthy food staples. 193 Lahainaluna Rd. ✆ 808/667-2855.

KAANAPALI

On a recent trip we were somewhat disappointed with upscale **Whalers Village,** 2435 Kaanapali Pkwy. (② **808/661-4567**). Although it offers everything from whale blubber to Prada and Ferragamo, it is short on local shops and parking at the nearby lot is expensive. The complex is home to the Whalers Village Museum with its interactive exhibits and 40-foot sperm whale skeleton, but shoppers come for the designer thrills and beachfront dining. You can find most of the items featured here in the shops in Lahaina and can avoid the parking hassle and the high prices by skipping this "not-worth-the-time-or-money" shopping center.

Our favorite shoe store, **Sandal Tree,** has its third store in Whalers Village. (you can skip Whaler's Village and shop at the other 2 stores, 1 at Hyatt Regency Maui and the other, Grand Wailea Resort in Wailea). **Martin & MacArthur,** a mainstay of the village, offers a dizzying array of Hawaii crafts: Hawaiian-quilt cushion covers, jewelry, soaps, books, and a stunning selection of woodworks. The always wonderful **Lahaina Printsellers** has a selection of antique prints, maps, paintings, and engravings, including 18th- to 20th-century cartography, all of which offer great browsing and gift potential. You can find award-winning **Kimo Bean** coffee at a kiosk, an expanded **Reyn's** for aloha wear, and **Cinnamon Girl,** a hit in Honolulu for its matching mother-daughter clothing. The return of **Waldenbooks** makes it that much easier to pick up the latest bestseller on the way to the beach. Once you've stood under the authentic whale skeleton at the **Whale Center of the Pacific** (see chapter 7), you can blow a bundle at **Tiffany, Prada, Chanel, Ferragamo, Vuitton, Coach, Dolphin Galleries, The Body Shop,** or any of the more than 60 shops and restaurants that have sprouted in this open-air shopping center. The posh Euro trend continues; despite obvious efforts to offer more of a balance between island-made and designer goods, the chain luxury stores still dominate.

Other mainstays: The **Eyecatcher** has an extensive selection of sunglasses; it's located just across from the busiest **ABC** store in the state. **Pizza Paradiso** has taken over the former **Maui Yogurt Company** and sells ice cream and smoothies in a food court of other dine-and-dash goodies, such as the terrific Japanese fare of **Ganso Kawara Soba,** a noodle's length away. Whalers Village is open daily from 9:30am to 10pm.

Ki'i Gallery Some of the works are large and lavish, such as the Toland Sand prisms for just under $5,000 and the John Stokes handblown glass. Those who love glass in all forms, from handblown vessels to jewelry, will enjoy a browse through Ki'i. We found Pat Kazi's work in porcelain and found objects, such as the mermaid in a teacup, inspired by fairy tales and mythology, both fantastic and compelling. The gallery is devoted to glass and original paintings and drawings; roughly half of the artists are from Hawaii. Hyatt Regency Maui, 200 Nohea Kai Dr. ② **808/661-4456.**

Sandal Tree It's unusual for a resort shop to draw local customers on a regular basis (add time and parking costs to that pair of sandals), but the Sandal Tree attracts a flock of footwear fanatics who come here from throughout the islands for rubber thongs and Top-Siders, sandals and dressy pumps, athletic shoes and hats, designer footwear, and much more. Sandal Tree also carries a generous selection of Mephisto and Arche comfort sandals, Donald Pliner, Anne Klein, Charles Jourdan, and beach wear and casual footwear for all tastes. Accessories range from fashionable knapsacks to avant-garde geometrical handbags—for town and country, day and evening, kids, women, and men. Prices are realistic, too. In Whalers Village, 2435 Kaanapali Pkwy. © **808/667-5330.** Also in the Grand Wailea Resort, 3850 Wailea Alanui Dr., Wailea; and in the Hyatt Regency Maui, 200 Nohea Kai Dr.

KAHANA/NAPILI/HONOKOWAI

Those driving north of Kaanapali toward Kapalua will notice the **Honokowai Marketplace** on Lower Honoapiilani Road, only minutes before the Kapalua Airport. There are restaurants and coffee shops, a dry cleaner, the flagship **Star Market, Hula Scoops** for ice cream, a gas station, a copy shop, a few clothing stores, and the sprawling **Hawaiian Interiorz.**

Nearby **Kahana Gateway** is an unimpressive mall built to serve the condominium community that has sprawled along the coastline between Honokowai and Kapalua. If you need women's swimsuits, however, **Rainbow Beach Swimwear** is a find. It carries a selection of suits for all shapes, at lower-than-resort prices, slashed even further during the frequent sales. **Hutton's Fine Jewelry** offers high-end jewelry from designers around the country (lots of platinum and diamonds), reflecting discerning taste for those who can afford it. Tahitian black pearls and jade (some hundreds of years old, all certified) are among Hutton's specialties.

KAPALUA

Honolua Store   Walk on the old wood floors peppered with holes from golf shoes and find your everyday essentials: bottled water, stationery, mailing tape, jackets, chips, wine, soft drinks, paper products, fresh fruit and produce, and aisles of notions and necessities. With picnic tables on the veranda and a take-out counter offering deli items—more than a dozen types of sandwiches, salads, and budget-friendly breakfasts—there are always long lines of customers. Golfers and surfers love to come here for the morning paper and coffee, when the ground is still aglow with dew. 502 Office Rd. (next to the Ritz-Carlton Kapalua). © **808/669-6128.**

Kapalua Shops   Shops have come and gone in this small, exclusive, and once-chic shopping center, now much quieter than in days past. The closing of elegant Mandalay is a big loss. The **Elizabeth Dole Gallery** has loads of Dale Chihuly studio glass, fabulous and expensive, a dramatic counterpoint to **South Seas Trading Post** and its exotic artifacts such as New Guinea masks, Balinese beads, tribal jewelry, lizard-skin drums, and coconut-shell carvings with mother-of-pearl inlay. Otherwise, it's slim pickings for shoppers in Kapalua, where logo wear, jewelry, and real-estate offices are the norm and the fabulous Sansei sushi bar reigns. Kapalua Bay Hotel and Villas. © **808/669-1029.**

Village Galleries   Maui's finest exhibit their works here and in the other two Village Galleries in Lahaina. Take heart, art lovers: There's no clichéd marine art here. Translucent, delicately turned bowls of Norfolk pine gleam in the light,

---

A Creative Way to Spend the Day

Make a bowl from clay or paint a premade one, then fire it and take it home. The **Art School at Kapalua** (© **808/665-0007**), in a charming 1920s plantation building that was part of an old cannery operation, features local and visiting instructors and is open daily for people of all ages and skill levels. This not-for-profit organization offers projects, classes, and workshops that highlight creativity in all forms, including photography, figure drawing, ceramics, landscape painting, painting on silk, and the performing arts (ballet, yoga, creative movement, Pilates). Classes are inexpensive. Call the school to see what's scheduled while you're on Maui.

and George Allan, Betty Hay Freeland, and Pamela Andelin are included in the pantheon of respected artists represented in the tiny gallery. Watercolors, oils, sculptures, handblown glass, Niihau shell leis, jewelry, and other media are represented. The Ritz-Carlton's monthly Artist-in-Residence program features gallery artists in demonstrations and special hands-on workshops that are free, including materials. In the Ritz-Carlton Kapalua, 1 Ritz-Carlton Dr. ✆ **808/669-1800.**

3 South Maui

KIHEI

Kihei is one long stretch of strip malls. Most of the shopping here is concentrated in the **Azeka Place Shopping Center** on South Kihei Road. Fast foods abound at Azeka, as do tourist-oriented clothing shops like **Crazy Shirts.** Across the street, **Azeka Place II** houses several prominent attractions, including **General Nutrition Center,** the **Coffee Store,** and a cluster of specialty shops with everything from children's clothes to shoes, sunglasses, beauty services, and swimwear. Also on South Kihei Road is the **Kukui Mall,** with movie theaters, **Waldenbooks,** and **Whaler's General Store.**

Hawaiian Moons Natural Foods   Hawaiian Moons is a health-food store, and a great one, but it's also a minisupermarket with one of the best selections of Maui products on the island. The Mexican tortillas are made on Maui (and good!), and much of the produce here, such as organic vine-ripened tomatoes and organic onions, is grown in the fertile upcountry soil of Kula. There's also locally grown organic coffee, gourmet salsas, Maui shiitake mushrooms, organic lemongrass and okra, Maui Crunch bread, free-range Big Island turkeys and chickens (no antibiotics or artificial nasties), and fresh Maui juices. Cosmetics are top-of-the-line: a staggering selection of sunblock, fragrant floral oils, and Island Essence made-on-Maui mango-coconut and vanilla-papaya lotions, the ultimate in body pampering. The salad bar is one of the most popular food stops on the coast. 2411 S. Kihei Rd. ✆ **808/875-4356.**

Pua's Lei Stand   Surprise—fresh plumeria lei in hot Kihei! Located at the far mauka (mountainside) end of the shopping village, Pua's Lei Stand is an oasis of fragrance, freshness, and the spirit of Hawaii. You'll see lavish wiliwili and seed lei, hula implements, Hawaiian-printed flaxseed eye pillows, Hawaiian angels made from fibers found in Kihei, and all manner of made-on-Maui gems. The hard-to-find Maui Herbal soaps are generous blocks in fabulous fragrances of pikake, tuberose, guavaberry, tropical sea, and—our favorite—plumeria. These soaps lather richly and contain pure ingredients; their simple packaging belies the fact that they are of top quality, and not widely available. In Kihei Kalama Village, 1941 S. Kihei Rd. No phone.

Tuna Luna   There are treasures to be found in this small cluster of tables and booths where Maui artists display their work. Ceramics, raku, sculpture, glass, koa-wood books and photo albums, jewelry, soaps, handmade paper, and fiber-art accessories make great gifts to go. Watch for Maui Metal handcrafted journals, aluminum books with designs of hula girls, palms, fish, and sea horses. Tuna Luna also has a new booth in the back pavilion. In Kihei Kalama Village, 1941 S. Kihei Rd. ✆ **808/874-9482.**

WAILEA

The Shops at Wailea   This is the big shopping boost that resort-goers have been awaiting for years. Chains still rule (**The Gap, Louis Vuitton, Banana Republic, Tiffany, Crazy Shirts, Honolua Surf Co.**), but there is still fertile ground for the inveterate shopper in the nearly 60 shops in the complex. **Martin & MacArthur** (furniture and gift gallery; see Whalers Village above) has landed in Wailea as part of a retail mix that is similar to Whalers Village. The high-end resort shops sell expensive souvenirs, gifts, clothing, and accessories for a life of perpetual vacations. 3750 Wailea Alanui. ✆ **808/891-6770.**

CY Maui   Women who like washable, flowing clothing in silks, rayons, and natural fibers will love this shop, formerly the popular Manikin in Kahului. If you don't find what you want on the racks of simple bias-cut designs, you can have it made from the bolts of stupendous fabrics lining the shop. Except for a few hand-painted silks, everything in the shop is washable. In The Shops at Wailea, 3750 Wailea Alanui Dr, A-30. ✆ **808/891-0782.**

Grand Wailea Shops   The sprawling Grand Wailea Resort is known for its long arcade of shops and galleries tailored to hefty pocketbooks. However, gift items in all price ranges can be found at Lahaina Printsellers (for old maps and prints), Dolphin Galleries, H. F. Wichman, Sandal Tree, and Napua Gallery, which houses the private collection of the resort owner. Ki'i Gallery is luminous with studio glass and exquisitely turned woods, and **Sandal Tree** (p. 226) raises the footwear bar. At Grand Wailea Resort, 3850 Wailea Alanui Dr. ✆ **808/875-1234.**

4 Upcountry Maui

MAKAWAO

Besides being a shopper's paradise, Makawao is the home of the island's most prominent arts organization, the **Hui No'eau Visual Arts Center,** 2841 Baldwin Ave. (✆ **808/572-6560**). Designed in 1917 by C. W. Dickey, one of Hawaii's most prominent architects, the two-story, Mediterranean-style stucco home that houses the center is located on a sprawling 9-acre estate called Kaluanui. A legacy of Maui's prominent *kamaaina* (old-timers) Harry and Ethel Baldwin, the estate became an arts center in 1976. Visiting artists offer lectures, classes, and demonstrations, all at reasonable prices, in basketry, jewelry making, ceramics, painting, and other media. Classes on Hawaiian art, culture, and history are also available. Call ahead for schedules and details. The exhibits here are drawn from a wide range of disciplines and multicultural sources, and include both contemporary and traditional art from established and emerging artists. The gift shop, featuring many one-of-a-kind works by local artists and artisans, is worth a stop. Hours are Monday through Saturday from 10am to 4pm.

Collections   This long-time Makawao attraction is showing renewed vigor after more than 2 decades on Baldwin Avenue. It's one of our favorite Makawao stops, full of gift items and spirited clothing reflecting the ease and color of island living. Its selection of sportswear, soaps, jewelry, candles, and tasteful, marvelous miscellany reflects good sense and style. Dresses (including up-to-the-moment Citron in cross-cultural and vintage-looking prints), separates, home and bath accessories, sweaters, and a shop full of good things make this a Makawao must. 3677 Baldwin Ave. ✆ **808/572-0781.**

Cuckoo for Coconuts   The owner's quirky sense of humor pervades every inch of this tiny shop, which is brimming with vintage collectibles, gag gifts, silly coconuts, 1960s and '70s aloha wear, tutus, sequined dresses, vintage wedding gowns, and all sorts of oddities. Things we've seen there: an Elvira wig, very convincing; a raffia hat looking suspiciously like a nest, with blue eggs on top; and some vintage aloha shirts that would make a collector drool. New items include crazy sunglasses, colored wigs, tie-dyes, and party hats. Vintage aloha wear comes and goes, and gets grabbed up fast. The new services—singing telegrams, balloon deliveries, costumes, make-up, and gag gifts—keep the laughs coming. 1158 Makawao Ave. Ⓒ 808/573-6887.

Gallery Maui Follow the sign down the charming shaded pathway to a cozy gallery of top-notch art and crafts. Most of the works here are by Maui artists, and the quality is outstanding. About 30 artists are represented: Wayne Omura and his Norfolk pine bowls, Pamela Hayes's watercolors, Martha Vockrodt and her wonderful paintings, a stunning Steve Hynson dresser of curly koa and ebony. The two- and three-dimensional original works reflect the high standards of gallery owners Deborah and Robert Zaleski (a painter), who have just added to their roster the talented ceramic artist David Stabley, a two-time American Craft Council juror. 3643-A Baldwin Ave. Ⓒ 808/572-8092.

Gecko Trading Co. Boutique The selection in this tiny boutique is eclectic and always changing: One day it's St. John's Wort body lotion and mesh T-shirts in a dragon motif, the next it's Provence soaps and antique lapis jewelry. We've seen everything from hair scrunchies to handmade crocheted bags from New York, clothing from Spain and France, collectible bottles, toys, shawls, and Mexican hammered-tin candleholders. The prices are reasonable, the service is friendly, and it's more homey than glammy, and not as self-conscious as some of the other local boutiques. 3621 Baldwin Ave. Ⓒ 808/572-0249.

Holiday & Co. Attractive women's clothing in natural fibers hangs from racks, while jewelry to go with it beckons from the counter. Recent finds include elegant fiber evening bags, luxurious bath gels, easygoing dresses and separates, Dansko clogs, shawls, shoes, soaps, aloha shirts, books, picture frames, and jewelry. 3681 Baldwin Ave. Ⓒ 808/572-1470.

Hot Island Glassblowing Studio & Gallery You can watch the artist transform molten glass into works of art and utility in this studio in Makawao's Courtyard, where an award-winning family of glassblowers built its own furnaces. It's fascinating to watch the shapes emerge from glass melted at 2,300°F (1,260°C). The colorful works displayed range from small paperweights to large vessels. Four to five artists participate in the demonstrations, which begin when the furnace is heated, about half an hour before the studio opens at 9am. 3620 Baldwin Ave. Ⓒ 808/572-4527.

Hurricane This boutique carries clothing, gifts, accessories, and books that are two steps ahead of the competition. Tommy Bahama aloha shirts and aloha print dresses; Sigrid Olsen's knitted shells, cardigans, and extraordinary silk tank dresses; hats; art by local artists; a notable selection of fragrances for men and women; and hard-to-find, eccentric books and home accessories are part of the Hurricane appeal. 3639 Baldwin Ave. Ⓒ 808/572-5076.

The Mercantile The jewelry, home accessories (especially the Tiffany-style glass-and-shell lamps), dinnerware, Italian linens, plantation-style furniture, and clothing here are a salute to the good life. The exquisite bedding, rugs, and furniture include hand-carved armoires, down-filled furniture and slipcovers, and a large selection of Kiehl's products. The clothing—comfortable cottons and upscale European linens—is for men and women, as are the soaps, which include Maui Herbal Soap products and some unusual finds from France. Maui-made jams, honey, soaps, and ceramics, and Jurlique organic facial and body products are among the new winners. 3673 Baldwin Ave. Ⓒ 808/572-1407.

Viewpoints Gallery   Maui's only fine-arts cooperative showcases the work of 20 established artists in an airy, attractive gallery located in a restored theater with a courtyard, glassblowing studio, and restaurants. The gallery features two-dimensional art, jewelry, fiber art, stained glass, paper, sculpture, and other media. This is a fine example of what can happen in a collectively supportive artistic environment. 3620 Baldwin Ave. ℂ **808/572-5979.**

EDIBLES

Working folks in Makawao pick up spaghetti, lasagna, sandwiches, salads, and wide-ranging specials from the **Rodeo General Store,** 3661 Baldwin Ave. (ℂ **808/572-7841**). At the far end of the store is the oenophile's bonanza, a superior wine selection housed in its own temperature-controlled cave.

   Down to Earth Natural Foods, 1169 Makawao Ave. (ℂ **808/572-1488**), always has fresh salads and sandwiches, a full section of organic produce (Kula onions, strawberry papayas, mangos, and litchis in season), bulk grains, beauty aids, herbs, juices, snacks, tofu, seaweed, soy products, and aisles of vegetarian and health foods. Whether it's a smoothie or a salad, Down to Earth has fresh, healthy, vegetarian offerings.

   In the more than 6 decades that the **T. Komoda Store and Bakery,** 3674 Baldwin Ave. (ℂ **808/572-7261**), has spent in this spot, untold numbers have creaked over the wooden floors to pick up Komoda's famous cream puffs. Old-timers know to come early, or they'll be sold out. Then the cinnamon rolls, doughnuts, pies, and chocolate cake take over. Pastries are just the beginning; poi, macadamia-nut candies and cookies, and small bunches of local fruit keep the customers coming.

FRESH FLOWERS IN KULA
(AT THE BASE OF HALEAKALA NATIONAL PARK)

Like anthuriums on the Big Island, proteas are a Maui trademark and an abundant crop on Haleakala's rich volcanic slopes. They also travel well, dry beautifully, and can be shipped with ease worldwide. Among Maui's most prominent sources is **Sunrise Protea** (ℂ **808/876-0200;** www.sunriseprotea.com), in Kula. It offers a walk-through garden and gift shops, friendly service, and a larger-than-usual selection. Freshly cut flowers arrive from the fields on Tuesday and Friday afternoons. You can order individual blooms, baskets, arrangements, or wreaths for shipping all over the world. (Next door, the Sunrise Country Market offers fresh local fruits, snacks, and sandwiches, with picnic tables for lingering.)

   Proteas of Hawaii (ℂ **808/878-2533;** www.proteasofhawaii.com), another reliable source, offers regular walking tours of the University of Hawaii Extension Service gardens across the street in Kula.

5 East Maui

ON THE ROAD TO HANA: PAIA

Biasa Rose Boutique   You'll find unusual gift items and clothing with a tropical flair: capri pants in bark cloth, floating plumeria candles, retro fabrics, dinnerware, handbags and accessories, and stylish vintage-inspired clothes for kids. If the aloha shirts don't get you, the candles and handbags will. You can also custom-order clothing from a selection of washable rayons. 104 Hana Hwy. ℂ **808/579-8602.**

Hemp House   Clothing and accessories made of hemp, a sturdy, ecofriendly, and sensible fiber, are finally making their way into the mainstream. The Hemp House has as complete a selection as you can expect to see in Hawaii, with "denim" hemp jeans, lightweight linenlike trousers, dresses, shirts, and a full range of sensible, easy-care wear. 16 Baldwin Ave. (© **808/579-8880.**

Maui Crafts Guild   The old wooden storefront at the gateway to Paia houses crafts of high quality and in all price ranges, from pit-fired raku to bowls of Norfolk pine and other Maui woods, fashioned by Maui hands. Artist-owned and -operated, the guild claims 25 members who live and work on Maui. Basketry, hand-painted fabrics, jewelry, beadwork, traditional Hawaiian stone work, pressed flowers, fused glass, stained glass, copper sculpture, banana bark paintings, pottery of all styles, and hundreds of items are displayed in the two-story gift gallery. Upstairs, sculptor Arthur Dennis Williams displays his breathtaking work in wood, bronze, and stone. Everything can be shipped. **Aloha Bead Co.** (© **808/ 579-9709**), in the back of the gallery, is a treasure trove for beadworkers. 43 Hana Hwy. (© **808/579-9697.**

Moonbow Tropics   If you're looking for a tasteful aloha shirt, go to Moonbow. The selection consists of a few carefully culled racks of the top labels in aloha wear, in fabrics ranging from the finest silks and linens to Egyptian cotton and spun rayons. Some of the finds: aloha shirts by Tori Richard, Reyn Spooner, Kamehameha, Paradise Found, Kahala, Tommy Bahama, and other top brands. Silk pants, silk shorts, vintage print neckwear, and an upgraded women's selection hang on neat, colorful racks. The jewelry pieces, ranging from tanzanite to topaz, rubies and moonstones, are mounted in unique settings made on-site. 36 Baldwin Ave. (© **808/579-8592.**

HANA

Hana Coast Gallery   This gallery is one main reason to go to Hana: It's an aesthetic and cultural experience that informs as it enlightens. Tucked away in the posh hideaway hotel, the gallery is known for its high level of curatorship and commitment to the cultural art of Hawaii. There are no jumping whales or dolphins here—and except for a section of European and Asian masters (Renoir, Japanese woodblock prints), the 3,000-square-foot gallery is devoted entirely to Hawaii artists. Dozens of well-established local artists display their sculptures, paintings, prints, feather work, stonework, and carvings in displays that are so natural they could well exist in someone's home. Director-curator Patrick Robinson (of impeccable artistic integrity) has expanded the selection of koa-wood furniture in response to the ongoing revival of the American Crafts Movement with a Hawaiian/Japanese influence. Stellar artists Tai Lake from the Big Island and Randall Watkins from Maui are among those represented.

Connoisseurs of hand-turned bowls will find the crème de la crème of the genre here: J. Kelly Dunn, Ron Kent, Todd Campbell, Ed Perrira, and Gary Stevens. You won't find a better selection elsewhere that exists under one roof. The award-winning gallery has won accolades from the top travel and arts magazines in the country and has steered clear of trendiness and unfortunate tastes. In the Hotel Hana-Maui. (© **808/248-8636.**

Hasegawa General Store   Established in 1910, immortalized in song since 1961, burned to the ground in 1990, and back in business in 1991, this legendary store is indefatigable and more colorful than ever in its fourth generation in business. The aisles are choked with merchandise: coffee specially roasted and blended for the store, Ono Farms organic dried fruit, fishing equipment, every tape and CD that mentions Hana, the best books on Hana to be found, T-shirts, beach and garden essentials, baseball caps, film, baby food, napkins, and other necessities. Hana Hwy., in Hana. (© **808/248-8231.**

9

Maui After Dark

Centered in the $32 million **Maui Arts and Cultural Center** in Kahului (© **808/242-7469;** www.mauiarts. org), the performing arts are alive and well on this island. The MACC remains the island's most prestigious entertainment venue, a first-class center for the visual and performing arts. Bonnie Raitt has performed here, as have Hiroshima, Pearl Jam, Ziggy Marley, Tony Bennett, the American Indian Dance Theatre, the Maui Symphony Orchestra, and Jonny Lang, not to mention the finest in local and Hawaiian talent. The center is as precious to Maui as the Met is to New York, with a visual-arts gallery, an outdoor amphitheater, offices, rehearsal space, a 300-seat theater for experimental performances, and a 1,200-seat main theater. The center's activities are well publicized locally, so check the *Maui News* or ask your hotel concierge what's going on during your visit.

People are still agog over **'Ulalena,** an extraordinary production that tells the story of Hawaii in chant, song, original music, acrobatics, and dance, using state-of-the-art technology and some of the most creative staging to be seen in Hawaii. There's nothing else like it in the state. A local and international cast performs this $9.5 million production at the comfy **Maui Myth & Magic Theatre** in Lahaina (see section 1 below).

IN SEARCH OF HAWAIIAN, JAWAIIAN & MORE

Nightlife options on this island are limited. Revelers generally head for **Casanova** in Makawao and **Maui Brews** in Lahaina. Because they are in different parts of this spread-out island, you'll either have to drive a great distance to these clubs or explore what's happening in the major hotels near you. The hotels generally have lobby lounges offering Hawaiian music, soft jazz, or hula shows beginning at sunset.

If **Hapa, Willie K., Amy Gilliom,** or the soloist **Keali'i Reichel** are playing anywhere on their native island, don't miss them; they're among the finest Hawaiian musicians around today. Most clubs with dance floors play a combination of Hawaiian and reggae, called Jawaiian, with a heated-up rhythm that young dancers love.

AT THE MOVIES

Movie buffs still rejoice over the infusion of celluloid at the 12-screen movie megaplex at the **Maui Mall,** 70 E. Kaahumanu Ave. (© **808/877-7559**), in Kahului, which comes complete with comfortable reclining seats. The megaplex features current releases. The **Maui Film Festival** presents "Academy House" films for the avant-garde, ultrahip movie buff Wednesday nights at the **Maui Art and Cultural Center,** 1 Cameron Way (just off Kahului Beach Rd.), Kahului (© **808/ 572-3456;** www.mauifilmfestival.com), usually followed by live music and poetry readings. In the summer, either around Memorial Day weekend or in June, the Maui Film Festival also puts on nights of cinema under the stars in Wailea.

Moments It Begins with Sunset...

Nightlife in Maui begins at sunset, when all eyes turn westward to see how the day will end. Sunset viewers seem to bond in the mutual enjoyment of a natural spectacle. And what better way to take it all in than over cocktails? Maui is a haven for lovers of both. With its view of Molokai to the northwest and Lanai to the west, Kaanapali and West Maui boast panoramic vistas unique to this island. In South Maui's resort areas of Wailea and Makena, tiny Kahoolawe and the crescent-shaped Molokini islet are visible as familiar forms on the horizon, and the West Maui Mountains look like an entirely separate island. No matter what your vantage point, you are likely to be treated to an astonishing view.

Sunset viewers along South and West Maui shorelines need only head for the ocean and find a seat. Our favorite sunset watering holes begin toward the north with **The Bay Club at Kapalua** (© 808/669-5656), where a pianist plays nightly and the northwesterly view of Molokai and Lanai is enhanced by the elegant surroundings. It's quiet here, removed from the hubbub that prevails in the more populated Kaanapali Beach Resort to the south.

In Kaanapali, park in Whalers Village and head for **Leilani's** (© 808/661-4495) or **Hula Grill** (© 808/667-6636), next to each other on the beach. Both have busy, upbeat bars and tables bordering the sand. These are happy places for great people watching, gazing at the lump of Lanai that looks to be a stone's throw away, and enjoying end-of-day rituals like mai tais and margaritas. Hula Grill's Barefoot Bar appetizer menu is a cut above. Leilani's has live music daily from 3:30 to 6pm, while at Hula Grill the happy hour starts at 3pm, live music at 6pm, and hula at 8pm.

Now, Lahaina: It's a sunset-lover's nirvana, lined with restaurants that hang over the ocean and offer fresh fish in a multitude of preparations—and mai tais elevated to an art form. If you love loud rock, head for **Cheeseburger in Paradise** (© 808/661-4855). A few doors away, the **Lahaina Fish Company** (© 808/661-3472) and **Kimo's** (© 808/661-4811) are magnets all day long and especially at sunset, when their open decks fill up with revelers. For the most part, you can expect great seafood appetizers at these oceanfront haunts. These three restaurants occupy the section of Front Street between Lahainaluna Road and Papalaua Street.

At the southern end of Lahaina, in the 505 Front Street complex, **Pacific'o** (© 808/667-4341) is a solid hit, with a raised bar, seating on the ocean, and a backdrop of Lanai across the channel. Besides the view and the friendly service, the food is notable, having won many awards for seafood. A few steps away from Pacific'o, sister restaurant **I'o** shares the

Film buffs can check the local newspapers to see what's playing at the other theaters around the island: the **Kaahumanu Theatres,** in the Kaahumanu Center in Kahului (© **808/873-3133**); the **Maui Theatre,** in the Kahului Shopping Center (© **808/877-3560**); the **Kukui Mall Theatre,** 1819 S. Kihei Rd., in same vista, with an appetizer menu and a techno-curved bar that will wow you as much as the drop-dead-gorgeous view.

Moving south toward Wailea, the harbor stop called Maalaea is famous for its whale sightings during the winter months. Year-round, **Buzz's Wharf** (© 808/244-5426) is a formula restaurant with a superb ocean view and continuous service between lunch and dinner. Those are the basic makings of a sunset-viewing way station. Add an ice-cold beer or mai tai, elegant fresh sashimi, or a steaming order of fish and chips, and the sunset package is complete.

In Wailea, the restaurants at the new Shops at Wailea, including the highly successful **Tommy Bahama** (© 808/875-9983), are a noteworthy addition to the beachfront retail and dining scene. **Ferraro's** and **Pacific Grill** (© 808/874-8000), both at the neighboring Four Seasons Resort Wailea, have great sunset views to go with their Italian and Pacific Rim menus. In Makena resort farther south, you can't beat the Maui Prince's **Molokini Lounge** (© 808/874-1111), with its casual elegance and unequaled view of Molokini islet on the ocean side and, on the mauka side, a graceful, serene courtyard with ponds, rock gardens, and lush foliage. Adding to the setting is the appetizer menu, which comes from the esteemed Prince Court kitchen. From 5 to 9:30pm nightly, the pupu menu features an exceptional Prince Court sampler platter: Kona lobster cakes, steamed clams, kalua duck lumpia, Pacific oysters on the half-shell, grilled tiger prawns, and grilled teriyaki steak poke. Live Hawaiian entertainment runs nightly from 6 to 10:30pm, beginning with a mini hula show from 6pm on Monday, Wednesday, and Friday and the contemporary Hawaiian melodies of Mele Ohana or Ron Kuala'au until 10:30pm. Ron Kuala'au plays Monday, Tuesday, Thursday, and Saturday; Mele Ohana plays nightly except Sunday.

Don't forget the upcountry view, a kick-ass way to end the day if you don't mind the drive. Even with its musical-chair chef scene, **Kula Lodge** (© 808/878-2517) has a good thing going: a phenomenal view that takes in central Maui, the West Maui Mountains (looking like Shangri-La in the distance), and the coastline. From 3:30 to 5pm, the appetizer-only menu includes everything from Maui onion soup to a host of gourmet salads (the farmers are a stone's throw away), plus pot stickers, summer rolls, seared ahi, and crab cakes. Dinner begins at 5pm, so you can take in the sunset over steamed clams, rack of lamb, Cajun ahi, New York steak, and other country-comfort fare. There's more glass than wood in the dining room, so the view encompasses Kihei, Kahului, and the West Maui Mountains—South and Central Maui in its jaw-dropping magnificence.

Kihei (© **808/875-4533**); and the Wallace Theatres (© **808/661-3347**), in Lahaina at the **Wharf Cinema Center,** 658 Front St., and the **Front Street Theatres** at the Lahaina Center, 900 Front St.

1 West Maui: Lahaina

Maui Brews, 900 Front St. (© **808/667-7794**), draws the late-night crowd to its corner of the Lahaina Center with swing, salsa, reggae, and jams—either live or with a DJ every night. The restaurant serves breakfast, lunch, and dinner beginning at 7:30am, and happy hour extends from 3 to 7pm, with $1 drafts and $1 wells. The nightclub opens at 9pm and closes at 2am. Depending on the entertainment, sometimes there's a cover charge after 9pm; generally if there is one it's $5. For recorded information on entertainment (which changes, so it's a good idea to call), call © **808/669-2739;** www.mauibrews.com.

At **Longhi's** (© **808/667-2288**), live music spills out into the streets from 9:30pm on weekends (with a cover charge of $5). It's usually salsa or jazz, but call ahead to confirm. Other special gigs can be expected if rock-and-rollers or jazz musicians who are friends of the owner happen to be passing through.

The **Hard Rock Cafe,** 900 Front St. (© **808/667-7400**), occasionally offers live music, so it wouldn't hurt to call them to see if something's up. Usually they feature mainland bands, normally on weekends after 10pm. Cover ranges from $3 to $5.

You won't have to ask what's going on at **Cheeseburger in Paradise** (© **808/ 661-4855**), the two-story green-and-white building at the corner of Front and Lahainaluna streets. Just go outside and you'll hear it. Loud, live tropical rock blasts into the streets and out to sea nightly from 4:30 to 11pm (no cover charge).

A NIGHT TO REMEMBER: LUAU, MAUI STYLE

Most of the larger hotels in Maui's major resorts offer luaus on a regular basis. You'll pay about $65 to attend one. To protect yourself from disappointment, don't expect it to be a homegrown affair prepared in the traditional Hawaiian way. There are, however, commercial luaus that capture the romance and spirit of the luau with quality food and entertainment in outdoor settings.

Maui's best luau is indisputably the nightly **Old Lahaina Luau** (© **800/ 248-5828** or 808/667-1998; www.oldlahainaluau.com). On its 1-acre site just ocean side of the Lahaina Cannery at 1251 Front St., the Old Lahaina Luau maintains its high standards in food and entertainment, in a peerless setting. Local craftspeople display their wares only a few feet from the ocean. Seating is provided on lauhala mats for those who wish to dine as the traditional Hawaiians did, but there are tables for everyone else. There's no fire dancing in the program, but you won't miss it (for that, go to the **Feast at Lele;** p. 128). This luau offers a healthy balance of entertainment, showmanship, authentic high-quality food, educational value, and sheer romantic beauty. (No watered-down mai tais, either; these are the real thing.)

The luau begins at sunset and features Tahitian and Hawaiian entertainment, including ancient hula, hula from the missionary era, modern hula, and an intelligent narrative on the dance's rocky course of survival into modern times. The entertainment is riveting, even for jaded locals. The food, served from an open-air thatched structure, is as much Pacific Rim as authentically Hawaiian: imu-roasted kalua pig, baked mahimahi in Maui onion cream sauce, guava chicken, teriyaki sirloin steak, lomi salmon, poi, dried fish, poke, Hawaiian sweet potato, sautéed vegetables, seafood salad, and the ultimate taste treat, taro leaves with coconut milk. The cost is $79 plus tax for adults, $49 plus tax for children.

'ULALENA: HULA, MYTH & MODERN DANCE

The highly polished **'Ulalena,** staged in the Maui Myth and Magic Theatre, 878 Front St. (© **877/688-4800** or 808/661-9913; www.ulalena.com), is the talk of the town, a riveting production that weaves Hawaiian mythology with drama, dance, and state-of-the-art multimedia capabilities in a brand-new, multimillion-dollar theater.

A local and international cast performs Polynesian dance, original music, acrobatics, and chant to create an experience that often leaves the audience speechless. It's interactive, with dancers coming down the aisles, drummers and musicians in surprising corners, and mind-boggling stage and lighting effects that draw the audience in. In one scene, sugar cane is shown growing on the stage, projected on mesh curtains as if by time-lapse photography. Some special moments: the goddess dancing on the moon, the white sail signaling the arrival of the first Europeans, the wrath of the volcano goddess, Pele (the stage effects depicting lava are brilliant), the despairing labors of the field-worker immigrants. The effects of the modern choreography and traditional hula, a fusion of genres, are surprisingly evocative and emotional. The story unfolds seamlessly and at the end, you'll be shocked to realize that not a single word of dialogue has been spoken. Performances are Tuesday at 6 and 8:30pm, and Wednesday to Saturday at 6pm only. Tickets are $48 to $58 for adults and $28 to $38 for children ages 3 to 10.

MAGIC—MAUI STYLE

A very different type of live entertainment is **Warren & Annabelle's,** 900 Front St. (near Ruth's Chris Steakhouse and Hard Rock Cafe), Lahaina (© **808/ 667-6244;** www.hawaiimagic.com), a mystery/magic cocktail show with illusionist Warren Gibson and "Annabella," a ghost from the 1800s who plays the grand piano (even taking requests from the audience) as Warren dazzles you with his sleight-of-hand magic. Preshow entertainment begins at 6:45pm nightly, tickets (book in advance) are $40, cocktails and food are extra. You must be 21 years old to attend, although they occasionally have a 5pm family show (minimum age is 6 years) without food or cocktails; call for details.

2 Upcountry Maui

Upcountry in Makawao, the party never ends at **Casanova,** 1188 Makawao Ave. (© **808/572-0220**), the popular Italian ristorante where the good times roll with the pasta. The newly renovated bar area has large booths, all the better for socializing around the stage and dance floor. If a big-name mainland band is resting up on Maui following a sold-out concert on Oahu, you may find its members setting up for an impromptu night here. DJs take over on Wednesday (ladies' night) and, on Thursday, Friday, and Saturday, live entertainment draws fun-lovers from even the most remote reaches of the island. Entertainment starts at 9:45pm and continues to 1:30am. Expect good blues, rock-and-roll, reggae, jazz, Hawaiian, and the top names in local and visiting entertainment. Elvin Bishop, the local duo Hapa, Los Lobos, and many others have filled Casanova's stage. The cover is usually $5. Come Sunday afternoons, 3 to 6pm, for excellent live jazz.

In the unlikely location of Paia, **Moanai Bakery & Café** (71 Baldwin Ave, © **808/579-9999**), not only has some of the best and most innovative cuisine around, but recently it has added live music: vintage Hawaiian from 6:30 to 9pm on Wednesday; smooth jazz and hot blues on from 6:30 to 9pm on Friday; and flamingo guitar and gypsy violin from 6 to 9pm on Sunday. There's no cover; just come and enjoy.

10

Molokai: The Most
Hawaiian Isle

Born of volcanic eruptions 1½ million years ago, Molokai remains a time capsule at the beginning of the 21st century. It has no deluxe resorts, no stoplights, and no buildings taller than a coconut tree. Fortunately for adventure travelers and peace seekers, Molokai is the least developed, most "Hawaiian" of all the islands.

Molokai lives up to its reputation as the most Hawaiian place chiefly through its lineage; there are more people here of Hawaiian blood than anywhere else. This slipper-shaped island was the cradle of Hawaiian dance (the hula was born here) and the ancient science of aquaculture. An aura of ancient mysticism clings to the land here, and the old ways still govern life. The residents survive by taking fish from the sea and hunting wild pigs and axis deer on the range. Some folks still catch fish in throw nets and troll the reef for squid.

Modern Hawaii's high-rise hotels, shopping centers, and other trappings of tourism haven't been able to gain a foothold here; one lone low-rise resort, Kaluakoi, built more than 25 years ago, is Molokai's token attempt at contemporary tourism. The only "new" developments since Kaluakoi are the Molokai Ranch's ecotourism project of pricey camping in semipermanent "tentalows" (a combination of a bungalow and a tent) and an upscale 22-room lodge on the 53,000-acre ranch, now managed by Sheraton. The focus of both is on outdoor recreation and adventure, with all the comforts of home.

The slow-paced, simple life of the people and the absence of contemporary landmarks attract those in search of the "real" Hawaii. But what makes these visitors stand in awe is this little island's diverse natural wonders: Hawaii's highest waterfall and greatest collection of fish ponds, the world's tallest sea cliffs, sand dunes, coral reefs, rainforests, hidden coves, and gloriously empty beaches.

EXPLORING THE "MOST HAWAIIAN" ISLE

Only 38 miles from end to end and just 10 miles wide, Molokai stands like a big green wedge in the blue Pacific. It has an east side, a west side, a backside, and a topside. This long, narrow island is like yin and yang: One side is a flat, austere, arid desert; the other is a lush, green, steepled tropical Eden. Three volcanic eruptions formed Molokai; the last produced the island's "thumb"—a peninsula jutting out of the steep cliffs of the north shore, like a punctuation mark on the island's geological story.

On the red-dirt southern plain, where most of the island's 6,000 residents live, the rustic village of **Kaunakakai** ✦ looks like the set of an old Hollywood western, with sun-faded clapboard houses and horses tethered on the side of the

Molokai

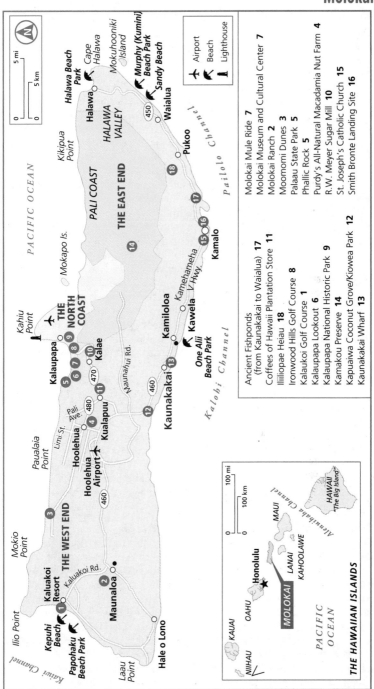

N

0 — 5 mi
0 — 5 km

Airport
Beach
Lighthouse

PACIFIC OCEAN

Ilio Point
Mokio Point
Paualaia Point
Kahiu Point
Kikipua Point
Mokapo Is.

THE NORTH COAST

Cape Halawa
Mokuhooniki Island

Murphy (Kumimi) Beach Park
Sandy Beach
Waialua

Halawa Beach Park
Halawa

HALAWA VALLEY

PALI COAST

THE EAST END

Pukoo

Kalaupapa

Kalae
Kualapuu
Hoolehua
Hoolehua Airport

Maunahui Rd.
Pali Ave.
Limi St.

Kamiloloa
Kawela
One Alii Beach Park
Kamehameha V Hwy.
Kamalo

Kalohi Channel
Kalohi Channel

Kaunakakai

Pailolo Channel

THE WEST END

Kaluakoi Resort
Kaluakoi Rd.
Maunaloa

Kepuhi Beach
Papohaku Beach Park
Hale o Lono
Laau Point

Kaiwi Channel

1 - 18 numbered markers

Molokai Mule Ride **7**
Molokai Museum and Cultural Center **7**
Molokai Ranch **2**
Moomomi Dunes **3**
Palaau State Park **5**
Phallic Rock **5**
Purdy's All-Natural Macadamia Nut Farm **4**
R.W. Meyer Sugar Mill **10**
St. Joseph's Catholic Church **15**
Smith Bronte Landing Site **16**

Ancient Fishponds
  (from Kaunakakai to Waialua) **17**
Coffees of Hawaii Plantation Store **11**
Iliiliopae Heiau **18**
Ironwood Hills Golf Course **8**
Kalaupapa Lookout **6**
Kalaupapa National Historic Park **9**
Kamakou Preserve **14**
Kapuaiwa Coconut Grove/Kiowea Park **12**
Kaunakakai Wharf **13**

THE HAWAIIAN ISLANDS

0 — 100 mi
0 — 100 km

PACIFIC OCEAN

NIIHAU
KAUAI
OAHU
Honolulu
MOLOKAI
LANAI
KAHOOLAWE
MAUI
HAWAII "The Big Island"

Kaieiewaho Channel
Alenuihaha Channel

road. Mile marker 0, in the center of town, divides the island into east and west; an arid cactus desert lies on one side, a lush coco-palm jungle on the other.

Eastbound, along the **coastal highway** ★★★ named for King Kamehameha V, are Gauguin-like, palm-shaded cottages set on small coves or near fish ponds; spectacular vistas that take in Maui, Lanai, and Kahoolawe; and a fringing coral reef visible through the crystal-clear waves.

Out on the sun-scorched West End is the island's lone destination resort, **Kaluakoi,** overlooking a gold-sand beach with water usually too rough to swim in. The old hilltop plantation town of **Maunaloa** has been razed and rebuilt as a gentrified plantation community, complete with an expensive country lodge with a pricey dining room. Cowboys still ride the range on **Molokai Ranch,** a 53,000-acre spread, while adventure travelers and outdoor-recreation buffs stay at the tentalows on the ranch property and spend their days mountain biking, kayaking, horseback riding, hiking, snorkeling, and just vegetating on the endless white-sand beaches.

Elsewhere around the island, in hamlets like **Kualapuu,** old farmhouses with pickup trucks in the yards and sleepy dogs under the shade trees stand amid row crops of papaya, coffee, and corn—just like farm towns in Anywhere, USA.

But that's not all there is. The "backside" of Molokai is a rugged wilderness of spectacular beauty. On the outskirts of **Kaunakakai,** the land rises gradually from sea-level fish ponds to cool uplands and the Molokai Forest, long ago stripped of sandalwood for the China trade. All that remains is an indentation in the earth that natives shaped like a ship's hull, a crude matrix that gave them a rough idea of when they'd cut enough sandalwood to fill a ship (it's identified on good maps as Luanamokuiliahi, or Sandalwood Boat).

The land inclines sharply to the lofty mountains and the nearly mile-high summit of Mount Kamakou, then ends abruptly with emerald-green cliffs, which plunge into a lurid aquamarine sea dotted with tiny deserted islets. These breathtaking 3,250-foot **sea cliffs,** the highest in the world, stretch 14 majestic miles along Molokai's north shore, laced by waterfalls and creased by five valleys (Halawa, Papalaua, Wailau, Pelekunu, and Waikolu) once occupied by early Hawaiians who built stone terraces and used waterfalls to irrigate taro patches.

Long after the sea cliffs were formed, a tiny volcano erupted out of the sea at their feet and spread lava into a flat, leaflike peninsula called **Kalaupapa**—the 1860s leper exile where Father Damien de Veuster of Belgium devoted his life to care for the afflicted. A few people remain in the remote colony by choice, keeping it tidy for the daily company that arrives on mules and by small planes.

WHAT A VISIT TO MOLOKAI IS *REALLY* LIKE

There's plenty of aloha on Molokai, but the so-called "friendly island" remains ambivalent about vacationers. One of the least visited Hawaiian islands, Molokai welcomes about 70,000 visitors annually on its own take-it-or-leave-it terms, and makes few concessions beyond that of gracious host; it never wanted to attract a crowd, anyway. A sign at the airport offers the first clue: SLOW DOWN, YOU ON MOLOKAI NOW—wisdom to heed on this island, where life proceeds at its own pace.

Rugged, red-dirt Molokai isn't for everyone, but those who like to explore remote places and seek their own adventures should love it. The best of the island can be seen only on foot, bicycle, mule, horseback, kayak, or boat. The sea cliffs are accessible only by sea in summer, when the Pacific is calm, or via a 10-mile trek through the Wailau Valley—an adventure only a handful of hardy hikers attempt each year. The great Kamakou Preserve is open just once a month, by special arrangement with the Nature Conservancy. Even Moomomi, which holds bony relics of prehistoric flightless birds and other creatures, requires a guide to divulge the secrets of the dunes.

Those in search of nightlife have come to the wrong place; Molokai shuts down after sunset. The only public diversions are softball games under the lights of Mitchell Pauole Field, movies at Maunaloa, and the few restaurants that stay open after dark, often serving local brew and pizza.

The "friendly" island may prove to be the real Hawaii of your dreams. On the other hand, you may leave shaking your head, never to return. Regardless of how you approach Molokai, remember our advice: Take it slow.

1 Orientation

ARRIVING

BY PLANE   Molokai has two airports, but you'll most likely fly into **Hoolehua Airport,** which everyone calls "the Molokai Airport." It's on a dusty plain about 6 miles from Kaunakakai town. Airlines offering service to Molokai include **Island Air** (© **800/323-3345** from the mainland, or 800/652-6541 interisland; www.alohaair.com), with 11 direct flights a day from Honolulu and four direct flights from Maui; **Molokai Air Shuttle** (© **808/545-4988**); **Hawaiian Airlines** (© **800/367-5320** or 808/553-3644; www.hawaiianair.com); and **Pacific Wings** (© **888/575-4546** from the mainland, or 808/873-0877 from Maui; www.pacific wings.com).

BY BOAT   You can travel across the seas from Maui's Lahaina Harbor to Molokai's Kaunakakai Wharf by ferry on the *Molokai Princess* (© **800/275-6969** or 808/667-6165; www.mauiprincess.com). The 110-foot yacht, certified for 149 passengers, is fitted with the latest generation of gyroscopic stabilizers, making the ride smoother. The ferry makes the 90-minute journey from Lahaina to Kaunakakai daily; the cost is $40 adults one-way and $20 children one-way. Or you can choose to tour the island from two different package options: Cruise-Drive, which includes round-trip passage and a rental car for $149 for the driver, $79 per additional adult passenger, and $45 for children; or the Alii Tour, which is a guided tour in an air-conditioned van plus lunch for $149 for adults and $89 for children.

They also offer ferry transportation and a hike-tour of the Kalaupapa Leprosy Settlement for $189 per person. See p. 266.

VISITOR INFORMATION

Look for a sun-faded, yellow building on Kamehameha V Highway (Hwy. 460— the main drag), on the right just past the town's first stop sign, at mile marker 0; it houses the **Molokai Visitors Association,** P.O. Box 960, Kaunakakai, HI 96748 (© **800/800-6367** from the U.S. mainland and Canada, 800/553-0404 interisland, or 808/553-3876; www.molokai-hawaii.com). The staff can give you all the information you need on what to see and do while you're on Molokai.

THE ISLAND IN BRIEF

KAUNAKAKAI ⊛   Dusty vehicles—mostly pickup trucks—are parked diagonally along Ala Malama Street. It could be any small town, except it's Kaunakakai, the closest thing Molokai has to a business district. Friendly Isle Realty and Friendly Isle Travel offer islanders dream homes and vacations; Rabang's Filipino Food posts bad checks in the window; antlered deer-head trophies guard the grocery aisles at Misaki's Market; and Kanemitsu's, the town's legendary bakery, churns out fresh loaves of onion-cheese bread daily.

Once an ancient canoe landing, Kaunakakai was the royal summer residence of King Kamehameha V. The port town bustled when pineapple and sugar were king, but those days, too, are gone. With its Old West–style storefronts laid out in a 3-block grid on a flat, dusty plain, Kaunakakai is a town from the past. At the end of Wharf Road is Molokai Wharf, a picturesque place to fish, photograph, and just hang out.

Kaunakakai is the dividing point between the lush, green East End and the dry, arid West End. On the west side of town stands a cactus and on the east side of town, there's thick, green vegetation.

THE NORTH COAST ☆☆   Upland from Kaunakakai, the land tilts skyward and turns green, with scented plumeria in yards and glossy coffee trees all in a row, until it blooms into a true forest—and then abruptly ends at a great precipice, falling 3,250 feet to the sea. The green sea cliffs are creased with five V-shaped crevices so deep that light is seldom seen (to paraphrase a Hawaii poet). The north coast is a remote, forbidding place, with a solitary peninsula—**Kalaupapa** ☆☆☆—once the home for exiled lepers (it's now a national historical park). This region is easy on the eyes, difficult to visit. It lies at a cool elevation, and frequent rain squalls blow in from the ocean. In summer, the ocean is calm, providing great opportunities for kayaking, fishing, and swimming, but during the rest of the year, giant waves come rolling onto the shores.

THE WEST END ☆   This end of the island, home to **Molokai Ranch,** is miles of stark desert terrain, bordered by the most beautiful white-sand beaches in Hawaii. The rugged rolling land slopes down to Molokai's only destination resort, **Kaluakoi,** a cul-de-sac of condos clustered around a 25-year-old seafront hotel (temporarily closed when we went to press) near 3-mile-long Papohaku, the island's biggest beach. On the way to Kaluakoi, you'll find **Maunaloa,** a 1920s-era pineapple plantation town that's in the midst of being transformed into a master-planned community, Maunaloa Village, with an upscale lodge, triplex theater, restaurants, and shops. Currently there is just one 22-room lodge with dining room, two stores, a theater, and a Kentucky Fried Chicken outlet. The West End is dry, dry, dry. It hardly ever rains, but when it does (usually in the winter), expect a downpour and a lot of red mud.

THE EAST END ☆☆☆   The area east of Kaunakakai becomes lush, green, and tropical, with golden pocket beaches and a handful of cottages and condos that are popular with thrifty travelers. With this voluptuous landscape comes rain. However, most storms are brief (15-min.) affairs that blow in, dry up, and disappear. Winter is Hawaii's rainy season, so expect more rain during January to March, but even then, the storms usually are brief and the sun comes back out.

Beyond Kaunakakai, the two-lane road curves along the coast past pigpens, palm groves, and a 20-mile string of fish ponds as well as an ancient heiau, Damien-built churches, and a few contemporary condos by the sea. The road ends in the glorious **Halawa Valley** ☆, one of Hawaii's most beautiful valleys.

FAST FACTS

Molokai and Lanai are both part of Maui County. For local emergencies, call © **911.** For nonemergencies, call the **police** at © **808/553-5355,** the **fire department** at © **808/553-5601,** or **Molokai General Hospital,** in Kaunakakai, at © **808/553-5331.**

Downtown Kaunakakai has a **post office** (© **808/553-5845**) and several banks, including the **Bank of Hawaii** (© **808/553-3273**), which has a 24-hour ATM.

2 Getting Around

Getting around Molokai isn't easy if you don't have a rental car, and rental cars are often hard to find here. On holiday weekends—and remember, Hawaii celebrates different holidays than the rest of the United States (p. 30)—car-rental agencies simply run out of cars. Book before you go. There's no municipal transit or shuttle service, but a 24-hour taxi service is available.

CAR-RENTAL AGENCIES Rental cars are available from **Budget** (© 808/567-6877) and **Dollar** (© 808/567-6156); both agencies are located at the Molokai Airport. We recommend trying **Island Kine** (© 808/553-5242; fishin @aloha.net); not only are the cars cheaper, but Barbara Shonely and her son, Steve, also give personalized service. They'll meet you at the Molokai Airport, take you to their office in Kaunakakai, and recommend specific outfitters for your activities. The used cars are in perfect condition ("I would drive every one of them with my grandkids," says Barbara) and are air-conditioned. Vans and pickup trucks are also available. You won't need a four-wheel-drive vehicle unless you're planning some specialized hiking, but if that's the case, Island Kine has it.

TAXI & TOUR SERVICES Molokai Off-Road Tours & Taxi (© 808/553-3369) offers regular taxi service, an airport shuttle ($7 per person, one-way, to Sheraton Molokai Lodge, based on 4 people; otherwise it is $28 for 2, one-way; and $7.50 per person to Kaunakakai, based on 3 people), and island tours (6 hours for $59 per person, 3 people minimum).

3 Accommodations

Molokai is Hawaii's most affordable island, especially for hotels. And because the island's restaurants are few, most hotel rooms and condo units come with kitchens, which can save you a bundle on dining costs.

There aren't a ton of accommodations options on Molokai—mostly B&Bs, condos, a few quaint oceanfront vacation rentals, an aging resort, and a very expensive lodge. For camping on Molokai, you have two options: the upscale tentalows offered by Sheraton Molokai Lodge and Beach Village, or, for hardy souls, camping with your own tent at the beach or in the cool upland forest (see "Hiking & Camping" later in this chapter). We've listed our top picks below; you may want to contact **Molokai Visitors Association** (see section 1 of this chapter) for additional options.

Note: Taxes of 11.42% will be added to your hotel bill. Parking is free at all the hotels listed below.

KAUNAKAKAI
MODERATE
Molokai Shores Suites *(Kids)* Bright, clean, basic units with kitchens and large lanais face a small gold-sand beach in this quiet complex of three-story Polynesian-style buildings, less than a mile from Kaunakakai. Alas, the beach is mostly for show (offshore, it's shallow mud flats underfoot), fishing, or launching kayaks, but the swimming pool and barbecue area come with an ocean view. Well-tended gardens, spreading lawns, and palms frame a restful view of fish ponds, offshore reefs, and neighbor islands. The central location can be a plus, minimizing driving time from the airport or town, and it's convenient to the mule ride, as well as the lush East End countryside. There's no daily maid service.

Kamehameha V Hwy. (P.O. Box 1037), Kaunakakai, HI 96748. © 800/535-0085 or 808/553-5954. Fax 808/553-5954. www.marcresorts.com. 102 units. $155 1-bedroom apt (sleeps up to 4); $199 2-bedroom apt (up to 6). Discounted rates for weekly and extended stays, plus corporate, military, and senior discounts. AE, DC, MC, V. **Amenities:** Putting green; salon; coin-op washer/dryers. *In room:* TV, kitchen, fridge, coffeemaker, iron.

INEXPENSIVE

A'ahi Place (Value) Just outside of the main town of Kaunakakai and up a small hill lies this dream vacation cottage, complete with a wicker-filled sitting area, a kitchen, and two full-size beds in the bedroom. Two lanais make great places to just sit and enjoy the stars at night. The entire property is surrounded by tropical plants, flowers, and fruit trees. You also get a great continental breakfast (home-grown Molokai coffee, fresh-baked goods, fruit from the property) in the kitchen, so you can enjoy it at your leisure. For those who seek a quiet place (no phone or TV to distract you), this is the place. And for those who wish to explore Molokai, the central location is perfect.

P.O. Box 2006, Kaunakakai, HI 96748. © 808/553-8033. www.molokai.com/aahi. 1 unit. $85–$95 double including continental breakfast, or $75–$85 double without breakfast Extra person $20. 2-night minimum for continental breakfast, 3-night minimum without breakfast. No credit cards. *In room:* Kitchen, fridge, coffeemaker, no phone.

Hotel Molokai ✦ This nostalgic Hawaiian motel complex is composed of a series of modified A-frame units, nestled under coco palms along a gray-sand beach with a great view of Lanai. The rooms are basic (be sure to ask for one with a ceiling fan), with a lanai. The mattresses are on the soft side, the sheets thin, and the bath towels rough, but you're on Molokai—and this is the only hotel in Kaunakakai. The kitchenettes, with coffeemaker, toaster, pots, and two-burner stove, can save you money on eating out. The front desk is open only from 7am to 8pm; late check-ins or visitors with problems have to go to security.

Kamehameha V Hwy. (P.O. Box 1020), Kaunakakai, HI 96748. © **800/367-5004** on the mainland, 800/272-5275 in Hawaii, or 808/553-5347. Fax 800/477-2329. www.hotelmolokai.com. 45 units. $82–$132 double; $137 suite with kitchenette (sleeps 4). Extra bed/crib $17. AE, DC, DISC, MC, V. **Amenities:** Restaurant (p. 250) with bar; outdoor pool; watersports equipment rentals; bike rental; activity desk; babysitting; coin-op washer/dryers. *In room:* A/C, TV, dataport, some kitchenettes, fridge, coffeemaker, hair dryer, iron, safe.

Ka Hale Mala Bed & Breakfast (Value) In a subdivision just outside town (off Kamehameha V Hwy., before mile marker 5) is this large four-room unit, with a private entrance through the garden and a Jacuzzi just outside. Inside, you'll find white rattan furnishings, room enough to sleep four, and a full kitchen. The helpful owners, Jack and Cheryl, meet all guests at the airport like long-lost relatives. They'll happily share their homegrown, organic produce; we recommend paying the extra $5 for the breakfast here. The owners can also supply a couple of bikes and snorkel and picnic gear.

7 Kamakana Place (P.O. Box 1582), Kaunakakai, HI 96748. © and fax **808/553-9009.** www.molokai-bnb.com. 1 unit. $70 double without breakfast, $80 double with breakfast. Extra person $10. No credit cards. **Amenities:** Jacuzzi. *In room:* TV, kitchen, fridge, coffeemaker.

THE WEST END
VERY EXPENSIVE

Sheraton Molokai Lodge & Beach Village ✦ Sheraton took over the beachside camping village (see "Believe it or Not: High-Priced Camping" below) and the quaint 22-room inn in Maunaloa in 2002, which was previously run by the Molokai Ranch, owner of 53,000 acres on the west side of the island. Located in a cool upcountry climate of the tiny village of Maunaloa, the attractive, two-story lodge sits on 8 nicely landscaped acres located 6 miles and a 20- to 25-minute shuttle ride to the nearest beach. Designed to resemble a 1930s-style Hawaii ranch

Molokai Accommodations & Dining

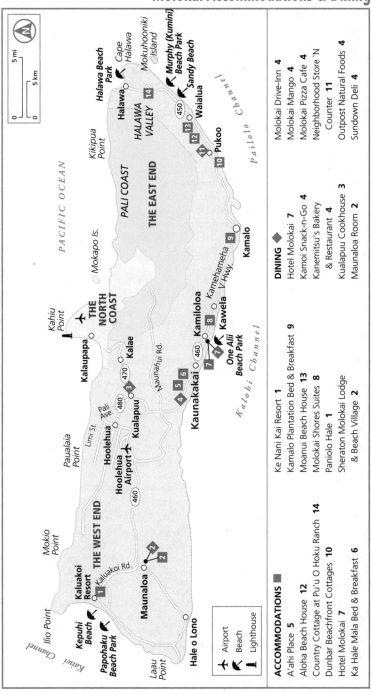

ACCOMMODATIONS ■

A'ahi Place **5**
Aloha Beach House **12**
Country Cottage at Pu'u O Hoku Ranch **14**
Dunbar Beachfront Cottages **10**
Hotel Molokai **7**
Ka Hale Mala Bed & Breakfast **6**

Ke Nani Kai Resort **1**
Kamalo Plantation Bed & Breakfast **9**
Moanui Beach House **13**
Molokai Shores Suites **8**
Paniolo Hale **1**
Sheraton Molokai Lodge
  & Beach Village **2**

DINING ◆

Hotel Molokai **7**
Kamoi Snack-n-Go **4**
Kanemitsu's Bakery
  & Restaurant **4**
Kualapuu Cookhouse **3**
Maunaloa Room **2**

Molokai Drive-Inn **4**
Molokai Mango **4**
Molokai Pizza Cafe **4**
Neighborhood Store 'N
  Counter **11**
Outpost Natural Foods **4**
Sundown Deli **4**

owner's private home, the Lodge features a giant fireplace, huge wooden beam construction, panoramic views, and lots of details—cuffed cowboy boots beside the door, old books lining the shelves—to make it look and feel like a real ranch. Guests step back in time to a Hawaii of yesteryear.

The guest rooms, each with individual country decor, are of two types: deluxe ($360) and luxury ($425). The luxury rooms are spacious corner units that feature either greenhouse-type skylights or a cozy king daybed nestled in a comfy alcove. Our luxury room was wonderful, with its free-standing four-poster bed, 270-degree view, and a TV that hydraulically lifted out of a credenza, then magically disappeared again.

Other amenities include a dining room, the option of dining at buffets at the beach pavilion, a small but practical spa (with massage treatments, men and women's sauna and locker facilities), outdoor heated swimming pool, and access to a host of activities. The Lodge is geared toward outdoorsy types, with complimentary shuttle to the beach and to activities (horseback riding, mountain biking, hiking, kayaking, snorkeling, beach activities, and more, ranging in price from $30–$125). There's also wonderful local entertainment in the Great Room in the evening; even if you don't stay here, come for the free entertainment.

This is the most expensive place to stay on Molokai and is priced as high as oceanfront resorts on Maui. Despite some nice features, it cannot compete with the amenities (not to mention the beach location) offered by other, similarly priced Hawaii resorts.

P.O. Box 259, Maunaloa, HI 96770. © **800/782-9488** or 808/660-2710. Fax 808/5520-2908. www.sheraton-hawaii.com. 22 units. $360–$425 double, plus $10 per day "resort fee" for transportation to beach, use of facilities at Lodge, and use of beach equipment at the beach camp. Extra person $45. AE, DC, DISC, MC, V. **Amenities:** Restaurant (Maunaloa Room, p. 252); bar with entertainment Tues–Sat evenings; gorgeous "infinity" pool heated to a perfect temperature for the cool climate; workout room; small spa with massage room; bike rental; game room; concierge; activity desk; car-rental desk; shopping arcade; massage; laundry service. *In room:* A/C, TV, dataport, fridge, coffeemaker, hair dryer, iron, safe.

MODERATE

Ke Nani Kai Resort ⚡ *(Kids)*   This place is great for families, who will appreciate the space. The large apartments are set up for full-time living with real kitchens, washer/dryers, VCRs, attractive furnishings, and breezy lanais. There's a huge pool, a volleyball court, tennis courts, and golf on the neighboring Kaluakoi course. These condos are farther from the sea than other local accommodations, but still just a brief walk from the beach. The two-story buildings are surrounded by parking and garden areas. The only downside: Maid service is only every third day.

In the Kaluakoi Resort development, Kaluakoi Rd., off Hwy. 460 (P.O. Box 289), Maunaloa, HI 96770. © **800/ 535-0085** or 808/552-2761. Fax 808/552-0045. www.marcresorts.com. 100 units. $155–$169 1-bedroom apt (sleeps up to 4); $189–$209 2-bedroom apt (up to 6). AE, DISC, DC, MC, V. **Amenities:** Outdoor pool; golf course; 2 tennis courts; Jacuzzi; washer/dryers in units. *In room:* TV, kitchen, fridge, coffeemaker.

Paniolo Hale ⚡⚡ *(Finds)*   This is far and away Molokai's most charming lodging, and probably its best value—be sure to ask about discounted weekly rates and special condo/car packages when making your reservations. The two-story, old Hawaii ranch-house design is airy and homey, with oak floors and walls of folding-glass doors that open to huge screened verandas, doubling your living space. The one- and two-bedrooms come with two bathrooms and accommodate three or four easily. Some units have hot tubs on the lanai. All are spacious, comfortably furnished, and well equipped, with full kitchens and washer/dryers.

Believe It or Not: High-Priced Camping

This was a great idea: a unique ecoadventure that combines camping and outdoor activities with the amenities of a resort. **Sheraton Molokai Lodge and Beach Village** (℃ **800/782-9488** or 808/660-2710; fax 808/552-2908; www.sheraton-hawaii.com) recently took over the Molokai Ranch's camping on an exclusive private beach, with very upscale "camping" accommodations. The Beach Village offers "tentalows" (safari-type tents mounted on wooden platforms). This is yuppie camping—with queen or twin beds, ceiling fans, solar-powered lights, private bathrooms with composting toilets, and solar hot-water showers, plus big decks with lounge chairs, personal hammocks for two, and picnic tables. There's even daily maid service! A big pavilion down at the beach has all-you-can-eat buffet meals three times a day, plus nightly entertainment under the stars.

When the Ranch first opened these camps, the price included meals and a large menu of outdoor activities (horseback riding, mountain biking, hiking, sailing, snorkeling, kayaking, and other adventures). It was quite a deal.

Today, the prices have risen to an astounding $275 (near the beach) and $320 (directly on the beach) double or single occupancy (plus the ubiquitous "resort fee" of $10 a day). Children 12 and under do stay free and eat free, when accompanied by an adult. Meal prices are: $12 for breakfast, $15 for lunch, and $29 for dinner. It starts to add up: Two adults staying in the least expensive room will spend $318 a day—including tax and $10 daily resort fee—just on the room! With meals, tax, and tip, it comes out to $452 a day for two—and that's not including any activities you may want to do. That's pretty expensive "camping."

The whole place overlooks the Kaluakoi Golf Course, a green barrier that separates these condos from the rest of Kaluakoi Resort. Out front, Kepuhi Beach is a scenic place to walk and beachcomb, although the seas are too hazardous for most swimmers. A pool, paddle tennis, and barbecue facilities are on the property, which adjoins open grassland countryside.

Next door to Kaluakoi Resort, Lio Place (P.O. Box 190), Maunaloa, HI 96770. ℃ **800/367-2984** or 808/ 552-2731. Fax 808/552-2288. www.paniolohaleresort.com. 77 units. $95–$155 double studio; $115–$230 1-bedroom apt (sleeps up to 4); $145–$265 2-bedroom apt (up to 6). Extra person $10. 2-night minimum, 1-week minimum Dec 20–Jan 5. AE, MC, V. **Amenities:** Outdoor pool; nearby golf course. In room: TV, kitchen, fridge, coffeemaker, washer/dryers.

THE EAST END
MODERATE

Aloha Beach House ★★ (Finds)   This is the place to stay on Molokai. Nestled on the lush East End of Molokai lies this Hawaiian-style beach house sitting right on the white-sand beach of Waialua. Perfect for families, this impeccably decorated two-bedroom, 1,600-square-foot beach house has a huge open living/dining/kitchen area that opens out to an old-fashioned porch for meals or just sitting in the comfy chairs and watching the clouds roll by. It's fully equipped, from the complete kitchen (including a dishwasher), to a VCR (plus a library of videos), to all the beach toys you can think of. It's located close to the Neighborhood Store in case you need to pick up something or don't feel like cooking and want to eat out.

Located just after mile marker 19. Reservations c/o The Rietows, P.O. Box 79, Kilauea, Hi 96754. ℂ **888/ 828-1008** or 808/828-1100. Fax 808/828-2199. www.molokaivacation.com. 1 2-bedroom house (sleeps up to 5). $180 (for up to 5) plus $95 cleaning fee. 3-night minimum. No credit cards. *In room:* TV, kitchen, fridge, coffeemaker, washer/dryer.

Dunbar Beachfront Cottages ★★ *Kids*   This is one of the most peaceful, comfortable, and elegant properties on Molokai's East End, and the setting is simply stunning. Each of these two green-and-white plantation-style cottages sits on its own secluded beach—you'll feel like you're on your own private island. The Puunana Cottage has a king bed and two twins, while the Pauwalu has a queen and two twins. Each has a full kitchen, VCR, ceiling fans, comfortable tropical furniture, large furnished deck (perfect for whale-watching in winter), and views of Maui, Lanai, and Kahoolawe across the channel.

Kamehameha V Hwy., at mile marker 25. Reservations: P.O. Box 1889, Kaunakakai, HI 96748. ℂ **808/673-0520** or 808/558-8153. Fax 808/558-8153. www.molokai-beachfront-cottages.com. 2 houses. $140 cottage, plus one-time $75 cleaning charge. 3-night minimum. No credit cards. **Amenities:** Pool. *In room:* TV/VCR available on request, kitchen, fridge, coffeemaker.

Moanui Beach House ★   If you're looking for a quiet, remote beach house, this is it. The genial Fosters, who have lived in the islands for many years, run the popular Kamalo Plantation Bed & Breakfast (see below). They recently purchased and renovated this two-bedroom beach house, right across the street from a secluded white-sand cove beach. The A-frame has a shaded lanai facing the ocean, a screened-in lanai on the side of the house, a full kitchen, and an ocean view that's worth the price alone. The Fosters leave a "starter supply" of breakfast foods for guests (fruit basket, home-baked bread, tropical fruit juices, tea, and coffee).

Kamehameha V Hwy., at mile marker 20. Reservations c/o Glenn and Akiko Foster, HC01, Box 300, Kaunakakai, HI 96748. ℂ and fax **808/558-8236**. www.molokai.com/kamalo. 1 2-bedroom unit. $140 double. Extra person $20. 3-night minimum. No credit cards. *In room:* TV, kitchen, fridge, coffeemaker, hair dryer, iron, washing machine.

INEXPENSIVE

Country Cottage at Pu'u O Hoku Ranch ★ *Kids*   Escape to a working cattle ranch! *Pu'u O Hoku* ("Star Hill") Ranch, which spreads across 14,000 acres of pasture and forests, is the last place to stay before Halawa Valley—it's at least an hour's drive from Kaunakakai along the shoreline. Two acres of tropically landscaped property circle the ranch's rustic cottage, which boasts breathtaking views of rolling hills and the Pacific Ocean. The wooden cottage features comfortable country furniture, a full kitchen, two bedrooms (1 with a double bed, 1 with two twins), two bathrooms, and a separate dining room on the enclosed lanai. TVs and VCRs are available on request. We recommend stargazing at night, watching the sunrise in the morning, and hiking, swimming, or a game of croquet in the afternoon. For larger parties, there's a four-bedroom, three-bathroom house on the property that sleeps eight. There's even an 11-room lodge available for family reunions or other large groups. Horseback riding is available at the ranch; see p. 262 for details.

Kamehameha V Hwy., at mile marker 25. Reservations: P.O. Box 1889, Kaunakakai, HI 96748. ℂ **808/558-8109.** Fax 808/558-8100. www.puuohoku.com. 2 houses. $125 double for 2-bedroom cottage or 4-bedroom house.

Kids Family-Friendly Accommodations

Molokai Shores Suites (p. 243)   At this great central location, just out-side Kaunakakai, families can choose from large one- and two-bedroom units in a tropical garden complex with great views of the fish ponds, offshore reefs, and neighbor islands. Amenities include a swimming pool and laundry facilities.

Ke Nani Kai Resort (p. 246)   Located in Kaluakoi Resort, these one-and two-bedroom condo units offer lots of space, with complete kitchens, washer/dryers, VCRs, and breezy lanais. For active families, there's a huge pool, a volleyball court, and tennis courts.

Country Cottage at Pu'u O Hoku Ranch (p. 248)   Take the kids to a working cattle ranch! *Pu'u O Hoku* ("Star Hill") has plenty of room for the kids to spread out and play, plus its own secluded, private beach. If you have a really big family (or you're staging a family reunion), there's an 11-room lodge on the property, too.

Dunbar Beachfront Cottages (p. 248)   These private two-bedroom cottages are located on the beach in the lush East End. Each cottage sits on its own secluded beach and features a complete kitchen, washer/dryer, VCR, large deck, and breathtaking views (great for watching whales in winter).

Extra person $20. $1100 for 11-room lodge (sleeps 22). 2-night minimum. No credit cards. **Amenities:** Pool. *In room:* TV/VCR available on request, kitchen, fridge, coffeemaker.

Kamalo Plantation Bed & Breakfast ★ *Value*   Glenn and Akiko Foster's (no relation to the author) 5-acre spread includes an ancient heiau ruin in the front yard, plus leafy tropical gardens and a working fruit orchard. Their lovely property is easy to find: It's right across the East End road from Father Damien's historic St. Joseph church. The plantation-style cottage is tucked under flowering trees and surrounded by swaying palms and tropical foliage. It has its own lanai, a big living room with a queen sofa bed, and a separate bedroom with a king bed, so it can sleep four comfortably. The kitchen is fully equipped (it even has spices), and there's a barbecue outside. A breakfast of fruit and freshly baked bread is served every morning. There's no TV reception, but the cottage does have a VCR, radio, and CD and cassette player.

Kamehameha V Hwy., just past mile marker 10 (HC01, Box 300), Kaunakakai, HI 96748. ℂ and fax **808/558-8236.** www.molokai.com/kamalo. 1 unit. $85 cottage. Rate includes continental breakfast. Extra person $10. 2-night minimum. No credit cards. *In room:* Kitchen, fridge, coffeemaker, hair dryer.

4 Dining

Molokai is strong on adventure, the outdoors, and the get-away-from-it-all feeling. No traffic lights and honking horns here, nor long lines at overbooked, self-important restaurants. But when it comes to dining and shopping, Molokai is not nirvana. Even with the first upscale hotel and dining room open in Maunaloa, Molokai's culinary and commercial offerings are spare.

A lot of people like it that way and acknowledge that the island's character is unchangeably rugged and natural. When the Molokai Ranch Lodge opened in

September 1999, it introduced two firsts: Molokai's first elevator and its first upscale restaurant, the Maunaloa Room, an attractive dining room with a deck, a view, and a menu featuring what the chef has dubbed "Molokai Regional Cuisine." Miles away in Kaunakakai, the reopening of the renovated Hotel Molokai unveiled a tropical fantasy of an oceanfront dining room, which has quickly become the island's busiest restaurant.

Even with these new developments, the pace of change on Molokai is glacial. The island is dominated by mom-and-pop eateries, nothing fancy, most of them fast-food or take-out places and many of them with a home-cooked touch. Lovers of the fast lane might consider this aspect of the island's personality a con rather than a pro, but they wouldn't choose to come here, anyway. Molokai is for those who want to get away from it all, who consider the lack of high-rises and traffic lights a welcome change from the urban chaos that keeps nibbling at the edges of the more popular and populated islands. Sybarites, foodies, and pampered oenophiles had best lower their expectations upon arrival, or turn around and leave the island's natural beauty to nature lovers.

Personally, we like the unpretentiousness of the island; it's an oasis in a state where plastic aloha abounds. Most Molokai residents fish, collect seaweed, grow potatoes and tomatoes, and prepare for backyard luaus. Unlike Lanai (see chapter 11), which is small and rural but offers some of the finest dining in the islands, Molokai provides no such mix of innocence and sophistication. Except for the significant cultural departure presented by the Sheraton Molokai Lodge, Molokai doesn't pretend to be anything more than a combination of old ways and an informal lifestyle that's closer to the land than to a chef's toque.

Although some of the best produce in Hawaii is grown on this island, you're not likely to find much of it served in its restaurants, other than in the take-out items at Outpost Natural Foods, or at the Molokai Pizza Cafe (one of the most pleasing eateries on the island), the Hotel Molokai, and the Maunaloa Room. The rest of the time, content yourself with ethnic or diner fare, or fresh fish from the Molokai Ice House—or by cooking for yourself. The many visitors who stay in condos find that it doesn't take long to sniff out the best sources of produce, groceries, and fresh fish to fire up at home when the island's other dining options are exhausted. Section 10 of this chapter, "Shopping," will point you to the places where you can pick up foodstuffs for your own island-style feast.

Except for the Maunaloa Room, Molokai's restaurants are inexpensive or moderately priced, and several of them do not accept credit cards. Regardless of where you eat, you certainly won't have to dress up. In most cases, we've listed just the town rather than the street address because, as you'll see, street addresses are as meaningless on this island as fancy cars and sequins. Reservations are not accepted unless otherwise noted.

To locate the following restaurants, see the map on p. 245.

KAUNAKAKAI

Hotel Molokai AMERICAN/ISLAND   On the ocean, with a view of Lanai, torches flickering under palm trees, and tiny fairy lights lining the room and the neighboring pool area, the Hotel Molokai's dining room evokes the romance of a South Seas fantasy. It's a casual room, and since its 1999 reopening, provides the only nightlife in Kaunakakai (see "Molokai After Dark" later in this chapter) and the most pleasing ambience on the island. Lunch choices stick to the basics; most promising are salads (Big Island organic greens) and sandwiches, from roast beef to grilled mahimahi. As the sun sets, the menu turns to heavier meats, ribs, fish, and pasta: fresh catch sautéed or broiled, Korean kalbi ribs, bar-becued pork ribs, New York steak, coconut shrimp, and garlic chicken. Temper your expectations of culinary excellence, and you're sure to enjoy a pleasing but not perfect dinner in an atmosphere that's unequaled on the island.

On Kamehameha V Hwy. Ⓒ 808/553-5347. Reservations recommended for dinner. Main courses $7–$8 lunch, $12–$19 dinner. AE, DC, MC, V. Daily 7–10am, 11am–2pm, and 6–9pm; bar until 10:30pm.

Kamoi Snack-N-Go ICE CREAM/SNACKS The Kamoi specialties are sweets and icy treats. Ice cream made by Dave's on Oahu comes in flavors such as green tea, litchi sherbet, *ube* (a brilliant purple color, made from Okinawan sweet potato), haupia, mango, and many other tropical and traditional flavors. Kids and their parents line up in the candy-filled aisles for the cones, shakes, floats, sundaes, and popular Icee floats served at this tiny snack shop (no tables).

In the Kamoi Professional Center. Ⓒ 808/553-3742. Ice cream $1.65–$3.40. MC, V. Mon–Sat 9am–9pm; Sun noon–9pm.

Kanemitsu's Bakery & Restaurant ⊛ BAKERY/DELI Morning, noon, and night, this local legend fills the Kaunakakai air with the sweet smells of bak-ing. Taro lavosh is the hot seller, joining Molokai bread (developed in 1935 in a cast-iron, kiawe-fired oven) as a Kanemitsu signature. Flavors range from apri-cot-pineapple to mango (in season), but the classics remain the regular white, wheat, cheese, sweet, and onion-cheese breads. For those who like their bread warm, the bread mixes offer a way to take Molokai home. In the adjoining cof-fee shop/deli, all sandwiches come on their own freshly baked buns and breads. The hamburgers, egg-salad sandwiches, mahi burgers, and honey-dipped fried chicken are popular and cheap.

Kanemitsu's has a life after dark, too. Whenever anyone on Molokai mentions "hot bread," they're talking about the hot-bread run at Kanemitsu's, the surreal late-night ritual for die-hard bread lovers. Those in the know line up at the bak-ery's back door beginning at 10:30pm, when the bread is whisked hot out of the oven and into waiting hands (see the box "A True Molokai Experience: The Hot Bread Run" later in this chapter). You can order your fresh bread with butter, jelly, cinnamon, or cream cheese, and the bakers will cut the hot loaves down the middle and slather on the works so it melts in the bread. *Hint:* The cream cheese and jelly bread makes a fine substitute for dessert.

79 Ala Malama St. Ⓒ 808/553-5855. Most items less than $5.50. No credit cards. Restaurant Wed–Mon 5:30–11:30am; bakery Wed–Mon 5:30am–6:30pm.

Molokai Drive-Inn AMERICAN/TAKEOUT It is a greasy spoon, but it's one of the rare drive-up places with fresh *akule* (mackerel) and ahi (when avail-able), plus fried saimin at budget-friendly prices. The honey-dipped fried chicken is a favorite among residents, who also come here for the floats, shakes, and other artery-clogging choices. But don't expect much in terms of ambience: This is a fast-food take-out counter with the smells of frying in the surrounding air—and it doesn't pretend to be otherwise.

Kaunakakai. Ⓒ 808/553-5655. Most items less than $7.75. No credit cards. Mon–Thurs 5:30am–10pm; Fri–Sun 6am–10:30pm.

Molokai Mango DELI/AMERICAN This video store and popular sandwich shop in downtown Kaunakakai sells sandwiches and nachos from the take-out counter. Turkey, ham, and roast beef (Angus beef) are served on five different breads, and all are popular. The inexpensive nachos are a hit, too, for those evenings at home with an old rented movie. Molokai Mango also rents and sells videos, games, and equipment, including TV sets.

93-D Ala Malama St. ☎ **808/553-3981**. Most items $2–$4. MC, V. Mon–Sat 9am–8pm.

Molokai Pizza Cafe ✦ PIZZA   This popular gathering place serves excellent pizzas and sandwiches that have made it a Kaunakakai staple as well as one of our favorite eateries on the island. The best-selling pies are the Molokai (pepperoni and cheese), the Big Island (pepperoni, ham, mushroom, Italian sausage, bacon, and vegetables), and the Molokini (plain cheese slices). Pasta, sandwiches, and specials round out the menu. Our personal fave is the vegetarian Maui pizza, but others tout the fresh-baked submarine and pocket sandwiches and the gyro pocket with spinach pie. Sunday is prime-rib day, Wednesday is Mexican, and Hawaiian plates are sold on Thursdays. Coin-operated cars and a toy airplane follow the children's theme, but adults should feel equally at home with the very popular barbecued baby-back rib plate and the fresh-fish dinners. Children's art and letters in the tiled dining room add an entertaining and charming touch. Free delivery to the Hotel Molokai is a welcome development.

In Kahua Center, on the old Wharf Rd. ☎ **808/553-3288**. Large pizzas $13–$23. No credit cards. Sun 11am–10pm; Mon–Thurs 10am–10pm; Fri–Sat 10am–11pm.

Outpost Natural Foods ✦ VEGETARIAN   The healthiest and freshest food on the island is served at the lunch counter of this health-food store, around the corner from the main drag on the makai (toward the sea) side of Kaunakakai town. The tiny store abounds in Molokai papayas, bananas, herbs, potatoes, watermelon, and other local produce, complementing its selection of vitamins, cosmetics, and health aids, as well as bulk and shelf items. But the real star is the closet-size lunch counter. The salads, burritos, tempeh sandwiches, vegetarian pot pie, tofu-spinach lasagna, and mock chicken, turkey, and meatloaf (made from oats, sprouts, seeds, and seasonings) are testament to the fact that vegetarian food need not be boring. A must for health-conscious diners and shoppers.

70 Makaena Place. ☎ **808/553-3377**. Most items less than $5. AE, DISC, MC, V. Sun–Fri 10am–3pm.

Sundown Deli DELI   From "gourmet saimin" to spinach pie, Sundown's offerings are home-cooked and healthy, with daily specials that include vegetarian quiche, spanakopita, vegetarian lasagna, and club sandwiches. The sandwiches (like smoked turkey and chicken salad) and several salads (Caesar, Asian, stuffed tomato) are served daily, with a soup of the day. Vitamins, T-shirts, and snacks are sold in this tiny cafe, but most of the business is takeout.

145 Puali St. (across the street from Veteran's Memorial Park). ☎ **808/553-3713**. Sandwiches, soups, and salads $3.95–$7.50. AE, MC, V. Mon–Fri 7am–4pm; Sat 10:30am–2pm.

THE WEST END

Maunaloa Room ✦ MOLOKAI REGIONAL   Molokai has never had anything resembling fine dining, but this restaurant changes the picture. It's in the island's first upscale hotel, a 22-room lodge fashioned after a ranch owner's private home in the cool hills of Maunaloa, where you can see Oahu (Diamond Head under the best of conditions) past the rolling ranchlands and the ocean. Fresh Molokai ingredients come in cross-cultural preparations. Breakfast features banana-stuffed Molokai sweetbread French toast or eggs with taro hash. The dinner menu includes entrees like fresh fish with roasted corn; Molokai prawns and Pacific snapper; lemon-grass mango chicken with avocado relish and spiced tortilla. The room's rustic, lodge-like ambience fits the paniolo surroundings, and Hawaiian proverbs stenciled on the walls are a nice cultural touch.

Sheraton Molokai Lodge & Beach Village, Maunaloa. © 808/660-2725. Reservations recommended for dinner. Breakfast entrees $6–$12; dinner main courses $20–$28. AE, DC, DISC, MC, V. Daily 7–10am and 6–9pm (Sunday brunch, 11am–1:30pm, $23). Lunch served 10am–4pm in the bar, most sandwiches under $10.

EN ROUTE TO THE NORTH COAST

Kualapuu Cook House ✿ AMERICAN   An old wagon in front of a former plantation house marks this down-home eatery, now takeout only. Local residents flock here for the oversize servings. Breakfasts feature giant omelets, homemade corned beef hash and, for those who dare, The Works—buttermilk pancakes, eggs, and home fries (you'll either be fueled for the day, or ready to take a nap). Lunch can be either a burger or sandwich or one of their humongous plate lunches of pork katsu or chicken, served up with rice, of course.

Farrington Hwy., 1 block west of Hwy. 470, Kalapuu. © 808/567-9655. Most items under $15. No credit cards. Mon–Sat 7am–3pm.

THE EAST END

Neighborhood Store 'N Counter ✿ AMERICAN   The Neighborhood Store is nothing fancy, and that's what we love about it. This store/lunch counter appears like a mirage near mile marker 16 in the Pukoo area en route to the East End. Picnic tables under a royal poinciana tree are a wonderful sight, and the food does not disappoint. Neighborhood Store serves omelets, Portuguese sausage, and other breakfast specials (brunch is very popular), then segues into sandwiches, salads, mahimahi plates, and varied over-the-counter lunch offerings. Favorites include the mahimahi plate lunch, the chicken katsu, and the Mexican plate, each one tried and true, with a home-cooked flavor. There are daily specials, ethnic dishes, and some vegetarian offerings, as well as burgers (including a killer veggie burger), saimin, and legendary desserts. Made-on-Maui Roselani ice cream is a featured attraction, and we hear raves over the Portuguese doughnut dessert, a deep-fried doughnut filled with ice cream. This is a great stop on the East End, a Molokai treasure. (Also see the store's entry under "Shopping" on p. 271.)

Pukoo. © 808/558-8498. Most items less than $6.95; bento $7.30. No credit cards. Daily 8am–6pm.

5 Beaches

With imposing sea cliffs on one side and lazy fish ponds on the other, Molokai has little room for beaches along its 106-mile coast. Still, a big gold-sand beach flourishes on the West End, and you'll find tiny pocket beaches on the East End. The emptiness of Molokai's beaches is both a blessing and a curse: The seclusion means no lifeguards.

KAUNAKAKAI
ONE ALII BEACH PARK

This thin strip of sand, once reserved for the *alii* (chiefs), is the oldest public beach park on Molokai. You'll find One Alii Beach Park (*One* is pronounced *o-nay*, not *won*) by a coconut grove on the outskirts of Kaunakakai. Safe for swimmers of all ages and abilities, it's often crowded with families on weekends, but it can be all yours on weekdays. Facilities include outdoor showers, restrooms, and free parking.

THE WEST END
PAPOHAKU BEACH ⭐⭐

Nearly 3 miles long and 100 yards wide, gold-sand Papohaku Beach is one of the biggest in Hawaii (17-mile Polihale Beach on Kauai is the biggest). It's great for walking, beachcombing, picnics, and sunset watching year-round. The big surf and rip currents make swimming risky except in summer, when the waters are calmer. Go early in the day when the tropic sun is less fierce and the winds calm. The beach is so big that you may never see another soul except at sunset, when a few people gather on the shore in hopes of spotting the elusive green flash, a natural wonder that takes place when the horizon is cloud-free. Facilities include outdoor showers, restrooms, picnic grounds, and free parking.

KEPUHI BEACH

Golfers see this picturesque golden strand in front of the Kaluakoi Resort and Golf Course as just another sand trap, but sunbathers like the semiprivate grassy dunes; they're seldom, if ever, crowded. Beachcombers often find what they're looking for here, but swimmers have to dodge lava rocks and risk rip currents. Watch out for errant golf balls. There are no facilities or lifeguards, but cold drinks and restrooms are handy at the resort.

THE EAST END
SANDY BEACH ⭐

Molokai's most popular swimming beach—ideal for families with small kids— is a roadside pocket of gold sand protected by a reef, with a great view of Maui and Lanai. You'll find it off the King Kamehameha V Highway (Hwy. 450) at mile marker 20. There are no facilities—just you, the sun, the sand, and the surf.

MURPHY BEACH PARK (KUMIMI BEACH PARK)

In 1970, the Molokai Jaycees wanted to create a sandy beach park with a good swimming area for the children of the East End. They chose a section known as Kumimi Beach, which was owned by the Pu'u o Hoku Ranch. The beach was a dump, literally. The ranch owner, George Murphy, immediately gave his permission to use the site as a park; the Jaycees cleaned it up and built three small pavilions, plus picnic tables and barbecue grills. Officially, the park is called the George Murphy Beach Park (shortened to Murphy Beach Park over the years), but some old-timers still call it Kumimi Beach, and, just to make things really confusing, some people call it Jaycees Park.

No matter what you call it, this small park is shaded by ironwood trees that line a white-sand beach. It's generally a very safe swimming area. On calm days, snorkeling and diving are great outside the reef. Fishermen are also frequently spotted here looking for papio and other island fish.

HALAWA BEACH PARK ⭐

At the foot of scenic Halawa Valley is this beautiful black-sand beach with a palm-fringed lagoon, a wave-lashed island offshore, and a distant view of the West Maui Mountains across the Pailolo Channel. The swimming is safe in the shallows close to shore, but where the waterfall stream meets the sea, the ocean is often murky and unnerving. A winter swell creases the mouth of Halawa Valley on the north side of the bay and attracts a crowd of local surfers. Facilities are minimal; bring your own water. To get here, take King Kamehameha V Highway (Hwy. 450) east to the end.

6 Watersports

The best places to rent beach toys (snorkels, Boogie Boards, beach chairs, fishing poles, and more) are **Molokai Rentals and Tours,** Kaunakakai (© 800/553-9071 or 808/553-5663; www.molokai-rentals.com), and **Molokai Outdoor Activities,** in the lobby of Hotel Molokai, just outside Kaunakakai (© 877/553-4477 or 808/553-4477; www.molokai-outdoors.com). Both operators not only have everything you need, but can also can give you advice on where to find a great swimming beach or where the waves are breaking. Another good place to check out is **Molokai Fish & Dive,** Kaunakakai (© 808/553-5926; http://molokai-aloha.com/fishdiv/), a mind-boggling store filled with outdoor gear. You can rent snorkels, fishing gear, and even ice chests here. This is also a hot spot for fishing news and tips on what's running where.

For general advice on the activities listed below, see "The Active Vacation Planner" in chapter 2.

BODY BOARDING (BOOGIE BOARDING) & BODYSURFING

Molokai has only three beaches that offer waves suitable for body boarding and bodysurfing: Papohaku, Kepuhi, and Halawa. Even these beaches are only for experienced bodysurfers, due to the strength of the rip currents and undertows. You can rent Boogie Boards with fins for $7 a day or $21 a week from **Molokai Rentals and Tours,** Kaunakakai (© 808/553-5663; www.molokai-rentals.com). Boards without fins go for just $2.95 a day at **Molokai Outdoor Activities,** in the lobby of Hotel Molokai, just outside Kaunakakai (© 877/553-4477 or 808/553-4477; www.molokai-outdoors.com).

OCEAN KAYAKING

During the summer months, when the waters on the north shore are calm, Molokai offers some of the most spectacular kayaking in Hawaii. You can paddle from remote valley to remote valley, spending a week or more exploring the exotic terrain. However, Molokai is for the experienced kayaker only. You must be adept in paddling through open ocean swells and rough waves. **Molokai Rentals and Tours,** Kaunakakai (© 808/553-5663; www.molokai-rentals.com), has a kayak tour of the south side of Molokai for $45 adults and $25 children under 16, which includes snorkeling. They also offer kayak rentals, singles $25 a day ($100 a week) and doubles $40 a day ($160 a week), which includes life jackets, roof rack, paddles, and leashes.

Molokai Outdoors Activities, in the lobby of Hotel Molokai, just outside Kaunakakai (© 877/553-4477 or 808/553-4477; www.molokai-outdoors.com), has sunset tours of the ancient Hawaii fish ponds and the inshore reefs for beginners or nature lovers ($45–$75 per person); a coastline tour for more experienced kayakers with snorkeling ($55–$75 per person). They also rent kayaks: from $10 a day.

On the West End, the **Sheraton Molokai Lodge and Beach Village** (© 800/ 782-9488 or 808/660-2710; www.molokai-ranch.com) offers ocean kayaking ($65 for nonguests, $45 for guests) and ocean expeditions ($35 nonguests, $30 guests).

SAILING

Molokai Charters ★ (© 808/553-5852) offers a variety of sailing trips on *Satan's Doll,* a 42-foot sloop: 2-hour sunset sails for $40 per person, a half day of sailing and whale-watching for $50, and a full-day sail to Lanai with swimming and snorkeling for $90 (which includes lunch, cold drinks, snacks, and all equipment).

Owners Richard and Doris Reed have been sailing visitors around Molokai's waters since 1975. They also offer **whale-watching cruises** from mid-December to mid-March, when humpback whales frequent the waters around Molokai.

SCUBA DIVING

Want to see turtles or manta rays up close? How about sharks? Molokai resident Bill Kapuni has been diving the waters around the island his entire life; he'll be happy to show you whatever you're brave enough to encounter. **Bill Kapuni's Snorkel and Dive,** Kaunakakai (✆ **808/553-9867**), can provide gear, a boat, and even instruction. Two-tank dives from his 22-foot Boston whaler cost $110 and include Bill's voluminous knowledge of the legends and lore of Hawaii.

SNORKELING

When the waters are calm, Molokai offers excellent snorkeling; you'll see a wide range of butterfly fish, tangs, and angelfish. Good snorkeling can be found—when conditions are right—at many of Molokai's beaches. **Molokai Rentals and Tours** (✆ **808/553-5663;** www.molokai-rentals.com) and **Molokai Outdoor Activities** (✆ **877/553-4477** or 808/553-4477; www.molokai-outdoors.com), offer the least-expensive snorkel gear for rent ($6 a day or $24 a week).

For snorkeling tours, contact **Bill Kapuni's Snorkel & Dive,** Kaunakakai (✆ **808/553-9867**), which charges $65 for a 2½-hour trip. They also rent snorkeling gear for $10 a day (see "Scuba Diving" above). Walter Naki of

---

 Molokai's Best Snorkel Spots

Most Molokai beaches are too dangerous for snorkeling in winter, when big waves and strong currents are generated by storms that sweep down from Alaska. From mid-September to April, stick to Murphy Beach Park (also known as Kumimi Beach Park) on the East End. In summer, roughly May to mid-September, when the Pacific Ocean takes a holiday and turns into a flat lake, the whole west coast of Molokai opens up for snorkeling. Mike Holmes, of Molokai Ranch & Fun Hogs Hawaii, says the best spots are as follows:

Kawaikiunui, Ilio Point, and **Pohaku Moiliili** (West End)   These are all special places seldom seen by even those who live on Molokai. You can reach Kawaikiunui and Pohaku Moiliili on foot after a long, hot, dusty ride in a four-wheel-drive vehicle, but it's much easier and quicker to go by sea.

Kapukahehu (Dixie Maru) Beach (West End)   This gold-sand family beach is well protected, and the reef is close and shallow. The name Dixie Maru comes from a 1920s Japanese fishing boat stranded off the rocky shore. One of the Molokai Ranch cowboys hung the wrecked boat's nameplate on a gate by Kapukahehu Beach, and the name Dixie Maru stuck. To get here, take Kaluakoi Road to the end of the pavement, and then take the footpath 100 yards to the beach.

Murphy (Kumimi) Beach Park 🏖 (East End)   This beach is located between mile markers 20 and 21, off Kamehameha V Highway. The reef here is easily reachable, and the waters are calm year-round.

Molokai Action Adventures (© **808/558-8184**) offers leisurely snorkeling, diving, and swimming trips in his 21-foot Boston whaler for $100 per person for a 4- to 6-hour custom tour.

SPORTFISHING

Molokai's waters can provide prime sporting opportunities, whether you're looking for big-game sportfishing or bottom fishing. When customers are scarce, Capt. Joe Reich, who has been fishing the waters around Molokai for decades, goes commercial fishing, so he always knows where the fish are biting. He runs *Alyce C.* **Sportfishing** out of Kaunakakai Harbor (© **808/558-8377**). A full day of fishing for up to six people is $400, three-quarters of a day is $350, and a half day is $300. You usually can persuade him to do a whale-watching cruise during the winter months.

For fly-fishing or light-tackle reef-fish trolling, contact Walter Naki at **Molokai Action Adventures** (© **808/558-8184**). Walter's been fishing his entire life and loves to share his secret spots with visiting fishermen—he knows *the* place for bonefishing on the flats. A full-day trip for up to four people in his 21-foot Boston whaler is $300.

Fun Hogs Hawaii (© **808/567-6789;** www.molokai-rentals.com/fun hogs.html) has deep-sea fishing excursions on a 27-foot, fully equipped sportfishing vessel. Prices are $350 for six passengers for 4 hours; $400 for a 6-hour excursion, and $450 for six people for the 8-hour trip.

If you just want to try your luck casting along the shoreline, **Molokai Outdoor Activities,** in the lobby of Hotel Molokai, just outside Kaunakakai (© **877/553-4477** or 808/553-4477; www.molokai-outdoors.com), rents fishing poles for $4.95 a day and can tell you where they're biting.

7 Hiking & Camping

HIKING MOLOKAI'S PEPEOPAE TRAIL

Molokai's most awesome hike is the **Pepeopae Trail** ★★, which takes you back a few million years. On the cloud-draped trail (actually a boardwalk across the bog), you'll see mosses, sedges, native violets, knee-high ancient ohias, and lichens that evolved in total isolation over eons. Eerie intermittent mists blowing in and out will give you an idea of what this island was like at its creation.

The narrow boardwalk, built by volunteers, protects the bog and keeps you out of the primal ooze. Don't venture off it; you could damage this fragile environment or get lost. The 3-mile round-trip takes about 90 minutes to hike—but first you have to drive about 20 miles from Kaunakakai, deep into the Molokai Forest Preserve on a four-wheel-drive road. *Don't try this with a regular rental car.* Plan a full day for this outing. Better yet, go on a guided nature hike with the **Nature Conservancy of Hawaii,** which guards this unusual ecosystem. For information, write to the Nature Conservancy at 1116 Smith St., Suite 201, Honolulu, HI 96817. No permit is required for this easy hike. Call ahead (© **808/537-4508** or 808/553-5236) to check on the condition of the ungraded four-wheel-drive red-dirt road that leads to the trailhead and to let people know that you'll be up there.

To get here, take Highway 460 west from Kaunakakai for 3½ miles and turn right before the Maunawainui Bridge onto the unmarked Molokai Forest Reserve Road (sorry, there aren't any road signs). The pavement ends at the cemetery; continue on the dirt road. After about 2 to 2½ miles, you'll see a sign telling you that you are now in the Molokai Forest Reserve. At the Waikolu Lookout and picnic area, which is just over 9 miles on the Molokai Forest Reserve Road, sign

Your Guide to Adventure

If it's action you crave, call **Molokai Action Adventures** (© 808/558-8184). Island guide Walter Naki will take you skin diving, reef trolling, kayaking, hunting, or hiking into Molokai's remote hidden valleys. Hiking tours are $50 per person for 4 hours; the number of participants is limited to no more than four. Not only does Walter know Molokai like the back of his hand, but he also loves being outdoors and talking story with visitors; he'll tell you about the island, the people, the politics, the myths, and anything else you want to know.

in at the box near the entrance. Continue on the road for another 5 miles to a fork in the road with the sign PU'U KOLEKOLE pointing to the right side of the fork. Do not turn right; instead, continue straight at the fork, which will lead to the clearly marked trailhead. The drive will take about 45 minutes.

HIKING THE WEST END

Molokai's entire West End, some 53,000 acres, is open to hiking tours through the **Sheraton Molokai Lodge and Beach Village** (© 800/782-9488 or 808/660-2710; www.molokai-ranch.com), which offers a range of hikes to fit different abilities. Prices range from $45 for nonguests ($30 for guests) for an easy 2- to 3-hour hike to $125 ($85 for guests) for advanced hikes along the sea cliff coast.

HIKING TO KALAUPAPA

This hike to the site of Molokai's famous leper colony is like going down a switchback staircase with what seems like a million steps. You don't always see the breathtaking view because you're too busy watching your step. Not surprisingly, it's easier going down—in about an hour, you'll go 2½ miles, from 2,000 feet to sea level. The trip up sometimes takes twice as long. The trailhead starts on the *mauka* (inland) side of Highway 470, just past the Mule Barn (you can't miss it). Check in here at 7:30am, get a permit, and go before the mule train departs. You must be 16 or older (it's an old state law that kept kids out of the leper colony) and should be in good shape. Wear good hiking boots or sneakers; you won't make it past the first turn in sandals.

CAMPING

Camping equipment is available for rent from **Molokai Rentals and Tours** (© 808/553-5663; www.molokai-rentals.com). A two-person camping package is $20 a day or $80 a week. **Molokai Outdoors Activities,** in the lobby of Hotel Molokai, just outside Kaunakakai (© 877/553-4477 or 808/553-4477; www.molokai-outdoors.com), also rents all kinds of tents and camping gear from $5 up.

AT THE BEACH

One of Molokai's best year-round campgrounds is **Papohaku Beach Park** , on the island's West End. This drive-up seaside site makes a great getaway. Facilities include restrooms, drinking water, outdoor showers, barbecue grills, and picnic tables. Groceries and gas are available in Maunaloa, 6 miles away. Kaluakoi Resort is a mile away. Get camping permits by contacting **Maui County Parks Department,** P.O. Box 526, Kaunakakai, HI 96748 (© 808/553-3204). Camping is limited to 3 days, but if nobody else has applied, the time limit is waived. The cost is $3 a person per night.

IN AN IRONWOOD FOREST

At the end of Highway 470 is **Palaau State Park** ★★, home to the Kalaupapa Lookout (the best vantage point for seeing the historic leper colony if you're not hiking or riding a mule in). It's airy and cool in the park's 234-acre ironwood forest, where many love to camp at the designated state campground. Camping is free, but you'll need a permit from the **State Division of Parks** (© 808/567-6618). For more on the park, see p. 263.

8 Golf & Other Outdoor Pursuits

GOLF

If you didn't bring your clubs, you can rent them from $6 a day ($24 for the week) from **Molokai Rentals and Tours,** Kaunakakai (© 808/553-5663; www.molokai-rentals.com).

Golf is one of Molokai's best-kept secrets; it's challenging and fun, tee times are open, and the rates are lower than your score will be. The 18-hole **Kaluakoi Golf Course** (© 808/552-0255) recently reopened in 2003 after extensive renovation (repairs to irrigation, new grass planted, redesigned bunkers and narrower fairways). Most of the work was cosmetic and the Ted Robinson–designed course is still as challenging as ever, especially the par 3, 16th hole, where you tee off over a gulch or the distraction of the incredible Papohaku Beach from the 3rd tee. Green fees are $35 without cart, $55 with cart or $45 each for two players with cart.

The real find is the **Ironwood Hills Golf Course,** off Kalae Highway (© 808/567-6000). It's located just before the Molokai Mule Ride Mule Barn, on the road to the Lookout. One of the oldest courses in the state, Ironwood Hills (named after the 2 predominant features of the course, ironwood trees and hills) was built in 1929 by Del Monte Plantation for its executives. This unusual course, which sits in the cool air at 1,200 feet, delights with its rich foliage, open fairways, and spectacular views of the rest of the island. If you play here, use a trick developed by the local residents: After teeing off on the sixth hole, just take whatever clubs you need to finish playing the hole and a driver for the seventh hole, and park your bag under a tree. The climb to the seventh hole is steep—you'll be glad that you're only carrying a few clubs. Greens fees are $15 for 9 holes, or $20 for 18 holes. Cart fees are $7 for 9 holes, or $14 for 18. You can also rent a hand cart for just $2.50. Club rentals are $7 for 9 holes and $12 for 18.

BICYCLING

Molokai is a great place to see by bicycle. The roads are not very busy and there are great places to pull off the road and take a quick dip. The best mountain biking in the state is on the trails of **Sheraton Molokai Lodge and Beach Village** (© 800/782-9488 or 808/660-2710; www.molokai-ranch.com). Imagine 53,000 acres with intercrossing trails that weave up and down the west end to the beach. Simply spectacular. The equipment is good, the guides excellent (they even have courses on how to mountain bike, which are given on specially constructed wooden trails). Guided tours range from $50 ($35 for guests) for 2 to 3 hours to $100 ($80 guests) for full-day rides with a guide and lunch.

Molokai Rentals and Tours, Kaunakakai (© 800/553-9071 or 808/553-5663; www.molokai-rentals.com) offers a great tour of the 500 cultivated acres of Coffee's of Hawaii fields. With numerous ups and downs, the tour rounds the perimeter of the coffee fields and ventures up to an overlook and back to

Frommer's Favorite Molokai Experiences

Riding a Mule into a Leper Colony. Don't pass up the opportunity to see this hauntingly beautiful peninsula. Buzzy Sproat's mules go up and down the 3-mile Kalaupapa Trail (with 26 switchbacks) to Molokai's famous leper colony. The views are breathtaking: You'll see the world's highest sea cliffs (taller than a 300-story skyscraper) and waterfalls plunging thousands of feet into the ocean. If you're afraid of heights, catch the views from the Kalaupapa Lookout.

Venture into the Garden of Eden. Drive the 30 miles along Molokai's East End. Take your time. Stop to smell the flowers and pick guavas by the side of the road. Pull over for a swim. Wave at every car you pass and every person you see. At the end of the road, stand on the beach at Halawa Valley and see Hawaii as it must have looked in A.D. 650, when the first people arrived in the islands.

Celebrate the Ancient Hula. Hula is the heartbeat of Hawaiian culture, and Molokai is its birthplace. Although most visitors to Hawaii never get to see the real thing, it's possible to see it here—once a year, on the third Saturday in May, when Molokai celebrates the birth of the hula at its **Ka Hula Pikoi Festival.** The daylong affair includes dance, music, food, and crafts.

Stroll the Sands at Papohaku. Go early, when the tropical sun isn't so fierce, and stroll this 3-mile stretch of unspoiled golden sand on Molokai's West End. It's one of the longest beaches in Hawaii. The big surf and rip currents make swimming somewhat risky, but Papohaku is perfect for walking, beachcombing, and sunset watching.

Travel Back in Time on the Pepeopae Trail. This awesome hike takes you through the Molokai Forest Reserve and back a few million years in time. Along the misty trail (actually a boardwalk across the bog), expect close encounters of the botanical kind: mosses, sedges, violets, lichens, and knee-high ancient ohias.

Soak in the Warm Waters off Sandy Beach. On the East End, about 20 miles outside Kaunakakai—just before the road starts to climb to Halawa Valley—lies a small pocket of white sand known as Sandy Beach. Submerging yourself here in the warm, calm waters (an outer reef protects the cove) is a sensuous experience par excellence.

Snorkel Among Clouds of Butterfly Fish. The calm waters off Murphy (Kumimi) Beach, on the East End, are perfect for snorkelers. Just don your

the plant where you get a walking tour of the process. Included in the tour are taste-testing of different varieties, a delicious Mocha Mama or Smoothie, and a complimentary 2 ounce bag of coffee. The 2½ hour tours are Monday to Friday at 8:30am, and cost $45 for adults and $25 for children under 16. The more adventurous may want to try their All Day Bike Tours which go either up to the Forest Reserve or along Molokai's off-the-beaten paths. Both tours start at 8:00am and just go until the tour has seen everything (usually finishing up around 3pm); lunch is also provided. Cost is $80 and includes bikes helmets and gear and head to the reef, where you'll find lots of exotic tropical fish, including long-nosed butterfly fish, saddle wrasses, and convict tangs.

Kayak Along the North Shore. This is the Hawaii of your dreams: waterfalls thundering down sheer cliffs, remote sand beaches, miles of tropical vegetation, and the sounds of the sea splashing on your kayak and the wind whispering in your ear. The best times to go are late March and early April, or in summer, especially August to September, when the normally galloping ocean lies down flat.

Watch the Sunset from a Coconut Grove. Kapuaiwa Coconut Beach Park, off Maunaloa Highway (Hwy. 460), is a perfect place to watch the sunset. The sky behind the coconut trees fills with a kaleidoscope of colors as the sun sinks into the Pacific. Be careful where you sit, though: Falling coconuts could have you seeing stars well before dusk.

Sample the Local Brew. Saunter up to the Espresso Bar at the Coffees of Hawaii Plantation Store in Kualapuu for a fresh cup of java made from beans that were grown, processed, and packed on this 450-acre plantation. While you sip, survey the vast collection of native crafts.

Taste Aloha at a Macadamia Nut Farm. It could be the owner, Tuddie Purdy, and his friendly disposition that make the macadamia nuts here taste so good. Or it could be his years of practice in growing, harvesting, and shelling them on his 1½-acre farm. Either way, Purdy produces a perfect crop. See how he does it on a short, free tour of Purdy's All-Natural Macadamia Nut Farm in Hoolehua, just a nut's throw from the airport.

Talk Story with the Locals. The number-one favorite pastime of most islanders is "talking story," or exchanging experiences and knowledge. It's an old Hawaiian custom that brings people, and generations, closer together. You can probably find residents more than willing to share their wisdom with you while fishing from the wharf at Kaunakakai, hanging out at Molokai Fish & Dive, or having coffee at any of the island's restaurants.

Post a Nut. Why send a picturesque postcard to your friends and family back home when you can send a fresh coconut? The Hoolelua Post Office will supply the free coconuts, if you'll supply the $3.95 postage fee.

water bottles. If you'd rather explore the island on your own, you can rent bikes for $20 a day or $80 a week.

Molokai Outdoors Activities, in the lobby of Hotel Molokai, just outside Kaunakakai (© **877/553-4477** or 808/553-4477; www.molokai-utdoors.com), offers a bike/kayak tour of the east end of Molokai, with snorkeling. All gear, lunch, guide and transportation is $135. Bike rentals range from a beach cruiser ($10 a day) to MTB front shocks ($35 a day), and include a complimentary bicycle rack for your rental.

HORSEBACK RIDING

One of the most scenic places to go riding on Molokai is **Puu-O-Hoku Ranch** (© 808/558-8109; www.puuohoku.com), about 25 miles outside Kaunakakai on the East End. Guided trail rides pass through green pasture on one of the largest working ranches on Molokai, then head up into the high mountain forest. Don't forget your camera: There are plenty of scenic views of waterfalls, the Pacific Ocean, and the islands of Maui and Lanai in the distance. Rates are $55 for a 1-hour ride, $75 for a 2-hour ride, and $120 for a 4-hour ride.

For those looking for a little more than just a horseback ride, **Sheraton Molokai Lodge and Beach Village** (© 800/782-9488 or 808/660-2710; www.molokai-ranch.com) offers a "Paniolo Roundup." You can learn horsemanship from the ranch's working cowboys and compete in traditional rodeo games; the half-day adventure is $105 ($80 guests). Trail rides range from $105 to $150 ($80–$125 for guests).

TENNIS

The only two tennis courts on Molokai are located at the **Mitchell Pauole Center** in Kaunakakai (© 808/553-5141). Both have night lights and are available free on a first-come, first-served basis, with a 45-minute time limit if someone is waiting. If you left your racket at home, you can rent one for just $4 a day ($16 a week) from **Molokai Rentals and Tours,** Kaunakakai (© 808/553-5663; www.molokai-rentals.com); they're the same price at **Molokai Outdoor Activities,** in the lobby of Hotel Molokai, just outside Kaunakakai (© 877/553-4477 or 808/553-4477; www.molokai-outdoors.com).

9 Seeing the Sights

IN & AROUND KAUNAKAKAI

Kapuaiwa Coconut Grove/Kiowea Park ★ *Kids*   This royal grove—1,000 coconut trees on 10 acres planted in 1863 by the island's high chief Kapua'iwa (later King Kamehameha V)—is a major roadside attraction. The shoreline park is a favorite subject of sunset photographers and visitors who delight in a hand-lettered sign that warns: DANGER: FALLING COCONUTS. In its backyard, across the highway, stands Church Row: seven churches, each a different denomination—clear evidence of the missionary impact on Hawaii.

Along Maunaloa Hwy. (Hwy. 460), 2 miles west of Kaunakakai.

Post-A-Nut ★   Postmaster Margaret Keahi-Leary will help you say "Aloha" with a dried Molokai coconut. Just write a message on the coconut with a felt-tip pen, and she'll send it via U.S. mail over the sea. Coconuts are free, but postage is $3.95 for a mainland-bound 2-pound coconut.

Hoolehua Post Office, Puu Peelua Ave. (Hwy. 480), near Maunaloa Hwy. (Hwy. 460). © 808/567-6144. Mon–Fri 7:30–11:30am and 12:30–4:30pm.

Purdy's All-Natural Macadamia Nut Farm (Na Hua O'Ka Aina) ★ *Finds*
The Purdys have made macadamia-nut buying an entertaining event, offering tours of the 1½-acre homestead and giving lively demonstrations of nutshell cracking in the shade of their towering trees. The tour of the 70-year-old nut farm explains the growth, bearing, harvesting, and shelling processes, so that by the time you bite into the luxurious macadamia nut, you'll have more than a passing knowledge of its entire life cycle.

Lihi Pali Ave. (behind Molokai High School), Hoolehua. © 808/567-6601. www.visitmolokai.com. Free admission. Mon–Fri 9:30am–3:30pm; Sat 10am–2pm; closed on holidays.

THE NORTH COAST

Even if you don't get a chance to see Hawaii's most dramatic coast in its entirety—not many people do—you shouldn't miss the opportunity to glimpse it from the **Kalaupapa Lookout** at Palauu State Park. On the way, there are a few diversions (arranged here in geographical order).

EN ROUTE TO THE NORTH COAST

Coffees of Hawaii Plantation Store   The defunct Del Monte pineapple town of Kualapuu is rising again—only this time, coffee is the catch, not pineapple. Located in the cool foothills, Coffees of Hawaii has planted coffee beans on 600 acres of former pineapple land. The plantation is irrigating the plants with a high-tech, continuous water and fertilizer drip system. You can see it all on the walking tour; call 24 hours in advance to set it up. The Plantation Store sells arts and crafts from Molokai. Stop by the Espresso Bar for a Mocha Mama (Molokai coffee, ice, chocolate ice cream, chocolate syrup, whipped cream, and chocolate shavings on top). It'll keep you going all day—maybe even all night.

Hwy. 480 (near the junction of Hwy. 470). © **800/709-BEAN** or 808/567-9241, www.molokaicoffee.com. Walking tour $7 adults, $3.50 children 5–12. Tours Mon–Sat. 9:30am and 11:30am; Sun 11:30am only. Store open Mon–Fri 7am–4pm; Sat 8am–4pm; Sun 10am–4pm.

Molokai Museum and Cultural Center   En route to the California Gold Rush in 1849, Rudolph W. Meyer, a German professor, came to Molokai, married the high chieftess Kalama, and began to operate a small sugar plantation near his home. Now on the National Register of Historic Places, this restored 1878 sugar mill, with its century-old steam engine, mule-driven cane crusher, copper clarifiers, and redwood evaporating pan (all in working order), is the last of its kind in Hawaii. The mill also houses a museum that traces the history of sugar growing on Molokai and features special events, such as wine tastings every 2 months, taro festivals, an annual music festival, and occasional classes in ukulele making, loom weaving, and sewing. Call for a schedule.

Meyer Sugar Mill, Hwy. 470 (just after the turnoff for the Ironwood Hills Golf Course, and 2 miles below Kalaupapa Overlook), Kalae. © **808/567-6436.** Admission $2.50 adults, $1 students. Mon–Sat 10am–2pm.

Palauu State Park ⭑   This 234-acre piney-woods park, 8 miles out of Kaunakakai, doesn't look like much until you get out of the car and take a hike,

---

Kids Especially for Kids

Flying a Kite (p. 271)   Not only can you get a guaranteed-to-fly kite at the **Big Wind Kite Factory** (© 808/552-2634) in Maunaloa, but kite designer Jonathan Socher offers free kite-flying classes to kids, who'll learn how to make their kites soar, swoop, and, most important, stay in the air for more than 5 minutes.

Spending the Day at Murphy (Kumimi) Beach Park (p. 254)   Just beyond Wailua on the East End is this small wayside park that's perfect for kids. You'll find safe swimming conditions, plenty of shade from the ironwood trees, and small pavilions with picnic tables and barbecue grills.

Watching Whales (p. 255)   From mid-December to mid-March, kids of all ages can go whale-watching on Molokai Charters's 42-foot sloop, *Satan's Doll.*

which really puts you between a rock and a hard place: Go right, and you end up on the edge of Molokai's magnificent sea cliffs, with its panoramic view of the well-known Kalaupapa leper colony; go left, and you come face to face with a stone phallus.

If you have no plans to scale the cliffs by mule or on foot (see "Hiking & Camping" earlier in this chapter), the **Kalaupapa Lookout** ✮✮✮ is the only place from which to see the former place of exile. The trail is marked, and historic photos and interpretive signs will explain what you're seeing.

It's airy and cool in the ironwood forest, where camping is free at the designated state campground. You'll need a permit from the **State Division of Parks** (✆ **808/ 567-6618**). Not many people seem to camp here, perhaps because of the legend associated with the **Phallic Rock** ✮. Six feet high, pointed at an angle that means business, Molokai's famous Phallic Rock is a legendary fertility tool that appears to be working today. According to Hawaiian legend, a woman who wishes to become pregnant need only spend the night near the rock and, voilà! It's probably just a coincidence, of course, but Molokai does have a growing number of young, pregnant women.

Phallic Rock is at the end of a well-worn uphill path that passes an ironwood grove and several other rocks that vaguely resemble sexual body parts. No mistaking the big guy, though. Supposedly, it belonged to Nanahoa, a demigod who quarreled with his wife, Kawahuna, over a pretty girl. In the tussle, Kawahuna was thrown over the cliff, and both husband and wife were turned to stone. Of all the phallic rocks in Hawaii and the Pacific, this is the one to see. It's featured on a postcard with a tiny, awestruck Japanese woman standing next to it.

At the end of Hwy. 470.

THE LEGACY OF FATHER DAMIEN: KALAUPAPA NATIONAL HISTORIC PARK ✮✮✮

An old tongue of lava that sticks out to form a peninsula, Kalaupapa became infamous because of man's inhumanity to victims of a formerly incurable contagious disease.

King Kamehameha V sent the first lepers—nine men and three women—into exile on this lonely shore, at the base of ramparts that rise like temples against the Pacific, on January 6, 1866. More than 11,000 lepers arrived between 1866 and 1874, dispatched to disfigure and die in one of the world's most beautiful—and lonely—places. They called Kalaupapa "The Place of the Living Dead."

Leprosy is actually one of the world's least contagious diseases, transmitted only by direct, repetitive contact over a long period of time. It's caused by a germ, *Mycobacterium leprae,* that attacks the nerves, skin, and eyes, and is found mainly, but not exclusively, in tropical regions. American scientists found a cure for the disease in the 1940s.

Before science intervened, there was Father Damien. Born to wealth in Belgium, Joseph de Veuster traded a life of excess for exile among lepers; he devoted himself to caring for the afflicted at Kalaupapa. Father Damien, as he became known, volunteered to go out to the Pacific in place of his ailing brother. Horrified by the conditions in the leper colony, Father Damien worked at Kalaupapa for 11 years, building houses, schools, and churches, and giving hope to his patients. He died on April 15, 1889, in Kalaupapa, of leprosy. He was 49.

A hero nominated for Catholic sainthood, Father Damien is buried not in his tomb next to Molokai's St. Philomena Church, but in his native Belgium. Well, most of him anyway. His hand was recently returned to Molokai and reinterred at Kalaupapa as a relic of his martyrdom.

This small peninsula is probably the final resting place of more than 11,000 souls. The sand dunes are littered with grave markers sorted by the religious affiliation—Catholic, Protestant, Lutheran, or Buddhist—of those who died here. But so many are buried in unmarked graves that no accurate census of the dead exists.

Kalaupapa is now a National Historic Park (© **808/567-6802;** www.nps. gov/kala) and one of Hawaii's richest archaeological preserves, with sites that date from A.D. 1000. About 60 former patients chose to remain in the tidy village of whitewashed houses with statues of angels in their yards. The original name for their former affliction, leprosy, was officially banned in Hawaii by the state legislature in 1981. The name used now is "Hansen's disease," for Dr. Gerhard Hansen of Norway, who discovered the germ in 1873. The few remaining residents of Kalaupapa still call the disease leprosy, although none are too keen on being called lepers.

Kalaupapa welcomes visitors who arrive on foot, by mule, or by small plane. Father Damien's St. Philomena church, built in 1872, is open to visitors, who can see it from a yellow school bus driven by resident tour guide Richard Marks, an ex-seaman and sheriff who survived the disease. You won't be able to roam freely, and you'll be allowed to enter only the museum, the craft shop, and the church.

MULE RIDES TO KALAUPAPA   The first turn's a gasp, and it's all downhill from there. You can close your eyes and hold on for dear life, or slip the reins over the pommel and sit back, letting the mule do the walking down the precipitous path to Kalaupapa National Historic Park.

Even if you have only 1 day to spend on Molokai, spend it on a mule. This is a once-in-a-lifetime ride. The cliffs are taller than a 300-story skyscraper, but Buzzy Sproat's mules go safely up and down the narrow 3-mile trail daily, rain or shine. Starting at the top of the nearly perpendicular ridge (1,600 ft. high), the surefooted mules step down the muddy trail, pausing often on the 26 switchbacks to calculate their next move—and always, it seems to us, veering a little too close to the edge. Each switchback is numbered; by the time you get to number four, you'll catch your breath, put the mule on cruise control, and begin to enjoy Hawaii's most awesome trail ride.

The mule tours are offered once daily starting at 8am, and they last until about 3:30pm. It costs $150 per person for the all-day adventure, which includes the round-trip mule ride, a guided tour of the settlement, a visit to Father Damien's church and grave, lunch at Kalawao, and souvenirs. To go, you must be at least 16 years old and physically fit, and you must weigh no more than 250 pounds. Contact **Molokai Mule Ride** ★★★, 100 Kalae Highway, Suite 104, on Highway 470, 5 miles north of Highway 460 (© **800/567-7550,** or 808/567-6088 between 8 and 10pm; www.muleride.com). Advance reservations (at least 2 weeks ahead) are required.

SEEING KALAUPAPA BY PLANE   The fastest and easiest way to get to Kalaupapa is by hopping on a plane and zipping to Kalaupapa airport. From here, you can pick up the same Kalaupapa tour that the mule riders and hikers take. **Father Damien Tours** (© and fax **808/567-6171**) picks you up at Kalaupapa airport and takes you to some of the area's most scenic spots, including Kalawao, where Father Damien's church still stands, and the town of Kalaupapa. Packages including a round-trip flight to Kalaupapa, entry permits, historical park tour with Damien Tours, and a light picnic lunch cost $119 from the Molokai Airport, $279 from

Maui; and $215 from Honolulu. All visitors must be at least 16 years old. From Maui (either Kahului, Kapalua or Hana), call **Paragon Air** (© 808/244-3356 or www. paragon-air.com). For flights from either Maui or Honolulu to both the Molokai airport and to Kalaupapa, call **Pacific Wings** (© 888/575-4546 or 808/873-0877 or www.pacificwings.com).

SEEING KALAUPAPA BY FERRY/HIKING From Maui take the *Molokai Princess* Ferry to Molokai (© 800/275-6969 or 808/667-6165; www.maui princess.com), where you are met and transported by van to the top of the 1,600-foot sea cliffs. Here you hike down the 3-mile trail to the Kalaupapa National Historic Park; at the park you are met by Damien tours and given a van tour of the peninsula, during which you'll visit Father Damien's St. Philomena Church, his early grave site, and hear the stories of struggle and courage of the residents of Kalaupapa. The only catch is you have to hike back up the cliffs, where you are picked up by the van and returned to the ferry dock for the trip back to Maui. This fabulous experience really should only be undertaken by the physically fit (it will take about an hour hiking down and another 1½ hr. to hike back up). Cost for ferry, transportation, tour, and lunch is $215 (participants must be 16 years and older).

THE WEST END
MAUNALOA
In the first and only urban renewal on Molokai, the 1920s-era pineapple-plantation town of Maunaloa is being reinvented. Streets are getting widened and paved, and curbs and sidewalks are being added to serve a new tract of houses. Historic Maunaloa is becoming Maunaloa Village—there's already a town center with a park, a restaurant, a triplex movie theater, a gas station, a KFC, and an upscale lodge.

This master-planned village will also have a museum and artisans' studios—uptown stuff for Molokai. Jonathan Socher of **Big Wind Kite Factory** (p. 271) is keeping his kites and books wrapped in cellophane against constant clouds of red dust raised by construction crews.

ON THE NORTHWEST SHORE: MOOMOMI DUNES
Undisturbed for centuries, the Moomomi Dunes, on Molokai's northwest shore, are a unique treasure chest of great scientific value. The area may look like just a pile of sand as you fly over on the final approach to Hoolehua Airport, but Moomomi Dunes is much more than that. Archaeologists have found adz quarries, ancient Hawaiian burial sites, and shelter caves; botanists have identified five endangered plant species; and marine biologists are finding evidence that endangered green sea turtles are coming out from the waters once again to lay eggs here. The greatest discovery, however, belongs to Smithsonian Institute ornithologists, who have found bones of prehistoric birds—some of them flightless—that existed nowhere else on earth.

Accessible by Jeep trails that thread downhill to the shore, this wild coast is buffeted by strong afternoon breezes. It's hot, dry, and windy, so take water, sunscreen, and a windbreaker.

At Kawaaloa Bay, a 20-minute walk to the west, there's a broad golden beach that you can have all to yourself. *But, due to the rough seas, stay out of the water.* The 920-acre preserve is accessible via monthly guided nature tours led by the **Nature Conservancy of Hawaii;** call © 808/553-5236 or 808/524-0779 for an exact schedule and details.

To get here, take Highway 460 (Maunaloa Hwy.) from Kaunakakai; turn right onto Highway 470, and follow it to Kualapuu. At Kualapuu, turn left on Highway 480 and go through Hoolehua Village; it's 3 miles to the bay.

THE EAST END

The East End is a cool and inviting green place that's worth a drive to the end of King Kamehameha V Highway (Hwy. 450). Unfortunately, the trail that leads into the area's greatest natural attraction, Halawa Valley, is now off-limits.

A WAGON RIDE OR HORSEBACK RIDE TO ILIILIOPAE HEIAU

On horseback (where the elevated view is magnificent), you bump along a dirt trail through an incredible mango grove, bound for an ancient temple of human sacrifice. This temple of doom—right out of *Indiana Jones*—is Iliiliopae, a huge rectangle of stone made of 90 million rocks, overlooking the once-important village of Mapulehu and four ancient fish ponds. Your horse will trot under the perfumed mangoes, then head uphill through a kiawe forest filled with Java plums to the *heiau* (temple), which stands across a dry stream bed under cloud-spiked Kaunolu, the 4,970-foot island summit.

Hawaii's most powerful heiau attracted *kahuna* (priests) from all over the islands. They came to learn the rules of human sacrifice at this university of sacred rites. Contrary to Hollywood's version, historians say that the victims here were always men, not young virgins, and that they were strangled, not thrown into a volcano, while priests sat on lauhala mats watching silently. Spooky, eh?

This is the biggest, oldest, and most famous heiau on Molokai. The massive 22-foot-high stone altar is dedicated to Lono, the Hawaiian god of fertility. The heiau resonates with *mana* (power) strong enough to lean on. Legend says Iliiliopae was built in a single night by a thousand men who passed rocks hand over hand through the Wailau Valley from the other side of the island; each received a shrimp (*'opae*) in exchange for the rock (*ili'ili*). Others say it was built by *menehunes*, mythic elves who accomplished Herculean feats.

After the visit to the temple, your horse takes you back to the mango grove. Contact **Molokai Wagon Rides** (the wagon fell apart years ago, but they kept the name)**,** King Kamehameha V Highway (Hwy. 450), at mile marker 15, Kaunakakai, HI 96748 (© **808/558-8380**). The tour and horseback ride cost $50 per person. The hour-long ride goes up to the heiau, then beyond it to the top of the mountain for those breathtaking views, and finally back down to the beach.

KAMAKOU PRESERVE

It's hard to believe, but close to the nearly mile-high summit here, it rains more than 80 inches a year—enough to qualify as a rainforest. The Molokai Forest, as it was historically known, is the source of 60% of Molokai's water. Nearly 3,000 acres from the summit to the lowland forests of eucalyptus and pine are now held by the Nature Conservancy, which has identified 219 Hawaiian plants that grow here exclusively. The preserve is also the last stand of the endangered Molokai thrush (*olomao*) and Molokai creeper (*kawawahie*).

To get to the preserve, take the Forest Reserve road from Kaunakakai. It's a 45-minute, four-wheel-drive trip on a dirt trail to Waikolu Lookout Campground; from here, you can venture into the wilderness preserve on foot for a 1½-hour hike across a boardwalk on the **Pepeopae Trail** (p. 257). For more information, contact the **Nature Conservancy** (© **808/553-5236**).

EN ROUTE TO HALAWA VALLEY

No visit to Molokai is complete without at least a passing glance at the island's **ancient fish ponds,** a singular achievement in Pacific aquaculture. With their hunger for fresh fish and lack of ice or refrigeration, Hawaiians perfected aquaculture around 1400, before Christopher Columbus "discovered" America. They built gated, U-shaped stone and coral walls on the shore to catch fish on the incoming tide then raised them in captivity. The result: a constant, ready supply of fresh fish.

The ponds, which stretch for 20 miles along Molokai's south shore and are visible from Kamehameha V Highway (Hwy. 450), offer insight into the island's ancient population. It took something like a thousand people to tend a single fish pond, and more than 60 ponds once existed on this coast. All the fish ponds are named; a few are privately owned. Some are silted in by red-dirt runoff from south coast gulches; others have been revived by folks who raise fish and seaweed.

The largest, 54-acre **Keawa Nui Pond,** is surrounded by a 3-foot-high, 2,000-foot-long stone wall. **Alii Fish Pond,** reserved for kings, is visible through the coconut groves at One Alii Beach Park (p. 253). From the road, you can see **Kalokoeli Pond,** 6 miles east of Kaunakakai on the highway.

Our Lady of Sorrows Catholic Church, one of five built by Father Damien on Molokai and the first outside Kalaupapa, sits across the highway from a fish pond. Park in the church lot (except on Sun) for a closer look.

St. Joseph's Catholic Church

The afternoon sun strikes St. Joseph's Church with such a bold ray of light that it looks as if God is about to perform a miracle. This little 1876 wood-frame church is one of four Father Damien built "topside" on Molokai. Restored in 1971, the church stands beside a seaside cemetery, where feral cats play under the gaze of a Damien statue amid gravestones decorated with flower leis.

King Kamehameha V Hwy. (Hwy. 450), just after mile marker 10.

Smith Bronte Landing Site

In 1927, Charles Lindbergh soloed the Atlantic Ocean in a plane called *The Spirit of St. Louis* and became an American hero. On July 14 of that same year, Ernie Smith and Emory B. Bronte took off from Oakland, California, in a single-engine Travelair aircraft named *The City of Oakland* and headed across the Pacific Ocean for Honolulu, 2,397 miles away. The next day, after running out of fuel, they crash-landed upside-down in a kiawe thicket on Molokai, but emerged unhurt to become the first civilians to fly to Hawaii from the U.S. mainland. The 25-hour, 2-minute flight landed Smith and Bronte a place in aviation history—and on a roadside marker on Molokai.

King Kamehameha V Hwy. (Hwy. 450), at mile marker 11, on the *makai* (ocean) side.

HALAWA VALLEY 👁

Of the five great valleys of Molokai, only Halawa, with its two waterfalls, golden beach, sleepy lagoon, great surf, and offshore island, is easily accessible. Unfortunately, the trail through fertile Halawa Valley, which was inhabited for centuries, and on to the 250-foot Moaula Falls has been closed for some time. There is one operator who conducts very expensive tours, but we have received so many letters of complaint (and have been personally stood up by him after a confirmed reservation) that we no longer recommend you use him.

You can spend a day at the county beach park, but do not venture into the valley on your own. In a kind of 21st-century *kapu,* the private landowners in the valley, worried about slip-and-fall lawsuits, have posted NO TRESPASSING signs on their property.

To get to Halawa Valley, drive north from Kaunakakai on Highway 450 for 30 miles along the coast to the end of the road, which descends into the valley past Jersalema Hou Church. If you'd just like a glimpse of the valley on your way to the beach, there's a scenic overlook along the road: After Puu o Hoku Ranch at mile marker 25, the narrow two-lane road widens at a hairpin curve, and you'll find the overlook on your right; it's 2 miles more to the valley floor.

10 Shopping

KAUNAKAKAI

Molokai Surf, Molokai Island Creations, Molokai Imports (which has great, inexpensive lauhala bags and local lemons), and **Lourdes** are clothing and gift shops in close proximity to one another in downtown Kaunakakai, where most of the retail shops sell T-shirts, muumuus, surf wear, and informal apparel. For food shopping, there are several good options (since many visitors stay in condos, knowing the grocery stores is especially important). Other than that, serious shoppers will be disappointed, unless they love kites or native wood vessels.

Imamura Store Wilfred Imamura, whose mother founded this store, recalls the old railroad track that stretched from the pier to a spot across the street. "We brought our household things from the pier on a hand-pumped vehicle," he recalls. His store, appropriately, is a leap into the past, a marvelous amalgam of precious old-fashioned things. Rubber boots, Hawaiian-print tablecloths, Japanese tea plates, ukulele cases, plastic slippers, and even coconut bikini tops line the shelves. But it's not all nostalgia: The Molokai T-shirts, jeans, and palaka shorts are of good quality and inexpensive, and the pareu fabrics are a find. Kaunakakai. ② 808/553-5615.

Molokai Drugs David Mikami, whose father-in-law founded the pharmacy in 1935, has made this more than a drugstore. It's a gleaming, friendly stop full of life's basic necessities, with generous amenities such as a phone and a restroom for passersby. You'll find the best selection of guidebooks, books about Molokai, and maps here, as well as greeting cards, paperbacks, cassette players, flip-flops, and every imaginable essential. The Mikamis are a household name on the island not only because of their pharmacy, but also because the family has shown exceptional kindness to the often economically strapped Molokaians. Kamoi Professional Center. ② 808/553-5790.

Molokai Fish & Dive Here you'll find the island's largest selection of T-shirts and souvenirs, crammed in among fishing, snorkeling, and outdoor gear that you can rent or buy. Find your way among the fishnets, Boogie Boards, diving equipment, bamboo rakes, beach towels, postcards, soft drinks, and disposable cameras. One entire wall is lined with T-shirts, and the selection of Molokai books and souvenirs is extensive. The staff is happy to point out the best snorkeling spots of the day. Kaunakakai. ② 808/553-5926.

Molokai Surf In a new wooden building at the edge of central Kaunakakai, you'll find skateboards, surf shorts, sweatshirts, sunglasses, T-shirts, footwear, Boogie Boards, backpacks, and a broad range of clothing and accessories for life in the surf and sun. 130 Kamehameha V Hwy. ② 808/553-5093.

Take's Variety Store If you need luggage tags, buzz saws, toys, candy, cloth dolls, canned goods, canteens, camping equipment, hardware, batteries, candles, fishing supplies—whew!—and other products for work and play, this 53-year-old variety store is the answer. You may suffer from claustrophobia in the crowded, dusty aisles, but Take's carries everything. Kaunakakai. © 808/553-5442.

EDIBLES

Another good source of healthy foods is **Outpost Natural Foods,** 70 Makaena Place (© 808/553-3377); see p. 252 for details.

Friendly Market Center   You can't miss this salmon-colored wooden storefront on the main drag of "downtown" Kaunakakai, where people of all generations can be found just talking story in the Molokai way. Friendly's has an especially good selection of produce and healthy foods—from local poi to Glenlivet. Blue-corn tortilla chips, soy milk, organic brown rice, a good selection of pasta sauces, and Kumu Farms macadamia-nut pesto, the island's stellar gourmet food, are among the items that surpass standard grocery-store fare. Kaunakakai. © 808/553-5595.

Misaki's Grocery and Dry Goods   Established in 1922, this third-generation local legend is one of Kaunakakai's two grocery stores. Some of its notable items: chopped garlic from Gilroy, California, fresh luau leaves (taro greens), fresh okra, Boca Burgers, large Korean chestnuts in season, gorgeous bananas, and an ATM. The fish section includes akule and ahi, fresh and dried, but the stock consists mostly of meats, produce, baking products, and a humongous array of soft drinks. Liquor, stationery, candies, and paper products round out the selection of this full-service grocery. Kaunakakai. © 808/553-5505.

Molokai Wines & Spirits   This is your best bet on the island for a decent bottle of wine. The shop offers 200 labels, including Caymus, Silver Oak, Joseph Phelps, Heitz, Bonny Doon, and a carefully culled European selection. *Wine Spectator* reviews are tacked to some of the selections, which always helps, and the snack options include imported gourmet cheeses, salami, and Carr's biscuits. Kaunakakai. © 808/553-5009.

EN ROUTE TO THE NORTH COAST

Coffees of Hawaii Plantation Store and Espresso Bar   This is a fairly slick—for Molokai—combination coffee bar, store, and gallery for more than 30 artists and craftspeople from Molokai, Maui, and the Big Island. Sold here are the Malulani Estate and Muleskinner coffees that are grown, processed, and packed on the 500-acre plantation surrounding the shop, as well as Hawaii-grown flavored coffees. (See p. 263 for details on plantation tours.) You may find better prices on coffee at other retail outlets, but the gift items are worth a look: pikake and plumeria soaps from Kauai, perfumes and pure beeswax candles from Maui, koa bookmarks and hair sticks, and pottery, woods, and baskets. Hwy. 480 (near the junction of Hwy. 470), Kualapuu. © 800/709-BEAN or 808/567-9023.

Kualapuu Market   This market, in its third generation, is a stone's throw from the Coffees of Hawaii store. It's a scaled-down, one-stop shop with wine, food, and necessities—and a surprisingly presentable, albeit small, assortment of produce, from Molokai sweet potatoes to Ka'u navel oranges in season. The shelves are filled with canned goods, propane, rope, hoses, paper products, and baking goods, reflecting the uncomplicated, rural lifestyle of the area. Kualapuu. © 808/567-6243.

Molokai Museum Gift Shop   This restored 1878 sugar mill sits 1,500 feet above the town of Kualapuu (for a review of the museum, see p. 263). It's a considerable drive from town, but a good cause for those who'd like to support the museum and the handful of local artisans who sell their crafts, fabrics, cookbooks, quilt sets, and other gift items in the tiny shop. There's also a modest selection of cards, T-shirts, coloring books, and, at Christmas, handmade ornaments made of lauhala and koa. Meyer Sugar Mill, Hwy. 470 (just after the turnoff for the Ironwood Hills Golf Course, and 2 miles below Kalaupapa Overlook), Kalae. © 808/567-6436.

THE WEST END

A Touch of Molokai   We were pleasantly surprised by the selection of gift items in this hotel shop. The surf shorts and aloha shirts are better than the norm, with attractive, up-to-date choices by Jams, Quiksilver, and other name brands. Tencel dresses, South Pacific shell necklaces (up to $400), and a magnificent, hand-turned milo bowl also caught our attention. Most impressive are the wiliwili, kamani, and soap-berry leis and a handsome array of lauhala bags, all made on Molokai. In the Kaluakoi Hotel & Golf Club. © 808/552-0133.

MAUNALOA

Big Wind Kite Factory & the Plantation Gallery   Jonathan and Daphne Socher, kite designers and inveterate Bali-philes, have combined their interests in a kite factory/import shop that dominates the commercial landscape of Maunaloa. The natural windiness here makes the area ideal for kite-flying classes, which are offered free when conditions are right. The adjoining Plantation Gallery features local handicrafts such as milo-wood bowls, locally made T-shirts, Hawaii-themed sandblasted glassware, baskets of lauhala and other fibers, and Hawaiian-music CDs. There are also many Balinese handicrafts, from jewelry to clothing and fabrics. Maunaloa. © 808/552-2634.

Maunaloa General Store   Maunaloa's only general store sells everything from paper products to batteries, dairy products, frozen and fresh meats, wine, canned goods, and other necessities. Maunaloa. © 808/552-2346.

Sheraton Molokai Lodge & Beach Village Logo Shop   Located between the front desk check-in and the bike rentals in a recently renovated wooden building, this shop can outfit you for life's great adventures. Heavy-duty sweat shirts, Bullfrog sunscreens, sandals, swimwear, T-shirts, walking sticks, and fashionable dresses line the shelves. The food items and souvenirs are also diverse: mugs, magnets, CDs and cassettes, Molokai jams and jellies, mobiles, toys, plastic buckets, lidded koa boxes, fine wines, cold beer, Muleskinner coffees, coconut-shell soap dishes, picture frames, and other attractive gifts to go. Maunaloa. © 808/552-2791.

THE EAST END

The Neighborhood Store 'N Counter   The Neighborhood Store, the only grocery on the East End, sells batteries, film, aspirin, cookies, beer, Molokai produce, candies, paper products, and other sundries. There's great food pouring out of the kitchen for the breakfast and lunch counter, too. Pukoo. © 808/558-8498.

11 Molokai After Dark

Hotel Molokai, in Kaunakakai (© 800/367-5004 or 808/553-5347), offers live entertainment from local musicians, poolside and in the dining room, on Friday from 4 to 11pm and on Saturday from 6 to 10pm. With its South Seas ambience and poolside setting, it's become the island's premier venue for local and visiting entertainers.

(Moments) The Hot Bread Run

For years, local residents have lined up outside Kanemitsu Bakery waiting for freshly baked bread to be taken from the oven. Molokai Bread—developed in 1935 in a cast-iron, kiawe-fired oven— is Kanemitsu Bakery's signature. Flavors range from apricot-pineapple to mango (in season), but the classics remain the regular white, wheat, cheese, sweet, and onion-cheese breads. Kanemitsu's is part of Molokai's night life, too. Whenever anyone on Molokai mentions "hot bread," he's talking about the hot-bread run at Kanemitsu's, the surreal late-night ritual for die-hard bread lovers. Those in the know line up at the bakery's back door beginning at 10:30pm, when the bread is whisked hot out of the oven and into waiting hands. You can order your fresh bread with butter, jelly, cinnamon, or cream cheese, and the bakers will cut the hot loaves down the middle and slather on the works so it melts in the bread. The cream cheese and jelly bread makes a fine substitute for dessert.

If you are a little hesitant to venture out by yourself for this only-on-Molokai experience, now you can go on a tour with **Molokai Outdoors Activities,** in the lobby of Hotel Molokai, just outside Kaunakakai (© **877/553-4477** or 808/553-4477; www.molokai-outdoors.com). The Hot Bread Run "tour" starts at 9:30pm, when guides whisk you through the back streets of Kaunakakai to line up in a dimly lit alley to wait for the bread to come out. After getting the still-hot bread, they take you on a night tour of the town and down to the wharf, where you can enjoy a cup of hot cocoa and your hot bread. The cost of the tour ($25) includes a loaf of the Molokai bread of your choice.

Molokai musicians to watch for include **Pound for Pound,** a powerful group of artists, each over 250 pounds. The members are lead vocalist Jack Stone, Shane Dudoit, Danny Reyes, John Pele, and Alika Lani. As popular off-island as on, they perform Hawaiian, reggae, country, and contemporary Hawaiian numbers, many of them originals. Their CD, *100% Molokai,* has become a local legend.

Darryl Labrado is a teen phenom and the island's rising star; he sings and plays the ukulele to a huge local following. And **Pa'a Pono,** with its contemporary Hawaiian and reggae sounds, is a familiar name on the local nightlife circuit. *Molokai Now,* a CD anthology of original music from Molokai, is a terrific memento for those who love the island and its music.

Movie buffs, too, finally have a place to call their own on Molokai. **Maunaloa Cinemas** (© **808/552-2707**) is a triplex theater that shows first-run movies in the middle of Maunaloa town—four screenings a day at each of the three theaters.

Also in Maunaloa, the lounge at the **Sheraton Molokai Lodge and Beach Village** (© **800/782-9488** or 808/660-2710; fax 808/552-2908; www.sheraton-hawaii.com) offers live music Friday and Saturday from 7 to 9pm, ranging from Phil Stevens and his lively Hawaiian songs and stories about the Hawaiian cowboys to keiki hula, acoustic classical guitar, and contemporary Hawaiian music.

11

Lanai: A Different Kind of Paradise

Lanai is not an easy place to reach. There are no direct flights from the mainland. It's almost as if this quiet, gentle oasis—known, paradoxically, for both its small-town feel and its celebrity appeal—demands that its visitors go to great lengths to get here in order to ensure that they will appreciate it.

Lanai (pronounced lah-*nigh*-ee), the nation's biggest defunct pineapple patch, now claims to be one of the world's top tropical destinations. It's a bold claim, since so little is here. Don't expect a lot of dining or accommodations choices (Lanai has even fewer than Molokai). There are no stoplights here and barely 30 miles of paved road. This almost virgin island is unspoiled by what passes for progress, except for a tiny 1920s-era plantation village—and, of course, the village's fancy new arrivals: two first-class luxury hotels where room rates hover around $400 a night.

As soon as you arrive on Lanai, you'll feel the small-town coziness. People wave to every car; residents stop to "talk story" with their friends; fishing and working in the garden are considered priorities in life; and leaving the keys in the car's ignition is standard practice.

For generations, Lanai was little more than a small village, owned and operated by the pineapple company, surrounded by acres of pineapple fields. The few visitors to the island were either relatives of the mainly Filipino residents or occasional weekend hunters. Life in the 1960s was pretty much the same as in the 1930s. But all that changed in 1990, when the Lodge at Koele, a 102-room hotel resembling an opulent English Tudor mansion, opened its doors, followed a year later by the 250-room Manele Bay Hotel, a Mediterranean-style luxury resort overlooking Hulopoe Bay. Overnight, the isolated island was transformed: Corporate jets streamed into the tiny Lanai Airport, former plantation workers were retrained in the art of serving gourmet meals, and the population of 2,500 swelled with transient visitors and outsiders coming to work in the island's new hospitality industry. Microsoft billionaire Bill Gates chose the island for his lavish wedding, buying up all of its hotel rooms to fend off the press—and uncomplicated Lanai went on the map as a vacation spot for the rich and powerful.

But this island is also a place where people come looking for dramatic beauty, quiet, solitude, and an experience with nature away from the bright lights of Waikiki, the publicity of Maui, and the hoopla surrounding most resorts. The sojourners who find their way to Lanai come seeking the dramatic views, the tropical fusion of stars at night, and the chance to be alone with the elements.

They also come for the wealth of activities: snorkeling and swimming in the marine preserve known as Hulopoe Bay; hiking on 100 miles of remote trails; talking story with the friendly locals; and beachcombing and whale-watching along stretches of otherwise deserted sand. For the adventurous, there's horseback riding in the forest, scuba diving in caves, playing golf on courses with stunning ocean views, or renting a four-wheel-drive vehicle for the day and discovering wild plains where spotted deer run free.

In a single decade, a plain red-dirt pineapple patch has become one of Hawaii's top fantasy destinations. But the real Lanai is a multifaceted place that's so much more than a luxury resort—and it's the traveler who comes to discover the island's natural wonders, local lifestyle, and other inherent joys who's bound to have the most genuine island experience.

THE PINEAPPLE ISLAND'S UNUSUAL PAST

This old shield volcano in the rain shadow of Maui has a history of resisting change in a big way. Early Polynesians, fierce Hawaiian kings, European explorers, 20th-century farmers—the island has seen them all and sent most of them packing, empty-handed and broken. The ancient Hawaiians believed that the island was haunted by spirits so wily and vicious that no human could survive here. The "cannibal spirits" were finally driven off around A.D. 1400, and people settled in.

But those spirits never really went away, it seems. In 1778, just before Captain Cook "discovered" Hawaii, the king of the Big Island, Kalaniopuu, invaded Lanai in what was called "the war of loose bowels." His men slaughtered every warrior, cut down trees, and set fire to all that was left except a bitter fern whose roots gave them all dysentery.

In 1802, Wu Tsin made the first attempt to harvest on the island, but he ultimately abandoned his cane fields and went away. Charles Gay acquired 600 acres at public auction to experiment with pineapple as a crop, but a 3-year drought left him bankrupt. Others tried in vain to grow cotton, sisal, and sugar beets; they started a dairy and a piggery, and raised sheep for wool. But all enterprises failed, mostly for lack of water.

Harry Baldwin, a missionary's grandson, was the first to do well for himself. He bought Lanai for $588,000 in 1917, developed a 20-mile water pipeline between Koele and Manele, and sold the island 5 years later to Jim Dole for $1.1 million.

Dole planted and irrigated 18,000 acres of pineapple, built Lanai City, blasted out a harbor, and turned the island into a fancy fruit plantation. For a half-century, he enjoyed great success. Even Dole was ultimately vanquished, however; cheaper pineapple production in Asia brought an end to Lanai's heyday.

The island still resembles old photographs taken in the glory days of Dole. Any minute now, you half expect to look up and see old Jim Dole himself rattling up the road in a Model-T truck with a load of fresh-picked pineapples. Only now, there's a new lord of the manor, and his name is David Murdock.

Of all who have looked at Lanai with a gleam in their eye, nobody has succeeded quite like David Murdock, a self-made billionaire who acquired the island in a merger more than a decade ago. About 97% of it is now his private holding.

After declaring Lanai's plantation era over, Murdock spent $400 million to build two grand hotels on the island: the Lodge at Koele, which resembles an English country retreat, and the Manele Bay Hotel, a green tile-roofed Mediterranean palazzo by the sea. Murdock recycled the former field hands into wait staff, even summoning a London butler to school the natives in the fine art of service, and carved a pair of daunting golf courses out of the island's interior and along the wave-lashed coast. He then set out to attract tourists by touting Lanai as "the private island."

Lanai

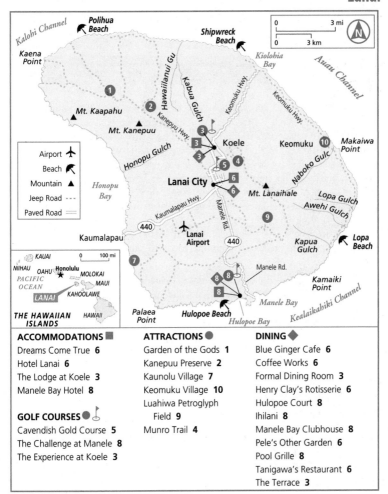

ACCOMMODATIONS ■

Dreams Come True **6**
Hotel Lanai **6**
The Lodge at Koele **3**
Manele Bay Hotel **8**

GOLF COURSES ● ⛳

Cavendish Gold Course **5**
The Challenge at Manele **8**
The Experience at Koele **3**

ATTRACTIONS ●

Garden of the Gods **1**
Kanepuu Preserve **2**
Kaunolu Village **7**
Keomuku Village **10**
Luahiwa Petroglyph
   Field **9**
Munro Trail **4**

DINING ◆

Blue Ginger Cafe **6**
Coffee Works **6**
Formal Dining Room **3**
Henry Clay's Rotisserie **6**
Hulopoe Court **8**
Ihilani **8**
Manele Bay Clubhouse **8**
Pele's Other Garden **6**
Pool Grille **8**
Tanigawa's Restaurant **6**
The Terrace **3**

Murdock is now trying to make all this pay for itself by selling vacation homes and condos next door to the two resorts. Hardly Thoreau's cabin in the woods, the homes and condos cost from $500,000 to upwards of $3 million.

The redevelopment of this tiny rock should have been a pushover for the big-time tycoon, but island-style politics have continually thwarted his schemes. GO SLOW, a sun-faded sign at Dole's old maintenance shed once said. Murdock might have heeded the warning, because his grandiose plans are taking twice as long to accomplish as he had expected. Every permit he has sought has stuck in the tropic heat like a damp cotton shirt. Lanai is under the political thumb of many who believe that the island's precious water supply shouldn't all be diverted to championship golf courses and Jacuzzis, and there remains opposition from Lanaians for Sensible Growth, who advocate affordable housing, alternative water systems, and civic improvements that benefit residents.

Lanai residents, who might have lived in a rural setting, certainly haven't been isolated. Having watched the other islands in Hawaii attempt the balancing act of economic growth and the maintenance of an island lifestyle, the residents of Lanai are cautiously welcoming visitors, but at a pace that is still easy for this former plantation community to digest.

1 Orientation

ARRIVING

BY PLANE No matter which island you're coming from, you'll have to make a connection in Honolulu, where you can easily catch a small plane for the 25-minute flight to Lanai's airport. Jet service to Lanai is now available, but only on Hawaiian Airlines (© 800/367-5320 or 808/565-6977; www.hawaiianair.com), which offers two flights a day. Twin-engine planes take longer and are sometimes bumpier, but they offer great views because they fly lower. **Island Air** (© 800/ 652-6541 or 808/565-6744; www.alohaair.com) offers 9 to 12 flights a day. For more details on these airlines—including details on how to get the cheapest fares—see "Getting There" in chapter 2.

Prop or jet, you'll touch down in Puuwai Basin, once the world's largest pineapple plantations; it's about 10 minutes by car to Lanai City and 25 minutes to Manele Bay.

BY BOAT A round-trip on **Expeditions Lahaina/Lanai Passenger Ferry** (© 808/661-3756) takes you between Maui and Lanai for $50. The ferry service runs five times a day, 365 days a year, between Lahaina and Lanai's Manele Bay harbor. The ferry leaves Lahaina at 6:45am, 9:15am, 12:45pm, 3:15pm, and 5:45pm; the return ferry from Lanai's Manele Bay Harbor leaves at 8am, 10:30am, 2pm, 4:30pm, and 6:45pm. The 9-mile channel crossing takes 45 minutes to an hour, depending on sea conditions. Reservations are strongly recommended. Baggage is limited to two checked bags and one carry-on.

VISITOR INFORMATION

Destination Lanai (© 800/947-4774 or 808/565-7600; fax 808/565-9316; www.visitlanai.net) and the **Hawaii Visitors and Convention Bureau** (© 800/ GO-HAWAII or 808/923-1811; www.gohawaii.com) will both provide brochures, maps, and island guides. For a free *Road and Site Map* of hikes, archaeological sites, and other sights, contact the **Castle and Cooke Resorts**, P.O. Box 310, Lanai, HI 96763 (© 808/565-3000; www.lanai-resorts.com).

THE ISLAND IN BRIEF

Inhabited Lanai is divided into three parts—Lanai City, Koele, and Manele—and two distinct climate zones: hot and dry, and cool and misty.

Lanai City (pop. 2,800) sits at the heart of the island at 1,645 feet above sea level. It's the only place on the island where you'll find services. Built in 1924, this plantation village is a tidy grid of quaint tin-roofed cottages in bright pastels, with roosters penned in tropical gardens of banana, lilikoi, and papaya. Many of the residents are Filipino immigrants who worked the pineapple fields and imported the art, culture, language, food, and lifestyle of the Philippines. Their clapboard homes are excellent examples of historic preservation; the whole town looks like it's been kept under a bell jar.

Around Dole Park Square, a charming village square lined with towering Norfolk and Cook Island pines, plantation buildings house general stores with basic necessities, as well as a post office (where people stop to chat), two banks, and a police station with a jail that consists of three blue-and-white wooden outhouse-size cells with padlocks.

In the nearby cool upland district of **Koele** is the Lodge at Koele, standing alone on a knoll overlooking pastures and the sea at the edge of a pine forest, like a grand European manor. The other bastion of indulgence, the Manele Bay Hotel, is on the sunny southwestern tip of the island at **Manele.** You'll get more of what you expect from Hawaii here—beaches, swaying palms, mai tais, and the like.

FAST FACTS

Lanai is part of Maui County. In case of **emergencies,** call the police, fire department, or ambulance services at ℂ 911, or the **Poison Control Center** at ℂ 800/362-3585. For nonemergencies, call the **police** (ℂ 808/565-6428).

For emergency dental care, call **Dr. Nick's Family Dentistry** (ℂ 808/565-7801). If you need a doctor, contact the **Lanai Family Health Center** (ℂ 808/565-6423) or the **Lanai Community Hospital** (ℂ 808/565-6411).

For a weather report, call the **National Weather Service** at ℂ 808/565-6033.

2 Getting Around

With so few paved roads here, you'll need a four-wheel-drive vehicle if you plan on exploring the island's remote shores, its interior, or the summit of Mount Lanaihale. Even if you only have 1 day on Lanai, rent one and see the island. You can also arrange a 4×4 adventure tour from **Adventure Lanai Ecocentre** (ℂ **808/565-7737** or 808/565-7373; www.adventurelanai.com), which offers 3- to 4-hour off-road tours.

Both cars and four-wheel-drive vehicles are available at the **Dollar Rent A Car** desk at **Lanai City Service,** 1036 Lanai Ave. (ℂ **800/588-7808** for Dollar reservations, or 808/565-7227 for Lanai City Service). Expect to pay about $60 a day for the least expensive car available, a Nissan Sentra, and $129 to $145 a day for a four-wheel-drive Jeep or SUV (both these rates drop 10% if you rent for a week or more). **Adventure Lanai EcoCentre** (ℂ **808/565-7373;** www.adventurelanai.com) rents Safari Jeeps (with towels, masks, fins, snorkels, ice chest, and an island map) for $104 and Suburbans for $179. *Be warned:* Gas is expensive on Lanai, and those four-wheel-drive vehicles get terrible mileage. Since everything in Lanai City is within walking distance, it makes sense to rent a Jeep only for the days you want to explore the island.

Though it's fun to rent a car and explore the island, it's possible to stay here and get to the beach without one. The two big resort hotels run shuttle vans around the island, but only for their guests. If you are staying at The Lodge at Koele or Hotel Lanai, the free shuttles to Manele Bay Hotel run every hour. From the Manele Bay Hotel, you walk over to Hulopoe Beach. When you want to return, you just catch the hourly shuttle (it may run on the half-hour from Manele Bay Hotel) back to Lanai City.

If you're staying elsewhere, you can walk to everything in Lanai City and take a taxi to the beach. **Lanai City Service** (ℂ **808/565-7227**) will provide transportation from Lanai City to Hulopoe Beach for $10 per person one-way (you can arrange with them when you want to be picked up, or walk over to the Manele Bay Hotel and phone them to come and get you—or you can most likely get a ride back up to Lanai City with a local). Whether or not you rent a car, sooner or later you'll find yourself at Lanai City Service. This all-in-one grocery store, gas station, rental-car agency, and souvenir shop serves as the island's Grand Central Station; here you can pick up information, directions, maps, and all the local gossip.

3 Accommodations

The majority of the accommodations are located "in the village," as residents call Lanai City. Above the village is the luxurious Lodge at Koele, while down the hill at Hulopoe Bay are two options: the equally luxurious Manele Bay Hotel, or tent camping under the stars at the park.

In addition to the choices listed below, also consider the B&B accommodations offered by **Delores Fabrao** (✆ **808/565-6134;** dmfabrao@hotmail.com), who has two guest rooms in her home: a double with a shared bathroom, and a family room that sleeps up to six ($55 double, $100 for 4) with a private bathroom; she doesn't provide breakfast, but you'll have the run of the entire house, including the kitchen. At **Hale Moe** (✆ **808/565-9520**), host and Lanai native Momi Suzuki makes three bedrooms in her Lanai City home available to guests; all have private bathrooms ($80–$90 double). Guests are welcome to use the entertainment center, large deck, and Momi's two bicycles. For a fully equipped, two-bedroom vacation rental that sleeps up to six, call **Hale O Lanai,** in Lanai City (✆ **808/247-3637;** www.hibeach.com); rates range from $95 to $125.

Don't forget to add 11.42% in taxes to all accommodation bills. Parking is free.

VERY EXPENSIVE

The Lodge at Koele ✮   In the past few years, we have been dismayed to watch this once grand resort (one of the best in the state) start to slip from its once very high standards, especially in the area of maintenance of the grounds and the hotel itself. At this property, once sterling in every respect, the management appears to be not as diligent as it once was (the carpet was torn in our room, housekeeping had missed cleaning a couple of spider webs, furniture on the outside lanai had seen better days, and weeds grew in the once pristine landscape); not to mention we had to have a "not so loving" discussion with the front desk over large Internet fees. For $375 a night (and up), we expect higher standards.

It still is a great place to stay for a quiet vacation in the cool mist of the mountains. Most guests here are looking for relaxation: sitting out on the porch, reading, or watching the turkeys mosey across the manicured lawns, strolling through the Japanese hillside garden, or watching the sun sink into the Pacific and the stars light up at night. The Lodge, as folks here call it, stands in a 21-acre grove of Norfolk Island pines at 1,700 feet above sea level, 8 miles inland from any beach. The atmosphere is informal during the day, more formal after sunset (jackets are required in the Formal Dining Room; see p. 280).

The 102-room resort resembles a grand English country estate. Inside, heavy timbers, beamed ceilings, and the two huge stone fireplaces of the Great Hall complete the look. Overstuffed furniture sits invitingly around the fireplaces, richly patterned rugs adorn the floor, and museum-quality art hangs on the walls. Cushioned wicker chairs on the long porches are perfect for a long afternoon with a good book. The guest rooms continue the English theme with four-poster beds, sitting areas (complete with window seats), flowery wallpaper, formal writing desks, and luxury bathrooms with oversize tubs. There are plenty of activities here and at the sister resort down the hill, Manele Bay, so you'll get the best of both hotels. Other pluses: complimentary shuttle to the golf courses, beach, and Manele Bay Hotel; complimentary coffee and tea in the lobby; formal tea every afternoon; twice-daily maid service; turndowns; and some rooms have butler service. Additional activities include croquet lawns, horse riding stables, upcountry hiking trails, and garden walks.

The hotel sponsors periodic guest appearances by celebrities who chat informally about their work in a drawing-room setting (see the box "'Talk Story' with the Greats" later in this chapter).

P.O. Box 630310, Lanai City, HI 96793. ℭ 800/321-4666 or 808/565-7300. Fax 808/565-4561. www.lanai-resorts.com. 102 units. $375–$725 double; $725–$2,200 suite. Extra person $75. Children under 15 stay free in parent's room. Numerous packages (such as 5th night free, adventure, golf, and wedding) available. AE, DC, MC, V. Airport shuttle $15 round-trip. **Amenities:** 2 restaurants (both reviewed below); bar (w/quiet live music, hula, and occasional talks by celebrities); outdoor pool; golf at the 18-hole championship Greg Norman/Ted Robinson–designed Experience at Koele course and executive putting green; tennis courts; fitness room; Jacuzzi; watersports equipment rentals at sister hotel Manele Bay Hotel; bike rental; children's program; game room; concierge; activity desk; car-rental desk; business center; shopping arcade; room service; massage; babysitting; laundry; dry cleaning. *In room:* A/C, TV, dataport, minibar, fridge, coffeemaker, hair dryer, iron, safe.

Manele Bay Hotel ⭐   We have the same complaints at this oceanside property as we do with the resort's sister property, the Lodge at Koele (reviewed above): In the past we have given both properties high marks, but we have been disappointed over the last few years at the downturn in the level of maintenance and housekeeping at both properties. We hope this trend will reverse itself in the coming year. General Manager Mark Vinsko assured us that several improvements were in the making, including new marble tile in the guest bathrooms, upgrading the showers with "rain maker" shower heads, and upholstering of the furniture in the lobbies.

Located on a sun-washed southern bluff overlooking Hulopoe Beach, one of Hawaii's best stretches of golden sand, this U-shaped hotel steps down the hillside to the pool and that great beach, then fans out in oceanfront wings separated by gardens with lush flora, manmade waterfalls, lotus ponds, and stream. On the other side, it's bordered by golf greens on a hillside of dry land scrub. The place is a real oasis against the dry Arizona-like heat of Lanai's arid South Coast.

Designed as a traditional luxury beachfront hotel, the Manele Bay features open, airy rooms situated so that every room has a peek of the big blue Pacific. The lobby is filled with murals depicting scenes from Hawaiian history, sea charts, potted palms, soft camel-hued club chairs, and hand-woven kilim rugs. The oversize guest rooms are done in the style of an English country house on the beach: sunny chintz fabrics, mahogany furniture, Audubon prints, huge marble bathrooms, and semiprivate lanais. This resort is much less formal than the Lodge up the hill. It attracts more families, and because it's warmer here, people wander through the lobby in shorts and T-shirts.

The 10-year-old small spa was given a facelift in 2001 with a redesign of the six treatment rooms. In addition to a variety of massages, facials, and wraps, the center, open from 8am to 8 pm daily, also has a fitness center with cardiovascular equipment, free weights, a multistation gym and yoga classes.

P.O. Box 630310, Lanai City, HI 96793. ℭ 800/321-4666 or 808/565-7700. Fax 808/565-2483. www.lanai-resorts.com. 250 units. $375–$795 double; $750–$3,00 suite. Additional person $75. Children under 15 stay free in parent's room. Numerous packages (such as 5th night free, adventure, golf, and wedding) available. AE, DC, MC, V. Airport shuttle $15 round-trip. **Amenities:** 2 restaurants (the acclaimed Ihilani and Hulopoe Court, both reviewed below); bar with breathtaking views; large outdoor pool; golf at the Jack Nicklaus–designed Challenge at Manele; tennis courts; fitness room; small spa; Jacuzzi; watersports equipment rentals; children's program; game room; concierge; activity desk; business center; shopping arcade; salon; room service; massage; babysitting; laundry; dry cleaning. *In room:* A/C, TV, dataport, minibar, coffeemaker, hair dryer, iron, safe.

MODERATE

Hotel Lanai ⭐ *Kids*   This hotel lacks the facilities of the two resorts described above, but it's perfect for families and other vacationers who can't afford to spend $400 to $500 a night. Until recently, the Hotel Lanai, on a rise overlooking Lanai

City, was the only place to stay and eat unless you knew someone who lived on the island. Built in the 1920s for VIP plantation guests, this clapboard planta-tion-era relic has retained its quaint character and lives on as a country inn. A well-known chef from Maui, Henry Clay Richardson, is the inn's owner and the dining room's executive chef.

The guest rooms are extremely small, but clean and newly decorated, with Hawaiian quilts, wood furniture, and ceiling fans (but no TVs). The most pop-ular are the lanai units, which feature a shared lanai with the room next door. All rooms have ceiling fans and private, shower-only bathrooms. The small, one-bedroom cottage, with a TV and bathtub, is perfect for a small family.

The hotel serves as a down-home crossroads where total strangers meet local folks on the lanai to drink beer and talk story, or play the ukulele and sing into the dark, tropic night. Often, a curious visitor in search of an authentic experi-ence will join the party and discover Lanai's very Hawaiian heart. Guests have the use of the complimentary shuttle to the Lodge at Koele, the Manele Bay Hotel, the golf courses (at which they get the same low rates given to guests at the 2 resorts), and the beach.

828 Lanai Ave. (P.O. Box 630520), Lanai City, HI 96763. ℰ **800/795-7211** or 808/565-7211. Fax 808/565-6450. www.hotellanai.com. 11 units. $98–$115 double; $150 cottage double. Nearby 2-bedroom house (sleeps 6) $250. Rates include continental breakfast. Extra person $10. AE, MC, V. Airport shuttle $15 round-trip. **Ameni-ties:** Excellent restaurant (Henry Clay's Rotisserie, reviewed below); intimate bar; access to 2 resort courses on the island and the 9-hole golf course in town; nearby tennis courts; complimentary snorkeling equipment.

INEXPENSIVE

Dreams Come True ⟨ (Finds) This quaint plantation house is tucked away among papaya, banana, lemon, and avocado trees in the heart of Lanai City, at 1,620 feet. Hosts Susan and Michael Hunter have filled their house with Southeast Asian antiques collected on their travels. Both are jewelers, and they operate a work-ing studio on the premises. Two of the three bedrooms feature a four-poster canopied bed, with an additional single bed (perfect for a small family), while the third has just one queen bed. The common area looks out on the garden and is equipped with both TV and VCR. Breakfast usually consists of freshly baked bread with homemade jellies and jams, tropical fruit, juice, and coffee. The Hunters also rent nearby two-, three-, and four-bedroom homes for $250 to $350 a night.

547 12th St. (P.O. Box 525), Lanai City, HI 96763. ℰ **800/566-6961** or 808/565-6961. Fax 808/565-7056. 4 units. $98.50 double. Rates include continental breakfast. Extra person $25. AE, DISC, MC, V. *In room:* No phone.

4 Dining

Lanai is a curious mix of innocence and sophistication, with strong cross-cul-tural elements that liven up its culinary offerings. On this island of three hotels, a handful of stores, and fewer than 3,000 residents, you can go from a greasy-spoon breakfast to a five-star dinner in less than a mile and a few hundred feet in altitude. You can dine like a sultan on this island, but be prepared for high prices. The tony hotel restaurants require deep pockets (or bottomless expense accounts), and there are only a handful of other options.

VERY EXPENSIVE

Formal Dining Room ⟨⟨ RUSTIC AMERICAN/UPCOUNTRY HAWAIIAN The setting: a roaring fire, bountiful sprays of orchids, sienna-colored walls, and well-dressed women in pearls sitting across from men in jackets, with wine buck-ets table side. The menu highlights American favorites with intense flavors. Foie gras has a strong presence on the seasonally changing menu, as do venison, local seafood, wild mushrooms, rack of lamb, and the vaunted threadfish. During fall and winter months, expect to see pumpkins, beans, ragouts, and braised items offered in creative seasonal preparations. The Dining Room is known for its use of fresh herbs, vegetables, and fruit grown on the island, harvested just minutes away.

In the Lodge at Koele. © **808/565-4580.** Reservations required. Jackets requested for men. Main courses $42–market price. AE, DC, MC, V. Daily 6–9:30pm.

Ihilani ✸✸ MEDITERRANEAN   Master chef Edwin Goto, ranked at the top in national surveys, has left his post at the Manele Bay Hotel's formal dining room. His replacement, Executive Chef Mark Tsuchiyama, has continued Goto's style of melding Mediterranean with Island cuisine. Standouts include appetizers like homemade goat cheese and spinach ravioli with roasted eggplant and asparagus salad, in a sun-dried tomato cilantro sauce ($13.00) or terrine of foie gras with pear d'anjou, Madeira wine gelee, and warm toasted black truffle brioche ($23.00). Entrees include baked onaga and citrus in a seasalt crust ($38) and lavender-honey glazed duck breast ($34). The prix fixe menu is very complete and comes with selected wines.

In the Manele Bay Hotel. © **808/565-2296.** Reservations strongly recommended. Jackets requested for men. Main courses $21–$40; set menu $100 without wine, $150 with wine. AE, DC, MC, V. Tues–Sat 6–9:30pm.

EXPENSIVE

Hulopoe Court ✸ HAWAII REGIONAL   Hulopoe is casual compared to the hotel's fine dining room, Ihilani, but more formal than the Pool Grille, the hotel's lunchtime spot. The 17th-century palanquin in the adjoining lower lobby, the Asian accents, the tropical murals by gifted Lanai artists, and the high vaulted ceilings add up to an eclectic ambience. The new menu showcases local ingredients such as Maui asparagus, hearts of palm, locally caught fresh fish, and gourmet breakfasts, including an impressive buffet. If crab-coconut soup is on the menu, or mahimahi on poblano mashed potatoes, they're a good bet.

In the Manele Bay Hotel. © **808/565-2290.** Reservations recommended. Collared shirt required for men. Main courses $20–$29. AE, DC, MC, V. Daily 7–11am and 6–9:30pm.

The Terrace ✸ AMERICAN   Located next to the Formal Dining Room in the Lodge at Koele, between the 35-foot-high Great Hall and a wall of glass looking out over prim English gardens, the Terrace is far from your typical hotel dining room. The menu may be fancy for comfort food, but it does, indeed, comfort. Hearty breakfasts of waffles and cereals, fresh pineapple from the nearby Palawai Basin, frittata, and eggs Polihua (on blue-crab cakes with watercress-tomato hollandaise) are a grand start to the day. At lunch, the fresh catch is presented on flavorful nori bread, served with bacon chips, fries, and a coleslaw too elegant for its name; vegetable wraps and turkey burgers are other options. Dinner choices are the American classics, with some Mediterranean touches: skillet-roasted chicken; polenta "pizza" with roasted eggplant, leeks, portobellos, and goat cheese; grilled and roasted vegetables; and seafood, venison, and pork entrees.

In the Lodge at Koele. © **808/565-4580.** Reservations recommended. Main courses $12–$15 breakfast, $21–$34 dinner. AE, DC, MC, V. Daily 6am–9:30pm.

MODERATE

Henry Clay's Rotisserie ✸✸ COUNTRY CUISINE   Henry Clay Richardson, a New Orleans native, has made some welcome changes to Lanai's dining landscape with his rustic inn in the middle of Lanai City. It's very popular and always full. Maybe that's because it's the only option on Lanai that occupies the vast gap between deli-diner and upscale-luxe.

The menu focuses on French country fare: fresh meats, seafood, and local produce in assertive preparations. Appetizers and entrees reflect Cajun, regional, and international influences, particularly the Rajun Cajun Clay's shrimp, a fiery concoction of hefty shrimp in a spiced tomato broth. The meats, which could be rabbit, duck, quail, venison, *osso buco,* beef, or chicken, are spit-roasted on the rotisserie. Gourmet pizzas and salads occupy the lighter end of the spectrum. Diners rave about the fresh catch in lemon butter caper sauce; we loved the eggplant Creole, presented with perfect sugar snap peas on a bed of herbed angelhair pasta. The decor consists of plates on the pine-paneled walls, chintz curtains, peach tablecloths, and hunter-green napkins, and fireplaces in both rooms.

In the Hotel Lanai. 828 Lanai Ave., Lanai City. ℂ 808/565-7211. Main courses $14–$38. MC, V. Daily 5:30–9pm.

Manele Bay Clubhouse ✿ PACIFIC RIM   The view from the alfresco tables here may be the best on the island, encompassing Kahoolawe, Haleakala on Maui, and, on an especially clear day, the peaks of Mauna Kea and Mauna Loa on the Big Island. Lighter fare prevails at lunch: salads and sandwiches, burgers, Caesar with chicken, herbed chicken sandwich on sourdough, fish-and-chips, and excellent dim sum and calamari salad. The clubhouse is casual, specializing in cold and warm pupu (appetizers), which can be enjoyed as a light meal or can be combined to create a large feast, such as soft shell crab sushi rolls ($12), crispy calamari with fried seagreens ($10), Chinese barbecue chicken salad ($11) and pan seared foie gras with sushi rice ($14).

In the Challenge at Manele Clubhouse. ℂ 808/565-2230. Reservations recommended. Main courses $10–$16. AE, DC, MC, V. Daily 11am–9pm.

Pool Grille ECLECTIC   At this, the most casual of the hotel's restaurants, you'll dine poolside under beach umbrellas, feasting on huge hamburgers (homemade buns, of course) and gourmet salads. Salad choices include spicy chicken ($13), grilled tiger prawns ($15) and Cobb salad ($14). Lanai venison pastrami sandwich ($12) and grilled Hawaiian taro burger ($10.50) are among the popular sandwich choices. Even nonguests drop by, as this is one of only two restaurants on the beach open for lunch.

In the Manele Bay Hotel. ℂ 808/565-7700. Main courses $11–$16. AE, DC, MC, V. Daily 11am–5pm.

INEXPENSIVE

Blue Ginger Cafe COFFEE SHOP   Famous for its mahimahi sandwiches and inexpensive omelets, Blue Ginger is a very local, very casual, and moderately priced alternative to Lanai's fancy hotel restaurants. The four tables on the front porch face the cool Norfolk pines of Dole Park and are always filled with locals who talk story from morning to night. The tiny cafe is often jammed from 6 to 7am with construction workers on their way to work. The offerings are solid, no-nonsense, everyday fare: fried saimin (no MSG, a plus), very popular hamburgers on homemade buns, and mahimahi with capers in a white-wine sauce. Blue Ginger also serves a tasty French toast of homemade bread, vegetable lumpia (the Filipino version of a spring roll), and Mexican specials. The stir-fried vegetables—a heaping platter of fresh, perfectly cooked veggies, including summer squash and fresh mushrooms—are a hit.

409 Seventh St. (at Lilima St), Lanai City. ℂ 808/565-6363. Breakfast items under $6.50, lunch under $10, and dinner less than $12. No credit cards. Daily 6am–8pm.

Coffee Works ✿ COFFEEHOUSE   Oahu's popular Ward Warehouse coffeehouse has opened a new branch in Lanai City with a menu of espresso coffees and drinks, ice cream, and a small selection of pastries. It's Lanai City's new gathering place, a tiny cafe with tables and benches on a pleasing wooden deck surrounded by tall pines, a stone's throw from Dole Park. Formerly a plantation house, the structure fits in with the surrounding plantation homes in the heart of Lanai City. The gift items here are promising: T-shirts, tea infusers, chai, prepared pasta sauces, teapots and cookies, and gourmet coffees. On my last visit, I spotted some great Lanai T-shirts for $9 and some beautiful Thai wooden spoons.

604 Ilima, Lanai City (across from post office). ✆ 808/565-6962. Most items under $5. MC, V. Mon–Fri 7am–6pm; Sat 7am–2pm.

Pele's Other Garden ✪ DELI/PIZZERIA/JUICE BAR This popular Lanai City eatery has added a patio with umbrella tables outside and expanded the kitchen in the back, so there's a lot more seating—and a fuller menu to match. Pele's Other Garden is now a full-scale New York deli, and you can also get box lunches and picnic baskets to go. Dinner is now served on china, not paper, with tablecloths under sconces—a real dining room! At lunch the pizzas and sandwiches are still top-drawer and popular; in the evening you can also order pastas (like butterfly pasta with garlic shrimp or fettuccine with smoked salmon) and salads. Daily soup and menu specials, excellent pizza, fresh organic produce, fresh juices, and special touches such as top-quality black-bean burritos, roasted red peppers, and stuffed grape leaves are some of the features that make Pele's Other Garden a Lanai City must. Sandwiches are made with whole-wheat, rye, sourdough, or French bread, baked on the island and delivered fresh daily; the turkey is free-range. The fire-truck-yellow building is easy to spot along tree-shaded Dole Park.

Dole Park, 811 Houston St., Lanai City. ✆ 808/565-9628. Most items less than $7. AE, DISC, MC, V. Mon–Sat 9:30am–3pm and 5–9pm.

Tanigawa's Restaurant LOCAL Formerly S. T. Properties, Tanigawa's has changed its name but remains the landmark that it's been since the 1920s. In those days, the tiny storefront sold canned goods and cigarettes; the 10 tables, hamburgers, and Filipino food came later. Jerry Tanigawa has kept his hole-in-the-wall a local institution, with a reputation for serving local-style breakfasts. The fare—fried rice, omelets, short stack, and simple ham and eggs—is more greasy-spoon than gourmet, but friendly to the pocketbook.

419 Seventh St., Lanai City. ✆ 808/565-6537. Reservations not accepted. Breakfast less than $7.50, lunch sandwiches $2.50–$7, burgers $2–$4.75. No credit cards. Thurs–Tues 6:30am–1pm.

5 Beaches

If you like big, wide, empty gold-sand beaches and crystal-clear, cobalt-blue water full of bright tropical fish—and who doesn't?—go to Lanai. With 18 miles of sandy shoreline, Lanai has some of Hawaii's least crowded and most interesting beaches. One spot in particular is perfect for swimming, snorkeling, and watching spinner dolphins play: Hulopoe Beach, Lanai's best.

HULOPOE BEACH ✪✪✪
In 1997, Stephen Leatherman of the University of Maryland (a professional beach surveyor who's also known as "Dr. Beach") ranked Hulopoe the best beach in the United States. It's easy to see why. This palm-fringed, gold-sand beach is bordered by black-lava fingers, protecting swimmers from the serious ocean currents that sweep around Lanai. In summer, Hulopoe is perfect for swimming,

snorkeling, or just lolling about; the water temperature is usually in the mid-70s. Swimming is usually safe, except when swells kick up in winter. The bay at the foot of the Manele Bay Hotel is a protected marine preserve, and the schools of colorful fish know it. So do the spinner dolphins that come here to play, and the humpback whales that cruise by in winter. Hulopoe is also Lanai's premier beach park, with a grassy lawn, picnic tables, barbecue grills, restrooms, showers, and ample parking. You can camp here, too.

HULOPOE'S TIDE POOLS   Some of the best lava-rock tide pools in Hawaii are found along the south shore of Hulopoe Bay. These miniature SeaWorlds are full of strange creatures such as asteroids (sea stars) and holothurians (sea cucumbers), not to mention spaghetti worms, Barber Pole shrimp, and Hawaii's favorite local delicacy, the opihi, a tasty morsel also known as the limpet. Youngsters enjoy swimming in the enlarged tide pool at the eastern edge of the bay. When you explore tide pools, do so at low tide. Never turn your back on the waves. Wear tennis shoes or reef walkers—the wet rocks are slippery. Collecting specimens in this marine preserve is forbidden, so don't take any souvenirs home.

SHIPWRECK BEACH 🐦
This 8-mile-long windswept strand on Lanai's northeastern shore—named for the rusty ship *Liberty,* stuck on the coral reef—is a sailor's nightmare and a beachcomber's dream. The strong currents yield all sorts of flotsam, from Japanese handblown-glass fish floats and rare pelagic paper nautilus shells to lots of junk. This is also a great place to spot whales from December to April, when the Pacific humpbacks cruise in from Alaska to winter in the calm offshore waters. The road to the beach is paved most of the way, but you really need four-wheel-drive to get down here.

POLIHUA BEACH 🐦
So many sea turtles once hauled themselves out of the water to lay their eggs in the sunbaked sand on Lanai's northwestern shore that Hawaiians named the beach here *Polihua,* or "egg nest." Although the endangered green sea turtles are making a comeback, they're seldom seen here now. You're more likely to spot an offshore whale (in season) or the perennial litter that washes up onto this deserted beach at the end of Polihua Road, a 4-mile Jeep trail. There are no facilities except fishermen's huts and driftwood shelters. Bring water and sunscreen. Beware the strong currents, which make the water unsafe for swimming. This strand is ideal for beachcombing (those little green-glass Japanese fishing-net floats often show up here), fishing, or just being alone.

6 Watersports
Lanai has Hawaii's best water clarity because it lacks major development, has low rainfall and runoff, and because its coast is washed clean daily by the sea current known as "The Way to Tahiti." But the strong sea currents pose a threat to swimmers, and there are few good surf breaks. Most of the aquatic adventures—swimming, snorkeling, scuba diving—are centered on the somewhat protected south shore, around Hulopoe Bay.

BODY BOARDING (BOOGIE BOARDING), BODYSURFING & BOARD SURFING
When the surf's up on Lanai, it's a real treat. Under the right conditions, Hulopoe and Polihua are both great for catching waves. Boogie Boards ($10 a

Frommer's Favorite Lanai Experiences

Snorkeling Hulopoe Beach. Crystal-clear waters teem with brilliant tropical fish off one of Hawaii's best beaches. There are tide pools to explore, waves to play in, and other surprises—like a pod of spinner dolphins that often makes a splashy entrance.

Exploring the Garden of the Gods. Eroded by wind, rain, and time, these geologic badlands are worth visiting at sunrise or sunset, when the low light plays tricks on the land—and your mind.

Hiking the Munro Trail. The 11-mile Munro Trail is a lofty, rigorous hike along the rim of an old volcano. You'll get great views of the nearby islands. Take a four-wheel-drive vehicle if you want to spend more time on top of the island.

Four-wheeling it. Four-wheeling is a way of life on Lanai, since there are only 30 miles of pavement. Plenty of rugged trails lead to deserted beaches, abandoned villages, and valleys filled with wild game. No other island offers off-road adventures like this one.

Camping under the stars. The campsites at Hulopoe Beach Park are about as close to the heavens as you can get. The sound of the crashing surf will lull you to sleep at night, and the chirping of the birds will wake you in the morning. If you're into roughing it, this is a great way to experience Lanai.

Watching the whales at Polihua Beach. Located on the north shore, this beach—which gets its name from the turtles that nest here—is a great place to spend the day scanning the ocean for whales during the winter months.

day) are available through **Adventure Lanai Ecocentre** (© **808/565-7737** or 808/565-7373; www.adventurelanai.com). The beach shack at Hulopoe Beach has complimentary Boogie Boards for hotel guests (Manele Bay and the Lodge at Koele) only.

OCEAN KAYAKING

Adventure Lanai Ecocentre (see contact information above), offers half-day sea kayak/snorkel adventures (as well as kayak/scuba trips; see below) aimed at introducing beginners to the world of ocean kayaking. The center provides state-of-the-art kayaks (with lightweight graphite paddles and full back-support seats), life vests, the latest in snorkel equipment, dry bags, towels, water, and snacks. After receiving instruction on how to kayak, your group will set off to explore the waters around Lanai, with stops for snorkeling, snacks, and beachcombing. The 4-hour trip costs $89. Rental kayaks are also available, starting at $49 a day or $10 an hour.

SAILING

Trilogy ⊛ (see contact information below), which has built a well-deserved reputation as the leader in sailing/snorkeling cruises in Hawaii, has a morning snorkel sailing trip on board their luxury custom sailing catamarans. The trips along Lanai's protected coastline including sailing past hundreds of spinner dolphins and into some of the best snorkeling sites in the world. The $110 price (1/2 price for children 3–15) includes breakfast, lunch, sodas, snacks, snorkel gear and instruction. Trips run Monday, Wednesday and Friday from 8:45am to 1pm and Saturday from 10am to 2:30pm

SCUBA DIVING/SNORKELING

Two of Hawaii's best-known dive spots are found in Lanai's clear waters, just off the south shore: **Cathedrals I** and **II,** so named because the sun lights up an underwater grotto like a magnificent church. **Trilogy** ☆ (② **888/628-4800** or 808/565-9303; www.sailtrilogy.com) offers sailing, diving, and snorkeling trips on catamarans, from 8:45am to 1pm, and includes continental breakfast, deli lunch with fresh pasta salad and homemade cookies, and all snorkeling equipment. The cost for a sailing/snorkeling cruise is $95; it's an additional $45 for a one-tank dive. Trilogy offers two-tank scuba diving charters every Tuesday, Thursday, and Saturday for $140.

   Adventure Lanai Ecocentre (see contact information above), offers two-tank scuba adventures for $119. Its store in Lanai City, 338 Eighth St., has scuba gear for rent from $69.

SNORKELING

Hulopoe is Lanai's best snorkeling spot. Fish are abundant and friendly in the marine-life conservation area. Try the lava-rock points at either end of the beach and around the lava pools. Snorkel gear is free to guests of the two resorts, and also can be rented from **Adventure Lanai Ecocentre;** see above for information on the center's ocean kayaking/snorkeling trips and contact information.

   On Sundays from 7:45am to 1pm, **Trilogy** (see contact information above) offers an extraordinary adventure, **In the Footsteps of Royalty,** where Captain Dustin Kaopuiki, a direct descendent of Lanai's royalty, takes a group on a snorkeling exportation of the waters around the southern coast of Lanai, where King Kamehameha the Great had his summer retreat. The pristine waters are teaming with tropical fish and lava tubes, and spinner dolphins are usually present. Masks, fins, juice, sodas and lunch are included in the $125 price (half price for children 3–15).

SPORTFISHING

Jeff Menze will take you out on the 28-foot Omega boat **Spinning Dolphin** (② **808/565-6613**). His fishing charters cost $400 for six people for 4 hours, or $600 for six people for 8 hours. He also offers exclusive 4-hour whale-watching/snorkeling charters, which cost $400 for six passengers.

SURFING

Adventure Lanai Ecocentre (see contact information above), specializes in teaching everyone from small kids to grandparents how to surf using lightweight wooden long boards. The 4-hour "Surf Safari" is $89; surfboard rental is $35 a day or $10 an hour.

WHALE-WATCHING

Year-round, **Trilogy** offers 1½-hour adventures on a 32-foot, 26-passenger rigid-hulled inflatable boat. From late December through April they are on the look-out for whales, but the remainder of the year schools of spinner dolphins are featured on this Blue Water Marine Mammal Watch. The cost is $75 (half price for children 3–15).

7 Hiking & Camping

HIKING
A LEISURELY MORNING HIKE

The 3-hour **Koele Nature Hike** starts by the reflecting pool in the backyard of the Lodge at Koele and takes you on a 5-mile loop through a cathedral of Norfolk Island pines, into Hulopoe Valley, past wild ginger, and up to Koloiki Ridge, with its panoramic view of Maunalei Valley and Molokai and Maui in the distance. You're welcome to take the hike even if you're not a guest at the Lodge. The trailhead isn't obvious—just keep going mauka (inland) toward the trees—and the path isn't clearly marked, but the concierge will give you a free map. We suggest doing this hike in the morning; the clouds usually roll in by afternoon, marring visibility at the top and increasing your chance of being caught in a downpour.

THE CHALLENGING MUNRO TRAIL

This tough, 11-mile round-trip uphill climb through the groves of Norfolk pines is a lung-buster, but if you reach the top, you'll be rewarded with a breathtaking view of Molokai, Maui, Kahoolawe, the peaks of the Big Island, and—on a really clear day—Oahu in the distance. Figure on 7 hours. The trail begins at Lanai Cemetery along Keomoku Road (Hwy. 44) and follows Lanai's ancient caldera rim, ending up at the island's highest point, Lanaihale. Go in the morning for the best visibility. After 4 miles, you'll get a view of Lanai City. The weary retrace their steps from here, while the more determined go the last 1⅓ miles to the top. Diehards head down Lanai's steep south-crater rim to join the highway to Manele Bay. For more details on the Munro Trail—including information on four-wheel-driving it to the top—see "Five Islands at a Single Glance: The Munro Trail" under "Seeing the Sights" below.

A SELF-GUIDED NATURE TRAIL

This self-guided nature trail in the Kanepuu Preserve is about a 10- to 15-minute walk through eight stations, with interpretive signs explaining the natural or cultural significance of what you're seeing. The trailhead is clearly marked on the Polihua Road on the way to the Garden of the Gods. Kanepuu is one of the last remaining examples of the type of forest that once covered the dry lowlands throughout the state. There are some 49 plant species here that are found only in Hawaii. The **Nature Conservancy** (✆ 808/565-7430) conducts guided hikes every month; call for details.

GUIDED HIKES

Adventure Lanai Ecocentre (✆ 808/565-7373; www.adventurelanai.com), offers a 4×4 Adventure Trek that combines hiking and four-wheeling. The trips include such destinations as the Munro Trail, Poiaiwa Gulch, Garden of the Gods, and more. The cost is $89 per person, which includes fruit, drinks, snacks, and transportation.

The **Lodge at Koele** (✆ 808/5657300; www.lanai-resorts.com) has a 2½-hour Koloiki Ridge Nature hike through 5 miles of the upland forests of Koele at 11am daily. The fee is $15, and snacks and drinks are included.

The **Manele Bay Hotel** (✆ 808/565-7700; www.lanai-resorts.com) has a 1½-hour fitness hike along an old fisherman's trail at 9am every morning. The fee is $20.

CAMPING AT HULOPOE BEACH PARK

There is only one "legal" place to camp on Lanai: Hulopoe Beach Park, which is owned by Castle and Cooke Resorts. To camp in this exquisite beach park, with its crescent-shaped, white-sand beach bordered by kiawe trees, contact **Castle and Cooke Resorts,** P.O. Box 310, Lanai City, HI 96763 (© **808/565-3978;** www. lanai-resorts.com). There's a $5 registration fee, plus a charge of $5 per person, per night. Hulopoe has six campsites, each of which can accommodate up to six people. Facilities include restrooms, running water, showers, barbecue areas, and picnic tables.

You can rent camping equipment from **Adventure Lanai Ecocentre** (see address above), which has everything from backpacks to tents. Castle and Cooke Resorts recommends a tent (rain can be expected year-round), a cooking stove or hibachi (the number of barbecues is limited), and insect repellent (mosquitoes are plentiful).

8 Golf & Other Outdoor Pursuits

GOLF

Cavendish Golf Course (Finds) This quirky par-36, nine-hole public course has not only no clubhouse or club pros, but also no tee times, scorecards, or club rentals. To play, just show up, put a donation into the little wooden box next to the first tee ($5–$10 would be nice), and hit away. The 3,071-yard, E. B. Cavendish–designed course was built by the Dole plantation in 1947 for its employees. The greens are a bit bumpy, but the views of Lanai are great, and the temperatures usually quite mild.

Next to the Lodge at Koele in Lanai City. No phone.

The Challenge at Manele ★★ This target-style, desert-links course, designed by Jack Nicklaus, is one of the most challenging courses in the state. Check out the local rules: "No retrieving golf balls from the 150-foot cliffs on the ocean holes 12, 13, or 17," and "All whales, axis deer, and other wild animals are considered immovable obstructions." That's just a hint of the uniqueness of this course, which is routed among lava outcroppings, archaeological sites, kiawe groves, and ilima trees. The five sets of staggered tees pose a challenge to everyone from the casual golfer to the pro. Facilities include a clubhouse, a pro shop, rentals, a practice area, lockers, and showers.

Next to the Manele Bay Hotel in Hulopoe Bay. © **800/321-4666** or 808/565-2222. Greens fees $200 ($150 for guests). Twlight play after 2pm, guests only, $80.

The Experience at Koele ★★ This traditional par-72 course, designed by Greg Norman with fairway architecture by Ted Robinson, has very different front and back 9 holes. Mother Nature reigns throughout: You'll see Cook Island and Norfolk pines, indigenous plants, and water—lots of water, including seven lakes, flowing streams, cascading waterfalls, and one green (the 17th) completely surrounded by a lake. All goes well until you hit the signature hole, number eight, where you tee off from a 250-foot elevated tee to a fairway bordered by a lake on the right and trees and dense shrubs on the left. After that, the back 9 holes drop dramatically through ravines filled with pine, koa, and eucalyptus trees. The grand finale, the par-five 18th, features a green rimmed by waterfalls that flow into a lake on the left side. To level the playing field, there are four different sets of tees. Facilities include a clubhouse, a pro shop, rentals, a practice area, lockers, and showers.

Next to the Lodge at Koele in Lanai City. ℭ 800/321-4666 or 808/565-4653. Greens fees $200 ($150 for guests). Twlight play after 2 pm, guests only, $80.

BICYCLING

Road-bike treks are available through **Adventure Lanai Ecocentre** (ℭ **808/565-7373;** www.adventurelanai.com), for $89 per person for half day and $119 per person for a full day. The half day, 3½-hour tours are perfect for beginners, because they're all downhill. A 4×4 van meets you at the bottom with snacks, takes you on a tour of the petroglyphs, and then gives you a ride back up to the top. Trips for more advanced riders are also available. The center rents 21-speed suspension mountain bikes starting at $25 a day or $10 an hour.

The **Lodge at Koele** (ℭ **808/565-7300**) also has mountain bikes to rent. They charge $8 an hour, $35 for 4 hours, and $40 to $55 for 8 hours.

For general information about bike trails, check out **www.bikehawaii.com**.

HORSEBACK RIDING

Horses can take you to many places in Lanai's unique landscape that are otherwise unreachable, even in a four-wheel-drive vehicle. The **Stables at Koele** (ℭ **808/565-4424**) offers various rides, including group rides that are a slow, gentle walk, starting at $50 for a 1½-hour trip. We recommend the 2-hour **Paniolo Trail Ride,** which takes you into the hills surrounding Koele. You'll meander through guava groves and patches of ironwood trees; catch glimpses of axis deer, quail, wild turkeys, and Santa Getrudis cattle; and end with panoramic views of Maui and Lanai. The cost is $75. Private rides (where you can canter, gallop, and trot) are $75 per person for 1 hour and $130 per person for 2 hours. Long pants and shoes are required; safety helmets are provided. Bring a jacket—the weather is chilly and rain is frequent. Children must be at least 9 years old and 4 feet tall. Riders must weigh less than 250 pounds.

TENNIS

Public courts, lit for night play, are available in Lanai City at no charge; call ℭ **808/565-6979** for reservations. Guests staying at the Lodge at Koele or the Manele Bay Hotel have tennis privileges at either the Tennis Center at Manele, with its six Plexi-paved courts, a fully equipped pro shop, and tournament facilities; or at the courts at Koele. Instruction is available for $25 for a clinic, $65 for a private 1-hour lesson. Court fees are $25 an hour. For information, call ℭ **808/565-2072.**

Perfect for a Rainy Day: Lanai Arts Program

A perfect activity for a rainy day in Lanai City is the Lanai Arts Program, 339 Seventh St., located in the heart of the small town. Frequently, top artists from across Hawaii visit this home-grown art program and teach a variety of classes ranging from raku (Japanese pottery), silk printing, silk screening, pareo making (creating your own design on this islanders' wrap), gyotaku (printing a real fish on your own T-shirt), and watercolor drawing to a variety of other island crafts. The cost is usually in the $60 range for the 2- to 3-hour classes and includes all materials. For more information call ℭ **808/565-7503.**

---

9 Seeing the Sights

You'll need a four-wheel-drive vehicle to reach all the sights listed below. Renting a Jeep is an expensive proposition on Lanai—from $129 to $145 a day—so we suggest that you rent one just for the day (or days) you plan on sightseeing; otherwise, it's easy enough to get to the beach and around Lanai City without your own wheels. For details on vehicle rentals, see "Getting Around" earlier in this chapter.

For a guided 4×4 tour, contact **Adventure Lanai Ecocentre** (© **808/565-7373;** www.adventurelanai.com), which offers 3- to 4-hour off-road tours for $89 per person.

GARDEN OF THE GODS

A four-wheel-drive dirt road leads out of Lanai City, through the now uncultivated pineapple fields, past the Kanepuu Preserve (a dry-land forest preserve teeming with rare plant and animal life) to the so-called Garden of the Gods, out on Lanai's north shore. This place has little to do with gods, Hawaiian or otherwise. It is, however, the ultimate rock garden: a rugged, barren, beautiful place full of rocks strewn by volcanic forces and shaped by the elements into a variety of shapes and colors—brilliant reds, oranges, ochers, and yellows.

Ancient Hawaiians considered this desolate, windswept place an entirely supernatural phenomenon. Scientists, however, have other, less colorful explanations. Some call the area an "ongoing posterosional event"; others say it's just "plain and simple badlands." Take a four-wheel-drive ride out here and decide for yourself.

Go early in the morning or just before sunset, when the light casts eerie shadows on the mysterious lava formations. Drive west from the Lodge on Polihua Road; in about 2 miles, you'll see a hand-painted sign that points you to the left, down a one-lane, red-dirt road through a kiawe forest and past sisal and scrub to the site.

FIVE ISLANDS AT A SINGLE GLANCE: THE MUNRO TRAIL

In the first golden rays of dawn, when lone owls swoop over abandoned pineapple fields, hop into a 4×4 and head out on the two-lane blacktop toward Mount Lanaihale, the 3,370-foot summit of Lanai. Your destination is the Munro Trail, the narrow, winding ridge trail that runs across Lanai's razorback spine to the summit. From here, if you're lucky, you'll get a rare Hawaii treat: On a clear day, you can see all of the main islands in the Hawaiian chain except Kauai.

When it rains, the Munro Trail becomes slick and boggy with major washouts. Rainy-day excursions often end with a rental Jeep on the hook of the island's lone tow truck—and a $250 tow charge. You could even slide off into a major gulch and never be found, so don't try it. But in late August and September, when trade winds stop and the air over the islands stalls in what's called a *kona* condition, Mount Lanaihale's suddenly visible peak becomes an irresistible attraction.

When you're on Lanai, look to the summit. If it's clear in the morning, get a four-wheel-drive vehicle and take the Munro Trail to the top. Look for a red-dirt road off Manele Road (Hwy. 440), about 5 miles south of Lanai City; turn left and head up the ridgeline. No sign marks the peak, so you'll have to keep an eye out. Look for a wide spot in the road and a clearing that falls sharply to the sea.

From here you can see Kahoolawe, Maui, the Big Island of Hawaii, and Molokini's tiny crescent. Even the summits show. You can also see the silver domes of Space City on Haleakala in Maui; Puu Moaulanui, the tongue-twisting

---

Kids **Especially for Kids**

Exploring Hulopoe Tide Pools (p. 284) An entire world of marine life lives in the tide pools on the eastern side of Hulopoe Bay. Everything in the water, including the tiny fish, is small—kid-size. After examining the wonders of the tide pool, check out the larger swimming holes in the lava rock, perfect for children.

Hunting for Petroglyphs (p. 291) The Luahiwa Petroglyphs Field, located just outside Lanai City, is spread out over a 3-acre site. Make it a game: Whoever finds the most petroglyphs gets ice cream from the Pine Isle Market.

Listening to Storytellers Check with the Lanai Library, Fraser Avenue near Fifth Street, Lanai City (© **808/565-6996**), to see if any storytelling or other children's activities are scheduled. The events are usually free and open to everyone.

---

summit of Kahoolawe; and, looming above the clouds, Mauna Kea on the Big Island. At another clearing farther along the thickly forested ridge, all of Molokai, including the 4,961-foot summit of Kamakou, and the faint outline of Oahu (more than 30 miles across the sea) are visible. You actually can't see all five in a single glance anymore, because a thriving pine forest blocks the view. For details on hiking the trail, see p. 287.

LUAHIWA PETROGLYPH FIELD

With more than 450 known petrogylphs in Hawaii at 23 sites, Lanai is second only to the Big Island in its wealth of prehistoric rock art, but you'll have to search a little to find it. Some of the best examples are on the outskirts of Lanai City, on a hillside site known as Luahiwa Petroglyph Field. The characters you'll see incised on 13 boulders in this grassy 3-acre knoll include a running man, a deer, a turtle, a bird, a goat, and even a rare, curly tailed Polynesian dog (a latter-day wag has put a leash on him—some joke).

To get here, take the road to Hulopoe Beach. About 2 miles out of Lanai City, look to the left, up on the slopes of the crater, for a cluster of reddish-tan boulders (believed to form a rain *heiau*, or shrine, where people called up the gods Ku and Hina to nourish their crops). A cluster of spiky century plants marks the spot. Look for the Norfolk pines on the left side of the highway, turn left on the dirt road that veers across the abandoned pineapple fields, and after about 1 mile, take a sharp left by the water tanks. Drive for another half mile and then veer to the right at the V in the road. Stay on this upper road for about a third of a mile; you'll come to a large cluster of boulders on the right side. It's just a short walk up the cliffs (wear walking or hiking shoes) to the petroglyphs. Exit the same way you came. Go between 3pm and sunset for ideal viewing and photo ops.

KAUNOLU VILLAGE

Out on Lanai's nearly vertical, Gibraltar-like sea cliffs is an old royal compound and fishing village. Now a national historic landmark and one of Hawaii's most treasured ruins, it's believed to have been inhabited by King Kamehameha the

Great and hundreds of his closest followers about 200 years ago. It's a hot, dry, dusty, slow-going 3-mile 4×4 drive from Lanai City to Kaunolu, but the mini-expedition is worth it. Take plenty of water, don a hat for protection against the sun, and wear sturdy shoes.

Ruins of 86 house platforms and 35 stone shelters have been identified on both sides of Kaunolu Gulch. The residential complex also includes the Halulu Heiau temple, named after a mythical man-eating bird. His Majesty's royal retreat is thought to have stood on the eastern edge of Kaunolu Gulch, over-looking the rocky shore facing Kahekili's Leap, a 62-foot-high bluff named for the mighty Maui chief who leaped off cliffs as a show of bravado. Nearby are burial caves, a fishing shrine, a lookout tower, and many warriorlike stick figures carved on boulders. Just offshore stands the telltale fin of little Shark Island, a popular dive spot that teems with bright tropical fish and, frequently, sharks.

Excavations are underway to discover more about how ancient Hawaiians lived, worked, and worshiped on Lanai's leeward coast. Who knows? The royal fishing village may yet yield the bones of King Kamehameha. His burial site, according to legend, is known only to the moon and the stars.

KANEPUU PRESERVE

Don't expect giant sequoias big enough to drive a car through; this ancient forest on the island's western plateau is so fragile, you can only visit once a month, and even then, only on a guided hike. Kanepuu, which has 48 species of plants unique to Hawaii, survives under the Nature Conservancy's protective wing. Botanists say the 590-acre forest is the last dry lowland forest in Hawaii; the others have all vanished, trashed by axis deer, agriculture, or "progress." Among the botanical marvels of this dry forest are the remains of *olopua* (native olive), *lama* (native ebony), *mau hau hele* (a native hibiscus), and the rare *'aiea* trees, which were used for canoe parts.

Due to the forest's fragile nature, guided hikes are led only 12 times a year, on a monthly, reservations-only basis. Contact the **Nature Conservancy Oahu Land Preserve** manager at 1116 Smith St., Suite 201, Honolulu, HI 96817 (© **808/ 537-4508**), to reserve.

OFF THE TOURIST TRAIL: KEOMOKU VILLAGE

If you're sunburned lobster red, have read all the books you packed, and are starting to get island fever, take a little drive to Keomoku Village, on Lanai's east coast. You'll really be off the tourist trail. All that's in Keomoku, a ghost town since the mid-1950s, is a 1903 clapboard church in disrepair, an overgrown graveyard, an excellent view across the 9-mile Auau Channel to Maui's crowded Kaanapali Beach, and some very empty beaches that are perfect for a picnic or a snorkel. This former ranching and fishing village of 2,000 was the first non-Hawaiian settlement on Lanai, but it dried up after droughts killed off the Mau-nalei Sugar Company. The village, such as it is, is a great little escape from Lanai City. Follow Keomoku Road for 8 miles to the coast, turn right on the sandy road, and keep going for about 6 miles.

10 Shopping

Central Bakery   This is the mother lode of the island's baked delights. If you've noshed on the fantastic sandwiches at Lodge at Koele's Terrace or any of the stel-lar desserts at its Formal Dining Room or at Manele Bay Hotel, you've enjoyed the good-time goodies from Central Bakery. The bakery supplies all breads, pastries, specialty ice creams and sorbets, all banquet desserts, and restaurant desserts on the island. Although it's not your standard retail outlet, you can call in advance, place your order, and pick it up. They prefer as much notice as possible, and it's worth it. The guava chiffon and chocolate chantilly cakes are in great demand, and the breads are legendary. 1311 Fraser Ave., Lanai City. ✆ **808/565-3920.**

Gifts with Aloha   Phoenix and Kimberly Dupree's store of treasures has blossomed since they moved to a larger location on the other side of Dole Park. They are now shipping minigardens, fountains, and lamps to the mainland, and are selling fabulously stylish hats and hatbands, T-shirts, swimwear, quilts, Jams World dresses, children's books and toys, Hawaii-themed books, pareus, candles, aloha shirts, picture frames, handbags, ceramics, dolls, and art by local artists (some of the most beautiful wooden bowls in the islands). The sumptuous white lehua honey from the Big Island is available here, as are jams and jellies by Lanai's Fabrao House. The made-on-Maui soaps and bath products—in gardenia, pikake, and plumeria fragrances—make great gifts to go. Dole Park, 363 Seventh St. (at Ilima St.) ✆ **808/565-6589.**

International Food & Clothing   This store carries the basics: groceries, housewares, T-shirts, hunting and fishing supplies, over-the-counter drugs, wine and liquor, paper goods, and hardware. We were pleasantly surprised by the extraordinary candy and bubble-gum section, the beautiful local bananas in the small produce section, the surprisingly extensive selection of yuppie soft drinks, and the best knife-sharpener we've seen—handy for the Lanai lifestyle. 833 Ilima Ave. ✆ **808/565-6433.**

Lanai Marketplace   Everyone on Lanai, it seems, is a backyard farmer. From 7 to 11am or noon on Saturday, they all head to this shady square to sell their dewy-fresh produce, home-baked breads, plate lunches, and handicrafts. This is Lanai's version of the green market: petite in scale (like the island), but charming, and growing.

Dolores Fabrao's jams and jellies, under the **Fabrao House** label (✆ **808/565-6134** if you want to special-order), are a big seller at the market and at the resort gift shops where they're sold. The exotic flavors include pineapple-coconut, pineapple-mango, papaya, guaivi (strawberry guava), poha (gooseberry) in season, passion fruit, Surinam cherry, and the very tart karamay jelly. All fruits are grown on the island. Dole Square.

The Local Gentry   Jenna Gentry's wonderful boutique is the first of its kind on the island, featuring clothing and accessories that are not the standard resort-shop fare. (Visitors and local women alike make a beeline for this store.) You'll find fabulous silk aloha shirts by Iolani, mahogany wood lamps, mermaids and hula girls, Putumayo separates (perfect for Hawaii) in easy-care fabrics, a fabulous line of silk aloha shirts by Tiki, top-quality hemp-linen camp shirts, inexpensive sarongs, fabulous socks, and the Tommy Bahama line for men and women. There are also great T-shirts, swimwear, jewelry, bath products, picture frames, jeans, chic sunglasses, and offbeat sandals. 363 Seventh St. (behind Gifs of Aloha, facing Ilima St.) ✆ **808/565-9130.**

Pele's Garden   Even if nothing ails you, Pele's Garden is the Eden of the island for health products, with an assortment of vitamins, herbs, homeopathics, and supplements. Shop here for health-related reference books, greeting cards and magazines, natural and organic groceries, baby food, natural pet products, organic seeds, and natural health and beauty aids. With the addition of **Pele's**

"Talk Story" with the Greats: Lanai's Visiting Artists Program

Not so very long ago, before CNN, e-mail, faxes, and modems, news spread in person, on the lips of those who chanced by these remote islands. Visitors were always welcome, especially if they had a good story to tell. The *ha'i mo'olelo,* or storyteller, was always held in high regard; Hawaii's kings invited them to the grass palace to discuss topics of contemporary life. Maybe you've seen the pictures in history books: King Kalakaua and Robert Louis Stevenson sitting on the beach at Waikiki, the famous author regaling His Majesty with bons mots. Or jaunty Jack London describing the voyage of his *Snark* to Queen Lili-uokalani. In Hawaiian pidgin, it's called "talk story."

The tradition continues. When the Lodge at Koele opened, David Murdock invited a few friends over. The "friends" just happened to be the late Henry Mancini, Sidney Sheldon, and Michael York, and they all had a fabulous time in the Great Hall, singing, playing the piano, and reciting poetry. Kurt Matsumoto, general manager at the Lodge then, liked what he saw and scheduled more informal gatherings of creative people. "We never had anything like this on this island before," said Matsumoto, who was born and reared on Lanai.

Today, the **Lanai Visiting Artists Program** ✹✹✹ is dedicated to bringing the literati of America to Lanai, in a new version of "talk story." On any given weekend, you could find yourself in the company of poets, musicians, writers, actors, filmmakers, chefs, and other creative types. You might find yourself vacationing with, say, classical pianist Andre Watts, humorist Dave Barry, author Tom Robbins, "A Prairie Home Companion" host Garrison Keillor, or who knows which Pulitzer Prize or Academy Award winner, each sharing his or her talent and insights in a casual, living-room atmosphere.

The program takes place about 14 or 15 times a year at both the Lodge and the Manele Bay Hotel. It's free and open to everyone. There's a constantly changing schedule, so contact either of those resorts to see who's visiting while you're on Lanai (✆ **800/321-4666;** www.lanai-resorts.com).

Other Garden, the deli that serves up guiltless gourmet fare in the front of the store (p. 283), this corner of Lanai is a place you'll want to find. 811 Houston St. ✆ 808/565-9629.

Petroglyphs Located between Richard's and Pine Isle on Dole Park, the former Akamai, under new ownership, sells espresso, Icee floats, T-shirts, Lanai jams and jellies, coffee mugs, newspapers and magazines, fresh pastries, and souvenirs. Plans call for a pizza bar. 408 Eighth St. ✆ 808/565-6587.

Pine Isle Market A local landmark for two generations, Pine Isle specializes in locally caught fresh fish, but you can also find fresh herbs and spices, canned goods, electronic games, ice cream, toys, zoris, diapers, paint, cigars, and other basic essentials of work and play. The fishing section is outstanding, with every lure imaginable. 356 Eighth St. ✆ 808/565-6488.

Richard's Shopping Center · The Tamashiros' family business has been on the square since 1946, and not much has changed over the years. This "shopping center" is, in fact, a general store with a grocery section, paper products, ethnic foods, meats (mostly frozen), liquor, toys, film, cosmetics, fishing gear, sunscreens, clothing, kitchen utensils, T-shirts, and other miscellany. Half a wall is lined with an extraordinary selection of fish hooks and anglers' needs. Aloha shirts, aloha-print zoris, inexpensive brocade-covered writing tablets, fold-up lauhala mats, and gourmet breads from the Central Bakery (see above) are among the countless good things at Richard's. 434 Eighth St. ⓒ 808/565-6047.

11 Lanai After Dark

Except for special programs such as the annual **Pineapple Festival** in May, when some of Hawaii's best musicians arrive to show their support for Lanai (see the Calendar of Events in chapter 2), the only regular nightlife venues are the Lanai Playhouse, at the corner of Seventh and Lanai avenues in Lanai City, and the two resorts, the Lodge at Koele and Manele Bay Hotel.

The **Lanai Playhouse** (ⓒ 808/565-7500) is a historic 1920s building that has won awards for its renovations. When it opened in 1993, the 150-seat venue stunned residents by offering first-run movies with Dolby sound—quite contemporary for anachronistic Lanai. Lanai Playhouse usually, but not always, shows two movies each evening from Friday to Tuesday (to Wed in summer), at 6:30 and 8:30pm, with occasional Sunday and Monday matinees; if a 3-hour movie is on, it's shown at 7:30pm. Tickets are $7 for adults and $4.50 for kids and seniors. The playhouse is also the venue for occasional special events.

The **Lodge at Koele** has stepped up its live entertainment. In the lodge's **Great Hall,** in front of its manorial fireplaces, visiting artists bring contemporary Hawaiian, jazz, Broadway, classical, and other genres to listeners who sip port and fine liqueurs while sinking into plush chairs. The special programs are on weekends, but throughout the week, some form of nightly entertainment takes place from 7 to 10pm.

Both the Lodge at Koele and Manele Bay Hotel are known for their **Visiting Artists Program** (see the box called "'Talk Story' with the Greats" above), which brings acclaimed literary and performing artists from across the country to this tiny island. These are scheduled throughout the year, usually on a monthly or bimonthly basis.

Other than that, what happens after dark in Lanai is really up to you. You can linger over your evening meal, letting dinner become leisurely extended entertainment. Afterwards, you can find an after-dinner crowd in the Tea Room at Koele or a game of billiards at Manele. And the local folks out on the veranda of the Hotel Lanai will be happy to welcome you.

Appendix A:
Maui in Depth

Maui is the only island in the Hawaiian chain named after a god—well, actually a demigod (half man, half god). Hawaiian legends are filled with the escapades of Maui, who had a reputation as a trickster. In one story, Maui is credited with causing the birth of the Hawaiian Islands when he threw his "magic" fishhook down to the ocean floor and pulled the islands up from the bottom of the sea. Another legend tells how Maui lassoed the sun to make it travel more slowly across the sky—so that his mother could more easily dry her clothes. Maui's status as the only island to carry the name of a deity seems fitting, considering its reputation as the perfect tropical paradise, or as Hawaiians say, *Maui no ka oi* ("Maui is the best").

1 History 101

IN THE BEGINNING   The ancestors of today's Hawaiians followed the stars, the wind, and the waves, trusting we know not what, but just knowing that their journey's destination was "the land of raging fire." Those first settlers were part of the great Polynesian migration that settled the vast triangle of islands stretching from New Zealand in the southwest to Easter Island in the east to Hawaii in the north. No one is sure when they arrived in Hawaii from Tahiti and the Marquesas Islands, some 2,500 miles to the south, but a dog-bone fish hook found at the southernmost tip of the Big Island has been carbon-dated to A.D. 700. Some recent archaeological digs at the Maluuluolele Park in Lahaina even pre-date that.

All we have today are some archaeological finds, some scientific data, and ancient chants to tell the story of Hawaii's past. The chants, especially the *Kumulipo,* which is the chant of creation and the litany of genealogy of the *alii* (high-ranking chiefs) who ruled the islands, talk about comings and goings between Hawaii and the islands of the south, presumed to be Tahiti. In fact, the channel between Maui, Kahoolawe, and Lanai is called *Kealaikahiki* or "the pathway to Tahiti."

Around 1300, the transoceanic voyages stopped for some reason, and Hawaii began to develop its own culture in earnest. The settlers built temples, fishponds, and aqueducts to irrigate taro plantations. Sailors became farmers and fishermen. Each island was a separate kingdom. The alii created a caste system and established taboos. Violators were strangled. High priests asked the gods Lono and Ku for divine guidance. Ritual human sacrifices were common.

Maui's history, like the rest of Hawaii, was one of wars and conquests of one king taking over another king's land. The rugged terrain of Maui and the water separating Maui, Molokai, Lanai, and Kahoolawe made for natural boundaries of kingdoms. In the early years, there were three kingdoms on Maui: Hana, Waikulu, and Lahaina. The chants are not just strict listings of family histories, but some are specific about such philosophies as how a ruler's pride and arrogance can destroy a community. For example, according to the chants, Hana's

King Hua killed a priest in the 12th century, and as a result, the gods sent a severe drought to Hana as a punishment.

Three centuries later, another ruler came out of Hana who was to change the course of Maui's history: Piilani was the first ruler to unite all of Maui. His rule was a time of not only peace, but Piilani built fish ponds, irrigation fields, and began creating a paved road some 4 to 6 feet wide around the entire island. Piilani's sons and his grandson continued these projects and completed the *Alalou,* the royal road that circled the united island. They also completed Hawaii's largest *heiau* (temple) to the god of war, Piilanihale; it still stands today.

Maui was a part of a pivotal change in Hawaii's history: Kamehameha uniting all of the islands. It started in 1759, when yet another battle over land was going on. This time Kalaniopuu, a chief from the Big Island, had captured Hana from the powerful Maui chief Kahikili. Kahikili was busy overtaking Molokai when the Big Island chief stole Hana from him. The Molokai chief escaped and fled with his wife to Hana, where the Big Island chief welcomed him. A few years later, the Molokai chief and his wife had a baby girl in Hana, named Kaahumanu, who later married Kamehameha and during her lifetime would make major changes in Hawaii's culture, like breaking the tabu of women eating with men and converting to Christianity, which lead the way for thousands of Hawaiians to adopt the religion of their queen.

THE "FATAL CATASTROPHE"   No ancient Hawaiian ever imagined a *haole* (a person with "no breath") would ever appear on "a floating island." But on November 26, 1777, 50-year-old Capt. James Cook spotted Maui. He sailed past because he couldn't find a suitable anchorage, but in 1778 he finally dropped anchor in Waimea Bay on Kauai, where he was welcomed as the god Lono.

Cook was already famous in Britain for "discovering" much of the southern Pacific. Now on his third great voyage of exploration, Cook had set sail from Tahiti northward across uncharted waters to find the mythical Northwest Passage purportedly linking the Pacific and Atlantic oceans. On his way, Cook stumbled upon the Hawaiian Islands quite by chance. He named them the Sandwich Islands, for the Earl of Sandwich, first lord of the Admiralty, who bankrolled the expedition.

Overnight, Stone Age Hawaii entered the age of iron. Gifts were presented and trade established: nails for fresh water, pigs, and the affections of Hawaiian women. The sailors brought syphilis, measles, and other diseases to which the Hawaiians had no natural immunity, thereby unwittingly wreaking havoc on the native population.

After damaging the mast of his ship, Cook returned to Kealakekua on the Big Island to seek repairs. What happened next is debatable: Some say a fight broke out over guns; others say that Cook's return challenged the authority of a new ruling chief. What is sure is that the great navigator was killed by a blow to the head. After this "fatal catastrophe," the British survivors sailed home.

Hawaii was now on the sea charts. French, Russian, American, and other traders on the fur route between Canada's Hudson Bay Company and China anchored in Hawaii to get fresh water. More trade and more disastrous liaisons ensued.

The foreigners also had something the Hawaiians had never seen before: cannons and guns. Kamehamaha, at the time a rising chief on the Big Island, was able to get his hands on these weapons, and his use of them would change the course of history: Kamehamaha was the first ruler to unite all of the Hawaiian islands.

Did You Know?

- The aloha shirt that Montgomery Clift wore in his final scene in *From Here to Eternity* is worth $3,500 today.
- Honolulu is second only to San Francisco in restaurant spending — but the locals' favorite meat is Spam.
- There haven't been any billboards in Hawaii since 1926.
- Although it's the capital of the 50th state, Honolulu is closer to Tokyo than to Washington, D.C.
- The Big Island's 13,796-foot Mauna Kea volcano often wears a crown of snow between December and March — which makes Hawaii one of the few places in the world where you can ski and snorkel on the same day. One year, a late snow allowed a ski meet to be held on the Fourth of July.

Kamehameha used the weapons in 1790 while battling the warriors of Maui's chief Kahekili at Iao. Kamehameha used cannons from the ship *Fair America*, with seamen Issac Davis and John Young providing the technological advice on how to use these weapons. His troops followed up with a bloody battle in Iao where the Maui warriors were slaughtered. After finally conquering Maui 5 years later, Kamehameha made Lahaina the capitol of his new united kingdom, stopping there in 1801 with his fleet of Pelehu war canoes on his way to do battle on Oahu and Kauai. Kamehameha stayed in Lahaina for a year, constructing the "Brick Palace," Hawaii's first Western-style structure. Queen Kaahumanu would have nothing to do with it and slept in a grass hut nearby.

WHALERS & MISSIONARIES   On a bright, sunny day in 1819, the first whaling ship dropped anchor in Lahaina. Sailors on the *Bellina* were looking for fresh water and supplies, but found beautiful women, mind-numbing grog, and a tropical paradise. A few years later, in 1823, the whalers were to meet rivals for this hedonistic playground: the missionaries. The God-fearing missionaries arrived from New England bent on converting the pagans. They chose Lahaina because it was the capital of Hawaii.

Intent on instilling their brand of rock-ribbed Christianity in the islands, the missionaries clothed the natives, banned them from dancing the hula, and nearly dismantled their ancient culture. They tried to keep the whalers and sailors out of the bawdy houses, where a flood of whiskey quenched fleet-size thirsts and where the virtue of native women was never safe.

The missionaries taught reading and writing, created the 12-letter Hawaiian alphabet, started a printing press in Lahaina, and began writing the islands' history, until then only an oral account in half-remembered chants. They also started the first school in Lahaina, which still exists today: Lahainaluna High School.

In Lahaina's heyday, some 500 whaling ships a year dropped anchor in the Lahaina Roadstead. Finally the missionaries starting winning in their battle with the whalers. In 1845, King Kamehameha III moved the capital of Hawaii from Lahaina to Honolulu, where more commerce could be accommodated in the natural harbor there. Some whaling ships starting skipping Lahaina for the larger port of Honolulu. Fifteen years later was the beginning of the end of the whaling industry due to the depletion of whales and the emergence of petroleum as a more suitable oil.

KING SUGAR EMERGES   When the capital of Hawaii was moved to Honolulu, Maui might have taken a back seat to Hawaii's history had it not been for the beginning of a new industry—sugar. In 1849 George Wilfong, a cantankerous sea captain, built a mill in Hana and planted some 60 acres of sugar cane, creating Hawaii's first sugar plantation. The Gold Rush was on in California, and sugar prices were wildly inflated. Wilfong's harsh personality and the demands he placed on plantation workers did not sit well with the Hawaiians. In 1852, he imported Chinese immigrants to work in his fields. By the end of the 1850s the Gold Rush had begun to diminish, and the inflated sugar prices dropped. When Wilfong's mill burned down, he finally called it quits.

Sugar production continued in Hana, however. In 1864, two Danish brothers, August and Oscar Unna, started the Hana Plantation. Four years later they imported Japanese immigrants to work the fields.

Some 40 miles away, in Haiku, two sons of missionaries, Samuel Alexander and Henry Baldwin, planted 12 acres of this new crop. The next year, Alexander and Baldwin added some 5,000 acres in Maui's central plains and started Hawaii's largest sugar company. They quickly discovered that without the copious amounts of rainfall found in Hana, they would need to get water to their crop, or it would fail. In 1876 they constructed an elaborate ditch system that took water from rainy Haiku some 17 miles away to the dry plains of Wailuku, a move which cemented the future of sugar in Hawaii.

Around the same time, another sugar pioneer, Claus Spreckels, bought up land in the arid desert of Puunene from the Hawaiians who sold him the "cursed" lands at a very cheap price. The Hawaiians were sure they had gotten the better part of the deal because they believed that the lands were haunted by the souls of the dead who were unsuccessful at making the leap at Black Rock in Kaanapali from this world to the next. Instead, these poor souls were condemned to "hell" in the arid wasteland of Puunene.

Spreckels was a gambler. He was gambling that these "cursed" lands could be very productive, if he could get water rights up in the rainy hills and bring that water to Puunene, just as Alexander and Baldwin had done. But first he needed that water. Thus began a series of late-night poker games with the then-King Kalakaua. Spreckels's gamble paid off: Not only did he beat the king at poker (some say "cheated"), but he built the elaborate 30-mile Haiku Ditch system, which transported 50 million gallons of water a day from rainy Haiku to dry Puunene.

The big boost to sugar not only on Maui, but across the entire state, came in 1876 when King Kalakaua negotiated the Sugar Reciprocity Treaty with the United States, giving the Hawaiian sugar industry a "sweet" deal on price and tariff.

In 1891, King Kalakaua visited chilly San Francisco, caught a cold, and died in the royal suite of the Sheraton Palace. His sister, Queen Liliuokalani, assumed the throne.

A SAD FAREWELL   On January 17, 1893, a group of American sugar planters and missionary descendants, with the support of gun-toting U.S. Marines, imprisoned Queen Liliuokalani in her own palace in Honolulu; later she penned the sad lyric *"Aloha Oe,"* Hawaii's song of farewell. The monarchy was dead.

A new republic was established, controlled by Sanford Dole, a powerful sugar cane planter. In 1898, Hawaii became an American territory ruled by Dole and his fellow sugar cane planters and the Big Five, a cartel that controlled banking, shipping, hardware, and every other facet of economic life in the islands.

Planters imported more contract laborers from Puerto Rico (in 1900), Korea (in 1903), and the Philippines (from 1907–31). Most of the new immigrants stayed on to establish families and become a part of the islands. Meanwhile, the native Hawaiians became a landless minority in their homeland.

For nearly 75 years, sugar was king, generously subsidized by the U.S. federal government. The sugar planters dominated the territory's economy, shaped its social fabric, and kept the islands in a colonial plantation era with bosses and field hands.

BOMBS AWAY   On December 7, 1941, Japanese Zeros came out of the rising sun to bomb American warships based at Pearl Harbor. It was the "day of infamy," which plunged the United States into World War II and gave the nation its revenge-laced battle cry, "Remember Pearl Harbor!"

The aftermath of the attack brought immediate changes to the islands. Martial law was declared, thus stripping the Big Five cartels of their absolute power in a single day. Feared to be spies, Japanese-Americans were interned in Hawaii as well as in California. Hawaii was "blacked out" at night, Waikiki Beach was strung with barbed wire, and Aloha Tower was painted in camouflage. Only young men bound for the Pacific came to Hawaii during the war years. Some came back to graves in a cemetery called The Punchbowl.

During the postwar years, the men of Hawaii returned after seeing another, bigger world outside of plantation life and rebelled. Throwing off the mantle of plantation life, the workers struck for higher wages and improved working conditions. Within a few short years after the war, the white, Republican leaders who had ruled since the overthrow of the monarchy were voted out of office, and labor leaders in the Democratic Party were suddenly in power.

TOURISM & STATEHOOD   In 1959, Hawaii became the last star on the Stars and Stripes, the 50th state of the union. But that year also saw the arrival of the first jet airliners, which brought 250,000 tourists to the fledgling state.

Tourism had already started on Maui shortly after World War II when Paul I. Fagan, an entrepreneur from San Francisco who had bought the Hana Sugar Co., became the town's angel.

Fagan wanted to retire to Hana, so he focused his business acumen on this tiny town with big problems. First, he recognized that growing sugar in isolated Hana was no longer economically feasible. He looked at the community and realized that there were other opportunities. Years ahead of his time, he thought tourism might have a future in Hana, so he built a small six-room inn, called Kauiki Inn, which later became the **Hotel Hana-Maui.** When he opened it in October 1946, he said it was for first-class, wealthy travelers (just like his friends). Not only did his friends come, but he pulled off a public relation coup that is still talked about today. Fagan also owned a baseball team, the San Francisco Seals. He figured they needed a spring training area, so why not use Hana? He brought out the entire team to train in Hana, and, more important, he brought out the sports writers. Not only did the sports writers love Hana and write glowing reports about the town, but one writer gave the town a name that stuck: "Heavenly Hana."

It would be another 3 decades before Maui became a popular visitor destination in Hawaii. Waikiki was king in the tourism industry, seeing some 16,000 visitors by the end of the 1960s, and some 4 million by the end of the 1970s.

Meanwhile, Maui was taking a different approach. In 1960, Amfac, owner of Pioneer Sugar Company, looked at the area outside of Lahaina that was being used to dump sugar cane refuse, and saw another use for the beachfront land. The company decided to build a manicured, planned luxury resort in the Kaanapali area. They built it, and people came.

A decade later, Alexander & Baldwin, now the state's largest sugar company, looked at the arid land they owned south of Keihi and also saw possibilities: The resort destination of Wailea was born.

By the mid-1970s, some 1 million visitors a year were coming to Maui. Ten years later the number was up to 2 million.

At the close of the 20th century, the visitor industry has replaced agriculture as Maui's number-one industry. Maui is the second largest visitors' destination in Hawaii. For nine years in a row, the readers of *Condé Nast Traveler* and *Travel and Leisure* magazines have voted Maui the "Best Island in the World."

2 Maui Today

Since the 1970s, Maui has seen a rapid increase in the number of visitors to this sleepy, agrarian community, which found itself suddenly designated the in place to visit. The islanders spent the 1970s trying to adjust not only to this sudden influx of visitors, but also to the fact that the visitors liked what they saw and wanted to stay. Seemingly overnight, a massive building campaign began, with condominiums mushrooming along the coastline.

By the 1980s, the furious pace of building had slowed, but the new visitors to the island were no longer content to just sit on the beach: They wanted snorkeling and sailing trips, bike rides down Haleakala, and guided tours to Hana. A new industry developed to service these action-oriented vacationers.

In the 1990s, Hawaii's state economy went into a tailspin following a series of events: First, the Gulf War severely curtailed air travel to the island; then, Hurricane Iniki slammed into Kauai, crippling its infrastructure; and finally, sugar cane companies across the state began shutting down, laying off thousands of workers. Maui, however, seemed to be able to weather this turbulent economic storm. As the rest of the state struggled with the stormy economy, the outlook remained sunny and clear on Maui.

What did Maui have that the other islands didn't? According to experts, the farsightedness to build up the island's name recognition in the fickle tourism industry, coupled with a diversified economy. Not only had Maui started planning "destination resort areas" in the 1960s, with Kaanapali the first planned resort area outside of Waikiki, but the island's tourism industry also knew that a reputation for the ability to deliver was the key to success. Or as one expert put it: "Maui has been unbelievably successful at name recognition. You'd be hard-pressed to find someone in the U.S. or Canada over 20 years old who has not heard of Maui."

In addition, Maui did not put all its eggs into the visitor-industry basket. Island leaders continued to nurture Maui's agricultural roots, but instead of wooing giant agribusiness, they courted small-niche farming: organic farmers, the flower industry, and herb growers. The island also branched out into various

Marijuana

This not-so-rare-and-unusual plant — called *pakalolo,* or "crazy weed," in Hawaiian — is grown throughout the islands, despite years of police efforts to eradicate the plant. You probably won't see it as you drive along the roads, but if you go hiking, you may glimpse the feathery green leaves with tight clusters of buds. Don't be tempted to pick a few buds; the captains of this nefarious industry don't take kindly to poaching.

---

high-tech fields, including the Internet industry. It's no coincidence that just as the World Wide Web was starting to become a household word, Maui's visitor industry—from tiny, two-bedroom B&Bs to megaresorts—had one of the highest rates of websites per capita in the United States.

Maui has seen centuries of change since Captain Cook first cruised by. The island, once populated only by Hawaiians, is today home to a diverse mix of Asians, Pacific Islanders, Caucasians, and African Americans. L.A.-style traffic jams and strip malls have arrived, but the island still maintains its natural beauty, with golden beaches, tropical waterfalls, and misty upcountry hills. The population continues to learn lessons in balance: how to nurture the visitor industry without destroying the very product that visitors come to see.

3 Life & Language

Plantations brought so many different people to Hawaii that the state is now a rainbow of ethnic groups. No one group is a majority; everyone's a minority. Living here are Caucasians, African Americans, Native Americans, Eskimos, Aleuts, Japanese, Chinese, Filipinos, Koreans, Tahitians, Asian Indians, Vietnamese, Hawaiians, Samoans, Tongans, and other Asian and Pacific Islanders. Add to that a few Canadians, Dutch, English, French, German, Irish, Italians, Portuguese, Scottish, Puerto Ricans, and Spanish.

In combination, it's a remarkable potpourri. Many people seem to retain an element of the traditions of their homeland. Some Japanese Americans of Hawaii, even three and four generations removed from the homeland, are more traditional than the Japanese of Tokyo. And the same is true of many Chinese, Koreans, Filipinos, and the rest of the 25 or so ethnic groups that make Hawaii a living museum of various Asian and Pacific cultures.

THE HAWAIIAN LANGUAGE

Almost everyone here speaks English, so except for pronouncing place names, you should have no trouble communicating on Maui. Many folks in Hawaii now speak Hawaiian as well, because the ancient language is making a comeback. Everybody who visits Hawaii, in fact, will hear the words *aloha* and *mahalo* (thank you). If you've just arrived, you're a *malihini.* Someone who's been here a long time is a *kamaaina.* When you finish a job or your meal, you are *pau* (over). On Friday, it's *pau hana* (work over). When you go *pau hana,* you put *pupu* in your mouth (that's Hawaii's version of hors d'oeuvres).

The Hawaiian alphabet, created by the New England missionaries, has only 12 letters—the five regular vowels (*a, e, i, o,* and *u*) and seven consonants (*h, k, l, m, n, p,* and *w*). The vowels are pronounced in the Roman fashion, that is, *ah, ay, ee, oh,* and *oo* (as in "too")—not *ay, ee, eye, oh,* and *you,* as they are in English. For example, *huhu* is pronounced *who-who*. Almost all vowels are sounded separately, although some are pronounced together, as in *Kalakaua: Kah-lah-cow-ah*.

WHAT *HAOLE* MEANS When Hawaiians first saw Western visitors, they called the pale-skinned, frail men *haole*, because they looked so out of breath. In Hawaiian, *ha* means breath, while *ole* means an absence of what precedes it: In other words, a lifeless-looking person. Today, the term *haole* is generally a synonym for Caucasian or foreigner; it's used casually without intending any disrespect. However, if uttered by an angry stranger who adds certain adjectives like "stupid" or "dumb," the term *haole* can be construed as a mild racial slur.

SOME HAWAIIAN WORDS Here are some basic Hawaiian words that you'll often hear in Hawaii and see throughout this book. For a more complete list of Hawaiian words, point your Web browser to www.geocities.com/~olelo/hltableofcontents.html or www.hisurf.com/hawaiian/dictionary.html.

akamai smart
alii Hawaiian royalty
aloha greeting or farewell
halau school
hale house or building
heiau Hawaiian temple or place of worship
hui club, assembly
kahuna priest or expert
kamaaina old-timer
kapa tapa, bark cloth
kapu taboo, forbidden
keiki child
lanai porch or veranda
lomilomi massage
mahalo thank you
makai a direction, toward the sea
malihini stranger, newcomer
mana spirit power
mauka a direction, toward the mountains
muumuu loose-fitting gown or dress
nene official state bird, a goose
ono delicious
pali cliff
wiki quick

PIDGIN: 'EH FO'REAL, BRAH

If you venture beyond the tourist areas, you might hear another local tongue: pidgin English. A conglomeration of slang and words from the Hawaiian language, pidgin was developed by sugar planters as a method to communicate with their Chinese laborers in the 1800s. Today it's used by people who grew up in Hawaii to talk with their peers.

"Broke da mouth" (tastes really good) is the favorite pidgin phrase and one you might hear; "'Eh fo'real, brah" means "It's true, brother." You could be invited to hear an elder "talk story" (relating myths and memories), or to enjoy local treats like "shave ice" (a tropical snow cone) and "crack seed" (highly seasoned preserved fruit). But since pidgin is really the province of the locals, you may not hear much of it during your visit to Maui.

4 A Taste of Maui

On Maui, a great lunch or dinner can lure a foodie halfway across the island. Whether it's haute cuisine, local-style diners, small mom-and-pops, or sunset appetizers in Kaanapali and Wailea, dining matters a lot on this island made for sybarites. Although Maui's restaurant kitchens are at the leading edge of Hawaii's maturing regional cuisine, the small-town charms remain, and countless gastronomic discoveries await the adventurous.

THE NEW GUARD: HAWAII REGIONAL CUISINE

Since the mid-1980s, when Hawaii Regional Cuisine (HRC) ignited a culinary revolution, Hawaii has elevated its standing on the global epicurean map to bona-fide star status. Fresh ideas and sophisticated menus have made the islands a culinary destination, applauded and emulated nationwide. (In a tip of the toque to island tradition, *ahi*—a word ubiquitous in Hawaii—has replaced *tuna* on many chic New York menus.)

Waves of new Asian residents have planted the food traditions of their homelands in the fertile soil of Hawaii, resulting in unforgettable taste treats true to their Thai, Vietnamese, Japanese, Chinese, and Indo-Pacific roots. Like the peoples of Hawaii, traditions are mixed and matched—and when combined with the fresh harvests from sea and land for which Hawaii is known, these ethnic and culinary traditions take on renewed vigor and a cross-cultural, uniquely Hawaiian quality.

This is good news for the eager palate. From the five-star restaurant to the informal neighborhood gathering place, from the totally eclectic to the purely Japanese to the multiethnic plate lunch, dining in Hawaii is one great culinary joy ride.

Expect to encounter Indonesian sates, Polynesian imu-baked foods, and guava-smoked meats in sophisticated presentations in the finest dining rooms on Maui. If there's pasta or risotto or rack of lamb on the menu, it could be nori (seaweed) linguine with opihi (limpet sauce), or risotto with local seafood served in taro cups, or a rack of lamb in cabernet and hoisin sauce (fermented soybean, garlic, and spices), or with macadamia nuts and coconut. Watch for ponzu sauce, too; it's lemony and zesty, much more flavorful than the soy sauce it resembles, and a welcome new staple on local menus.

While on Maui, you'll encounter many labels that embrace the fundamentals of HRC and the sophistication, informality, and nostalgia it encompasses. Euro-Asian, Pacific Rim, Pacific Edge, Euro-Pacific, fusion cuisine, hapa cuisine—by whatever name, Hawaii Regional Cuisine has evolved as Hawaii's singular cooking style, what some say is this country's current gastronomic, as well as geographic, frontier. It highlights the fresh seafood and produce of Hawaii's rich waters and volcanic soil, the cultural traditions of Hawaii's ethnic groups, and the skills of well-trained chefs who broke ranks with their European predecessors to forge new ground in the 50th state. Among those in the vanguard of HRC are Peter Merriman (Merriman's on the Big Island and Hula Grill on Maui), Beverly Gannon (Haliimaile General Store), Roy Yamaguchi (Roy's on Oahu, Maui, Hawaii, and Kauai), George Mavrothalassitis (Chef Mavro Restaurant in Honolulu), and Jean-Marie Josselin (A Pacific Cafe on Kauai).

Fresh ingredients are foremost, and farmers and fishermen work together to provide steady supplies of just-harvested seafood, seaweed, fern shoots, vine-ripened tomatoes, goat cheese, lamb, herbs, taro, and gourmet lettuces. Countless harvests from land and sea wind up in myriad forms on ever-changing menus, prepared in Asian and Western culinary styles. Exotic fruits introduced by recent Southeast Asian immigrants, such as sapodilla, mangosteen, soursop, and rambutan, are beginning to appear regularly in Chinatown markets. Aqua-cultured seafood, from seaweed to salmon to lobster, is a staple on many menus. Additionally, fresh-fruit salsas and sauces (mango, litchi, papaya, pineapple, guava), ginger-sesame-wasabi flavorings, corn cakes with sake sauces, tamarind and fish sauces, coconut-chile accents, tropical-fruit vinaigrettes, and other local and newly arrived seasonings from Southeast Asia and the Pacific impart unique qualities to the preparations.

Here's a sampling of what you can expect to find on a Hawaii Regional menu: seared Hawaiian fish with lilikoi shrimp butter; taro-crab cakes; Molokai sweet-potato or breadfruit vichyssoise; Ka'u orange sauce and Kahua Ranch lamb; Hawaiian bouillabaisse with fresh snapper, Kona crab, and fresh aquacultured shrimp; blackened ahi summer rolls; and gourmet Waimanalo or Kula greens, picked that day. Menus often change daily, and since the leading chefs have an unquenchable appetite for cooking on the edge, possibilities abound on Maui for once-in-a-lifetime dining adventures.

PLATE LUNCHES & MORE: LOCAL FOOD

At the other end of the spectrum is the vast and endearing world of "local food." By that we mean plate lunches and poke, shave ice and saimin, bento lunches and manapua—cultural hybrids all.

Reflecting a polyglot population of many styles and ethnicities, Hawaii's idio-syncratic dining scene is eminently inclusive. Consider surfer chic: barefoot in the sand, in a swimsuit, you chow down on a plate lunch ordered from a lunch wagon, consisting of fried mahimahi, "two scoops rice," macaroni salad, and a few leaves of green, typically julienned cabbage or iceberg lettuce. (Generally, teriyaki beef or shoyu chicken are options, too.) Heavy gravy is often the accom-paniment of choice, accompanied by a soft drink in a paper cup. Like saimin—the local version of noodles in broth topped with scrambled eggs, green onions, and, sometimes, pork—the plate lunch is Hawaii's version of high camp.

Because this is Hawaii, at least a few licks of *poi*—the Hawaiian staple of cooked, pounded taro (the local tuber)—and other examples of indigenous cui-sine are de rigueur, if not at a corny luau, then at least in a Hawaiian plate lunch. The native samplers include foods from before and after Western contact, such as *laulau* (pork, chicken, or fish steamed in ti leaves); *kalua* pork (pork cooked in a Polynesian underground oven known here as an *imu*); *lomi* salmon (salted salmon with tomatoes and green onions); squid *luau* (octopus cooked in coconut milk and taro tops); *poke* (cubed raw fish seasoned with onions and seaweed, and the occasional sprinkling of roasted *kukui* nuts); *haupia* (creamy coconut pudding); and *kulolo* (steamed pudding of coconut, brown sugar, and taro).

Bento, another popular choice for the dine-and-dash set, is also available throughout Hawaii. The compact, boxed assortment of picnic fare usually con-sists of neatly arranged sections of rice, pickled vegetables, and fried chicken, beef, or pork. Increasingly, however, the bento is becoming more streamlined and health-conscious, as in macrobiotic bento lunches or vegetarian brown-rice bentos. A derivative of the modest lunch box for Japanese immigrants who once labored in the sugar and pineapple fields, bentos are dispensed ubiquitously throughout Hawaii, everywhere from Long's Drugs and Japanese stores to cor-ner delis and supermarkets.

Ahi, Ono & Opakapaka: A Hawaiian Seafood Primer

The fresh seafood in Hawaii has been described as the best in the world. In the pivotal book *The New Cuisine of Hawaii,* by Janice Wald Henderson, acclaimed chef Nobuyuki Matsuhisa (chef/owner of Matsuhisa in Beverly Hills and Nobu in Manhattan and London) writes, "As a chef who specializes in fresh seafood, I am in awe of the quality of Hawaii's fish; it is unparalleled anywhere else in the world." And why not? Without a doubt, the islands' surrounding waters, the waters of the remote northwestern Hawaiian Islands, and a growing aquaculture industry are fertile grounds for this most important of Hawaii's food resources.

The reputable restaurants in Hawaii buy fresh fish daily at predawn auctions or from local fishermen. Some chefs even spear-fish their ingredients themselves. "Still wiggling" is the ultimate term for freshness in Hawaii. The fish can then be grilled over *kiawe* (mesquite) or prepared in innumerable ways—wrapped in ti leaves and baked, encrusted in nori or Hawaiian salt, wrapped, rolled, tempura-fried, skewered, topped with ogo sauces and fruit salsas, you name it.

Although many menus include the Western description for the fresh fish used, most often the local nomenclature is listed, turning dinner for the uninitiated into a confusing, quasi-foreign experience. To help familiarize you with the menu language of Hawaii, here's a basic glossary of island fish:

ahi   yellowfin or bigeye tuna, important for its use in sashimi and poke, at sushi bars, and in Hawaii Regional Cuisine

aku   skipjack tuna, heavily used by local families in home cooking and poke

ehu   red snapper, delicate and sumptuous, yet lesser known than opakapaka (see below)

hapuupuu   grouper, a sea bass whose use is expanding from ethnic to nonethnic restaurants

hebi   spearfish, mildly flavored and frequently featured as the "catch of the day" in upscale restaurants

---

Also from the plantations come *manapua,* a bready, doughy round with tasty fillings of sweetened pork or sweet beans. In the old days, the Chinese "manapua man" would make his rounds with bamboo containers balanced on a rod over his shoulders. Today, you'll find white or whole-wheat manapua containing chicken, vegetables, curry, and other savory fillings.

The daintier Chinese delicacy, dim sum, is made of translucent wrappers filled with fresh seafood, pork hash, and vegetables, served for breakfast and lunch in Chinatown restaurants. The Hong Kong–style dumplings are ordered fresh and hot from bamboo steamers from invariably brusque servers who move their carts from table to table. Much like hailing a taxi in Manhattan, you have to be quick and loud for dim sum.

TASTY TREATS: SHAVE ICE & MALASSADAS

For dessert or a snack, the prevailing choice is shave ice, the island version of a snow cone. Particularly on hot, humid days, long lines gather for the rainbow-colored

kajiki Pacific blue marlin, also called *au*, with a firm flesh and high fat content that make it a plausible substitute for tuna in some raw fish dishes, and as a grilled item on menus

kumu goatfish, a luxury item on Chinese and upscale menus, served en papillote or steamed whole, Asian style, with sesame oil, scallions, ginger, and garlic

mahimahi dolphin fish (the game fish, not the mammal) or dorado, a classic sweet, white-fleshed fish requiring vigilance among purists because it is often disguised as fresh when it's actually "fresh-frozen"—a big difference

monchong big-scale or sickle pomfret, an exotic, tasty fish, scarce but gaining a higher profile on Hawaiian Island menus

nairagi striped marlin, also called *au;* good as sashimi and in poke, and often substituted for ahi in raw-fish products

onaga ruby snapper, a luxury fish, versatile, moist, and flaky; top-of-the-line

ono wahoo, firmer and drier than the snappers, often served grilled and in sandwiches

opah moonfish, rich, fatty, and versatile—cooked, raw, smoked, and broiled

opakapaka pink snapper, light, flaky, and luxurious, suited for sashimi, poaching, sautéing, and baking; the best-known upscale fish

papio jack fish, light, firm, and flavorful, and favored in island cookery

shutome broadbill swordfish, of beeflike texture and rich flavor

tombo albacore tuna, with a high fat content, suitable for grilling and sautéing

uhu parrot fish, most often encountered steamed, Chinese style

uku gray snapper of clear, pale-pink flesh, delicately flavored and moist

ulua large jack fish, firm-fleshed and versatile.

cones heaped with finely shaved ice and topped with sweet tropical syrups. (The sweet-sour *li hing mui* flavor is a current rage.) The fast-melting mounds requiring prompt, efficient consumption are quite the local summer ritual for those with a sweet tooth. Aficionados order shave ice with ice cream and sweetened adzuki beans plopped in the middle.

You might also encounter *malassadas,* the Portuguese version of doughnuts, and if you do, it's best to eat them immediately. A leftover malassada has all the appeal of a heavy, lumpen, cold doughnut. When fresh and hot, however, as at school carnivals (where they attract the longest lines), or at bakeries and road-side stands, the sugary, yeasty doughnut-without-a-hole is enjoyed by many as one of the enduring legacies of the Portuguese in Hawaii.

PINEAPPLES, PAPAYAS & OTHER ISLAND FRUITS

Lanai isn't growing pineapples commercially anymore, but low-acid, white-fleshed, wondrously sweet Hawaiian Sugar Loaf pineapples are being commercially grown,

A Summary of Everyday Hawaiian Food Terms

Here's a handy list of foods discussed in this section, plus a few extras. All the following foods are common in plate lunches and at luaus. A number of them will also pop up on gourmet menus—usually with expensive ingredients and prepared with a twist, of course:

- **Bento:** This box lunch is a descendent of the modest box lunches once eaten by Japanese laborers in the sugar or pineapple fields. Usually they consist of rice, pickled vegetables, and fried chicken, beef, or pork.
- **Haupia** (how-*pee*-ah): Creamy coconut pudding, usually served in squares.
- **Kalua pork:** Pork slow-cooked in an *imu,* or underground oven; listed on menus as "luau pig" on occasion. Sometimes it's served in a pulled kalua pork sandwich, much like barbecue pork might be in the southeast United States or Texas.
- **Kiawe** (kee-*ah*-vay): An aromatic mesquite wood often used to fire the wood-burning ovens.
- **Kulolo:** Steamed coconut pudding made with brown sugar and taro.
- **Laulau:** Pork, chicken, or fish wrapped in ti leaves and steamed.
- **Lilikoi** (lil-ee-koy): Passion fruit.
- **Lomi salmon:** Salted salmon marinated, ceviche-like, with tomatoes and green onions.
- **Lumpia** (lum-*pee*-ah): The Portuguese version of a spring roll, but spicier, doughier, and deep-fried (and usually stuffed with pork and veggies).
- **Malassada** (mah-lah-*sah*-da): The Portuguese version of a doughnut, usually round, deep-fried, and generously sprinkled with powdered sugar. Best when eaten hot.

on a small scale, on Kauai as well as the Big Island. That's just one of the developments in the rapidly changing agricultural landscape in Hawaii. The litchilike Southeast Asian *rambutan; longan* (Chinese dragon's-eye litchis); 80-pound Indian jackfruits; the starfruit; the luscious, custardy mangosteen; and the usual mangoes, papayas, guava, and *lilikoi* (passion fruit) make up the dazzling parade of fresh island fruits that come and go with the seasons.

Papayas, bananas, and **pineapples** grow year-round, but pineapples are always sweetest, juiciest, and most yellow in the summer. Although new papaya hybrids are making their way into the marketplace, the classic bests include the fleshy, firm-textured Kahuku papayas, the queen of them all; the Big Island's sweet Kapoho and Puna papayas; and the fragile, juicy, and reddish-orange Sunrise papayas from Kauai. Those who have transferred their allegiance from Puna to Sunrise claim they're sweeter, juicier, and more elegant than all others. Also called strawberry papayas, the Sunrise variety is easily misjudged and often served overripe; delicate inside and out, these papayas are easily bruised and fragile in texture, yet robust in flavor. Apple bananas are smaller, firmer, and tarter than the standard, and they are a local specialty that flourish throughout the islands.

- **Manapua** (man-ah-*pòo*-ah): A doughy bun usually filled with sweetened pork or sweet beans.
- **Ohelo** (oh-*hay*-low): A berry very similar to a cranberry that commonly appears in Hawaii Regional Cuisine sauces.
- **Panko:** Japanese bread crumbs, most commonly used to prepare *katsu* (deep-fried pork or chicken cutlet). Creative chefs often use it for other purposes, most commonly as a tempura-like crust on sushi-grade ahi rolls.
- **Poi:** The root of the taro pounded into a purple, starchy paste; a staple of the island diet, but generally tasteless to most outsiders.
- **Poke** (*po*-kay): Cubed raw fish—usually ahi or marlin—seasoned with onions, soy, and seaweed.
- **Ponzu:** A soy-and-citrus dipping sauce popular with Hawaii Regional Cuisine chefs.
- **Saimin** (*sai*-min): A brothy soup with ramen-like noodles, topped with bits of fish, chicken, pork, scrambled eggs, and/or vegetables. Saimin is served almost everywhere in Hawaii, from plate-lunch stands to museum cafes to McDonald's.
- **Shave Ice:** The island version of a snow cone, best enjoyed with ice cream and sweet *azuki* (red) beans.
- **Squid luau:** Octopus cooked in coconut milk and taro tops.
- **Taro:** A green leafy vegetable grown in Hawaii; the root is used to make poi (mentioned earlier in this list), and the leafy part of the vegetable is often steamed like spinach.

Litchis and **mangoes** are long-awaited summer fruit. Mangoes begin appearing in late spring or early summer and can be found at roadside fruit stands, markets, and health-food stores (where the high prices may shock you). Our favorite is the white pirie—rare and resinous, fiberless, and so sweet and juicy it makes the high-profile Hayden seem prosaic. A popular newcomer is the Rapoza mango, a fiberless, 2-pound fruit fairly new to the islands, yet already earning raves for its sweetness and resilience.

Watermelons are a summer hit and a signature of Molokai and Oahu. The state of Hawaii, where more watermelons are consumed per capita than in any other state, produces top-notch fruit for its loyal clientele. Kahuku watermelons, available in the summer months, give the popular Molokai variety a run for its money. Juicy, fleshy, and sweet, Kahuku watermelons are now grown primarily in Waialua on Oahu's north shore, while production of the Molokai variety has expanded to central Oahu. Most markets sell these bulging orbs of refreshment throughout summer and early fall.

In the competitive world of **oranges,** the Kau Gold navel oranges from the southern Big Island put Sunkist to shame. Grown in the volcanic soil and sunny conditions of the South Point region (the southernmost point in the United

States), the "Ugly Orange" is brown, rough, and anything but pretty. But the browner and uglier they look, the sweeter and juicier they taste. Because the thin-skinned oranges are tree-ripened, they're fleshy and heavy with liquid, and they will spoil you for life. Although these oranges have traditionally been a winter fruit, they're appearing more abundantly year-round.

5 The Natural World: An Environmental Guide to Maui

Born of violent volcanic eruptions from deep beneath the ocean's surface, the first Hawaiian islands emerged about 70 million years ago—more than 200 million years after the major continental land masses formed. Two thousand miles from the nearest continent, Mother Nature's fury began to carve beauty from barren rock. Untiring volcanoes spewed forth curtains of fire that cooled into stone, while severe tropical storms, some with hurricane-force winds, battered and blasted the cooling lava rock into a series of shapes. Ferocious earthquakes flattened, shattered, and reshaped the islands into precipitous valleys, jagged cliffs, and recumbent flatlands. Monstrous surf and gigantic tidal waves rearranged and polished the lands above and below the reaches of the tide.

It took millions upon millions of years for nature to chisel the familiar form of Maui's majestic Haleakala peak, to create the waterfalls on Molokai's northern side, to shape the reefs of Hulopoe Bay on Lanai, and to establish the lush rainforests of the Hana coastline. The result is an island-chain-within-a-chain like no other on the planet—rich in unique flora and fauna, surrounded by a vibrant underwater world that will haunt you forever.

THE FLORA OF MAUI

Maui radiates with the sweet smell of flowers, lush vegetation, and exotic plant life.

AFRICAN TULIP TREES   Even from afar, you can see the flaming red flowers on these large trees, which can grow to be more than 50 feet tall. Children in Hawaii love them because the buds hold water—they use the flowers as water pistols.

ANGEL'S TRUMPETS   These small trees can grow up to 20 feet tall, with an abundance of large (up to 10 in. in diameter) pendants—white or pink flowers that resemble, well, trumpets. The Hawaiians call them *nana-honua,* which means "earth gazing." The flowers, which bloom continually from early spring to late fall, have a musky scent. *But beware:* All parts of the plant are poisonous and contain a strong narcotic.

ANTHURIUMS   One of Hawaii's most popular cut flowers, anthuriums originally came from the tropical Americas and the Caribbean islands. There are more than 550 species, but the most popular in Hawaii are the heart-shaped red, orange, pink, white, and even purple flowers with tail-like spathes. Look for the heart-shaped green leaves in shaded areas. These exotic plants have no scent but will last several weeks as cut flowers.

BIRDS OF PARADISE   These natives of Africa have become something of a trademark of Hawaii. They're easily recognizable by the orange and blue flowers nestled in gray-green bracts, looking somewhat like birds in flight.

BOUGAINVILLEA   Originally from Brazil and named for the 18th-century French explorer Louis Antoine de Bougainville, these colorful, tissue-thin bracts (ranging in color from majestic purple to fiery orange) hide tiny white flowers.

BROMELIADS   The pineapple plant is the best-known bromeliad; native to tropical South America and the islands of the Caribbean, bromeliads comprise more than 1,400 species. "Bromes," as they're affectionately called, are generally spiky plants ranging in size from a few inches to several feet in diameter. They are popular not only for their unusual foliage but also for their strange and wonderful flowers, which range from colorful spikes to delicate blossoms resembling orchids. Bromeliads are widely used in landscaping and as interior decoration, especially in resort areas.

COFFEE   Hawaii is the only state that commercially produces coffee. Coffee is an evergreen shrub with shiny, waxy, dark-green, pointed leaves. The flower is a small, fragrant white blossom that develops into half-inch berries that turn bright red when ripe. Look for coffee plants in Kaanapali on Maui and in Kualapuu on Molokai.

GINGER   Some of the most fragrant flowers in Hawaii are white and yellow ginger. Usually found in clumps, and growing 4 to 7 feet tall in areas blessed by rain, these sweet-smelling, 3-inch-wide flowers are composed of three dainty petal-like stamens and three long, thin petals. Both white and yellow ginger are so prolific that many people assume they are native to Hawaii; actually, they were introduced in the 19th century from the Indonesia-Malaysia area. Look for white and yellow ginger from late spring to fall. If you see them on the side of the road (especially on the Hana Hwy.), stop and pick a few blossoms—your car will be filled with a divine fragrance for the rest of the day. The only downside is that, once picked, the flowers will live only briefly.

Other members of the ginger family frequently seen in Hawaii (there are some 700 species) include red, shell, and torch gingers. Red ginger consists of tall, green stalks with foot-long red "flower heads." The red "petals" are actually bracts; inch-long white flowers are protected by the bracts and can be seen if you look down into the red head. Red ginger, which does not share the heavenly smell of white ginger, will last a week or longer when cut. Look for red ginger from spring through late fall. Cool, wet mountain forests are ideal conditions for shell ginger; natives of India and Burma, these plants, with their pearly white, clamshell-like blossoms, bloom from spring to fall.

Perhaps the most exotic ginger is the red or pink torch ginger. Cultivated in Malaysia as seasoning (the young flower shoots are used in curries), torch ginger rises directly out of the ground; the flower stalks, which are about 5 to 8 inches in length, resemble the fire of a lighted torch. This is one of the few types of ginger that can bloom year-round.

HELICONIA   Some 80 species of the colorful heliconia family came to Hawaii from the Caribbean and Central and South America. The bright yellow, red, green, and orange bracts overlap and appear to unfold like origami birds. The most obvious heliconia to spot is the lobster claw, which resembles a string of boiled crustacean pincers—the brilliant crimson bracts alternate on the stem. Another prolific heliconia is the parrot's beak; growing to about hip height, it's composed of bright-orange flower bracts with black tips, not unlike the beak of a parrot. Look for parrot's beak in the spring and summer, when it blooms in profusion.

HIBISCUS   One variety of this year-round blossom, the yellow hibiscus, is the official state flower. The 4- to 6-inch hibiscus flowers come in a range of colors, from lily white to lipstick red. The flowers resemble crepe paper, with stamens and pistils protruding spire-like from the center. Hibiscus hedges can grow up to 15 feet tall. Once plucked, the flowers wither quickly.

JACARANDA   Beginning around March and sometimes lasting until early May, these huge, lacy-leafed trees metamorphose into large clusters of spectacular lavender-blue sprays. The bell-shaped flowers drop quickly, leaving a majestic purple carpet beneath the tree.

NIGHT-BLOOMING CEREUS   Look along rock walls for this spectacular night-blooming flower. Originally from Central America, this vinelike member of the cactus family has green scalloped edges and produces foot-long white flowers that open as darkness falls and wither as the sun rises. The plant also bears a red fruit that is edible.

ORCHIDS   To many minds, nothing says Hawaii more than orchids. The orchid family is the largest in the entire plant kingdom. The most widely grown variety—and the major source of flowers for leis and garnish for tropical libations—is the vanda orchid. The vandas used in Hawaii's commercial flower industry are generally lavender or white, but they grow in a rainbow of colors, shapes, and sizes. The orchids used for corsages are the large, delicate cattleya; the ones used in floral arrangements—you'll probably see them in your hotel lobby—are usually dendrobiums.

PLUMERIA   Also known as frangipani, this sweet-smelling, five-petal flower, found in clusters on trees, is the most popular choice of lei makers. The Singapore plumeria has five creamy-white petals, with a touch of yellow in the center. Another popular variety, ruba—with flowers from soft pink to flaming red—is also used in leis. When picking plumeria, be careful of the sap from the flower—it is poisonous and can stain clothes.

PROTEAS   Originally from South Africa, this unusual plant comes in more than 40 varieties. Proteas are shrubs that bloom into a range of flower types. Different species of proteas range from those resembling pincushions to a species that looks just like a bouquet of feathers. Proteas are long-lasting cut flowers; once dried, they will last for years.

FRUIT TREES

BANANA   Edible bananas are among the oldest of the world's food crops. By the time Europeans arrived in the islands, the Hawaiians had planted more than 40 types of bananas. Most banana plants have long green leaves hanging from the tree, with the flowers giving way to fruit in clusters.

BREADFRUIT   A large tree, more than 60 feet tall, with broad, sculpted, dark-green leaves, the famous breadfruit produces a round, head-size green fruit that is a staple in the diets of all Polynesians. When roasted or baked, the whitish-yellow meat tastes somewhat like a sweet potato.

LITCHI   This evergreen tree, which can grow to well over 30 feet across, originated in China. Small flowers grow into panicles about a foot long in June and July. The round, red-skinned fruit appears shortly afterward.

MACADAMIA   A transplant from Australia, macadamia nuts have become a commercial crop in recent decades in Hawaii, especially on Maui and the Big Island. The large trees, up to 60 feet tall, bear a hard-shelled nut encased in a leathery husk, which splits open and dries when ripe.

MANGO   From Indonesia and Malaysia comes the delicious mango, a fruit with peachlike flesh. Mango season usually begins in the spring and lasts through the summer, depending on the variety. The trees can grow to more than

100 feet tall. The tiny reddish flowers give way to a green fruit that turns red-yellow when ripe. Some people enjoy unripe mangoes, either thinly sliced or in chutney, a traditional Indian preparation. Note that mango sap can cause a skin rash on some people.

PAPAYA   One of the sweetest of all tropical fruits, the pear-shaped papaya turns yellow or reddish pink when ripe. They are found at the base of the large, scalloped-shaped leaves on a pedestal-like, nonbranched tree whose trunk is hollow. Papayas ripen year-round.

OTHER TREES & PLANTS

BANYAN   Among the world's largest trees, banyans have branches that grow out and away from the trunk, forming descending roots that grow down to the ground to feed and form additional trunks, making the tree very stable during tropical storms. The banyan in the courtyard next to the old Court House in Lahaina is an excellent example of a spreading banyan—it covers ⅔ acre.

MONKEYPOD   The monkeypod is one of Hawaii's most majestic trees; it grows more than 80 feet tall and 100 feet across. Seen near older homes and in parks, the leaves of the monkeypod drop in February and March. The wood is a favorite of woodworking artisans.

SILVERSWORD   This very uncommon and unusual plant is seen only on the Big Island and in the Haleakala Crater on Maui. Once a year, this rare relative of the sunflower family blooms between July and September. Resembling a pine cone more than a sunflower, the silversword in bloom is a fountain of red-petaled, daisylike flowers that turn silver soon after blooming.

TARO   Around pools, near streams, and in neatly planted fields, you'll see the green heart-shaped leaves of taro, whose dense roots are a Polynesian staple. The ancient Hawaiians pounded the roots into poi. Originally from Sri Lanka, taro is grown not only as a food crop, but also as an ornamental.

MARIJUANA   This not-so-rare-and-unusual plant—called *pakalolo,* or "crazy weed"—is grown throughout the islands. You probably won't see it as you drive along the roads, but if you go hiking, you might glimpse the feathery green leaves with tight clusters of buds. Despite years of police effort to eradicate the plant, the illegal industry continues. Don't be tempted to pick a few buds; the purveyors of this nefarious industry don't take kindly to poaching.

THE FAUNA OF MAUI

When the first Polynesians arrived in Hawaii between A.D. 500 and 800, scientists say they found some 67 varieties of endemic Hawaiian birds, a third of which are now believed to be extinct. What's even more astonishing is what they didn't find—there were no reptiles, amphibians, mosquitoes, lice, fleas, or even cockroaches.

There were only two endemic mammals: the hoary bat and the monk seal. The small **hoary bat** must have accidentally blown to Hawaii at some point, from either North or South America. It can still be seen today on its early evening forays.

The **Hawaiian monk seal,** a relative of warm-water seals found in the Caribbean and Mediterranean, was nearly slaughtered into extinction for its skin and oil during the 19th century. These seals have recently experienced a minor population explosion, forcing relocation of some males from their protected

Leapin' Lizards!

Geckos are harmless, soft-skinned, insect-eating lizards that come equipped with suction pads on their feet, enabling them to climb walls and windows to reach tasty insects like mosquitoes and cockroaches. You'll see these little guys on windows outside a lighted room at night or hear their cheerful chirp.

homes in the islets north of the main Hawaiian Islands. Periodically, these endangered animals turn up at various beaches throughout the state. They are protected under federal law by the Marine Mammals Protection Act. If you're fortunate enough to see a monk seal, just look; don't disturb one of Hawaii's living treasures.

The first Polynesians brought a few animals from home: dogs, pigs, and chickens (all were for eating), as well as rats (stowaways). All four animals are still found in the Hawaiian wild today.

BIRDS

More species of native birds have become extinct in Hawaii in the past 200 years than anywhere else on the planet. Of the 67 native species, 23 are extinct and 30 are endangered. Even the Hawaiian crow, **alala,** is threatened.

The **aeo,** or Hawaiian stilt, a 16-inch-long bird with a black head, a black coat, a white underside, and long pink legs, can be found in protected wetlands like the Kanaha Wild Life Sanctuary (where it shares its natural habitat with the Hawaiian coot) and the Kealia Pond.

Endemic to the islands, the **nene** is Hawaii's state bird. It's currently being brought back from the brink of extinction through captive breeding and by strenuous protection laws. A relative of the Canada goose, the nene stands about 2 feet high and has a black head and yellow cheek, a buff neck with deep furrows, a grayish-brown body, and clawed feet. It gets its name from its two-syllable, high nasal call, "nay-nay." The approximately 500 nenes in existence can be seen at Haleakala National Park.

The Hawaiian short-eared owl, **pueo,** which grows to between 12 and 17 inches in size, can be seen at dawn and dusk, when the black-billed, brown-and-white bird goes hunting for rodents. Pueos are highly regarded by Hawaiians; according to legend, spotting a pueo is a good omen.

SEA LIFE

Approximately 680 species of fish are known to inhabit the waters around the Hawaiian Islands. Of those, approximately 450 species stay close to the reef and inshore areas.

CORAL   The reefs surrounding Hawaii are made up of various coral and algae. The living coral grows through sunlight that feeds a specialized algae, which in turn allows the development of the coral's calcareous skeleton. The reefs, which take thousands of years to develop, attract and support fish and crustaceans, which use them for food, habitat, mating, and raising their young. Mother Nature can batter the fragile reefs with a strong storm or large waves, but humans, through seemingly innocuous acts such as touching the coral, have proven far more destructive.

The corals most frequently seen around Maui are hard, rocklike formations named for their familiar shapes: antler, cauliflower, finger, plate, and razor coral.

Wire coral looks just like its name—a randomly bent wire growing straight out of the reef. Some corals appear soft, such as tube coral, which can be found in the ceilings of caves. Black coral, which resembles winter-bare trees or shrubs, is found at depths of more than 100 feet.

REEF FISH   Of the approximately 450 reef fish, about 27% are native to Hawaii and are found nowhere else in the world. As the islands were born from erupting volcanoes, evolving over millions of years, ocean currents, mainly from Southeast Asia, carried the larvae of thousands of marine animals and plants to Hawaii's reef. Of those, approximately 100 species not only adapted, but thrived.

Some species are much bigger and more plentiful than their Pacific cousins, and many developed unique characteristics. Some, like the lemon or milletseed butterfly fish, are not only particular to Hawaii but also unique within their larger, worldwide family in their specialized schooling and feeding behaviors. Another surprising thing about Hawaii endemics is how common some of the native fish are; you can see the saddleback wrasse, for instance, on virtually any snorkeling excursion or dive in Hawaiian waters. You're likely to spot one or more of the following reef fish while underwater.

Angel fish, often mistaken for butterfly fish, can be distinguished by the spine, located low on the gill plate. Angel fish are very shy; several species live in colonies close to coral for protection.

Blennies are small, elongated fish, ranging from 2 to 10 inches long, with the majority in the 3- to 4-inch range. Blennies are so small that they can live in tide pools; you might have a hard time spotting one.

Butterfly fish, among the most colorful of the reef fish, are usually seen in pairs (scientists believe they mate for life) and appear to spend most of their day feeding. There are 22 species of butterfly fish, of which three (blue-stripe, lemon or milletseed, and multiband or pebbled butterfly fish) are endemic. Most butterfly fish have a dark band through the eye and a spot near the tail resembling an eye, meant to confuse their predators (the moray eel loves to lunch on them).

Moray and conger **eels** are the common eels seen in Hawaii. Morays are usually docile unless provoked, or if there's food or an injured fish around. Unfortunately, some morays have been fed by divers and, being intelligent creatures, associate divers with food; thus, they can become aggressive. But most morays like to keep to themselves, hidden in their hole or crevice. While morays may look menacing, conger eels look downright happy, with big lips and pectoral fins (situated so they look like big ears) that give them the appearance of a perpetually smiling face. Conger eels have crushing teeth so they can feed on crustaceans; in fact, since they're sloppy eaters, they usually live with shrimp and crabs that feed off the crumbs they leave.

One of the largest and most colorful of the reef fish, the **parrot fish** can grow up to 40 inches long. Parrot fish are easy to spot—their front teeth are fused together, protruding like buck teeth and resembling a parrot's beak. These unique teeth allow them to feed by scraping algae from rocks and coral. The rocks and coral pass through the parrot fish's system, resulting in fine sand. In fact, most of the white sand found in Hawaii is parrot-fish waste; one large parrot fish can produce a ton of sand a year. Hawaiian native parrot-fish species include yellowbar, regal, and spectacled.

Scorpion fish are what scientists call "ambush predators." They hide under camouflaged exteriors and ambush their prey when they come along. Several sport a venomous dorsal spine. These fish don't have a gas bladder, so when they stop swimming, they sink—that's why you usually find them "resting" on ledges and on the ocean bottom. Although they're not aggressive, an inattentive snorkeler or diver could feel the effects of those venomous spines—so be very careful where you put your hands and feet in the water.

Surgeonfish, sometimes called *tang,* get their name from the scalpel-like spines located on each side of their bodies near the base of their tails. Some surgeonfish have a rigid spine, while others have the ability to fold their spine against their body until it's needed for defense purposes. Some surgeonfish, like the brightly colored yellow tang, are boldly colored; others are adorned in more conservative shades of gray, brown, or black. The only endemic surgeonfish—and the most abundant in Hawaiian waters—is the convict tang, a pale white fish with vertical black stripes (like a convict's uniform).

Wrasses are a very diverse family of fish, ranging in size from 2 to 15 inches. Several wrasses are brilliantly colored and change their colors through aging and sexual dimorphism (sex changing). Wrasses have the ability to change gender with maturation, from female (when young) to male. Several types are endemic to Hawaii: the Hawaiian cleaner, shortnose, belted, and gray (or old woman).

GAME FISH   Hawaii is known around the globe as *the* place for big-game fish—marlin, swordfish, and tuna—but its waters are also great for catching other offshore fish, such as mahimahi, rainbow runner, and wahoo; coastal fish, such as barracuda and scad; bottom fish, such as snappers, sea bass, and amberjack; and inshore fish, like trevally and bonefish.

Six kinds of **billfish** are found in the offshore waters around the islands: Pacific blue marlin, black marlin, sailfish, broadbill swordfish, striped marlin, and shortbill spearfish. Hawaii billfish range in size from the 20-pound shortbill spearfish and striped marlin to a 1,805-pound Pacific blue marlin, the largest marlin ever caught on rod and reel anywhere in the world.

Tuna ranges in size from small (a pound or less) mackerel tuna used as bait (Hawaiians call them *oioi*) to 250-pound yellowfin ahi tuna. Other species of tuna found in Hawaii are bigeye, albacore, kawakawa, and skipjack.

Some of the best fish for eating are also found in offshore waters: **mahimahi** (also known as dolphin fish or dorado), in the 20- to 70-pound range; **rainbow runner** (*kamanu*), from 15 to 30 pounds; and **wahoo** (*ono*), from 15 to 80 pounds. Shoreline fishers are always on the lookout for **trevally** (the state record for giant trevally is 191 lb.), **bonefish, ladyfish, threadfin, leatherfish,** and **goatfish.** Bottom fishers pursue a range of **snappers**—red, pink, gray, and others—as well as **sea bass** (the state record is a whopping 563 lb.) and **amberjack,** which weigh up to 100 pounds.

WHALES   The most popular visitors to Hawaii come every year around December and stay until April or so, when they return to their summer home in Alaska. Humpback whales—some as big as a city bus and weighing many tons—migrate to the warm, protected Hawaiian waters in the winter to mate and calve.

You can take whale-watching cruises that will let you observe these magnificent leviathans up close, or you can spot their signature spouts of water from shore as they expel water off in the distance. Humpbacks grow to up to 45 feet long, so when they breach (propel their entire body out of the water) or even wave a fluke, you can see it for miles.

Humpbacks are among the biggest whales found in Hawaiian waters, but other whales—like pilot, sperm, false killer, melon-headed, pygmy killer, and beaked—can be seen year-round. These whales usually travel in pods of 20 to 40 animals and are very social, interacting with one another on the surface.

SHARKS   Yes, there *are* sharks in Hawaii, but more than likely you won't see a shark unless you specifically go looking for one. The ancient Hawaiians had great respect for these animals and believed that some sharks were reincarnated relatives who had returned to assist them.

About 40 different species of shark inhabit the waters surrounding Hawaii, ranging from the totally harmless whale shark (at 60 ft., the world's largest fish), which has no teeth and is so docile that it frequently lets divers ride on its back, to the not-so-docile, infamous, and extremely uncommon, great white shark. The most common sharks seen in Hawaii are white-tip reef sharks, gray reef sharks (both about 5 ft. long), and black-tip reef sharks (about 6 ft. long).

MAUI'S ECOSYSTEM PROBLEMS

Maui might be paradise, but even paradise has its problems. The biggest threat facing Maui's natural environment is human intrusion—simply put, too many people want to experience paradise firsthand. From the magnificent underwater world to the breathtaking rainforest, the presence of people isn't always benign, no matter how cautious or environmentally aware they may be.

MARINE LIFE   Hawaii's beautiful and abundant marine life has attracted so many visitors that they threaten to overwhelm it. A great example of this over-enthusiasm is **Molokini,** a small, partially submerged, half-moon–shaped crater off the coast of Maui. In the 1970s, residents made the area a conservation district to protect the unique aquarium-like atmosphere of the waters inside the arms of the crater. Unfortunately, once it was protected, everyone wanted to come here just to see what was worth special protection. Twenty-five years ago, one or two small six-passenger boats made the trip once a day to Molokini; today, it's not uncommon to see 20 or more boats, each carrying 20 to 49 passengers, moored inside the tiny crater. One tour operator has claimed that on some days, it's so crowded that you can actually see a slick of suntan oil floating on the surface of the water.

People who fall in love with the colorful **reef fish** and want to see them all the time back home are also thought to be impacting the health of Hawaii's reefs. Because of the popularity of home and office aquariums, more and more collectors are taking a growing number of reef fish from Hawaiian waters.

The **reefs** themselves have faced increasing ecological problems over the years. Runoff of soil and chemicals from construction, agriculture, erosion, and even heavy storms can blanket and choke a reef, which needs sunlight to survive. In addition, the intrusion of foreign elements, like breaks in sewage lines, can cause problems for Hawaii's reef. Human contact with the reef can upset the ecosystem as well. Coral, the basis of the reef system, is very fragile; snorkelers and divers grabbing onto it can break off pieces that took decades to form. Feeding the fish can also upset the balance of the ecosystem (not to mention upsetting the digestive systems of the fish). One glass-bottom boat operator reported that divers fed an eel for years, considering it their "pet" eel. One day the eel decided that it wanted more than just the food being offered and bit the diver's fingers. Divers and snorkelers report that in areas where the fish are fed, the fish have become more aggressive; clouds of normally shy reef fish surround divers, demanding food.

FLORA   One of Hawaii's most fragile environments is the rainforest. Any intrusion—from a hiker carrying seeds on his shoes to the rooting of wild boars—can upset the delicate balance in these complete ecosystems. In recent years, development has moved closer and closer to the rainforest.

FAUNA   The biggest impact on the fauna in Hawaii is the decimation of native birds by feral animals, which have destroyed the birds' habitats, and by mongooses that have eaten the birds' eggs and young. Government officials are vigilant about snakes because of the potential damage tree snakes can do to the remaining bird life.

Appendix B: Useful Toll-Free Numbers & Websites

AIRLINES

Air Canada
☎ 888/247-2262
www.aircanada.ca

Air New Zealand
☎ 800/262-1234 or -2468 in the U.S.
☎ 800/663-5494 in Canada
☎ 0800/737-767 in New Zealand
www.airnewzealand.com

All Nippon Airways
☎ 800/235-9262 in U.S.
☎ 0120/029-222 in Japan
www.fly-ana.com

Aloha Airlines
☎ 800/367-5250 in Continental
U.S. and Canada
☎ 808/484-1111 in Oahu; 244-9071
in Maui; 935-5771 in Hilo and Kona;
245-3691 in Kauai
www.alohaairlines.com

American Airlines
☎ 800/433-7300
www.aa.com

American Trans Air
☎ 800/225-2995
www.ata.com

China Airlines
☎ 800/227-5118 in U.S.
☎ 02/2715-1212 in Taiwan
www.china-airlines.com

Continental Airlines
☎ 800/525-0280
www.continental.com

Delta Air Lines
☎ 800/221-1212
www.delta.com

Hawaiian Airlines
☎ 800/367-5320
www.hawaiianair.com

Japan Airlines
☎ 800/525/3663 in U.S.
☎ 0120/25-5971 in Japan
www.jal.co.jp

Korean Air
☎ 800/438-5000 in U.S.
☎ 1588-2001 in Korea
www.koreanair.com

Northwest Airlines
☎ 800/225-2525
www.nwa.com

Qantas
☎ 800/227-4500 in the U.S.
☎ 612/9691-3636 in Australia
www.qantas.com

United Airlines
☎ 800/241-6522
www.united.com

US Airways
☎ 800/428-4322
www.usairways.com

CAR-RENTAL AGENCIES

Advantage
☎ 800/777-5500
www.advantagerentacar.com

Alamo
☎ 800/327-9633
www.goalamo.com

Avis
☎ 800/331-1212 in Continental U.S.
☎ 800/TRY-AVIS in Canada
www.avis.com

Budget
☎ 800/527-0700
www.budget.com

Dollar
© 800/800-4000
www.dollar.com

Enterprise
© 800/325-8007
www.enterprise.com

Hertz
© 800/654-3131
www.hertz.com

National
© 800/CAR-RENT
www.nationalcar.com

Payless
© 800/PAYLESS
www.paylesscarrental.com

Rent-A-Wreck
© 800/535-1391
www.rentawreck.com

Thrifty
© 800/367-2277
www.thrifty.com

MAJOR HOTEL & MOTEL CHAINS

Best Western International
© 800/528-1234
www.bestwestern.com

Doubletree Hotels
© 800/222-TREE
www.doubletree.com

Four Seasons
© 800/819-5053
www.fourseasons.com

Hampton Inn
© 800/HAMPTON
www.hampton-inn.com

Hilton Hotels
© 800/HILTONS
www.hilton.com

Holiday Inn
© 800/HOLIDAY
www.basshotels.com

Hyatt Hotels & Resorts
© 800/228-9000
www.hyatt.com

Marriott Hotels
© 800/228-9290
www.marriott.com

Radisson Hotels International
© 800/333-3333
www.radisson.com

Renaissance
© 800/228-9290
www.renaissancehotels.com

Ritz Carlton
© 800/241-3333
www.ritzcarlton.com

Sheraton Hotels & Resorts
© 800-325-3535
www.sheraton.com

Westin Hotels & Resorts
© 800-937-8461
www.westin.com

Index

See also Accommodations and Restaurant indexes, below.

A AA (American Automobile Association), 76–77
AARP, 43
Access-Able Travel Source, 41–42
Access America, 37
Accessible Vans of Hawaii, 42
Accommodations, 81–122
  avoiding unpleasant surprises, 60
  bargaining on prices, 60–61
  best bed and breakfasts, 15–16
  best luxury hotels and resorts, 12–13
  best moderately priced, 13–14
  best resort spas, 17
  booking agencies, 61
  Central Maui, 81–82
  East Maui, 114–117
  family-friendly, 88–89
  Haiku, 114–116
  Hana, 117–122
  Honokowai, 92, 94–97
  Kaanapali, 86–91
  Kahana, 91–92, 94–96
  Kapalua, 97–99
  Kihei, 99–106
  Kula, 112–114
  Lahaina, 82–86
  Lanai, 278–280
  Maalaea, 99
  Makawao, Olinda, Haliimaile, 109–112
  Makena, 109
  Molokai, 243–249
    family-friendly, 249
  Napili, 92, 94–97
  package deals at hotel chains, 52–53
  "resort fee" at, 97
  shopping online for, 53–54
  South Maui, 99–109
  tipping, 80
  tips on, 58–61
  types of, 58–60
  Upcountry Maui, 109–114
  Wailea, 106–109
  West Maui, 82–99
  what's new, 1
Active vacations, 62–64
Activities and Attractions Association of Hawaii Gold Card, 63
Activities desks, 63–64
Activity Warehouse, 152, 158, 161, 164, 166, 176, 179
Admission Day, 34
Adventure Lanai Ecocentre, 277, 285–290
Adventure on Horseback, 179
Adventure vacations, best, 9–10
Aeo (Hawaiian stilt), 312
Aerial tours
  Molokai, 265–266
  over West Maui Mountains, 9
A-1 Foreign Exchange, 74
African tulip trees, 310
Agricultural screening at the airports, 48
Ahihi-Kinau Natural Preserve, 11, 164
Air Canada, 75, 76
Air Canada Vacations, 52
Airfares, 45–46
  shopping online for, 52
Airlines, 45
  interisland flights, 49–51
  to Molokai, 186, 241
Air New Zealand, 76
Air Pacific, 76
Airports
  agricultural screening at, 48
  security procedures, 46–48
Air travel
  jet lag, 46
  staying comfortable, 48–49
Alalakeiki Channel, 167, 198
Alamo car rentals, 57
Alexander, Samuel, 184, 299
Alexander & Baldwin, 198, 301

Alexander & Baldwin Sugar Museum (Puunene), 184
Alii Cab Co., 58
Alii Fish Pond (Molokai), 268
All Nippon Airways (ANA), 76
All Stings Considered (Thomas), 38, 40, 41
Aloha Airlines, 45, 50
  nonstop service to California, 1
Aloha Bead Co. (Paia), 232
Aloha Classic World Wave-sailing Championship (Hookipa Beach), 35
Aloha Festivals, 34
Aloha Guide to Accessibility, 41
Aloha Lahaina Dentists, 68
Aloha wear
  Kahului, 220
  Lahaina, 224
  Makawao, 229
  Wailuku, 222
Alyce C. Sportfishing (Molokai), 257
America II (yacht), 159
American Airlines, 45
American Airlines FlyAway Vacations, 52
American Express, 68
  traveler's checks, 28
American Trans Air (ATA), 45
Angel fish, 315
Angel's trumpets, 310
Animal Quarantine Facility, 42
Annual Lei Day Celebration, 32
Annual Ritz-Carlton Kapalua Celebration of the Arts, 31
Annual Trash Art Show, 32
Anthuriums, 308
Antiques (Wailuku), 221–222
Apricot Rose (Kahului), 220
Aquarium, Maui Ocean Center, 197–198
Area code, 68

Art galleries
  Hana, 232
  Kaanapali, 226
  on Kahekili Highway, 197
  Kapalua, 227
  Lahaina, 224, 225
  Makawao, 229–231
Art Maui 2004, 31
Art Night (Lahaina), 223
Arts and crafts
  Hana, 232
  Kaanapali, 226
  Kahului, 220
  Kihei, 228
  Molokai, 271
  Paia, 232
Art School at Kapalua, 227
**Art shows and festivals,
  31–32**
Aston chain, 52
ATA (American Trans Air), 45
**Atlantis Submarines, 5, 8,
  183**
**ATMs (automated teller
  machines), 28**
**Automobile organizations,
  76**
Automobile rentals, 57, 77
  Molokai, 243
  shopping online for, 54
**Avis, for travelers with dis-
  abilities, 42**
Avis car rentals, 57

B abson, Ann and Bob,
  61–62
Baby's Away, 43
Baggage. *See* Luggage
**Bailey House Gift Shop
  (Wailuku), 21, 221**
**Bailey House Museum
  (Wailuku), 184**
Baldwin, Henry, 299
**Baldwin Beach (Baldwin
  Park), 160**
**Baldwin Home (Lahaina),
  223**
**Baldwin Home Museum
  (Lahaina), 187, 191–192**
Baldwin Park, 157
**Bamboo Forest, 172–173,
  209**
Banana plants, 312
**Banyan Tree Birthday Party
  (Lahaina), 32**
**Banyan Tree (Lahaina), 33,
  187, 193**
Banyan trees, 313
**The Base Camp (Makawao),
  168**
**Basketball Tournament, Maui
  Invitational, 35**

Bath and beauty products
  Kahului, 220
  Kihei, 228
**The Bay Club at Kapalua,
  234**
Beaches, 152–158
  Baldwin Park, 157
  best, 4–5
  D. T. Fleming Beach Park, 4,
    152
  Halawa Beach Park
    (Molokai), 254
  Hamoa Beach, 5, 158, 216
  Hana, 215–216
  Honomanu Bay County
    Beach Park, 209
  Hookipa Beach Park,
    157–158
  Hulopoe Beach (Lanai),
    160, 283–285
  Kaanapali Beach, 4, 153
  Kamaole III Beach Park,
    156, 160
  Kapalua Beach, 4, 153
  Kapukahehu (Dixie Maru)
    Beach (Molokai), 256
  Kepuhi Beach (Molokai),
    254
  Koki Beach, 215–216
  Lanai, 5, 283–284
  Launiupoko County Way-
    side Park, 153, 156
  Little Beach, 157
  Maluaka Beach (Makena
    Beach), 5, 157
  Molokai, 253–254
  Murphy (Kumimi) Beach
    Park (Molokai), 254
  One Alii Beach Park
    (Molokai), 253
  Oneloa Beach (Big Beach),
    157
  Papohaku Beach Park
    (Molokai), 254, 258, 260
  Pinaau, 210
  Polihua Beach (Lanai), 284,
    285
  Red Sand Beach, 215
  Sandy Beach (Molokai),
    254, 260
  Shipwreck Beach
    (Lanai), 284
  snorkeling, 164
  South Maui, 156–157
  surfing, 166
  Ulua Beach, 156
  Wahikuli County Wayside
    Park, 153
  Waianapanapa State Park,
    5, 158, 211
  Wailea Beach, 4–5, 156
  Waioka Pond, 216

  West Maui, 152–156
**Bed & breakfasts (B&Bs),
  59–61.** *See also* Accommo-
  dations; Accommodations
  Index
  etiquette, 85
**Biasa Rose Boutique
  (Paia), 231**
BiddingForTravel, 53
**Big Beach (Oneloa Beach),
  157, 160**
**Big Wind Kite Factory
  (Molokai), 263, 266, 271**
**Biking and mountain biking,
  178–179**
  Lanai, 289
  Molokai, 259–261
Billfish, 314
**Bill Kapuni's Snorkel and
  Dive (Molokai), 256**
**Bird of Paradise Unique
  Antiques (Wailuku),
  221–222**
Birds, 312
Birds of paradise, 308
**Bird-watching, Kealia Pond
  National Wildlife Preserve,
  183, 198**
Black Rock, 10, 153, 164
Blennies, 315
Blue Hawaiian, 182
Blue Pool, 216, 217
Boat excursions. *See* Ferries
  and boat trips
**Body boarding (boogie
  boarding) and body-
  surfing, 160**
  Lanai, 284–285
  Molokai, 255
**Bon Dance and Lantern
  Ceremony (Lahaina), 34**
Books, recommended, 66–68
Bookstores
  Kaanapali, 226
  Lahaina, 225
Botanical gardens
  Iao Valley Botanic Garden,
    185
  Kahanu Garden, 216
Both Sides Now, 42
Bougainvillea, 310
Box jellyfish, 40
Breadfruit, 312
Brewer, C., 212
Brick Palace (Lahaina), 192
**The Brig Carthaginian
  (Lahaina), 187, 192**
Bromeliads, 311
Bronte, Emory B., 268
**Brown-Kobayashi (Wailuku),
  22, 222**
Bucket shops, 45–46
Buddha Day, 31

Buddhist Church (Lahaina), 195

Budget car rentals, 57
    Molokai, 243

Buns of Maui, 56

Business hours, 68

Butterfly fish, 315

Cabs, 58
    Molokai, 243
    tipping, 80

Calendar of events, 30–35

Calling cards, 79

Camping, 168
    Haleakala National Park, 171
    Kanaha Beach Park, 174
    Lanai, 285
    Molokai, 247, 258–259
    Polipoli Springs State Recreation Area, 173
    Waianapanapa State Park, 174

Camp Trilogy, 2

Campus Travel, 76

Canal (Lahaina), 193

Canoe paddling, special events, 32

Capt. Steve's Rafting Excursions, 167

Car rentals, 57, 77
    Molokai, 243
    shopping online for, 54

Carthaginian, The Brig (Lahaina), 187, 192

Car travel
    automobile organizations, 76–77
    driving safety, 75

Casanova (Makawao), 233, 237

Castle and Cooke Resorts (Lanai), 276, 288

Cathedrals I and II (Lanai), 286

Cavendish Golf Course (Lanai), 288

Cellphones, 56

Centipedes, 37

Central Bakery (Lanai), 292–293

Central Maui
    accommodations, 81–82
    golf, 176
    restaurants, 123–126
        family-friendly, 130
    shops and galleries, 219–223
    sights and attractions, 183–185

The Challenge at Manele (Lanai), 12, 288

The Chamber of Commerce of Hawaii, 27

Cheap Seats, 46

Cheap Tickets, 46

Cheeseburger in Paradise (Lahaina), 236

Chevron Service Station (Hana), 215

Children, families with
    accommodations, 88–89
        Molokai, 249
    information and resources, 43
    restaurants, 130–131
    sights and attractions
        Lanai, 291
        Molokai, 263
    sun protection, 39
    what's new, 2

China Airlines, 76

Chinese New Year, 31

Churches
    Buddhist Church (Lahaina), 195
    Holy Ghost Catholic Church, 204
    Holy Innocents Episcopal Church (Lahaina), 193
    Huialoha Congregationalist "Circuit" Church (near Kaupo), 218
    Kaenae Congregational Church, 210
    Keawali Congregational Church (Makena), 199
    Our Lady of Sorrows Catholic Church (Molokai), 268
    Palapala Hoomau Congregational Church (Hana), 217
    St. Joseph's Catholic Church (Molokai), 268
    St. Philomena church (Molokai), 265
    Wainee Church (Lahaina), 194
    Wananalua Congregation Church, 214

Cinder Desert Hike, 171

Cirrus, 28

The City of Oakland (aircraft), 268

Climate, 29

Coconut Grove, Kapuaiwa (Molokai), 262

Coffee, 309
    Molokai, 261, 263, 270

Coffees of Hawaii Plantation Store and Espresso Bar (Molokai), 261, 263, 270

Collections (Makawao), 229

Columbus Direct, 74

Compadres Taquería (Lahaina), 223

Condominium Rentals Hawaii, 99

Condo rentals, 59, 61. *See also* Accommodations; Accommodations Index
    for families, 43
    Lahaina, 82

Consolidators, 45–46

Consulates, 77–78

Continental Airlines, 45

Continental Airlines Vacations, 52

Cook, Capt. James, 297

Coral, 314–315

Coral cuts, 41

Coral Miracle Church (Wailua), 210–211

Cost Less Imports (Kahului), 220

Council Travel, 46

County parks, 28

Courthouse (Lahaina), 193

Credit cards, 29, 75
    frequent-flier, 46

Crime, 69

Cuckoo for Coconuts (Makawao), 229–230

Cuisine, 303–308

Curbside check-in, 48

Currency and currency exchange, 74

Customs regulations, 72–74

Cuts, 41

CY Maui (Wailea), 229

Damien, Father, 264

David Lee Galleries (Lahaina), 224

David Malo Day, 32

David Malo's Home (Lahaina), 195

Delta Airlines, 45

Delta Dream Vacations, 52

Dentists, 68
    Lanai, 277

Destination Lanai, 276

Destination Resorts Hawaii, 106

Disabilities, travelers with, 41–42

Discount Car Rental, 57

Discount-tickets.com, 76

Dixie Maru (Kapukahehu) Beach (Molokai), 256

Doctors, 68

Dollar Rent A Car, 57, 211
    Lanai, 277
    Molokai, 243

Dolphin Dream Weddings, 45

Down to Earth Natural Foods (Kahului), 221, 225
Down to Earth Natural Foods (Makawao), 231
A Dream Wedding: Maui Style, 44
Driver's licenses, foreign, 71
Driving safety, 75
Dr. Nick's Family Dentistry (Lanai), 277
D. T. Fleming Beach Park, 4, 152

East End (Molokai), 242, 253, 260
  accommodations, 247–249
  beaches, 254
  shopping, 271
  sights and attractions, 267
East Maui
  accommodations, 114–117
  beaches, 157–158
  brief description of, 26–27
  restaurants, 148–151
    map, 145
  shopping, 231–232
East Maui Taro Festival, 31
Ecosystem problems, 317–318
Edibles. See Food and food markets
Ed Robinson's Diving Adventures, 162
Eels, 315
Ekahi Tours, 169, 183
Elderhostel, 43
Electricity, 77
Elizabeth Dole Gallery (Kapalua), 227
Elleair Maui Golf Club (Kihei), 177
Embassies and consulates, 77–78
Emergencies, 68, 78
Enenue Side, 162–163
Entry requirements, 70–71
Episcopal Cemetery (Lahaina), 195
Etiquette, outdoor, 64
Eucalyptus, 173, 208–209, 267
Europ Assistance's "Worldwide Healthcare Plan," 74
Expedia, 46, 52, 53
Expeditions Lahaina/Lanai Passenger Ferry, 159–160, 276
The Experience at Koele (Lanai), 12, 288–289

Fabrao, Delores, 278
Fabrao House jams and jellies, 293
Fagan, Paul I., 212, 300
Fagan's Cross, 214
  hiking to, 174
The Fairmont Kea Lani Maui, Spa Kea Lani at, 17
Families with children
  accommodations, 88–89
    Molokai, 249
  information and resources, 43
  restaurants, 130–131
  sights and attractions
    Lanai, 291
    Molokai, 263
  sun protection, 39
  what's new, 2
Farmers markets (Kahului), 221
Fashions (clothing). See also Aloha wear
  Kahului, 220, 221
  Lahaina, 225
  Lanai, 293
  Makawao, 229, 230
  Molokai, 269
  Paia, 231–232
  Wailuku, 222
Father Damien Tours (Molokai), 265
Fauna of Maui, 311–316
  books on, 67
Ferries and boat trips, 159–160
  Kalaupapa National Historic Park (Molokai), 266
  Lanai, 276
  Molokai, 241
  snorkel cruises, 160, 164–165
Festival of Art & Flowers (Lahaina), 35
Festival of Lights, 35
Festivals and special events, 30–35
Fiction, Hawaii in, 66
Film, flying with, 47
Film Festival, Hawaii International, 35
Film Festival, Maui, 32–33
Film Safety for Traveling on Planes (FSTOP), 47
First Light 2004, 35
Fish
  game, 316
  reef, 315–316, 317
Fishing, 165–166
  Lanai, 286
  Molokai, 257

Fish ponds (Molokai), 268
Flora of Maui, 308–311, 315–316
  books on, 67
Flowers (Kula), 231
1-800-FLY-CHEAP, 46
Food and food markets. See also Farmers markets; Health-food stores
  Kahului, 220–221
  Kapalua, 227
  Keanae, 210
  Lanai, 293, 294–295
  Molokai, 270
  special events and festivals, 31, 32, 34
  Wailuku, 222–223
Foreign visitors, 70–80
  customs regulations, 72–74
  entry requirements, 70–71
  health insurance, 74
  money matters, 74–75
  passport information, 71–72
Fort (Lahaina), 193
Four Seasons Resort Maui, Health Centre at, 17
14-mile marker (Olowalu), 164, 186
Fourth of July (Kaanapali), 34
Four-wheeling, Lanai, 285
Four Winds II (catamaran), 165
Frequent-flier clubs, 46
Friday Night Is Art Night (Lahaina), 33
Friendly Market Center (Molokai), 270
Frommers.com, 54
Front Street Theatres (Lahaina), 235
Fruits, 307–310
Fruit trees, 312–313
Fun Hogs Hawaii (Molokai), 257

Galleries. See Art galleries
Gallery Maui (Makawao), 230
Game fish, 316
Garden of the Gods (Lanai), 290
Gardens
  Iao Valley Botanic Garden, 185
  Kahanu Garden, 216
Gary's Island (Lahaina), 224
Gasoline, 78
Gay and lesbian travelers, 42

Gay Men's Health Crisis, 71
GayWired Travel Services, 42
Geckos, 314
Gecko Trading Co. Boutique
    (Makawao), 230
Getting Married, 44
Gifts. *See* Hawaiiana and
    gift items
Gifts with Aloha (Lanai), 293
Ginger, 311
Golden Age Passport, 43
Golden Week, 29
Golf, 175–178
    best courses, 11–12
    Lanai, 288–289
    Molokai, 3, 259
    South Maui, 177–178
    tournaments, 30, 31
    Upcountry Maui, 178
    West Maui, 176
Golf Club Rentals, 176
Gottling Ltd. (Wailuku), 222
Government Market
    (Lahaina), 193
Grand Wailea Resort
    American Express office, 68
    Spa Grande at, 17
Grand Wailea Shops, 229
Guava trees, 207, 208, 289

Haiku, 27, 207
    accommodations, 114–116
Halawa Beach Park
    (Molokai), 254
Halawa Valley (Molokai),
    242, 268–269
Haleakala Bike Company, 179
Haleakala Crater Road
    (Highway 378), 202
Haleakala National Park, 26,
    28, 168
    access points, 200, 202
    cabins, 171
    camping, 171–172
    driving to the summit,
        202–204
    Headquarters, 202
    hiking and camping,
        170–173
    on horseback, 179
    Kipahulu section of, 202
    map, 201
    origin of name, 203
    ranger programs, 202
    sights and attractions,
        199–204
    stargazing from, 9
    sunrise over, 8, 200
    visitor information and
        visitor centers, 202
    when to go, 200

Haleakala Observatories,
    204
Haleakala Ridge, 173
Haleakala Summit, 200
Haleakala Visitor Center,
    202, 204
Hale Aloha (Lahaina), 195
Hale Imua Internet Café
    (Kihei), 56
Hale Kahiko, 224
Halekii and Pihanakalani
    Heiau, 197
Halemauu Trail, 170, 171
Hale Pai (Lahaina), 187–188
Hale Piula (Lahaina), 194
Haliimaile
    accommodations, 109, 110
    restaurant, 144, 146
Halloween in Lahaina, 35
Hamoa Beach (Hana), 5, 158,
    216
Hana
    accommodations, 117–122
    beaches, 215–216
    brief description of, 27
    hiking, 174, 216–217
    restaurant, 151
    on the road to
        accommodations,
            114–117
        restaurants, 148–151
        sights and attractions,
            205–212
    shopping, 232
    sights and attractions,
        212–218
Hana Airport, 49, 211
Hana Bay, 214
Hana Coast Gallery, 22, 232
Hana District Police Station
    and Courthouse., 214
Hana Farmer's and Crafter's
    Market, 33
Hana Highway, 27
Hana-Maui Sea Sports, 161,
    166, 215
Hana Medical Center, 69
Hana Museum Cultural
    Center, 214
Hana Ranch Center, 214
Hana Relays, 34
Hana-Waianapanapa Coast
    Trail, 174
Handicrafts
    Hana, 232
    Kaanapali, 226
    Kahului, 220
    Kihei, 228
    Molokai, 271
    Paia, 232
Hard Rock Cafe (Lahaina),
    236

Hasegawa General Store
    (Hana), 214, 232
Hauola Stone (Lahaina), 192
Hawaiiana and gift items
    Lahaina, 225
    Lanai, 293
    Makawao, 229, 230
    Molokai, 269–271
    Wailea, 229
    Wailuku, 221, 222
Hawaiian Airlines, 45, 51,
    241, 276
Hawaiian Islands Humpback
    Whale National Marine
    Sanctuary, 168
Hawaiian Island Surf and
    Sport, 168
Hawaiian language, 302–303
The Hawaiian Language
    Website, 55
Hawaiian monk seal,
    313–314
Hawaiian Moons Natural
    Foods (Kihei), 228
Hawaiian music
    radio station, 69
    special events and
        festivals, 31–35
Hawaiian Ocean Raft, 161
Hawaiian Reef, 10, 162
Hawaiian Sailboarding Tech-
    niques, 168
Hawaiian Slack-Key Guitar
    Festival, 33
Hawaii Beachfront Vacation
    Homes, 62
Hawaii Center for Indepen-
    dent Living, 41
Hawaii Chapter of the Sierra
    Club, 62, 169
Hawaii Condo Exchange, 62
Hawaii International Film
    Festival, 35
Hawaii Marriage Project,
    42, 44
Hawaii Nature Center, 185
Hawaii's Best Bed & Break-
    fasts, 61
Hawaii State Department of
    Land and Natural
    Resources, 28, 168
Hawaii State Windsurf
    Championship (Kanaha
    Beach Park), 34
Hawaii Visitors and Conven-
    tion Bureau (HVCB), 27, 55
Health Canada, 74
Health concerns, 37
Health-food stores
    Kahului, 221
    Kihei, 228
    Lahaina, 225

Health insurance, 37, 41
  for foreign visitors, 74
Heliconia, 311
Helicopter rides, 182–183
Hemp House (Paia), 231–232
Hertz, for travelers with disabilities, 42
Hertz car rentals, 57
Hibiscus, 311
High season, 29
Highway 378 (Haleakala Crater Road), 202
Hike Maui, 169
Hiking and walking, 168–175. *See also specific trails*
  to Fagan's Cross, 174
  guided hikes, 169
  Haleakala National Park, 170–173, 202
  Hana, 174, 216–217
  information and maps, 168
  Kalaupapa National Historic Park (Molokai), 266
  Keanae Arboretum, 174–175
  Lanai, 287
  Makena, 199
  Molokai, 257–258
  Polipoli Springs State Recreation Area, 173
  Polipoli State Park, 173
  rental gear, 168
  safety, 38, 169
  Waianapanapa State Park, 174
  Waihee Ridge, 175
  Wailea, 198
  to a waterfall, 9
History
  of Lanai, 274–276
  of Maui, 8, 296–301
History of Hawaii, books on, 67–68
HIV-positive visitors, 71
Hoary bat, 313
Holiday & Co. (Makawao), 230
Holidays, 30
Holua Campground, 171
Holy Ghost Catholic Church (Kula), 204
Holy Innocents Episcopal Church (Lahaina), 193
Home decor
  Kahului, 220
  Makawao, 230
  Wailuku, 222
Hongwanji Mission (Lahaina), 194–195
Honoapiilani Highway (Hwy. 30), 57

Honokowai, 33
  accommodations, 92, 94–97
  brief description of, 24
  restaurants, 136–137
  shopping, 227
Honokowai Marketplace, 227
Honolua Bay, 166, 196
Honolua Store (Kapalua), 227
Honolulu International Airport, currency services at, 74
Honomanu Bay County Beach Park, 209
Hookipa Beach Park, 27, 157–158, 166, 167, 206–207
Hoolehua Airport (Molokai), 241
Horseback riding, 179–180
  Lanai, 289
  Molokai, 262
    Iliiliopae Heiau, 267
Hosmer Grove, 171
Hosmer Grove Nature Trail, 171
Hospitals, 69
  Molokai, 242
Hoteldiscounts. com, 53
Hotel Hana-Maui, 213, 214
Hotel Molokai, live entertainment, 271
Hotels.com, 53
Hot Island Glassblowing Studio & Gallery (Makawao), 230
Hotwire, 53
Huelo, 27
  sights and attractions, 208
Huialoha Congregationalist "Circuit" Church (near Kaupo), 218
Hui No'eau Visual Arts Center (Makawao), 22, 229
Hula
  Molokai, 260
  special events, 32, 33
Hula Bowl Football All-Star Classic, 31
Hula Grill (Kaanapali), 234
Hula O Na Keiki (Kaanapali Beach), 35
Hulopoe Bay tide pools, 291
Hulopoe Beach Park (Lanai), 5, 160, 283–284
  camping at, 288
Hurricane (Makawao), 230
HVCB (Hawaii Visitors and Convention Bureau), 27

Hwy. 30 (Honoapiilani Highway), 57
Hwy. 311 (Mokulele Highway), 57
Hyatt Regency Maui Resort & Spa
  "Beach Boot Camp," 2
  entertainment, 2–3
  Spa Moana at, 17

Iao Needle, 185
Iao Stream, 185
Iao Valley
  brief description of, 23
  sights and attractions, 185
Iao Valley Botanic Garden, 185
Iao Valley State Park, 185
IGLTA (International Gay & Lesbian Travel Association), 42
Iliiliopae Heiau (Molokai), 267
Ilio Point (Molokai), 256
Imamura Store (Molokai), 269
In Celebration of Canoes, 32
Information sources, 27–28
Insurance
  car rental, 57–58
  travel, 36–37
Interior design. *See* Home decor
International Driving Permit, 77
International Food & Clothing (Lanai), 293
International Gay & Lesbian Travel Association (IGLTA), 42
International visitors, 70–80
  customs regulations, 72–74
  entry requirements, 70–71
  health insurance, 74
  money matters, 74–75
  passport information, 71–72
Internet access, 55–56
Internet Hawaii Radio, 55
In the Footsteps of Royalty (Lanai), 286
InTouch USA, 56
Ironwood Hills Golf Course (Molokai), 259
Island Air, 49, 50–51, 241, 276
Island Kine (Molokai), 243
Island Riders, 58
Itinerary, suggested, 64–65

J acaranda, 312
Japan Air Lines, 76
Jellyfish, 40
Jet lag, 46

K aahumanu, Queen, 192, 214, 297, 298
Kaahumanu Shopping Center, 33
Kaahumanu Theatres (Kahului), 234
Kaaiea Bridge, 209
Kaanapali
accommodations, 86–91
map, 83
brief description of, 24
restaurants, 133–136
map, 127
shopping, 226–227
sights and attractions, 196
Kaanapali Beach, 4, 153
Kaanapali Beach Resort Association, 27
Kaanapali Courses, 11, 176
Kaenae Congregational Church, 210
Kahakuloa, 197
Kahana
accommodations, 91–92, 94–96
brief description of, 24
restaurants, 136–137
shopping, 227
Kahana Gateway, 227
Kahanu Garden, 216
Kahekili Highway, 9–10, 196–197
Kahikinui Forest Reserve, 173
Ka Hula Pikoi Festival (Molokai), 260
Kahului
accommodations, 81
brief description of, 23
restaurants, 123–125
shopping, 219–221
sights and attractions, 183
Kahului Airport, 45, 49
Kahului Shopping Center, 33
Kalahaku Overlook, 203
Kalaupapa Lookout (Molokai), 259, 263, 264
Kalaupapa (Molokai), 240, 242
hiking to, 258
Kalaupapa National Historical Park (Molokai), 28, 264–265
aerial tours, 265–266
hiking, 266
mule rides to, 10, 186, 265

Kaloa Point Trail, 172
Kalokoeli Pond (Molokai), 268
Kaluakoi Golf Course (Molokai), 3, 259
Kaluakoi (Molokai), 240, 242
Kamakou Preserve (Molokai), 267
Kamaole III Beach Park, 156, 160, 164
Kamehameha I, King, 192–194, 197, 297–298
Kamehameha III, King, 186, 188, 189, 192–194, 298
Kamehameha V, King, 240, 242, 262, 264
Ka Molokai Makahiki, 31
Kanaha, 167
Kanaha Beach Park
camping, 174
Hawaii State Windsurf Championship, 34
Kanaha Wildlife Sanctuary (Kahului), 183
Kanemitsu Bakery (Molokai), 272
Kanepuu Preserve (Lanai), 292
Kapalua
accommodations, 97–99
brief description of, 24–25
restaurants, 137–138
shopping, 227
Kapalua Beach, 4, 153, 164
Kapalua Resort Courses, 11, 176–177
Kapalua Shops (Kapalua), 227
Kapalua Tennis Garden and Village Tennis Center, 180–181
Kapalua-West Maui Airport, 49
Kapalua Wine and Food Festival, 34
Kapuaiwa Coconut Grove/Kiowea Park (Molokai), 262
Kapukahehu (Dixie Maru) Beach (Molokai), 256
Kauiki Hill, 214
Kaukini Gallery, 197
Kaulanapueo Church (Huelo), 208
Kaumahina State Wayside Park, 209
Kaunakakai (Molokai), 238, 240, 241–242
accommodations, 243–244
beach, 253
restaurants, 250–252
shopping, 269
sights and attractions, 262

Kaunolu Village (Lanai), 291–292
Kaupo, 218
Kaupo Gap, 172
Kaupo Road (Old Piilani Highway), 218
Kaupo Store, 218
Kawaikiunui (Molokai), 256
Kayaking, 9, 160–161
Lanai, 285
Molokai, 255, 261
Kealia Pond National Wildlife Preserve (Kihei), 183, 198
Keanae, 210
Keanae Arboretum, 174–175, 210
Keanae Lookout, 210
Keanae Peninsula, 210
Keawali Congregational Church (Makena), 199
Keawa Nui Pond (Molokai), 268
Keomoku Village (Lanai), 292
Kepaniwai Heritage Garden, 185
Kepuhi Beach (Molokai), 254
Kids
accommodations, 88–89
Molokai, 249
information and resources, 43
restaurants, 130–131
sights and attractions
Lanai, 291
Molokai, 263
sun protection, 39
what's new, 2
Kihei, 167
accommodations, 99–106
brief description of, 25
Internet access, 56
restaurants, 139–142
shopping, 228
sights and attractions, 198–199
Kihei Coast, 160–161
Kihei Dental Center, 68
Kihei Maui Vacation, 99
Kihei Taxi, 58
Ki'i Gallery (Kaanapali), 226
King Kamehameha Celebration, 32
Kiowea Park (Molokai), 262
Kipahulu, 172, 200, 202
Kipahulu Ranger Station, 172, 217
Kite-flying, Molokai, 263
Koele (Lanai), 277
Koele Nature Hike (Lanai), 287
Koki Beach (Hana), 215–216

Koolau Forest Reserve, 208–209
Korean Airlines, 76
Kualapuu Market (Molokai), 270
Kualapuu (Molokai), 240
Kuau, 206
  accommodations, 114
Kukui Mall Theatre (Kihei), 234–235
Kula, 204
  accommodations, 112–114
  brief description of, 26
  restaurants, 146–148
  shopping, 231
Kula Botanical Garden, 204
Kumimi (Murphy) Beach Park (Molokai), 254, 256, 263

L abrado, Darryl, 272
Lahaina
  accommodations, 82–86
  brief description of, 23–24
  maps, 188, 191
  nightlife, 235, 236
  parking, 190
  restaurants, 126–133
  shopping, 223–225
  sights and attractions, 186–196
  walking tour, 190–196
Lahaina Arts Society Galleries (Lahaina), 224
Lahaina Cannery Mall, 223
Lahaina Center, 223–224
Lahaina Harbor, 166
Lahaina Jodo Mission (Lahaina), 188
Lahaina Printsellers (Kaanapali), 226
Lahaina Printsellers (Lahaina), 223
Lahaina Restoration Foundation, 187
Lanai, 273–295
  accommodations, 278–280
  arriving in, 276
  beaches, 283–284
  camping, 288
  day cruises to, 159–160
  day trip to, 8
  dental and medical emergencies, 277
  Frommer's favorite experiences, 285
  hiking, 287
  history of, 274–276
  for kids, 291
  nightlife, 295
  outdoor activities (land-based), 288–289
  restaurants, 280–283

  shopping, 292–295
  sights and attractions, 290–292
  transportation, 277
  visitor information, 276
  watersports, 284–286
Lanai Arts Program, 289
Lanai City, 276
Lanai City Service, 160, 277
Lanai Community Hospital, 277
Lanai Courses, 12
Lanai Family Health Center, 277
Lanai Playhouse, 295
Lanai Visiting Artists Program, 294, 295
L & L Drive-Inn (Lahaina), 223
Lanilili Peak, 175
La Pérouse Monument (Makena), 199
La Pérouse Pinnacle, 11, 163, 165
Last-minute.com, 53
Laundry facilities, 36
Launiupoko County Wayside Park, 153, 156
Lava tubes, 9, 215
Legal aid, 78
Leg room, on airplanes, 48
Leilani's (Kaanapali), 234
Leis, 50
  Annual Lei Day Celebration, 32
Lei Spa Maui (Lahaina), 224
Leleiwi Overlook, 203
Leper colony. See Kalaupapa National Historic Park
Lesbians. See Gay and lesbian travelers
Lightning Bolt Maui Inc. (Kahului), 220
Liliuokalani, Queen, 68, 299
Lindbergh's Grave (Hana), 217
Liquor laws, 69
Litchi trees, 310
Little Beach, 157
The Local Gentry (Lanai), 293
Lodge at Koele (Lanai), 289, 295
  guided hikes, 287
Longhi's (Lahaina), 236
Lost-luggage insurance, 37
Lowestfare.com, 46
Luahiwa Petroglyph Field (Lanai), 291
Luakini Street (Lahaina), 195
Luaus, 21, 236
Luggage
  lost-luggage insurance, 37
  not locking your, 48

M aalaea, 166, 197
  accommodations, 99
  brief description of, 25
  restaurants, 139–142
Maalaea Bay, 197
Macadamia nuts, Molokai, 261, 262
Macadamia trees, 312
McGregor Point, 166
Mahimahi, 316
Mahinahina, brief description of, 24
Mail, 78
Mail2web, 56
Makahiku Falls, 172
Makawao, 204
  accommodations, 109, 110, 112
  brief description of, 26
  restaurants, 146
  shopping, 229–231
Makawao Parade and Rodeo, 34
Makee Sugar Mill, 205
Makena
  accommodations, 109
  brief description of, 25–26
  restaurant, 144
  sights and attractions, 199
Makena Beach (Maluaka Beach), 157
Makena Courses, 11–12, 177
Makena Kayak Tours, 161
Makena Landing, 199
Malassadas, 307, 308
Maliko Bay, 207
Maliko Gulch, 207
Malo, David, Home (Lahaina), 195
Maluaka Beach (Makena Beach), 5, 157
Maluuluolele Park (Lahaina), 188–189, 194
Manele Bay Hotel (Lanai), guided hikes, 287
Manele (Lanai), 277
Mangoes, 309
Mango trees, 312–313
Marathon, Maui, 34
Marijuana, 313
Marine life, 314–317
Markets, 33
Marriage License Office, 44
Marriages, 43–45
  gay, 42
Martin & MacArthur (Kaanapali), 226
Martin & MacArthur (Wailea), 229
Martin Lawrence Galleries (Lahaina), 225

MasterCard, traveler's checks, 28
Masters' Reading Room (Lahaina), 187, 191
Maui Art and Cultural Center (Kahului), 233
Maui Brews (Lahaina), 233, 236
Maui Cave Adventures, 9, 180
Maui Central Cab, 58
Maui Classic Charters, 165
Maui County Fair (Wailuku), 34–35
Maui County Parks and Recreation, 28, 168, 174, 180
Maui Crafts Guild (Paia), 232
Maui Dive Guide, 163
Maui Dive Shop, 163
Maui Downhill, 178
Maui Eco-Adventures, 169, 183
Maui Film Festival (Kahului), 32–33, 233
Maui Grown Market and Deli (Haiku), 207
Maui Hands
    Kahului, 220
    Makawao, 220
    Paia, 220
Maui Hiking Safaris, 169
Maui Invitational Basketball Tournament, 35
Maui Island Currents, 55
Maui Magic (catamaran), 165
Maui Mall (Kahului), 219, 233
Maui Marathon, 34
Maui Memorial Hospital (Wailuku), 69
Maui Menehune Golf, miniature golf course, 2
Maui Mountain Cruisers, 178
Maui Myth & Magic Theatre (Lahaina), 233, 236–237
Maui Net, 55
Maui Ocean Center, 197–198
    brief description of, 25
Maui Onion Festival (Kaanapali), 34
Maui Swap Meet (Kahului), 33, 220–221
Maui Theatre (Kahului), 234
Maui Tropical Plantation (Waikapu), 184
Maui Visitors Bureau, 27
Maui Windsurf Co., 168
Maui Writer's Conference (Wailea), 34
Maunaloa, 266

Maunaloa Cinemas (Molokai), 272
Maunaloa General Store (Molokai), 271
Maunaloa (Molokai), 240, 242
    shopping, 271
Medic Alert Identification Tag, 37, 41
Medical insurance, 37, 41
Medical requirements for entry, 71
Medications, prescription, 41
Mendes Ranch & Trail Rides (near Wailuku), 180
The Mercantile (Makawao), 230
Michener, James A., 66, 118, 158, 191
Microclimates, 30
Mile marker 14 (Olowalu), 164, 186
Misaki's Grocery and Dry Goods (Molokai), 270
Mitchell Pauole Center (Molokai), 262
Moanai Bakery & Café (Paia), 237
Mokuleia Bay, 196
Mokuleia Beach, 160
Mokulele Highway (Hwy. 311), 57
Molokai, 238–272
    accommodations, 243–249
        family-friendly, 249
    arriving in, 241
    day trips to, 159, 186
    exploring, 238, 240
    golf, 3
    hiking and camping, 257–259
    for kids, 263
    mule rides to Kalaupapa, 10, 186, 265
    nightlife, 271–272
    outdoor activities (land-based), 259–262
    post office, 242
    restaurants, 249–253
    shopping, 269–271
    sights and attractions, 262–269
    transportation, 243
    visitor information, 241
    watersports, 255–257
    website, 55
Molokai Action Adventures, 257, 258
Molokai Air Shuttle, 241
Molokai Charters, 255–256
Molokai Drugs, 269

Molokai Earth Day, 32
Molokai Fish & Dive, 255, 269
Molokai Hawaiian Paniolo Heritage Rodeo, 31
Molokai Ka Hula Piko, 32
Molokai Mule Ride, 10, 265
Molokai Museum and Cultural Center, 263
Molokai Museum Gift Shop, 270–271
Molokai Off-Road Tours & Taxi, 243
Molokai Outdoor Activities, 255–258, 262, 272
Molokai Princess (yacht), 159, 186, 241, 266
Molokai Ranch, 240, 242
Molokai Rentals and Tours, 255, 256, 258, 259, 262
Molokai Surf (Molokai), 269
Molokai Visitors Association, 241, 243
Molokai Wagon Rides, 267
Molokai Wines & Spirits (Molokai), 270
Molokini, 11, 160, 315
    day trips to
        snorkel cruises, 164–165
        whale-watching cruises, 165, 167
Molokini Crater, 162
Money matters, 28–29
    for foreign visitors, 74–75
Money-saving package deals, 51–52
Monkeypod, 311
Moomomi Dunes (Molokai), 266–267
Moonbow Tropics (Paia), 232
Mopeds, 58
More Hawaii For Less, 52
Mosquitoes, 37
Moss Rehab ResourceNet, 41
Mother's Day Orchid Show, 32
Motorcycle rentals, 58
Mountain biking. *See* Biking and mountain biking
Mountain Riders Bike Tours, 178
Movies, 233–235
Mule rides to Kalaupapa, 10, 186, 265
Munro Trail (Lanai), 285, 287, 290–291
Murphy (Kumimi) Beach Park (Molokai), 254, 256, 263
Music, Hawaiian
    radio station, 69
    special events and festivals, 31–35

Nahiku, 211
Na Hua O'Ka Aina (Purdy's All-Natural Macadamia Nut Farm; Molokai), 262
Na Mea Hawaii (Lahaina), 225
Na Mele O Maui, Student Song and Art Competition, 35
Nancy Emerson School of Surfing, 166
Napili
  accommodations, 92, 94–97
  brief description of, 24
  restaurants, 136–137
  shopping, 227
Narcotics, 71
National car rentals, 57
National Center for HIV, 71
National Marine Fisheries Service, 168
National Public Radio, 69
National Weather Service, 38
Nature Conservancy Oahu Land Preserve, 292
Nature Conservancy of Hawaii, 62, 257
The Neighborhood Store 'N Counter (Molokai), 271
Neil Pryde Slalom, 32
Nene, 314
Newspapers, 69
Night-blooming cereus, 312
Nightlife and entertainment, 233–237
  Lanai, 295
  Molokai, 271–272
  what's new, 2–3
Nonfiction books, 66–67
North Coast (Molokai), 242
  sights and attractions, 263–266
Northwest Airlines, 45

Ocean Activities Center, 165, 167
Ocean kayaking, 9, 160–161
  Lanai, 285
  Molokai, 255, 261
Ocean rafting, 161
Ocean safety, 38
Off seasons, 29
Ohana Farmers Market (Kahului), 221
Oheo Campground, 172
Oheo Gulch (Seven Sacred Pools), 172, 179, 217
Oheo Stables, 179, 215
Ohukai Park, 167

Old Daze (Wailuku), 222
Old-Fashioned Holiday Celebration (Lahaina), 35
The Old Lahaina Book Emporium, 225
Old Lahaina Luau (Lahaina), 236
Old Prison (Lahaina), 195
Olinda, accommodations, 109, 110
Olowalu, 10, 164, 186
Olowalu Reef, 167
One Alii Beach Park (Molokai), 253
Oneloa Beach (Big Beach), 157, 160
Ooka Super Market (Wailuku), 222–223
Oranges, 309–310
Orbitz, 52
Orchids, 312
Our Lady of Fatima Shrine (Wailua), 210–211
Our Lady of Sorrows Catholic Church (Molokai), 268
Out and About, 42
Outdoor activities (land-based). See also Beaches; specific activities
  biking, 178–179
  golf, 175–178
  hiking and camping, 168–175
  horseback riding, 179–180
  Lanai, 288–289
  spelunking, 180
  tennis, 180–181
Outdoor etiquette, 64
Outdoor markets, 33
Outfitters, 62–63
Outpost Natural Foods (Molokai), 270
Outrigger canoe races, 32
Outrigger Hotels and Resorts, 52
Outrigger Wailea Resort, whale-watching from, 166

Pa'a Pono (Molokai), 272
Pacific Money Exchange, 74
Pacific Ocean Holidays, 42
Pacific Whale Foundation, 167
Pacific Wings, 49, 51, 186, 211, 241, 266
Package deals, 51–52
Packing tips, 36
Paia, 26–27, 167, 205–206
  restaurants, 148–149
  shopping, 231–232

Palaau State Park (Molokai), 259, 263–264
Palapala Hoomau Congregational Church (Hana), 217
Paliku Campground, 171
Paniolo (cowboy) heritage, 31
Paniolo Trail Ride (Lanai), 289
Papayas, 308
Papaya trees, 313
Papohaku Beach Park (Molokai), 254, 258, 260
Paragon Air, 186, 266
Parasailing, 161
Parrot fish, 315
Passport information, 71–72
Pele's Garden (Lanai), 293–294
Pele's Other Garden (Lanai), 293
People Attentive to Children (PATCH), 43
Pepeopae Trail (Molokai), 257, 260, 267
Petroglyphs (Lanai), 291
Petrol, 78
PGA Kapalua Mercedes Championship, 30
Phallic Rock (Molokai), 264
Philippine Airlines, 76
Pic-nics (Paia), 149, 206
Pidgin English, 303
Piilani, 212, 217, 297
Piilanihale Heiau, 212, 216–217
Pinaau, 210
Pineapple Festival (Lanai), 34, 295
Pineapples, 307
Pine Isle Market (Lanai), 294
Pioneer Inn (Lahaina), 192
Planet Hawaii, 55
Plantation Course (Kapalua), 177
Plantation Gallery (Molokai), 271
Plate lunches, 306
Pleasant Hawaiian Holidays, 53
Plumeria, 310
Plum Trail, 173
PLUS ATM network, 28
Pocket Guide to Hawaii, 42
Pohaku Moiliili (Molokai), 256
Poison Control Center, 68
Police, 68
  Lanai, 277
  Molokai, 242
Polihua Beach (Lanai), 284, 285
Polipoli Loop, 173

Polipoli Springs State Recreation Area, 173
Polipoli State Park, 173
Polo Season, 33–34
Pony Express Tours, 179
Portuguese man-of-war, 40
Post-A-Nut (Molokai), 262
Post offices, 69
Pound for Pound (Molokai), 272
Prescription medications, 41
Priceline, 53
Pride of Maui, 165
Proteas, 312
Proteas of Hawaii (Kula), 231
Puaa Kaa State Wayside Park, 211
Pua's Lei Stand (Kihei), 228
Pueo, 314
Pukalani, restaurants, 146
Pukalani Country Club, 178
Punctures, 40–41
Puohokamoa Falls, 209
Purdy's All-Natural Macadamia Nut Farm (Na Hua O'Ka Aina; Molokai), 262
Puunene, 183–184
Puu-O-Hoku Ranch (Molokai), 262
Puu Olai, 167
Puu Ulaula Overlook (Red Hill), 204

Qantas, 76
Queen Kaahumanu Center (Kahului), 220

Radio stations, 69
Rafting, ocean, 161
Rainbow runner, 316
Rainforests, 8
Ranch rides, 180
Red Hill (Puu Ulaula Overlook), 204
Red Sand Beach (Hana), 215
Redwood Trail, 173
Reef fish, 315–316, 317
Reefs, 314–315
Reef's End, 163
Regions of Maui, 23–27
Rental cars, 54
Resorts, 59
Restaurants, 123–151
    best, 17–21
    Central Maui, family-friendly, 130
    East Maui, 148–151
    family-friendly, 130
    Hana, 151
    Honokowai, Kahana and Napili, 136–137
    Kaanapali, 133–136
    Kahului, 123–125
    Kapalua, 137–138
    Kihei/Maalaea, 139–142
    Kula, 146–148
    Lahaina, 126–133
    Lanai, 280–283
    Makawao and Pukalani, 146
    Makena, 144
    Molokai, 249–253
    Paia, 148–149
    South Maui, 139–144
        family-friendly, 131
    tipping, 80
    Upcountry Maui, 144–148
        family-friendly, 131
    Wailea, 142–144
    Wailuku, 125–126
    West Maui, 126–138
        family-friendly, 130–131
    what's new, 1–2
Richards House (Lahaina), 192
Richard's Shopping Center (Lanai), 295
Ritz-Carlton Kapalua, Spa at, 17
Rodeo General Store (Makawao), 231
Rodeos, 31, 34
Roland's (Lahaina), 223
A Romantic Maui Wedding, 44–45
Run to the Sun, 31

Safety, 69
    for foreign visitors, 75
    hiking, 38
    hiking and camping, 169
    ocean, 38
Sailing (yachting), 159–160
    Lanai, 285–286
    Molokai, 255–256
St. Gabriel's Church (Wailua), 210–211
St. Joseph's Catholic Church (Molokai), 268
St. Philomena church (Molokai), 265
Sandal Tree (Kaanapali), 226–227
Sandal Tree (Wailea), 229
Sandy Beach (Molokai), 254, 260
Satan's Doll (sloop), 255
Science City, 204
Scorpion fish, 315–316
Scorpions, 38
Scotch Mist Sailing Charters, 159
Scuba diving, 9, 161–163
    best places for, 10–11, 162–163
    Lanai, 286
    Molokai, 256
Sea life, 314–317
Seasickness, 38, 40
Seasons, 29
Seeing Eye dogs, 42
Seniors, 42–43
Senior Skins Tournament, 31
Seven Sacred Pools (Oheo Gulch), 172, 179, 217
Severns Diving, 163
Sharks, 317
Shave ice, 306–307
Sheraton Molokai Lodge and Beach Village
    accommodations, 244, 246, 247
    bicycling, 259
    hiking, 258
    horseback riding, 262
    kayaking, 255
    live music, 272
    Logo Shop, 271
Shipwreck Beach (Lanai), 284
Shoes (Kaanapali), 226
Shopping, 219–232
    best shops and galleries, 21–22
    Hana, 232
    Kaanapali, 226–227
    Kahului, 219–221
    Lahaina, 223–225
    Lanai, 292–295
    Makawao, 229–231
    South Maui, 228–229
    Upcountry Maui, 229–231
    Wailea, 228–229
    Wailuku, 221–223
    West Maui, 223–228
    what's new, 2
The Shops at Wailea, 2, 219, 228–229
Side-Step, 52
Sierra Club, Hawaii Chapter of the, 62, 169
Sights and attractions, 182–218
    Central Maui, 183–185
    ecotours, 183
    Haleakala National Park, 199–204
    helicopter rides, 182–183
    Kahekili Highway, 196–197
    Lanai, 290–292

Sights and attractions (cont.)
    Molokai, 262–269
    on the road to Hana, 205
    South Maui, 197–199
    submarine rides, 183
    Upcountry Maui, 204–205
    West Maui, 186–197
Sig Zane Designs Wailuku,
    22, 222
Silversword, 203
Simply Married, 45
Sir Wilfred's Coffee House
    (Lahaina), 223
Site59.com, 53
Skyline Trail, 173
Sliding Sands Trail, 170, 171
Smarter Living, 53
Smith, Ernie, 268
Smith Bronte Landing Site
    (Molokai), 268
Smoking, 69
Snorkel Bob's, 158, 164
Snorkeling, 160, 164
    best places for, 10–11
    Hulopoe Beach (Lanai),
        285
    Lanai, 8, 286
    mile marker 14 (Olowalu),
        164, 186
    Molokai, 256–257,
        260–261
South Maui
    accommodations, 99–109
        family-friendly, 89
    beaches, 156–157
    brief description of, 25
    golf, 177–178
    restaurants, 139–144
        family-friendly, 131
    shopping, 228–229
    sights and attractions,
        197–199
South Pacific Kayaks, 161
South Seas Trading Post
    (Kapalua), 227
Spas
    best, 17
    Lei Spa Maui (Lahaina),
        224
    treatments offered by, 18
Special events and festivals,
    30–35
SpeediShuttle, 49, 58
Spelunking, 180
Spinning Dolphin (Omega
    boat), 286
Sportfish Hawaii, 165–166
Sportfishing. See Fishing
Stables at Koele (Lanai), 289
Stand-by Golf, 176
Stargazing, from Haleakala, 9

State Division of Forestry
    and Wildlife, 168
Statehood, 300
State parks, 28
Stings, 40
Storytelling, 261, 291, 294
Submarine rides, 183
Suda Store, 33
Sugar production, 299
Summer, 29
Summerhouse (Kahului), 21,
    221
Sun protection, 36, 39
Sunrise Protea (Kula), 231
Sunscreen, 39
Sunset viewing, 234–235
    Molokai, 261
Sunshine Helicopters,
    182–183
Surfing, 166
    Lanai, 286
Surgeonfish, 316

Takamiya Market
    (Wailuku), 223
Take's Variety Store
    (Molokai), 269–270
"Talking story," 261, 291,
    294
Tanning tips, 39
Taro, 313
Taro Patch (Lahaina), 192
A Taste of Lahaina, 34
Taxes, 69, 78
Taxis, 58
    Molokai, 243
    tipping, 80
Tedeschi Vineyards and
    Winery, 204
Telephone, 78–79
    area code, 68
Telephone directories, 79
Temptation Tours, 180
Tennis, 180–181
    Lanai, 289
    Molokai, 262
That Ulupalakua Thing!
    Maui County Agricultural
    Trade Show and Sampling,
    32
Third Tank, 10–11, 162
This Week Maui, 49
Tide pools, Hulopoe Bay
    (Lanai), 284, 291
Time zone, 69
Tipping, 79–80
T. Komoda Store and Bakery
    (Makawao), 231
Toilets, 80
Tom Barefoot's Cashback
    Tours, 64

Tony n' Tina's Wedding, 2
Totally Hawaiian Gift Gallery
    (Lahaina), 225
Totem pole, Kihei, 198
A Touch of Molokai, 271
Tourist information, 27–28
Tours, package, 51–52
Transportation, 56–58
TravelAxe, 53–54
Traveler's checks, 28, 75
Travelex Insurance Services,
    37
Travel Guard International, 37
Traveling
    to Maui, 45–51
    to the United States, 75–76
Travel insurance, 36–37
Travel Insured International,
    37
Travelocity, 46, 52, 53
Tree Lighting Ceremony
    (Kapalua), 35
Trevally, 316
Trilogy Excursions, 8, 160
    "Eco-Enrichment Kids
        Camp," 2
    Lanai, 285–286
Trip-cancellation insurance,
    36–37
Tuna, 316
Tuna Luna (Kihei), 228
Twin Falls, 208
    accommodations, 116

UFO Parasail, 161
'Ulalena (Lahaina), 233,
    236–237
Ulua Beach, 156, 160, 164
Ulupalakua Ranch, 204–205,
    218
Uncle Harry's (Keanae), 210
United Airlines, 45
United Vacations, 52
Unna, August and Oscar,
    212, 299
Upcountry Maui, 8. See also
    Haleakala National Park
    accommodations, 109–114
        family-friendly, 89
    brief description of, 26
    golf, 178
    nightlife, 237
    restaurants, 144–148
        family-friendly, 131
    shopping, 229–231
    sights and attractions,
        204–205
Urgent Care, 68

Vacation rentals, 60, 61
Video, flying with, 47
Viewpoints Gallery
    (Makawao), 22, 231
Village Course
    (Kapalua), 177
Village Galleries in Lahaina,
    22, 225
Village Galleries (Kapalua),
    227–228
Visas, 70–71
Visa traveler's checks, 28
Visa Waiver Program, 70
Vision-impaired travelers
    with Seeing Eye dogs, 42
Visiting Artists Program
    (Lanai), 294, 295
Visitor information, 27–28
Visit USA, 76
Vog, 38

Wagon rides, to Iliiliopae
    Heiau (Molokai), 267
Wahikuli County Wayside
    Park, 153
Wahoo (ono), 314
Waianapanapa Beach, 211
Waianapanapa State Park,
    158, 174, 211–212
    beach, 5
Waiehu Municipal Golf
    Course, 176
Waihee Cemetery (Lahaina),
    194
Waihee Ridge, 175
Waikamoi Cloud Forest Hike,
    171
Waikamoi Ridge Trail, 209
Waikani Falls, 211
Waikapu Golf and Country
    Club, 184
Waikapu sights and attrac-
    tions, 184
Wailea
    accommodations, 106–109
    brief description of, 25
    restaurants, 142–144
    shopping, 228–229
    sights and attractions, 198
Wailea Beach, 4–5, 156
Wailea Courses, 11, 177–178
Wailea Taxi, 58
Wailea Tennis Club, 181
Wailua sights and attrac-
    tions, 210–211
Wailua Valley State Wayside
    Park, 211
Wailuku
    accommodations, 81–82

brief description of, 23
    restaurants, 125–126
    shopping, 221–223
    sights and attractions, 184
Waimoku Falls, 9, 172, 173
Wainee Church
    (Lahaina), 194
Waioka Pond (Hana), 216
Wananalua Congregation
    Church, 214
Warren & Annabelle's
    (Lahaina), 237
Waterfalls, 9
    Makahiku Falls, 172
    Oheo Gulch (Seven Sacred
        Pools), 172, 179, 217
    Puohokamoa Falls, 209
    Twin Falls, 208
    Waikani Falls, 211
    Waimoku Falls, 9, 172
Watermelons, 309
Watersports, 158–168
    Lanai, 284–286
    Molokai, 255–257
Weather, 30, 36
    hiking and camping, 170
    information numbers, 69
Websites
    best Hawaii-specific, 55
    travel-planning and
        booking, 52–55
A Wedding Made in Par-
    adise, 44
Wedding planners, 44–45
Weddings, 43–45
West End (Molokai), 242
    accommodations, 244–247
    beaches, 254
    hiking, 258
    restaurants, 252–253
    shopping, 271
    sights and attractions, 266
Westin Maui, American
    Express office, 68
West Maui
    accommodations, 82–99
        family-friendly, 88–89
    beaches, 152–156
    brief description of, 23–24
    golf, 176
    nightlife, 236–237
    restaurants, 126–138
        family-friendly,
            130–131
    shopping, 223–228
    sights and attractions,
        186–197
West Maui Healthcare
    Center, 68
West Maui Mountains, 9
Whale Center of the Pacific
    (Kaanapali), 2, 196

Whalefest Week, 31
Whalers Village (Kaanapali),
    24, 196, 226
    live cooking demonstra-
        tion, 1
Whales, 316–317
Whale-watching, 168
    cruises, 159, 165, 167
    Lanai, 286
    Molokai, 256, 263
    by kayak and raft, 167
    from land, 8
    Lanai, 285
    from shore, 166–167
Wharf Cinema Center
    (Lahaina), 235
Wheelchair accessibility,
    41–42
Wheels USA, 58
Wilfong, George, 212, 299
Wind and Surf Report, 168
Windsurfing, 8, 167–168
    Aloha Classic World Wave-
        sailing Championship
        (Hookipa Beach), 35
    Hawaii State Windsurf
        Championship (Kanaha
        Beach Park), 34
    Hookipa Beach Park,
        206–207
    Maalaea Bay, 197
    Neil Pryde Slalom, 32
Wo Hing Temple (Lahaina),
    189
Word of Mouth Rent-a-Used-
    Car, 57
Worldwide Assistance Ser-
    vices, 74
WOW (Wailea on Wednes-
    day), 2
Wrasses, 316

Yahoo! Mail, 56
Yahoo! Travel, 46

ACCOMMODATIONS

A'ahi Place (Kaunakakai),
    244
Aloha Beach House
    (Molokai), 16, 247–248
Aloha Cottages (Hana), 120
Aloha Journeys (Kihei), 102
Aloha Maui B&B (Haiku),
    115–116
Aloha Pualani (Kihei), 102
Ann and Bob Babson's Bed
    & Breakfast and Sunset
    Cottage (Kihei), 102–103
Aston at the Maui Banyan
    (Kihei), 99

Baby Pigs Crossing Bed & Breakfast (Hana), 120

Bamboo Mountain Sanctuary (Haiku), 115

Banana Bungalow Maui (Wailuku), 82

Banyan Tree House (Makawao), 110, 112

Best Western Pioneer Inn (Lahaina), 82

Blue Horizons (Kahana), 96

Cheeseburger in Paradise (Lahaina), 234

Country Cottage at Pu'u O Hoku Ranch (Molokai), 248, 249

Delores Fabrao (Lanai), 278

Dreams Come True (Lanai), 280

Dunbar Beachfront Cottages (Molokai), 248, 249

Ekena (Hana), 16, 118

The Fairmont Kea Lani Maui (Wailea), 13, 106–107

Four Seasons Resort Maui at Wailea, 13, 89, 107

Garden Gate Bed and Breakfast (Lahaina), 86

Gildersleeve's Vacation Rentals (Kula), 113

Grand Wailea Resort Hotel & Spa, 13, 107–108

Guest House (Lahaina), 15, 86

Hale Akua Shangri-la B&B Retreat Center (Huelo), 117

Hale Ho'okipa Inn Makawao, 112

Hale Kai (Honokowai), 88, 92

Hale Kumulani (Kihei), 103

Hale Maui Apartment Hotel (Honokowai), 95–96

Hale Moe (Lanai), 278

Hale O Lanai, 278

Halfway to Hana House (Twin Falls), 116

Hamoa Bay Bungalow (Hana), 16, 118

Hana Hale Malamalama, 119

Hana Kai Maui Resort, 119

Hana Oceanfront, 119

Hana's Heaven, 120–121

Hana's Tradewinds Cottage, 121

Heavenly Hana Inn, 16, 119–120

Honokeana Cove, 92, 94

Honopou Lodge (Haiku), 114

Hotel Hana-Maui, 1, 13, 117–118

Hotel Lanai, 14, 279–280

Hotel Molokai (Kaunakakai), 244

House of Fountains Bed & Breakfast (Lahaina), 82, 84

Hoyochi Nikko (Honokowai), 95

Huelo Point Flower Farm, 116–117

Hyatt Regency Maui (Kaanapali), 12–13, 90

The Inn at Mama's Fish House (Kuau), 114

I'o (Lahaina), 234–235

Joe's Place (Hana), 121

Kaanapali Alii, 12, 87

Kaanapali Beach Hotel, 91

Ka Hale Mala Bed & Breakfast (Kaunakakai), 244

Kahana Sunset, 13–14, 94

Kailua Maui Gardens, 117

Kaleialoha (Honokowai), 96

Kamalo Plantation Bed & Breakfast (Molokai), 249

Kamaole Nalu Resort (Kihei), 100

Kapalua Bay Hotel & Ocean Villas, 97–98

Kapalua Villas, 99

Kealia Resort (Kihei), 103

Ke Nani Kai Resort (Maunaloa), 246

Ke Nani Kai Resort (Molokai), 249

Kihei Beach Resort, 100

Kihei Kai, 102

Kili's Cottage (Kula), 16, 113

Kimo's (Lahaina), 234

Koa Resort (Kihei), 89, 100

Kula Cottage, 113

Kula Lynn Farm Bed & Bath, 113

Kulani's Hideaway in Hana, Maui, 121

Kula View B&B, 114

Lahaina Fish Company, 234

Lahaina Inn, 14, 84

Lahaina Roads, 82

Lahaina Shores Beach Resort, 82

Leinaala (Kihei), 103–104

The Lodge at Koele (Lanai), 278–279

Luana Kai Resort (Kihei), 102

Maalaea Surf Resort (Kihei), 99

Malu Manu (Kula), 16, 112

Mana Kai Maui Resort (Kihei), 89, 104

Manele Bay Hotel (Lanai), 279

Mauian Hotel on Napili Beach, 94–95

Maui Beach Hotel, 81

Maui Coast Hotel (Kihei), 14, 100

Maui Dream Cottages (Haiku), 116

Maui Eldorado Resort (Kaanapali), 90–91

Maui Hill (Kihei), 99

Maui Kamaole (Kihei), 102

Maui Marriott Resort and Ocean Club (Kaanapali), 86–87

Maui Prince Hotel (Makena), 109

Maui Sands (Honokowai), 94

Menehune Shores (Kihei), 104

Moanui Beach House (Molokai), 248

Molokai Shores Suites (Kaunakakai), 243–244, 249

Napili Bay, 96

Napili Kai Beach Resort, 13, 92

Napili Sunset, 96–97

Napili Surf Beach Resort, 95

Noelani Condominium Resort (Kahana), 88, 95

Nona Lani Cottages (Kihei), 15, 104–105

Northwind Inn (Wailuku), 82

Ohana Maui Islander (Lahaina), 84

Old Lahaina House, 86

Old Wailuku Inn at Ulupono, 15, 81

Olinda Country Cottages & Inn, 15–16, 110

Pacific'o (Lahaina), 234

Paniolo Hale (Maunaloa), 14, 246–247

Papakea (Honokowai), 97

Papalani (Hana), 120

Peace of Maui (Haliimaile), 110

Penny's Place in Paradise (Lahaina), 84

Pilialoha B&B Cottage (Haiku), 114–115

The Plantation Inn (Lahaina), 14, 84

Polynesian Shores (near Kahana), 92

Pualani Paradise Island Cottage (Kihei), 105

Puamana (Lahaina), 85

Punahoa Beach Apartments (Kihei), 14, 105

Renaissance Wailea Beach Resort, 108

Ritz-Carlton Kapalua, 12, 88, 98

Royal Lahaina Resort (Kaanapali), 86

Sands of Kahana, 91–92
Sheraton Maui (Kaanapali), 12, 87, 88
Sheraton Molokai Lodge and Beach Village, 244, 246, 247
Silver Cloud Ranch (Kula), 112–113
Sunseeker Resort (Kihei), 102
Tea House Cottage (Twin Falls), 116
Two Mermaids on the Sunnyside of Maui B&B (Kihei), 15, 105–106
Waianapanapa State Park Cabins (Hana), 121–122
Wailea Marriott, an Outrigger Resort, 108–109
Wai Ola Vacation Paradise on Maui (Lahaina), 85–86
Westin Maui, 88–90
The Whaler on Kaanapali Beach, 91
What a Wonderful World B&B (Kihei), 15, 106
Wild Ginger (Haiku), 15, 115

RESTAURANTS

Aloha Mixed Plate (Lahaina), 132
Aunty Aloha's Breakfast Luau (Kaanapali), 135
The Bay Club (Kapalua), 19–20, 137
Beachside Grill and Leilani's on the Beach (Kaanapali), 133–134
Blue Ginger Cafe (Lanai), 282
Bubba's Burgers (Kihei), 140
Buzz's Wharf (Maalaea), 139, 235
Cafe des Amis (Paia), 148–149
Cafe 808 (Kula), 147
Cafe O'Lei (Makawao), 19, 146
Café O'Lei on Main (Wailuku), 125
Caffe Ciao (Wailea), 143–144
Casanova Italian Restaurant (Makawao), 20, 146, 237
Charlie's Restaurant (Paia), 148, 206
Cheeseburger in Paradise (Lahaina), 132
Chez Paul (Lahaina), 128
Class Act (Wailuku), 125–126
Coffee Store (Kahului), 124
The Coffee Store (Kihei), 140

Coffee Works (Lanai), 282–283
Compadres Bar & Grill (Lahaina), 129
Cow Country Cafe (Pukalani), 146
David Paul's Lahaina Grill, 19, 128, 130
Down to Earth (Lahaina), 132
Edo Japan (Kahului), 124
The Feast at Lele (Lahaina), 128
Ferraro's at Seaside (Wailea), 142, 235
Fish & Game Brewing Co. & Rotisserie (Kahana), 136–137
Five Palms (Kihei), 139
Formal Dining Room (Lanai), 280–281
Gerard's (Lahaina), 19, 128–129
Grandma's Coffee House (Kula), 147
Haliimaile General Store, 20, 131, 144, 146
Hana Ranch Restaurant, 151
Hard Rock Cafe (Lahaina), 126
Henry Clay's Rotisserie (Lanai), 20–21, 281–282
Hotel Molokai, 250–251
Hula Grill (Kaanapali), 130–131, 134
Hulopoe Court (Lanai), 281
Ichiban (Kahului), 124
Ihilani (Lanai), 281
I'o (Lahaina), 129
Jameson's Grill & Bar at Kapalua, 138
Joe's Bar & Grill (Wailea), 20, 142–143
Kaahumanu Center (Kahului), 124
Kamoi Snack-N-Go (Molokai), 251
Kanemitsu's Bakery & Restaurant (Molokai), 251
Kimo's (Lahaina), 129
Koho Grill & Bar, 130
Kualapuu Cook House (Molokai), 253
Kula Lodge, 146–147, 235
Kula Sandalwoods Restaurant, 147–148
Lahaina Coolers, 133
Lahaina Fish Company, 130–131
Longhi's (Wailea), 143
Mama's Fish House (Kuau), 150

Mañana Garage (Kahului), 17, 19, 123
Manele Bay Clubhouse (Lanai), 282
Marco's Grill & Deli (Kahului), 123–124
Maui Bake Shop (Wailuku), 126
Maui Mixed Plate (Kahului), 124
Maui Swiss Cafe (Lahaina), 133, 196
Maui Tacos (Kahului), 124, 131
Maui Tacos (Kihei), 139
Maui Tacos (Lahaina), 126, 131
Maui Tacos (Napili), 137
Maunaloa Room (Molokai), 252–253
Milagros Food Company (Paia), 149
Moanai Bakery & Cafe (Paia), 20, 148, 237
Molokai Drive-Inn, 251
Molokai Mango, 251–252
Molokai Pizza Cafe, 252
Molokini Lounge (Wailea), 235
Nahiku Coffee Shop, Smoked Fish Stand, and Ti Gallery (near Hana), 150
Neighborhood Store 'N Counter (Molokai), 253
Nick's Fishmarket Maui (Wailea), 143
Old Lahaina Luau, 21, 65, 236
Outpost Natural Foods (Molokai), 252
Pacific Grill (Wailea), 235
Pacific'o Restaurant (Lahaina), 129
Paia Fish Market, 149
Panda Cuisine (Kahului), 124
Pauwela Cafe (Haiku), 150–151
Peggy Sue's (Kihei), 131, 140
Pele's Other Garden (Lanai), 21, 283
Pic-nics (Paia), 149
Pizza Paradiso Italian Caffe (Honokowai), 137
Pizza Paradiso (Kaanapali), 135–136
Plantation House Restaurant (Kapalua), 20, 138
Pool Grille (Lanai), 282
Prince Court (Makena), 144
Restaurant Matsu (Kahului), 124–125

Roy's Kahana Bar &
   Grill/Roy's Nicolina
   Restaurant, 19, 136
A Saigon Cafe (Wailuku),
   19, 125
Sam Sato's (Wailuku), 126
Sansei Seafood Restaurant
   and Sushi Bar (Kapalua),
   20, 138
Sea House Restaurant
   (Napili), 136
SeaWatch (Wailea), 144
Shaka Sandwich & Pizza
   (Kihei), 140, 142

Spago (Wailea), 142
Stella Blues Cafe (Kihei),
   139–140
Sundown Deli (Molokai),
   252
Swan Court (Kaanapali),
   19, 133
Tanigawa's Restaurant
   (Lanai), 283
The Terrace (Lanai), 281
Tiki Terrace (Kaanapali),
   134–135
Tommy Bahama (Wailea),
   235

The Vegan (Paia), 149
The Waterfront at Maalaea,
   139
Wei Wei BBQ and Noodle
   House (Wailuku), 126
Whalers Village (Kaanapali),
   135
Woody's Island Grill
   (Lahaina), 131–132
Yummy Korean B-BQ
   (Kahului), 124

TRAVEL AROUND THE WORLD IN STYLE
– WITHOUT BREAKING THE BANK –
WITH FROMMER'S DOLLAR-A-DAY GUIDES!

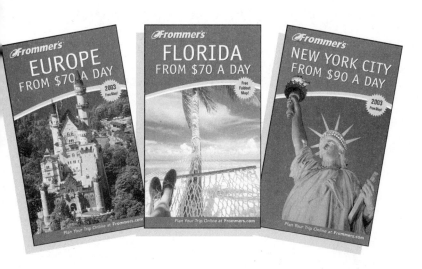

THE ULTIMATE GUIDES TO COMFORTABLE LOW-COST TRAVEL.

OTHER DOLLAR-A-DAY TITLES

Australia from $50 a Day
California from $70 a Day
Caribbean from $70 a Day
England from $75 a Day
Europe from $70 a Day
Florida from $70 a Day
Hawaii from $80 a Day

Ireland from $60 a Day
Italy from $70 a Day
London from $85 a Day
New York City from $90 a Day
Paris from $80 a Day
San Francisco from $70 a Day
Washington, D.C. from $80 a Day

Frommer's®

WITH KIDS

Traveling with kids ages 2 to 14 has never been this easy!

Frommer's Chicago with Kids
Frommer's Las Vegas with Kids
Frommer's New York City with Kids
Frommer's Ottawa with Kids

Frommer's San Francisco with Kids
Frommer's Toronto with Kids
Frommer's Vancouver with Kids
Frommer's Washington, D.C. with Kids

"Every page of this comprehensive book is full of tips."
—*Parenting*

Frommer's
Portable Guides
Complete Guides for the Short-Term Traveler

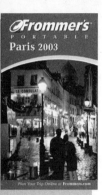

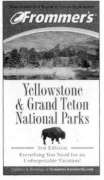
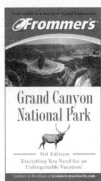

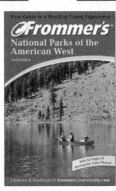
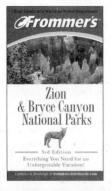

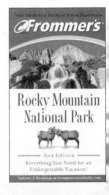

ROMMER'S® COMPLETE TRAVEL GUIDES

aska
aska Cruises & Ports of Call
nsterdam
gentina & Chile
izona
lanta
ustralia
ustria
hamas
rcelona, Madrid & Seville
ijing
lgium, Holland & Luxembourg
rmuda
ston
azil
itish Columbia & the Canadian
  Rockies
ussels & Bruges
idapest & the Best of Hungary
ulifornia
anada
uncún, Cozumel & the Yucatán
upe Cod, Nantucket & Martha's
  Vineyard
aribbean
aribbean Cruises & Ports of Call
aribbean Ports of Call
arolinas & Georgia
nicago
nina
olorado
osta Rica
uba
enmark
enver, Boulder & Colorado Springs
agland
urope
uropean Cruises & Ports of Call

Florida
France
Germany
Great Britain
Greece
Greek Islands
Hawaii
Hong Kong
Honolulu, Waikiki & Oahu
Ireland
Israel
Italy
Jamaica
Japan
Las Vegas
London
Los Angeles
Maryland & Delaware
Maui
Mexico
Montana & Wyoming
Montréal & Québec City
Munich & the Bavarian Alps
Nashville & Memphis
New England
New Mexico
New Orleans
New York City
New Zealand
Northern Italy
Norway
Nova Scotia, New Brunswick &
  Prince Edward Island
Oregon
Paris
Peru
Philadelphia & the Amish Country
Portugal

Prague & the Best of the Czech
  Republic
Provence & the Riviera
Puerto Rico
Rome
San Antonio & Austin
San Diego
San Francisco
Santa Fe, Taos & Albuquerque
Scandinavia
Scotland
Seattle & Portland
Shanghai
Sicily
Singapore & Malaysia
South Africa
South America
South Florida
South Pacific
Southeast Asia
Spain
Sweden
Switzerland
Texas
Thailand
Tokyo
Toronto
Tuscany & Umbria
USA
Utah
Vancouver & Victoria
Vermont, New Hampshire & Maine
Vienna & the Danube Valley
Virgin Islands
Virginia
Walt Disney World® & Orlando
Washington, D.C.
Washington State

ROMMER'S® DOLLAR-A-DAY GUIDES

ustralia from $50 a Day
ulifornia from $70 a Day
agland from $75 a Day
urope from $70 a Day
orida from $70 a Day
awaii from $80 a Day

Ireland from $60 a Day
Italy from $70 a Day
London from $85 a Day
New York from $90 a Day
Paris from $80 a Day

San Francisco from $70 a Day
Washington, D.C. from $80 a Day
Portable London from $85 a Day
Portable New York City from $90
  a Day

ROMMER'S® PORTABLE GUIDES

apulco, Ixtapa & Zihuatanejo
nsterdam
uba
ustralia's Great Barrier Reef
hamas
rlin
g Island of Hawaii
ston
ulifornia Wine Country
uncún
ayman Islands
narleston
nicago
sneyland®
ublin
orence

Frankfurt
Hong Kong
Houston
Las Vegas
Las Vegas for Non-Gamblers
London
Los Angeles
Los Cabos & Baja
Maine Coast
Maui
Miami
Nantucket & Martha's Vineyard
New Orleans
New York City
Paris
Phoenix & Scottsdale

Portland
Puerto Rico
Puerto Vallarta, Manzanillo &
  Guadalajara
Rio de Janeiro
San Diego
San Francisco
Savannah
Seattle
Sydney
Tampa & St. Petersburg
Vancouver
Venice
Virgin Islands
Washington, D.C.

ROMMER'S® NATIONAL PARK GUIDES

inff & Jasper
mily Vacations in the National
  Parks

Grand Canyon
National Parks of the American West
Rocky Mountain

Yellowstone & Grand Teton
Yosemite & Sequoia/Kings Canyon
Zion & Bryce Canyon

FROMMER'S® MEMORABLE WALKS

| Chicago | New York | San Francisco |
| London | Paris | |

FROMMER'S® WITH KIDS GUIDES

Chicago	Ottawa	Vancouver
Las Vegas	San Francisco	Washington, D.C.
New York City	Toronto	

SUZY GERSHMAN'S BORN TO SHOP GUIDES

Born to Shop: France	Born to Shop: Italy	Born to Shop: New York
Born to Shop: Hong Kong,	Born to Shop: London	Born to Shop: Paris
Shanghai & Beijing		

FROMMER'S® IRREVERENT GUIDES

Amsterdam	Los Angeles	San Francisco
Boston	Manhattan	Seattle & Portland
Chicago	New Orleans	Vancouver
Las Vegas	Paris	Walt Disney World®
London	Rome	Washington, D.C.

FROMMER'S® BEST-LOVED DRIVING TOURS

Britain	Germany	Northern Italy
California	Ireland	Scotland
Florida	Italy	Spain
France	New England	Tuscany & Umbria

HANGING OUT™ GUIDES

| Hanging Out in England | Hanging Out in France | Hanging Out in Italy |
| Hanging Out in Europe | Hanging Out in Ireland | Hanging Out in Spain |

THE UNOFFICIAL GUIDES®

Bed & Breakfasts and Country
  Inns in:
  California
  Great Lakes States
  Mid-Atlantic
  New England
  Northwest
  Rockies
  Southeast
  Southwest
Best RV & Tent Campgrounds in:
  California & the West
  Florida & the Southeast
  Great Lakes States
  Mid-Atlantic
  Northeast
  Northwest & Central Plains

Southwest & South Central
  Plains
  U.S.A.
Beyond Disney
Branson, Missouri
California with Kids
Central Italy
Chicago
Cruises
Disneyland®
Florida with Kids
Golf Vacations in the Eastern U.S.
Great Smoky & Blue Ridge Region
Inside Disney
Hawaii
Las Vegas
London
Maui

Mexio's Best Beach Resorts
Mid-Atlantic with Kids
Mini Las Vegas
Mini-Mickey
New England & New York with
  Kids
New Orleans
New York City
Paris
San Francisco
Skiing & Snowboarding in the West
Southeast with Kids
Walt Disney World®
Walt Disney World® for
  Grown-ups
Walt Disney World® with Kids
Washington, D.C.
World's Best Diving Vacations

SPECIAL-INTEREST TITLES

Frommer's Adventure Guide to Australia &
  New Zealand
Frommer's Adventure Guide to Central America
Frommer's Adventure Guide to India & Pakistan
Frommer's Adventure Guide to South America
Frommer's Adventure Guide to Southeast Asia
Frommer's Adventure Guide to Southern Africa
Frommer's Britain's Best Bed & Breakfasts and
  Country Inns
Frommer's Caribbean Hideaways
Frommer's Exploring America by RV
Frommer's Fly Safe, Fly Smart

Frommer's France's Best Bed & Breakfasts and
  Country Inns
Frommer's Gay & Lesbian Europe
Frommer's Italy's Best Bed & Breakfasts and
  Country Inns
Frommer's Road Atlas Britain
Frommer's Road Atlas Europe
Frommer's Road Atlas France
The New York Times' Guide to Unforgettable
  Weekends
Places Rated Almanac
Retirement Places Rated
Rome Past & Present